Awakening to China's Rise

Awakening to China's Rise

European Foreign and Security Policies towards the People's Republic of China

HUGO MEIJER

Great Clarendon Street, Oxford, OX2 6DP,
United Kingdom

Oxford University Press is a department of the University of Oxford.
It furthers the University's objective of excellence in research, scholarship,
and education by publishing worldwide. Oxford is a registered trade mark of
Oxford University Press in the UK and in certain other countries

© Hugo Meijer 2022

The moral rights of the author have been asserted

Impression: 1

All rights reserved. No part of this publication may be reproduced, stored in
a retrieval system, or transmitted, in any form or by any means, without the
prior permission in writing of Oxford University Press, or as expressly permitted
by law, by licence or under terms agreed with the appropriate reprographics
rights organization. Enquiries concerning reproduction outside the scope of the
above should be sent to the Rights Department, Oxford University Press, at the
address above

You must not circulate this work in any other form
and you must impose this same condition on any acquirer

Published in the United States of America by Oxford University Press
198 Madison Avenue, New York, NY 10016, United States of America

British Library Cataloguing in Publication Data
Data available

Library of Congress Control Number: 2021952586

ISBN 978-0-19-886553-7

DOI: 10.1093/oso/ 9780198865537.001.0001

Printed and bound by
CPI Group (UK) Ltd, Croydon, CR0 4YY

Links to third party websites are provided by Oxford in good faith and
for information only. Oxford disclaims any responsibility for the materials
contained in any third party website referenced in this work.

Acknowledgements

The research for such a monograph is the result of personal dedication and passion. Yet, this book could not have come to fruition without the precious contribution and help of several colleagues and academic institutions who share my curiosity and interests in the global ramifications of China's rise, European foreign and security policies towards Beijing, and the role of Europeans in world politics amidst mounting Sino-American strategic competition. *Awakening to China's Rise* is the endpoint of a long journey that has taken me to many countries and enabled me to meet exceptional people. Over more than eight years, numerous research trips brought me to Washington, DC, Beijing, Brussels, Florence, Paris, Berlin, London, Seoul, and New Delhi where I conducted archival research and more than 200 interviews with senior policymakers.

The central idea of this book—comparing the foreign and security policies of Europe's three major powers towards China both in the Asia-Pacific and in Europe—emerged during a writing retreat in my beloved Tuscan countryside, first in the hills of Vellano and in subsequent writing sessions in Antella. But I had first started developing the building blocks of this project at King's College London (KCL) in the United Kingdom, where I was Lecturer in Defence Studies, and then as Research Fellow at the Institute for Strategic Research of the French Military Academy (IRSEM) in Paris. At KCL, together with Matthew Uttley and other European colleagues, Lucie Béraud-Sudreau and Paul Holtom, we focused on a specific dimension of US and European policies towards China, namely the transfer of defence-related technologies and the thorny transatlantic controversy over the EU arms embargo on China. At IRSEM, I then broadened the scope of my research to explore European foreign and security policies in the Asia-Pacific. I am grateful to the Director of IRSEM Jean-Baptiste Jeangène Vilmer for his backing and for enabling me to conduct research trips in the US and South Korea, and to attend the Shangri-La Dialogue, the annual security forum organized by the International Institute for Strategic Studies (IISS) in Singapore, which gathers defence ministers and military chiefs of Asian-Pacific states, the United States, France, and the United Kingdom, among others.

I was then able to fully delve into the book's topic thanks to research funding provided by the European Union, namely a Marie Curie Fellowship at the European University Institute (EUI) in Florence, Italy. This project received funding from the EU's Horizon 2020 Research and Innovation Programme under the

Marie Skłodowska-Curie grant agreement No. 752790. I am very grateful to Ulrich Krotz for his steadfast support and friendship, and for allowing me to present my project in the seminar series of the *Europe in the World* programme at the EUI's Robert Schuman Centre for Advanced Studies, where I benefitted from excellent feedback. I finalized the manuscript of this book at Sciences Po's Centre for International Studies (CERI), where I was recruited as CNRS Research Fellow in 2019. There, as a founding member of the Franco-German Observatory of the Indo-Pacific co-organized by Sciences Po-CERI and the German Institute for Global and Area Studies (GIGA), I greatly profited from such a stimulating academic environment and from the seminar series organized by the Observatory.

Along this journey, I also immensely benefitted from the input and feedback of numerous colleagues and friends. With Stephen G. Brooks we collaborated on a project on European defence and security policies, distinct from this book, which nonetheless displayed several overlapping areas and themes with this monograph, including European threat perceptions and defence capabilities. This collaboration considerably sharpened my capacity to construct the architecture of a scholarly argument and, more broadly, to thoroughly think and write about international security issues. Likewise, at various stages of the writing process, I have been lucky to be able to count on advice and feedback from Nicolas Blarel, Pietro Castelli Gattinara, Natalia De Lima Bracarense, Benjamin Dodman, Mario Del Pero, Samuel Faure, Caterina Froio, Mauro Gilli, Francesca Ghiretti, Clément Godbarge, Frédéric Grare, John Hemmings, Van Jackson, Jean Joana, Alexander Lanoszka, Mélissa Levaillant, Meia Nouwens, Avinash Paliwal, Alessio Patalano, Giulio Pugliese, Luis Simón, Bruno Tertrais, Jurek Wille, and Marco Wyss. Needless to say, all errors and omissions are my responsibility only. I am also very grateful to Konstantin Jannone and Maximilian Reinold for their outstanding research assistance.

At Oxford University Press, I wish to thank Dominic Byatt, Commissioning Editor for Politics and International Relations, who embraced this project from its inception and offered invaluable support throughout the writing and production process. Céline Louasli, Ryan Morris and Sharmila Radha guided me smoothly through the final stages of the process and Susan Frampton meticulously copy-edited the entire volume. Last but not least, I am thankful to all the current and former officials who were interviewed for this book for accepting to share their views and experience, and for their availability.

Contents

List of Figures and Tables ix
List of Acronyms x

Introduction: Europe's Awakening to the Rise of China 1

I. CONFRONTING CHINA'S ASSERTIVENESS IN THE ASIA-PACIFIC

Introduction: China in the Asia-Pacific: From Peaceful Rise to Regional Hegemony 17

1. Pulled East: French Foreign and Security Policy in the Asia-Pacific 22

2. The Reluctant European Power: Germany in Asian-Pacific Security 61

3. Ripples of Empire: China's Rise and British Regional Policy to the East of Suez 88

II. RESPONDING TO CHINA'S ASSERTIVENESS IN EUROPE

Introduction: Inroads into Europe: Beijing's Deepening Foothold on the Continent 127

4. France and the Rise of China: From Open Door to Clear-Eyed 137

5. Germany's 'China Policy': Engagement, Resilience, Leverage 169

6. The China Challenge: Rebalancing Economics and National Security in UK Foreign Policy 195

Conclusion: Europe in the Midst of the United States–China Rivalry 226

APPENDICES

Appendix A. Data, Sources, and Chart on France and the
United Kingdom's Naval Deployments in the Asia-Pacific   245

Appendix B. Data, Sources, and Charts on FDIs, Trade, and
Arms Transfers   249

Bibliography   257
Index   311

List of Figures and Tables

Figures

1.1.	Deployments of French navy's capital ships in the Indian and Pacific Oceans, 2012–2019	44
3.1.	Deployments of Royal Navy's capital ships in the Indian and Pacific Oceans, 2009–2019	114
A.1.	Big Three's power-projection units capable of deployments in the Asia-Pacific, 2018	248
B.1.	The Big Three's total trade (exports + imports) with China and the Asia-Pacific (US$ bn)	254
B.2.	The Big Three's FDIs to and from China	255
B.3.	The European Union (27 + United Kingdom) FDIs to and from China	256

Tables

1.1.	French navy's capital ships deployed in the Indian and Pacific Oceans, 2012–2019	45
3.1.	UK MoD personnel in the Asia-Pacific and Indian Ocean Region, 2021	92
3.2.	Royal Navy's capital ships and naval support helicopters in the Indian and Pacific Oceans, 2009–2019	115

List of Acronyms

Note on acronyms: for the purpose of clarity and simplicity, the book refers to the same name of a ministry even if the name changed during the 1990–2020 timeframe.

21CN	21st Century Network
ACG	American Council on Germany
ADIZ	Air Defence Identification Zone
ADMM+	ASEAN Defence Ministers Meeting Plus
AEI	American Enterprise Institute
AFII	French Agency for International Investments
AIIB	Asia Infrastructure Investment Bank
ALPACI	French command of the Pacific Ocean maritime zone
ANSSI	French national cybersecurity agency
APT 10	Advanced Persistent Threat 10
ARCEP	Postal and Print Media Distribution Regulatory Authority
ARF	ASEAN Regional Forum
ASEAN	Association of Southeast Asian Nations
ASEM	Asia–Europe Meeting
ASIAPAC	Directorate for Asia and the Pacific
ASL	Anti-Secession Law
AUKMIN	Australia–United Kingdom Ministerial Consultations
AUKUS	Australia, United Kingdom, United States Enhanced Trilateral Security Partnership
AVIC	Aviation Industry Corporation of China
BOP	Balance of Payment Principle
BDI	Federation of German Industries
BDSSU	British Defence Singapore Support Unit
BEIS	Department for Business, Energy and Industrial Strategy
BIOT	British Indian Ocean Territory
BMI	Federal Ministry of the Interior
BND	Federal Intelligence Service
BRI	Belt and Road Initiative
BSI	Federal Office for Information Security
C2	Command and Control
C&ESAR	Computer & Electronics Security Applications Rendez-vous
CADN	Centre of Diplomatic Archives in Nantes
CAI	Comprehensive Agreement on Investment
CASIC	China Aerospace and Industry Group

CASIL	China Airport Synergy Investment Limited
CBBC	China-Britain Business Council
CBM	Cross Border Monitor
CCP	Chinese Communist Party
CEO	Chief Executive Officer
CERI	Centre for International Studies, Sciences Po
CFSP	Common Foreign and Security Policy
CGN	China General Nuclear Power Group
CIC	China Investment Corporation
CLCS	Commission on the Limits of the Continental Shelf
CMC	Central Military Commission
CMF	Combined Maritime Force
CMI	commercial-military integration
CMP	Coordinated Maritime Presences
COASI	Asia-Oceania Working Party
COREPER	Committee of Permanent Representatives
CORDIS	Community Research and Development Information Service
CPS	cyber-physical system
CRG	China Research Group
CRIMARIO II	Critical Maritime Routes in the Indian Ocean II
CSDP	Common Security and Defence Policy
CSIRT	Computer Security Incident Response Team
CWG	China Working Group
DCMS	Department for Culture, Media and Sport
DGRIS	Directorate General for International Relations and Strategy
DISP	Defence and International Security Partnership
DIT	Department for International Trade
DSEI	Defence and Security Equipment International
DTIB	Defence and Technological Industrial Base
DW	Deutsche Welle
EAS	East Asia Summit
EEAS	European External Action Service
EC	European Community
ECFR	European Council on Foreign Relations
EDF	Électricité de France
EEAS	European External Action Service
EEZ	Exclusive Economic Zone
ENISA	European Union Agency for Cybersecurity
EPA	European Union–Japan Economic Partnership Agreement
EPRS	European Parliamentary Research Service
EUI	European University Institute
EUNAVFOR	European Naval Force
FA/APS	Private Secretary for Foreign Affairs to the Prime Minister
FCO/FCDO	Foreign and Commonwealth Office/Foreign, Commonwealth & Development Office

FDI	Foreign Direct Investment
FFO	Federal Foreign Office
FMEA	Federal Ministry of Economic Affairs
FMI	Federal Ministry of the Interior
FMoD	Federal Ministry of Defence
FOIA	Freedom of Information Act
FOI	Freedom of Information Request
FONOPs	Freedom of Navigation Operations
FPDA	Five Power Defence Arrangement
GAO	Government Accountability Office
GCHQ	Government Communications Headquarters
GDP	gross domestic product
GIGA	German Institute for Global and Area Studies
HCSEC	Huawei Cyber Security Evaluation Centre
HMG	Her Majesty's Government
HoC	House of Commons
HQ IADS	Integrated Area Defence System Headquarters
HRV	high-risk vendor
HR/VP	High Representative/Vice-President
ERC	Huawei European Research Center
ICT	Information and Communications Technology
IFC	Information Fusion Centre
IFC-IOR	Information Fusion Centre for the Indian Ocean Region
IFRI	French Institute of International Relations
IGPDE	Institute for Public Management and Economic Development
IISS	International Institute for Strategic Studies
INDOPACOM	US Indo-Pacific Command
IONS	Indian Ocean Naval Symposium
IORA	Indian Ocean Rim Association
IoT	Internet of Things
IRSEM	Institute for Strategic Research
ISC	Intelligence and Security Committee
ISR	Intelligence, Surveillance, and Reconnaissance
JIC	Joint Intelligence Committee
JDFPG	Joint Defence Facility Pine Gap
JMCGS	Joint Military Communications Ground Station
JMSDF	Japan Maritime Self-Defence Force
KfW	Kreditanstalt für Wiederaufbau
M&A	Mergers and Acquisitions
MAICC	Maritime Area of Interest Coordination Cell
MEF	Ministry for the Economy and Finance
MERICS	Mercator Institute for China Studies
MFA	Ministry of Foreign Affairs
MFEA	Federal Ministry of Economic Affairs
MiC 2025	Made in China 2025

MoD	Ministry of Defence
MOFCOM	Chinese Ministry of Commerce
MOST	Ministry of Science and Technology
MoU	Memorandum of Understanding
MP	Member of Parliament
NAO	National Audit Office
NATO	North Atlantic Treaty Organization
NBS	National Bureau of Statistics of China
NCSC	National Cyber Security Centre
NIS	Network and Information Systems
NSA	National Security Agency
NSL	National Security Law
OECD	Organisation for Economic Co-operation and Development
ONISTS	National Security Science and Technology Observatory
OSD	Office of the Secretary of Defence
PAAA	Political Archive of the German Federal Foreign Office
PACOM	US Pacific Command
PACTE	Action Plan for Business Growth and Transformation
PAFMM	People's Armed Forces Maritime Militia
PLA	People's Liberation Army
PMO	Prime Minister's Office
PPS	Policy Planning Staff
PREM	Prime Minister's Office Record
PRC	People's Republic of China
R&D	research and development
RAFBP	Royal Air Force Butterworth and Penang Association
RAN	Radio Access Network
ReCAAP	Regional Cooperation Agreement on Combating Piracy and Armed Robbery against Ships in Asia
RHG	Rhodium Group
RIMPAC	Rim of the Pacific Exercise
RMAF	Royal Malaysian Air Force
RMB	Renminbi
S&T	Science and Technology
SEPEP	Société Européenne de Production d'Écrans Plats
SGAE	General Secretariat for European Affairs
SGDN	Secretariat-General for National Defence
SGDSN	Secretariat-General for National Defence and Security
SAIC	Shanghai Automotive Industrial Corporation
SIGINT	signals intelligence
SIPRI	Stockholm International Peace Research Institute
SLD	Shangri-La Dialogue
SLOCs	Sea Lines of Communication
SOE	State-owned enterprise
SPDMM	South Pacific Defence Ministers' Meeting

TKMS	ThyssenKrupp Marine Systems
TEU	Treaty on European Union
TIV	Trend-Indicator Value
TNA	The National Archives
TSR	Telecoms Security Requirements
UN Comtrade	United Nations International Trade Statistics Database
UNCTAD	United Nations Conference on Trade and Development
UNSD	United Nations Statistics Division
UKUSA	United Kingdom-United States of America Agreement
USNS	US Naval Ship
WITS	World Bank's World Integrated Trade Solution
WTO	World Trade Organization

Introduction

Europe's Awakening to the Rise of China

For a long time, the major European powers looked at China through predominantly economic lenses, as a faraway market that offered tremendous opportunities. In the 1990s, France's relations with the People's Republic of China (PRC) found their 'main and perhaps only raison d'être', as a declassified diplomatic cable puts it, 'in the pursuit of our economic interests and our influence on a huge market with great potential'.[1] Accordingly, the aerospace corporation Airbus agreed to transfer dual-use manufacturing technologies and production lines used in the making of A320 wings components to the state-owned China Aviation Industry Corporation (AVIC).[2] Germany, for its part, aggressively pursued economic opportunities in this vast, emerging market, becoming the economically most successful European country in China and, more broadly, in the Asia-Pacific.[3] A case in point was the German car company Volkswagen (VW) which enjoyed the first-mover advantage in China and, by the mid-2000s, reached a local market share of more than 30 per cent, becoming China's leading carmaker.[4] Likewise, after the retrocession of Hong Kong to the PRC in 1997, the United

---

[1] French Embassy in China to Ministry of Foreign Affairs, 'Relations bilatérales franco-chinoises', 30 January 1992a, French Centre of Diplomatic Archives in Nantes (CADN), 513PO/2004038.
[2] See 'Airbus Celebrates Technology Transfer to China', China.org, 1 April 2005, www.china.org.cn/english/scitech/124458.htm; and Sören Eriksson, 'China's Aircraft Industry: Collaboration and Technology Transfer—The Case of Airbus', *International Journal of Technology Transfer and Commercialisation 9*, no. 4 (2010): pp. 306–325. Dual-use refers to commodities, software, or technologies that have both commercial and military applications. They may be developed for military purposes and then be applied commercially or vice versa.
[3] On the economic opportunities offered by the Chinese market, see Federal Government, *The Federal Government's Concept on Asia*, 22 September 1993, https://www.asienhaus.de/public/archiv/brdasia.htm.
[4] VW established two joint ventures in China, one with Shanghai Automotive Industrial Corporation (SAIC) in 1983, and one with First Automotive Work (FAW) in 1991, subsequently creating the Volkswagen Group China, in 2004, for coordination and management of activities of the Volkswagen Group within China. Data for 2003 retrieved from Shenxue Li, Mark Easterby-Smith, and Marjorie A. Lyles, 'Overcoming Corporate Rigidities in the Dynamic Chinese Market', *Business Horizons 51* (2008), p. 501; see also 'China Sector Watch: Automobiles', *China Briefing*, 29 May 2009, https://www.china-briefing.com/news/china-sector-watch-automobiles/; and Jörg Mull, Executive Vice President for Finance, Presentation on the Volkswagen Group China, Beijing, 27 November 2012, p. 3, https://www.volkswagenag.com/presence/investorrelation/publications/presentations/2012/03-march/Presentation_Dr_Mull.pdf (accessed 9 June 2021).

Kingdom's approach towards Beijing was, in the words of one official, 'one of engagement, engagement, engagement'.[5]

Fast-forward two decades later, however, and Europe's three major powers had all developed an 'Indo-Pacific' strategy, bolstered their diplomatic and security presence in the region, hardened their stance towards Beijing, established screening mechanisms to monitor and block Chinese investments in Europe, and imposed restrictions on the supply of 5G telecommunications equipment by Chinese companies like Huawei. What explains this stark policy shift? To address this question, this book examines how Europe's major powers (France, Germany, and the United Kingdom) have responded to the national security challenges posed by the rise of China since 1989.[6]

The re-emergence of China as a great power and the intensifying United States–China competition have marked the return of great power rivalry in world politics, with wide-ranging implications for Europeans. In particular, three overarching trends have provided the context within which the major European powers have confronted China's rise. For one, in light of the shifting centre of strategic gravity of world politics from the Atlantic to the Asia-Pacific, the gradual retrenchment of the United States from Europe since the end of the Cold War—coupled with growing doubts about the credibility of US commitments to the continent—has incited Europe's major powers to increasingly provide for their own security.[7] Furthermore, sustained by expanding economic, military, and technological capabilities, the PRC has displayed an ever more assertive foreign policy both in the Asia-Pacific and in Europe since the 2010s, which impinges upon a broad range of European diplomatic, security, and economic interests.[8] Thirdly, the rising global

---

[5] Parliamentary Under-Secretary of State for Foreign and Commonwealth Affairs Denis MacShane, in House of Commons (HoC), *China*, HoC Hansard, Vol. 387, 18 June 2002, https://publications.parliament.uk/pa/cm200102/cmhansrd/vo020618/halltext/20618h01.htm.

[6] 1989 witnessed both the fall of the Berlin Wall and the crackdown on the students' demonstration on Tiananmen Square in Beijing which, combined, marked a major turning point in the relations between Europe's major powers—and the then European Community (EC) more broadly—and the PRC. See Mary Elise Sarotte, *1989: The Struggle to Create Post-Cold War Europe* (Princeton, NJ: Princeton University Press, 2009); Jeffrey A. Engel, ed., *The Fall of the Berlin Wall: The Revolutionary Legacy of 1989* (Oxford: Oxford University Press, 2009); Kristina Spohr, *Post Wall, Post Square: Rebuilding the World after 1989* (London: William Collins, 2009).

[7] See, for instance, Jolyon Howorth, 'Implications of the US Rebalance toward Asia: European Security and NATO', in *Origins and Evolution of the US Rebalance toward Asia: Diplomatic, Military, and Economic Dimensions*, edited by Hugo Meijer (New York: Palgrave Macmillan, 2015), pp. 197–222; Hugo Meijer and Stephen G. Brooks, 'Illusions of Autonomy: Why Europe Cannot Provide for its Security If the United States Pulls Back', *International Security* 45, no. 4 (Spring 2021): pp. 7–8; Luis Simón, 'Europe, the Rise of Asia and the Future of the Transatlantic Relationship', *International Affairs* 91, no. 5 (2015): pp. 969–989.

[8] On Chinese assertiveness after 2009, see the Introductions of Part I and Part II as well as, among others, Michael Yahuda, 'China's New Assertiveness in the South China Sea', *Journal of Contemporary China* 22, no. 81 (2013): pp. 446–459; Nien-Chung Chang Lao, 'The Sources of China's Assertiveness: The System, Domestic Politics or Leadership Preferences?', *International Affairs* 92, no. 4 (2016): pp. 817–833; Janka Oertel, 'The New China Consensus: How Europe Is Growing Wary of Beijing', *ECFR Policy Brief*, September 2020; Julianne Smith and Torrey Taussig, 'The Old World and the Middle Kingdom: Europe Wakes up to China's Rise', *Foreign Affairs*, September/October 2019; Peter Ferdinand,

competition between the United States and China has become a structural feature of great power politics in the twenty-first century, with ramifications across different regions, including Europe.⁹ In short, stuck between a rock and a hard place, the major European powers increasingly doubt the robustness of the US ally's commitment to their security while grappling with China's expanding clout and influence in the larger context of mounting Sino-American rivalry—and they are thus compelled to define their own position therein.

Yet, we know little about how Europeans have dealt with the security implications of China's rise. The existing scholarly literature has often assumed that European foreign policies towards the PRC have been driven by a 'naïve' and self-interested focus on the economic opportunities offered by this large and emerging market, largely ignoring security considerations.¹⁰ This book challenges such conventional wisdom. Through a detailed examination of the policies of France, Germany and the United Kingdom it shows that China's shifting foreign policy behaviour, as an exogenous driver, has affected their national threat perceptions and economic interests which, in turn, has influenced the policy goals and the policy instruments mobilized in the pursuit of these goals. In the 1990s and 2000s, in light of China's restrained and low-key foreign policy, Europeans displayed a low threat assessment and indeed looked at the PRC primarily through economic lenses. However, China's growing assertiveness after 2009—and national policymakers' perceptions of it—has been the key driver of change in their policies toward Beijing.¹¹ Throughout the 2010s, heightened threat perceptions of China, coupled with increasingly competitive bilateral economic relations with the PRC, have gradually and cumulatively caused the hardening of their policy goals which,

---

'Westward Ho—The China Dream and "One Belt, One Road": Chinese Foreign Policy under Xi Jinping', *International Affairs* 92, no 4 (2016): pp. 941–957. For a different periodization, see Andrew Chubb, 'PRC Assertiveness in the South China Sea: Measuring Continuity and Change, 1970–2015', *International Security* 45, no. 3 (2021): pp. 79–121. For a contrarian perspective arguing that China did not become more assertive, see Alastair Iain Johnston, 'How New and Assertive Is China's New Assertiveness?', *International Security* 34, no. 4 (2013): pp. 35–45; and Dingding Chen, Xiaoyu Pu, and Alastair Iain Johnston, 'Debating China's Assertiveness', *International Security* 38, no. 3 (2014): pp. 176–183.

⁹ On US-China competition, see, e.g., Aaron L. Friedberg, 'Competing with China', *Survival* 60, no. 3 (2018): pp. 7–64; Aaron L. Friedberg, *A Contest for Supremacy: China, America, and the Struggle for Mastery in Asia* (New York: W.W. Norton & Company, 2011); Iskander Rehman (chair), 'Policy Roundtable: Are the United States and China in a New Cold War?', *Texas National Security Review*, 15 May 2018b; Huiyun Feng and Kai He, eds, *US–China Competition and the South China Sea Disputes* (New York: Routledge, 2018); Yuen Foong Khong, 'Primacy or World Order? The United States and China's Rise—A Review Essay', *International Security* 38, no. 3 (2013/14): pp. 153–175; David Shambaugh, *Where Great Powers Meet: America and China in Southeast Asia* (New York: Oxford University Press, 2021); Minghao Zhao, 'Is a New Cold War Inevitable? Chinese Perspectives on US–China Strategic Competition', *The Chinese Journal of International Politics* 12, no. 3 (2019): pp. 371–394; Michael Beckley and Hal Brands, 'Competition with China Could Be Short and Sharp', *Foreign Affairs*, 17 December 2020.

¹⁰ See the section 'Contribution to the Literature'.

¹¹ On Chinese assertiveness after 2009, see the Introductions of Part I and Part II as well as footnote 8.

in turn, translated into the formulation of new, more stringent policy instruments to confront such a challenge. In short, as a result of Beijing's growing assertiveness in the Asia-Pacific, in Europe and beyond, the major European powers have awakened to the security challenges posed by the rise of China.

To substantiate this argument, the book relies upon a large body of previously undisclosed primary written and oral sources to examine the evolution of the policies of Europe's major powers vis-à-vis China since 1989 in two key regions. First, it analyses their response to China's increasingly muscular regional posture in the Asia-Pacific through the development of diplomatic and security initiatives with partners in the region. Second, it delineates how they have confronted China's inroads into Europe, looking at the measures that they have taken to tackle the security challenges posed by Chinese investments in, and supply of, technologies in strategic sectors such as critical national infrastructures, dual-use technologies, and in the digital domain, including 5G networks.

Admittedly, the question of how Europe's major powers wrestle with the security challenges posed by China's rise goes beyond these two regions. How they respond to China's growing influence in Africa, the Middle East, or Central Asia as well as in global governance issues (e.g. climate change or non-proliferation) is certainly relevant. Yet, this book focuses on a circumscribed but crucial dimension of this larger question, namely two key regions in which China's behaviour impinges upon the national security of Europe's major powers.[12]

In the Asia-Pacific, Beijing's territorial disputes and contested sovereignty claims in the East and South China Seas, its growing regional might, and the ensuing geopolitical tensions threaten to destabilize the regional balance of power as well as vital sea lines of communication (SLOCs) upon which Europe's economic prosperity increasingly relies. Although China's contestation of the regional order in the Asia-Pacific may not be seen as crucial to European security, this region is today a pivot of international politics—where China's leverage and influence are the most robust and direct—and is thus central to any discussion about the foreign and security policies of European major powers and about their role in world politics.

The second area explored in this book is a mirror image of the first. China's inroads in the European continent itself through aggressive investments in sensitive

---

[12] While this book does touch upon the economic policy instruments developed by the three countries (such as free-trade agreements, the EU Connectivity Strategy or the EU–China Comprehensive Investment Agreement), its organizing compass specifically revolves around how they have confronted the perceived national security challenges posed by China's rise. Rather than providing an in-depth analysis of their economic policies, it therefore focuses (i) on their political-military engagement in the Asia-Pacific and (ii) on the policy instruments developed by the three countries in response to China's growing presence in Europe's strategic sectors, i.e. investment screening mechanisms and restrictions on telecoms suppliers of concern.

technologies is where the rise of China has been most directly felt by Europeans in that it has fuelled rising national security concerns over the protection of strategic sectors. China's foothold on the continent has widened through, among others, increased foreign direct investments (FDIs)—including in sensitive areas such as dual-use sectors and critical national infrastructures—and the supply of advanced telecommunications equipment for Europe's digital infrastructure by companies linked to the Chinese state, such as Huawei. And while this domain may not be considered as key to the larger debate about the geopolitical implications of China's rise in world politics, it is increasingly central to any European discussions on how to confront the PRC.

The common denominator in both regions is that China has displayed an increasingly assertive behaviour in the aftermath of the 2008 financial crisis and especially after 2009, as shown by a large body of literature.[13] Undeniably, as further detailed in this book, Chinese assertiveness has exhibited partly different characteristics in the two regions. In the Asia-Pacific, Beijing moved away from the low-key regional posture of the 1990s and 2000s and sought to expand its geopolitical and economic clout within its home region with the goal of establishing a Sino-centric regional order. In faraway Europe, Chinese assertiveness has largely taken the form of a deeper and more pervasive economic foothold on the continent, with aggressive acquisitions in strategic sectors, and in the resulting enhanced political leverage over some European countries. Yet, in both regions, Chinese behaviour has stemmed from a common driver: the growing capabilities and the ambition of the leadership in Beijing to expand the country's reach and influence globally. The cross-regional analysis put forward in this book aims to shed light on how the major European powers have perceived the security challenges posed by China's rising assertiveness and to compare the combination of diplomatic, military, and industrial policy instruments they have mobilized, in response thereto, both in Europe and in the Asia-Pacific.

Rather than primarily focusing on the relations between the European Union and China, *Awakening to China's Rise* takes as its analytical compass the comparative study of national foreign and security policies. As detailed below, most of the existing studies on European foreign and security policy towards the PRC tend to concentrate on European Union-China relations, overlooking the thorough analysis of the national policies that underpin the EU Common Foreign and Security Policy (CFSP), if and when such common policy exists.[14] Yet, the management of European foreign and security policies towards China, especially in policy areas linked to national security like those examined in this book, largely

---

[13] For details on the drivers and characteristics of Chinese assertiveness in the Asia-Pacific and in Europe after 2009, see the Introductions of Part I and II respectively and footnote 8.
[14] See the section 'Contribution to Literature'.

remains the prerogative of nation-states rather than of the European Union. As stated by the Treaty on European Union (TEU), which sets out the EU's goals and principles, 'national security remains the sole responsibility of each Member State' (Art. 4).[15] Therefore, it is necessary to turn the dominant analytical lens of the literature upside down and to give analytical precedence to the comparative study of national foreign and security policies.[16] To be sure, since some competences that are relevant for the purpose of this study are located at the EU level (such as in the domain of FDIs), this book also examines those instances in which the major European powers have sought to cooperate through or with EU institutions. Nonetheless, it gives analytical precedence to the comparative analysis of national foreign and security policies and then examines whether, and to what extent, individual countries have channelled their policies and cooperated through (and with) EU institutions.

In this comparative endeavour, the book does not examine the policy responses of all European states to China's rise but rather focuses on Europe's three major powers—i.e. France, Germany, and the United Kingdom (the 'Big Three'). These three countries are the major diplomatic, economic, and military powers in Europe and are all NATO allies. Furthermore, they are the only European countries with the diplomatic, economic, and military capabilities that would be required to sustain a political-military engagement in the Asia-Pacific region, and they have also been the largest recipients of Chinese FDIs in Europe.[17]

Contribution to the Literature

Despite the rise of China as a major world power and its substantial national security ramifications for Europe, this dimension of European foreign and security policy has long been neglected in the international relations (IR) and security studies literature. A voluminous body of scholarship has investigated when and how the United States rebalanced its foreign and security policy towards the Asia-Pacific as well as the reordering of Washington's alliances and security partnerships in the region to confront the PRC.[18] The response by Asia-Pacific

---

[15] Eur-Lex, 'Consolidated version of the Treaty on European Union—Title I Common Provisions—Article 4', https://eur-lex.europa.eu/legal-content/EN/TXT/?uri=CELEX%3A12012M004.

[16] On the need to give analytical precedence to the comparative study of national policies before focusing on the EU-level, see Hugo Meijer and Marco Wyss, 'Upside Down: Reframing European Defence Studies', *Cooperation and Conflict 54*, no. 3 (2019): pp. 378–406.

[17] See Thilo Hanemann, Mikko Huotari, and Agatha Kratz, *Chinese FDI in Europe: 2018 Trends and Impact of New Screening Policies*, Report by Rhodium Group (RHG) and the Mercator Institute for China Studies (MERICS), March 2019, p. 7 (2018 figures); and Agatha Kratz, Max J. Zenglein, and Gregor Sebastian, *Chinese FDI in Europe—2020 Update*, MERICS/Rhodium Group, June 2021. For more details on Chinese investments in Europe, see the introduction and chapters of Part II and Appendix B.

[18] See for instance Kurt M. Campbell, *The Pivot: The Future of American Statecraft in Asia* (New York: Basic Books, 2016); Victor D. Cha, *Powerplay: The Origins of the American Alliance System in*

countries to China's expanding regional clout and ambitions, and their alignment behaviour, have similarly been the subject of a burgeoning literature.[19] By contrast, the question of how Europe's major powers have sought to confront the security implications of China's rise—comparing their policies both in Europe and in the Asia-Pacific—largely remains a blind spot in the scholarly literature.

Most existing studies on European foreign and security policies focus on transatlantic relations[20] or on Europe's 'near abroad', namely Russia and the Eastern neighbourhood[21] or the Middle East and Northern Africa.[22] And while a growing body of literature has touched upon various aspects of European foreign and security policies towards China and in the Asia-Pacific, these works nonetheless display several major shortcomings.

For one, as previously mentioned, they focus almost exclusively on European Union–China or European Union–Asia relations, largely neglecting the in-depth analysis of national foreign and security policies.[23] Secondly, the few studies that

---

Asia (Princeton, NJ: Princeton University Press, 2016); Nina Silove, 'The Pivot before the Pivot: U.S. Strategy to Preserve the Power Balance in Asia', *International Security* 40, no. 4 (2016): pp. 45–88; Luis Simón, Alexander Lanoszka, and Hugo Meijer, 'Nodal Defence: The Changing Structure of U.S. Alliance Systems in Europe and East Asia', *Journal of Strategic Studies* 44, no. 3 (2021): pp. 360–388; Hugo Meijer, 'Shaping China's Rise: The Reordering of U.S. Alliances and Defense Partnerships in East Asia', *International Politics* 57, no. 2 (2020): pp. 166–184.

[19] Michael Beckley, 'The Emerging Military Balance in East Asia: How China's Neighbours Can Check Chinese Naval Expansion', *International Security* 42, no. 2 (2017): pp. 78–119; John D. Ciorciari, *The Limits of Alignment: Southeast Asia and the Great Powers since 1975* (Washington, DC: Georgetown University Press, 2010); Adam P. Liff, 'Whither the Balancers? The Case for a Methodological Reset', *Security Studies* 25, no. 3 (2016): pp. 420–459; Darren J. Lim and Zack Cooper, 'Reassessing Hedging: The Logic of Alignment in East Asia', *Security Studies* 24, no. 4 (2015): pp. 696–727; David Shambaugh, 'U.S.–China Rivalry in Southeast Asia: Power Shift or Competitive Coexistence?', *International Security* 42, no. 4 (2018): pp. 85–127; Hugo Meijer and Luis Simón, 'Covert Balancing: Great Powers, Secondary States and US Balancing Strategies against China', *International Affairs* 82, no. 2 (2021): pp. 463–481.

[20] See, e.g. Ulrich Krotz, *History and Foreign Policy in France and Germany* (New York: Palgrave Macmillan, 2015); Janne Haaland Matlary and Magnus Petersson, eds, *NATO's European Allies Military Capability and Political Will* (Basingstoke: Palgrave Macmillan, 2013); Luis Simón, *Geopolitical Change, Grand Strategy and European Security: The EU-NATO Conundrum* (New York: Palgrave Macmillan, 2013).

[21] See, among others, Tuomas Forsberg and Hiski Haukkala, *The European Union and Russia* (New York: Palgrave Macmillan, 2016); Beatrix Futák-Campbell, *Practising EU Foreign Policy: Russia and the Eastern Neighbours* (Manchester: Manchester University Press, 2017).

[22] On EU foreign policy in the Middle East and Northern Africa, see e.g. Maurizio Carbone, *The European Union in Africa: Incoherent Policies, Asymmetrical Partnership, Declining Relevance?* (New York: Palgrave Macmillan, 2013); and Patrick Müller, ed., *EU Foreign Policymaking and the Middle East Conflict: The Europeanization of National Foreign Policy* (New York, Routledge, 2012).

[23] See for example, Nicola Casarini, *Remaking Global Order: The Evolution of Europe–China Relations and its Implications for East Asia and the United States* (Oxford: Oxford University Press, 2009); Nicola Casarini, ed., *Brussels-Beijing: Changing the Game* (Paris, EUISS, 2013); Nicola Casarini, 'Rising to the Challenge: Europe's Security Policy in East Asia amid US–China Rivalry', *The International Spectator* 55, no. 1 (2020): pp. 78–92; Thomas Christiansen, Emil Kirchner, and Philomena B. Murray, eds, *The Palgrave Handbook of EU–Asia Relations* (London: Palgrave Macmillan, 2013); Andrew Cottey, 'Europe and China's Sea Disputes: Between Normative Politics, Power Balancing and Acquiescence', *European Security* 28, no. 4 (2019): pp. 473–492; Emil J. Kirchner, Thomas Christiansen, and Han Dorussen, eds, *Security Relations between China and the European Union: From Convergence to Cooperation?* (Cambridge: Cambridge University Press, 2016); Thomas Christiansen, Emil Kirchner, and Uwe Wissenbach, *The European Union and China* (London: Red Globe Press, 2019); Thomas Christiansen,

have focused on the foreign and security policies towards China of individual European states have often been limited to one discrete dimension, most notably arms exports.[24] Likewise, whereas Chinese investments in European strategic sectors have attracted scholarly attention,[25] no monograph has scrutinized the foreign and security policies of European states in the Asia-Pacific in the face of

---

Emil Kirchner, and See Seng Tan, eds, *The European Union's Security Relations with Asian Partners* (Cham, Switzerland: Palgrave Macmillan, 2021); David Kerr and Liu Fei, eds, *The International Politics of EU–China Relations* (Oxford: Oxford University Press, 2007); Frans-Paul van der Putten and Chu Shulong, eds, *China, Europe and International Security: Interests, Roles and Prospects* (London: Routledge, 2011); Eva Pejsova, ed., *Guns, Engines and Turbines: The EU's Hard Power in Asia* (Paris: EUISS, 2018); Michael Reiterer, 'The EU's Comprehensive Approach to Security in Asia', *European Foreign Affairs Review* 19, no. 1 (2014): pp. 1–22; Robert S. Ross, Øystein Tunsjø, and Tuosheng Zhang, eds, *US–China–EU Relations: Managing the New World Order* (London: Routledge, 2010); David Shambaugh, Eberhard Sandschneider, and Zhou Hong, eds, *China–Europe Relations: Perceptions, Policies, and Prospects* (New York: Routledge, 2007); May-Britt Stumbaum, *The European Union and China: Decision-Making in EU Foreign and Security Policy towards the People's Republic of China* (Baden-Baden: Nomos, 2009); Reuben Y. Wong, *The Europeanization of French Foreign Policy: France and the EU in East Asia* (New York: Palgrave, 2006). On EU–US cooperation on China and the Asia-Pacific, see, for instance, Fidel Sendagorta, 'The Triangle in the Long Game: Rethinking Relations between China, Europe, and the United States in the New Era of Strategic Competition', Belfer Center for Science and International Affairs, Harvard Kennedy School, 19 June 2019; Andrew Small, 'Transatlantic Cooperation on Asia and the Trump Administration', *GMF Policy Paper*, 30 October 2019; Andrew Small, Bonnie S. Glaser, and Garima Mohan, 'Closing the Gap: US-European Cooperation on China and the Indo-Pacific', Policy Paper, German Marshall Fund, February 2022; and Erik Brattberg and Philippe Le Corre, *The Case for Transatlantic Cooperation in the Indo-Pacific* (Washington, DC: Carnegie Endowment for International Peace, 2019). National perspectives on the EU's role amidst mounting US–China strategic competition were explored in a think tank report: Mario Esteban et al., eds, *Europe in the Face of US–China Rivalry*, European Think-tank Network on China, January 2020.

[24] On European arms transfers to China and on the EU arms embargo on the PRC, see Hugo Meijer, 'Transatlantic Perspectives on China's Military Modernization: The Case of Europe's Arms Embargo against the People's Republic of China', *Paris Paper no. 12*, Strategic Research Institute (IRSEM), 2014; Hugo Meijer, *Trading with the Enemy: The Making of US Export Control Policy toward the People's Republic of China* (New York: Oxford University Press, 2016), ch. 7; Hugo Meijer, Lucie Béraud-Sudreau, Paul Holtom, and Matthew Uttley, 'Arming China: Major Powers' Arms Transfers to the People's Republic of China', *Journal of Strategic Studies* 41, no. 6 (2018): pp. 850–886; Oliver Bräuner, Mark Bromley, and Mathieu Duchâtel, *Western Arms Exports to China* (Stockholm: SIPRI, 2015); Stumbaum, 2009, ch. 6; Scott A. W. Brown, *Power, Perception and Foreign Policymaking: US and EU Responses to the Rise of China* (New York, NY: Routledge, 2018), ch. 5. On European arms transfers to the Asia-Pacific, see Mathieu Duchâtel and Mark Bromley, 'Influence by Default: Europe's Impact on Military Security in East Asia', *ECFR Policy Brief*, May 2017.

[25] See, e.g. James Reilly, *Orchestration: China's Economic Statecraft Across Asia and Europe* (New York: Oxford University Press, 2021); Philippe Le Corre and Alain Sepulchre, *China's Offensive in Europe* (Washington, DC: Brookings Institution Press, 2016); Erik Brattberg et al., *China's Influence in Southeastern, Central, and Eastern Europe: Vulnerabilities and Resilience in Four Countries* (Washington, DC: Carnegie Endowment for International Peace, 2021); Sophie Meunier, 'Divide and Conquer? China and the Cacophony of Foreign Investment Rules in the EU', *Journal of European Public Policy* 21, no. 7 (2014): pp. 996–1016; Nicola Casarini, 'When All Roads Lead to Beijing: Assessing China's New Silk Road and its Implications for Europe', *The International Spectator* 51, no. 4 (2016): pp. 95–108; Ramon Pacheco Pardo, 'Europe's Financial Security and Chinese Economic Statecraft: The Case of the Belt and Road Initiative', *Asia-Europe Journal* 16, no. 3 (2018): pp. 237–250; Tim Wenniges and Walter Lohman, *Chinese FDI in the EU and the US: Simple Rules for Turbulent Times* (Singapore: Palgrave Macmillan, 2019). See also Dragan Pavlićević and Anastas Vangeli, 'New Perspectives on China–Central and Eastern Europe Relations', *Asia-Europe Journal* 17, no. 4 (2019), Special Issue.

a rising China.[26] Existing works have mostly focused on Europeans' approaches towards 'non-traditional' security issues in the Asia-Pacific (e.g. climate change or humanitarian disasters) rather than towards China's rise.[27] Finally, and crucially, the existing literature has stressed how European foreign policies towards the PRC have been mainly driven by economic interests rather than by security concerns—what Nicola Casarini refers to as 'the prioritization of commercial relations' as 'the basis for the upgrading of political relations'; a point also emphasized by numerous other scholars.[28] Yet, as shown in this book, in the 2010s, because of China's rising assertiveness, the major European powers' threat perceptions of the PRC intensified and—combined with increasingly competitive economic relations with Beijing—produced a significant policy shift.

Accordingly, through a novel cross-regional comparison, *Awakening to China's Rise* delivers the first post-Cold War history of how the main European powers have responded to the national security challenges posed by the rise of China looking at both Europe and the Asia-Pacific. By investigating this strategically crucial yet neglected dimension of the foreign and security policy of Europe's major powers, this book thus fills an important gap in the scholarly literature on both European and Asia-Pacific security dynamics. Its findings also shed new light on the assets that Europe's major powers can bring to bear in the formulation of a

---

[26] Only a limited number of scholarly and think-tank articles and policy papers have addressed this issue such as, for instance, Brattberg and Le Corre, 2019; Liselotte Odgaard, 'European Engagement in the Indo-Pacific: The Interplay between Institutional and State-Level Naval Diplomacy', *Asia Policy 14*, no. 4 (2019): pp. 129–159; Simón, 2015; Luis Simón and Stephan Klose, 'European Perspectives towards the Rise of Asia: Contextualising the Debate', *Asia-Europe Journal 14*, no. 3 (2016): pp. 239–260; and James Rogers, 'European (British and French) Geostrategy in the Indo-Pacific', *Journal of the Indian Ocean Region 9*, no. 1 (2013): pp. 69–89; Sharon Stirling, ed., *Mind the Gap: Naval Views of the Free and Open Indo-Pacific* (Washington, DC: The German Marshall Fund, 2019).

[27] On the EU and non-traditional security challenges in the Asia-Pacific, see for instance: Christiansen, Kirchner, and Tan, 2021; Thomas Christiansen, Emil Kirchner, and See Seng Tan, 'EU–Asia Security Relations—Cooperation against the Odds?', Paper presented at the 16th Biennial Conference of EUSA, Denver, May 2019; May-Britt Stumbaum, 'Impact of the Rebalance on Europe's Interest in East Asia: Consequences for Europe in Economic, Diplomatic, and Military/Security Dimensions', in *Origins and Evolution of the US Rebalance toward Asia: Diplomatic, Military, and Economic Dimensions*, edited by Hugo Meijer (New York: Palgrave Macmillan, 2015), pp. 223–252; Odgaard, 2019; Michael Reiterer, 'The EU's Comprehensive Approach to Security in Asia', *European Foreign Affairs Review 19*, no. 1 (2014): pp. 1–22.

[28] Casarini, 2009, p. 57. A comprehensive presentation of this argument can also be found in Scott Brown; he argues that the European Union has been characterized by a high degree of convergence around the perception that China opened significant economic and political opportunities for the European Union, rather than being a potential national security challenge (Brown, 2018, pp. 5, 30, 108, 197, 199, and 200, among others). Likewise, according to Kirchner, Dorussen, and Christiansen, although the political and security dimensions of the bilateral relationship have partly increased over time, 'the main drivers of EU–China relations have undoubtedly been of an economic nature, meaning primarily concerns with trade, investment, monetary and intellectual property issues' (Kirchner, Christiansen, and Dorussen, 2016, p. 1). Michael Yahuda concurs stressing that, historically, the relationship between Europeans and China has been characterized by 'the primacy of trade as the main conduit for and substance of their relationship' (Michael Yahuda, 'The Sino-European Encounter: Historical Influences on Contemporary Relations', in Shambaugh, Sandschneider, and Hong, 2007, p. 13).

common European policy towards China, on the repercussions of Brexit, and on the implications thereof for the prospect of a joint transatlantic strategy vis-à-vis China.

Primary Sources

To do so, the book relies on a broad and unique collection of primary written and oral sources (the written sources are presented in the Bibliography by category of source). For one, it draws on a large range of interviews: 223 interviews were conducted with senior officials in Europe (Berlin, Brussels, London, Paris), in the United States (Washington, DC), and in Asia (Beijing, Shanghai, New Delhi, Seoul) between January 2013 and December 2021. The interviewees include civilians and military policymakers with responsibilities for relations with China and the Asia-Pacific, political-military affairs, digital technology, and/or investment screening mechanisms in the ministries of foreign affairs, defence, interior, and economics/industry, in embassies in the Asia-Pacific and in the United States, in the interagency coordinating bodies in charge of politico-military affairs, in the respective intelligence communities and in the national military staffs (including chiefs of defence staffs). They also include advisers in the Offices of the British Prime Minister, of the French President and Prime Minister, and of the German Chancellor and President as well as officials in the European Commission and the European External Action Service (EEAS), the European Union's diplomatic service.[29] Interviews were also conducted with representatives of the high-tech industry, of its business associations, and of the national chambers of commerce in China.

Second, the book relies upon previously undisclosed declassified archival documents retrieved in various national archives located in France, Germany, and the United Kingdom. Specifically, these archives include: the French Centre of Diplomatic Archives in Nantes (CADN);[30] the Political Archive of the German Federal Foreign Office (PAAA);[31] and the National Archives (TNA) of the United Kingdom.[32] Data on the United Kingdom's military presence in the Asia-Pacific were

---

[29] For each direct quote, the interviewees were asked for a prior written approval; those who declined were anonymized. The degree of anonymization was agreed upon with the interviewees (e.g. with or without reference to their job title, Ministry, etc.). Quotes from interviews in French were translated by the author. Because of the restrictions linked to the Covid-19 pandemic, some interviews were conducted through virtual meetings or by telephone. Given the particular empirical focus of this book, as well as the practical constraints of conducting research on this topic in China, the interviews in the PRC have been mainly conducted with officials in European embassies and with Chinese experts in universities and think tanks both in Beijing and Shanghai.

[30] Folder 'Ambassade de France à Pékin, 1989–1992', 513PO/2004038, CADN.

[31] Folder 'Bilaterale politische Beziehungen', in *Süd- und Ostasien, Australien, Neuseeland und Ozeanien*, 1989, Politisches Archiv des Auswärtigen Amts (PAAA), B 37-ZA/161825.

[32] Folder 'Foreign Policy: EU/Asia Summit', Prime Minister's Office Record (PREM) 19/5633, TNA.

also obtained from the British Ministry of Defence through several Freedom of Information requests under the Freedom of Information Act (FOIA) as well as in the MoD's *Annual Location Statistics for UK Regular Service and Civilian Personnel*.[33]

Third, this study leverages a large body of diplomatic cables leaked by Wikileaks/Cablegate (1990–2010). These cables bring to light the debates (and the key considerations therein) between the diplomats of the three European countries and their American counterparts over their respective foreign and security policies towards China. Dozens of relevant cables were found in the Wikileaks/Cablegate archive, including documents to and from the State Department and the US embassies in Beijing, Brussels, The Hague, Madrid, Paris, Rome, Stockholm, Vienna, the American Institute in Taiwan, and the US Mission to the European Union. The data gathered through these leaked diplomatic cables provide valuable evidence on British, French, and German policymakers' threat perceptions of China, on their policy responses thereto, and on their consultations with the US over the PRC especially in the 2000s and early 2010s (2010). In this book, only part of this large body of documents is referenced.

Fourth, this monograph draws upon a comprehensive examination of more than 540 executive branch publications, parliamentary reports, national policymakers' speeches and their statements in front of parliamentary committees and subcommittees with responsibilities for the Asia-Pacific, European affairs, and investments.[34] For the United Kingdom, public statements were also found in the House of Commons' Hansard, i.e. the verbatim reports of what is said in Parliament. While the bulk of the executive branch and parliamentary publications used in this book revolves around the Big Three and the European Union, these sources encompass a much wider range of countries that also include Australia, India, Japan, the Netherlands, the People's Republic of China, Singapore, the United States, as well as international and regional organizations such as the North Atlantic Treaty Organization (NATO) or the Association of Southeast Asian Nations (ASEAN), among others.

Finally, the book provides new data on the naval deployments in the Asia-Pacific by the capital ships of the three European powers' navies by combining the available primary and secondary sources. The data include the type and name of these capital ships and the missions (and dates) in which they were deployed. For France, the data were retrieved from the magazine of the French Navy, *Cols Bleus*. For the United Kingdom and Germany, they were both obtained from the websites of their respective Ministries of Defence and from existing secondary sources (for more details, see Appendix A which also includes a chart comparing the Big Three's naval assets capable of deployment in the Asia-Pacific). This study also

---

[33] The author submitted six separate Freedom of Information Requests: FOI2021/0869, FOI2021/08470, FOI2021/09732, FOI2021/11244, FOI2021/13563, and FOI2021/15256.
[34] Quotes from documents in French and German were translated by the author.

systematically gathered and presents data from a variety of existing databases on trade, investments, and arms transfers between the Big Three and China and in the Asia-Pacific, and on European Union–China investment ties (Appendix B includes charts visualizing these data as well as details on the available data, their limitations, and the choice of sources).

To be sure, each of these primary sources entails specific challenges and limitations. Interviewees may distort facts either willingly to hide certain details or to bolster their image, or unwillingly because of imprecise memories. Likewise, the available archival sources are partly fragmentary especially because, given the timeframe examined in this book, only few have so far been declassified. Furthermore, government publications and public speeches and statements by policymakers may seek to provide an 'official' version of events with a view to influencing domestic and/or foreign audiences. And although the diplomatic cables leaked by Wikileaks provide unredacted and still classified primary sources, they are produced by one specific, individual bureaucracy, namely the US Department of State headquarters or one of its embassies, and the views presented in the diplomatic cable might well differ from those of other bureaucracies. Additionally, it is not possible to gauge, simply from reading a cable, its relative importance in the decision-making process within that department or within the whole government, or whether the descriptions of Europeans' policy positions in such cables are accurate.

To address the challenges posed by each type of source, the validity and reliability of the information provided by individual sources was corroborated by triangulating and contextualizing them with a broad variety of other written and oral sources. Furthermore, the 223 interviews conducted for this book offer a critical mass that allows verifying and cross-checking the reliability of a single source or piece of evidence.[35] By leveraging such a wide range of primary sources, the ambition of this book is to provide the most comprehensive analysis to date of the three major European powers' foreign and security policies towards the People's Republic of China since the end of the Cold War.

Outline of the Book

Awakening to China's Rise is divided into two parts, each one examining how the major European powers have coped with China's growing might and ambitions in one key region, i.e. the Asia-Pacific and Europe respectively. Part I analyses

---

[35] On the methods adopted for gathering and using oral and written sources, see, among others, Marc Trachtenberg, *The Craft of International History: A Guide to Method* (Princeton, NJ: Princeton University Press, 2006); and Robert Loring Allen and Jan Vansina, *Oral Tradition: A Study in Historical Methodology*, 2nd edition (Abingdon: Routledge, 2017). On Wikileaks, see Gabriel Michael, 'Who's Afraid of WikiLeaks? Missed Opportunities in Political Science Research', *Review of Policy Research 32*, no. 2 (2015): pp. 175–199.

the range of bilateral diplomatic and security ties with Asian partners, multilateral security regimes, and defence capabilities that have been leveraged by the Big Three to confront China's increasingly muscular regional posture in the Asia-Pacific. Part II focuses on the measures taken by these three countries to tackle China's mounting foreign direct investments in sensitive sectors and its supply of technologies for digital infrastructures in Europe. In particular, it looks at their screening mechanisms of Chinese FDIs and at the measures taken to protect Europe's digital infrastructure from suppliers of concern, notably telecommunications companies with ties to the Chinese state and its intelligence services, such as Huawei. For analytical purposes, the book thus separately scrutinizes how the Big Three have confronted China in each region. Yet, their policies towards the PRC in Europe and in the Asia-Pacific are clearly intertwined; they are but two sides of the same coin. Through this cross-regional comparison, Part I and Part II combinedly aim to provide an all-round picture of how Europe's major powers have grappled with the re-emergence of China as a major power in world politics.

Each part is sub-divided into a short introduction that outlines the drivers and characteristics of China's rising assertiveness in the region under investigation, and three country-focused chapters then examine the policy response by each major European power. The Conclusion of the book synthesizes its core findings on the policies of Europe's three major powers towards China across both continents and, based upon such findings, discusses new important avenues for future research at a time when the European Union and NATO have recalibrated their approaches towards the PRC amidst mounting United States-China strategic competition, and the implications of Brexit therefore.

In each chapter, *Awakening to China's Rise* addresses four standardized questions, each one corresponding to a section: (i) *Economic interests*: What are the country's economic interests at play?; (ii) *Threat perceptions*: What is the national assessment of the security implications of China's rise?; (iii) *Policy goals*: What are the policy goals devised in light of such threat assessments and economic interests?; (iv) *Policy instruments*: What policy instruments have been mobilized to achieve these policy goals? Structuring each chapter around these four specific themes allows to substantiate the central argument of the book through a structured comparison and cumulation of findings. It also enables readers interested in just one (or more) of these countries or themes to easily compare them across cases. In each section, the timeframe is divided into two periods: having first provided an overview of the first two post-Cold War decades, the chapter then conducts an in-depth analysis of the 2010s.

Through this thematic and temporal organization, the book offers a systematic analysis of the historical evolution and current state of how each major European power has confronted the security implications of China's rise and demonstrates why and how the 2010s witnessed a major policy shift. It will be shown that whereas growing economic interests have provided the underlying impetus for the three countries' growing attention to the PRC and the Asia-Pacific, their threat perceptions of China—coupled with increasingly competitive bilateral economic relations—have been the key driver of change in their policy goals towards Beijing and in the policy instruments leveraged to achieve such goals in the Asia-Pacific and in Europe.

PART I
CONFRONTING CHINA'S ASSERTIVENESS IN THE ASIA-PACIFIC

Introduction

China in the Asia-Pacific: From Peaceful Rise to Regional Hegemony

China's foreign and security policy in the Asia-Pacific has markedly evolved since the end of the Cold War, with 2009 marking a turning point towards an increasingly assertive regional behaviour. During the first two decades of the post-Cold War era, the PRC abided by Deng Xiaoping's so-called 'twenty-four-character strategy' of hiding its capacities, keeping a low profile, and refraining from claiming leadership.[1] Admittedly, Beijing displayed an aggressive stance vis-à-vis Taiwan, most notably during the 1995-1996 Taiwan Strait Crisis.[2] Nonetheless, during these two decades, it pursued a restrained regional foreign policy in the context of what former President Hu Jintao labelled China's 'peaceful rise'.[3] This regional posture rested on several pillars, namely a growing engagement with regional organizations (e.g. ASEAN+3 and the ASEAN Regional Forum), the establishment of strategic partnerships across the region, and the expansion of regional economic ties coupled with a variety of confidence-building measures.[4]

Starting in the late 2000s, however, and increasingly so in the 2010s, Beijing's behaviour in the Asia-Pacific became more muscular and confrontational. Examples abound: the 2009 harassment of the US Naval Ship (USNS) *Impeccable* ocean surveillance ship by Chinese vessels which almost caused a collision and triggered significant Sino-American diplomatic frictions; the 2009 presentation to the United Nations of China's formal claims over the so-called 'nine-dash line',

---

[1] This guideline can be translated as: 'Observe calmly; secure our position; cope with affairs calmly; hide our capacities and bide our time; be good at maintaining a low profile; and never claim leadership'. For a discussion, see Ronald C. Keith, *Deng Xiaoping and China's Foreign Policy* (New York: Routledge, 2017), ch. 1: 'Judging Deng Xiaoping's Foreign Policy "Pragmatism"', pp. 1–67.
[2] Robert S. Ross, 'The 1995–96 Taiwan Strait Confrontation: Coercion, Credibility, and the Use of Force, *International Security* 25, no. 2 (2000): pp. 87–123.
[3] 'Full Text: China's Peaceful Development Road', *The People's Daily*, 22 December 2005, en.people.cn/200512/22/eng20051222_230059.html.
[4] ASEAN refers to the Association of Southeast Asian Nations. See, e.g. Cheng-Chwee Kuik, 'Multilateralism in China's ASEAN Policy: Its Evolution, Characteristics, and Aspiration', *Contemporary Southeast Asia* 27, no. 1 (2005): pp. 102–122; Sujian Guo, *China's 'Peaceful Rise' in the 21st Century Domestic and International Conditions* (New York: Routledge, 2006); David Shambaugh, 'China Engages Asia: Reshaping the Regional Order', *International Security* 29, no. 3 (Winter, 2004/2005): pp. 64–99.

a large area which covers 80 per cent of the maritime space of the South China Sea and over which Beijing claims sovereignty; the 2012 tensions with Japan over the disputed Diaoyu/Senkaku islands and with the Philippines over the Scarborough Shoal; the 2013 establishment of the air defence identification zone (ADIZ) over the East China Sea, including airspace over the Diaoyu/Senkaku islands; the 2014 China–Vietnam 'oil rig crisis' in which the state-owned China National Offshore Oil Corporation moved an oil platform into waters near the disputed Paracel Islands thereby causing major tensions between Beijing and Hanoi; the 2014 interception of US Navy planes conducting routine patrols over the South China Sea which raised fears over a potential incident or collision; China's rejection of the landmark 2016 Arbitral Tribunal's ruling on its territorial dispute with the Philippines; the substantial expansion of its land reclamation activities (i.e. the construction of artificial islands) in the South China Sea throughout the decade, and the militarization of these islets with the construction of airstrips, radars, and missile batteries, among others; China's erosion of the 'one country, two systems' status quo in Hong Kong, including through the National Security Law (NSL) passed in 2020; or the growing use of state-controlled Chinese Coast Guard and the People's Armed Forces Maritime Militia (PAFMM), complementing the People's Liberation Army (PLA) Navy, for tailored forms of coercion to pursue China's maritime claims vis-à-vis Vietnam, the Philippines and others.[5]

While the drivers of China's rising assertiveness after 2009 remain a matter of contention, they likely resulted from a combination of international and domestic factors.[6] In the aftermath of the 2008 financial crisis and of China's surpassing of Japan as the world's second-largest economy soon thereafter, policymakers in Beijing came to consider that the United States was on the decline whereas the PRC was in the ascendance.[7] This, in turn, spurred the PRC to gradually adopt a

---

[5] See footnote 8 in the introduction of the book as well as, on this last point, Patrick M. Cronin et al., *Tailored Coercion: Competition and Risk in Maritime Asia* (Washington, DC: Center for New American Security, 2014), p. 9; Andrew S. Erickson and Conor M. Kennedy, 'China Maritime Report no. 1: China's Third Sea Force, The People's Armed Forces Maritime Militia: Tethered to the PLA', *CNSI China Maritime Report*, 2017; Suisheng Zhao, 'East Asian Disorder: China and the South China Sea Disputes', *Asian Survey* 60, no. 3 (2020): pp. 490–509.

[6] For diverging views on the main explanatory factors see, e.g. Nien-Chung Chang Lao, 'The Sources of China's Assertiveness: The System, Domestic Politics or Leadership Preferences?', *International Affairs* 92, no. 4 (2016): pp. 817–833; Andrew Scobell and Scott W. Harold, 'An "Assertive" China? Insights from Interviews', *Asian Security* 9, no. 2 (2013): pp. 111–131; Kai He and Huiyun Feng, 'Debating China's Assertiveness: Taking China's Power and Interests Seriously', *International Politics* 49, no. 5 (2012): pp. 633–644; Robert S. Ross, 'The Domestic Sources of China's "Assertive Diplomacy," 2009–2010: Nationalism and Chinese Foreign Policy', in *China across the Divide: The Domestic and Global in Politics and Society*, edited by Rosemary Foot (Oxford: Oxford University Press, 2013), pp. 72–96. For a different periodization, see Andrew Chubb, 'PRC Assertiveness in the South China Sea: Measuring Continuity and Change, 1970–2015', *International Security* 45, no. 3 (2021): pp. 79–121. For a contrarian perspective arguing that China did not become more assertive, see Alastair Iain Johnston, 'How New and Assertive is China's New Assertiveness?', *International Security* 34, no. 4 (2013): pp. 35–45; and Dingding Chen, Xiaoyu Pu, and Alastair Iain Johnston. 'Debating China's Assertiveness', *International Security* 38, no. 3 (2014): pp. 176–183.

[7] Scobell and Harold, 2013, pp. 115–116.

more forceful behaviour in the region and towards the United States.[8] This self-confidence was also partly fuelled by China's steadily growing defence capabilities over the previous decades, which resulted from its ongoing military modernization effort, and more broadly by its reemergence as a major power in world politics.[9] Domestically, Xi Jinping's rise to power was accompanied by a more ambitious foreign policy, one aspiring to establish a Sino-centric regional order in the Asia-Pacific.[10] In 2007, Xi was elected to the Politburo Standing Committee; then, in 2012, he was named General Secretary of the Chinese Communist Party (CCP) and head of the Central Military Commission (CMC); and, one year later, he became President of the People's Republic of China.[11] President Xi's rhetoric of the 'China Dream' of 'Great Rejuvenation' has aimed to transform China into a powerful and prosperous nation and to thereby restore the glory of five thousand years of Chinese civilization which, in his view, had been stolen during the so-called 'century of humiliation' at the hands of imperial powers from the mid-nineteenth century to the establishment of the PRC in 1949.[12]

Part I analyses how Europe's three major powers have sought to confront China's expanding clout and ambitions in the Asia-Pacific since the end of the Cold War (to ensure consistency and avoid anachronisms, the book refers to the 'Asia-Pacific' when discussing the Big Three's policies from the early 1990s to the mid-2010s, and uses the larger 'Indo-Pacific' label for the post-2018 period, when they began adopting this new policy framework; for the sake of simplicity, when generically discussing the decade of the 2010s, the book refers to the Asia-Pacific).[13] In

---

[8] Scobell and Harold, 2013, pp. 115–116.
[9] He and Feng, 2012.
[10] On China's contestation of the US-led hegemonic order in the region, see Rosemary Foot, 'China's Rise and US Hegemony: Renegotiating Hegemonic Order in East Asia?', *International Politics* 57, no. 2 (2020): pp. 150–165; Evelyn Goh, 'Contesting Hegemonic Order: China in East Asia', *Security Studies* 28, no. 3 (2019): pp. 614–644.
[11] On Xi and his foreign policy, see Jean-Marc F. Blanchard, 'The People's Republic of China Leadership Transition and its External Relations: Still Searching for Definitive Answers', *Journal of Chinese Political Science* 20, no. 1 (2015): pp. 1–16; Angela Poh and Mingjiang Li, 'A China in Transition: The Rhetoric and Substance of Chinese Foreign Policy under Xi Jinping', *Asian Security* 13, no. 2 (2017): pp. 84–97; Kai He and Huiyun Feng, 'Xi Jinping's Operational Code Beliefs and China's Foreign Policy', *The Chinese Journal of International Politics* 6, no. 3 (2013): pp. 209–231; and Shaun Breslin and Pan Zhongqi, 'Introduction: A Xi Change in Policy? *The British Journal of Politics and International Relations* 23, no. 2 (2021), doi:10.1177/1369148121992499.
[12] 'Full Text of Xi Jinping's Report at 19th CPC National Congress', *China Daily*, 18 October 2017, https://www.chinadaily.com.cn/china/19thcpcnationalcongress/2017-11/04/content_34115212.htm. For an analysis, see Maria Adele Carrai, 'Chinese Political Nostalgia and Xi Jinping's Dream of Great Rejuvenation', *International Journal of Asian Studies* 18, no. 1 (2020): p. 7 doi:10.1017/S1479591420000406.
[13] Specifically, the book distinguishes three geographical groupings. The 'Asia-Pacific' encompasses the region from Myanmar to Australia and to Japan (excluding India and Russia). 'Asia and Oceania' embraces the Asia-Pacific and South Asia (Bangladesh, India, and Pakistan). The 'Indo-Pacific' is a more recent label developed by various governments in the late 2010s; although different governments have adopted different definitions, it generally refers to a larger region which includes Asia-Oceania and the broader Indian and Pacific Oceans areas. As discussed in Part I, the 'Indo-Pacific' label was adopted in 2018 by France, in 2020 by Germany, and in 2021 by the United Kingdom. The data used in the

particular, it focuses on the three countries' bilateral, minilateral, and multilateral diplomatic and security arrangements in the Asia-Pacific, their cooperation with other Western (US and European powers) as well as their naval deployments and forward deployed forces.

To be sure, China's rise is one among several security challenges that the three major European powers have faced in the region which also include North Korea's nuclear programme, the proliferation of weapons of mass destruction, piracy, or terrorism in South East Asia. Yet, it will be shown that China's rising regional assertiveness after 2009—and national policymakers' perceptions thereof—has been the key driver of the change, in the 2010s, in the foreign and security policies of Europe's three major powers in the Asia-Pacific.

In the first two decades of the post-Cold War era, because of low threat perceptions of China and of expanding economic interests, they overwhelmingly focused on economic engagement with the PRC and the broader region. In the subsequent decade, however, France, Germany, and the United Kingdom have come to regard China's behaviour in the Asia-Pacific as posing a mounting challenge to their regional diplomatic, security, and economic interests. In particular, gradually and cumulatively, they have all displayed growing concerns over how Chinese assertiveness could undermine regional stability (raising risks of unintended escalation and conflict), the resilience of 'rules-based' order, as well as regional sea lines of communication.[14] Because of heightened threat perceptions in the 2010s, the three European powers have recalibrated their policy goals, giving greater prominence to national security considerations, and broadened the scope of their policies to the larger 'Indo-Pacific' region, encompassing both the Indian and Pacific Oceans regions. Their new regional policy frameworks have specifically revolved around the following goals: preserving regional stability and upholding key norms of the rules-based order (e.g. freedom of navigation and the peaceful resolution of disputes) while furthering their economic interests in the region. The formulation of these new policy frameworks, in turn, has caused them

---

book (e.g. on trade, naval deployments, forward-deployed forces, etc.) refer to different geographical groupings because it was sometimes not possible, based upon publicly available figures, to disaggregate the data for the various (sub-)groupings. On the differing national interpretations of the geographical area covered by the Indo-Pacific construct, see for instance: Franco-German Observatory of the Indo-Pacific, Sciences Po, 'Maps of the Indo-Pacific', Center for International Studies (CERI), http://www.sciencespo.fr/ceri/observatory-indo-pacific; and Rory Medcalf, *Contest for the Indo-Pacific: Why China Won't Map the Future* (Melbourne: La Trobe University Press, 2020).

[14] A rules-based 'regional order' can be defined as rule-governed interactions among states in a given region in which 'shared norms, rules, and expectations constitute, regulate, and make predictable international life'; in the Asia-Pacific, these norms and rules include the respect of sovereignty, free trade, and international law (and in particular freedom of navigation and the peaceful resolution of disputes). Quote from Evelyn Goh, *The Struggle for Order: Hegemony, Hierarchy, and Transition in Post-Cold War East Asia* (Oxford: Oxford University Press, 2013), p. 7. See also Barry Buzan and Yongjin Zhang, 'Introduction: Interrogating Regional International Society in East Asia', in *Contesting International Society in East Asia*, edited by Barry Buzan and Yongjin Zhang (Cambridge: Cambridge University Press, 2014), pp. 1–28.

to adapt and strengthen the policy instruments leveraged to achieve such goals. Specifically, they have sought to increase their political-military engagement in the region by strengthening and diversifying their networks of bilateral diplomatic and security partnerships, by bolstering their involvement in Asian multilateral security regimes, and by expanding their naval engagement—although with significantly discrepant capabilities. They have also fostered greater cooperation with the United States and with other European powers, promoting the development of more cohesive EU policies towards China and in the Asia-Pacific, although after Brexit the United Kingdom abandoned such an objective. Through these endeavours, the three major European powers have not aimed to balance China, an unviable objective given their capability shortfalls, the tyranny of distance, and their desire to continue to bilaterally engage Beijing.[15] Rather, they have pursued the 'milieu goal' of seeking to shape the regional environment in which China's rise has unfolded, defining a distinct position for themselves in the context of the growing United States–China rivalry in the region.[16]

To substantiate this argument, the chapters of Part I—each one focusing on one major European power—are organized as follows. First, the Introduction provides an overview of the country's colonial history in the Asia-Pacific and of how decolonization shaped its post-colonial diplomatic and military footprint in the region. The first two sections of each chapter then examine the two central drivers of the country's foreign and security policy in the Asia-Pacific, namely its regional economic interests and its threat assessment of China respectively. The two subsequent sections show how these drivers have, in turn, caused the country's policy goals and instruments to change over time. As each country has adapted its policy goals to evolving threat assessments of China and to growing regional economic interests, the diplomatic and security instruments mobilized in the Asia-Pacific to achieve those goals have evolved accordingly. The timeframe covered in each section is divided in two periods: after an overview of the first two post-Cold War decades, the chapter offers an in-depth analysis of the 2010s. Thereby, the chapters of Part I shed light on how each major European power has confronted the security implications of Chinese assertiveness in the Asia-Pacific and demonstrates why a major policy shift occurred in the 2010s.

---

[15] On the concept of tyranny of distance, see Geoffrey Blainey, *The Tyranny of Distance: How Distance Shaped Australia's History* (Sydney: Macmillan, 2001).
[16] On the concept of 'milieu goals', see Arnold Wolfers, *Discord and Collaboration: Essays on International Politics* (Baltimore: Johns Hopkins University Press, 1965), pp. 73–74. See also Christopher Hill, *Foreign Policy in the Twenty-first Century*, 2nd edition (Basingstoke: Palgrave Macmillan, 2015), pp. 54, 131, and 312.

1
Pulled East

French Foreign and Security Policy in the Asia-Pacific

Introduction

Among Europe's three major powers, France retains the largest foothold in the Asia-Pacific in the form of overseas territories, exclusive economic zones (EEZ), and forward-deployed forces—largely as the by-product of its colonial history.[1] Building upon these assets, France has responded to China's rising assertiveness by bolstering its political-military engagement in the region, thereby developing the most robust strategic presence in the Asia-Pacific among Europe's major powers.

During the first French colonial empire (sixteenth to early nineteenth century), the island of La Réunion became a French colony in the Indian Ocean (1642). But it is during its second colonial empire (nineteenth and twentieth centuries) that France expanded the most into the region by taking possession, in the Indian Ocean, of the islands of Mayotte (1853), of the Scattered Islands (1896) and of the Southern and Antarctic Lands (between 1772 and 1843) as well as, in the South Pacific, of New Caledonia (1853), French Polynesia (1881), Wallis and Futuna (1841) and Clipperton (discovered in 1711 but a French possession since 1931).[2]

---

[1] On French foreign and security policy in the Asia-Pacific, see among others Andrea Gilli, 'France's New Raison d'Être in the Indo-Pacific', in *Mind the Gap: Naval Views of the Free and Open Indo-Pacific*, edited by Sharon Stirling (Washington, DC: The German Marshall Fund, 2019), pp. 18–21; Céline Pajon, 'France's Indo-Pacific Strategy and the Quad Plus', *The Journal of Indo-Pacific Affairs* 3, no. 5 (Winter 2020/21): pp. 165–178; Nicolas Regaud, 'France and Security in the Asia-Pacific: From the End of the First Indochina Conflict to Today', Australian Strategic Policy Institute, *Strategic Insights* 12 (December 2016); Nicolas Regaud, 'France's Indo-Pacific Strategy and its Overseas Territories in the Indian and Pacific Oceans: Characteristics, Capabilities, Constraints and Avenues for Deepening the Franco-Australian Strategic Partnership', *Australian Strategic Policy Institute*, 25 June 2021, https://www.aspi.org.au/report/frances-indo-pacific-strategy-and-its-overseas-territories-indian-and-pacific-oceans; Iskander Rehman, 'The Indian Ocean in France's Global Defense Strategy', CNA Roundtable Proceedings, 18 January 2018a, pp. 21–26; David Scott, 'France's "Indo-Pacific" Strategy: Regional Power Projection', *Journal of Military and Strategic Studies* 19, no. 4 (2019): pp. 76–103.

[2] On French colonialism in the Indian and Pacific Oceans, see Robert Aldrich, *The French Presence in the South Pacific, 1842–1940* (Basingstoke: Macmillan, 1990); Denise Fisher, *France in the South Pacific: Power and Politics* (Canberra: ANU Press, 2013), ch. 1; Edmond Maestri, *Les îles du Sud-Ouest de l'Océan Indien et la France de 1815 à nos jours* (Paris: L'Harmattan, 1994).

France also established itself as a colonial empire in South East Asia between 1874 and 1954. Through the Indochinese Union it ruled over Laos, Cambodia, Tonkin, Annam, and Cochinchina (the last three constituting present-day Vietnam).[3] With Indochina becoming its largest colony, Paris became embroiled in the territorial disputes in the South China Sea. Beginning in the 1920s, France began occupying the Paracel and the Spratly archipelagos; in 1933, it asserted its sovereignty by taking possession of these islands, thereby causing frictions with Beijing which also claimed sovereignty over them. France offered to take the dispute to international courts, which China refused.[4] After its defeat at Dien Bien Phu in 1954, Paris withdrew from South East Asia, thereby also disentangling itself from territorial disputes with Beijing.[5]

As a result of its colonial heritage and of these overseas territories, France's regional presence encompasses more than 1.6 million French nationals as well as the largest forward deployed force stationed in the region among Europe's major powers—with a total of 7,000 permanent military personnel across the Pacific and Indian Ocean regions. Specifically, it deploys military personnel in the Indian Ocean (La Réunion and the Mayotte islands) and in the South Pacific (New Caledonia and French Polynesia) as part of its 'sovereign forces', and further maintains 'presence forces' (i.e. in foreign military bases) in the northern quadrant of the Indian Ocean, namely in the United Arab Emirates and Djibouti (these forces were incorporated in the larger 'Indo-Pacific' framework in the late 2010s, as discussed below).[6] In addition to managing a network of signals intelligence stations (in Mayotte, La Réunion, New Caledonia, and French Polynesia),[7] France also

---

[3] On French colonialism in South East Asia, see Pierre Brocheux and Daniel Hémery, *Indochina: An Ambiguous Colonization, 1858-1954* (Berkeley, CA: University of California Press, 2009).

[4] In 1939, Japan occupied the Spratly and Paracel archipelagoes. With the defeat of Japan after World War II, both colonial France and the Republic of China sought to gain a foothold in the Paracels. On France's involvement in territorial disputes in the South China Sea, see Thi Lan Anh Nguyen, 'Origins of the South China Sea Dispute', in *Territorial Disputes in the South China Sea: Navigating Rough Waters*, edited by Jing Huang and Andrew Billo (New York: Palgrave Macmillan, 2014), pp. 15–35.

[5] Denise Artaud and Laurence Kaplan (eds), *Diên Biên Phu. L'alliance atlantique et la défense du Sud-Est asiatique* (Lyon: La Manufacture, 1989).

[6] As detailed below, since 2018, these forces are officially included as part of the so-called Indo-Pacific strategy which broadened the geographical scope of French policy from the Asia-Pacific to the Indo-Pacific, thereby also including the Indian Ocean. In 2019, 4,100 of these 7,000 military personnel were stationed throughout the Indian Ocean region and 2,900 in the Pacific Ocean regions (MoD, *France and Security in the Indo-Pacific*, 2019b, p. 6). For details on French military equipment deployed in the region, see 'Appendix: France's Military Presence and Naval Deployments in the Asia-Pacific' in Hugo Meijer, 'Pulled East: The Rise of China, Europe and French Security Policy in the Asia-Pacific', *Journal of Strategic Studies* (2021a), available at https://ndownloader.figstatic.com/files/30687660.

[7] Satellite pictures of French signals intelligence stations can be found on Google Earth, at https://www.google.com/maps/d/viewer?mid=1956kVWOYQEh7e5S302am5oxjD0U&hl=fr&usp=sharing (retrieved from Jean-Marc Manach, 'Comment on peut, en trois clics, découvrir la carte des stations d'écoute des espions de la DGSE', *Slate*, 7 May 2014). The Senate's draft finance law for 2013 stated that France's "forward (or autonomous) signal detachments" ("détachements avancés, ou autonomes, des transmissions," DAT) form a "network able to monitor the activities in the areas in which we have overseas interests or that would have a relevant role in the event of a crisis." A list of France's "forward signal detachments" was also made available in a 2013 decree (now abrogated by a subsequent 2014

possesses the world's second-largest EEZ (after that of the United States), 93 per cent of which is located in the Indian and Pacific Oceans.[8]

This chapter shows that China's growing assertiveness—and French policymakers' perceptions of it—has been the central driver of change in French foreign and security policy in the region. Specifically, rising economic interests in the region and a heightened threat assessment of the People's Republic of China (PRC) have pulled France strategically into the Asia-Pacific.[9] Throughout the 1990s and 2000s, France displayed low threat perceptions of China and its regional policy overwhelmingly revolved around the pursuit of its economic interests. It sought to foster economic and diplomatic engagement with China and other emerging powers in the broader Asia-Pacific region, largely relying on a loose patchwork of diplomatic and economic initiatives. After 2009, however, because of growing economic interests in the region and, crucially, mounting threat perceptions of the PRC, Paris reassessed the national security implications of China's rise. French policymakers displayed mounting concerns over how China's regional behaviour could undermine regional stability, the resilience of the 'rules-based order', as well as regional sea lines of communication (SLOCs) (while they concomitantly also grew wary of Chinese inroads into Europe's strategic sectors, as discussed in Chapter 4).[10] Consequently, Paris forged a new regional policy framework for the larger Indo-Pacific regions through which it pursued several interrelated goals, namely protecting its sovereign overseas territories, upholding foundational norms of the regional order (sovereignty, freedom of navigation and the peaceful settlement of disputes), and promoting regional stability to reduce the potential for escalation and conflict—thereby also furthering its regional economic interests. To achieve these objectives, Paris bolstered its regional presence through several lines of effort. It expanded naval deployments, broadened its network of bilateral diplomatic and security partnerships, and strengthened its engagement in the region's multilateral security architecture. Concomitantly, it fostered multinational cooperation with both regional states and with other Western (US and European) powers, spurring the formulation of a more cohesive EU policy towards the region. Thereby, France sought to define a distinct and autonomous position for itself,

---

law). See Senate, *Projet de loi de finances pour 2013 – Défense : équipement des forces*, 22 november 2012b, Section II.B.2 www.senat.fr/rap/a12-150-8/a12-150-812.html; and Légifrance, "Arrêté du 2 janvier 2013 relatif aux formations et aux unités relevant du ministère de la défense pouvant bénéficier de l'avance de trésorerie pour l'activité des forces," 18 January 2013b, Annex I, https://www.legifrance.gouv.fr/loda/id/LEGIARTI000026953778/2013-01-19/

[8] MFA, 'The Indo-Pacific Region: A Priority for France', *Country Files*, August 2019b. See also MFA, 'The Indo-Pacific: A Priority for France, April 2021a, https://www.diplomatie.gouv.fr/en/country-files/asia-and-oceania/the-indo-pacific-region-a-priority-for-france/ (accessed on 1 December 2021).

[9] To be sure, France has had overseas territories in the region for several centuries. Yet, the Asia-Pacific's importance in the hierarchy of French diplomatic priorities had declined with decolonization; and it is only in the 2010s, as shown in this chapter, that greater attention and resources were again devoted to the region, mainly because of the regional ramifications of China's rising assertiveness.

[10] For a definition of a 'rules-based regional order' see the Introduction of Part I.

and for the European Union, in the context of the mounting United States–China rivalry in the region.

The remainder of the chapter proceeds as follows. The first two sections examine the key drivers of France's foreign and security policy in the Asia-Pacific, namely its economic interests in the region and its threat assessment of China respectively. The subsequent two sections show how these drivers have, in turn, caused Paris's policy goals and instruments to change over time.

Economic Interests

French economic interests in the Asia-Pacific have steadily grown throughout the post-Cold War period, including trade, investment, strategic supplies, arms sales, and the exploitation of its EEZ. As the region emerged as an increasingly central hub for the world economy, its importance for France expanded. These growing economic interests drove the desire to deepen France's diplomatic and economic engagement with the PRC and across the region. Yet, it is only when its threat assessment of China's rise intensified in the 2010s that France developed a cohesive regional strategy with a strengthened political-military dimension. Overall, whereas economic interests have provided the underlying impetus for France's growing attention to the Asia-Pacific, security considerations and, specifically, threat perceptions of China have been the key driver of change shaping French foreign and security policy in the region.

A New El Dorado? The Rising Economic Potential of the Asia-Pacific

Although France's trade and investment in the region increased in the 1990s and 2000s, in these decades Paris was driven more by the potential for economic expansion than by its actual business deals which remained limited to a few countries, most notably the PRC.

French overall trade with the Asia-Pacific did rise between 1995 and 2009, but from a low basis (from $49bn to $112bn),[11] while its trade with China expanded from $8bn to $52bn in the same timeframe.[12] Likewise, although French FDIs in the Asia-Pacific increased, they remained relatively modest, representing 6.5 per cent of France's global FDIs in 2000.[13] The value of the utilized FDIs in China then merely rose from $550m to $650m between 2000 and 2009.[14] During this decade,

---

[11] World Bank's World Integrated Trade Solution (WITS), https://wits.worldbank.org.
[12] UN Comtrade—International Trade Statistics Database, https://comtrade.un.org.
[13] UN Comtrade—International Trade Statistics Database, https://comtrade.un.org.
[14] The value of actually utilized investments refers to the investments ultimately used by companies in China, in contrast to the values of agreed investments in contracts (for more details on the

France ranked second and third among EU member states in terms of exports to, and FDIs in, China respectively—far behind Germany which exported roughly as much as the whole European Union into China (see the comparative charts on the Big Three's trade and investment ties with China and in the Asia-Pacific in Appendix B).[15] French bilateral economic relations with the PRC thus remained, according to then President Jacques Chirac (1995–2007), 'below the potential of the two economies'.[16] Overall, it was therefore the potential for further expansion that drove Paris's desire to engage the region and the emerging powers therein.

Paris also maintained significant economic interests in the region due to its large EEZ in the Indian and Pacific Oceans. While France did not produce oil therein, the seabed in the EEZ was (and remains) rich in rare metals and polymetallic nodules (i.e. rocky concretions resting on the ocean floor that contain manganese, copper, cobalt, or nickel) that play an integral role in the manufacture of modern electronic equipment.[17] In the South Pacific, for instance, France's major exploration and investments focused on nickel assets in New Caledonia which represented around 20–25 per cent of the world's nickel reserves in 2008.[18]

Besides civilian economic interests, another economic driver of Paris's rising attention to the Asia-Pacific was the potential to boost arms exports. France was highly dependent on arms exports to support its defence and technological industrial base (DTIB), exporting an average 38 per cent of the total turnover of its DTIB between 2002 and 2010 (based on available data).[19] As a result, Paris faced strong incentives to expand its arms sales to the region to allow for longer production runs and help to reduce the unit cost of military equipment.[20] As explained by the former Head of the Bureau for Strategy of the MoD's Directorate General of Armaments (DGA, 2007–2011), 'the Asia-Pacific was becoming one of the largest clients of the French defence industry; we saw this regional market overtaking our traditional customers who tended to be located in the Middle East.'[21] The share of the Asia-Pacific in overall French arms exports more than doubled between 1998–2002 and 2008–2012, rising from 12 per cent to 28 per cent.[22]

---

data, see Appendix B). For data on FDI stock, which rose from €1.8bn to €8.4bn in the same timeframe, see Banque de France, 'Flux d'investissements directs par pays et par secteur, données annuelles (2000-2020)', 2020, https://www.banque-france.fr/statistiques/balance-des-paiements-et-statistiques-bancaires-internationales/les-investissements-directs/investissements-directs-series-annuelles.

[15] National Assembly, *Les échanges commerciaux entre la Chine et la France*, Committee on Finance, General Economics and the Plan, Report no. 2473, 13 July 2005a, p. 55.

[16] President Jacques Chirac, interview with the New China Agency (Xinhua), 14 May 1997a.

[17] Senate, *Zones économiques exclusives ultramarines*, Report no. 430, 9 April 2014c, pp. 50–60.

[18] Central Intelligence Agency, *The World Factbook 2008* (Washington, DC: US Government Printing Office, 2008), p. 420.

[19] Hugo Meijer, Lucie Béraud-Sudreau, Paul Holtom, and Matthew Uttley, 'Arming China: Major Powers' Arms Transfers to the People's Republic of China', *Journal of Strategic Studies* 41, no. 6 (2018): p. 869.

[20] MoD, *French White Paper on Defence and National Security*, 2008, p. 267.

[21] Guillaume Lagane, interview, 29 January 2020.

[22] MoD, *France and Security in the Asia-Pacific*, 2014, p. 14.

Asia as the New Global Economic Hub

During the 2010s, the weight of the Asia-Pacific in the world economy and for French interests further expanded. By the end of the decade, the region produced 45 per cent of the world's GDP, generated 60 per cent of global economic growth, included two thirds of the world's population, and concentrated critical sea trade routes as well as one-third of international trade.[23] The emergence of the Asia-Pacific as a core hub of the global economy substantially magnified its importance for French economic interests.

As the region became ever more central to international value chains and global economic flows, France reoriented its external trade thereto. Between 2010 and 2018, its overall trade with the Asia-Pacific expanded from $134 bn to $168 bn, reaching 14% of France's total trade.[24] At the end of the decade, 30 per cent of its exports to the region revolved around the aeronautic sector,[25] while the PRC gradually became France's fifth-largest trading partner.[26] Meanwhile, the stock of FDI assets held by France in Asia-Oceania expanded sevenfold between 2000 and 2016, while its investment flows increased at an average of €4bn per year in the same timeframe.[27] By the latter half of the decade, France ranked second among Europeans (after Germany) in terms of turnover generated in the region.[28]

As a result of the growth in France's external trade with the Asia-Pacific, the sea lines of communication (SLOCs) in the Pacific and Indian Oceans—with 30 per cent of Asia-Europe trade passing through the South China Sea[29]—became increasingly 'vital'.[30] France came to depend ever more on maritime supplies for its imports (hydrocarbons, ores, industrial components, finished products) as well as for its exports (cereals, agricultural products, manufactured goods).[31] The containerized routes from the South China Sea to France represented more than 67 per cent of the total containerized traffic concerning France.[32] In short, the South

---

[23] See, among others, MFA, *White Paper—2030 French Strategy in Asia-Oceania: Towards an Inclusive Asian Indo-Pacific Region*, 2018a, p. 1; and MFA, 2019b.
[24] UN Comtrade—International Trade Statistics Database, https://comtrade.un.org.
[25] MFA, 'Les relations économiques entre la France et la région Asie-Océanie', *Country Factsheet*, June 2018b (2017 data).
[26] MFA, 'Fiche Pays—Repères économiques', Direction de la diplomatie économique, April 2021b, https://www.diplomatie.gouv.fr/fr/politique-etrangere-de-la-france/diplomatie-economique-et-commerce-exterieur/la-france-et-ses-partenaires-economiques-pays-par-pays/asie/article/chine.
[27] MFA, 2018b.
[28] MFA, 2018b.
[29] MoD, *Strategic Update*, January 2021, p. 35.
[30] MoD, *France and Security in the Asia-Pacific*, 2014, foreword by the Minister of Defence.
[31] Senate, *La France face à l'émergence de l'Asie du Sud-Est*, Committee on Foreign Affairs, Defence and Armed Forces, Report no. 723, 14 July 2014a, p. 199. See also Senate, *Reprendre pied en Asie du Sud-Est*, Committee on Foreign Affairs, Defence and Armed Forces, Report no. 723, 2014b, I.C.1.
[32] Luc Viellard, Mathieu Anquez, and Jean-Pierre Histrimont, *Vulnérabilités de la France face aux flux maritimes*, European Company of Strategic Intelligence, Report Commissioned by the MoD, 31 January 2012, p. 124.

China Sea and, more broadly, the SLOCs in the Indian and Pacific Oceans emerged as a 'strategic chokepoint' for world trade and for France.[33]

Finally, as in previous decades, France remained highly dependent on arms exports—which represented, depending on the year, between 25 per cent and 40 per cent of its output.[34] Arms transfers were thus considered, as a Senate report puts it, as 'the necessary precondition for the survival of [the French] defence industry'.[35] High arms export dependence and rising imports of military equipment from the Asia-Pacific combinedly fuelled French economic interest in further expanding arms sales to the region.[36] Between 2008 and 2017, Asia-Oceania represented almost 30 per cent of total French arms exports.[37] As a defence official succinctly puts it, 'it is there, in the Asia-Pacific, that the potentially fastest growing arms markets are.'[38]

Overall, France's economic interests in the Asia-Pacific thus grew amid considerable opportunities for further expansion. For Philippe Errera, Director General for International Relations and Strategy at the MoD (2015–2018) and later Director General for Political and Security Affairs at the Ministry of Foreign Affairs (MFA, since 2019), France's engagement in the region has been, at least in part, driven by 'the immense opportunities offered by this vast geopolitical complex, which has been the main engine of global economic growth in recent decades'.[39]

Threat Perceptions

Whereas French economic interests in the region have steadily grown since the end of the Cold War, its threat assessment of China only changed in the 2010s. In the first two post-Cold War decades, France displayed a low threat perception of the PRC, viewing it mainly as a distant and lucrative emerging market. It is in the 2010s that Paris's threat assessment markedly intensified because of China's rising assertiveness and that France reconsidered the national security implications of China's rise. This, in turn, drove a significant shift in French foreign and security policy towards the region.

---

[33] National Assembly, *Enjeux stratégiques en mer de Chine méridionale*, Committee on Foreign Affairs, Report no. 1868, 10 April 2019a, p. 48.
[34] MoD, *French White Paper on Defence and National Security*, 2013, p. 118. See also Meijer et al., 2018.
[35] Senate, 2014a, p. 169.
[36] Arms export dependence refers to the share of arms exports in the total turnover of its defence and technological industrial base (Meijer et al., 2018, p. 857). On regional arms imports, see SIPRI (Stockholm International Peace Research Institute), 'Trends in international arms transfers, 2018', *Fact Sheet*, March 2019, p. 9.
[37] MoD, 2019b, p. 17.
[38] MoD official, interview, 13 October 2017.
[39] Philippe Errera, 'Présentation de la politique de défense et de sécurité', Speech at the Hôtel de la Marine, 10 April 2014, p. 2.

Low Threat Perceptions: China's Peaceful Rise

From the end of the Cold War to the late 2000s, French policymakers considered that China followed Deng Xiaoping's so-called 'twenty-four-character strategy', which can be summarized as hiding its capacities, maintaining a low profile, and refraining from claiming leadership.[40] As such, they adhered to the view that the PRC was a peaceful rising power.

As explained by General Henri Bentégeat, former Deputy Chief of the Personal Military Staff of Presidents François Mitterrand and Jacques Chirac (1993–2006), Chief of the Personal Military Staff of President Chirac (1999–2002), and then Chief of Defence Staff (2002–2006), President Chirac 'considered that China did not pose a real danger in the region, he was convinced that China had always been a peaceful major power; at a fundamental level, he considered that China had no expansionist ambitions'.[41] Likewise, according to another senior adviser to President Chirac, 'China's economic rise had become a major and unavoidable fact, and we duly drew all the necessary consequences for our own foreign policy. By contrast, China's military power was still in its infancy, it was not really a cause for concern.'[42]

Paris did monitor closely the trajectory of China's military modernization. Throughout the 1990s and 2000s, Beijing's rising regional influence and the sustained increase in its defence budget (10 per cent over the 1989–2007 period) were scrutinized, especially since Chinese spending figures lacked transparency.[43] Yet, although French defence officials acknowledged qualitative and quantitative improvements in China's military capabilities, they saw the People's Liberation Army (PLA) as remaining, overall, twenty years behind top-end Western military systems.[44] In the conventional realm, despite its numerical size, the PLA was seen as under-equipped and with little actual combat experience.[45] As a result, French defence planners considered that, in case a conflict emerged in the Taiwan Strait, US material preponderance vis-à-vis the PRC was such that Washington could rely on standoff weapons without having to deploy ground forces; and, in their view, a potential occupation of Taiwan by the PRC was 'the problem of the United States, it was not France's problem'.[46]

---

[40] Interviews with a former senior diplomat and with former MoD officials in office in the 1990s and 2000s, January–December 2017 and March 2020. On Deng's strategy, see Ronald C. Keith, *Deng Xiaoping and China's Foreign Policy* (New York: Routledge, 2017), ch. 1. See also the Introduction of Part I.
[41] Interview, 16 March 2020.
[42] Interview, 20 March 2020.
[43] See MoD, 1994, p. 10; MoD, 2008, p. 34.
[44] Interviews with MoD officials in office in the 1990s and 2000s, January–March 2020.
[45] Interviews with MoD officials in office in the 1990s and 2000s, January–March 2020.
[46] Senior adviser to President Chirac, interview, May 2017.

Accordingly, the re-emergence of China in world politics was believed to have very little national security ramifications for French interests, with one main exception being the nuclear domain. When the PRC developed intercontinental ballistic missiles capable of reaching France's mainland territory in the late 1990s, President Chirac decided, according to one of his close advisers, to revise France's nuclear posture by enlarging the concept of deterrence to include a crisis scenario with the PRC and to adapt the reach and precision of French M51 submarine-launched ballistic missiles accordingly.[47] As detailed in Chapter 4, policymakers in Paris also witnessed the growth in Chinese espionage in sensitive sectors such as dual-use technologies, including through cyber means; but the gap between French and Chinese technological capabilities was deemed so profound that such practices raised relatively few concerns.

In short, during the first two decades after the end of the Cold War, French policymakers assessed that the PLA lagged far behind Western military standards and posed little security concerns (with one exception in the nuclear domain). Overall, Paris exhibited a low threat perception of China.

Heightened Threat Assessment: China's Assertiveness

The turn of the decade marked a critical juncture in France's threat assessment of the PRC. Because of China's increasingly ambitious regional posture after 2009, French policymakers gradually and cumulatively began to re-evaluate the security implications of China's rise in the 2010s. They came to see Beijing's regional behaviour as ever more assertive, which, in turn, had major implications for French interests in the region.

Foreign and defence policy officials have pointed to a variety of markers of China's rising assertiveness, including China's harassment of the USNS *Impeccable* ocean surveillance ship, the expansion of Beijing's land reclamation activities in the South China Sea, intensifying tensions between the PRC and its neighbours, as well as, more broadly, its naval modernization programme.[48] As stressed by a report of the National Assembly's Committee on Foreign Affairs, China's 'massive land reclamation' and the militarization of islets in the South China Sea displayed

---

[47] Senior adviser to then President Chirac, interview, May 2017. The only indirect public reference to this decision is to be found in a speech by former Prime Minister Lionel Jospin (1997–2002) in which he referred to the role of nuclear deterrence in countering threats 'whatever their origin, even distant' (Address to the Institute for Higher National Defence Studies, Paris, 22 October 1999). See also Bruno Tertrais, 'French Nuclear Deterrence Policy, Forces, and Future: A Handbook', *FRS Research & Documents 4* (2020), p. 31. An additional concern was related to China's proliferation of missile and nuclear technologies (interview with a former official in the Secretariat-General for National Defence and Security, in the Prime Minister's Office, 20 April 2021).

[48] Interviews with officials in the MFA and MoD, January–December 2017 and January–March 2020.

a 'very clear acceleration' through the construction of airstrips, hangars, logistics buildings, installation of radars, and the deployment of anti-aircraft and anti-ship missile batteries on the Paracel and Spratly islands.[49] In 2009 China also formalized its claims in the South China Sea by presenting to the United Nations the map of the so-called 'nine-dash line' over which Beijing claims sovereignty in the South China Sea.[50] Concomitantly, Paris monitored China's naval modernization with mounting apprehension as Beijing produced, in only four years, the equivalent of the entire French Navy's fleet in terms of number of vessels and submarines.[51]

In line with an international pattern of mounting disquiet vis-à-vis China's behaviour, senior French officials therefore grew increasingly concerned by Beijing's expanding capabilities and ambitions in the Asia-Pacific in the 2010s (as well as by China's growing clout in Europe, as discussed in Chapter 4). Specifically, while the PRC was not deemed to pose a direct military threat to France—unlike for other regional powers—the chief concerns of French policymakers revolved around China's challenge to the balance of power in the Asia-Pacific, its contestation of foundational norms of the rules-based order and the ensuing risk of escalation and regional instability which, in turn, impacted French diplomatic, economic, and security interests in the region and beyond.

China's Challenge to the Regional Balance of Power

French civilian and military leaders became increasingly wary of how the PLA's military modernization programme and its growing military (especially naval) capabilities were altering the regional balance of power in a context of rising United States–China competition. For Nicolas Regaud, former Assistant Director for Defence Policy at the MoD's Directorate for Strategic Affairs (DAS, 2008–2014) and later Special Representative to the Indo-Pacific of the MoD's DGRIS (2015–2019), whereas in the 2000s the Chinese military was considered a 'paper tiger—the PRC was 20 years behind us—today, it certainly depends on what sector you examine, but we have seen a phenomenal and highly concerning progress.'[52]

The MoD assessed that 'there had been a game changer between 2005 and 2010' in China's military modernization.[53] Accordingly, in 2010, a working group on

---

[49] National Assembly, 2019a, p. 22.
[50] National Assembly, 2019a, p. 19.
[51] Chief of the Staff of the Navy Admiral Christophe Prazuck, Testimony before the National Assembly's Committee on National Defence and Armed Forces, 26 July 2017, pp. 2–3. See also Chief of the Staff of the Navy Christophe Prazuck, Testimony before the National Assembly's Committee on National Defence and Armed Forces, 3 October 2019.
[52] Interview, 6 July 2013. DGRIS stands for Directorate General for International Relations and Strategy.
[53] Interview, 6 July 2013. This point was confirmed in interviews with officials in the Office of the President, MFA, and MoD, January–December 2017.

'Chinese power' was created within the MoD—with representatives also from the MFA, the Ministry of Economics and Finance, and the external intelligence agency, the Directorate-General for External Security (DGSE)—to assess China's rising economic, technological, and military capabilities. Among other things, the working group's classified report evaluated the PRC's defence and technological capabilities across a variety of areas including power projection, naval, space, and cyber capabilities (the report was finalized in 2011 and then updated in 2014).[54]

In subsequent years, French policymakers continued to display rising concerns over the pace of China's military modernization.[55] As a former MoD official succinctly puts it, 'we had a wake-up call, things really started to accelerate. China's power suddenly became much more concretely visible.'[56] By 2017, the *Strategic Review of Defence and National Security* stressed that the Chinese defence budget was 'four times that of France' compared to similar levels in the mid-2000s, and that China's military modernization had specifically focused on 'high-end technologies' with 'the objective of dominating the South China Sea'.[57] As a consequence of this military build-up, according to a MoD strategy report, China's expanding regional might had 'substantially shift[ed] the balance of power in Northeast and South East Asia, as well as in the Indian Ocean and the South Pacific'.[58]

China's Contestation of the Rules-Based Order

In addition to reshaping the regional balance of power, China's behaviour was also seen as directly challenging key norms of the rules-based order, most notably the peaceful resolution of disputes, freedom of navigation, and sovereignty.

French policymakers considered that China's unilateral actions in the South China Sea—such as large-scale land reclamation, the militarization of contested archipelagos, the establishment of an air defence identification zone or the rejection of the 2016 Arbitral Tribunal's ruling on the territorial dispute between the PRC and the Philippines—violated the peaceful resolution of disputes. In their view, through the use of force and *fait accompli* tactics, China was altering the status quo and raising regional tensions.[59]

---

[54] Interviews with former MoD officials, October–December 2017 and January–March 2020.
[55] See for instance MoD, 2013, pp. 34–35.
[56] Interview, 6 July 2017.
[57] MoD, *Strategic Review of Defence and National Security*, 2017a, p. 42. On China's defence budget and power projection capabilities, see also MoD, *Strategic Update*, January 2021, pp. 18–22.
[58] MoD, *France's Defence Strategy in the Indo-Pacific*, 2019a, p. 8. See also Ministry of Foreign Affairs, *France's Indo-Pacific Strategy*, July 2021e, p. 9, https://franceintheus.org/IMG/pdf/Indopacifique_web.pdf
[59] See, e.g. Minister of the Armed Forces Florence Parly, Speech at the Shangri-La Dialogue, Singapore, 3 June 2018; Senate, 2014a, p. 71; MoD, 2017a, p. 26.

They also considered that any Chinese attempt at controlling or prohibiting the access of commercial or military assets in international waters or airspace 'threatened the security of navigation'.[60] As explained by Admiral Anne Cullerre, former Head of the Defence Staff's Bureau of International Military Relations with the Asia-Pacific (2011–2012) and then Joint Commander of French Armed Forces in French Polynesia and Commander of the French Naval Forces in the Pacific (2012–2014), although China's military build-up and its regional posture was 'not perceived as a direct military threat to our country', it was seen as 'a threat to freedom of navigation'; 'we do not accept restrictions on naval traffic and in the air because that is a direct attack on the freedom of navigation, and that is a red line.'[61]

China was also deemed to contest French sovereignty through so-called 'grey zone' activities. The combination of regular and irregular forces (e.g. the Chinese Coast Guard and the People's Armed Forces Maritime Militia) used by the PRC to advance its interests—as well as Chinese illegal fishing practices—were seen by French policymakers as potentially challenging France's sovereignty over its EEZ.[62] A former Asia-hand at the MoD stresses that, since France has the second largest EEZ in the Asia-Pacific, 'every nibble of international law on the part of China impacts our own sovereignty in our exclusive economic zones.'[63] The concern, the official adds, 'is not that China will come and invade Polynesia, but rather its regular intrusions into France's EEZ; we must uphold our sovereignty, we must protect this huge EEZ.'[64]

In light of China's contestation of norms such as the peaceful resolution of disputes, freedom of navigation, and sovereignty, the Asia-Pacific in general and the South China Sea in particular were viewed as a '"test-case" for the future of the rules-based international order'.[65]

Rising Risks of Escalation and Regional Crisis

The combination of China's challenge to the Asian-Pacific balance of power and to key norms of the regional order was perceived by French policymakers as potentially fuelling the risk of unintended escalation and crises and, more broadly, as nurturing regional instability. The risk of incidents, escalation spirals, and regional

---

[60] MoD, *France and Security in the Asia-Pacific* 2016, p. 2. See also Office of the Prime Minister, *National Strategy for the Security of Maritime Areas*, 2015, p. 8.
[61] Interview, 27 March 2017.
[62] MoD, 2018a, p. 8; MoD, 2019a, p. 13.
[63] Interview, 6 July 2017.
[64] Interview, 3 February 2020.
[65] National Assembly, 2019a, p. 6

crises would, in turn, affect France's diplomatic, economic, and security interests in the Asia-Pacific.

For one, a regional crisis would have major implications for French economic interests in the Asia-Pacific. As a testament to Paris's rising threat perception of China, in 2012 the MoD commissioned a study on France's dependence on SLOCs which assessed, among other things, the economic impact for France of a crisis in the South China Sea.[66] It specifically focused on the establishment of an exclusion zone for maritime traffic by the PRC. The report concluded that the adverse impact of such a crisis would be 'very significant' in that it would provoke the paralysis of many industries (in particular automobile and information and communication technology) as well as the cessation in the supply of certain consumer goods, thereby causing inflationary pressures.[67] Accordingly, as emphasized by a MFA official, 'China's military modernization does not impact directly our vital interests, but it does impact indirectly our economic interests'; France, therefore, 'does not have an interest in the destabilization of the region because this would harm our own economic interests'.[68]

But a regional crisis or conflict would also have larger ramifications for Paris's diplomatic and security interests in the Asia-Pacific. It would both hinder France's capacity to deploy naval forces and impact its security relations with regional partners, including military exercises, training, and capacity-building efforts.[69] Furthermore, a regional crisis would likely mobilize France as a member of the UN Security Council.[70] As explained by a former MoD official, 'you cannot decorrelate what happens in the East and South China Seas from the rest of the international relations that France conducts as a middle power and as a member of the UN Security Council. You have to consider such scenario in the larger context of France's international role, of the regional balance of power, and of the maintenance of international law'.[71]

Overall, as a defence official in charge of strategic affairs succinctly puts it, in previous decades 'there was no real threat; there were commercial exchanges with the Asia-Pacific, and this trade steadily grew. But there was no threat.'[72] Thereafter, 'the rise of China changed the strategic equilibria in the region, so we are adapting to it'.[73]

---

[66] Viellard, Anquez, and Histrimont, 2012.
[67] Viellard, Anquez, and Histrimont, 2012, pp. 113 and 121–126.
[68] Interview, 14 November 2013.
[69] Interviews with MoD officials, January–March 2020.
[70] MoD, 2013, p. 35; MoD, 2017a, p. 26.
[71] Interview, 6 July 2017.
[72] Interview, 11 October 2017.
[73] Interview, 11 October 2017. A 2021 MoD report similarly concluded that, 'this basic trend marks a turning point in the development of Chinese power: now endowed with unprecedented capabilities, Beijing intends to weigh more directly on global issues and to assert its strategic aspirations.' MoD, 2021,

Policy Goals

As a result of these rising economic interests and a changing threat assessment, France's policy goals in the Asia-Pacific shifted accordingly. In the 1990s and 2000s, major economic interests and low threat perceptions drove the desire to diplomatically engage China (and other emerging regional powers) and to fervently pursue economic opportunities in the region. Yet, the policy remained fickle and fragmented, with no clearly defined overarching framework and with little emphasis on security considerations. It is only when Paris's threat assessment of China's rise shifted in the 2010s—while its regional economic interests continued to expand—that France gradually developed a cohesive foreign policy framework, the Indo-Pacific strategy, and bolstered the political-military dimension of its presence in the region.

Muddling Through: France's Diplomatic and Economic (Re)Engagement with the Asia-Pacific

Beginning in the 1990s, the proclaimed ambition of the French government to make the Asia-Pacific 'the new frontier of French diplomacy'[74] translated into a variety of initiatives that laid the foundations for an uptick in France's diplomatic and economic engagement with the region in the subsequent decade.

The 1995/1996 cessation of French nuclear tests in the South Pacific—on the Mururoa and Fangataufa atolls—marked a turning point in France's relations with the region. In 1996, Paris signed the Treaty of Rarotonga, establishing a nuclear-weapon-free zone in the South Pacific, and the Comprehensive Nuclear-Test-Ban Treaty prohibiting nuclear weapons tests.[75] Two years later it closed the Pacific Experimental Centre which had overseen the French nuclear test programme in the South Pacific since 1966.[76] The end of French nuclear tests in the region removed a major issue of contention in France's relations with South Pacific countries (e.g. Australia and New Zealand) and, more broadly, across the Asia-Pacific (including Japan)—thereby enabling greater diplomatic and economic cooperation in the following decade.[77]

---

p. 21. See also National Assembly, *L'espace indopacifique : enjeux et stratégie pour la France*, Committee on Foreign Affairs, Report no. 5041, 2022.
[74] Minister of Foreign Affairs, Hervé de Charette, in Session of the Senate, 31 October 1996, https://www.senat.fr/seances/s199610/s19961031/s19961031_mono.html.
[75] Bernard Dumortier, *Les Atolls de l'atome* (Paris: Marine éditions, 2004), pp. 167–169; and Senate, Bill Authorizing the Ratification of the CTBT, Committee on Foreign Affairs, Defence and Armed Forces, Report no. 330, 1997–1998.
[76] Dumortier, 2004.
[77] Senate, *Australie : quelle place pour la France dans le Nouveau monde ?*, Committee on Foreign Affairs, Defence and Armed Forces, Report no. 222, 2016, pp. 87–88.

President Chirac stressed how his 'goal [was] simple: to triple, in ten years, our market shares in Asia'.[78] Similarly, according to General Bentégeat, a close military advisor to the President, 'France's policy in the Asia-Pacific was largely driven by mercantilist interests'.[79] Within this regional economic objective, France's 'China policy' specifically revolved around three central goals (further detailed in Chapter 4): pursuing trade and investment opportunities in this vast, emerging market; broadening the areas of diplomatic engagement with Beijing so as to integrate China in the international system in what was seen as the emerging multipolar world order; and to thereby encourage the 'Westernization' of China through domestic political and economic reforms.

Besides such objectives, Paris's initiatives in the Asia-Pacific lacked a clearly defined policy framework and received little prioritization in France's overall foreign policy.[80] In the words of General Bentégeat, 'unlike our policy vis-à-vis the Arab world, Africa, or Europe', 'France did not have a constructed, coherent, and constant policy towards the Asia-Pacific', the region was 'never a front-burner issue but there nonetheless were economic interests; there were very strong economic interests'.[81] A former official in the Secretariat-General for National Defence (SGDN), the coordinating body for political-military affairs in the Prime Minister's Office, similarly stresses that 'France had no strategy in the Asia-Pacific. We managed the crumbs of the Empire'.[82]

Towards the Indo-Pacific Strategy

During the 2010s, however, the combination of rising economic opportunities in the region and, more decisively, a heightened threat assessment of China led Paris to gradually recalibrate its foreign and security policy towards the Asia-Pacific. This led, over time, to the formulation of a more cohesive policy framework, the Indo-Pacific strategy, with a strengthened political-military dimension.

---

[78] President Jacques Chirac, Speech in Singapore, 29 February 1996.
[79] General Henri Bentégeat, Deputy Chief of the Personal Military Staff of Presidents François Mitterrand and Jacques Chirac (1993–2006), Chief of the Personal Military Staff of President Chirac (1999–2002) and then Chief of the Defence Staff (2002–2006), interview, 16 March 2020.
[80] François Godement, 'Une politique française pour l'Asie-Pacifique ?', *Politique étrangère 60*, no. 4 (1995): pp. 959 and 967. For a similar assessment, see also René Dorient, 'Un septennat de politique asiatique : quel bilan pour la France ?', *Politique étrangère 67*, no. 1 (2002): pp. 173–188; Paul Stares and Nicolas Regaud, 'Europe's Role in Asia-Pacific Security', *Survival 39*, no. 4 (1997): pp. 117 and 131; and Hadrienne Terres, 'La France et l'Asie : l'ébauche d'un "pivot" à la française', French Institute of International Relations (IFRI), April 2015, p. 9.
[81] Interview, 16 May 2017.
[82] Nicolas Regaud, Deputy Assistant Director for Regional Affairs at the MoD's DAS (1997–1999) and then Deputy Director for International Crises and Conflict at the SGDN (2000–2005), interview, 21 March 2017.

Having finalized the first 2010 MoD working group on Chinese power—which, as discussed above, assessed China's growing economic, technological, and military power—the MoD organized another working group, between December 2012 and April 2013, tasked with developing an action plan for France in the Asia-Pacific. Its report assessed the Asia-Pacific's strategic environment and French interests therein, discussed the extant presence of French armed forces in the region, and outlined policy recommendations.[83] Building upon this report, the MoD then published a non-classified document, the 2014 *France and Security in the Asia-Pacific* (which was then regularly updated).[84] In parallel, the 2013 *White Paper on Defence and National Security* significantly expanded, in comparison to previous white papers, the emphasis on the Asia-Pacific—now considered as 'a region where the risks of tension and conflict are among the highest in the world'.[85] Subsequent policy papers and strategy reports further clarified the contours of France's policy in the region.[86]

In 2018, the geographical scope of the overall policy was reframed and refocused on the larger 'Indo-Pacific' so as to combine the two main areas of French involvement in the region, the Indian and the Pacific Oceans.[87] It thereby followed a larger trend among several Asian countries and the United States of expanding the focus of their policy around the Indo-Pacific; France became the first European power to adopt an Indo-Pacific strategy.[88] In the framework of this strategy, Paris's core policy goals revolved around protecting its sovereign territories in the region, upholding key norms of the rules-based order (sovereignty, freedom of navigation and the peaceful resolution of disputes) as well as promoting regional stability to reduce the risk of escalation to a regional crisis or conflict, thereby also sustaining its economic interests in the region, e.g. trade, investment, strategic supplies, and its EEZ.[89]

Overall, Paris aimed to establish its role as a 'mediating power' in the region—in the context of mounting United States–China competition—and to promote 'the emergence of a stable, multipolar regional equilibrium' to prevent the advent

---

[83] Interviews with MoD officials January–December 2017 and January–March 2020.
[84] MoD, *France and Security in the Asia-Pacific*, 2014.
[85] MoD, 2013.
[86] These reports included, among others, MoD, 2013, 2017a; MFA, 2018a; MFA, *The French Strategy in the Indo-Pacific*, 2019a; MoD, 2014; MoD, *France and Security in the Asia-Pacific*, 2016; MoD, 2018a; MoD, 2019a. See also the speeches by French Defence Ministers at the SLD listed in the Bibliography.
[87] President's Office, 'Discours à Garden Island', Sydney, Australia, 3 May 2018; MFA, 2018a, 2019a; and MoD, 2018a.
[88] See, e.g. Rory Medcalf, *Contest for the Indo-Pacific: Why China Won't Map the Future* (Melbourne: La Trobe University Press, 2020) and Robert G. Patman, Patrick Köllner, and Balazs Kiglics, eds., *From Asia-Pacific to Indo-Pacific: Diplomacy in a Contested Region* (Cham, Switzerland: Palgrave Macmillan, 2022). On the German and British policies towards the 'Indo-Pacific', see Chapters 2 and 3 respectively.
[89] President's Office, 'Discours à Garden Island'; MFA, 2018a, pp. 1–4; MFA, 2019a, pp. 5 and 35; MoD, 2019a, pp. 5 and 12–14; Minister of Defence Jean-Yves Le Drian, Speech at the Shangri-La Dialogue, Singapore, 5 June 2016a; Minister of the Armed Forces Florence Parly, 2018; MFA, 2021e, pp. 55-64.

of regional hegemonic powers.[90] In the words of an MoD official, Paris hoped to contribute 'to channelling the rise of China so as to avoid having a region that would completely fall under Chinese influence' as well as 'to the management of the frictions induced by the United States–China competition—by this moving tectonic plate—and to minimize the ensuing shakes'.[91] As detailed later, France thereby sought to forge a distinct and autonomous role for itself, and for the European Union more broadly, in the midst of the rising Sino-American strategic competition.[92]

Policy Instruments

As France redefined and sharpened its regional policy goals, the instruments leveraged to implement such goals also evolved. In the first two post-Cold War decades, because of the absence of a clearly defined overarching policy framework, Paris's engagement with the Asia-Pacific remained a 'patchwork' of largely uncoordinated diplomatic and economic endeavours, with little emphasis on the security dimension of its regional presence.[93] By contrast, as France gradually formulated a more cohesive policy framework in the 2010s, its posture in the region transitioned from this loose patchwork into a more systematic set of initiatives, with an enhanced political-military footprint in the region.

An Unwieldy Patchwork of Initiatives

From the early 1990s to the late 2000s, French engagement in the region largely focused on developing bilateral diplomatic and economic ties with China and other regional powers, most notably Japan and India. In this timeframe, also referred to as the 'honeymoon' of France–China relations,[94] Paris aimed to position itself as the key political partner of Beijing within the European Union and to vigorously expand bilateral economic opportunities, including arms sales. In parallel, France sought, with only partial success, to increase its participation in the emerging Asian multilateral structures as a complement to these bilateral efforts. What

---

[90] MFA, 2018a, pp. 4–6. See also MFA, 2019a, pp. 31 and 35; and President Macron quoted in 'Macron Wants a Balance against China in the Pacific', *Radio New Zealand*, 7 May 2018.
[91] Interview, 13 December 2016.
[92] On France's promotion of the EU strategy for the Indo-Pacific, see the section entitled 'Policy Instruments' later in this chapter. On the formulation of a more cohesive EU policy towards the PRC, see also Chapter 4.
[93] The concept of 'patchwork' as applied to France's policy in the region was first used by Stares and Regaud, 1997.
[94] Lawrence R. Sullivan, *Historical Dictionary of the People's Republic of China* (Boulder, CO: Rowman and Littlefield, 2016), p. 258.

gradually emerged was a loose patchwork of bilateral and multilateral initiatives but with little centralized coordination.

Bilateral Ties: Major Power Focus (China, Japan, and India)
The repression on Tiananmen Square, in June 1989, marked, according to a declassified document, a 'turning point'[95] in Franco-Chinese relations which were thereafter 'greatly degraded', at least temporarily.[96] Paris reacted by combining a freeze on bilateral diplomatic visits and meetings, on military cooperation, and on government loans to Beijing with the pursuit of normal economic relations.[97] Importantly, at the Madrid Summit on 27 June 1989, France established, together with the other European Community (EC) members, an embargo on arms sales to China, which became a major irritant in French-Chinese relations. Paris's sale of six La Fayette frigates and of sixty Mirage 2000-5 to Taiwan, in 1991-1992, further damaged bilateral ties with Beijing,[98] despite the efforts by French diplomats to persuade their Chinese counterparts that France's economic 'interest in the Taiwanese market had no political significance.'[99]

After the subsequent stabilization of their relations in the mid-1990s,[100] the two countries established a 'long-term global partnership', in 1997, which focused on strengthening bilateral economic ties as well as diplomatic cooperation in areas such as the reform of the UN Security Council, the promotion of disarmament, or development aid.[101] In 2001, Paris and Beijing instituted a 'strategic dialogue' to foster cooperation in three overarching areas: dialogue on political and strategic issues, military cooperation (e.g. peacekeeping operations, exchange of officers, military medicine), and armaments cooperation.[102] Key strategic items in the bilateral partnership included nuclear equipment (such as nuclear reactors), aeronautics (e.g. Airbus's production of A320 in China), and space technology

---

[95] MFA to French Embassy in China, 'Relations franco-chinoises', 15 September 1989, CADN, 513PO/2004038.
[96] French Embassy in China to MFA, 'Relations bilatérales entre la France et la Chine en 1989', 4 January 1990, CADN, 513PO/2004038.
[97] MFA to French Embassy in China, 'Situation intérieure en Chine et relations franco-chinoises', 24 April 1990, CADN, 513PO/2004038. See also MFA, 1989.
[98] Jean-Pierre Cabestan, 'France's Taiwan Policy: A Case of Shopkeeper Diplomacy', Paper presented at the conference The Role of France and Germany in Sino-European Relations, Hong Kong Baptist University, 22-23 June 2001, pp. 5-9.
[99] French Embassy in China to MFA, 'La Chine de 1991 à 1992: relations bilatérales franco-chinoises', 30 January 1992b, CADN, 513PO/2004038.
[100] MFA, 'Communiqué conjoint franco-chinois sur le rétablissement de relations de coopération entre la France et la Chine', 12 January 1994, https://www.vie-publique.fr/discours/133004-communique-conjoint-franco-chinois-en-date-du-12-janvier-1994-sur-le-r.
[101] Government, 'Déclaration conjointe franco-chinoise pour un partenariat global', signed by Jacques Chirac and Jiang Zemin, Beijing, 16 May 1997.
[102] National Assembly, Chine, Committee on Foreign Affairs, Report no. 1597, 4 December 2013, Section II; National Assembly, Report by the Delegation of the France–China Friendship Group, August 2010, https://www.assemblee-nationale.fr/13/pdf/rap-dian/dian003-2012.pdf (accessed 2 June 2010), p. 10, fn. 1.

transfers.[103] The partnership was then elevated to a 'global strategic partnership' in 2004, reinforcing consultations across all levels of the two countries' MFAs.[104]

Concomitantly, in the first half of the 2000s, France was the EU country to advocate for the lifting of the EU embargo on arms sales to China most vehemently, thereby causing a major rift in transatlantic relations.[105] In contrast to the 1989 US arms embargo on China, the EU arms embargo is a non-legally binding political declaration which requires an EU-wide consensus to be lifted.[106] From Paris's perspective, the rationale for lifting the embargo was three-fold.

First, lifting the EU arms embargo was seen as a deliverable—a 'symbolic gesture'[107]—to be provided to Beijing so as to remove a significant obstacle to the deepening of their bilateral diplomatic and economic ties. As shown in leaked US diplomatic cables, maintaining an arms embargo on a rising power such as China was viewed in Paris as being both discriminatory and politically harmful.[108] Second, in the view of the French government, if the embargo was lifted, the 1998 EU Code of Conduct on arms exports and the existing export controls systems would prevent an increase in defence exports to China and would therefore have no impact on China's military modernization nor on regional stability in the Asia-Pacific.[109] Third, Paris considered that the EU arms embargo on China was actually counterproductive in that it had spurred China to indigenously develop its defence and technological industrial base.[110]

By 2005, however, the political landscape of the European debate on the 'China embargo' had changed. Under the combined impact of intense US pressures on EU member states, of persistent intra-European fragmentation on this issue, and of China's adoption of the Anti-Secession Law (ASL) in March 2005, the push

---

[103] National Assembly, 2013; and Presidency's Office, 'Déclaration conjointe du Président de la République française et du Président de la République populaire de Chine', 10 January 2018. On Sino-French space cooperation, see Hugo Meijer, *Trading with the Enemy: The Making of US Export Control Policy toward the People's Republic of China* (New York: Oxford University Press, 2016), pp. 283–287.

[104] Presidency's Office, 'Déclaration conjointe Chine–France', 27 January 2004.

[105] Hugo Meijer, 'Transatlantic Perspectives on China's Military Modernization: The Case of Europe's Arms Embargo against the People's Republic of China', *Paris Paper no. 12*, Strategic Research Institute (IRSEM), 2014, pp. 49–50.

[106] European Council, Presidency Conclusions, Madrid, 26 and 27 June 1989, Appendix II. For a detailed analysis, see Meijer, 2014.

[107] Former MoD official, interview, 16 July 2013.

[108] US Embassy in France, 'MOD Advisor Upbeat on Bilateral Relationship; Sees Rapprochement on Middle East; No Change on EU China Arms Embargo', Confidential, Wikileaks Cablegate, 18 March 2005b; US Embassy in France, 'Codel Smith Meets Chirac, French Officials', Confidential, Wikileaks Cablegate, 31 January 2005a.

[109] Interviews with former MFA official, 24 September 2013; and with former MoD officials on 23 July, 29 July, and 12 December 2013. See also, e.g. US Embassy in France, 2005a; US Embassy in France, 'France/GAERC: Agreement on Most Issues except China Embargo', Confidential, 8 December 2006, Wikileaks/Cablegate. For details on the revisions to 1998 EU Code of Conduct on arms exports, see Meijer, 2014, pp. 22–24.

[110] MoD official, interview, 29 July 2013. See also, e.g. then Minister of Defence Michèle Alliot-Marie (2002–2007) quoted in Peter Spiegel and John Thornhill, 'France Urges End to China Arms Embargo', *Financial Times*, 15 February 2005.

to lift the embargo lost considerable momentum.[111] Furthermore, as discussed in Chapters 2 and 3, London and Berlin's policy positions shifted, and they decided to oppose such a move.[112] By the second half of the 2000s, the issue of the EU arms embargo on China had thus been shelved.[113] Thereafter, France maintained talking points indicating its official support for lifting the EU embargo on China while de facto abandoning the endeavour, taking no concrete initiative to achieve this goal. This approach allowed reaping diplomatic benefits for the Franco-Chinese bilateral relationship while avoiding the political costs and fallouts that would result from actively pursuing this effort given the existing intra-European and transatlantic disagreements on this issue.[114]

Besides the PRC, France bolstered its political and economic ties also with other major regional powers, namely Japan and India. Paris and Tokyo established a 'strategic partnership' in 1995 and the two countries started holding bilateral consultations at the working group level between the respective MFAs and MoDs.[115] Through the 1990s and 2000s, however, political-military cooperation was considerably constrained by the almost complete monopoly of the United States on defence cooperation with Japan, by Tokyo's concerns regarding France's advocacy for lifting the EU arms embargo on the PRC, and by Japan's own stringent regulations on arms trade.[116] In this timeframe, Franco-Japanese relations thus largely revolved around fostering greater bilateral political engagement and expanding trade relations.

With India, France developed, from 1998, a 'strategic partnership' structured around three main pillars, namely cooperation in the defence, space, and civil nuclear areas.[117] Over time, bilateral cooperation came to also encompass counter-terrorism, counter-piracy, maritime security, military exercises, and arms

---

[111] The ASL declared that, in case of Taiwan's secession from the PRC, Beijing could employ military means 'to protect China's sovereignty and territorial integrity'. See 'Full Text of China's Anti-Secession Law', *People's Daily Online*, 14 March 2005. On the implication of the ASL and on the US pressures on EU member states on the 'China embargo', see Meijer, 2014, pp. 26–34.

[112] Furthermore, the Chinese government had come to realize the growing unlikelihood of the lifting of the European arms embargo and had therefore decreased its diplomatic pressures on the European Union on this specific issue. Interviews with Chinese experts in Beijing and Shanghai, July–November 2013. See also Meijer, 2016, p. 250.

[113] See, e.g. US Embassy in Belgium, 'Is the EU Retreating on the China Arms Embargo?', Confidential, Wikileaks Cablegate, 24 March 2005.

[114] For more details, see Meijer, 2014, pp. 39–48; and Meijer, 2016, pp. 248–250.

[115] National Assembly, 2019a, p. 52. See also Kazuhiko Tōgō, *Japan's Foreign Policy, 1945–2009: The Quest for a Proactive Policy* (Leiden: Brill, 2010), pp. 272–273.

[116] Interviews with current and former MoD officials, January–December 2017. See also François Godement, 'France's "Pivot" to Asia', European Council on Foreign Relations (ECFR), *Policy Brief*, May 2014, p. 5.

[117] One year later, they established a 'strategic dialogue'. On the strategic partnership and strategic dialogue see, e.g. National Assembly, *La place de la France en Inde*, Committee on Foreign Affairs, Report no. 4187, 18 January 2012, p. 48; Indian MFA, 'India-France Bilateral Relations', Indian Embassy in Paris, April 2018a.

transfers, among others.[118] In 2005, a major contract was finalized for France's sale of six Scorpène diesel-electric attack submarines to India.[119] Building upon ties dating back to the early Cold War, France and India also bolstered their cooperative relations in the space and civilian nuclear sectors.[120] The depth and breadth of such cooperation made it one of France's most robust bilateral defence relationships in the region.

Asian Multilateralism: France and the Asia–Europe Meeting

Complementing these bilateral endeavours, France sought to nurture its political relations with China and other regional powers by contributing to the development of Asian multilateralism. In particular, after its unsuccessful attempt to apply—independently from the European Union—to the Association of Southeast Asian Nations (ASEAN) Regional Forum (ARF) in 1995,[121] Paris contributed to launching the Asia–Europe Meeting (ASEM) while it held the EU Presidency thereby opting to engage ASEAN multilateralism through the European Union.[122] The initiative jointly developed by France and Singapore gave birth, in 1996, to ASEM as a format for intergovernmental political and economic dialogue between Asians and Europeans.[123]

Christian Lechervy, the former Head of the Asia Pacific Bureau of the MoD's Directorate of Strategic Affairs (1992–1996) and then Advisor for International Affairs to the Minister of Defence (1997–2002) later argued that China was the 'unspoken' factor in the ASEM process: the ASEM format was, in his view, a way to resume talks with Beijing—after the significant frictions between EU member states and the PRC that had followed the 1989 Tiananmen Square repression—and, thereby, to politically re-engage China.[124] From Paris's perspective, contributing to the launch of the ASEM multilateral framework complemented the deepening of

---

[118] French Embassy in India, 'Relations franco-indiennes', 18 September 2019, https://in.ambafrance.org/-Relations-franco-indiennes- (accessed on 1 December 2021). On their bilateral military exercises, see Nicolas Regaud, 'France and Security in the Asia-Pacific', p. 7.

[119] National Assembly, 2012, p. 59.

[120] On space cooperation, see Embassy in India, 'Coopération spatiale', *Factsheet*, 14 July 2018. On nuclear cooperation and on French support to India's bid to the Nuclear Suppliers Group, see Presidency's Office, 'Déclaration commune publiée à l'occasion du Sommet franco-indien', 30 September 2008; National Assembly, 2012, p. 48.

[121] Rodolfo Severino, *The ASEAN Regional Forum* (Singapore: Institute of Southeast Asian Studies, 2009), pp. 22–23.

[122] Frédéric Bozo, *La politique étrangère de la France depuis 1945* (Paris: Flammarion, 2012), pp. 230–231.

[123] Christian Lechervy, 'La France, l'Europe et l'Asie-Pacifique', Institute for Strategic Research, *Lettre de l'IRSEM*, no. 2, 2013, p. 1.

[124] Christian Lechervy, 'L'ASEM : le début d'un (mini-)pivot européen vers l'Asie-Pacifique ?', *Relations internationales 4*, no. 168 (2016): p. 126.

France's bilateral political and economic relations with China and other regional powers.

Bolstering France's Regional Political-Military Footprint

It is during the 2010s, as France gradually developed a more cohesive policy framework—which was formalized in the 2018 Indo-Pacific strategy—that it strengthened the political-military dimension of its regional presence. It did so through several lines of effort: expanding its naval deployments in the region, broadening the range of bilateral diplomatic and security partnerships, increasing France's participation in the regional multilateral architecture, while enhancing multinational cooperation with both regional and Western (US and European) powers. In the words of a MoD official in charge of strategic affairs, China was 'the key driver of change of the strategic environment' and that required 'a more muscular French presence in the region'.[125]

Naval Deployments and Bilateral Partnerships

During the 2010s, while Paris did not increase the volume of its permanently forward-deployed forces in the region—largely because of resource constraints and competing regional priorities[126]—it intensified its naval deployments.

Even though France retained the largest European military presence in the region, it faced delicate trade-offs in the allocation of scarce resources to different regions and theatres, such as Afghanistan, Libya, Mali, or reinforcing NATO deterrence after the 2014 Ukrainian crisis. In fact, the Asia-Pacific remained subordinated to other regions within the hierarchy of its defence-planning priorities, most notably Europe, the Middle East, and Northern and sub-Saharan Africa.[127] As explained by an MoD official, although the Defence Staff did not 'explicitly refer to a system of concentric circles, it is all the same'; the Defence Staff assessed that French armed forces had an operational range for high-end military interventions of roughly 5,000 km, thus reaching the north-western quadrant of

---

[125] Interview, 20 March 2017.

[126] On French forward-deployed forces in the region, 'Appendix: France's Military Presence and Naval Deployments in the Asia-Pacific' in Meijer, 2021a, available at https://ndownloader.figstatic.com/files/30687660. See also the analysis of French capability shortfalls and how they affect its regional presence in Regaud, 2021, p. 20; and Senate, *Australie : quelle place pour la France dans le Nouveau monde ?*, Committee on Foreign Affairs, Defence and Armed Forces, Report no. 222, 2016, pp. 78–80 and 117–118.

[127] Both the 2013 *White Paper* and the 2017 *Strategic Review*, for instance, ranked European security, sub-Saharan Africa, the Middle East, and the Persian Gulf before the Asia-Pacific. MoD, *French White Paper on Defence and National Security*, 2013, ch. 4; MoD, *Strategic Review of Defence and National Security*, 2017a, ch. 2.

the Indian Ocean.[128] It was, therefore, within this radius that France had the capability to maintain robust defence commitments in the framework of a military coalition. By contrast, in the Asia-Pacific, France's 'defence commitments are not at the high-end of the spectrum; rather, France contributes to security through greater regional presence and influence.'[129] Accordingly, the expanding emphasis on the Asia-Pacific and the greater policy cohesiveness in French foreign and security policy did not substantially alter the overall regional prioritization in French defence-planning.

Yet, within the limits of available resources, France increased its naval deployments in the Asia-Pacific.[130] Based upon available data, Figure 1.1 shows the number of the French navy's capital ships that were deployed in the Indian and Pacific Oceans between 2012 and 2019, with an average of 3.9 deployments per year (of which on average 2 deployments were conducted with US and/or other European navies per year, as discussed later).[131] The type and name of these capital ships—and the missions for which they were deployed—are listed in Table 1.1. In 2021, France also deployed for the first time the nuclear attack submarine (SSN) Émeraude to the South China Sea as well as a signals intelligence (SIGINT) ship,

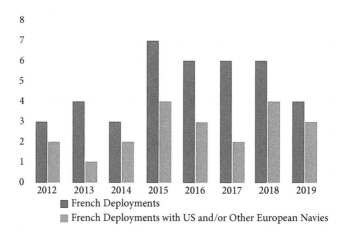

Fig. 1.1 Deployments of French navy's capital ships in the Indian and Pacific Oceans, 2012–2019

Source: French Navy, *Cols Bleus*, 2012–2019 (for details, see Appendix A).

---

[128] MoD official, interview, 13 October 2017.
[129] MoD official, interview, 13 October 2017.
[130] The procedures followed by French deployments differ from those of US so-called freedom of navigation operations (FONOPs). On France's position on FONOPs, see 'Appendix: France's Military Presence and Naval Deployments in the Asia-Pacific' in Meijer, 2021a, available at https://ndownloader.figstatic.com/files/30687660.
[131] The data refer to the deployments of capital ships, not to total deployments in the Asia-Pacific. This allows us to focus on major deployments and to set aside minor deployments, e.g. for hydrographic missions. For details, see Appendix A.

Table 1.1 French navy's capital ships deployed in the Indian and Pacific Oceans, 2012–2019

Name of ship	Type and description of ship	Missions involved
Charles de Gaulle	French aircraft carrier and flagship of the Marine Nationale	2014: Bois Belleau; 2015: Operation Chammal; 2015: Mission Arromanches; 2016: Operation Chammal; 2019: Mission Clémenceau
BPC Tonnerre	Amphibious assault helicopter carrier	2013: Mission Jeanne d'Arc; 2016: Mission Jeanne d'Arc; 2018: Bois Belleau 100; 2019: Bois Belleau 100; 2019: Mission Jeanne d'Arc
Dixmude	Amphibious assault helicopter carrier	2012: Operation Atalanta; 2012: EAOM; 2015: Jeanne d'Arc; 2018: Jeanne d'Arc
Mistral	Amphibious assault ship and helicopter carrier	2017: Jeanne d'Arc
Auvergne	FREMM multipurpose frigate	2017: Maritime Surveillance; 2017: Long Term Deployment
Cassard	Anti-aircraft frigate	2012: Operation Enduring Freedom; 2015: CTF 150; 2015: Operation Chammal; 2018: Maritime Surveillance; 2018: TF 55; 2019: TF 150
Chevalier Paul	Frigate, escort, and protection of a carrier strike group	2013: Operation Enduring Freedom; 2013: Deployment; 2015: Operation Chammal; 2015: Mission Arromanches; 2016: Operation Chammal; 2018: Bois Belleau
Forbin	Anti-air frigate	2014: Bois Belleau; 2016: TF 150; 2017: Operational Preparation; 2017: Operation Chammal; 2019: Mission Clémenceau
Jean Bart	Anti-air frigate	2014: Operation Enduring Freedom; 2015: NA; 2015: Operation Enduring Freedom; 2017: Support to TF 150; 2019: Maritime Surveillance
Jean de Vienne	Anti-submarine frigate	2014: Bois Belleau; 2018: Maritime Surveillance; 2018: TF 150
La Fayette	Multi-mission stealth frigate	2016: Operational Preparation; 2016: TF 465; 2018: TF 150; 2019: Jeanne d'Arc
Motte Picquet	Anti-submarine frigate	2012: Operation Enduring Freedom; 2016: Operation Chammal
Provence	FREMM anti-submarine frigate	2016: Operation Chammal; 2016: TF 150; 2016: Maritime Surveillance; 2019: Mission Clémenceau
Vendémiaire	Surveillance frigate	2012: Mission Asie, Maritime Surveillance; 2014: Mission Asie, Maritime Surveillance; 2015: Mission Asie, Maritime Surveillance; 2016: Mission Asie; 2017: Maritime Surveillance; 2018: Mission Asie, Maritime Surveillance; 2019: Maritime Surveillance

Source: French Navy, *Cols Bleus*, 2012–2019; and website of French MoD (https://www.defense.gouv.fr).

the Dupuy de Lôme, through the Taiwan Strait.[132] And, one year later, during the Mission Jeanne d'Arc, France led the La Pérouse multinational naval exercise with assets from Australia, India, Japan and the United States.[133]

A second line of effort was the deepening and broadening of its network of bilateral partnerships.[134] Paris strengthened its existing ties with Tokyo and New Delhi while rebalancing its bilateral relationship with Beijing; but it also diversified its diplomatic and security partnerships with medium and lesser regional powers through strategic dialogues, military operational cooperation, and arms transfers.

For one, Paris continued to broaden the areas of bilateral cooperation with the PRC by establishing, among others, a financial and economic dialogue, in 2013, and a high-level dialogue on scientific, academic, and cultural exchanges, as well as on human rights.[135] At the same time, as further detailed in Chapter 4, it sought to recalibrate its relationship with Beijing by establishing a more stringent screening mechanism on FDI inflows from China (and other countries) and by tightening the restrictions on telecommunications suppliers of concern like Huawei, first on 4G then on 5G technology. It also abandoned any attempt at lifting the EU arms embargo on China, further confirming the central role of rising threat perceptions of the PRC.[136]

As it rebalanced its bilateral relationship with Beijing, Paris reinforced and diversified its political-military ties in East Asia, South East Asia, and into the Indian Ocean. The political-military dimension of the Franco-Japanese relationship—relabelled as an 'exceptional partnership' in 2013 (with annual 2+2 ministerial consultations since 2014)—was subsequently expanded through a variety of initiatives, including on information-sharing, military technology transfers, cyber, maritime security, and military exercises, among others.[137] Similarly, France and India further deepened their defence and security cooperation in areas such as logistics support, maritime security, the exchange of classified information, space cooperation, military exercises, and through large arms sales, including thirty-six

---

[132] Sébastien Seibt, 'France Wades into the South China Sea with a Nuclear Attack Submarine', *France24*, 12 February 2021; Xavier Vavasseur, 'French SIGINT ship Dupuy de Lôme Makes Rare Taiwan Strait Transit', *Naval News*, 13 October 2021b, https://www.navalnews.com/naval-news/2021/10/french-sigint-ship-dupuy-de-lome-taiwan/.

[133] Xavier Vavasseur, 'Australia, France, India, Japan and the United States Take Part in Exercise La Pérouse', *Naval News*, 6 April 2021a.

[134] See for instance, MFA, *France's Partnerships in the Indo-Pacific*, 2021c, https://www.diplomatie.gouv.fr/IMG/pdf/en_a4_indopacifique_16p_2021_v4_cle4b8b46.pdf.

[135] MFA, 'Relations bilatérales—China', *Country Factsheet*, 28 June 2019f, https://www.diplomatie.gouv.fr/fr/dossiers-pays/chine/relations-bilaterales/.

[136] Interviews with MFA and MoD officials, January–December 2017 and January–March 2020. Additional considerations that persuaded Paris to abandon the goal of lifting the embargo included the risk of major transatlantic frictions that such a move would entail; furthermore, intra-European fragmentation on this issue continued to preclude reaching the consensus required within the European Union to lift the embargo. For more details, see Meijer, 2014, pp. 39–46.

[137] See Japanese MFA, 'Japan-France Relations (Archives)', https://www.mofa.go.jp/region/europe/france/archives.html. See also Jeffrey W. Hornung, *Allies Growing Closer: Japan–Europe Security Ties in the Age of Strategic Competition* (Santa Monica, CA: RAND Corporation, 2020), pp. 39–57.

Rafale fighter jets.[138] As one diplomat puts it, 'China is an implicit factor in France's capacity building with India.'[139]

Besides strengthening its existing ties with major regional powers, Paris also broadened its network of bilateral partnerships by cultivating enhanced defence ties with Australia as well as with South East Asian countries.[140] Building upon their 2009 defence cooperation and status of forces (SOF) agreement,[141] Paris and Canberra developed a 'strategic partnership' in 2012—then elevated to an 'enhanced' strategic partnership (in 2017)—with the goal of promoting 'a stable Indo-Pacific region'.[142] In 2016, the Australian Government selected Naval Group (then called DCNS) for the SEA 1000 Future Submarine Program, i.e. the design of twelve Shortfin Block 1A diesel-electric submarines (SSK) for the Royal Australian Navy.[143] This agreement was the largest defence contract ever awarded by Canberra and the largest contract ever granted to a European defence company ($34.5bn).[144] The first submarine was supposed to commence service in the early 2030s, the construction of the last submarine was scheduled for the 2050s, and sustainment would continue until the 2080s.[145] Paris thereby expected to considerably tighten its long-term political and defence relationship with Canberra. In September 2021, however, Australia, the United States, and the United Kingdom announced a new, enhanced trilateral security partnership (labelled AUKUS) which included, among other things, the delivery of a fleet of at least eight nuclear-powered submarines for Australia.[146] By scrapping the previous bilateral

---

[138] See, among others, MFA, 'Indo-French Dialogue on Maritime Cooperation and Signing of White Shipping Agreement', French Embassy in India, New Delhi, 19 January 2017a; Indian MFA, 'India-France Bilateral Relations', Embassy of India in Paris, April 2018a.

[139] Interview, New Delhi, 12 December 2018.

[140] On the diversification of French security partnerships in Southeast Asia, see among others Senate 2014a, 2014b.

[141] Australian Government, *Agreement between the Government of Australia and the Government of the French Republic Regarding Defence Cooperation and Status of Forces*, Paris, France, 14 December 2006 (ratified in 2009).

[142] MFA, 'Joint Statement of Enhanced Strategic Partnership between Australia and France', 3 March 2017b. See also Australian Government, 'Joint Statement of Enhanced Strategic Partnership between Australia and France', 19 January 2012; Senate, 2016, pp. 96–103.

[143] In addition to Naval Group, the tender also opposed competitive offers by Germany's ThyssenKrupp Marine Systems (TKMS) and a Japanese consortium comprising Mitsubishi Heavy Industries and Kawasaki Shipbuilding Corporation. Xavier Vavasseur, 'France and Australia Reaffirm Commitment to the Attack-class Submarine Program', *Naval News*, 18 February 2020b.

[144] Xavier Vavasseur, 'Naval Group Inks Major "Attack-class" Submarine Contract with Australia', *Naval News*, 1 February 2020a.

[145] Julian Kerr, 'Attack Class—-Plan of Action', *Australian Defence Magazine*, 10 October 2019.

[146] Office of the Prime Minister of Australia, 'Australia to Pursue Nuclear-Powered Submarines through New Trilateral Enhanced Security Partnership', *Media Statement*, 16 September 2021, https://www.pm.gov.au/media/australia-pursue-nuclear-powered-submarines-through-new-trilateral-enhanced-security; The White House, 'Remarks by President Biden, Prime Minister Morrison of Australia, and Prime Minister Johnson of the United Kingdom Announcing the Creation of AUKUS', *Briefing Room*, 15 September 2021a, https://www.whitehouse.gov/briefing-room/speeches-remarks/2021/09/15/remarks-by-president-biden-prime-minister-morrison-of-australia-and-prime-minister-johnson-of-the-united-kingdom-announcing-the-creation-of-aukus/; The White House, 'Background

deal between Paris and Canberra, AUKUS caused a significant diplomatic rift between France and the three countries. French senior policymakers were caught by surprise and felt they had been 'stabbed in the back',[147] especially since just two weeks prior to the AUKUS announcement the French and Australian Ministers of Foreign Affairs and Defence had jointly 'underlined the importance of the future submarine program'.[148] Canberra's reversal of the previous Franco-Australian submarine contract weakened what was considered by Paris as one of the pillars of its regional strategy.

In South East Asia, Paris elevated the bilateral relationship with Singapore to a 'strategic partnership' in 2012, fostering cooperation in areas such as cybersecurity, joint military exercises, military-to-military exchanges, and training of fighter pilots, among others.[149] It also engaged in significant arms sales to the city-island throughout the 2010s (e.g. H225M helicopters, A330 MRTT air-to-air refuelling aircraft, and Aster SAMP/T missiles), becoming Singapore's second largest arms supplier after the United States.[150] Singapore also emerged as one of France's largest partners in the field of defence research and development in areas such as radars and submarine detection.[151]

Malaysia was France's second main security partner in South East Asia.[152] Although the two countries did not establish a formal 'strategic partnership', they built upon previous arms sales—most notably Kuala Lumpur's acquisition of two Scorpène-class diesel-electric submarines in the 2000s—to further develop their political-military ties.[153] Armaments cooperation and the institutionalization of military, technical, and training cooperation were seen by French officials as mutually feeding one another, and thus helped strengthening bilateral ties over time.[154] The two countries significantly deepened their armaments cooperation to the point that, in the 2009–2018 period, France became Malaysia's first arms supplier

---

Press Call on AUKUS', *Briefing Room*, 15 September 2021b, https://www.whitehouse.gov/briefing-room/press-briefings/2021/09/15/background-press-call-on-aukus.

[147] 'Jean-Yves Le Drian dénonce "un coup dans le dos" après la rupture du contrat des sous-marins par l'Australie', *France Info*, 16 September 2021.

[148] Australian DoD, 'Inaugural Australia–France 2+2 Ministerial Consultations', 30 August 2021, https://www.foreignminister.gov.au/minister/marise-payne/media-release/inaugural-australia-france-22-ministerial-consultations.

[149] Senate, 2014a, p. 171; Singaporean MoD, 'Singapore and France Strengthen Defence Relations through 18th Defence Policy Dialogue', *News Releases*, 1 February 2019.

[150] Imports from France represented between 16 per cent and 21 per cent of total Singaporean arms imports between 2009 and 2018 (and imports from the US between 46 and 57 per cent). SIPRI, 2019, p. 6.

[151] Interview with a former official posted in Singapore, 28 April 2017.

[152] Senate, 2014a, p. 57.

[153] Interviews with a former defence official, 28 June 2017, and with a former official in the MFA's Directorate of Defence and Security Cooperation, 19 April 2017.

[154] Interviews with MFA and MoD officials, Paris, January–December 2017.

and transferred systems such as Gowind corvettes, A400M military transport aircraft, and EC725 helicopters.[155]

Besides Singapore and Malaysia, the two key hubs of its diplomatic and military presence in South East Asia, France also sought to foster the development of ties with Vietnam and Indonesia. Yet, while Paris and Hanoi established a 'strategic partnership' in 2013 and signed a bilateral framework to facilitate intelligence cooperation,[156] their defence cooperation remained constrained by Hanoi's heavy reliance on Russia for its arms imports.[157] With Jakarta, Paris established a 'strategic partnership', in 2011, which focused on capacity-building, training, and exchange of defence officials; they subsequently strengthened their bilateral cooperation in areas such as maritime security, joint training, military education, and armaments—including Indonesia's acquisition of forty-two Rafale fighter jets.[158]

The 'China Factor' in France's Regional Partnerships

Overall, France thus significantly strengthened and diversified its network of diplomatic and security partnerships in the region. A central driver of this effort was China's rising assertiveness (and France's perceptions thereof) as well as the resulting demand pull from regional states which requested greater French engagement and capacity-building efforts. In fact, France's threat assessment and the demand pull from regional partners were two sides of the same coin. The PRC's assertiveness caused French threat perceptions to intensify which, in turn, led Paris to bolster and diversify its network of regional partnerships. At the same time, China's muscular regional posture also caused the threat assessments of French regional partners to heighten which, in turn, drove a 'demand pull', i.e. a growing demand by these partners for more French security cooperation and capability-building efforts.

As explained by a MoD official working on Asian-Pacific security, although Paris does 'not build a bilateral partnership exclusively in reaction to the behaviour of one country', China's behaviour 'does shape our bilateral partnerships through

---

[155] Senate, 2014a, p. 171; Airbus, 'Malaysia Takes Delivery of its First Airbus A400M', Media, 10 March 2015; Defence Industry Daily Staff, 'Malaysia Ordering EC725 SAR Helicopters', *Defence Industry Daily*, 3 June 2019; Giovanni de Briganti, 'DCNS Confirms Sale of 10 Gowind Corvettes, Expects More', *Defence Aerospace*, 31 October 2014; National Assembly, 2019a, p. 59.

[156] MFA, 'Présentation de la Mission de Défense', French Embassy in Hanoi, 4 October 2018c; National Assembly, 2019a, p. 59; Senate, 2014a, p. 176.

[157] National Assembly, 2019a, p. 59.

[158] See MFA, 'Indonésie——Relations bilatérales', *Country Factsheet*, August 2019c; Francis Striby, 'L'Indonésie et la France prêts à signer un accord de coopération en matière de défense', *Portail de l'intelligence économique*, 23 January 2020; Dassault Aviation, 'Indonesia purchases the Rafale', Press Kit, 10 February 2022, https://www.dassault-aviation.com/en/group/press/press-kits/indonesia-purchases-the-rafale/.

the willingness of our regional partners to develop, for instance, their naval capabilities'.[159] Christian Lechervy, former Personal Advisor for Strategic Affairs and the Asia-Pacific to President François Hollande (2012–2014), further expounds the 'China factor' in France's network of bilateral partnerships—and specifically in its arms transfers—as follows:

> Obviously the China factor is always sitting somewhere. When Taiwan buys Mirage fighter jets from France, it is not to confront US armed forces; when Malaysia buys submarines, it is not to protect fishermen in the South China Sea; and when we export submarines to Australia, we know very well that it is not to ensure Canberra against an attack from New Zealand. So, from the moment France supplies equipment of strategic superiority—e.g. combat aircraft, submarines, satellites, cruise missiles, etc.—China becomes an implicit factor.[160]

An MoD official confirms that, 'although this enhanced political-military engagement in the Indo-Pacific is not "anti-Chinese"—it is not geared against China—clearly the actor who is changing the regional strategic environment, who is altering the balance of power, and who is pushing regional states to increase their defence spending is China. So our policy response is not "anti-Chinese", also because we would not have the resources to achieve such goal. But, on the other hand, we are compelled to adapt to this changing regional security environment.'[161]

In short, China's rising assertiveness and the ensuing demand pull from regional states played an important, though not always explicit, role in driving the strengthening and diversification of French bilateral partnerships in the region and its capacity-building efforts.

Consolidating the Regional Security Architecture: Multilateral Regimes and Western Security Cooperation

Paris complemented these bilateral undertakings by expanding its engagement in the regional security architecture both through greater involvement in mini- and multilateral regional initiatives as well as through enhanced—though still modest—cooperation with other Western powers in the Asia-Pacific (and, since 2018, in the larger Indo-Pacific region). The main purpose of these endeavours was, as part of the emerging Indo-Pacific strategy, to foster regional cooperation to uphold the key norms of the regional order and to preserve regional stability in the face of China's rise.

---

[159] Interview, 21 March 2017.
[160] Interview, 23 March 2017.
[161] Interview, 10 May 2021.

Multilateral Security Regimes and Multinational Military Exercises

France's engagement with multilateral regimes in the Asia-Pacific had begun, as previously shown, in the mid-1990s and had continued in the 2000s (with limited success).[162] In the subsequent decade, Paris further expanded its activities in a wide variety of regional political-security regimes, technical-functional institutions, and ad hoc fora.

It did so, among other things, by annually attending the Shangri-La Dialogue (SLD) in Singapore,[163] the Raisina Dialogue (since 2016) in New Delhi, as well as the South Pacific Defence Ministers Meeting which focused on security challenges in the South Pacific. French defence officials also regularly participated in fora such as the Asia-Pacific Chief of Defence Conference, the Western Pacific Naval Symposium, the Indian Ocean Naval Symposium, and in other functional organizations and minilateral groupings in the South Pacific, while attempting to join two working groups of the ASEAN Defence Ministers Meeting Plus (ADMM+) and the Regional Cooperation Agreement on Combating Piracy and Armed Robbery against Ships in Asia (ReCAAP) (for details, see the Appendix in Meijer 2021a).

Combined with this engagement in the region's multilateral security architecture, Paris expanded its participation in multinational military exercises in the region, including on the Korean peninsula (Ulchi Freedom Guardian and Key Resolve), in the Pacific Ocean (e.g. RIMPAC, Multinational Planning Augmentation Team, Southern Katipo, etc.) and in the Indian Ocean (Papangue, Diana, Cutlass Express).[164] France itself has organized several multinational exercises, most notably the Croix du Sud in the South Pacific which gathers two-thousand soldiers (including from the United States and United Kingdom).[165]

Western Security Cooperation in the Asia-Pacific

In order to contribute to regional stability and to uphold key norms of the regional order, Paris concurrently sought to deepen its diplomatic and security cooperation, although from a modest starting point, with other Western powers in the Asia-Pacific, i.e. the United States and European countries. Largely because of intra-European disagreements and capability shortfalls, however, these efforts have remained relatively modest and produced only limited operational cooperation.

---

[162] In 2007, France became the first EU country to accede to ASEAN's Treaty of Amity and Cooperation in Southeast Asia.
[163] Although the French Defence Minister attended for the first time the SLD in 2008, regular (i.e. annual) attendance only started in 2012.
[164] Regaud, 2016, p. 7; and MoD, 2019b, p. 8.
[165] MoD, 'FANC: bilan de l'exercice Croix du Sud', 25 May 2018b.

Franco-American Security Cooperation Beginning in the early 2010s, Paris and Washington explored ways to expand their military and intelligence cooperation in the region. As explained by the former US Assistant Secretary of Defence for Asian and Pacific Security Affairs (2012–2013), and then Chief of Staff of the Secretary of Defence Chuck Hagel (2013–2014), Mark Lippert, the Pentagon worked 'with the French bilaterally on Asia-Pacific issues', hoping to 'increase their salience in our overall bilateral relationship with the French' while encouraging US allies and partners, such as India, Japan and Australia, 'to bring the French in more effectively'.[166]

The two countries established a bilateral dialogue in 2016, the Asia-Pacific Security Dialogue (relabelled as Indo-Pacific Security Dialogue in 2018) between officials of the French MoD'S DGRIS and the US Office of the Secretary of Defence (OSD). Its goal was to exchange assessments on regional security dynamics, e.g. China's behaviour in the South China Sea and in the Indian Ocean, and its challenge to freedom of navigation, among other issues.[167]

Paris and Washington also expanded their operational military cooperation bilaterally as well as minilaterally with other regional powers, most notably India, Japan, and Australia. From 2015 onward, the French and US navies have conducted deployments through the so-called Task Force (TF) 473 formed around the aircraft carrier Charles de Gaulle, through the mission Bois Belleau 100 in the Indian Ocean, and through the Jeanne d'Arc mission, which every year ensures the operational training of the officer-cadets of the French navy (see Figure 1.1 and Table 1.1; for details, see also the Appendix in Meijer 2021a).

At the minilateral level, France conducted the first trilateral amphibious exercise with the United States and Japan in 2017;[168] and it pursued greater trilateral cooperation with Australia and India in a variety of areas such as maritime security, including through trilateral information consultations on maritime domain awareness held at the Information Fusion Centre for the Indian Ocean Region (IFC-IOR).[169] New quadrilateral military exercises began to emerge such as the French-led joint military exercise with the United Kingdom, the United States, and

---

[166] Lippert then became US Ambassador to South Korea (2014–2017). Interview, Seoul, 20 October 2016.
[167] Interviews with MoD officials, December 2016 and January 2020.
[168] MoD, 'Mission Jeanne d'Arc: des manœuvres amphibies encore jamais réalisées', 1 June 2015a, http://www.defense.gouv.fr/english/marine/a-la-une/mission-jeanne-d-arc-des-manoeuvres-amphibies-encore-jamais-realisees; 'Japan, France and the United States Conducted a Joint Amphibious Exercise for the 1st Time', *DefesaNet*, 1 June 2015.
[169] French MFA, 'India–France–Australia Joint Statement on the Occasion of the Trilateral Ministerial Dialogue', *News*, 4 May 2021d, https://www.diplomatie.gouv.fr/en/country-files/asia-and-oceania/news/article/india-france-australia-joint-statement-on-the-occasion-of-the-trilateral; MFA, 2021c, p. 7; Australian Department of Foreign Affairs and Trade, 'Vision Statement on the Australia–France Relationship', 2 May 2018; and Jean-Baptiste Vey and Michel Rose, 'Macron Wants Strategic Paris–Delhi–Canberra Axis amid Pacific Tension', *Reuters*, 2 May 2018. France and Australia have also cooperated trilaterally with New Zealand through the FRANZ arrangement and quadrilaterally with New Zealand and the United States through the QUAD. See 'Appendix: France's Military Presence

Japan practicing amphibious landings (in 2017 and again in subsequent years)[170] and quadrilateral naval exercises between France, Japan, Australia, and the United States in the Indian Ocean.[171] In 2021, the Australian, Indian, Japanese, and US navies trained with France in the Bay of Bengal in the French-led exercise La Pérouse.[172] The AUKUS trilateral agreement between Australia, the United Kingdom, and the United States—which, as discussed earlier, weakened France's relations with Australia—was followed by diplomatic efforts to repair Franco-American diplomatic ties, with Washington reaffirming the strategic importance of French and European engagement in the Indo-Pacific region.[173]

Finally, France and the United States strengthened their intelligence cooperation. In addition to establishing a framework for enhanced intelligence cooperation between the French command of the Pacific Ocean maritime zone (ALPACI) and the US Pacific Command (PACOM, later relabelled Indo-Pacific Command, INDOPACOM),[174] since 2018 France also deployed a liaison officer to the US INDOPACOM. According to Admiral Cullerre who first discussed the proposal with the then-Commander of PACOM, Admiral Samuel J. Locklear (2012–2015), establishing a liaison officer would have two main purposes. First, a French presence 'in the heart of the US Defence Staff which deals with China' would facilitate intelligence-sharing.[175] Second, it would give greater influence and visibility to France's activities in the Asia-Pacific 'in the eyes of the Americans'.[176]

Promoting Intra-European Diplomatic and Security Cooperation in the Region
The expanded engagement with the United States went hand in hand with Paris's attempts to foster greater intra-European cooperation in the Asia-Pacific, both at the military/operational and diplomatic levels.

At the 2016 SLD, then Defence Minister Jean-Yves Le Drian (2012–2017) first called for European navies to 'coordinate in order to ensure as regular and as visible

---

and Naval Deployments in the Asia-Pacific' in Meijer, 2021a, available at https://ndownloader.figstatic.com/files/30687660.

[170] In 2021, France participated in an amphibious exercise with the United States and Japan aiming at testing their ability to defend remote islands. 'France Leads Naval Exercise with US, UK and Japan in American Territory of Guam in the Pacific', *South China Morning Post*, 12 May 2017; 'Japan, US, France Joint Military Drills Set for Kyushu in May', *Nikkei Asia*, 23 April 2021.

[171] Tim Kelly, 'U.S., France, Japan and Australia Hold First Combined Naval Drill in Asia', *Reuters*, 16 May 2019; Vavasseur, 2021a.

[172] US Navy, 'Multinational Naval Forces Conduct Exercise La Perouse', 6 April 2021, https://www.navy.mil/Press-Office/News-Stories/Article/2562180/multinational-naval-forces-conduct-exercise-la-perouse/.

[173] The White House, 'Joint Statement on the Phone Call between President Biden and President Macron', *Briefing Room*, 22 September 2021c, https://www.whitehouse.gov/briefing-room/statements-releases/2021/09/22/joint-statement-on-the-phone-call-between-president-biden-and-president-macron/; Minister of Foreign Affairs Jean-Yves Le Drian, Testimony before the National Defence and Armed Forces Committee, National Assembly, 6 October 2021.

[174] Interviews with MoD officials, January–December 2017.

[175] Interview, 27 March 2017.

[176] Interview, 27 March 2017.

a presence as possible in the maritime areas of Asia'.[177] The proposal was reiterated by his successors in subsequent SLDs.[178] Beginning in the mid-2010s, the French and the British thus started conducting naval deployments in the region, with British Navy personnel and helicopters included onboard during the Mission Jeanne d'Arc, with the Combined Task Force 150 in the Indian Ocean, and with deployments in the South China Sea (see Figure 1.1 and Table 1.1; for further details, see the Appendix in Meijer 2021a). For France, one advantage of conducting naval deployments in the South China Sea in combination with other European states was to 'defuse the tensions' with the PRC and the risk of retaliation from Beijing which regularly resulted from such deployments.[179]

Besides the United Kingdom, Paris also explored, bilaterally, the possibility of enlisting other European countries to conduct deployments in the Indian and Pacific Oceans, such as Germany, Norway, Denmark, Sweden, Belgium, the Netherlands, Portugal, or Spain, but only with marginal success (on German naval deployments, see Chapter 2).[180] According to French officials, many countries have been reluctant to build a stronger EU naval presence in the region because of a lack of interests therein, insufficient naval capabilities, and/or by fear of alienating China, with whom many maintain close economic ties.[181] One notable example is the development of the EU Coordinated Maritime Presences (CMP), of which France has been one of the most forceful advocates within the European Union. The CMP aims to strengthen EU maritime security engagement by enhancing coordination of naval and air assets among EU member states (although these assets remain under national rather than EU command).[182] While the first CMP pilot initiative has taken place closer to Europe, i.e. in the Gulf of Guinea, France advocated for several years for an expansion of the CMP into the Indo-Pacific, but this proposal faced resistance by several EU member states.[183] As explained by a MFA official, 'when we try to move forward EU cooperation

---

[177] Minister of Defence, 2016.
[178] See the Minister of the Armed Forces Sylvie Goulard at the Shangri-La Dialogue, Singapore, 3 June 2017; and the Minister of the Armed Forces Florence Parly, 2018.
[179] MFA official, interview, 6 March 2020.
[180] Senior MoD official, interview, 20 January 2020; and MFA official, 6 March 2020.
[181] Interviews with senior MoD official, 20 January 2020, and with MFA officials (6 March 2020 and 3 October 2020). This point was also raised in interviews with a senior EU official, Brussels, 6 March 2020; with British diplomats (24 November 2014, 15 January 2018, and 8 October 2018); and with a German MFA official, 19 March 2020.
[182] CMP also aims to bolster information sharing between member states through the Maritime Area of Interest Coordination Cell (MAICC) established within the EU military staff. See EU High Representative/Vice-President Federica Mogherini, Remarks at the Press Conference Following the Informal Meeting of EU Defence Ministers, 29 August 2019; EEAS, 'Coordinated Maritime Presences', Factsheets, 25 January 2021c, http://eeas.europa.eu/sites/default/files/coordinated_maritime_presences.pdf.
[183] Interviews with MFA officials, March 2020 and October 2021. On the pilot initiative in the Gulf of Guinea, see EEAS 2021c.

efforts in the Indo-Pacific—especially on hard defence and security operational initiatives—we regularly face an outcry by several Indo-Pacific sceptics. These are mostly countries from Northern and Eastern Europe for whom the priority is the Baltic region, the Black Sea, or the eastern flank, and countries in southern Europe that prioritize instability in the Mediterranean Sea; they tend to stress that the Indo-Pacific is a French priority, not theirs.'[184] Furthermore, according to French officials, many countries maintain deep economic relations with China which often makes them reluctant to join initiatives that might irritate Beijing and hinder their bilateral relationships with the PRC.[185] Nonetheless, at the time of writing, the expansion of the CMP was finally agreed upon, and the Council decided to launch the implementation of the CMP in the North-Western Indian Ocean.[186]

At the diplomatic level, discussions on how to foster greater European cooperation in the Asia-Pacific have taken place bilaterally, through informal minilateral groupings (outside EU institutional structures), as well as through formal EU channels. The minilateral groupings have comprised, for instance, the E3 (France, Germany, and the United Kingdom) that produced a joint statement as well as a 'note verbale' for the United Nations stressing the need to uphold regional stability and enforce international law in the South China Sea.[187] Likewise, through the Quad, France, the United Kingdom, Germany, and the United States (together with representatives of the European External Action Service, EEAS) have exchanged on China's foreign policy and rising regional tensions, and on how to seek political support for greater cooperation or coordination in the Asia-Pacific (these exchanges were also conducted through the Quint, which additionally includes Italy).[188] And, at the EU level, the formal channels have included the Asia-Oceania Working Party (COASI) or the Committee of Permanent Representatives (COREPER).[189]

The exit of the United Kingdom from the European Union gave new impetus to the *moteur franco-allemand* ('Franco-German engine'). Having laid out their respective national strategic documents for the Indo-Pacific (in 2018 and 2020 respectively), Paris and Berlin intensified their diplomatic cooperation—albeit with little underlying operational security cooperation—with the purpose

---

[184] MFA official, interview, 3 October 2021.
[185] Interviews with MFA and MEF officials, March 2020.
[186] Council of the EU, 'Coordinated Maritime Presences: Council Extends Implementation in the Gulf of Guinea for Two Years and Establishes a new Maritime Area of Interest in the North-Western Indian Ocean', *Press Release*, 21 February 2022.
[187] Permanent Mission of France to the United Nations, 'Note verbale' to the Commission on the Limits of the Continental Shelf, no. BF N° 2020-0343647, New York, 16 September 2020; MFA, 'Déclaration conjointe de la France, de l'Allemagne et du Royaume-Uni—Situation en mer de Chine méridionale', 30 August 2019e, https://www.diplomatie.gouv.fr/fr/dossiers-pays/asie-oceanie/evenements/article/declaration-conjointe-de-la-france-de-l-allemagne-et-du-royaume-uni-situation.
[188] Interviews with former French diplomats involved in these discussions, January–December 2020 and October 2021.
[189] Interviews with French, British, and German diplomats, and with EU officials, January–December 2020.

of developing a common bilateral approach to the 'Indo-Pacific' which was intended, over time, to lay the foundations for a common EU strategy for the region.[190] In particular, the two countries cooperated both bilaterally and with the Netherlands—who published its own Indo-Pacific guidelines in 2020[191]—as a core group of countries advocating for the development of an EU Indo-Pacific strategy. As stressed by a MFA official, 'it is this small core group—France, Germany, and the Netherlands—that mostly pushed for this initiative.'[192]

Specifically, the formulation of the European Union's Indo-Pacific strategy proceeded in three main steps. First, leveraging Germany's presidency of the Council of the European Union (July–December 2020), the three countries jointly wrote a non-paper proposing the development of such strategy. In the summer of 2020 France had sent the first draft of the non-paper to Germany, who amended it, and once the two countries finalized a document they then shared it with the Netherlands with whom they consolidated a final version; the non-paper was then circulated by Germany to other member states and subsequently co-signed by seven member states (the Czech Republic, Croatia, Greece, Italy, Poland, Portugal, and Slovenia, in addition to these three countries).[193]

Secondly, France, Germany, and the Netherlands—together with other countries—sought to ensure that the Council of the European Union's Foreign Affairs Council, which brings together the Ministers of Foreign Affairs of individual EU member states, would adopt a common stance on an EU Indo-Pacific strategy, building upon this non-paper. To that end, through bilateral endeavours, they aimed to persuade those countries that were initially less enthusiastic about this effort as well as the EEAS to come on board.[194] Some countries in Northern, Eastern and Southern Europe initially considered that the Indo-Pacific was less a priority than other regions closer to Europe (e.g. the Eastern neighbourhood and the Mediterranean region), and they also feared that the adoption of such a concept

---

[190] On the 2020 German guidelines for the Indo-Pacific, see Chapter 2. On the desire to foster greater Franco-German coordination in the Indo-Pacific, see MFA, 'Conseil des ministres franco-allemand: Feuille de route ministérielle "Affaires étrangères"', 16 October 2019d.

[191] Government of the Netherlands, *Indo-Pacific: Een Leidraad voor Versterking van de Nederlandse en EU-Samenwerking met Partners in Azië*, 13 November 2020, https://open.overheid.nl/repository/ronl-84107ff4-e66b-4aa2-a7a9-07fec3e3601b/1/pdf/indo-pacific-een-leidraad-voor-versterking-van-de-nederlandse-en-eu-samenwerking-met-partners-in-azie.pdf. See also Government of the Netherlands, *Jaarverslag en slotwet Ministerie van Buitenlandse Zaken 2020*, 35830-V-1, 22 June 2021, https://www.rijksoverheid.nl/binaries/rijksoverheid/documenten/jaarverslagen/2021/05/19/buitenlandse-zaken-2020/V%20Buitenlandse%20Zaken.pdf; and, on the Dutch policy towards China, see Dutch MFA, *The Netherlands and China: A New Balance*, 14 May 2019a, https://www.government.nl/documents/policy-notes/2019/05/15/china-strategy-the-netherlands—china-a-new-balance; and Dutch MFA, 'Kabinetsreactie Op Advies "China en de Strategische Opdracht voor Nederland in Europa"', 9 September 2019b, https://www.rijksoverheid.nl/binaries/rijksoverheid/documenten/kamerstukken/2019/09/09/kamerbrief-kabinetsreactie-op-advies-china-en-de-strategische-opdracht-voor-nederland-in-europa/kamerbrief-kabinetsreactie-op-advies-china-en-de-strategische-opdracht-voor-nederland-in-europa.pdf.

[192] Interview, 3 October 2021.
[193] Interviews with government officials, 3, 5, 21 October and 11 November 2021.
[194] Interviews with MFA officials, October 2021.

might antagonize Beijing and hamper their bilateral relationships with the PRC.[195] Likewise, the Directorate for Asia and the Pacific of the EU's diplomatic service (the EEAS) was, at first, hesitant (if not reluctant) to adopt the 'Indo-Pacific' construct; this label—and the related strategy—was seen by the EEAS, as explained by a French official, as an 'anti-China concept' linked to what the EEAS viewed as a 'US containment strategy of China'.[196]

Ultimately, however, a consensus was reached among members states, with the support also of the EEAS, and the Council of the European Union's Foreign Affairs Council adopted the Conclusions on an 'EU Strategy for Cooperation in the Indo-Pacific' in April 2021.[197] Reaching such consensus was possible partly because, in the view of an EU official, the Conclusions 'made clear that this was a "strategy for cooperation" as opposed to confrontation; the fact we put the word "cooperation" in the title was precisely to stress that the strategy was non-confrontational, inclusive, and not directed against China.'[198] Likewise, the fact that the initial non-paper had been co-signed by ten EU member states had the added benefit of helping the EEAS overcome its initial reluctance vis-à-vis the formulation of an EU Indo-Pacific strategy.[199] Furthermore, 'the less enthusiastic countries—including in Northern, Eastern, and Southern Europe—could accept being drawn into this', according to a French government official, also because 'the EU Indo-Pacific strategy, as outlined in the Conclusions, entailed little operational cooperation in defence and security; the security and defence aspects—which are undoubtedly the most sensitive—remained very limited.'[200] Accordingly, these countries 'saw the EU strategy for the Indo-Pacific as just a label to be put on non-controversial initiatives, such as in the economic domain'.[201] A senior EU official confirms this point: 'apart from France, Germany, and the Netherlands, most other member states may have a broad political interest in the Indo-Pacific but it pales in comparison to other issues such as Russia, Ukraine, the Mediterranean, or Turkey, that they deem to be much higher priorities.'[202] He adds that 'the Indo-Pacific strategy remains fairly generic on defence and security issues' and, in the European Union's policy-making process, 'when you do not touch hard security issues, it is easier to reach a common position.'[203]

---

[195] Interviews with MFA officials, October 2021.
[196] Government official, interview, 5 October 2021.
[197] European Commission, 'The EU Strategy for Cooperation in the Indo-Pacific', Joint Communication JOIN(2021) 24 final, 16 September 2021c. See also MFA, 2021c, p. 10.
[198] Interview, 8 October 2021.
[199] The adoption by ASEAN of the *Outlook on the Indo-Pacific* further helped the EEAS overcome its initial reticence. Government official, interview, 11 November 2021. See also ASEAN, *Outlook on the Indo-Pacific*, June 2021, https://asean.org/speechandstatement/asean-outlook-on-the-indo-pacific/.
[200] Interview, 3 October 2021.
[201] Interview, 3 October 2021.
[202] Interview, 7 October 2021.
[203] Interview, 7 October 2021.

As a third step, the Council Conclusions invited the European Commission and the EU High Representative for Foreign Affairs and Security Policy to present a Joint Communication that would build upon these Council Conclusions and detail a specific action plan. One rationale for doing so was that all the key external relations of the European Union with major powers—such as those with the United States and China, among others—are formalized through Joint Communications.[204] Furthermore, from Paris's perspective, establishing a Joint Communication would ensure that all the key EU actors, including the European Commission, would be supporting the Indo-Pacific strategy, rather than merely the member states in the Council.[205] It was therefore, in the words of one official, 'a matter of ambition'.[206]

The Joint Communication, 'The EU Strategy for Cooperation in the Indo-Pacific', was presented by the European Commission and the EU High Representative for Foreign Affairs and Security Policy Josep Borrell (HR/VP, since 2019) in September 2021.[207] It revolved around a variety of issue areas, namely fostering prosperity through new trade agreements and other economic instruments, ocean governance, the green transition, digital governance, connectivity, defence and security, and human security (e.g. addressing the Covid-19 pandemic).[208] The initiatives in the field of defence and security, however, remained largely limited to 'non-traditional' security issues, such as maritime security, malicious cyber activities, disinformation, as well as countering and improving resilience to terrorism, violent extremism, organized crime, and illicit trafficking.[209] Furthermore, in the defence and security realm, the concrete operational proposals put forward in the strategy were modest. The European Union would seek greater participation by Indo-Pacific countries (such as Japan) in missions and operations of the EU's Common Security and Defence Policy (CSDP), including EUNAVFOR Atalanta which nonetheless remained confined to counter-piracy operations and, geographically, to the Gulf of Aden.[210] Partly in response to French advocacy, as discussed above, the Union would also 'explore ways to ensure enhanced naval deployments by its Member States' in the Indo-Pacific, and 'assess the opportunity' of extending the CMP into the Indo-Pacific.[211] Finally, the strategy stressed the desire to expand the

---

[204] European Commission and the High Representative of the Union for Foreign Affairs and Security Policy (HR/VP), *A New EU-US Agenda for Global Change*, Brussels, JOIN(2020) 22 final, 2 December 2020; European Commission and HR/VP, *EU–China: A Strategic Outlook*, 12 March 2019.
[205] Interviews with MFA officials, October 2021.
[206] Government official, interview, 5 October 2021.
[207] European Commission, 'The EU Strategy for Cooperation in the Indo-Pacific', Joint Communication JOIN(2021) 24 final, 16 September 2021c. See also MFA, 2021a, p. 10. See also EEAS, 'EU Strategy for Cooperation in the Indo-Pacific', *Factsheet*, 19 April 2021a.
[208] European Commission, 2021c, p. 5.
[209] European Commission 2021c, p 14; see also Council of the European Union, 'EU Strategy for Cooperation in the Indo-Pacific', Council Conclusions, 16 April 2021c, p. 8.
[210] European Commission, 2021c, p. 13.
[211] European Commission, 2021c, p. 13.

geographical scope of the European Union's Critical Maritime Routes in the Indian Ocean II (CRIMARIO II) initiative. CRIMARIO II had sought to strengthen information exchange, analysis, and crisis/incident management in the Indian Ocean and South East Asia by supporting coastal countries' maritime situational awareness capacity.[212] The European Union would now explore the possibility of replicating the CRIMARIO experience in the South Pacific.[213]

Overall, France—together with Germany, the Netherlands, and other member states—had thus spurred the development of an EU strategy for the Indo-Pacific, although the strategy was underpinned by little EU-wide operational cooperation and few defence capabilities.

Conclusion

France has been pulled into the Asia-Pacific by steadily growing economic interests in the region and, crucially, by heightened threat perceptions in reaction to China's rising assertiveness. As a result, Paris has come to develop an overarching policy framework, the Indo-Pacific strategy, which has translated into a strengthened political-military engagement in the region. Specifically, it has intensified its naval deployments, widened its network of bilateral security partnerships, and stepped up its participation in the region's multilateral security architecture. As a complement to these endeavours, it has fostered multinational cooperation with the United States and with other European powers, promoting the development of a common EU policy towards the region. By doing so, France has sought to contribute to regional stability through an enhanced political-military presence and capacity-building efforts, to uphold the rules-based order, and thereby to also protect its regional economic interests. Overall, through these endeavours, Paris has aimed to shape the regional environment in which China's rise has unfolded. Whereas in the first two post-Cold War decades France mostly pursued mercantilist interests in the region, it has now awakened to the national security implications of China's rise.

To be sure, despite this renewed activism, resource limitations have continued to constrain French foreign and security policy in the region. Even the European country with the largest military footprint in the Asia-Pacific faces severe capability shortfalls which, coupled with competing regional priorities and defence requirements in other regional theatres, have substantially inhibited France's capacity to project power in the Asia-Pacific. Likewise, although Paris increased the number of its naval deployments, deepened its political-military ties in the region, and broadened its engagement with multilateral regional security regimes, it did

---

[212] Critical Maritimes Route Programme, 'CRIMARIO: Indo-Pacific 2015–2024', https://criticalmaritimeroutes.eu/projects/crimario/.
[213] European Commission, 2021c, p. 13.

not substantially alter the overall regional prioritization in French defence planning. Yet, notwithstanding these limitations, France is the European country that has developed the most robust strategic presence in the Asia-Pacific and has concurrently sought to foster the formulation of a more cohesive EU approach to the region.

2
The Reluctant European Power
Germany in Asian-Pacific Security

Introduction

In sharp contrast to France, Germany has no direct foothold in the Asia-Pacific. Its lack of overseas territories and forward-deployed forces in the region is largely the result of German colonial history. The legacy of World War II (WWII)—coupled with severely declining defence capabilities since the end of the Cold War—further constrained the use of defence means in the pursuit of Berlin's foreign policy goals. Yet, as it gradually became Europe's largest economic power in the post-Cold War era, Germany has adopted an increasingly proactive foreign policy.[1] As shown in this chapter, within such constraints, Berlin has responded to China's rising assertiveness by bolstering its diplomatic and security engagement in the Asia-Pacific.

Germany's colonial trajectory in the Asia-Pacific differs markedly from that of the other European major powers for its relative brevity and its limited geographical scope. In China, through a lease agreement, Berlin established the German Protectorate of Kiautschou (1898) on the Shandong Peninsula—with Tsingtau as its administrative centre hosting an important naval base—while also obtaining concessions in Hankou and Tianjin.[2] In the South Pacific, the German Protectorate of New Guinea initially comprised Kaiser Wilhelmsland (north eastern New Guinea), the Bismarck Archipelago (New Britain and New Ireland), and the German Solomon Islands that were annexed in the mid-1880s. Further additions to the Protectorate were made with the annexation of the Marshall Islands (1885) and

---

[1] On this point, see Ulrich Krotz and Richard Maher, 'Europe's Crises and the EU's "Big Three"', *West European Politics 39*, no. 5 (2016): pp. 1053–1072; Ina Kraft, 'Germany', in *The Handbook of European Defence Policies and Armed Forces*, edited by Hugo Meijer and Marco Wyss (Oxford: Oxford University Press, 2018), pp. 52–70. On Germany's economic clout in Europe, see, e.g. Christian Dustmann et al., 'From Sick Man of Europe to Economic Superstar: Germany's Resurgent Economy', *Journal of Economic Perspectives 28*, no. 1 (2014): pp. 167–188; Hans Kundnani, 'Germany as a Geo-Economic Power', *The Washington Quarterly 34*, no. 3 (2011): pp. 31–45.

[2] Orazio Coco, 'German Imperialism in China: The Leasehold of Kiaochow Bay (1897–1914)', *The Chinese Historical Review 26*, no. 2 (2019): pp. 156–174; Fion Wai Ling So, *Germany's Colony in China: Colonialism, Protection, and Economic Development in Qingdao and Shandong, 1898–1914* (New York: Routledge, 2019).

with the 1899 purchase of the Caroline, Palau, and Mariana islands from Spain, in the wake of the Spanish-American War, thereby constituting German Micronesia. That same year, through the 'Tripartite Treaty' with the United States and the United Kingdom, Germany assumed control of the western Samoan islands, thus creating German Samoa.[3]

World War I brought an end to the colonial presence of Imperial Germany in the Asia-Pacific. During the war, as Japan cooperated with the British Empire against Germany in the region—and in light of the Royal Navy's preponderant focus on the North Sea, Atlantic, and Mediterranean—Japan occupied German territories north of the equator as well as Kiautschou, while Australia and New Zealand took control of those to the south.[4] After the war, Japan, Australia and New Zealand received Germany's Pacific territories as League of Nations 'C' Class Mandates, thereby turning their military rule into colonial administration.[5] Germany had been eliminated as a player in the 'Far Eastern Game'.

Coupled with this colonial heritage, the legacies of WWII further restrained the course of German foreign and security policy in the Asia-Pacific. The concurrent domestic taboo against unilateralism and military rearmament that emerged in Germany from the ashes of WWII has translated not only into a strong preference for multilateral endeavours over unilateral policies but also into a reluctant attitude towards the use of military force embracing instead non-military instruments for achieving its policy goals.[6] This, combined with the severe downsizing of German defence capabilities since reunification and the end of the Cold War, including in the naval domain, considerably limited the range of capabilities that Germany could bring to bear in the Asia-Pacific.

This chapter shows that, despite these longstanding constraints, Germany has both expanded and diversified its diplomatic and security engagement in the Asia-Pacific in response to growing economic interests in the region and, crucially, to rising threat perceptions of the PRC. Chinese assertiveness after 2009

---

[3] Germany also ceded territories in the Solomons to Britain in compensation for the latter's surrender of all rights in Samoa while the United States took over the eastern Samoan islands. Charles Stephenson, *Germany's Asia-Pacific Empire: Colonialism and Naval Policy, 1885-1914* (Woodbridge: Boydell Press, 2009), chs. 5–9.

[4] Hermann Hiery, *The Neglected War: The German South Pacific and the Influence of World War I* (Honolulu: University of Hawaii Press, 1995); Hew Strachan, *The First World War* (London: Penguin Books, 2004), pp. 203–218; Irmline Veit-Brause, 'Australia and Germany in the Pacific: Aspects of the "New Imperialism"', in *The German Empire and Britain's Pacific Dominions, 1871-1919: Essays on the Role of Australia and New Zealand in World Politics in the Age of Imperialism*, edited by John A. Moses and Christopher Pugsley (Claremont, CA: Regina Books, 2000), pp. 309–336.

[5] On the League of Nation's mandatory system, see Susan Pedersen, *The Guardians: The League of Nations and the Crisis of Empire* (Oxford: Oxford University Press, 2015).

[6] See, e.g. Ulrich Krotz, *History and Foreign Policy in France and Germany* (Basingstoke: Palgrave Macmillan, 2015), Chapter 4; Thomas U. Berger, 'The Past in the Present: Historical Memory and German National Security Policy', *German Politics* 6, no. 1 (1997): pp. 39–59; Hanns W. Maull, 'Germany and Japan: The New Civilian Powers', *Foreign Affairs* 69, no. 5 (1990): pp. 91–106. For a discussion of how this military restraint has partly receded since the end of the Cold War, see Kraft, 2018.

has been the main driver of change, prompting a significant policy shift in German foreign and security policy. Whereas in the first two decades after the Cold War German policymakers saw the PRC as a vast emerging market that posed few (if any) security challenges, during the 2010s they displayed rising security concerns over how China's behaviour challenged the rules-based order and regional stability in the Asia-Pacific (while they also became more wary of Chinese investments into strategic sectors in Europe, as discussed in Chapter 5).[7] As a result, Germany gradually revised its policy goals and forged a new regional policy framework for the broader Indo-Pacific region, putting greater emphasis on security considerations. This policy framework revolved around upholding regional stability and preserving foundational norms of the rules-based order (freedom of navigation and the peaceful resolution of disputes), thereby also furthering German economic interests. To be sure, given its lack of direct military footprint in the region, major capability shortfalls, and competing regional priorities, German regional engagement revolved primarily around political and economic endeavours. Yet, Berlin also reinforced its security engagement in the Asia-Pacific through several channels. It moved beyond its previous 'China-centric' approach by broadening its network of bilateral diplomatic and security partnerships across the region, enhanced its participation in Asian multilateral security regimes, and promoted greater intra-European cooperation so as to forge an autonomous role for the European Union in the context of the mounting United States–China strategic rivalry—while also agreeing to conduct naval deployments in the Indian and Pacific Oceans. In short, after two decades in which it focused almost exclusively on economic opportunities, the traditionally 'reluctant' European power has awakened to the security implications of China's rise and has therefore sought to strengthen its role in Asian-Pacific security.

In order to substantiate this argument, the first two sections of this chapter examine the evolution of German economic interests in the region and of its threat assessment of China, two key drivers of Berlin's foreign and security policy in the Asia-Pacific. The subsequent two sections show how rising economic interests and shifting threat perceptions have, in turn, led Germany to sharpen its policy goals and to strengthen the diplomatic and security instruments leveraged to achieve such goals.

Economic Interests

As the world's centre of economic gravity gradually shifted towards the Asia-Pacific in the post-Cold War era, Germany's economic ties with the region, and

---

[7] For a definition of a 'rules-based regional order' see the Introduction of Part I.

with China in particular, considerably deepened and broadened. Berlin pursued trade, investment, and arms sales opportunities in the Asia-Pacific, and the PRC became a key engine for Germany's economic growth after reunification (while the economic relationship with the PRC concurrently became more competitive in the 2010s, as detailed in Chapter 5).

Germany in the Asian-Pacific Economy

The reunification of Germany entailed a significant subsequent reordering of its domestic economic structure and of its foreign economic relations in the first two decades of the post-Cold War era.[8] Investments and exports in the Asia-Pacific became key sources of economic growth, while Berlin also increased its arms transfers to the region.

Starting in the 1990s, the Federal Government came to see the Asia-Pacific as 'the most dynamic growth region in the world' which offered German companies 'tremendous opportunities today and for the future'.[9] The region, and most notably Japan and China, emerged as an important engine of foreign demand. Throughout the 1990s and 2000s, Germany became increasingly dependent on foreign trade to sustain its economic growth and to absorb the costs of reunification; and as China gradually opened up to international markets, the Sino-German trade relationship significantly expanded.[10] German exports to China soared from $2.5bn to $52bn between 1991 and 2009, and by the end of the decade China had overtaken Japan as Germany's largest trading partner in the region.[11] Concomitantly, Sino-German investment ties deepened, although asymmetrically and from a low basis. Whereas Chinese FDIs in Germany remained extremely limited (as discussed in Chapter 5), German investment stocks in the PRC massively increased between 1990 and 2009, from $100m to $26bn,[12] with Germany thereby becoming the biggest European investor in the PRC.[13] Overall, Germany became

---

[8] Dustmann et al., 2014; Kundnani, 2011.
[9] Federal Government, *The Federal Government's Concept on Asia*, 22 September 1993, https://www.asienhaus.de/public/archiv/brdasia.htm.
[10] The contribution of exports to Germany's GDP rose from 33 per cent to 48 per cent between 2000 and 2010. Hans Kundnani, *The Paradox of German Power* (Oxford: Oxford University Press, 2015), p. 76.
[11] Data retrieved from United Nations (UN) Comtrade—International Trade Statistics Database, https://comtrade.un.org. On China's overtaking Japan as Germany's main trading partner, see Deutsche Bundesbank, 'Germany's External Relations with the People's Republic of China', *Monthly Report*, July 2005, p. 44.
[12] Deutsche Bundesbank. 'Direktinvestitionen und Auslandsunternehmenseinheiten (FATS)' https://www.bundesbank.de/de/statistiken/aussenwirtschaft/direktinvestitionen (the numbers are based on the average annual exchange rates for Deutsche Marks to US dollar and for euros to US dollar in the respective years).
[13] Gudrun Wacker, 'Changes and Continuities in EU–China Relations: A German Perspective', in *US–China–EU Relations: Managing the New World Order*, edited by Robert S. Ross, Øystein Tunsjø, and Zhang Tuosheng (New York: Routledge, 2010), p. 84.

the most successful of Europe's three major powers in the Asia-Pacific markets as well as the PRC's main trading partner in the European Union (see the comparative charts on the Big Three's economic relations with China and in the Asia-Pacific in Appendix B).[14]

Berlin also pursued its economic interests by exporting defence equipment in the Asia-Pacific even though, overall, its arms export volumes remained relatively limited (with the exception of a few destinations).[15] During the 2000s, Germany transferred, among other systems, Alpha Jet combat aircraft to Thailand; underwater detection and ship navigation equipment as well as attack helicopters to South Korea; Leopard 2 main battle tanks and anti-tank weapons to Singapore; underwater detection equipment and components for frigates and submarines to India; and corvettes, sonar devices and navigation equipment to Malaysia.[16] The volume of German arms transfers to countries in the Asia-Pacific more than tripled, although from a low basis, from $271m to $909m between 2000 and 2009.[17] Yet, according to a former official in the Federal Foreign Office's (FFO) Policy Planning Staff in charge of Asian affairs (1996–2001) and then Deputy Head of the Policy Planning Staff (2004–2006), Heinrich Kreft, 'German arms sales to the Asia-Pacific were very small in comparison to other trade and investment interests in that region. Arms sales never influenced German policy vis-à-vis Asia as, for example, in the case of France. There was more interest in the region in buying German arms than the German government was willing to allow, given our restrictions on arms sales.'[18]

Asia as the Global Centre of Economic Gravity

With the Asia-Pacific emerging as an increasingly central hub for the global economy in the 2010s, its importance for Germany continued to expand while China became an ever more important trade and investment partner (as well as an economic competitor, as detailed in Chapter 5).[19] Throughout the 2010s, German trade in goods with the countries in the Asia-Pacific and South Asia rose constantly

---

[14] Wacker, 2010, pp. 78–79; and Reuben Y. Wong, *The Europeanization of French Foreign Policy: France and the EU in East Asia* (New York: Palgrave Macmillan, 2006), p. 69.
[15] Interviews with former Federal Foreign Office (FFO) officials, December 2020.
[16] See the annual reports of the Federal Ministry for Economic Affairs, *Report of the Government of the Federal Republic of Germany on its Policy on Exports of Conventional Military Equipment*, 1999–2009.
[17] Data retrieved from SIPRI, https://www.sipri.org/databases/armstransfers (for more detail on the data, see Appendix B).
[18] Interview, 6 March 2021.
[19] As the PRC gradually transitioned from being the world's manufacturing workshop to a value-added high-tech economy, the competition between German and Chinese companies intensified, thereby altering the character of the bilateral economic relationship. This point is discussed in Chapter 5.

to the point that, by the end of the decade, it represented over 20 per cent of Germany's total trade in goods,[20] reaching almost double the size of German trade in goods with the United States.[21] Concomitantly, German bilateral trade with the PRC increased from $175bn to $232bn between 2010 to 2019.[22] In addition to being a key market and a production hub, China became the most important supplier for the German economy outside Europe as well as a research and development (R&D) location for German companies.[23] As a result, by the end of the decade, not only did Germany continue to be the commercially most successful European country in China, but the PRC superseded the United States as Germany's first trading partner in the world.[24]

As the share of the Asia-Pacific in Germany's external trade expanded, the regional SLOCs became increasingly important, with 25 per cent of seaborne world trade passing through the Strait of Malacca.[25] Germany came to depend ever more on maritime routes passing in the Indian and Pacific Oceans, whose stability became crucial for sustaining trade flows with the region.[26] As stressed by a Federal Government's report, 'a disruption to these maritime trade routes and thus to the supply chains to and from Europe would have serious consequences for the prosperity of and provision for our population.'[27]

German FDIs in the Asia-Pacific also significantly increased during the 2010s.[28] The most conspicuous evolution took place in the Sino-German investment relationship. As Chinese investments in Germany soared during this decade (see Chapter 5), the value of actually utilized German FDI in China rose from $900m to $1.6bn between 2010 and 2019, with a focus on transport manufacturing (including automotive).[29] Germany continued to dominate the ranking of EU investor

---

[20] Federal Government, *Policy Guidelines for the Indo-Pacific: Germany—Europe—Asia. Shaping the 21st Century Together*, 2020a, p. 9.

[21] Data retrieved from UN Comtrade—International Trade Statistics Database, https://comtrade.un.org (for details see Appendix B). For a comparison of the share of Germany's trade with the Asia-Pacific and with the United States, see German Chamber of Commerce in China, *German Businesses in China: Business Confidence Survey 2019/2020*, p. 19.

[22] Data retrieved from UN Comtrade—International Trade Statistics Database, https://comtrade.un.org (for details see Appendix B). On Sino-German economic ties, see also Federal Foreign Minister Guido Westerwelle, 'Four Decades of Dynamic Development', interview with the *China Daily*, 11 October 2012c; and Federal Statistical Office, 'Ranking of Germany's Trading Partners in Foreign Trade—2019', 17 August 2020.

[23] Federal Ministry for Economic Affairs, 'Facts about German Foreign Trade', September 2019b, p. 2; Federation of German Industries (BDI), 'Systemic Competitor—How Do We Deal with China's State-Controlled Economy?', *BDI Policy Paper*, January 2019, p. 4.

[24] Federal Statistical Office, 2020; and FFO, 'China: A Land with Many Faces', at https://www.auswaertiges-amt.de/en/aussenpolitik/regionaleschwerpunkte/asien/-/231348.

[25] Federal Government, 2020a, p. 9.

[26] Federal Chancellor Angela Merkel, Speech during the Event Hosted by the Newspaper *Asahi Shimbun*, Tokyo, 9 March 2015.

[27] Federal Government, 2020a, p. 9.

[28] Federal Government, 2020a, p. 9.

[29] Actually utilized FDIs refer to the investments ultimately used by companies in China, in contrast to the values of agreed investments in contracts (for more details, see Appendix B). Data retrieved from National Bureau of Statistics of China, *Statistical Yearbooks of China*, http://www.stats.gov.cn/english/

countries in China, accounting for over 50 per cent of EU completed investment in the PRC.[30]

Berlin further pursued arms sales opportunities to the Asia-Pacific, which became a region of substantial interest for its arms industry. Out of Germany's total arms exports, those that went to Asia-Oceania reached 30 per cent in the 2015–2019 period making it, by the late 2010s, the main destination for German arms transfers ahead of Europe, the Middle East, and the Americas.[31] Overall, throughout the post-Cold War era, the Asia-Pacific region—and China in particular—had become of vital economic importance to Germany.[32]

Threat Perceptions

While Germany's economic interests in the Asia-Pacific steadily expanded throughout the post-Cold War period, its threat assessment of the PRC shifted only in the 2010s. In the first two decades of the post-Cold War period, Berlin displayed low threat perception of China, perceiving it mainly as a vast emerging market which posed few security challenges. In the 2010s, however, German policymakers exhibited rising security concerns over Beijing's intentions and growing capabilities. This, in turn, drove Berlin to gradually formulate a new policy framework for the broader Indo-Pacific region and to put greater emphasis on national security considerations.

China as a Peaceful Emerging Market

In the first two decades after the Cold War, German policymakers perceived the PRC as a faraway, peaceful rising power mostly preoccupied with domestic priorities. While Berlin paid scant attention to China's military modernization during the 1990s,[33] by the mid-2000s it came to assess that the PRC had 'undergone

---

Statisticaldata/AnnualData/ (for details, see Appendix B). See also Chinese Ministry of Commerce, *German Investment in China: Changing Opportunities and Trends,* China International Investment Promotion Agency—Germany (CIIPAG), 2019, pp. 3 and 11.

[30] Rhodium Group, 'People's Republic of China—European Union Direct Investment', *Cross Border Monitor* (CBM), 16 January 2019, p. 6. See also the comparative charts on the Big Three's economic ties with China and in the Asia-Pacific in Appendix B.

[31] SIPRI, 'Trends in International Arms Transfers 2015', *SIPRI Fact Sheet*, February 2016, p. 3; and SIPRI, 'Trends in International Arms Transfers 2019', *SIPRI Fact Sheet*, March 2020, p. 5. For more details, see the annual reports of the Federal Ministry for Economic Affairs, *Report of the Government of the Federal Republic of Germany on its Policy on Exports of Conventional Military Equipment,* 2010–2019.

[32] On the concurrent concerns in Berlin over the increasingly direct competition between German and Chinese companies, see Chapter 5.

[33] See FMoD, *White Paper on the Security of the Federal Republic of Germany and the Situation of the Future Bundeswehr*, 4 May 1994, ch. II.

a breath-taking development process' and that, 'due to its economic, political and military potential', China's growing clout was bound to 'have a significant impact on the future of the Asian-Pacific area and international politics'.[34] Yet, despite the quantitative size of Chinese armed forces, German officials—similarly to their French counterparts—viewed the PLA as equipped with outdated military capabilities and as being poorly trained.[35] Furthermore, in light of American predominance in the Pacific, they concluded that Beijing would be deterred from attacking Taiwan.[36] In the words of Volker Stanzel, former FFO's Director for Asian and Pacific Affairs (2001–2002), then FFO's Director General for Political Affairs in charge of relations with the Asia-Pacific (2002–2004), and subsequently German Ambassador to the PRC (2004–2007), the 'East China Sea, the South China Sea, Taiwan, and the Korean peninsula were all under the US security umbrella; the US was the major guarantor of security in East Asia, so why care?'[37] As such, as explained by the former Chief of the German Fleet (2000–2003) and then Chief of German Naval Staff Vice Admiral Lutz Feldt (2000–2006), 'China's military modernization was noticed neither by the German armed forces as a whole nor by foreign policymakers, it was something which was far away.'[38]

One area in which German policymakers did perceive some security challenges was Beijing's theft of advanced technology, including cyber espionage, to sustain its military and economic modernization efforts.[39] Yet, according to the former Consul General in Chengdu (2004–2006) and then Deputy Head of the FFO's East Asia Division (2006–2008), Thomas Gerberich, Berlin assessed that the superior innovation capabilities of German companies would enable them to maintain the technological edge vis-à-vis the PRC despite its illicit technology acquisitions and forced technology transfers; a point confirmed by other former officials and business representatives.[40]

Overall, throughout this period, German policymakers thus saw China and the Asia-Pacific region through a predominantly economic lens, perceiving its rise as posing few, if any, geostrategic challenges. According to the FFO of the 1990s, 'German interest [in the region] still focused primarily on the economic

---

[34] FMoD, *White Paper on German Security Policy and the Future of the Bundeswehr*, 2006, p. 48
[35] Interviews with FFO and FMoD officials, and with former high-ranking military officers, January–December 2020.
[36] Ambassador Heinrich Kreft, FFO's Policy Planning Staff (PPS) in charge of Asian affairs (1996–2001) and then Deputy Head of the PPS (2004–2006), interview, 19 October 2020. This assessment was confirmed in interviews with former FFO and FMoD officials in office in the 1990s and 2000s, January–December 2020.
[37] Volker Stanzel, interview, 12 November 2020.
[38] Interview, 26 October 2020.
[39] Interviews with FFO officials, January–December 2020. Germany's concerns in the cyber domain are further discussed in Chapter 5.
[40] Interview, 15 October 2020. This point was confirmed by a former Asia-hand at FFO in office in the 2000s (interview, 11 January 2021), and by a former representative of the BDI (17 December 2020). For further details on this point, see Chapter 5.

side of German-Asian cooperation', namely 'integrating German businesses more effectively into the Asia-Pacific economic area' and 'establishing a market economy structure in the region's economies'.[41] Likewise, during the 2000s, Berlin considered that 'the main risks to stability and security in this Asian region [did] not stem from interstate disputes' but rather from 'international cross-border problems' such as transnational terrorist movements.[42]

Chinese Assertiveness, Regional Stability, and the Rules-Based Order

It is only in the 2010s that Berlin's threat perceptions of the PRC intensified because of China's rising assertiveness in the Asia-Pacific. German officials became increasingly concerned over how China's regional behaviour and extending global reach could affect German interests in the Asia-Pacific and beyond. They grew wary of Beijing's muscular regional posture under Xi Jinping, its rejection of the 2016 Arbitral Tribunal ruling on the Chinese-Philippines maritime dispute, and its land reclamation activities in the South China Sea, among other issues (on the concurrent mounting concerns over Chinese investments in sensitive sectors in Germany and over its cyber-espionage practices, see Chapter 5).[43] As a result, as explained by Thomas Bagger, former Head of Policy Planning at the FFO (2011–2017) and then Director of Foreign Policy in the Office of President Frank-Walter Steinmeier (since 2017), China came to be perceived as 'more aggressive in its own positions and in its own interactions with other countries in the region and around the globe'.[44]

Whereas German policymakers considered that the PRC posed no direct military threat to Germany, their core concerns revolved around China's challenge to the foundational norms of the rules-based order, the ensuing risks of regional instability, and the consequences thereof for German economic interests.

For one, a major source of apprehension in Berlin was, according to a FFO official, 'that the international rules-based order was coming under strain' and that, 'as a result of China's rise, the theatre where this takes place is first and foremost the Asia-Pacific.'[45] Specifically, policymakers in Berlin were alarmed by China's challenge to the peaceful resolution of disputes and to freedom of navigation (and more broadly international maritime law).[46] In the words of former Chancellor

---

[41] FFO, 'Asia in German Foreign Policy', https://www.auswaertiges-amt.de/en/aussenpolitik/regionaleschwerpunkte/asien/-/231344.
[42] FFO, *Tasks of German Foreign Policy: Southeast Asia, Australia, New Zealand and Pacific Islands*, 2002b, pp. 7 and 11.
[43] Interviews with FFO and MoD officials, January–July 2020.
[44] Interview, 6 May 2020. On this point see also BDI, 2019, p. 6.
[45] Interview, 23 April 2020.
[46] Interviews with FFO officials, January–July 2020. On the government's preoccupation with the peaceful resolution of disputes in the region, see also FFO, 'Antwort der Bundesregierung zur sicherheitspolitischen Lage in Ost- und Südostasien', *German Parliament*, 8 February 2012b, p. 2; and Federal

Angela Merkel (2005–2021), 'our primary concern is that the naval routes (in the South and East China Seas) remain free and safe.'[47]

Concomitantly, German officials expressed disquiet over how China's increasingly muscular regional posture and the ensuing tensions with neighbouring countries—coupled with rising Sino-American strategic competition—could alter the regional balance of power and fuel instability.[48] According to the Federal Ministry of Defence (FMoD), in the context of the emerging 'struggles for regional hegemony', the combination of regional territorial disputes with expanding power projection capabilities entailed growing 'risk[s] of escalating interstate conflict' in the Asia-Pacific.[49] Furthermore, instability in that region and the resulting risk of unintended escalation to a conflict could potentially have major consequences for German trade in the Asia-Pacific.[50]

In short, in the 2010s, Berlin's assessment of the PRC shifted considerably. For German policymakers, China's challenge to the rules-based order, the rising risks of regional instability, and its potentially adverse consequences for German economic interests were closely intertwined.[51]

Policy Goals

Berlin's policy goals shifted as a result of these rising economic interests and a heightened threat assessment. During the 1990s and the 2000s, major economic interests and low threat perceptions led Germany to eagerly pursue economic opportunities in the Asia-Pacific while seeking to integrate China in the international system so as to foster its convergence towards Western market economies. In the 2010s, however, mounting threat perceptions of the PRC, coupled with steadily increasing economic interests in the region, drove Berlin to gradually formulate

---

Foreign Minister Sigmar Gabriel, Speech at the 97th Liebesmahl of the German Asia-Pacific Business Association, Hamburg, 3 March 2017.

[47] Federal Government, 'Rede von Bundeskanzlerin Merkel beim Bergedorfer Gesprächskreis', 29 October 2015. See also Federal Government, 2020a, p. 11; FFO, 'Joint Declaration by the Minister for Foreign Affairs of the Republic of Singapore Vivian Balakrishnan and the Minister for Foreign Affairs of the Federal Republic of Germany Heiko Maas', 28 September 2018.

[48] See, e.g. Federal Government, 2020a, p. 9; Federal Minister of Defence Annegret Kramp-Karrenbauer, Speech at the Bundeswehr University Munich, 7 November 2019; Federal Foreign Minister Heiko Maas, Speech at the National Graduate Institute for Policy Studies, Tokyo, Japan, 25 September 2018; and Federal Foreign Minister Guido Westerwelle (2009–2013), Speech by at the CDU/CSU Conference on 'Asia's New Global Players', 13 June 2012a.

[49] Federal Ministry of Defence, *White Paper on German Security Policy and the Future of the Bundeswehr*, 2016, p. 38. The same point was stressed in interviews with FFO officials, January–July 2020.

[50] Interviews with FFO officials, January–December 2020. On this point, see also Federal Government, 2020a, p. 9; and Torrey Taussig, 'Germany's Incomplete Pivot to the Indo-Pacific', in *Mind the Gap: National Views of the Free and Open Indo-Pacific*, edited by Sharon Sterling (Washington, DC: German Marshall Fund of the United States, 2019), p. 25.

[51] Interviews with FFO officials, January–December 2020.

an overarching policy framework for the larger Indo-Pacific region and to give more prominence to national security considerations.

Trade, Integration, and Convergence

In the first two decades of the post-Cold War, Germany's Asia-Pacific policy predominantly revolved around the advancement of its economic interests while seeking to embed China in the international system through expanded diplomatic and economic interactions.

'The Federal Government's objective', as a policy document of the 1990s clearly indicates, was 'to give the impetus for the further development of economic cooperation with Asia and the Pacific'.[52] Likewise, in the 2000s, the overarching goal in the region remained to 'secure and promote our economic interests' and to make use of 'the opportunities offered by the huge growth potential in the region'.[53]

In the context of this region-wide economic objective, Germany pursued three specific policy goals vis-à-vis China. For one, Berlin intended to expand trade and investment opportunities with the PRC. As stressed by the Office of the Federal Chancellor, Germany's 'aim' was to 'focus on economic relations' and 'to boost German exports and investment' ties with China.[54] According to a former Asia-hand in the FFO, 'the economy was basically the only issue on the agenda of the Sino-German relationship; it was pure economics'.[55] A second 'major foreign policy concern' was, as indicated in a FFO policy document, to 'integrate China, a country rapidly growing in political and economic significance, into the international community' and to convince Beijing that 'it bore increasing responsibility' for both the 'stability in the Asia-Pacific region' and 'for global concerns'.[56] For former Foreign Minister Frank-Walter Steinmeier (2005–2009), the underlying assumption was that 'the more closely integrated we are into the global information and trade flows, the less able we are to evade our responsibilities with regard to jointly facing up to the global challenges'.[57] Third, Germany hoped that broadening economic ties and enabling China's integration

---

[52] Federal Government, 1993.

[53] FFO, *Tasks of German Foreign Policy: East Asia*, 2002a, p. 17. On this point, see also FFO, 'Asia in German Foreign Policy', https://www.auswaertiges-amt.de/en/aussenpolitik/regionaleschwerpunkte/asien/-/231344.

[54] Office of the Federal Chancellor, 'Chancellor Visits the Far East: China and Japan', 26 August 2007, https://www.bundeskanzlerin.de/bkin-en/news/chancellor-visits-the-far-east-china-and-japan-607408.

[55] Ambassador Heinrich Kreft, official in the FFO's PPS in charge of Asian affairs (1996–2001) and then Deputy Head of the PPS (2004–2006), interview, 19 October 2020.

[56] FFO, 2002a, p. 8. The same point was also stressed in Federal Government, 1993.

[57] Federal Foreign Minister Frank-Walter Steinmeier (2005–2009), Speech at the Opening of the Hamburg Summit "China Meets Europe', Hamburg Chamber of Commerce, 10 September 2008.

in the international system would foster domestic reforms in the PRC and its 'convergence' towards Western open market, liberal economies—what former Chancellor Gerhard Schröder (1998–2005) labelled the 'change through trade' policy.[58]

An Emerging Policy Framework for the Indo-Pacific

In the 2010s, however, the combination of growing economic interests in the Asia-Pacific and a heightened threat assessment of the PRC drove Berlin's policy goals to evolve. Germany revised the goals of its 'China policy' and hardened its stance vis-à-vis Beijing (as further detailed in Chapter 5) while gradually formulating a new regional policy framework with an expanded scope onto the larger Indo-Pacific and a partly strengthened political-military dimension.

Given the previously discussed geopolitical and economic trends in the Asia-Pacific, the region was now perceived by German policymakers as 'key to shaping the international order in the twenty-first century',[59] and was thus elevated to a 'priority of German foreign policy'.[60] As one FFO official puts it, 'the Asia-Pacific is a region where our future—and the global security architecture—will be shaped'; 'the growing importance of the region itself just reflects how much importance China has gained in the last decade.'[61]

Accordingly, after Berlin began to put growing emphasis on engaging the world's emerging powers (including China and India) with its 2012 *New Players Concept*, it then gradually forged a new policy framework to steer its foreign and security policy in the region.[62] In line with a concurrent trend in the United States, in the Asia-Pacific region, and in some other European states (including France and subsequently the United Kingdom), the policy was subsequently reframed around the larger 'Indo-Pacific'; the geographical scope of the policy was broadened to encompass the maritime and land components of both the Indian and Pacific regions.[63]

---

[58] Interviews with former FFO officials, September–December 2020. On this point see also Hans Kundnani and Jonas Parello-Plesner, 'China and Germany: Why the Emerging Special Relationship Matters for Europe', European Council on Foreign Relations, *Policy Brief*, 2012, p. 3; Christoph Schnellbach and Joyce Man, 'Germany and China: Embracing a Different Kind of Partnership?', Center for Applied Policy Research, *CAP Working Paper*, September 2015, pp. 2–17.

[59] Federal Government, 2020a, p. 8.

[60] FFO, 'Foreign Minister Maas on the Adoption of the German Government Policy Guidelines on the Indo-Pacific Region', *Press Release*, 2 September 2020b.

[61] Interview, 16 April 2020.

[62] On the *New Players Concept*, see FFO, *Globalisierung gestalten—Partnerschaften ausbauen—Verantwortung teilen. Konzept der Bundesregierung*, 2012a, pp. 9 and 12.

[63] According to the Federal Government, while the label 'Indo-Pacific' embraces 'the entire region characterized by the Indian Ocean and the Pacific', its specific geographical contours remain 'not clearly delineated in geographical terms' since they are 'defined variously by different actors' (FFO, *Germany—Europe—Asia: Shaping the 21st Century Together: The German Government Adopts Policy Guidelines on*

The Federal Government's *2020 Guidelines for the Indo-Pacific* outlined Germany's core policy goals in the region: promoting regional stability and upholding freedom of navigation and the peaceful resolution of disputes which, in turn, would jointly enable the advancement of its economic interests.[64] Overall, sustaining the resilience of the rules-based order in the face of China's contestation of it, promoting regional stability, and protecting German economic interests were seen as interwoven and mutually reinforcing goals.[65]

Policy Instruments

As Berlin revised its policy goals vis-à-vis China and in the Asia-Pacific, the instruments mobilized to achieve those goals also evolved. In the first two decades after the Cold War, German foreign policy in the Asia-Pacific remained focused on deepening diplomatic and economic ties with emerging regional powers (with a strong focus on China) through bilateral and multilateral channels. It is only in the 2010s, as it gradually forged a new regional policy framework, that Berlin strengthened and diversified its diplomatic and security engagement across the Asia-Pacific, albeit within the constraints imposed by severe capability shortfalls and competing regional priorities.

Economic Engagement with China and Other Regional Powers

During the 1990s and 2000s, Germany's policy towards the Asia-Pacific centred primarily around economically and diplomatically engaging the PRC and other regional powers. To that end, Berlin developed bilateral partnerships with these

---

the Indo-Pacific Region, 1 September 2020e). German policymakers stress a central difference between the German Indo-Pacific construct and those developed by France and the United Kingdom. In their view, whereas the British and French focus on the maritime domain, Germany's construct also encompasses a land component; thereby, they seek to devise a response to Chinese attempts at challenging the rules-based order not only in maritime spaces but also 'on land', e.g. the Belt and Road Initiative (interviews with FFO officials, January–June 2020).

[64] Federal Government, 2020a, Preface by Foreign Minister Heiko Maas and pp. 35–40. On these policy guidelines, see also Rafał Ulatowski, 'Germany in the Indo-Pacific Region: Strengthening the Liberal Order and Regional Security', *International Affairs* 98, no. 2 (2022): pp. 383–402. On Germany's overall foreign policy goals in the region, see also Federal Foreign Minister Heiko Maas, Speech at the Luncheon Held by the American Council on Germany (ACG) on 'Germany, Europe and the United States: A Strategic Partnership Facing New Challenges?', 1 April 2019a; and FFO, 'Germany and China: Fostering Fairness in Business and Politics', 24 November 2016a; Federal Minister of State for Europe at the FFO Michael Roth, 'Speech at the Asia Pacific Lunch 'Europe at the Crossroads: The Challenges Europe Is Facing in 2017', 18 May 2017; and State Secretary Stephan Steinlein, 'Speech at the Asia-Pacific Conference of German Business: "Political Stability and Security in Asia-Pacific"', Ho Chi Minh City, 22 November 2014; and Vice Admiral Kay-Achim Schönbach, 'The Future of Indo-Pacific Maritime Security', Speech by the German Chief of Navy, 42nd IISS Fullerton Lecture, 21 December 2021, https://www.iiss.org/events/2021/12/42nd-iiss-fullerton-lecture.

[65] Interviews with FFO officials, January–June 2020. On this point, see State Secretary at the FFO Andreas Michaelis, 'Welcome Remarks at the Regional Ambassadors' Conference on ASEAN', 22 May 2019.

countries and promoted, through multilateral channels, a greater role for the European Union in the Asian multilateral regional architecture—although with limited success.

Bilateral Ties: China, Japan, India

The Chinese government's repression of the demonstrations on Tiananmen Square in June 1989 'triggered', as one declassified document puts it, 'a heavy perturbation' in the Sino-German bilateral relationship.[66] Furthermore, according to a former FFO official, 'there was a huge fear that what we had seen just a few weeks before in Tiananmen Square could happen in Leipzig and East Berlin because of a similar reaction by the Soviets; this was very present in the German discussions at that time.'[67] Together with the other European Community (EC) members, Germany thus imposed a freeze on senior bilateral diplomatic contacts, on military cooperation, and on government loans while also imposing an embargo on arms sales to China.[68] In 1992, however, Berlin ended what then Foreign Minister Klaus Kinkel (1992–1998) labelled the 'ice age' of the bilateral relationship which was deemed to harm German economic interests in China; it resumed diplomatic contacts and helped to lift EC sanctions—with the exception of the arms embargo—thus paving the way for the development of closer ties in subsequent decades.[69] Having established a 'strategic partnership in global responsibility' in 2004, the two countries thereafter engaged in a strategic dialogue to further deepen the bilateral political and economic relationship.[70]

To that end, Berlin also initially pushed for lifting the EU embargo on arms sales to China in the early 2000s, together with Paris and London.[71] From a German perspective, a key underlying rationale was that the embargo was politically

---

[66] FFO, 'Deutschland-Besuch PM Li Peng', 13 June 1989b, Politisches Archiv des Auswärtigen Amts (PAAA), B 37-ZA/161,825. See also FFO, 'Deutschland-Besuch PM Li Peng', 9 June 1989c, PAAA, B 37-ZA/161,825; and Klaus Rupprecht, 'Germany's Policy towards China and the SARs of Hong Kong and Macau', in *Europe, China and the Two SARs: Towards a New Era*, edited by Miguel Santos Neves and Brian Bridges (Basingstoke: Palgrave Macmillan, 2000), p. 64.

[67] Interview, 19 October 2020. See also Qinna Shen, 'Tiananmen Square, Leipzig, and the "Chinese Solution": Revisiting the Wende from an Asian-German Perspective', *German Studies Review 42*, no. 1 (2019): pp. 37–56.

[68] European Council, Presidency Conclusions, Madrid, 26 and 27 June 1989, Appendix II. For details on the measures taken by Berlin in response to the Tiananmen massacre, see FFO, 1989b; and FFO, 'Deutschland-Besuch PM Li Peng', 6 June 1989a, Politisches Archiv des Auswärtigen Amts, B 37-ZA/161,825.

[69] Rupprecht, 2000, p. 64 The economic rationale that drove Berlin's desire to remove its sanctions on the PRC was highlighted in interviews with former German diplomats stationed in the region, September–December 2020.

[70] See Office of the Federal Chancellor, 'Germany and China: Strategic Partnership in Global Responsibility', 22 May 2006; and Mikko Huotari, 'Germany's China Policy: No Honeymoon Forever', in *Mapping Europe–China Relations: A Bottom-Up Approach*, edited by Mikko Huotari, Miguel Otero-Iglesias, John Seaman, and Alice Ekman (Berlin: Joint Report by MERICS/IFRI/Elcano, 2015), p. 30.

[71] See also Chapters 1 and 3.

counterproductive in that it harmed the development of bilateral diplomatic and economic relations with a major rising power.[72] Furthermore, German officials considered that lifting the embargo would not alter the quality or quantity of military equipment being sold to China given the existing export control systems.[73] In the words of Chancellor Gerhard Schröder, one of the main proponents of lifting the embargo, the arms ban was an outdated 'political-symbolic instrument' which was, in his view, 'dispensable'.[74]

Germany's position, however, shifted in 2005 when Chancellor Schröder was replaced by Angela Merkel—who had long criticized this initiative—and Berlin came to oppose the lifting of the embargo.[75] Thereafter, as evidenced in leaked diplomatic cables, Germany became disinclined to support an end to the arms embargo on China.[76] London concomitantly also reversed its position, largely out of fear of damaging its relationship with Washington.[77] The combination of intense US pressures on EU member states, Beijing's adoption of the 2005 Anti-Secession Law, and intra-European fragmentation on this issue—which was further reinforced by the German and British policy shift—resulted in the issue of the EU arms embargo on China being de facto abandoned.[78]

Besides China, Germany deepened its bilateral diplomatic and economic ties with other regional powers, most notably Japan as well as, to a lesser extent, India.[79] Before being overtaken by Beijing, Tokyo had been Berlin's first economic partner in the region until the turn of the twentieth century.[80] In 2000, Germany and Japan agreed to a policy document which identified key areas to advance the bilateral relationship, including bolstering economic ties as well as political cooperation on disarmament and non-proliferation, the reform of the UN Security Council, and

---

[72] Interviews with FFO officials in office in the 2000s, January–December 2020.
[73] Interviews with FFO and MoD officials in office in the 2000s, January–December 2020.
[74] Federal Chancellor Gerhard Schröder, 'Rede vor dem Deutschen Bundestag zum Waffenembargo gegen China', Berlin, 14 April 2005.
[75] Francis Miko, 'Germany's "Grand Coalition" Government: Prospects and Implications', Congressional Research Service, *CRS Report*, 17 January 2006, p. 16.
[76] US Embassy in Germany, 'German Views on The December Foreign Ministers Meeting', Confidential, Wikileaks Cablegate, 8 December 2006b. On this point, see also US Embassy in China, 'EU Arms Embargo Unlikely to Be Lifted during the German EU Presidency', Confidential, Wikileaks Cablegate, 9 November 2006; US Embassy in Germany, 'German Foreign Minister Steinmeier Talks UNSC Reform, Iran, ROK and East Asian Security with GOJ', Confidential, Wikileaks Cablegate, 27 February 2006a; US Embassy in Germany, 'Germany Looks Eastward: Chancellor Merkel's Trip to China, Japan', Confidential, Wikileaks Cablegate, 8 December 2006c.
[77] See Chapter 3.
[78] For a detailed analysis, see Hugo Meijer, *Trading with the Enemy: The Making of US Export Control Policy toward the People's Republic of China* (New York: Oxford University Press, 2016), pp. 248–250; and Hugo Meijer, 'Transatlantic Perspectives on China's Military Modernization: The Case of Europe's Arms Embargo against the People's Republic of China', *Paris Paper no. 12*, Strategic Research Institute (IRSEM), 2014.
[79] As detailed below, Berlin also sought to expand its economic relations with South East Asian nations and, in particular, with ASEAN countries. See also FFO, 2002b.
[80] FFO, 2002a, p. 4.

enhanced dialogue through the ASEAN Regional Forum, among other areas.[81] In 2004, they then agreed to further their scientific and technological cooperation.[82] Overall, although the bilateral relationship developed during the 2000s, it remained largely limited to political and economic affairs, with little emphasis on defence cooperation.

Berlin also intensified its relations with India. In 2000, the two countries agreed to an 'Agenda for German-Indian Partnership in the 21st Century' which laid the foundations for greater economic, political, and technological cooperation.[83] One year later they forged a 'strategic partnership' which was complemented by a bilateral agreement, in 2006, that established a framework for defence cooperation—especially in the armaments sector.[84] During the 2000s, German arms transfers to India included licensing arrangements for anti-submarine sonar, the further production of Dornier aircraft in India, and the delivery of diesel engines for India's submarines, surface naval vessels, and Arjun tanks.[85]

Promoting Asian Multilateralism through the European Union

As a complement to these bilateral initiatives, and consistently with its propensity for multilateral engagement, Germany cultivated its political and economic ties with China and other regional powers by fostering—through the European Union—the development of Asian multilateralism.

Berlin decided to make 'greater use of the instruments for interregional cooperation between Europe and Asia' considering, as emphasized in a policy paper of the mid-1990s, that a 'fundamental aspect of an active policy towards Asia and the Pacific must be the development of relations between the European Community and the countries and regions of Asia and the Pacific'.[86] Likewise, in the 2000s, the FFO stressed that Germany could 'only achieve [its] objectives' of enhanced political, trade, and investment ties with regional powers through 'cooperation with our European partners'.[87] Nurturing intra-European cooperation and engaging multilateral regimes in the Asia-Pacific thus went hand in hand.

Germany therefore advocated for and supported greater EU involvement in the Association for Southeast Asian Nations (ASEAN), the ASEAN Regional Forum (ARF) and the ASEM.[88] In 2007, at a meeting hosted by the German EU

---

[81] Japanese MFA, 'Japan and Germany in the 21st Century: Seven Pillars of Cooperation', 30 October 2000.

[82] Japanese MFA, 'Japanese-German Science, Technology and Academic Cooperation and Exchanges', 9 December 2004.

[83] FFO, 'Agenda for the Indo-German Partnership in the 21st Century', 18 May 2000.

[84] Indian MFA, 'India–Germany Relations', August 2013; and Indian MFA, 'India–Germany Relations', 5 January 2018b.

[85] SIPRI, 'Trade Register', https://www.sipri.org/databases/armstransfers. See also Dhruva Jaishankar, 'India and Germany: Realising Strategic Convergence', Brookings Institution, 31 January 2017, p. 4.

[86] Federal Government, 1993.

[87] FFO, 2002b, p. 16. See also FFO, 'Germany and ASEAN to Cooperate on Strengthening ASEAN Institutions', 27 February 2008.

[88] See, e.g. Federal Government, 1993; FFO, 2002a, pp. 2 and 16.

Presidency, the so-called 'Nuremberg Declaration' promoted enhanced political dialogue between the European Union and ASEAN (including the ARF).[89] Two years later, Germany accredited its first Permanent Representative to ASEAN.[90]

Yet, despite its attempts at strengthening political and economic ties between the European Union and the Asia-Pacific through multilateral institutions, conflicting regional priorities and rivalling economic interests within the European Union undermined the prospect of a common EU foreign policy in the region. German policymakers in office during the 1990s and 2000s stress a profound lack of political interest within the European Union with regards to the Asia-Pacific, especially because other priorities dominated the diplomatic agenda such as the Balkans, the expansion of the European Union in Central and Eastern Europe, and the invasions in Afghanistan and Iraq.[91] In the words of Volker Stanzel, a Asia-hand at the FFO and then German Ambassador to the PRC (2004–2007), the EU members states 'lacked the incentive to act forcefully and we lacked our own cohesion on these matters'; 'the EU was of insignificant importance in the Asia-Pacific.'[92]

Furthermore, although Germany was the most economically successful European power in China—and was thus less concerned than France and the United Kingdom by intra-European economic competition—the desire of the Big Three to deepen their respective economic ties with Beijing further weakened the capacity of the European Union to forge a common policy vis-à-vis China and in the Asia-Pacific.[93] As the former Head of the FFO's East Asia Division Thomas Gerberich (2006–2008) puts it, 'the problem was the ambivalence of German, British, and French bilateral policies vis-à-vis China which were based on economic and trade relationships; so, there was always a competition between Germany, Britain, and France in the field of trade and the economy.'[94] Likewise, in the words of another foreign policy official, while 'within the European Union we were partners, when it came to China—on concrete business endeavours—we were very much competitors.'[95] He adds that the 2004 enlargement of the European Union further complicated the achievement of consensus around a EU common policy in the Asia-Pacific: it 'greatly contributed to making cohesiveness within the European Union difficult; the more countries that are members, the more different positions

---

[89] Commissioner for Disarmament and Arms Control Friedrich Gröning, Opening Speech at the ASEAN Regional Forum Workshop on 'Confidence-Building Measures and Preventive Diplomacy in Asia and Europe, 13 March 2008.
[90] FFO, 'German Government Accredits First Ambassador to the ASEAN', 12 February 2009.
[91] Interviews with former FFO and FMoD officials, January–December 2020.
[92] Volker Stanzel, former FFO's Director for Asian and Pacific Affairs (2001–2002), then FFO's Director General for Political Affairs in charge of relations with the Asia-Pacific (2002–2004) and subsequently German Ambassador to the PRC (2004–2007), interview, 12 November 2020.
[93] Interviews with former FFO officials in office in the 2000s, September–December 2020. For a comparison of the Big Three's exports and investments in China, see the charts in Appendix B.
[94] Thomas Gerberich, Consul General in Chengdu (2004–2006) and then Deputy Head of the FFO's East Asia Division (2006–2008), interview, 15 October 2020.
[95] Interview, 17 November 2020.

you find, and the more difficult it is to come up with a cohesive position.'[96] Accordingly, while there were working-level diplomatic consultations between Berlin, London, and Paris, there was no high-level political coordination around joint policies in the Asia-Pacific.[97]

Enhanced Political-Military Engagement

As the Asia-Pacific's importance for Germany grew, and as Berlin gradually developed a new regional policy framework during the 2010s, it bolstered its diplomatic and security engagement in the region. To be sure, as detailed later, Germany displayed a markedly feebler regional undertaking than France and the United Kingdom because of profound capability shortfalls and conflicting regional priorities. Yet, within such constraints, it strengthened and diversified its bilateral diplomatic and security arrangements, promoted greater intra-European cooperation in the region in order to better cope with the security ramifications of China's rise, and partly expanded its naval engagement in the region.

Capability Shortfalls, Naval Deployments, and the Expanded Network of Bilateral Security Partnerships

Since the end of the Cold War, the capabilities of the Bundeswehr (the German armed forces) sharply declined and displayed profound readiness deficiencies—with less than 50 per cent of its major weapons systems being ready for training or deployment in 2017.[98] The navy reported that, that same year, none of its six Type 212A submarines were working and that, even if they did, only three trained crews would be available to man them.[99] Likewise, two years later, the Parliamentary Commissioner for the Armed Forces concluded that the navy had 'never been smaller than it is now' (with a fleet of merely nine large combat vessels).[100] Furthermore, the German navy maintained, as its main areas of engagement, the North Atlantic, the North Sea, and the Baltic Sea, as well as the Mediterranean.[101]

---

[96] Interview, 17 November 2020.
[97] Interviews with former FFO officials in office in the 2000s, September–December 2020.
[98] Data from the classified FMoD's *Report on the Operational Readiness of the Bundeswehr's Primary Weapons Systems 2017*, quoted in 'Limited Number of Weapons in German Military Ready for Action: Report', *DW News*, 27 February 2018. See also Parliamentary Commissioner for the Armed Forces, *Annual Report to the Bundestag—2017*, 20 February 2018, p. 41; and FMoD, *Bericht zur Materiellen Einsatzbereitschaft der Hauptwaffensysteme der Bundeswehr*, 2019.
[99] Quoted in Sven Rascke, 'Marine-Misere: Deutschlands U-Boote Sind alle Kaputt', *SHZ.de*, 20 October 2017. See also Sebastian Roblin, 'Germany Does Not Have One Working Submarine', *The National Interest*, 16 December 2017.
[100] Parliamentary Commissioner for the Armed Forces, *Annual Report to the Bundestag—2019*, 28 February 2020, p. 43. To address the capabilities shortfalls, Berlin has invested, among others, in naval capabilities such as new F125-class frigates, multi-purpose combat ships MKS 180, and new submarines currently under development together with Norway. Andreas Krause, 'German Navy Chief of Staff: The Naval Force is Preparing for Challenges Beyond 2020', *Defense News*, 2 December 2019.
[101] Krause, 2019.

The combination of severe capability shortfalls and competing regional priorities—coupled with the lack of forward-deployed forces in the region—considerably constrained the naval capabilities that Germany could deploy in the Asia-Pacific. Accordingly, throughout the 2010s, the German navy provided only minor contributions to existing multinational naval deployments in the Indian and Pacific Oceans. For instance, it deployed naval officers in the Rim of the Pacific (RIMPAC) multinational military exercise as well as in deployments of the US-led Combined Task Force 151 and of the EU-Naval Force Somalia.[102] Then, in order to concretize its 2020 *Indo-Pacific Guidelines*, Germany decided to deploy a Bayern frigate in the Asia-Pacific, from August 2021 to February 2022, thereby marking an important (though modest) shift in its regional posture.[103] And while Berlin announced an increase of 100bn euros for defence spending and a pledge to spend more than 2 percent of its GDP on defence after Russia's invasion of Ukraine in 2022, it remains to be seen whether such increase will be sufficient to address Germany's severe capability shortfalls and bolster its naval regional presence.[104]

Despite its thin naval engagement, Germany nonetheless deepened and broadened its network of diplomatic and security ties across the Asia-Pacific. Thereby, it sought to move beyond the China-centric approach that had characterized previous decades and to diversify its political and security relations across the region.[105] Although the priority remained the economic component of these relationships, Germany also expanded their political dimension, 'including closer cooperation in the area of security'.[106] Not only did Berlin develop its existing bilateral relationships (with the PRC, Japan, and India) but it also widened the range of its diplomatic and security partnerships with medium and small regional powers.[107]

For one, Germany recalibrated its bilateral relationship with the PRC. On the one hand, having upgraded the relationship to a 'comprehensive strategic partnership' in 2014, the two countries intensified their economic relations and intergovernmental consultations to the point that, by the end of the decade, they held

---

[102] Dzirhan Mahadzir, 'PACFLEET Commander: RIMPAC 2020 Will Be More Complex, Feature More Countries', *USNI News*, 6 March 2020; Combined Maritime Force (CMF), 'CTF 151 Leads Focused Operation (FO) "DYNAMIC KHARIF" in Further Successful Collaboration with EU NAVFOR', 5 October 2017, at https://combinedmaritimeforces.com/2017/10/05/ctf-151-leads-focused-operation-fo-dynamic-kharif-in-further-successful-collaboration-with-eu-navfor/; EU Naval Force Somalia, 'EU NAVFOR Force Commander Thanks German Maritime Air Patrol Team for Invaluable Contribution to Operation Atalanta off Coast of Somalia', 13 June 2017, at https://eunavfor.eu (accessed 1 December 2021).
[103] On the deployment of the Bayern frigate, see Federal Minister of Defence quoted in Abhijnan Rej, 'Germany to Deploy a Frigate to Patrol the Indo-Pacific', *The Diplomat*, 3 November 2020; and Shogo Akagawa, 'Germany to Send Naval Frigate to Japan with Eye on China', *Nikkei Asia*, 25 January 2020.
[104] Christophe Schuetze, 'Russia's Invasion Prompts Germany to Beef Up Military Funding', *The New York Times*, 27 February 2022.
[105] Interviews with FFO officials, January–June 2020. See also Federal Foreign Minister Sigmar Gabriel, 2017.
[106] Federal Government, 2020a, p. 3.
[107] Federal Government, 2020a, p. 9; and Federal Foreign Minister Guido Westerwelle, 2012a.

some eighty dialogue mechanisms ranging from trade and investment relations to cultural and scientific cooperation.[108] On the other hand, in line with its rising security concerns and the resulting more cautious engagement with the PRC, Berlin strengthened its screening mechanisms on Chinese investments in sensitive sectors and tightened its scrutiny over telecommunications vendors of concern like Huawei (as detailed in Chapter 5), while also continuing to oppose the lifting of the EU arms embargo on China, stressing that it had 'no intention' to 'change the status quo'.[109]

As it hardened its bilateral relationship with Beijing, Germany concomitantly developed closer ties with Japan. Although the German-Japanese relationship remained centred around bilateral economic issues and the establishment of the European Union–Japan Economic Partnership Agreement (EPA, entered into force in 2019),[110] Berlin and Tokyo expanded their bilateral defence cooperation—albeit from a low level—through agreements on defence equipment and technology transfers, the exchange of classified information, and cyber cooperation.[111] The Japanese government further stressed that, although Berlin allocated most of its military assets for NATO and EU missions outside the Asia-Pacific, German efforts to enhance its naval engagement in the region would 'attract attention'.[112]

Building upon their 2006 strategic partnership, Berlin also intensified its high-level security engagement with New Delhi through foreign secretary-level consultations and the high defence committee, stressing the importance of freedom of navigation and the peaceful resolution of disputes.[113] The two countries deepened

---

[108] FFO, 'Joint Declaration: Establishment of a Comprehensive Strategic Partnership between Germany and China', 28 March 2014; FFO, 'Germany and China: Bilateral Relations China', 17 August 2020c.

[109] US Embassy in Germany, 'German Views on the EU Arms Embargo against China and the February 22 EU Foreign Affairs Council', Confidential, Wikileaks Cablegate, 19 February 2010. This point is confirmed by interviews with FFO officials, January–June 2020; and in FFO, 2018b, p. 11.

[110] See Japanese MFA, 'Japan–Germany Summit Meeting', 4 February 2019; Federal Government, 'Angela Merkel in Japan: Long-Standing Friendship is an "Incentive to Cooperate More Closely"', 5 February 2019a, https://www.bundesregierung.de/breg-en/search/long-standing-friendship-is-an-incentive-to-cooperate-more-closely--1577310; and Federal Ministry for Economic Affairs (MEA) and Japanese MEA, 'Joint Statement on Economic Policy and Cooperation', 6 November 2019a.

[111] FFO, 'Sign of Mutual Trust: Japan and Germany Sign Agreement on the Security of Information', 22 March 2021, https://www.auswaertiges-amt.de/en/aussenpolitik/laenderinformationen/japan-node/japan-agreement-security-information/2449392; Japanese Embassy in Germany, 'Premierminister Abe besucht Deutschland', 5 May 2016, https://www.de.emb-japan.go.jp/presse/pm_160505.html.; Japanese Embassy in Germany, 'Japanisch-Deutsches Gipfeltreffen', 4 February 2019, https://www.de.emb-japan.go.jp/presse/pm_190204.html.; Japanese MFA, 2019; Japanese MoD, *White Paper: Defense of Japan*, 2018, p. 373. See also Jeffrey W. Hornung, *Allies Growing Closer: Japan–Europe Security Ties in the Age of Strategic Competition* (Santa Monica, CA: RAND Corporation, 2020), pp. 59–74.

[112] Japanese MoD, *White Paper: Defense of Japan*, 2020, p. 152.

[113] Indian Embassy in Germany, 'India–Germany Relations', 30 March 2020, https://indianembassyberlin.gov.in/pages?id=eyJpdiI6ImZrK2FvcOJDNXNBZ1YxSWdCQXNRYXc9PSIsInZhbHVlIjoicOxsaFY5eTcwZXhjUDQ5dk1ISVF5Zz09IiwibWFjIjoiOTgwYzc2YjI1NjkxOTA3YmM3MjU2ZDY5YTM2ZmVhZDkyZWE0NzA5ZDk2ZWY2NDhmMzg1NTBmNThiZjU5NmNlOCJ9 (accessed on 1 December 2021); Indian MFA, 'Joint Statement—Third India Germany Inter-Governmental Consultations', 5 October 2015; and Indian MFA, Joint Statement 'Strategic Partnership for Sustainable Growth and a Reliable International Order', 1 November 2019.

their military-to-military engagement and their defence industrial cooperation in the areas of defence manufacturing, defence technology, and R&D as well as in the cyber and space domains.[114] Berlin committed to facilitating defence exports and technology-sharing with India, including co-development and co-production of military equipment,[115] e.g. transferring maritime patrol aircraft and diesel engines, while planning to upgrade India's Shishumar-class attack submarines.[116]

Besides developing existing partnerships with regional powers, Germany also broadened and diversified the range of bilateral ties across the region, including with Australia and South East Asian countries. Berlin and Canberra developed a 'strategic partnership' in 2013 which was elevated three years later through the establishment of '2+2 consultations' (between their respective MFAs and MoDs).[117] The two countries thereby fostered greater political-military consultations on China's challenge to freedom of navigation and regional stability in the South China Sea, among other issues.[118] Although the main areas of cooperation revolved around economics, science and technology (S&T), and energy, the two countries sought to deepen defence cooperation, although only modestly, through an arrangement to protect the exchange of classified information, enhanced cooperation in cyberspace, and joint training.[119] Germany also supplied Australia with, among other systems, offshore patrol vessels, infantry fighting vehicles, and armoured personnel carriers, and agreed to deliver Type 218SG submarines.[120] The two countries then upgraded their relationship to an 'enhanced strategic partnership' in 2021, committing to enhance their security and defence cooperation, including through training and exercises, and to work together on capacity-building projects in the region.[121]

In South East Asia, building upon a previous 2005 arrangement, Germany and Singapore established a 'enhanced defence cooperation agreement' in 2018, bolstering ties through high-level consultations, technological collaboration, and military exercises (such as Panzer Strike) while strengthening cooperation in

---

[114] Indian MFA, 'India–Germany Joint Statement during the Visit of Prime Minister to Germany', 30 May 2017, https://www.mea.gov.in/bilateral-documents.htm?dtl/28496/IndiaGermany.; Indian MFA, 2019; Indian Embassy in Germany, 2020.
[115] Indian MFA, 2019.
[116] SIPRI, 'Trade Register'. See also Franz-Stefan Gady, 'Germany to Upgrade Two Indian Attack Submarines', *The Diplomat*, 14 June 2016.
[117] FFO, 'Berlin–Canberra Declaration of Intent on a Strategic Partnership', 28 January 2013; Australian Department of Foreign Affairs and Trade, 'Joint Ministerial Media Release: Inaugural German-Australian 2+2 Ministerial Meeting in Berlin', 6 September 2016.
[118] Australian Department of Foreign Affairs and Trade, 2016.
[119] FMoD, 'Ministerin betont enge Kooperation mit australischen Streitkräften', 24 October 2018; Federal Government, 2020a, p. 16; FFO, 2013.
[120] SIPRI, 'Trade Register'.
[121] Australian Government, 'Enhanced Strategic Partnership between Australia and the Federal Republic of Germany', 10 June 2021, https://www.dfat.gov.au/about-us/publications/international-relations/enhanced-strategic-partnership-between-australia-and-federal-republic-germany.

cyberspace.[122] Likewise, they developed their armaments cooperation: Germany transferred to Singapore systems such as the Leopard 2 main battle tank and planned the delivery of four Type 218SG submarines.[123]

Germany also developed its ties with Vietnam and Indonesia. Berlin and Hanoi elevated their relationship to a 'strategic partnership' in 2011, expanding defence cooperation in areas such as training and defence industrial cooperation, then agreed to appoint a permanent resident German defence attaché to Vietnam and to raise the level of their political-military consultations (establishing a deputy ministerial-level defence policy dialogue).[124] The 'strategic partnership' with Indonesia, agreed to in 2012, was subsequently reinforced through enhanced defence cooperation on military training, defence R&D, military logistics, as well as on maritime security cooperation.[125] In the armament domain, Germany transferred Leopard 2 main battle tanks and Marder armoured infantry fighting vehicles to Jakarta.[126]

The 'China Factor' in Germany's Network of Regional Partnerships

Overall, within the limits of its capability constraints, Germany thus developed and diversified its network of partnerships across the Asia-Pacific, and thereby moved beyond the China-centred approach that had characterized previous decades. Chinese growing assertiveness—and the resulting demand pulls from regional partners—was an important driver in Berlin's endeavour to diversify its diplomatic and security engagement in the region.

As the Head of the FFO's China Division Joern Beissert (since 2019) explains, 'Chinese assertiveness resulted in greater coherence of interests with our partners in the Asia-Pacific and so, in a way, it facilitates this progress. And the more assertive China will become, the greater this trend towards coherence will be.'[127] Similarly, according to the Minister of Defence Kramp-Karrenbauer (2019–2021), 'our partners in the Indo-Pacific are feeling increasingly harassed by China's claim to power', and thus 'want a clear sign of solidarity' in upholding freedom of

---

[122] Singaporean MoD, 'Singapore and Germany Strengthen Defence Ties through New Agreement on Defence Cooperation', *News Releases*, 2 June 2018a; Singaporean MFA, 'Joint Declaration on the Sidelines of the UN General Assembly', 28 September 2018; Prashanth Parameswaran, 'Military Exercise Highlights Singapore–Germany Defense Ties', *The Diplomat*, 24 March 2018; and Prashanth Parameswaran, 'What's in the New Singapore–Germany Cyber Pact?', *The Diplomat*, 11 July 2017.

[123] SIPRI, 'Trade Register'.

[124] Prashanth Parameswaran, 'What's Next for Germany–Vietnam Military Cooperation?', *The Diplomat*, 18 June 2019; 'Vietnam, Germany Expand Defense Cooperation', *People's Army Newspaper*, 15 June 2019.

[125] Elly Burhaini Faizal, 'Lawmakers Ratify Defense Agreements with Germany, China', *The Jakarta Post*, 21 March 2016; Jan Senkyr, 'Germany–Indonesia Strategic Dialogue', Event Reports, Konrad Adenauer Stiftung, 4 December 2018.

[126] See the annual reports of the Federal Ministry for Economic Affairs, *Report of the Government of the Federal Republic of Germany on its Policy on Exports of Conventional Military Equipment*, 2010–2019.

[127] Interview, 2 December 2020.

navigation and international law; 'the time has come for Germany to give such a sign and to be present in the region together with our allies'.[128]

A senior adviser to President Frank-Walter Steinmeier confirms that the diversification of German diplomatic and security partnerships in the Asia-Pacific was 'more or less the direct consequence of a more critical appraisal of China, not just on the economic level, but also geopolitically', which resulted in an effort to 'shape China's environment by engaging with the region and with China's neighbours'.[129]

Multinational Cooperation: Asian Multilateral Regimes and Enhanced European Coordination

Berlin complemented these bilateral initiatives by bolstering its engagement with the regional security architecture through both greater participation in Asian multilateral security regimes and expanded cooperation with other European powers in the Asia-Pacific.

Regional Security Regimes

During the 2010s, in light of the 'growing power rivalries and tensions' in the Asia-Pacific, Berlin came to see Asian multilateral security institutions as an ever more central venue for strengthening multinational coordination and resilience in the face of China's regional behaviour.[130] To that end, in addition to promoting a loosely defined 'alliance for multilateralism' together with France, Germany sought to expand its presence in various political and security fora in the Asia-Pacific.[131]

It promoted the strengthening of ASEAN, and in particular of ARF, which was seen as the most important security forum in the Asia-Pacific region.[132] Furthermore, in addition to attending the Shangri-La Dialogue in 2018,[133] it participated in the Indian Ocean Rim Association (IORA) in areas such as maritime security and in the Indian Ocean Naval Symposium (IONS, as an observer); and it further maintained a liaison officer to the Information Fusion Centre (IFC) in Singapore, which is dedicated to the surveillance of maritime spaces and the SLOCs in the Indian and Pacific Oceans.[134] It also joined the Regional Cooperation Agreement on Combating Piracy and Armed Robbery against Ships in Asia (ReCAAP) in

---

[128] Federal Minister of Defence Annegret Kramp-Karrenbauer, 2019.
[129] Thomas Bagger, interview, 20 January 2021.
[130] On Germany's engagement with regional multilateral institutions, see Federal Government, 2020a, p. 23; and State Secretary Andreas Michaelis, 2019.
[131] On the 'alliance for multilateralism', Federal Foreign Minister Heiko Maas, 2018.
[132] See FFO, 2018b, p. 9; and Secretary Stephan Steinlein, 2014. In 2020, Berlin acceded to the Treaty of Amity and Cooperation in Southeast Asia. See Federal Government, 2020a, p. 25.
[133] Federal Minister of Defence Ursula von der Leyen, Speech at Shangri-La Dialogue, Singapore, 3 June 2018.
[134] Federal Government, 2020a, pp. 13 and 36. Federal Government, 2020a, pp. 25 and 36.

2021 and applied to become observer of the ASEAN Defence Ministers' Meeting Plus (ADMM+)—which it attended at ministerial level as guest for the first time in December 2020—in order to 'actively contribute to a regional security architecture'.[135]

Promoting EU Cooperation in the Region

In conjunction with its expanded security cooperation with Asian partners through bilateral and multilateral channels, Germany sought to foster a greater role for the European Union in Asian-Pacific security and, after 2020, in the broader Indo-Pacific region. Unlike France and the United Kingdom, Berlin did not engage in any significant security cooperation with the United States in the region, largely because of German capability constraints. It therefore prioritized intra-EU diplomatic and security cooperation in the Asia-Pacific.

For German policymakers, a central rationale for doing so was that only 'through a united and coherent approach the European Union and its member states can better protect and enforce their interests' in the Indo-Pacific region.[136] Specifically, through a coordinated European policy, Germany hoped to carve out a distinct role for itself—and for the European Union—in the context of the growing strategic rivalry between the United States and China, one which would 'differ markedly' from what German policymakers saw as a US 'containment' strategy of China.[137] According to a senior foreign policy adviser to President Steinmeier (since 2017):

> The main concern is the growing confrontation between the US and China. You do not want to be in a position of having to choose between your major economic partner and your existential security guarantee; yet, with no EU unity, it becomes ever more difficult to define a space for Europe that is not simply taking sides in this growing US–China competition. To avoid a patchwork of different national responses, you need to empower a more coordinated European position so as to create a third place for Europe where it can maintain both a functional relationship with the United States as its main security provider and with China as a major economic partner and as a partner on global issues. It is not a position of equidistance because on many policy issues and on the fundamental question of how we organize our societies we are clearly more aligned with Washington, but

---

[135] FMoD, 'For Stability, Prosperity and a Rules-Based Order in the Indo-Pacific Region', *News*, 9 December 2020.
[136] Federal Government, 2020a, p. 11.
[137] State Secretary at the FFO Andreas Michaelis, 'Keynote Speech: EU Retreat on China: A Strategic Approach for Dealing with China', *Federal Foreign Office News Room*, 2 March 2020. See also Federal Government, 2020a, pp. 11–12.

that does not automatically translate into full consensus and joint action when it comes to China.[138]

Germany therefore supported closer coordination with EU partners as well as the expansion of European engagement in the Indo-Pacific since 'only a unified European policy' could effectively meet these goals.[139] It sought to gather traction for these efforts through a variety of venues: bilateral exchanges, formal EU channels, and informal minilateral gatherings. The latter included, among others, the E3 (with France and the United Kingdom) that produced joint statements on the South China Sea; the Quad (with France, the United States, and the United Kingdom) and the Quint which also included Italy (as well as EEAS representatives); or the Big Five which gathered Germany, France, Italy, Poland, and Spain (and, before Brexit, the United Kingdom, making it the Big Six).[140]

Berlin devised a three-pronged approach. The first consisted in developing a unified interagency position on Germany's policy in the Indo-Pacific, formalized in the 2020 *Guidelines*, as a 'point of departure' for closer cooperation among Europeans in the region.[141] Second, building upon the Franco-German Treaty of Aachen and the previous Élysée Treaty,[142] German policymakers aimed to foster greater bilateral consultations and coordination with France to develop a joint approach to the region—which, at a later stage, could potentially also include additional countries.[143] This, in turn, would lay the foundations for the third step, namely 'to promote a European Indo-Pacific strategy'.[144]

Specifically, as already detailed in Chapter 1, Germany worked, together with France and the Netherlands, on a non-paper advocating for the development of an EU strategy for the Indo-Pacific. Berlin then circulated this non-paper among

---

[138] Thomas Bagger, Director of Foreign Policy in the Office of the President (since 2017), interview, 6 May 2020.
[139] Federal Government, 2020a, p. 49.
[140] Interviews with FFO officials, September–December 2020. On the outputs of the E3, see British FCO, 'E3 Joint Statement on the Situation in the South China Sea', *Press Release*, 29 August 2019c; and Permanent Mission of the Federal Republic of Germany to the United Nations, 'Note verbale' to the Commission on the Limits of the Continental Shelf, no. 324/2020, New York, 16 September 2020.
[141] FFO, '*Germany—Europe—Asia: Shaping the 21st Century Together*': The German Government Adopts Policy Guidelines on the Indo-Pacific Region, 1 September 2020e, https://www.auswaertiges-amt.de/en/aussenpolitik/regionaleschwerpunkte/asien/german-government-policy-guidelines-indo-pacific/2380510.
[142] The Treaty on Cooperation and Integration (or Aachen Treaty) is a Franco-German bilateral agreement which complemented the 1963 Élysée Treaty and aimed to deepen bilateral defence cooperation, among other areas. On the Élysée Treaty, see Ulrich Krotz, *Shaping Europe: France, Germany, and Embedded Bilateralism from the Elysee Treaty to Twenty-First Century Politics* (Oxford: Oxford University Press, 2013). See also FFO, 'Treaty between the Federal Republic of Germany and the French Republic on Franco-German Cooperation and Integration', 22 January 2019a.
[143] Interviews with FFO officials, January–June 2020. See also FFO, 'Erklärung der Außenminister anlässlich des Deutsch-Französischen Ministerrats', 16 October 2019b; and FFO, 2020b.
[144] Federal Government, 2020a.

member states, and it was then co-signed by seven additional member states. Germany's EU Presidency gave Berlin, Paris and The Hague, in the words of one official, 'greater leverage on the agenda-setting'.[145] To be sure, Germany was less supportive than France of specific initiatives in the defence and security realm, such as extending the Coordinated Maritime Presences (CMP) into the Indo-Pacific.[146] As one official puts it with regard to the European Union's role in Asian-Pacific security:

> In general, Germany shares the line of thought about the importance to be more engaged militarily in the region but, realistically, the European Union does not have the capabilities to really make a difference in the region; as we stand now, this is not possible. It is a question of capabilities, not policy. Germany is not necessarily less supportive [than France] of an EU military role in the Indo-Pacific region because it deems such activities to be less important, but rather because it has limited naval capabilities. So, from our point of view, there is no special emphasis on military aspects, on hard power.[147]

Yet, despite this different emphasis from the French approach, Germany supported the formulation of Council Conclusions on an EU policy towards the Indo-Pacific, one that would be 'inclusive and not aimed at containing China'.[148] Partly as a result of these efforts and building upon this non-paper, the Council of the European Union adopted the Conclusions on an 'EU Strategy for Cooperation in the Indo-Pacific' in April 2021.[149] And these Conclusions, in turn, invited the European Commission and the EU High Representative for Foreign Affairs and Security Policy Josep Borrell (HR/VP, since 2019) to develop the Joint Communication on the European Union's Indo-Pacific Strategy, which was then presented in September 2021.[150] Germany had thus coalesced with France and the Netherlands to form a core group of countries pushing for an EU-wide approach to the Indo-Pacific.

Conclusions

Although Germany has long been the most 'reluctant' major European power in the field of foreign and security policy after its reunification, since the 2010s it has sought to respond to China's rising assertiveness by strengthening and diversifying

---

[145] Government official, interview, 5 October 2021.
[146] Interviews with German and French diplomats, October 2021.
[147] Government official, interview, 20 October 2021.
[148] Government official, interview, 20 October 2021.
[149] Council of the European Union, 'EU Strategy for Cooperation in the Indo-Pacific', Council Conclusions, 16 April 2021c.
[150] European Commission, 'The EU Strategy for Cooperation in the Indo-Pacific', Joint Communication JOIN(2021) 24 final, 16 September 2021c; and EEAS, 'EU Strategy for Cooperation in the Indo-Pacific', *Factsheet*, 19 April 2021a.

its diplomatic and security engagement in the region. In light of its major regional economic interests and of heightened threat perceptions of the PRC, Germany has developed a more cohesive policy framework for the larger Indo-Pacific region and given greater prominence to security considerations. It has broadened its network of bilateral partnerships, expanded its involvement in the regional security architecture, and actively promoted a larger role for the European Union in regional security while also deciding to conduct naval deployments in the Indian and Pacific Oceans. Certainly, Germany faces even more constraints than the other major European powers in the pursuit of this effort. For one, not only does it lack any military footprint in the Asia-Pacific, but its capabilities have experienced the most severe decline—among the Big Three's armed forces—since the end of the Cold War. Today, Berlin faces profound capability shortfalls, readiness deficiencies, and budgetary gaps. Furthermore, coupled with its post-WWII predisposition for multilateral diplomacy and for non-military instruments for achieving foreign policy goals, competing regional priorities have put additional strains on its limited resources. Yet, within the confines of these capability constraints, Berlin has sought to step up its contribution to upholding regional stability and the foundational norms of the rules-based order, and to thereby also sustain its economic interests in the Asia-Pacific. Through its multipronged efforts, Germany has aimed to shape the strategic, normative, and economic regional environment within which China's rise has unfolded.

3
Ripples of Empire

China's Rise and British Regional Policy to the East of Suez

Introduction

Building upon a distinct colonial trajectory, British foreign and security policy in the Asia-Pacific has experienced a major shift in response to China's rise akin to that of the other major European powers. Whereas the United Kingdom had possessed the largest European colonial empire in Asia, spanning from India to South East Asia and from China to the South Pacific, decolonization fundamentally curtailed its presence in the region. London's regional footprint became smaller than that of post-colonial France but larger than that of Germany. This, in turn, shaped the relative breadth of its strategic and economic interests and the course of its regional policy. On these grounds, and within the confines of limited capabilities, the United Kingdom has sought to cope with China's rising regional assertiveness by intensifying and broadening its political-military engagement in the Asia-Pacific through greater diplomatic and security cooperation with both Asian and Western powers.

The United Kingdom's colonial encounters with the Indian and Pacific Oceans date back at least to the seventeenth century when the East India Company began establishing trading posts in India and commercial contacts in the Indonesian archipelago.[1] As the British presence gradually transformed into a territorial power in India during the eighteenth and nineteenth centuries, and with the loss of the North American colonies, the centre of gravity of the whole Empire gradually shifted from the Atlantic to the Indian Ocean.[2] For both strategic and economic reasons, the Raj thereafter became the cornerstone of the British Empire in the East.

---

[1] Philip J. Stern, *The Company-State: Corporate Sovereignty and the Early Modern Foundations of the British Empire in India* (Oxford: Oxford University Press, 2011).

[2] P. J. Marshall, *Problems of Empire: Britain and India, 1757–1813* (London: George Allen and Unwin Ltd., 1968).

Beginning in the late seventeenth century, the Crown also developed and later entrenched its colonial power in South East Asia, especially in Burma, the Malay States, and Borneo.³ The First and Second Opium Wars with China, in the nineteenth century, provided Great Britain with an opportunity to further expand its foothold in the Far East. By imposing a range of international treaties, it gradually developed an 'informal empire' in several major Chinese cities and ports, while also acquiring Hong Kong (1842) and the Kowloon Peninsula (1860), subsequently leasing the New Territories (1898) for a period of ninety-nine years.⁴ In the South Pacific, the British arrived in the second half of the eighteenth century and gradually developed a colonial rule over Australia, New Zealand, and Fiji, as well as over smaller outposts, including the Gilbert and Ellice Islands Colony, Pitcairn, the Kingdom of Tonga, the British Solomon Islands Protectorate, and the British-French Condominium of the New Hebrides.⁵ The United Kingdom thus ruled over the largest European colonial empire in Asia and beyond.

Yet, decolonization in the twentieth century shattered the United Kingdom's role and presence in the region. The dissolution of the Raj in 1947 resulted in the partition of the subcontinent into India and Pakistan. In South East Asia, London fostered the creation of the Federation of Malaya in 1957—with which it established the Anglo-Malayan Defence Agreement—that was then joined in 1963 by Singapore, Sarawak, and North Borneo to form the new state of Malaysia (from which Singapore was then expelled in 1965).⁶ The retreat of the United Kingdom to the 'East of Suez' and the withdrawal of its military forces from Malaysia and Singapore in the late 1960s and early 1970s marked a watershed in British presence in the Asia-Pacific.⁷ London lost its last remaining major territories and military bases in the region, with the exception of the Pitcairn Islands in the South Pacific and of the British Indian Ocean Territory (BIOT), including Diego Garcia (leased to the United States).⁸ Decolonization in the Pacific occurred later than in other regions,

---

³ A. J. Stockwell, 'British Expansion and Rule in South-East Asia', in *The Oxford History of the British Empire, Vol. 3: The Nineteenth Century*, edited by Andrew Porter (Oxford: Oxford University Press, 1998), pp. 371–394.

⁴ See Jürgen Osterhammel, 'Semi-Colonialism and Informal Empire in Twentieth-Century China: Towards a Framework of Analysis', in *Imperialism and After: Continuities and Discontinuities*, edited by Wolfgang Mommsen and Jürgen Osterhammel (London: Allen & Unwin for the German Historical Institute, 1986), pp. 297–298.

⁵ Glyndwr Williams, 'The Pacific: Exploration and Exploitation', in *The Oxford History of the British Empire, Vol. 2: 'The Eighteenth Century'*, edited by P. J. Marshall and Alaine Low (Oxford: Oxford University Press, 1998), pp. 552–575.

⁶ Karl Hack, *Defence and Decolonisation in South-East Asia: Britain, Malaya and Singapore 1941–1968* (Richmond, Surrey: Curzon Press, 2001).

⁷ See Philip Darby, *British Defence Policy East of Suez, 1947–1960* (New York: Oxford University Press, 1973); Saki Dokrill, *Britain's Retreat from East of Suez: The Choice between Europe and the World?* (Basingstoke: Palgrave Macmillan, 2002).

⁸ London is, however, under pressure to bring an end to its administration of the BIOT. James Griffith, 'UN Court Ruling Puts Future of Strategic US Military Base Diego Garcia into Question', *CNN World*, 26 February 2019; Andrew Harding, 'UN Court Rules UK Has No Sovereignty over Chagos Islands', *BBC News*, 28 January 2021.

with Australia and New Zealand gradually achieving formal independence from Britain between the early twentieth century and the 1980s, and most South Pacific islands gaining independence during the 1970s.[9] Hong Kong was the last remaining Crown colony in the Far East. The management of the transfer of Hong Kong to Beijing in the 1980s and 1990s constituted a distinct specificity of the United Kingdom's relations with China which set it apart from those of the other major European powers. The 1997 handover of the former colony to the People's Republic of China marked the final chapter of the British imperial venture in Asia.[10]

The ripples of empire and decolonization profoundly shaped Great Britain's post-Cold War role in the Asia-Pacific.[11] London's 'direct involvement in the region's security', as the Foreign and Commonwealth Office (FCO) put it, had 'declined with Empire'.[12] Thereafter, its regional footprint shrunk to the point that, today, London only fields a modest permanent military presence in the Asia-Pacific. This presence encompasses: a garrison in Brunei for the protection of the Sultan with an infantry battalion of Gurkhas; a naval-repair and logistic-support facility at Sembawang Dockyard in Singapore (the British Defence Singapore Support Unit, BDSSU); a light presence in Australia consisting of liaison and exchange officers with the Australian Defence Force and the Australian Department of Defence as well as personnel in the intelligence and science and technology areas; and a small military staff at the Integrated Area Defence System Headquarters (HQ IADS) at Butterworth in Malaysia.[13] HQ IADS is part of the Five Power

---

[9] Frank Bongiorno, 'British Empire: Australasia and Pacific', in *The Encyclopedia of Empire, Vol. 4*, edited by John MacKenzie (Chichester, UK: John Wiley & Sons, 2016), pp. 1–7; David W. McIntyre, *British Colonization, 1946-1997: When, Why, and How Did the British Empire Fall?* (New York: St. Martin's Press, 1998), ch. 1.

[10] James T. H. Tang, 'From Empire Defence to Imperial Retreat: Britain's Postwar China Policy and the Decolonization of Hong Kong', *Modern Asian Studies* 28, no. 2 (1994): pp. 317–337.

[11] This image was borrowed from Charles Hawksley and Rowena Ward, 'Ripples of Decolonisation in the Asia-Pacific', *Journal of Multidisciplinary International Studies* 16, no. 1/2 (2019): pp. 1–10. On British post-Cold War foreign and security policy in the Asia-Pacific see, among others, Andrea Gilli, 'The United Kingdom and the Indo-Pacific: Return of Global Britain?', in *Mind the Gap: Naval Views of the Free and Open Indo-Pacific*, edited by Sharon Stirling (Washington, DC: The German Marshall Fund, 2019), pp. 44–48; Jürgen Haacke and John H. Breen, 'From Benign Neglect to Effective Re-engagement? Assessing British Strategizing and Policies towards Southeast Asia Since 2010', *Contemporary Southeast Asia* 41, no. 3 (2019): pp. 329–363; Alessio Patalano, 'Days of Future Past? British Strategy and the Shaping of Indo-Pacific Security', *Policy Exchange*, 1 April 2019; Alessio Patalano, 'UK Defence from the "Far East" to the "Indo-Pacific"', *Policy Exchange*, 24 July 2019; Alessio Patalano, 'The United Kingdom and Indo-Pacific Security', in IISS, *Asia-Pacific Regional Security Assessment 2021* (London: IISS, 2021), 9–26.

[12] FCO, 'Written Evidence Submitted by the Foreign and Commonwealth Office', in House of Commons, *East Asia*, Foreign Affairs Committee, Vol. II, 2006, Ev. 121.

[13] The majority of British defence personnel in Australia are posted to Army, Navy and Air Force units, in particular those linked to capabilities which are also operated by (or under development in) the British Armed Forces; other positions are found in intelligence and science and technology areas (exchanges with defence officials in Canberra, December 2021). British personnel are stationed in signal intelligence facilities in Australia such as the Joint Military Communications Ground Station (JMCGS) and the Joint Defence Facility Pine Gap (JDFPG), operated under the 'Five Eyes' (UKUSA) agreement.

Defence Arrangements (FPDA) created in 1971 together with Australia, Malaysia, New Zealand and Singapore to replace the previous 1957 Anglo-Malayan Defence Agreement.[14] The United Kingdom also maintains operational headquarters in Qatar, a logistics support base in Oman, and a naval support facility in Bahrain that jointly enable operational reach into the Indian Ocean (more recently, they were included in the 'Indo-Pacific' policy framework, as discussed below).[15]

In order to obtain precise data on British military personnel stationed in the region, which was previously not publicly disclosed, the author filed several Freedom of Information Requests (FOIs) and obtained relevant data from the UK Ministry of Defence.[16] Additional data were gathered from the MoD's *Annual Location Statistics for UK Regular Service and Civilian Personnel* and through exchanges with defence officials in Malaysia and with the British Defence Staff Asia-Pacific in Singapore. As detailed in the Table 3.1, these data indicate that, in 2021, the United Kingdom maintained 1,490 regular forces and MoD personnel (civilian and military) in the Asia-Pacific and the Eastern Indian Ocean, and 160 in the Western Indian Ocean, for a total of around 1,650 defence personnel across the region. Overall, the United Kingdom thus displays a relatively thinner military presence than France in the Asia-Pacific and the Indian Ocean region though substantially larger than that of Germany which has no forward-deployed forces therein.

This chapter shows that Beijing's rising assertiveness in the 2010s—and British policymakers' perceptions of it—led the United Kingdom to strategically re-engage the East of Suez. In particular, growing regional economic interests and, crucially, rising threat perceptions of China caused the hardening of the United Kingdom's policy goals and, in turn, a strengthening of the policy instruments leveraged to achieve such goals in the region. In the first two decades after the

---

[14] On the FPDA, see Ralf Emmers, 'The Five Power Defence Arrangements and Defense Diplomacy in Southeast Asia', *Asian Security* 8, no. 3 (2012): pp. 271–286; Tim Huxley, 'The Future of the FPDA in an Evolving Regional Strategic Environment', in *The Five Power Defence Arrangements at Forty*, edited by Ian Storey, Ralf Emmers, and Daljit Singh (Singapore: Institute of Southeast Asian Studies, 2011), pp. 119–120.

[15] Since the late 2010s, and formally since 2021, these facilities and military personnel have been incorporated in the larger 'Indo-Pacific' construct (analysed later) which broadened the geographical scope of British policy from the Asia-Pacific to the Indo-Pacific, thus also including the Indian Ocean.

[16] The author filed six Freedom of Information requests to the UK Ministry of Defence (FOI2021/0869, FOI2021/08470, FOI2021/09732, FOI2021/11244, FOI2021/13563, and FOI2021/15256) on the precise number of British military personnel in the Asia-Pacific as well as in Qatar, Oman, and Bahrain. According to the data initially released by the MoD in response to these FOIs, the number of British military personnel deployed in the Asia-Pacific between March 1 and April 30 was: none in 2019, ten in 2020, and none in 2021; and the number of British military personnel deployed in Qatar, Oman, and Bahrain (in the same timeframe) was 560 in 2019, 1,060 in 2020, and 820 in 2021. The problem with such data was that the MoD's definition of 'overseas deployments' refers to 'contingency operations, wartime operations, UN peacekeeping operations and humanitarian operations' but excludes 'personnel stationed' in these countries, thus distorting the numbers. After several exchanges with the MoD, the Ministry subsequently indicated that requested data could be found in the *Annual Location Statistics for UK Regular Service and Civilian Personnel*, which is thus one of the sources used to compile Table 3.1. These data were also discussed and corroborated in interviews with current and former MoD officials, January-June 2021.

Table 3.1 UK MoD personnel in the Asia-Pacific and Indian Ocean Region, 2021

	UK regular forces	MoD military personnel	MoD civilian personnel	Gurkhas	Total
Brunei	150	140	360	620**	1,270
British Indian Ocean Territory	40	40	–	–	80
Malaysia*	11	–	–	–	11
Singapore	0	10	30	–	40
Australia	20	50	10	–	80
New Zealand	0	10	0	–	10
Total Asia-Pacific and Eastern Indian Ocean	220	250	400	620	**1,490**
Oman	20	90	–	–	110
Bahrain	20	20	–	–	40
Qatar	0	10	–	–	10
Total Western Indian Ocean	40	120	–	–	**160**
Total	260	370	400	620	**1,650**

Source: Data compiled by the author based on data retrieved from: MoD, *Annual Location Statistics for UK Regular Service and Civilian Personnel*—1 April 2021, https://assets.publishing.service.gov.uk/government/uploads/system/uploads/attachment_data/file/998488/Annual_location_statistics_1_April_2021.xlsx (accessed 1 November 2021); author's Freedom of Information Requests FOI2021/13563 and FOI2021/15256 to the UK MoD; and author's exchanges with the Integrated Area Defence System Headquarters (HQ IADS) at Butterworth in Malaysia and with the British Defence Staff Asia-Pacific in Singapore.

UK regular forces include both trained and untrained personnel but—in the definition of the MoD's *Annual Location Statistics for UK Regular Service and Civilian Personnel*—exclude Gurkhas, full-time reserve service personnel and mobilized reservists.
MOD personnel: *MoD military personnel* includes officers and other ranks of military personnel. *MoD civilian personnel* include industrial, non-industrial, trading funds, and locally engaged civilians.
* **Malaysia:** The MoD's *Annual Location Statistics* do not include data for Malaysia. The author thus filed a Freedom of Information Request (FOI2021/15256) to obtain such data. The MoD's response indicates that the number of UK Regular Forces in Malaysia in 2021 was ten. To corroborate this figure, the author then contacted the Integrated Area Defence System Headquarters (HQ IADS) at Butterworth in Malaysia and the British Defence Staff Asia-Pacific in Singapore (in December 2021 and January 2022 respectively). The latter stated that in 2021 the UK had four military personnel in its Defence Section in Kuala Lumpur and six personnel in HQ IADS.
** **Gurkhas:** The British Army in Brunei comprises an infantry battalion of Gurkhas and an Army Air Corps Flight of Bell 212 helicopters. The infantry battalion is supported by the small British garrison, which provides all logistic and administrative support. Furthermore, the Jungle Warfare Division in Brunei is the Army's jungle warfare school which runs courses for all members of the British Army, ranging from Jungle Warfare Instructor Courses to the Operational Tracking Instructor Course.
Given that the infantry battalion of Gurkhas is not included in the definition of regular forces of the *Annual Location Statistics for UK Regular Service and Civilian Personnel*, the number of Gurkhas was obtained separately. To that end, the author filed a Freedom of Information Request to the UK MoD (FOI2021/135639) which is the source of the number indicated in Table 3.1. See also UK Army, 'The British Army in Brunei', https://www.army.mod.uk/deployments/brunei/.

Cold War, London perceived China as a peaceful rising power and its regional engagement was overwhelmingly driven by economic considerations—with the exception of Hong Kong, which absorbed considerable diplomatic capital during the 1990s. In the 2010s, however, British policymakers displayed mounting concerns over how China's increasingly muscular posture in the Asia-Pacific challenged the 'rules-based order', fuelled regional instability, and thereby also affected British prosperity (at a time when they also exhibited growing disquiet over Chinese investments into UK strategic sectors, as discussed in Chapter 6).[17] As a result, the United Kingdom gradually formulated a more coherent policy framework for the larger Indo-Pacific region, putting greater emphasis on national security considerations. These policy goals revolved around upholding central norms of the rules-based order (freedom of navigation and the peaceful resolution of disputes), promoting regional stability, and thereby also protecting its regional economic interests. In order to concretize these goals, London strengthened its political-military presence in the Asia-Pacific through enhanced naval deployments, a broadened network of bilateral partnerships, and greater engagement in regional minilateral and multilateral security arrangements. It concurrently sought to expand its cooperation with other Western (US and European) powers in the Asia-Pacific through a variety of venues. After its 2016 decision to withdraw from the European Union, however, the consultations and cooperation on Asian-Pacific security between the United Kingdom and other European states took place only bilaterally and minilaterally, outside EU channels.

The remainder of the chapter proceeds as follows. The first two sections analyse the evolution of London's economic interests in the region and of British policymakers' threat assessment of China as central drivers of the United Kingdom's foreign and security policy in the Asia-Pacific. The subsequent two sections show how rising economic interests and, decisively, a heightened threat assessment of China caused London to revise its policy goals and the resulting policy instruments, driving it to bolster its political-military engagement in the Asia-Pacific in the 2010s.

Economic Interests

British economic interests in the Asia-Pacific have grown considerably throughout the post-Cold War period, spanning from trade, investment, and finance to arms transfers. Especially after the handover of Hong Kong in 1997, the rise in the United Kingdom's economic interests in the region has been the main driver behind London's desire to engage the emerging powers in the Asia-Pacific economically and diplomatically. It is only when the British threat assessment

---

[17] For a definition of 'rules-based order' see the Introduction of Part I.

of China intensified in the 2010s that London put greater emphasis on security considerations and formulated a more cohesive policy toward the region.

Emerging Lucrative Markets in the Asia-Pacific

The expansion of British economic interests in the Asia-Pacific in the 1990s and 2000s was prompted as much by actual opportunities as by the potential for further expansion in the world's economically most dynamic region. From a trade perspective, beginning in the mid-1990s British policymakers came to see the region, as shown in declassified documents, as 'a hugely important commercial growth market'[18] and, therefore, as 'a top commercial priority'[19]—while expecting the further expansion of its growth potential over subsequent decades.[20] Especially after China's accession to the World Trade Organization (WTO) in 2001, Sino-British bilateral trade more than tripled, rising from $19bn to $60bn between 2001 and 2009;[21] the United Kingdom became China's third largest trading partner within the European Union after Germany and France.[22] By the end of the decade, the FCO stressed that, as 'the fastest growing market for UK exports', China had a 'huge economic potential' and presented 'more opportunities for our businesses than any other country' over the subsequent decade.[23]

London concomitantly grew significant investment ties in China and in the Asia-Pacific. In the mid-1990s, according to the Department of Trade and Industry, the United Kingdom was the largest European investor in the region—which represented 14.3 per cent of its global FDIs.[24] The value of the United Kingdom's FDIs that were utilized by Chinese companies rose from $38m to $701m between

---

[18] Private Secretary to the Prime Minister to FCO, 'Asia–Europe Meeting: Round 2', 2 December 1995, The National Archives (TNA), Prime Minister's Office Record (PREM) 19/5633. The same point is stressed in FCO to the Private Secretary for Foreign Affairs to the Prime Minister (FA/APS), 'Asia–Europe Meeting, Bangkok, 1–2 March 1996', Brief No. 21, 27 February 1996c, TNA, PREM 19/5633.

[19] FCO to FA/APS, 'Asia-Europe Meeting, Bangkok, 1–2 March 1996', Brief No. 5 'British Export Promotion in Asia', 27 February 1996a, TNL, PREM 19/5633.

[20] See House of Commons (HoC), *East Asia*, Foreign Affairs Committee, Volume I, 2006a, pp. 29-45; HoC, *Tenth Report: China*, Foreign Affairs Committee, 22 November 2000, Section 'Advancing British Commercial Interests, https://publications.parliament.uk/pa/cm199900/cmselect/cmfaff/574/57402.htm (accessed 2 June 2020); and FCO, Memorandum Submitted to the House of Commons Select Committee on Foreign Affairs Memoranda, 30 October 2000b, https://publications.parliament.uk/pa/cm199900/cmselect/cmfaff/uc574iv/574m01.htm.

[21] Data retrieved from United Nations (UN) Comtrade—International Trade Statistics Database, https://comtrade.un.org (for details on the data, see Appendix B).

[22] FCO, 'Written Evidence Submitted by the FCO', in HoC, *East Asia*, 2006, Vol. II, Ev. 112; and Matthew Ward, 'Statistics on UK Trade with China', HoC Library, *Briefing Paper*, 5 November 2019, p. 13.

[23] FCO, *The UK and China: A Framework for Engagement*, 2009, pp. 3, 7, and 9.

[24] Private Secretary of the Secretary of State for Trade and Industry to the PM Private Secretary, 'Prime Minister's Visit to the EU/Asia Summit, 28 February–2 March: Statistical Briefing', 23 February 1996, TNA, PREM 19/5633 (data retrieved from Table 5, removing data for India and Pakistan).

1991 and 2009; but Germany overtook the United Kingdom as the biggest European investor in the PRC after 1999 and the United Kingdom slipped to second position (see the comparative charts on the Big Three's economic relations with China in Appendix B).[25]

Finally, London explored arms sales opportunities in the Asia-Pacific. The United Kingdom was highly dependent on arms exports' revenues to sustain its defence and technological industrial base (DTIB), with an average arms export dependence of almost 60 per cent between 2002 and 2007 (based on available data).[26] At the same time, while the MoD expected in the 1990s that by the subsequent decade ten of its top twenty defence sales markets were going to be in the Asia-Pacific,[27] the region represented on average 18 per cent of its global arms exports between 2000 and 2009.[28] Accordingly, although other regions ranked first (such as the Middle East), the United Kingdom displayed growing interests in Asian arms markets,[29] transferring weapon systems such as Hawk-100 fighter jets to India and Australia, EH-101-400 transport helicopters to Japan, and Super Lynx-100 multipurpose helicopters to South Korea.[30]

The World's New Centre of Economic Gravity

As the Asia-Pacific became the 'engine of a globalizing world',[31] British economic interests there continued to expand.[32] The 2010s marked a significant increase in UK trade, investment, and financial ties with the region, as well as in its arms exports thereto, while London and Beijing entered what they labelled the 'Golden Era' of their bilateral relations.[33]

---

[25] National Bureau of Statistics of China, *Statistical Yearbooks of China*, http://www.stats.gov.cn/english/Statisticaldata/AnnualData/.

[26] Arms export dependence refers to the share of arms exports in the total turnover of its defence and technological industrial base. Hugo Meijer, Lucie Béraud-Sudreau, Paul Holtom, and Matthew Uttley, 'Arming China: Major Powers' Arms Transfers to the People's Republic of China', *Journal of Strategic Studies 41*, no. 6 (2018): p. 864.

[27] MoD to FCO, 'Follow-Up Meeting: UK Offer to Host?', 29 November 1995, TNA, PREM 19/5633.

[28] Stockholm International Peace Research Institute (SIPRI), TIV (trend-indicator value) Trade Register, https://www.sipri.org/databases/armstransfers.

[29] SIPRI, TIV Trade Register, https://www.sipri.org/databases/armstransfers.

[31] Minister of state for International Defence and Security (2008–2010), Baroness Ann Taylor, Speech at the Shangri-La Dialogue, 31 May 2009, p. 2.

[32] Her Majesty's Government (HMG), *Global Britain in a Competitive Age: The Integrated Review of Security, Defence, Development and Foreign Policy*, Presented to Parliament by the Prime Minister, March 2021, pp. 27 and 66.

[33] FCO, 'UK–China Joint Statement on Building a Global Comprehensive Strategic Partnership for the 21st Century', 22 October 2015a.

Although the Asia-Pacific ranked behind other major trading partners for the United Kingdom (i.e. the European Union and the United States), the region became its fastest growing export market.[34] By 2020, the Asia-Pacific accounted for 20 per cent of both UK exports and imports (whereas the Americas accounted for 25 per cent thereof).[35] In particular, British exports to the PRC almost tripled, rising from $11bn to $30bn between 2010 and 2019.[36] China then became the United Kingdom's third major trading partner while the latter was the PRC's second-largest trading partner in Europe after Germany (reaching almost $96bn).[37] Sino-British investment ties also substantially increased. The United Kingdom became the first recipient of Chinese FDIs in Europe, as detailed in Chapter 6. At the same time, the value of its actually utilized investments in the PRC similarly soared from $710m to $2.5bn between 2010 and 2018, making the United Kingdom the second-largest European investor in China after Germany.[38] During this decade, China thus became a 'vital' economic partner for the United Kingdom.[39]

As the importance of the Asia-Pacific for the world's economy and for British trade grew, the sea routes spanning through the East and South China Seas, the Malacca Straits, and into the Indian Ocean—across which two-thirds of global trade transited[40]—became crucial maritime trade and energy transportation routes.[41] The British economy was, and remains, highly dependent on trade (60 per cent of its GDP in 2016) of which 95 per cent relied upon the world's sea

---

[34] MoD, 'Written Evidence Submitted to the House of Commons', in response to HoC, *UK Defence and the Far East*, Defence Committee, HC 2035, 13 June 2019a, p. 1; and Wyelands Bank, *UK Trade Briefing*, 2018, pp. 3-4.

[35] Matthew Ward, 'Geographical Pattern of UK Trade', *Briefing Paper*, HoC Library, 25 November 2020, p. 6.

[36] Yet, China's overall importance as an export market remained relatively modest accounting for 6 per cent of all UK exports of goods and services in 2019 (UN Comtrade—International Trade Statistics Database, https://comtrade.un.org).

[37] Data retrieved from UN Comtrade—International Trade Statistics Database, https://comtrade.un.org. See also Daniel Workman, 'United Kingdom's Top Trading Partners', *World Top Exports*, 19 July 2020; Nick Gutteridge, '"Ahead of the Curve" British Trade with Global Giant China Booms as Rest of EU Lags Behind', *Express*, 3 November 2017; and Department for International Trade, 'Trade and Investment Factsheets: China', 18 June 2021, https://assets.publishing.service.gov.uk/government/uploads/system/uploads/attachment_data/file/993589/china-trade-and-investment-factsheet-2021-06-18.pdf (accessed on 1 December 2021).

[38] National Bureau of Statistics of China, *Statistical Yearbooks of China*, http://www.stats.gov.cn/english/Statisticaldata/AnnualData/ (for details on the data, including the comparative charts of the Big Three's FDIs in China, see Appendix B).

[39] Secretary of State for Foreign and Commonwealth Affairs, Philip Hammond (2014–2016), 'China: Diplomatic and Economic Relations', in House of Commons Hansard, *China: Diplomatic and Economic Relations*, Oral Answers to Questions, Vol. 604, 12 January 2016. See also HMG, 'Appendix: Memorandum from the Foreign and Commonwealth Office', in HoC, *Global Britain*, Foreign Affairs Committee, HC 780, 6 March 2018a, p. 24.

[40] Minister of State for Asia and the Pacific Mark Field (2017–2019), in HoC, *China and the International Rules-Based System*, Foreign Affairs Committee, HC 612, 15 January 2019a, Question 206.

[41] HMG, *The UK National Strategy for Maritime Security*, 2014, p. 52.

lines for its delivery.⁴² Accordingly, as the region gradually became the 'centre of gravity' of the global economy,⁴³ London developed a growing interest in the stability of the SLOCs in the Indian and Pacific Oceans.⁴⁴

Likewise, given the central role of the City of London as a world financial hub, the United Kingdom and the PRC further developed their financial ties which became, according to the FCO, 'a leading area in the bilateral relationship'.⁴⁵ After China designated London as an offshore trading centre for Renminbi (RMB) in 2011, the United Kingdom became the first offshore centre, outside of Asia, for RMB transactions (with 34 per cent of the world's RMB offshore foreign exchange transactions).⁴⁶ Concomitantly, London became an important market for 'dim sum bonds', i.e. RMB-denominated bonds outside the PRC.⁴⁷ Overall, in light of the prime importance of London as a financial centre for both the United Kingdom and the PRC and as a key platform for the internationalization of the RMB, the two countries grew very significant financial relations.⁴⁸

Finally, as the world's second-largest defence exporter after the United States, the United Kingdom continued to pursue arms export opportunities in the region.⁴⁹ Certainly, the Asia-Pacific ranked below the Middle East, North America, and Europe in British total arms transfers.⁵⁰ Yet, the region was considered important from a defence and security export perspective given that it was the world's second-largest importer of defence equipment behind the Middle East and that it significantly increased its defence imports in the 2010s.⁵¹ In particular, between 2009 and 2018, the Asia-Pacific accounted for 9 per cent of total UK defence exports and 13 per cent of its security exports.⁵²

Overall, in light of the growing importance of the Asia-Pacific for the global economy and for the United Kingdom, British economic interests in the region thus steadily expanded. As a senior FCO official puts it: 'The primary driver of

---

⁴² Wyelands Bank, 2018, p. 4; and Secretary of State for Defence Philip Hammond (2011-2014), Speech at the Shangri-La Dialogue, Singapore, 31 May 2014, p. 2.
⁴³ HMG, *National Security and Capability Review*, March 2018a, p. 30.
⁴⁴ Minister of State for Asia and the Pacific (2017-2019), Mark Field, 2019a, Question 206.
⁴⁵ FCO, 2015a.
⁴⁶ SWIFT, 'An Inside Look into London's Quest for the Renminbi', *RMB Tracker*, September 2019, p. 5.
⁴⁷ In 2019, 113 'dim sum' bonds were listed on the London Stock Exchange with a total size of RMB 32.85bn. City of London Corporation and The People's Bank of China, 'London RMB Business Quarterly', Issue 3, April 2019, p. 4.
⁴⁸ Kerry Brown, *Erase and Rewind: Britain's Relations with China* (Sydney: The Australia-China Relations Institute, 2015), p. 7.
⁴⁹ Between 2007 and 2016 the United Kingdom was the world's second largest defence exporter behind the United States but ahead of Russia. Noel Dempsey, 'UK Defence Industry Exports', HoC Library, 18 May 2018, p. 4.
⁵⁰ Department for International Trade (DIT), *UK Defence and Security Export Statistics for 2018*, 30 July 2019, p. 13.
⁵¹ MoD, 2019a, pp. 1-2.
⁵² DIT, 2019, p. 13 (for a definition of 'security exports', cf. p. 18).

[the] UK's growing attention to the Asia-Pacific is economic; and the economic driver is that half of global economic growth is in that region.'[53]

Threat Perceptions

While UK regional economic interests steadily grew throughout the post-Cold War era, London's threat assessment of China shifted only in the 2010s. During the 1990s and 2000s, the emergence of the PRC as a major regional power was regarded by British policymakers as having few security ramifications for UK interests. However, starting in the 2010s, Beijing's increasingly muscular behaviour in the Asia-Pacific drove London to revise its threat assessment of China and, in turn, to forge a more cohesive regional policy framework with an enhanced political-military dimension.

China as a Non-Hegemonic Rising Power

In the first two decades after the Cold War, British policymakers saw China as a peaceful rising power. During this period, they considered that China was operating under Deng Xiaoping so-called 'twenty-four-character strategy' of 'biding your time and hiding your might'.[54] In particular, as a former FCO official puts it, the PRC was seen as 'careful about the international projection of its interests' and as having 'neither a strong political position nor strong armed forces capable of projecting power'.[55] Similarly, according to the former MoD's Policy Director Simon Webb (2001–2004), China was largely 'preoccupied with internal stability and hence fundamentally non-hegemonistic' and, therefore, 'posed no threat to British interests in the region'.[56]

To be sure, throughout the 1990s and 2000s, Beijing modernized its armed forces, bolstered its missile and overall military capabilities vis-à-vis Taiwan, and begun to play a greater role in regional security affairs. Yet, its conventional military capabilities, though growing, were deemed by British policymakers to be outdated compared to Western armed forces.[57] The MoD considered that the qualitative and quantitative upgrade of the PLA constituted a 'normal military modernization process for an emerging power' which was 'essentially defensive

---

[53] Interview, London, 15 January 2018.
[54] Interviews with former FCO and MoD officials in office during the 1990s and 2000s, January–June 2020.
[55] Interview, June 2020.
[56] Simon Webb, interview, London, 25 November 2016.
[57] Interviews with former FCO and MoD officials in office during the 1990s and 2000s, January–June 2020.

rather than aggressive'; 'that was very much the majority view.'⁵⁸ A former diplomat similarly stresses how 'the Chinese military was still not far along the course of modernization and had not reached the point of having the capability to be very muscular in the South China Sea'; accordingly, 'there was no acute sense of threat arising from China's military modernization' and there were 'no subjects of immediate concern in China's security posture'.⁵⁹ And, according to British policymakers, US military preponderance vis-à-vis China was such that Beijing would be deterred from using force against Taiwan.⁶⁰

In the nuclear realm, as explained by the Former Director of the United Kingdom's signal intelligence agency, the Government Communications Headquarters (GCHQ, 1996–1997), and then Cabinet Office Intelligence and Security Coordinator (2002–2005), British and US intelligence services cooperated closely in monitoring China's nuclear modernization, including their nuclear tests, the introduction of a new class of ballistic missile submarine, the gradual expansion of the range of Chinese intercontinental ballistic missiles, as well as the development of China's space programme.⁶¹ However, the range and capability of the British submarine-launched Trident D5 ballistic missile system was judged sufficient for deterrence and London did not alter its nuclear posture.⁶²

Overall, except for Beijing's programme of intellectual property theft and its effort to secure technological advances by stealing secrets from Western economies,⁶³ the PRC was deemed by British policymakers to pose little security concerns to the United Kingdom and was predominantly perceived as an opportunity—a faraway lucrative market—rather than a threat.

China's Challenge to Regional Rules, Stability, and Prosperity

In the subsequent decade, however, the United Kingdom's threat assessment of the PRC evolved. Foreign and defence policy officials have pointed to a variety of key steps in the intensification of British threat perceptions of China, including Beijing's increasingly muscular posture in the Asia-Pacific after 2009; the accession of Xi Jinping to the position of General Secretary of the CCP in 2012 and Beijing's ensuing muscular foreign policy; the landmark rejection by the PRC of

---

⁵⁸ Former senior MoD official, interview, July 2020.
⁵⁹ Christopher Hum, former FCO's Assistant Under-Secretary of State for Northern Asia and the Pacific (1992–1995) and later British Ambassador to China (2002–2005), interview, 15 June 2020.
⁶⁰ Interviews with former FCO and MoD officials in office during the 1990s and 2000s, January–June 2020.
⁶¹ Sir David Omand, interview, 14 January 2021.
⁶² Sir David Omand, Former Director of the Government Communications Headquarters (GCHQ, 1996–1997) and then Cabinet Office Intelligence and Security Coordinator (2002–2005), interview, 14 January 2021; and MoD's Policy Director (2001–2004), Simon Webb, interview, 8 July 2020.
⁶³ These concerns are detailed in Chapter 6.

the Permanent Court of Arbitration's 2016 ruling on its territorial dispute with the Philippines; and mounting apprehension over the erosion of the 'one country, two systems' status quo in Hong Kong (on the concurrently rising concerns over Chinese investments in United Kingdom's strategic sectors and over its cyber-espionage practices, see Chapter 6).[64] Along this trajectory, the balance of forces between competing views within Whitehall substantially evolved.

Starting in the early 2010s, an upward trend of rising threat perceptions of China gradually and cumulatively developed within Whitehall, culminating in the latter half of the decade—as explained by several former high-ranking officials—in an overall shift in London's assessment of the security ramification of China's rise.[65] Until the mid-2010s, however (as further detailed in Chapter 6), the government's overall assessment of China was split between those who saw Beijing as a key economic partner and those who highlighted mounting security concerns.[66] The economically oriented agencies of the government advocating for engagement with China remained more influential than those stressing rising security concerns.[67] As a senior official puts it: 'National security concerns tended to play a secondary order in strategic policymaking.'[68]

It is after 2016—which marked a turning point—that the government's overall threat perceptions of the PRC substantially intensified. The new government of Theresa May (2016–2019) came to assess that China's behaviour in the region and beyond could adversely impact the United Kingdom's interests.[69] According to a senior MoD official, Beijing's rejection of the 2016 Permanent Court of Arbitration's ruling on its territorial dispute with the Philippines marked a 'pivot point' that 'made it much clearer—and much sharper—to people that there was a pattern of aggressive Chinese behaviour, whether it was the South China Sea or the East China Sea' that aimed to 'gradually squeeze the US out of the Asia Pacific'.[70] Theresa May's government thereafter became 'more balanced and realistic' in terms of how it saw the security implications of China's rise, and Whitehall's

---

[64] Interviews with officials in the FCO and MoD and with intelligence officials, November 2016, January 2018, January–June 2020.
[65] Interviews with Lord Peter Ricketts, former National Security Adviser (2010–2012), 3 June 2020; General Lord David Richards, former Chief of the Defence Staff (2010–2013), 3 June 2020; General Lord Nick Houghton, former Chief of the Defence Staff (2013–2016), 9 June 2020; senior MoD official, interview, 3 July 2020; and senior advisor to the Prime Minister, 26 June 2020.
[66] Interviews with Lord Peter Ricketts, former National Security Adviser (2010–2012), 3 June 2020; General Lord David Richards, former Chief of the Defence Staff (2010–2013), 3 June 2020; General Lord Nick Houghton, former Chief of the Defence Staff (2013–2016), 9 June 2020; senior MoD official, interview, 3 July 2020; and senior advisor to the Prime Minister, 26 June 2020.
[67] Interviews with Lord Peter Ricketts, former National Security Adviser (2010–2012), 3 June 2020; General Lord David Richards, former Chief of the Defence Staff (2010–2013), 3 June 2020; General Lord Nick Houghton, former Chief of the Defence Staff (2013–2016), 9 June 2020; senior MoD official, interview, 3 July 2020; and senior advisor to the Prime Minister, 26 June 2020.
[68] Interview, 26 June 2020.
[69] Interviews with FCO and MoD officials, January–December 2020.
[70] Former senior MoD official, interview, 17 February 2020.

attitude 'shifted from an approach that was very much driven by economic factors to one that was driven more by security concerns'.[71]

Accordingly, by the late 2010s, London considered that the previous Deng Xiaoping approach of 'hiding your might and biding your time' was 'now over',[72] and that China's rise had become 'the big geopolitical issue of our age'.[73] Specifically, although the PRC was not seen as posing a direct threat to UK armed forces, British policymakers considered that China's increasingly assertive posture in the Asia-Pacific challenged the foundational norms of the rules-based order, could fuel regional instability and, thereby, could also harm British prosperity.

Central Concerns: Rules-Based Order, Regional Stability, and Prosperity

For one, London grew increasingly wary of how Beijing's foreign and security policy challenged the regional rules-based order, including the peaceful resolution of disputes and, most notably, freedom of navigation.[74] As an island trading nation with a vested interest in stable and open SLOCs, a central concern in London was that China might seek 'to deny freedom of sea movement' in the South China Sea and around its 'militarised man-made islands'.[75] Furthermore, British officials considered that the PRC undermined the peaceful resolution of disputes by seeking to impose its unilateral claims in the South China Sea and East China Sea through *fait accompli* tactics.[76]

Secondly, London was concerned that China's expanding military capabilities and regional behaviour, as well as the ensuing tensions in the Asia-Pacific, were fuelling risks of unintended escalation and, potentially, regional conflict.[77] Since British policymakers considered that the preservation of the regional balance of power largely remained the purview of the United States,[78] they foresaw growing risks of regional instability associated with mounting United

---

[71] Former senior MoD official, interview, 17 February 2020.
[72] MoD, 2019a, p. 3. See also HoC, *Oral Evidence: China and the International Rules-Based System*, Foreign Affairs Committee, HC 612, 15 January 2019a, p. 7.
[73] Minister of State for Asia and the Pacific (2017–2019), Mark Field, 2019b. See also MoD, *Defence in a Competitive Age*, Presented to Parliament by the Secretary of State for Defence, March 2021, pp. 5–6 and 9.
[74] See, e.g. HMG, 'UK Foreign Policy in a Shifting World Order', Government Response to the House of Lords Select Committee on International Relations, 2018c, p. 4.
[75] Secretary of State for Defence (2014–2017), Michael Fallon, Speech at the Shangri-La Dialogue, Singapore, 30 May 2015, p. 3.
[76] Interviews with FCO and MoD officials, January–June 2020.
[77] Minister of State for the Armed Forces Nick Harvey (2010–2012), Speech at the Shangri-La Dialogue, Singapore, 3 June 2012; Secretary of State for Defence Philip Hammond (2011–2014), 2014; and HMG, March 2018a, p. 6.
[78] Interviews with FCO and MoD officials, January–June 2020.

States–China competition in the region.⁷⁹ A regional crisis could also have security ramifications for the United Kingdom as a permanent member of the UN Security Council and for the resilience of the rules-based order that underpinned British interests. London considered that, given the importance of the Asia-Pacific, it had 'a very strong interest in the region remaining stable and in avoiding potential conflict in the South China Sea or elsewhere'.⁸⁰ Accordingly, as explained by a senior FCO official, the United Kingdom viewed the stability of the Asia-Pacific region 'as a test-case for the integrity of the rules-based international system and for whether the different countries were going to play by those rules or were going to pursue a more traditional might-is-right approach'.⁸¹

Finally, this heightened risk of escalation and conflict could also impact British economic interests in the Asia-Pacific and beyond. As a former MoD official puts it, given that the 'region was the powerhouse of the global economy', 'if there were to be a drift towards confrontation or conflict in the Asia-Pacific, that would have a massive impact on world trade and on the economic interests of Britain and other European countries.'⁸²

Overall, London's rising concerns over the strategic consequences of Chinese behaviour for the resilience of the rules-based order, for regional stability, and for British economic interests were thus closely intertwined. As such, the 'significant impact' of China's 'growing international assertiveness' came to be seen as posing 'an increasing risk to UK interests'.⁸³

Policy Goals

As its threat assessment evolved and its economic interests steadily increased, London's policy goals shifted accordingly. While until 1997 its overarching objective had been the handover of Hong Kong, the United Kingdom thereafter focused on fostering economic and political engagement with the PRC and other emerging regional powers. It is only in the 2010s, when its threat perception of China heightened, that the United Kingdom sought to gradually recalibrate its policy towards

---

⁷⁹ Secretary of State for Foreign and Commonwealth Affairs Jeremy Hunt (2018–2019), in House of Lords, *Corrected Oral Evidence—UK Foreign Policy in Changed World Conditions*, Select Committee on International Relations, 15 November 2018a, http://data.parliament.uk/writtenevidence/committeeevidence.svc/evidencedocument/international-relations-committee/foreign-policy-in-changed-world-conditions/oral/92531.html.

⁸⁰ FCO official, interview, 18 November 2020.

⁸¹ Interview, London, 24 November 2016. On this point, see also MoD, *Global Strategic Trends. The Future Starts Today*, 2018, p. 190.

⁸² Former senior MoD official, interview, 3 July 2020. See also Secretary of State for Defence (2014–2017) Michael Fallon, 2015.

⁸³ HMG, *Global Britain in a Competitive Age: The Integrated Review of Security, Defence, Development and Foreign Policy*, Presented to Parliament by the Prime Minister, March 2021, pp. 26 and 29.

Beijing and to formulate a more coherent regional policy framework—with greater prominence given to security considerations.

Beyond Hong Kong: Engaging China and the Asia-Pacific

In the first two post-Cold War decades, the Asia-Pacific was mostly perceived as a distant region that offered tremendous economic opportunities. Declassified documents show that the United Kingdom's main foreign policy goal in the 1990s primarily revolved around 'strengthening trade and investment links with the Asia-Pacific'.[84] London aimed, according to another diplomatic cable, 'to maintain and, where possible, increase Britain's profile and activity in this area of fast expanding markets'.[85] Likewise, in the 2000s, London did not consider 'having [a] major security interest in the Asia-Pacific' besides economic interests, according to the former MoD's Policy Director Simon Webb (2001-2004).[86] As an FCO official puts it: 'Neither the UK nor Europe had much skin in the game in security issues in Asia. There wasn't any sort of direct UK, or EU, security interest in the region'.[87] Overall, besides economic interests, the region thus remained relatively low in the overall hierarchy of UK foreign policy priorities, with the exception of the PRC and Hong Kong.

The handover of Hong Kong to the PRC in 1997 marked a major turning point in London's 'China policy'. Prior to that, the dominant issue—and the overarching policy goal—in United Kingdom's relationship with the PRC had been the transfer of sovereignty over Hong Kong within the parameters of the 'One Country, Two Systems' formula sketched out in the 1984 Sino-British Declaration.[88] Until 1997, the two countries pursued intense negotiations over the status of Hong Kong, with London seeking to ensure the political stability in the transition of sovereignty, the autonomy of the former colony, and its economic interests therein.[89] In the words of a former FCO official, the United Kingdom's relations

---

[84] FCO to FA/APS, 1996a.
[85] Private Secretary for Foreign Affairs to the Prime Minister, 'Asia Manifesto', 18 January 1995, TNA, PREM 19/5633.
[86] Interview, London, 25 November 2016.
[87] Former FCO official, interview, June 2020.
[88] See among others Charles Moore, *Margaret Thatcher: The Authorized Bibliography, Vol. II* (New York: Penguin Press, 2015), ch. 4; and Peter Ferdinand. 'UK Policy towards China', in *Europe, China and the Two SARs: Towards a New Era*, edited by Miguel Santos Neves and Brian Bridges (Basingstoke: Palgrave Macmillan, 2000), pp. 29–62.
[89] Interviews with Lord Peter Ricketts, Head of FCO's Hong Kong Department (1991–1994) and later FCO's Deputy Political Director (1997–1999), 3 June 2020; and with Rod Wye, First Secretary at the British Embassy in Beijing (1995–1999), 1 June 2020. See also Secretary of State for Foreign and Commonwealth Affairs Robin Cook (1997–2001), in HoC, *Examination of Witnesses—Minutes of Evidence*, Select Committee on Foreign Affairs, 7 June 2020, Questions 180–199; and HoC, *China and Hong Kong*, and HoC Hansard, Vol. 258, 27 April 1995.

with China were 'dominated by the objective of facilitating the implementation of the Joint Declaration and a smooth handover in 1997'.[90]

After 1997, while Hong Kong remained a significant matter in the bilateral relationship, the overall trust of UK foreign policy towards the PRC markedly changed and Britain's economic relationship with China became the central focus. After a century and a half of British control, the retrocession of Hong Kong removed a major source of tensions in the bilateral relationship and thereby enabled the development of United Kingdom–China economic and diplomatic ties.[91] The incoming government of Prime Minister Tony Blair (1997–2007) established the so-called policy of 'engagement' with the PRC—which was then de facto continued by his successor Gordon Brown (2007–2010).[92]

This policy had three central goals (further discussed in Chapter 6). First, the United Kingdom aimed to expand its bilateral trade and investment ties with China, considering it, in the words of former Foreign Secretary David Miliband (2007–2010), 'an indispensable power economically'.[93] Furthermore, London sought to widen the domains of bilateral diplomatic and economic cooperation so as to foster 'China's emergence as a responsible global player'.[94] Third, British policymakers hoped that enmeshing the PRC into the international system through a wide range of bilateral and multilateral economic and diplomatic channels would spur 'modernisation and internal reform' in China, and over time result in political liberalization.[95]

Besides the goal of deepening economic and political ties with emerging regional powers—with a preponderant focus on China—London did not have a coherent overall policy for the Asia-Pacific. Whereas in the 1990s the centre of gravity of the United Kingdom's foreign and security policy had overwhelmingly revolved around the Balkans, by the 2000s it shifted to the Middle East and South Asia because of its military interventions in Iraq and Afghanistan, with the Asia-Pacific remaining a peripheral issue in the United Kingdom's foreign policy.[96] In the words of a former FCO Asia-hand, the United Kingdom 'lacked a real coherent

---

[90] Christopher Hum, Former Assistant Under-Secretary of State (Northern Asia and Pacific) (1992–1995) and later British Ambassador to the PRC (2002–2005), interview, 15 June 2020.

[91] Shaun Breslin, 'Beyond Diplomacy? UK Relations with China Since 1997', *The British Journal of Politics and International Relations* 6, no. 3 (2004): p. 409.

[92] Parliamentary Under-Secretary of State for Foreign and Commonwealth Affairs Denis MacShane (2001), in HoC, *China*, HoC Hansard, Vol. 387, 18 June 2002, https://publications.parliament.uk/pa/cm200102/cmhansrd/vo020618/halltext/20618h01.htm. See also Kerry Brown, 'Britain's Relations with China under New Labour: Engagement and Repulsion?', in *British Foreign Policy: The New Labour Years*, edited by Olivier Daddow and Jamie Gaskarth (New York: Palgrave Macmillan, 2011), pp. 170–187.

[93] Quoted in Julian Borger, 'David Miliband: China Ready to Join US as World Power', *The Guardian*, 17 May 2009. See also FCO, *The UK and China: A Framework for Engagement*, 2009, pp. 3, 5, 7, and 9.

[94] FCO, 2009, p. 13. See also HoC, 2000, Section 'Advancing British Commercial Interests'.

[95] FCO, 2009, p. 6.

[96] Interviews with former FCO and MoD officials, January–July 2020.

plan for the whole region; there was no clear, well worked out strategy towards the Asia Pacific region.'[97] Lord Peter Ricketts, former Head of FCO's Hong Kong Department (1991–1994), then FCO's Deputy Political Director (1997–1999), and subsequently FCO's Permanent Secretary (2006–2010), confirms that London maintained a set of 'essentially bilateral relationships but lacked a really coherent policy towards Asia-Pacific'.[98]

Recalibrating the United Kingdom's Regional Engagement: From 'All-of-Asia' to Indo-Pacific

In the subsequent decade, however, London recalibrated its regional policy in light of its rising economic interests in the Asia-Pacific and of its evolving threat assessment of China. While the pursuit of economic interests remained a primary policy goal, the United Kingdom nonetheless formulated a cohesive policy framework for its regional engagement with a strengthened political-military dimension.

Beginning in the early 2010s, as Britain had withdrawn its forces from Iraq (and later Afghanistan), an 'overriding objective was', according to a senior FCO official, 'to shift United Kingdom's foreign policy more towards the Asia-Pacific region; a very basic objective was to think more carefully about the rising strategic power in the world', namely China.[99] Reflecting the growing importance in the United Kingdom's foreign policy of emerging powers in general, and of China and the Asia-Pacific in particular, a variety of regular cross-government working groups were organized.[100] Led by the FCO, these groups were formed to assess how to further develop the United Kingdom's engagement with key emerging powers, namely China, India, Russia, Brazil, and South Africa;[101] and, among them, the 'Asia-Pacific element was more dominant'.[102]

In this context, the FCO, with the support of the MoD, decided to move beyond the China-centric approach that had characterized previous decades and to establish an 'All-of-Asia' policy.[103] As explained by several interviewees, internal discussions on this enhanced engagement and broader regional focus had begun in 2010 and the label 'All-of-Asia' was then coined in 2013 although publicly used

---

[97] Rod Wye, Head of the FCO's Asia Research Group (2002–2010), interview, 1 June 2020.
[98] Lord Peter Ricketts, interview, 3 June 2020.
[99] Interview, London, 15 January 2018.
[100] Interviews with a senior FCO official, 12 June 2020; and with senior MoD official, November 2016; and 24 June 2020.
[101] Interviews with a senior FCO official, 12 June 2020; and with senior MoD official, November 2016; and 24 June 2020.
[102] Former MoD official, interview, November 2016.
[103] Interviews with senior FCO officials, 15 January 2018, and 12 June 2020; and with senior MoD officials, 24 June 2020, and 3 July 2020.

only after 2016.[104] The government felt that the United Kingdom's policy had been too focused on the largest countries in the region, most notably China, to the exclusion of other regional states.[105] London 'recognized that you could not look at Asia-Pacific purely in terms of China's rise; China was necessary but not sufficient to our Asia-Pacific policy and we should therefore develop a much more coherent All-of-Asia approach.'[106] This policy encompassed the following main pillars: developing a more 'pragmatic engagement' policy towards the PRC, one that would be more balanced in terms of how it tackled the implications of China's rise;[107] deepening existing bilateral partnerships (including with Japan and Australia); and devoting greater attention to South East Asia and ASEAN as well as to the South Pacific.[108] Building upon this revised policy, London subsequently replaced the 'All-of-Asia' construct with the larger 'Indo-Pacific' policy framework in 2021.[109] Through this 'tilt' to the Indo-Pacific,[110] the United Kingdom followed a larger regional trend in Asia and the United States—as well as in other European countries (including France and Germany)—of broadening the geographical compass of its regional policy to also include the Indian Ocean region.[111]

As the United Kingdom formulated a more cohesive policy framework, it clarified and sharpened its regional policy goals, namely upholding the foundational norms of the rules-based order and sustaining regional stability, while pursuing expanded economic opportunities. As a senior FCO official puts it, the overarching policy goal was to foster 'a prosperous, stable Indo-Pacific anchored in the rules-based international system.'[112] For one, London aimed to defend such

[104] Interviews with FCO officials, January 2018 and January–June 2020. The first speech to articulate the United Kingdom's enhanced engagement across Asia—even though without using the All-of-Asia label—was delivered by William Hague in 2012; thereafter, the label was coined internally within the FCO in 2013, but it was used publicly only after 2016 in a speech by the FCO's Asia-Pacific Director, Stephen Lillie, and subsequently also by other government officials (interviews with senior FCO officials, 15 January 2018, 12 June, and 8 July 2020). See Secretary of State for Foreign and Commonwealth Affairs (2010–2015), William Hague, 'Britain in Asia', Speech, 26 April 2012; and FCO's Asia-Pacific Director (2013–2017), Stephen Lillie, 'The United Kingdom and the Asia-Pacific Region', Speech at the Carnegie Endowment in Washington, DC, 15 March 2016. See also Minister of State for Asia and the Pacific (2017–2019), Mark Field, 'The UK and All-of-Asia: A Modern Partnership', Speech at the Center for Strategic and International Studies, Jakarta, 14 August 2018.
[105] Minister of State for Asia and the Pacific (2017–2019), Mark Field, 2018.
[106] Senior FCO official, interview, London, 15 January 2018.
[107] For more details on the recalibration of UK's 'China policy', see Chapter 5.
[108] Interviews with seniors FCO and MoD officials, 24 November 2016, 15 January 2018, and 12 June 2020.
[109] HMG, 2021, p. 66. The British government defines the 'Indo-Pacific' region 'as covering most of South Asia and the Indian Ocean, Northeast and Southeast Asia, Oceania and the Pacific'. For more details, see House of Lords, *Oral Evidence: The UK's Security and Trade Relationship with China*, International Relations and Defence Committee, 9 June 2021, p. 18.
[110] HMG, 2021, pp. 66–68.
[111] See, e.g. Rory Medcalf, *Contest for the Indo-Pacific: Why China Won't Map the Future* (Melbourne: La Trobe University Press, 2020); and Robert G. Patman, Patrick Köllner, and Balazs Kiglics, eds, *From Asia-Pacific to Indo-Pacific: Diplomacy in a Contested Region* (Cham, Switzerland: Palgrave Macmillan, 2021). On France and Germany's policies toward the 'Indo-Pacific', see Chapters 1 and 2 respectively.
[112] Interview, 12 June 2020.

'order against irresponsible states that seek to erode it', most notably China.[113] This meant upholding its central norms, including the peaceful resolution of disputes and freedom of navigation.[114] The government stressed how, in particular, 'preserving freedom of navigation' was 'essential to the UK's national interests'.[115] Second, through greater political and military engagement across the region (detailed later), London intended to promote regional stability by ensuring that, 'in the face of the significant military modernisation being undertaken across the region, the scope for miscalculation or conflict within the region is minimised'.[116]

Overall, the resilience of the rules-based order, regional stability, and economic opportunities were seen as mutually interdependent goals. According to a senior FCO official, 'fundamentally our view is that the two—economic and security interests—are inseparable. Regional economic growth is contingent upon the region being stable and secure.'[117]

Policy Instruments

As London recalibrated its policy goals in the region, the instruments it leveraged to implement those goals also evolved. During the 1990s and 2000s, and especially after the handover of Hong Kong, the United Kingdom's engagement with the Asia-Pacific largely focused on fostering economic and diplomatic ties with regional emerging powers—most notably China—through bilateral and, to a lesser extent, multilateral channels, but with little centralized coordination. By contrast, in the 2010s, as London gradually formulated a more cohesive policy framework, it bolstered and diversified its political-military engagement across the region to better cope with the security challenges posed by China's expanding regional clout.

---

[113] Prime Minister Theresa May (2016–2019), Speech to the Lord Mayor's Banquet 2017, 13 November 2017. See also Secretary of State for Defence Gavin Williamson (2017–2019), Speech at the Shangri-La Dialogue, Singapore, 3 June 2018b; and FCO's Asia-Pacific Director Stephen Lillie (2013–2017), 2016.

[114] On this point, see MoD, 2019a, pp. 2–3; Minister of State for Asia and the Pacific Mark Field (2017–2019), in House of Commons Hansard, Wesminster Hall, Foreign Affairs Committee, 4 April 2019b, Vol. 657; and Minister of State for Asia and the Pacific, Mark Field, in HoC, 2019a, Question 207.

[115] HMG, 2021, p. 66.

[116] Minister of State for the Armed Forces Nick Harvey (2010–2012), 2012. See also HMG, 2021, pp. 66-67 and 72.

[117] Interview, London, 24 November 2016. On this point, see also HMG, 2021, p. 66.

Engaging the Asia-Pacific: A China-Centric Approach

During the first two decades of the post-Cold War era, the main thrust of London's engagement in the Asia-Pacific largely remained centred on China, consisting in deepening bilateral economic and diplomatic cooperation with the PRC (and, to a lesser extent, with Japan and Australia). The United Kingdom competed with France and Germany to become Beijing's main political and economic partner in Europe. At the same time, it put little effort into the region's multilateral security architecture, relying instead on minilateral arrangements such as the FPDA. As a result, British engagement in the Asia-Pacific remained piecemeal, mostly consisting of bilateral economic endeavours centred on few major powers and on Cold War-originated minilateral security arrangements.

Bilateral Ties with Emerging Markets

The United Kingdom's bilateral relationship with China had been appreciably damaged in the aftermath of the 1989 repression on Tiananmen Square, which had raised significant concerns—and complicated the ongoing negotiations—over the future of Hong Kong.[118] London, together with the other EC member states, suspended contacts at the senior level for two years (while working-level relations were maintained), suspended new aid projects, and imposed an embargo on arms sales to the PRC.[119] Yet, the United Kingdom was one of the first European countries to 'break ranks' and to pursue senior-level political engagement with the PRC, stressing the necessity to restore diplomatic ties with Beijing given the ongoing negotiations with Beijing over the status of Hong Kong.[120]

After the successful handover of Hong Kong, the United Kingdom and the PRC established a 'comprehensive partnership' in 1998 with the goal of 'opening a new chapter' in the bilateral relationship.[121] The two countries expanded political and military consultations through annual senior official-level talks and high-level military visits.[122] Yet, consistently with London's policy of engagement, the 'main stress was', as underscored by a House of Commons report, 'on economic ties and

---

[118] Interviews with James Hoare, former Consul-General and Head of Chancery in Beijing (1988–1991), 16 June 2020; Christopher Hum, former Assistant Under-Secretary of State for Northern Asia and Pacific (1992–1995), 15 June 2020; and Lord Peter Ricketts, former Head of FCO's Hong Kong Department (1991–1994) and later FCO's Deputy Political Director (1997–1999), 3 June 2020.
[119] European Council, Presidency Conclusions, Madrid, 26 and 27 June 1989, Appendix II.
[120] Interviews with former FCO officials in office in the late 1980s and early 1990s, January–July 2020. See also Kay Möller, 'Diplomatic Relations and Mutual Strategic Perceptions: China and the European Union', *The China Quarterly 169*, no. 169, Special Issue: China and Europe since 1978 (2002): p. 17.
[121] FCO, '1998 UK–China Joint Statement', in HoC, *Tenth Report: China*, Foreign Affairs Committee, 22 November 2000a, Annex B, https://publications.parliament.uk/pa/cm199900/cmselect/cmfaff/574/57402.htm.
[122] FCO, 2000a.

trade'.¹²³ The relationship was subsequently elevated to a 'comprehensive strategic partnership' in 2004, with London and Beijing agreeing to further intensify bilateral trade and investment, to increase the exchange of high-level visits, and to strengthen cooperation across a variety of areas, including finance, science, and technology, among others.¹²⁴

Concomitantly, in the early-to-mid 2000s, the United Kingdom—together with France and Germany—initially supported lifting the EU arms embargo on China.¹²⁵ The rationale for pursuing such a goal was twofold. For one, the embargo was seen, as one official puts it, 'as largely redundant, and lifting it was a good political gesture to make to the Chinese to show that they were now seen as part of the community of nations'.¹²⁶ Second, British policymakers considered that existing national and European export control systems ensured that the United Kingdom would not expand its arms sales to the PRC if the embargo was lifted.¹²⁷ Overall, lifting the arms embargo would thus remove a political obstacle to the deepening of UK-PRC economic and political relations without resulting in increased arms sales.¹²⁸

Washington grew highly concerned by the position of the UK government, as evidenced by US diplomatic cables.¹²⁹ According to Lincoln Bloomfield, then US Assistant Secretary of State for Political-Military Affairs (2000–2005), the United Kingdom 'was perceived as wanting to play a role as the bridge between Washington and Europe, the country with a foot in both continents. This was an issue that the United Kingdom expected to be resolved along the lines that the French desired, and that the Brits could be the ones to accomplish this.'¹³⁰ Washington therefore warned London that the lifting of the EU embargo could result in US suspension of US–UK defence industrial cooperation, including the bilateral defence

---

¹²³ HoC, 2000, 'Introduction: A New China Policy'.
¹²⁴ 'UK–China Joint Statement, 2004', in HoC, *East Asia*, 2006b, Vol. II, Ev. 127.
¹²⁵ On London's interpretation of what types of weapon systems were covered by the embargo, see the Minister of State Baroness Chalker of Wallasey (1989–1997), in HoC, *China: Arms Sales Embargo*, House of Commons Hansard, WA11, 4 April 1995. On the volume of British arms sales to China, see Meijer et al., 2018, pp. 862–866.
¹²⁶ Rod Wye, FCO's Head of the Asia Research Group (2002–2010), interview, 1 June 2020.
¹²⁷ Interviews with former FCO and MoD officials in office in the 2000s, January–July 2020.
¹²⁸ Interviews with former FCO and MoD officials in office in the 2000s, January–July 2020. According to Sebastian Wood, the former Political Counsellor in the British Embassy in Washington covering Asia-Pacific affairs (2001–2005), then FCO's Asia-Pacific Director (2005–2008) and later Ambassador to the PRC (2010–2015), a third consideration was that, after the transatlantic drift over the war in Iraq, lifting the EU arms embargo on China would provide a flagship joint initiative among Europe's three major powers that could partly 'repair some of the split' within Europe and the transatlantic relationship that had emerged over the military intervention in Iraq (interview, 12 June 2020).
¹²⁹ See, e.g. American Institute in Taiwan, 'Taiwan Pessimistic about EU Embargo', Cable from the American Institute in Taiwan, Confidential, Wikileaks Cablegate, 23 November 2004; US Embassy in Belgium, 'Is the EU Retreating on the China Arms Embargo?', Cable from the US Embassy in Brussels, Confidential, Wikileaks Cablegate, 24 March 2005.
¹³⁰ Lincoln Bloomfield, interview, Washington, DC, 26 March 2012.

trade agreement which was being negotiated.[131] Given its high degree of arms import dependence from Washington, London was therefore confronted with a stark choice between securing privileged bilateral cooperation with the US defence industrial base or pressing for lifting the embargo on arms sales to China and risking a major row with Washington.[132] The United Kingdom decided to modify its position and came to officially oppose the lifting of the embargo.[133] This, combined with Germany's concurrent shifting position (described in Chapter 2), persistently divergent positions within the European Union, and intense US pressures on other EU member states, effectively killed the prospect of lifting the embargo.[134]

Besides engaging the PRC, London also stepped up its engagement with other regional powers, most notably Japan and Australia. During the 1990s, the United Kingdom and Japan strengthened their diplomatic and economic ties and their bilateral politico-military consultations.[135] In 2006, Whitehall formulated a new United Kingdom-Japan strategy and, one year later, the two countries agreed to strengthen their cooperation in a variety of areas including defence procurement, peace support operations, naval cooperation—which dated back to the end of the nineteenth century—as well as arms sales.[136] Yet, since defence cooperation continued to be partly constrained by Japan's constitution and by its deep ties with the United States, trade and investment remained 'the dominant side' of the bilateral relationship.[137]

The United Kingdom concomitantly developed its longstanding diplomatic and security ties with Australia.[138] Although the two countries did not establish an overarching framework for defence cooperation in this period, they further developed the existing intricate amalgam of formal and informal ties, including the 'Five-Eyes' intelligence arrangement and the FPDA, while also establishing a variety of security arrangements and memoranda of understanding (MoUs) for the

---

[131] Former US State Department official, interview, Washington, DC, 16 September 2013. On the defence trade agreement, see HoC, *UK/US Defence Trade Cooperation Treaty*, HC107, 4 December 2007; and Claire Taylor, *UK–US Defence Trade Co-operation Treaty*, House of Commons Library, 17 February 2009.

[132] Between 1989 and 2015, the United States accounted for 79 per cent of the volume of British arms imports. Meijer et al., 2018, p. 866.

[133] On London's changing position on the embargo, see US Embassy in the United Kingdom, 'UK Views on December EU Foreign Ministers' Meeting (GAERC)', Confidential, Wikileaks Cablegate, 8 December 2006. See also Meijer et al., 2018, pp. 862–866.

[134] Meijer, 2016, pp. 248–250.

[135] Japanese MFA, 'UK/Japan Action Agenda: Special Partnership around the World', 2 September 1996; Japanese MFA, 'Action Agenda 21: The UK and Japan in the 21st Century', 1999. See also Japanese MFA, 'Japan–UK Joint Statement: A Framework for the Future', 9 January 2007, https://www.mofa.go.jp/region/europe/uk/joint0701.html.

[136] FCO, 'Submission from the Foreign and Commonwealth Office', in HoC, *Global Security: Japan and South Korea*, Foreign Affairs Committee, HC 449, 12 November 2008, Ev. 58 and 60.

[137] FCO, 2008, Ev. 56.

[138] Eugene Kevin Foley-Friel, 'Commonwealth Defence Cooperation during the Cold War, 1947–1982', Ph.D. dissertation, University of Bristol, 2019, ch. 4; Richard Higgot, 'Closing a Branch Office of Empire: Australian Foreign Policy and the UK at Century's End', *International Affairs* 70, no. 1 (1994): pp. 41–65.

reciprocal protection of classified information, logistics, defence science and technology, military capability harmonization, and equipment cooperation, among others.[139]

Minilateral Groupings and Feeble Multilateral Endeavours
While heavily relying on bilateral relationships, the United Kingdom also leveraged Cold War-originated minilateral arrangements, most notably the FPDA, but invested few resources into fostering greater multilateral cooperation in the region.

Beginning in the 1990s and continuing into the 2000s, the United Kingdom deepened its engagement with the FPDA through institutional reforms and by upgrading the FPDA's Integrated Air Defence System, located at the Royal Malaysian Air Force (RMAF) Base Butterworth, into an Integrated Area Defence System, combining air, naval, and land forces.[140] Furthermore, over this period, the United Kingdom and the other FPDA members moved towards greater combined joint exercises, including the Ocean Wave '97, Flying Fish, as well as subsequent deployments for the same exercise in 2000 and 2003.[141] Overall, as a residual arrangement dating back to the Cold War, the FPDA provided a rationale and a framework for continued, though limited, UK defence engagement in South East Asia.

Besides the FPDA, however, London put relatively less effort on promoting multilateral regimes in the Asia-Pacific. The United Kingdom, together with France, had 'lobbied for national membership of the ASEAN Regional Forum [ARF] to complement the existing EU representation'.[142] Yet, because of resistance among some ARF members as well as some European countries, these efforts were unsuccessful.[143] Accordingly, London (like Paris) thereafter shifted its support to the development of the ASEM, established in 1996. For London, a central goal of such multilateral framework was to 'strengthen political dialogue between Asia and Europe'[144] considering that the absence of 'links between Europe and Asia similar to those across the Atlantic and the Pacific' was 'an anomaly'.[145] Yet, despite these desultory attempts at engaging regional multilateral frameworks, the Asia-Pacific

---

[139] These agreements are listed in FCO, 'Treaty between the Government of the United Kingdom of Great Britain and Northern Ireland and the Government of Australia for Defence and Security Cooperation', Perth, 18 January 2013b; and in HoC, Written Answers to Questions—Column 1282W, *Daily Hansard*, 6 June 2013.
[140] In the mid-1990s, the FPDA Consultative Council and the FPDA Activities Coordinating Council were created. Emmers, 2012, p. 279; Carlyle A. Thayer, 'The Five Power Defence Arrangements: The Quiet Achiever', *Security Challenges* 3, no. 1 (2007): p. 83.
[141] See Singaporean MoD, '2nd FPDA's Defence Ministers' Informal Meeting', News Release, 7 June 2004; and Thayer, 2007: 92; HoC, 'Written Answers—Ocean Wave 97', 24 February 1997, House of Commons Hansard, Vol 291, https://api.parliament.uk/historic-hansard/written-answers/1997/feb/24/ocean-wave-97; and Thayer 2007, p. 87.
[142] FCO to the PM Private Secretary, 'Asia–Europe Meeting, Bangkok, 1–2 March 1996'; FCO to FA/APS, Brief No. 17, 27 February 1996b, TNA, PREM 19/5633. See also FCO to PM Private Secretary 'ASEAN Regional Forum', 23 February 1996e, TNA, PREM 19/5633.
[143] FCO to FA/APS, 1996b.
[144] FCO to FA/APS, 1996b.
[145] FCO to FA/APS, 'Proposed Asia–Europe Meeting', 15 May 1995, TNA, PREM 19/5633.

continued to be seen, as explained by a former FCO Asia-hand, as 'lacking an overarching forum for discussion on Asia-Pacific security issues'.[146]

Similarly, throughout this period, the United Kingdom put little emphasis on 'Europeanizing' its foreign and security policy in the region since the European Union was perceived by British officials as having no common foreign and security policy in the Asia-Pacific.[147] In fact, the United Kingdom robustly competed with France and Germany for who would become Beijing's main political and economic partner in Europe and would extract favourable economic and investment opportunities from China.[148] As emphasized by a 2006 House of Commons' report, the European Union's engagement with the Asia-Pacific displayed 'political passivity' because it was 'largely defined through Member States' economic interests in the region rather than [through] the political or security concerns of regional partners'.[149]

Enhanced Political-Military Engagement in the Asia-Pacific

It is only in the 2010s, in response to rising regional economic interests and heightened threat perceptions of China, that London took a series of initiatives aimed at bolstering British presence across the Asia-Pacific thereby concretizing its emerging regional policy framework (reframed around the larger Indo-Pacific after 2021).[150] In the words of a senior FCO official, 'the speed and the size of China's rise had strategic consequences and that meant we needed to step up our game in the region.'[151]

Certainly, limited resources and competing regional priorities—including the commitments in Afghanistan and the successive crises in Libya, Syria, and Ukraine—imposed significant constraints on this endeavour.[152] The National Audit Office (NAO) found that the MoD's equipment plan for the 2019–2029 period was 'unaffordable' and estimated a funding shortfall of close to £3bn.[153] It further concluded that the United Kingdom faced major risks to the timely delivery of nearly one-third of its most significant capabilities as well as skills and training shortages.[154] Given that the United Kingdom's armed forces were highly

---

[146] Rod Wye, former FCO's Head of the Asia Research Group (2002–2010), interview, 1 June 2020.
[147] Interviews with former FCO and MoD officials, January–July 2020.
[148] Interviews with former FCO and MoD officials, January–July 2020.
[149] HoC, 2006b, Ev. 123.
[150] On the United Kingdom's enhanced defence engagement in the Asia-Pacific, see among others Secretary of State for Defence Gavin Williamson (2017–2019), in HoC, *Defence*, Hansard, Volume 648, 22 October 2018a; and Secretary of State for Defence Michael Fallon (2014–2017), 2015.
[151] Interview, London, 15 January 2018.
[152] Interviews with NSC, FCO, and MoD officials, January–June 2020.
[153] NAO, *The Equipment Plan 2019 to 2029*, 27 February 2020a, p. 6.
[154] NAO, *Defence Capabilities: Delivering What Was Promised*, 18 March 2020b, pp. 8–11.

dependent on small numbers of highly expensive weapon systems, this made British capabilities 'extremely fragile'.[155]

Conflicting regional priorities, and the ensuing trade-offs in the allocation of resources, further constrained British capabilities. As a senior FCO official argues, 'our assets are not inconsiderable but they face constraints; in our overall hierarchy of strategic priorities, the Asia-Pacific may be the most important strategic centre of gravity in the long term, but in the day-to-day business the immediate threats come from Russia, the Eastern Mediterranean, and the Middle East.'[156] Likewise, according to former Chief of the Defence Staff General Lord Nick Houghton (2013–2016), the United Kingdom's 'ability to project force into the Asia-Pacific was hugely limited given the other standing tasks of our armed forces'.[157]

Within these constraints, the United Kingdom nonetheless sought to reinforce its political-military presence in the region by expanding naval deployments, by strengthening and diversifying its bilateral partnerships—with greater emphasis on South East Asia, the South Pacific and into the Indian Ocean—as well as through a more sustained engagement with regional multilateral security fora.

Naval Deployments and Bilateral Security Ties

After a hiatus between 2014 and 2017, largely due to more urgent contingencies, London increased the scale and frequency of its navy deployments to the region after 2018. Figure 3.1 displays the Royal Navy deployments of capital ships in the Indian and Pacific Oceans from 2009 to 2019, including in combination with US and/or other European navies (French in particular). Table 3.2 details the names, types, and missions of such capital ships as well as the deployments conducted in the region. Admiral Sir Philip Jones, First Sea Lord (2016–2019), also raised the possibility of permanently basing Type 31 frigates in South-East Asia,[158] and the United Kingdom then deployed a carrier strike group (CSG21) led by the HMS *Queen Elizabeth* aircraft carrier in the Indian and Pacific Oceans in 2021.[159] The MoD's *Defence Command Paper* further outlined the United Kingdom's plans to increase its maritime presence in the Indo-Pacific by deploying offshore patrol

---

[155] Memorandum by Sir Richard Barrons, Joint Forces Command, to the Secretary of State for Defence, Sir Michael Fallon, quoted in Sam Jones, 'Britain's "Withered" Forces Not Fit to Repel All-out Attack', *Financial Times*, 16 September 2016.
[156] Interview, 24 November 2016.
[157] General Lord Nick Houghton, interview, 9 June 2020.
[158] First Sea Lord Admiral Sir Philip Jones (2016–2019), Speech at the DSEI Maritime Conference, 11 September 2017.
[159] British Embassy in Tokyo, 'UK Carrier Strike Group Flagship HMS Queen Elizabeth to Arrive in Japan', 3 September 2021, https://www.gov.uk/government/news/uk-carrier-strike-group-flagship-hms-queen-elizabeth-to-arrive-in-japan; HMG, 2021, p. 5. See also Ben Barry, 'Posturing and Presence: The United Kingdom and France in the Indo-Pacific', *IISS Military Balance Blog*, 11 June 2021, https://www.iiss.org/blogs/military-balance/2021/06/france-uk-indo-pacific.

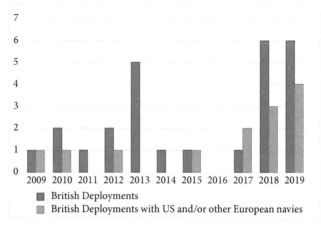

Fig. 3.1 Deployments of Royal Navy's capital ships in the Indian and Pacific Oceans, 2009–2019
Source: See Appendix A.

vessels from 2021 onward, the Littoral Response Group from 2023, and Type 31 frigates later in the decade.[160]

Besides its enhanced naval presence, London recalibrated its relationship with China and diversified its network of bilateral partnerships and capacity-building in the region through joint training, collaboration on defence capabilities and equipment, R&D, and information-sharing.[161] According to Secretary of State for Defence Michael Fallon (2014–2017), by 'investing more heavily in defence engagement' the United Kingdom was 'expanding [its] footprint' in the Pacific and Indian Ocean regions.[162]

First, London continued to deepen its political and economic ties with the PRC and established a 'global comprehensive strategic partnership', in 2015, which broadened the range of high-level exchanges on foreign policy and economic issues.[163] At the same time, in line with its more prudent engagement with Beijing (detailed in Chapter 6), London tightened its screening mechanisms of Chinese FDIs in sensitive sectors and decided to remove Huawei's equipment from the

---

[160] MoD, 2021, p. 32. See also Louisa Brooke-Holland, 'Integrated Review: The Defence Tilt to the Indo-Pacific', House of Commons Library, *Briefing Paper* no. 09217, 11 May 2021.

[161] These efforts began in the early 2010s. See for instance Secretary of State for Defence Liam Fox (2010–2011), Speech at the Shangri-La Dialogue, Singapore, 4 June 2011.

[162] Secretary of State for Defence Michael Fallon (2014–2017), Speech at the Shangri-La Dialogue, Singapore, 4 June 2016.

[163] FCO, 2015a; FCO, 'Written Evidence from the Foreign and Commonwealth Office (CIR0018)', in response to HoC, *China and the International Rules-Based System*, Foreign Affairs Committee, HC 612, 15 January 2019a.

Table 3.2 Royal Navy's capital ships and naval support helicopters in the Indian and Pacific Oceans, 2009–2019

Name of ship	Type and description of ship	Missions involved 2009–2019
HMS *Illustrious*	Aircraft carrier	Humanitarian aid after Typhoon Haiyan (2013)
HMS *Ocean*	Helicopter carrier	Taurus 09 deployment (2009)
HMS *Albion*	Amphibious assault ship	Enforce sanctions against North Korea (2018); Freedom of Navigation Operation (Franco-British) (2018); Freedom of Navigation Operation (2018)
HMS *Bulwark*	Amphibious assault ship	Taurus 09 deployment (2009)
HMS *Daring*	Destroyer	100th Anniversary of Australian Navy (2013); Exercise Bersama Lima (2013); Scientific trials in Pacific Ocean (2013); Humanitarian aid after Typhoon Haiyan (2013)
HMS *Argyll*	Frigate	Five Power naval exercise (2018); Exercise Bersama Lima (2018); Combined UK–US exercises in the South China Sea (2019)
HMS *Kent*	Frigate	Mission Arromanches (2015)
HMS *Montrose*	Frigate	UK–US maritime security and logistics operation (2019); Trilateral UK–US–Japan anti-submarine exercise (2019)
HMS *Enterprise*	Auxiliary support ship	Surveillance mission Taiwan Strait (2019)
HMS *Tireless*	Submarine	Search for MH370 (2014)
Typhoon	Jet	Exercise Bersama Lima (2014); Exercise Bersama Lima (2016); Exercise Guardian North (2016); Exercise Invincible Shield (2016)
Helicopter	Merlin MK2	Mission Jeanne d'Arc (2017)
Maritime Attack Helicopter	Wildcat	Mission Jeanne d'Arc (2018)

Source: See Appendix A.

United Kingdom's telecommunications network by 2027, while continuing to oppose the lifting of the EU arms embargo on China.[164]

As it rebalanced its bilateral relationship with Beijing, London strengthened and diversified its political and defence ties both with major regional powers and with lesser powers in South East Asia. The United Kingdom and Japan further intensified and widened their defence cooperation—a 'cornerstone' of the bilateral relationship—becoming 'each other's closest security partners in Asia and Europe respectively'.[165] Building upon the 2012 memorandum on defence cooperation, they soon thereafter concluded agreements on the joint development of defence equipment, on the exchange of classified information, and a defence logistics treaty while also deepening their political-military consultation mechanisms, e.g. '2+2' meetings; military-to-military visits, exchanges, and exercises; and deploying a British liaison officer in Japan to work with the US seventh fleet and Japan's Maritime Self-Defence Force.[166] Throughout the 2010s, British arms transfers to Japan considerably increased to the point that London became Tokyo's second-largest arms provider after the United States.[167]

London also substantially strengthened defence cooperation with its second main security partner in the region, namely Australia. London and Canberra expanded their political-military consultation mechanisms (through the Australia–United Kingdom Ministerial Consultations, AUKMIN) and established their first comprehensive framework for bilateral defence cooperation in 2013, which boosted collaboration in weapons procurement, joint research, exchanges of military and civilian personnel, the use of facilities, and information-sharing.[168] In parallel, they developed bilateral space cooperation including in communications technologies, space situational awareness, and satellite navigation,[169] while also

---

[164] On UK opposition to lifting the embargo, see Meijer et al., 2018, pp. 862–866.

[165] HMG, *National Security Capability Review*, 2018a, p. 38. See also PM's Office, 'Japan–UK Joint Declaration on Security Cooperation', 31 August 2017, https://www.gov.uk/government/publications/japan-uk-joint-declaration-on-security-cooperation.

[166] FCO, 'Agreement between the Government of the United Kingdom of Great Britain and Northern Ireland and the Government of Japan on the Security of Information', London, 4 July 2013a; Japanese MoD, *White Paper: Defense of Japan*, 2014, Part III, Section 7 'Japan–U.K. Defense Cooperation and Exchanges'. See also Philip Shetler-Jones, 'Britain's Quasi-Alliance with Japan', in *Natural Partners? Europe, Japan and Security in the Indo-Pacific*, edited by Luis Simón and Ulrich Speck (Madrid: Elcano Royal Institute, 2018), pp. 15–19; and Jeffrey W. Hornung, *Allies Growing Closer: Japan–Europe Security Ties in the Age of Strategic Competition* (Santa Monica, CA: RAND Corporation, 2020), pp. 19–38.

[167] Erik Brattberg and Philippe Le Corre, *The Case for Transatlantic Cooperation in the Indo-Pacific* (Washington, DC: Carnegie Endowment for International Peace, 2019), p. 19 (2013–2017 data).

[168] Australian Department of Foreign Affairs and Trade, 'Australia–United States Ministerial Consultations 2009 Joint Communiqué', 9 April 2009; FCO, 2013a. See also John Hemmings and Milia Hau, 'AUKMIN 2018: The Future of Global Britain?', *RUSI Commentary*, 14 August 2018.

[169] UK Space Agency, 'Britain and Australia Enter into Space Agreement', *News Story*, 3 October 2018.

expanding their cooperation in the South Pacific.[170] In the armament domain, Canberra selected BAE Systems in 2018 as prime contractor for the £20bn programme to build a new fleet of nine Type 26 frigates for advanced anti-submarine warfare missions,[171] the largest surface ship project in Australia's defence history.[172] Then, in 2021, the British government declared its intention to create a new British Defence Staff in Canberra to work alongside the existing Defence Staff in Singapore and coordinate defence engagement across the region.[173] That same year, the United Kingdom, Australia, and the United States announced a new trilateral security partnership (AUKUS) which, as discussed in Chapter 1, anticipated the delivery of a fleet of at least eight nuclear-powered submarines to Australia.[174] Through this partnership, the three countries also agreed to enhance their joint capabilities and interoperability in areas such as cyber capabilities, artificial intelligence, quantum technologies, and undersea capabilities, and to pursue integration of their security and defence-related science, technology, industrial bases, and supply chains.[175] AUKUS became, for the British government, a significant concretization of its 'tilt' to the Indo-Pacific.[176]

Besides these longstanding bilateral partnerships, the United Kingdom further developed its network of political-military cooperation in South East Asia.[177] It strengthened defence cooperation with Singapore, an important security partner in the sub-region. In 2016, London established the British Defence Staff for the Asia-Pacific in Singapore, a regional hub for the coordination of UK defence

---

[170] On the Enhanced Partnership in the South Pacific see FCO, 'The UK and Australia: A Dynamic Partnership for the 21st Century', 20 July 2018b.

[171] FCO, 2018b.

[172] They also pledged to reinforce their Anti-Submarine Warfare Strategic Partnership and explored broader defence industrial cooperation with respect to the F-35 Joint Strike Fighter and the P-8 Poseidon maritime patrol. See FCO, 2018b; and MoD, 'New Level of Australia–United Kingdom Defence Industry Partnership', 28 July 2017b; BAE Systems, 'Hunter Class Frigates', https://www.baesystems.com/en-aus/what-we-do/hunter.

[173] MoD, 2021, p. 32.

[174] Office of the Prime Minister of Australia, 'Australia to Pursue Nuclear-Powered Submarines through New Trilateral Enhanced Security Partnership', *Media Statement*, 16 September 2021, https://www.pm.gov.au/media/australia-pursue-nuclear-powered-submarines-through-new-trilateral-enhanced-security; The White House, 'Remarks by President Biden, Prime Minister Morrison of Australia, and Prime Minister Johnson of the United Kingdom Announcing the Creation of AUKUS', *Briefing Room*, 15 September 2021a, https://www.whitehouse.gov/briefing-room/speeches-remarks/2021/09/15/remarks-by-president-biden-prime-minister-morrison-of-australia-and-prime-minister-johnson-of-the-united-kingdom-announcing-the-creation-of-aukus/; The White House, 'Background Press Call on AUKUS', *Briefing Room*, 15 September 2021b, https://www.whitehouse.gov/briefing-room/press-briefings/2021/09/15/background-press-call-on-aukus.

[175] Prime Minister's Office (PMO), 'UK, US and Australia Launch New Security Partnership', 15 September 2021, https://www.gov.uk/government/news/uk-us-and-australia-launch-new-security-partnership.

[176] PMO, 2021.

[177] On the growing emphasis on Southeast Asia, see FCO, 'Appendix: Memorandum from the Foreign and Commonwealth Office', in HoC, *Global Britain*, Foreign Affairs Committee, HC 780, 6 March 2018a, p. 24; FCO and DIT, 'Building Prosperity and Supporting Security in South East Asia', 8 January 2016.

cooperation with regional partners, e.g. training and exercises.[178] Through a 2018 MoU the two countries then further developed their cooperation, on a ten-year basis, in joint research and technology development, testing of defence-related technologies, and in areas such as logistics management and maritime security.[179]

In the broader Indian Ocean region, the United Kingdom bolstered its defence engagement with India. London and New Delhi expanded their bilateral cooperation on maritime domain awareness, equipment collaboration (e.g. ship design), intelligence-sharing, and cybersecurity.[180] They subsequently agreed to further develop defence industrial cooperation and technology transfers,[181] while continuing to conduct land, air, and maritime bilateral exercises (e.g. Ajeya Warrior, Eastern Hawk, and Konkan, among others).[182] Yet, in the words of the former Foreign Secretary Jeremy Hunt (2018–2019) the bilateral relationship remained 'not near [its] full potential',[183] with India's share of UK arms exports declining by the late 2010s.[184]

The 'China Factor' in British Regional Partnerships

China's rising assertiveness—and the ensuing demand pull from regional states—was a central factor driving this thickening and diversification of British political-military ties across the region. British policymakers considered that strengthening capacity-building efforts across the region was key to signalling London's commitment to regional stability and the rules-based order in the face of China's expanding clout and ambitions.[185]

---

[178] MoD, 2019a. See also FCO, 'UK–ASEAN Factsheet', 6 January 2020; MoD, 'Britain Extends Global Defence Reach', 12 December 2016b, https://www.gov.uk/government/news/britain-extends-global-defence-reach.

[179] See Singaporean MoD, 'Singapore and UK Strengthen Long-Standing Defence Ties for Next Bound', 2 June 2018a; and Singaporean MoD, 'Singapore and the UK Affirm Long-Standing Defence Technology Relations with Renewal of MoU on Cooperative Defence Research', 28 June 2018b, https://www.mindef.sg/web/portal/mindef/news-and-events/latest-releases/article-detail/2018/june/28jun18_nr; British High Commission Singapore, 'Joint Statement by UK and Singapore at the Launch of Singapore–UK "Partnership for the Future"', 4 January 2020; UK Space Agency, 'UK Space Sector Lands in Singapore', 3 February 2020.

[180] On the UK–India 2015 Defence and International Security Partnership (DISP), see FCO, 'Written Evidence', in HoC, *Global Britain and India*, Foreign Affairs Committee, HC 1465, 19 March 2019b, p. 2; FCO, MoD, and PMO, 'UK–India Defence and International Security Partnership', 12 November 2015b, https://www.gov.uk/government/news/uk-india-defence-and-international-security-partnership.

[181] MoD, 'Joint Statement: India–UK Defence Partnership', 13 April 2017a, https://www.gov.uk/government/news/joint-statement-india-uk-defence-partnership.

[182] FCO, 2019b, p. 23; FCO, MoD, and PMO, 2015b. See also FCO, 'UK-India Joint Statement: Shared Values, Global Capability', 18 April 2018c.

[183] Secretary of State for Foreign and Commonwealth Affairs Jeremy Hunt (2018–2019), in HoC, 'Oral Evidence from the Foreign Secretary', HC 538, 31 October 2018b, Q354.

[184] See Minister of State for Asia and the Pacific Mark Field (2017–2019), and Head of South Asia Department and India Co-ordinator Fergus Auld (since 2017), in FCO, 2019b; HoC, *Building Bridges: Reawakening UK-India Ties*, Foreign Affairs Committee, HC 1465, 11 June 2019c, p. 10; Erik Brattberg, et al., 'Can France and the UK Pivot to the Pacific?', *Carnegie Endowment for International Peace*, 5 July 2018, https://carnegieendowment.org/2018/07/05/can-france-and-uk-pivot-to-pacific-pub-76732.

[185] Interviews with FCO and MoD officials, January–June 2020.

At the same time, this enhanced defence engagement was partly the result of demands from regional partners for greater capacity-building efforts. As explained by a senior FCO official, 'in becoming more engaged in Asia-Pacific', the United Kingdom was 'responding to a kind of strong demand signal—from Australia, from Japan, from the United States, and others—for greater involvement; and, to a significant extent, there was a sort of common assessment of the threat posed by China'.[186]

Through this expanded defence engagement in the Asia-Pacific, the United Kingdom therefore sought to ensure that its regional partners 'felt a strengthened degree of confidence in order to be able to deal with China'.[187] In particular, as explained by the MoD, these bilateral capacity-building efforts were intended to help regional powers 'develop organic abilities' including 'in key areas such as maritime domain awareness'.[188] An Asia-hand in the FCO confirms that a 'strategic objective in the Asia-Pacific' was to ensure 'the stability of the region'; 'so, encouraging the different countries of the region to step up to their responsibilities and doing whatever we could to assist in them having those capabilities was part of it.'[189]

Engaging the Regional Security Architecture: Multilateral Regimes and Western Cooperation

In combination with these bilateral endeavours, the United Kingdom stepped up its participation in the regional security architecture through greater multinational cooperation with both regional and Western powers. In particular, it aimed to expand its involvement with both minilateral groupings and multilateral regimes in the region, while exploring ways to deepen cooperation with both the United States and other European countries in the Asia-Pacific.

FPDA, Security Regimes, and Joint Military Exercises

During the 2010s, London sought to 'modernize' the FPDA by broadening its focus to encompass areas such as maritime security, while continuing to conduct sustained bilateral and multinational military exercises with FPDA partners, including Bersama Lima, Suman Warrior, and Bersama Shield.[190] The former UK Foreign Secretary Philip Hammond (2014–2016) suggested that, given the large amount of trade which passes through the South China Sea, 'the UK would be prepared to deploy armed forces as part of the FPDA should its interests and alliances

---

[186] Interview, 12 June 2020.
[187] Senior FCO official, interview, London, 15 January 2018.
[188] MoD, 2019a, pp. 7–8. On this point see also HMG, 2014, p. 41
[189] FCO official, interview, November 2016.
[190] Secretary of State for Defence Gavin Williamson (2017–2019), 2018b; MoD, 'Joint Exercises: Written Question—32484', HoC, 2016a, https://www.parliament.uk/business/publications/written-questions-answers-statements/written-question/Commons/2016-03-24/32484.

in the region be put at risk by regional security challenges.'[191] Considering that the FPDA had an important 'confidence-building role',[192] the United Kingdom thereby intended 'to signal a renewed interest in the region', while ensuring the continued interoperability of the armed forces of FPDA member states.[193]

London also pursued minilateral intelligence cooperation with the other members of the so-called 'Five Eyes' network with Australia, Canada, New Zealand, and the United States (the United Kingdom–United States of America Agreement, UKUSA).[194] In the 2010s, consultations and intelligence cooperation with regards to China's regional influence and behaviour, including in the South Pacific, gathered momentum.[195] As explained by one official, the five member states aimed to 'make sure that we were strategically aligned and that we were exchanging information but with a reorientation because the Asia-Pacific region was increasingly becoming a priority for us'.[196] The United Kingdom also reportedly invited Japan to join the Five Eyes arrangements.[197]

Together with these minilateral efforts, the United Kingdom expanded its engagement within the regional multilateral security architecture. Besides annually attending the Shangri-La Dialogue, London opened a mission to ASEAN, appointing its first dedicated ambassador thereto, and applied for observer status on two working groups of the ADMM+.[198] It also became a member of ReCAAP which aimed to counter piracy and to protect 'the trade-routes that are vital to [the UK's] economy'.[199] The other regional security regimes in which the United Kingdom

---

[191] Quoted in HoC, *Flexible Response? An SDSR Checklist of Potential Threats and Vulnerabilities*, Defence Committee, HC 493, 17 November 2015, p. 14.

[192] Singaporean MoD, 'Joint Statement of the 10th Five Power Defence Arrangements Defence Ministers' Meeting', Singapore, 22 August 2017, https://www.minister.defence.gov.au/minister/marise-payne/statements/joint-communique-10th-singapore-australia-joint-ministerial.

[193] Senior FCO official, interview, London, 15 January 2018. See also HMG, 2021, p. 73; and HMG, 'FPDA Defence Ministers' Joint Statement', *Press Release*, 27 November 2020, https://www.gov.uk/government/news/fpda-defence-ministers-joint-statement.

[194] Jeffrey T. Richelson, *The Ties that Bind. Intelligence Cooperation between the UKUSA Countries: The United Kingdom, the United States of America, Canada, Australia and New Zealand* (Sydney: Allen and Unwin, 1990).

[195] Anonymous US official quoted in 'Five Eyes Intelligence Alliance Builds Coalition to Counter China', *Reuters*, 12 October 2018. See also Austin Gee and Robert G. Patman, 'Small State or Minor Power? New Zealand's Five Eyes Membership, Intelligence Reforms, and Wellington's Response to China's Growing Pacific Role', *Intelligence and National Security* 36, no. 1(2021): pp. 38–42.

[196] Interview, London, January 2018.

[197] Okabe Noboru, 'The New Anglo-Japanese Alliance and the "Six Eyes"', *Nippon.com*, 29 October 2020.

[198] The expert working groups are those on Peacekeeping Operations and Military Medicine. See MoD, 2019a, p. 2; MoD, *Annual Report and Accounts, 2018–2019*, 31 March 2019b, p. 51. On the United Kingdom's larger engagement with ASEAN, see FCO, 2020. On the UK's first ambassador to ASEAN, see ASEAN, 'Ambassador of the United Kingdom of Great Britain and Northern Ireland to ASEAN Presents Credentials', 28 November 2019, https://asean.org/ambassador-of-the-united-kingdom-of-great-britain-and-northern-ireland-to-asean-presents-credentials.

[199] 'UK Joins the ReCAAP', ReCAAP, *Press Release*, 2 May 2012.

participated included, among others, the IORA, the Western Pacific Naval Symposium, and the SPDMM.²⁰⁰ Additionally, London expanded the range of bilateral and multinational exercises in the region in which British armed forces participated, including major FPDA exercises (both bilaterally and multinationally) and RIMPAC.²⁰¹

Western Cooperation in the Asia-Pacific
As it strengthened its engagement with Asian major and lesser partners, the United Kingdom concomitantly sought to expand its cooperation with other Western powers in the Asia-Pacific: the United States on the one hand, and European countries on the other.

Anglo-American Cooperation For one, London aimed to contribute—within the confines of its capabilities—to US foreign and security policies goals in the Asia-Pacific. According to the FCO, the United Kingdom saw the region 'as an area where the US and UK should, and would, cooperate more closely in future',²⁰² jointly facing 'the implications of an increasingly assertive China'.²⁰³ By strengthening and diversifying its regional presence and its capacity-building efforts, London sought to expand, as stressed by the MoD, the 'potential for greater burden-sharing in policing the global commons'.²⁰⁴

To do so, it bolstered its intelligence and security cooperation with Washington and expanded bilateral and minilateral operational and defence industrial cooperation. In 2016, the United Kingdom, the United States, and Japan signed a trilateral defence agreement to strengthen cooperation between their respective navies—e.g. conducting joint exercises and combined patrols—so as to enhance the operational effectiveness of their maritime forces in the region.²⁰⁵ In 2018, HMS *Argyll* and elements of the Japan Maritime Self-Defence Force (JMSDF) took

---

²⁰⁰ See e.g. SPDMM, 'Joint Communiqué', 1 May 2015, https://png.embassy.gov.au/files/pmsb/150508%20SPDMM%20-Agreed%20Joint%20Communique.pdf; Indian Ocean Rim Association, 'Dialogue Partners', https://www.iora.int/en/about/dialogue-partners; US Indo-Pacific Command, 'Western Pacific Naval Symposium Nations Begin Diving Exercise in Guam', *News*, 8 June 2017, https://www.pacom.mil/Media/News/News-Article-View/Article/1208639/western-pacific-naval-symposium-nations-begin-diving-exercise-in-guam/.
²⁰¹ Richard Williams, Written Evidence Submitted in Response to HoC, in *UK Defence and the Far East*, Defence Committee, HC 2035, 13 June 2019, http://data.parliament.uk/writtenevidence/committeeevidence.svc/evidencedocument/defence-committee/uk-defence-in-the-asiapacific-region/written/103172.html.
²⁰² FCO quoted in HoC, *Government Foreign Policy towards the United States*, Foreign Affairs Committee, 25 March 2014, ch. 4, https://publications.parliament.uk/pa/cm201314/cmselect/cmfaff/695/69502.htm (accessed 2 June 2021).
²⁰³ FCO, 2018a, pp. 21–22.
²⁰⁴ Secretary of State for Defence Philip Hammond (2011–2014), 2014.
²⁰⁵ Royal Navy, Japan Maritime Self-Defence Force, and US Navy, '2016 Trilateral Maritime Talks', 20 October 2016. See also Steven Stashwick, 'US, UK, and Japan Navies Sign First-Ever Trilateral Cooperation Agreement', *The Diplomat*, 1 November 2016. On the UK and the Quadrilateral Security Dialogue with the United Kingdom, Japan, and Australia, see John Hemmings and James Rogers, 'Britain and the Quadrilateral', *Journal of Indo-Pacific Affairs* 3, no. 5 (2020): pp. 118–130.

part in their first trilateral anti-submarine exercise with the US Navy and HMS *Montrose* participated in a second trilateral exercise in 2019 (Table 3.2).[206] Furthermore, in order to enhance UK–US military and intelligence ties, London also strengthened the role of its liaison officer to the US Pacific Command (which was relabelled Indo-Pacific Command in 2018) in Hawaii, by raising its rank.[207] The 2021 AUKUS partnership between the United Kingdom, the United States, and Australia, discussed earlier, significantly strengthened their trilateral defence and industrial cooperation.

Intra-European Diplomatic and Security Cooperation in the Region Enhanced cooperation with the United States went hand in hand with the United Kingdom's pursuit of greater intra-European cooperation in the Asia-Pacific. At the operational level, the British and French navies started conducting combined deployments in the Indian and Pacific Oceans in the second half of the 2010s. For instance, UK military personnel and helicopters were included in the Mission Jeanne d'Arc and the two navies deployed ships as part of the Combined Task Force 150 in the Indian Ocean and during deployments in the South China Sea (Table 3.2; see also Chapter 1 and Appendix A). The United Kingdom–France bilateral communiqué of the January 2018 Sandhurst summit pledged to further develop maritime cooperation in the region by supporting each other's future deployments of aircraft carriers as well as by deploying and operating ships and aircraft together in the Indian Ocean and the Asia-Pacific.[208]

London explored ways to strengthen intra-European cooperation in the Asia-Pacific also at the diplomatic level. Prior to Brexit, as explained by a senior FCO official, the United Kingdom tried 'to forge a more coherent European Union approach towards the Asia-Pacific and particularly vis-à-vis China.'[209] However, formal EU channels (e.g. the European Union's COASI or the COREPER) were deemed to be largely ineffective venues because of the diverging interests and perspectives on China among the (then) twenty-eight EU member states.[210] Several Northern, Eastern and Southern European countries, for instance, as stressed by various diplomats, were reluctant to forge strong diplomatic positions—let alone robust security policies—in the Asia-Pacific because of their economic dependence on China and lack of capabilities.[211] As one official puts it, it was doubtful 'whether COASI or other EU institutional settings were really ever going to deliver on greater diplomatic and security cooperation in the Asia-Pacific, not least

---

[206] MoD, 2019b.
[207] MoD official, interview, 17 February 2020.
[208] PMO, 'UK–France Summit Communiqué', Royal Military Academy Sandhurst, 18 January 2018, p. 3.
[209] Interview, London, 15 January 2018.
[210] Interviews with current and former FCO officials involved in these discussions, London, January–November 2018 and January, June, and December 2020.
[211] Interviews with British diplomats, London, November 2016 and January 2018.

because of the discrepancy in views of China'; for instance, it seemed 'far-fetched to believe that twenty-eight countries that could not agree on a less-than-robust statement on the South China Sea in 2016 would ever agree to something more substantive'.[212] In the words of another diplomat, 'the difficulty on EU-level coordination on Asia-Pacific was that it was becoming increasingly difficult to bring all [EU] member states together behind a common line because there is always a strong division with those countries over which Beijing has more leverage'; as a result, in his words: 'COASI is more form than substance'.[213]

Accordingly, the discussions on how to better align European foreign and security policies in the Asia-Pacific were mostly conducted bilaterally and through informal minilateral groupings (such as the E3, the Quad, or the Quint) rather than through the EU formal structures such as COASI.[214] Minilateral groupings were deemed to be more effective channels to discuss European cooperation in the Asia-Pacific among fewer countries with greater commonality of interests in the region. The E3 grouping, for instance, was used to produce joint statements on the importance of upholding regional stability and international law in the South China Sea.[215] Likewise, consultations on Asian-Pacific security were conducted through the Quad, a minilateral format which includes the United Kingdom, France, Germany, and the United States (as well as EEAS representatives) and through the Quint (which also includes Italy).[216]

The UK withdrawal from the European Union had thus only a relatively minor impact on London's pursuit of its foreign and security policy goals in the region. To be sure, the United Kingdom was henceforth deprived of the established EU institutional venues to consult other European powers on regional security dynamics and to foster greater intra-European cooperation in the Asia-Pacific. But British officials had long been sceptical about the effectiveness of these formal EU institutional venues. Furthermore, as it developed its 'vision of Global Britain' outside the European Union,[217] London continued to participate in informal minilateral

---

[212] Interview with UK official, 28 December 2020. On how the Council of the EU 'Declaration on the Award Rendered in the Arbitration between the Philippines and China' was diluted because of diverging interests across the European Union, see the book's Conclusion.
[213] Interview, 24 November 2016.
[214] Interviews with former FCO officials involved in the discussions, London, January–November 2018 and January–June 2020.
[215] FCO, 'E3 Joint Statement on the Situation in the South China Sea', *Press Release*, 29 August 2019c. See also the 'note verbale' submitted by the E3 to the UN Commission on the Limits of the Continental Shelf. Permanent Mission of the UK to the United Nations, 'Note verbale' to the UN Commission on the Limits of the Continental Shelf, no. 162/20, New York, 16 September 2020.
[216] Interviews with current and former FCO officials involved in these discussions, London, January–November 2018 and January, June, and December 2020.
[217] On Global Britain, see FCO, 2018a; and FCO, 'Written Evidence—-Foreign and Commonwealth Office (FPW0027)', 28 February 2018d, data.parliament.uk/writtenevidence/committeeevidence. svc/evidencedocument/international-relations-committee/foreign-policy-in-changed-world-conditions/written/79,900.html.

groupings such as the E3, the Quad, or the Quint (outside EU structures),[218] and stated its intention 'to work more closely with European partners, including France and Germany'.[219] Nevertheless, the trilateral AUKUS agreement with Australia and the United States—that scrapped the previous Franco-Australian contract for the delivery of submarines to Canberra—signalled the pursuit of potentially more antagonistic policies in the region between the United Kingdom and its continental neighbours, at least in the short term.

Conclusion

China's rising assertiveness has been a key driver of change in British foreign and security policy in the Asia-Pacific. While in the first two post-Cold War decades, London perceived little security challenges from the PRC and largely saw the region through economic lenses, since the 2010s, rising threat perceptions of China—coupled with shifting regional economic interests—have sparked a significant policy change. The United Kingdom has developed a policy framework for the larger Indo-Pacific region and taken concrete steps to strengthen its presence therein through naval deployments, enhanced bilateral partnerships, and multinational regional cooperation, including with the United States. And while the United Kingdom formally exited EU institutional structures after Brexit, it had nonetheless displayed scepticism vis-à-vis the European Union's capacity to forge a coherent and effective policy in the region well before Brexit. Certainly, major budgetary constraints and competing regional priorities have limited the range of capabilities that the United Kingdom could mobilize in support of these endeavours and its capacity to project power into the region. Financial difficulties, capability shortfalls, and the requirements imposed by contingencies in other regions, such as the Middle East, have entailed challenging trade-offs in the allocation of resources. Yet, through its enhanced political-military engagement, London has sought to step up its contribution to upholding the rules-based order and regional stability—while advancing its economic interests—in the face of China's increasingly muscular foreign policy. In doing so, an overarching ambition of the United Kingdom has thus revolved around shaping China's surrounding regional environment.

---

[218] Interviews with FCO officials, January and February 2021, and with EU officials, November 2021. The continued participation of the United Kingdom in these minilateral formats was confirmed in interviews with French and German officials (cf. Chapters 1 and 2). See also Daniel Lippman, 'Trump National Security Adviser Heading to Europe for Talks on China', *Politico EU*, 7 November 2020.

[219] HMG, 2021, p. 66.

PART II
RESPONDING TO CHINA'S ASSERTIVENESS IN EUROPE

Introduction

Inroads into Europe: Beijing's Deepening Foothold on the Continent

The central finding of Part I is that China's rising assertiveness after 2009 has sparked—gradually and cumulatively—a major shift in French, British, and German foreign and security policies in the Asia-Pacific in the 2010s. While rising economic interests have provided the underlying impetus for the three countries' growing attention to the region, threat perceptions of China have been the main driver of change. France, Germany, and the United Kingdom have thus largely been drawn into the Asia-Pacific by Beijing's increasingly muscular regional posture. It is in their home continent—Europe—however, that China's rise has been most directly felt. Beijing's political and economic footprint in Europe has substantially deepened and widened since the end of the Cold War. After 2009, as its economic and technological capabilities grew and its political ambitions expanded, the PRC became increasingly assertive not only in the Asia-Pacific, but also in Europe.[1] Enabled and supported by the government in Beijing, Chinese state-owned and private enterprises became entrenched in the European high-tech industrial landscape through increased FDIs and the supply of advanced telecommunications equipment. The thickening of this economic presence, in turn, translated into greater economic and political leverage that has enabled Beijing to exploit intra-European fragmentation and to drive a wedge among European states so as to prevent the European Union from forging unified policies. As a result, by the 2010s, China's rising clout in Europe—and its inroads into strategic sectors—have sparked a wake-up call among European policymakers over the security ramifications of China's rise.

---

[1] As discussed in the Introduction of this book, Chinese assertiveness has exhibited partly different characteristics in the two regions. In the Asia-Pacific it has revolved around a diplomatic, military, and economic posture geared towards the establishment of a Sino-centric regional order. In Europe, it has largely taken the form of a deeper and more robust economic footprint on the continent—with significant investments into Europe's strategic sectors—and in the ensuing political leverage over European countries. Yet, in Europe like in the Asia-Pacific, Chinese assertiveness has been driven by the country's growing capabilities and by the ambitions of the leadership in Beijing to expand the reach of China's power and influence.

During the 1990s and the 2000s, the PRC's developing economy mostly revolved around labour-intensive manufacturing and remained largely dependent upon the acquisition of foreign technology and know-how through inward direct investments and imports.[2] The promotion of the country's science and technology (S&T) capabilities overwhelmingly focused upon the absorption and 're-innovation' (or advanced imitation) of foreign technology.[3] Accordingly, whereas the PRC offered a major market for foreign high-tech capital equipment, Chinese companies made very few outward FDIs.[4] European FDI to China vastly overshadowed the PRC's investments on the continent: the accumulated value of completed Chinese FDI into EU countries between 2000 and 2009 reached $8bn;[5] over the same timeframe, the accumulated value of EU investments utilized by Chinese companies reached $45.7bn (see also the comparative charts on the investment ties between the Big Three and China and between the European Union and China in Appendix B).[6] China's economic presence in Europe—and its ensuing political influence—remained marginal.

From the late 2000s onward, and most markedly in the 2010s, however, as it strived to catch up with Western advanced industrial capabilities and establish itself as a major power, China increasingly turned away from labour-intensive manufacturing. It moved towards higher added-value, high-tech capital goods production, concomitantly shifting from an FDI import country to an FDI export country.[7] In line with the political and technological ambitions of the new leadership under Xi Jinping, Chinese companies considerably increased their outward FDIs and became key suppliers of advanced telecommunications equipment in Europe.[8] Thereby, China's foothold on the continent expanded substantially.

---

[2] See, e.g. Kathleen Walsh, *Foreign High-Tech R&D in China. Risks, Rewards, and Implications for US-China Relations* (Washington, DC: The Henry L. Stimson Center, 2003).

[3] Tai Ming Cheung et al., *Planning for Innovation: Understanding China's Plans for Technological, Energy, Industrial, and Defense Development*, Report prepared for the US–China Economic and Security Review Commission, 28 July 2016, p. 32. See also Tai Ming Cheung, 'Innovation in China's Defense Technology Base: Foreign Technology and Military Capabilities', *Journal of Strategic Studies* 39, no. 5–6 (2016): p. 732.

[4] On the definition of FDI and the data used in this book, see Appendix B.

[5] Data retrieved from Agatha Kratz, Max J. Zenglein, and Gregor Sebastian, *Chinese FDI in Europe—2020 Update*, MERICS/Rhodium Group, June 2021, p. 9 (currency converted at the average exchange rate for the respective year).

[6] Data retrieved from National Bureau of Statistics of China, *Statistical Yearbooks of China*, http://www.stats.gov.cn/english/Statisticaldata/AnnualData/ (for details, see Appendix B). See also Thilo Hanemann and Daniel H. Rosen, *China Invests in Europe: Patterns, Impacts and Policy Implications*, Rhodium Group, June 2012, p. 4; Rhodium Group, 'People's Republic of China/European Union Direct Investment', *Cross Border Monitor*, 16 January 2019.

[7] Ling Li, 'China's Manufacturing Locus in 2025: With a a Comparison of "Made-in-China 2025" and "Industry 4.0"', *Technological Forecasting & Social Change*, no. 135 (2018): pp. 66–74; Alexander B. Hammer and Shahid Yusuf, 'Is China in a High-Tech, Low Productivity Trap?', US International Trade Commission, *Working Paper 2020–07-B*, July 2020.

[8] On how Chinese outward FDI started expanding in the late 2000s as a result of the so-called 'Go Out' policy and then soared in the 2010s, see Yushan Li, 'China's Go Out Policy: A Review on China's Promotion Policy for Outward Foreign Direct Investment from a Historical Perspective', Centre for Economic and Regional Studies, HAS Institute of World Economics, *Working Paper no. 244*, September

President Xi's ambition to achieve the 'China Dream' of 'Great Rejuvenation' was laid out at the Third Plenary Session of the 18th Party Central Committee in 2013.⁹ He then outlined a 'two-stage development plan' for the period from 2020 to 2049 (the one-hundredth anniversary of the founding of the PRC): in the first stage between 2020 and 2035, the PRC would become 'a global leader in innovation'; and in the second stage the PRC would complete its modernization and become 'prosperous, strong, democratic, culturally advanced, harmonious, and beautiful.'¹⁰ Beijing sought to concretize these goals through a wide range of top-down, state-directed plans (as many as a hundred), the key ones including *Made in China 2025*, *Internet Plus*, and *Commercial-Military Integration*.¹¹

The *Made in China 2025* (MiC25) plan, presented in 2015, is a ten-year, comprehensive industrial policy that aims to reduce China's dependence on foreign technology, increase 'self-sufficiency' and indigenous innovation, and leverage the trends of advanced manufacturing—such as autonomous robots, the Internet of Things (IoT) and big data—to shift away from low-cost manufacturing and towards the production of value-added products.¹² The plan specifically prioritizes ten industrial sectors for policy and funding support, including new generation information technology, automated machine tools, and robotics, among others.¹³ *Internet Plus* complements the MiC25 by seeking to 'integrate mobile Internet, cloud computing, big data and the Internet of Things with modern manufacturing.'¹⁴ Concurrently, Beijing continued the promotion of commercial-military integration (CMI, referred to in China as 'civil-military fusion'), namely the exploitation of civil technological developments for military applications and the

---

2018; and EY, 'How Will Chinese Enterprises Navigate New Challenges when "Going Abroad" under the New Global Trade Landscape'?, *ChinaGoAbroad*, no. 9, October 2019, pp. 4 and 6.

⁹ 'Communiqué of the Third Plenary Session of the 18th Central Committee of the Communist Party of China', 12 November 2013, www.china.org.cn/china/third_plenary_session/2014-01/15/content_31203056.htm (accessed on 1 December 2021). On the 'China Dream', see also the Introduction of Part I of this book.

¹⁰ 'Full Text of Xi Jinping's Report at 19th CPC National Congress', *China Daily*, 18 October 2017, https://www.chinadaily.com.cn/china/19thcpcnationalcongress/2017-11/04/content_34115212.htm.

¹¹ According to Cheung et al., under President Xi the National Medium-and Long-Term Plan for Science and Technology Development and the Five-Year Plans, although relevant, have declined in importance. Cheung et al., 2016, pp. 34 and 38.

¹² State Council of the PRC, *Made in China 2025*, 7 July 2015b, http://www.cittadellascienza.it/cina/wp-content/uploads/2017/02/IoT-ONE-Made-in-China-2025.pdf. For an analysis, see Cheung et al., 2016, p. 55. The 'Internet of Things' (IoT) refers to the 'linkage of sensors and actuators embedded in physical objects through wireless networks, often using the same Internet protocol (IP) that connects the Internet' (p. 43).

¹³ The ten sectors are: new generation information technology, automated machine tools and robotics, space and aviation equipment, maritime equipment and high-tech shipping, modern rail transportation equipment, new energy vehicles and equipment, power generation equipment, agricultural equipment, new materials, and biopharma and advanced medical products. State Council of the PRC, 2015b, pp. 22–27.

¹⁴ State Council of the PRC, 'China Unveils Internet Plus Action Plan to Fuel Growth', 4 July 2015a, http://english.www.gov.cn/policies/latest_releases/2015/07/04/content_281475140165588.htm.

furthering of China's defence manufacturers' access to dual-use technologies.[15] To support these intertwined endeavours, the government incentivized R&D in these core areas through funds, subsidies, tax breaks, preferential loans, export subsidies, and guarantees so as to foster the creation of national champions in each sector.[16]

As a result of these new ambitions and of Beijing's financial and regulatory support, China's state-owned and private companies became noticeably more active internationally, and by the latter half of the 2010s the PRC was the world's second-largest outward investor after Japan.[17] This rise in Chinese investments paralleled President Xi's launch of a massive infrastructure development project, the One Belt One Road in 2013, later relabelled Belt and Road Initiative (BRI), which provided further momentum for Chinese firms to invest abroad.[18] In Europe, Chinese corporations both considerably expanded and diversified their FDIs in advanced technological assets and infrastructure projects and became increasingly central suppliers of equipment for Europe's digital infrastructure.

The Advent of Chinese FDIs in Europe

The European Union witnessed a burst in Chinese investments after the 2008 financial crisis and, most conspicuously, in the 2010s.[19] The annual value of

---

[15] See, e.g. Chinese Ministry of Science and Technology (MOST), 'The "13th Five-Year" Special Plan for S&T Military-Civil Fusion Development' (translated in English), 26 September 2017, https://cset.georgetown.edu/research/the-13th-five-year-special-plan-for-st-military-civil-fusion-development. For an analysis of China's CMI efforts, see Tai Ming Cheung, *Fortifying China: The Struggle to Build a Modern Defense Economy* (Ithaca, NY: Cornell University Press, 2009), ch 5; and Tai Ming Cheung and Eric Hagt, 'China's Efforts in Civil-Military Integration, its Impact on the Development of China's Acquisition System, and Implications for the United States', in *Proceedings of the 16th Annual Acquisition Research Symposium—Volume I* (Monterey, CA: Naval Postgraduate School, 2019), pp. 146–171.

[16] Meia Nouwens and Helena Legarda, 'China's Pursuit of Advanced Dual-Use Technologies', *IISS Research Papers*, 18 December 2018, https://www.iiss.org/blogs/research-paper/2018/12/emerging-technology-dominance.

[17] EY, 2019, p. 6 (2018 data).

[18] See State Council of the PRC, 'Full Text: Action Plan on the Belt and Road Initiative', 30 March 2015c, english.www.gov.cn/archive/publications/2015/03/30/content_281475080249035.htm; and 'Full Text: China's International Development Cooperation in the New Era', *XinhuaNet*, 10 January 2021, www.xinhuanet.com/english/2021-01/10/c_139655400.htm. BRI comprises both a land and a maritime component (the so-called Silk Road Economic Belt and the Maritime Silk Road) and is designed to strengthen China's economic ties with more than sixty-five countries through lending for infrastructure projects and investments totalling an estimated $200 billion (in 2020) that could reach an estimated $1.2–1.3 trillion by 2027. Andrew Chatzky and James McBride, 'China's Massive Belt and Road Initiative', Council on Foreign Relations, *Backgrounder*, 28 January 2020; see also Gisela Grieger, 'Foreign Direct Investment Screening: A Debate in Light of China–EU FDI Flows', *European Parliamentary Research Service (EPRS) Briefing*, May 2017, p. 3.

[19] In the aftermath of the 2008 financial crisis, many countries across Europe welcomed Chinese FDIs as an engine to revamp economic growth. Ramón Pacheco Pardo, 'Europe's Financial Security and Chinese Economic Statecraft: The Case of the Belt and Road Initiative', *Asia-Europe Journal 16*, no. 3 (2018): pp. 237–250.

completed Chinese FDIs in the EU-27 and the United Kingdom soared from virtually zero in the mid-2000s to a peak of $49 billion in 2016, then declining to $21bn in 2018;[20] they now outstripped EU FDIs in China ($10.4bn in 2018).[21] While in Northern, Eastern, and Southern Europe, Chinese investments largely revolved around infrastructure projects and large-scale privatization processes (e.g. in the context of the so-called '16+1' framework),[22] they focused on capital investments and on the acquisition of strategic assets and R&D networks in Western Europe.[23]

The bulk of Chinese FDIs (45 per cent) targeted the Big Three, mostly in high-tech sectors such as consumer products and services, information and communication technologies, and automotive—thus indicating a persistent interest of Chinese companies in European technology and know-how.[24] As they diversified their investment ties across the continent, Chinese mergers and acquisitions (M&A) increased in sensitive strategic areas such as dual-use sectors and critical infrastructures (e.g. energy, telecommunications, transport, health, or water supply), as explained by a report commissioned by the Danish Business Authority.[25] And, according to Datenna, a research group specialized in Chinese FDIs, out of the more than 650 Chinese acquisitions of European companies between 2010 and 2021, 40 per cent were completed by companies with medium-to-high level of influence by the Chinese State.[26]

---

[20] Data retrieved from Agatha Kratz, Max J. Zenglein, and Gregor Sebastian, 2021, p. 9 (currency converted at the average exchange rate for the respective year). The reduction in FDI flows after 2016 can be attributed to a combination of Chinese restrictions on capital outflows, an economic slowdown in the PRC and the establishment of stricter screening mechanisms in Europe (on this point, see Betty Huang et al., 'China: Five Facts about Outward Direct Investment and their Implication for Future Trend', *BBVA Research—China Economic Watch*, March 2019, p. 1). The challenges of gathering systematic and comparable FDI data and the book's data selection are discussed in Appendix B.

[21] Data retrieved from National Bureau of Statistics of China, *Statistical Yearbooks of China*, http://www.stats.gov.cn/english/Statisticaldata/AnnualData/ (for details, see Appendix B).

[22] The '16+1' mechanism was initially a cooperation framework between China and Central and Eastern European countries that included Albania, Bosnia and Herzegovina, Bulgaria, Croatia, Czech Republic, Estonia, Hungary, Latvia, Lithuania, North Macedonia, Montenegro, Poland, Romania, Serbia, Slovakia, and Slovenia. Subsequently, Greece joined the group in 2019, making it the '17+1'. Then Lithuania withdrew in 2021, and the framework went back to its original label: '16+1'. See François Godement and Abigaël Vasselier, *China at the Gates: A New Power Audit of EU–China Relations* (London: European Council on Foreign Relations, 2017), pp. 64–74; Stuart Lau, 'Lithuania Pulls Out of China's "17+1" Bloc in Eastern Europe', *Politico EU*, 21 May 2021.

[23] Philippe Le Corre, 'Chinese Investments in European Countries: Experiences and Lessons for the "Belt and Road" Initiative', in *Rethinking the Silk Road: China's Belt and Road Initiative and Emerging Eurasian Relations*, edited by Maximilian Mayer (Singapore: Palgrave Macmillan, 2017), pp. 161–176; and Valbona Zenelli, 'Mapping China's Investments in Europe', *The Diplomat*, 14 March 2019.

[24] Agatha Kratz, Mikko Huotari, Thilo Hanemann, and Rebecca Arcesati, *Chinese FDI in Europe: 2019 Update—Special Topic: Research Collaborations*, Report by Rhodium Group (RHG) and MERICS, April 2020, pp. 7 and 13–14.

[25] Eva Rytter Sunesen and Morten May Hansen, *Screening of FDI towards the EU*, Report Commissioned by the Danish Business Authority, January 2018, p. 34.

[26] Datenna, 'China–EU FDI Radar', https://www.datenna.com/china-eu-fdi-radar/ (accessed 12 May 2021). On this point, see also European Court of Auditors, *The EU's Response to China's State-Driven Investment Strategy*, Review no. 3, 2020, p. 22.

The growing involvement of Chinese corporations—sustained and funded by state-directed plans—in the European industrial fabric provoked widespread concerns among Europe's major powers. As shown in the subsequent chapters, policymakers in Berlin, Paris, and London grew increasingly wary over how Chinese companies could siphon advanced dual-use technology, acquire strategic assets in Europe's critical infrastructure, erode the technological edge of European high-tech companies through discriminatory practices and potentially hinder the security of supply in civilian, dual-use, and military domains. They also feared that China's deepening economic imprint on the continent provided Beijing with political leverage that it could exploit to advance its interests at the expense of Europeans (although, after the Brexit referendum, this concern faded away in the United Kingdom).

China Enters Europe's Digital Infrastructure

A second, related area in which the PRC expanded its influence in Europe has been the digital sector. Leading Chinese companies such as ZTE and, most notably, Huawei Technologies consolidated their position as key providers of advanced telecommunications in Europe, first of 4G and subsequently of 5G technology.[27] As a world leader in this sector, Huawei maintained a global market share of 29 per cent (in 2018), ranking first among the top seven global telecommunications equipment vendors, ahead of American Cisco and Ciena, Swedish Ericsson, Finnish Nokia, South Korean Samsung, and Chinese ZTE Corporation.[28] Huawei's 'most spectacular growth in Europe', according to the company itself, took place in the second half of the 2010s.[29] Having first established itself as a leading 4G supplier, Huawei became the main manufacturer of 5G trial equipment in Europe, supplying fifty-one out of 180 trials (ahead of Ericsson and Nokia, with forty-three and thirty-seven respectively).[30] A report carried out by Oxford Economics and commissioned by Huawei assessed that the company's contribution to Europe's

---

[27] 4G refers to the fourth generation of mobile technology which followed the 2G and 3G networks that came before it. The standards for 4G, set by the radio sector of the International Telecommunication Union, include the secure provision for mobile service users with bandwidth higher than 100 Mbps. As further detailed later, fifth generation (5G) technology refers to network infrastructure elements for mobile and wireless communications technology with advanced performance characteristics such as very high data rates and capacity, low latency communications, ultra-high reliability, and the capacity to support a high number of connected devices. This definition is provided in the Official Journal of the European Union, 'Commission Recommendation (EU) 2019/534: Cybersercurity of 5G Networks', L. 88/45, 26 March 2019a.

[28] Thomas D. Lairson, 'The International Political Economy of Huawei's Global and Domestic Environment', in *Huawei Goes Global, Vol. I: Made in China for the World*, edited by Wenxian Zhang, Ilan Alon, and Christoph Lattemann (Cham, Switzerland: Palgrave Macmillan, 2020), p. 23.

[29] Huawei, 'The Win–Win Relationship between the EU and Huawei', *Factsheet*, May 2020, p. 1.

[30] Kristin Shi-Kupfer and Mareike Ohlberg, 'China's Digital Rise: Challenges for Europe', *MERICS Papers on China no. 7*, April 2019, p. 25.

GDP had increased by an average of 19.1 per cent per year (in real terms) between 2015 and 2019, supporting more than 224,000 jobs.[31] Building upon its successes in the supply of 4G and then 5G technology, Huawei's economic footprint spread across every European country, with the largest contribution going to the GDP of Germany, the United Kingdom, and France (with €3.7bn, €3.6bn, and €1.8bn, respectively).[32] The Chinese corporation also significantly invested in R&D networks, spending $1bn on its Innovation Research Programme in Europe, operating twenty-three research sites in collaboration with more than a hundred research institutions and universities across the continent, and participating in EU-funded research projects in IT systems.[33]

The increasingly central role of Huawei in the supply of key technologies for Europe's digital infrastructure caused mounting disquiet among Europe's three major powers, as detailed in Part II, because of its implications in the commercial, military, and intelligence domains. For one thing, 5G technology was projected to considerably augment the speed of data transfer and to improve bandwidth over previous generation systems (e.g. 4G and 3G), thereby enabling a range of civilian and commercial applications.[34] It would have commercial uses—in sectors such as energy, transport, banking, and health—supporting interconnected or autonomous devices such as smart homes, self-driving vehicles, industrial machinery, and advanced robotics.[35] But 5G networks would also have significant military applications: for instance, they would substantially improve intelligence, surveillance, and reconnaissance (ISR) systems and the processing, exploitation, and dissemination of large volumes of information; and they would streamline command and control (C2) as well as logistics systems.[36]

Besides the dual-use nature of 5G networks, their specific technological features, which increased the overall attack surface and the number of potential entry points for attackers (e.g. antennas and sensors), also raised cybersecurity concerns in Europe over the potential compromise of the confidentiality, availability, and integrity of digital networks.[37] Specifically, key scenarios of concern involved

---

[31] Oxford Economics, *The Economic Impact of Huawei* (London: Oxford Economics, 2020), p. 5. On the methodology used to assess the company's direct, indirect, and induced contribution to national GDPs, see pp. 8–9.
[32] Oxford Economics, 2020, p. 14.
[33] Oxford Economics, 2020, p. 5 (2019 data). For the list of EU-funded projects involving Huawei, see European Commission—Community Research and Development Information Service (CORDIS), 'Huawei', https://cordis.europa.eu.
[34] John R. Hoehn and Kelley M. Sayler, 'National Security Implications of Fifth Generation (5G) Mobile Technologies', *Congressional Research Service In Focus*, 12 June 2019, p. 1.
[35] Hoehn and Sayler, 2019, p. 1. See also Network and Information Systems (NIS) Cooperation Group, *Cybersecurity of 5G Networks EU Toolbox of Risk Mitigating Measures*, Report for the European Commission, January 2020, p. 5.
[36] Hoehn and Sayler, 2019, p. 1. See also Andrea Gilli, 'NATO and 5G: What Strategic Lessons?', NATO Defense College, *Policy Brief no. 13*, July 2020.
[37] NIS Cooperation Group, 2020, p. 33.

cyberattacks intended to disrupt the network, to spy over the data flows, to modify or reroute the data traffic, or to destroy (or alter) digital infrastructures.[38]

Relatedly, Huawei's suspected ties with China's intelligence services, coupled with the fact that China's 2017 National Intelligence Law compels any company or citizen to 'support, provide assistance, and cooperate in national intelligence work',[39] led to suspicions among European powers over the degree of cooperation between Huawei and Chinese state security services, including with regard to the potential installation of backdoors.[40] Although it is formally a private company, Huawei was founded in 1987 by a former engineer in the People's Liberation Army (PLA) and had as its chairwoman (1999–2018) a former official in the Communications Division of the Ministry of State Security.[41] It is owned at 99 per cent by the Huawei Trade Union Committee which, like all trade unions in China, is subject to the Chinese Communist Party (CCP) authority, thus making the company an 'indirectly state-owned enterprise'.[42] And not only did the PRC provide Huawei with billions of dollars in loans and export credits through various state banks and credit institutions,[43] but the company reportedly also received funding from China's National Security Commission, the PLA, and a branch of the Chinese state intelligence network, according to the CIA.[44]

In light of the mounting security concerns fuelled by China's deepening foothold on the continent, Part II delineates how Europe's three major powers have confronted Beijing's rising clout and ambitions in Europe since the end of the Cold War. It focuses on the key policy instruments that they devised to confront the security challenges linked to China's investment in, and supply of, sensitive technologies, namely FDI screening mechanisms and the restrictions on telecommunications suppliers of concern, like Huawei, to protect Europe's digital infrastructure. Certainly, Europe's three major powers—as well as the European Union—have also promoted other policy tools, such as the EU

---

[38] NIS Cooperation Group, 2020, p. 12. On China's espionage practices, see William C. Hannas, James Mulvenon, and Anna B. Puglisi, *Chinese Industrial Espionage: Technology Acquisition and Military Modernization* (New York: Routledge, 2013).

[39] Standing Committee of the National People's Congress, 'National Intelligence Law of the People's Republic of China (2018 Amendment)', 2018, http://en.pkulaw.cn/display.aspx?cgid=313975&lib=law.

[40] NIS Cooperation Group, 2020, p. 33; Grieger, 2017, p. 2.

[41] Mathieu Duchâtel and François Godement, *Europe and 5G: The Huawei Case*, Institut Montaigne, Note, June 2019, p. 6.

[42] Lairson, 2020, p. 17. For an analysis of Huawei's ownership structure, see also Colin Hawes, 'Why is Huawei's Ownership So Strange? A Case Study of the Chinese Corporate and Socio-Political Ecosystem', *Journal of Corporate Law Studies 21*, no. 1 (2020): pp. 1–38, doi:10.1080/14,735,970.2020.1809161; Raymond Zhang, 'Who Owns Huawei? The Company Tried to Explain. It Got Complicated', *The New York Times*, 25 April 2019.

[43] Jean-Marc F. Blanchard, 'Helping Hands for Huawei: Dialing into China's Technology Policy to Understand Its Contemporary Support for Huawei', in *Huawei Goes Global, Vol. I: Made in China for the World*, edited by Wenxian Zhang, Ilan Alon, and Christoph Lattemann (Cham, Switzerland: Palgrave Macmillan, 2020), p. 74; Cheung et al., 2020, pp. 179–180.

[44] Reuters Staff, 'US Intelligence Says Huawei Funded by Chinese State Security: Report', *Reuters*, 20 April 2019.

Connectivity Strategy, the European Union–China Comprehensive Agreement on Investment, international public procurement or 'anti-coercive' instruments, among others.[45] Yet, given the focus of this book, Part II specifically examines these two measures (FDI screening mechanisms and restrictions of telecommunications suppliers) since they have been purposely devised to tackle the national security concerns posed by China's growing foothold in the European high-tech industrial landscape.

It will be shown that mounting threat perceptions of China's rise in the 2010s—coupled with increasingly competitive bilateral economic relations with the PRC—have caused the hardening of each country's policy goals, which, in turn, translated into new, more stringent policy instruments. Beijing's aggressive inroads into Europe's most sensitive high-tech sectors—and national policymakers' perceptions thereof—have been the key driver of the change in the 'China policies' of the Big Three (coupled with Chinese assertiveness in the Asia-Pacific which concomitantly spurred rising concerns, as discussed in Part I). Whereas in the first two decades after the Cold War they looked at China largely through economic lenses, during the 2010s they have come to perceive the PRC's rising clout in Europe as posing major security challenges. Specifically, they have become increasingly alarmed by the security ramifications of China's expanding foothold in Europe's industrial landscape, and by the resulting capacity of Beijing to use its economic and political ties across the continent to drive a wedge among Europeans and exploit intra-European fragmentation. Gradually and cumulatively, these heightened threat perceptions—coupled with increasingly competitive economic relations with China—have caused France, Germany, and the United Kingdom to recalibrate and harden their national policy goals vis-à-vis Beijing by putting greater emphasis on national security considerations. Likewise, at the EU level, they have promoted enhanced coordination in order to reduce their exposure to potential Chinese pressure and retaliation, and to acquire negotiating leverage over China (even though, as detailed in Chapter 6, the United Kingdom abandoned this objective after Brexit). In implementing these policy goals, the Big Three have mobilized a combination of national and EU policy instruments to strengthen their capacity to monitor and, if needed, to veto Chinese FDIs and to restrict 5G suppliers of concern such as Huawei—although the United Kingdom adopted an increasingly ambivalent position on EU instruments as it entered the process of exiting from the European Union. Thereby, they have neither opted to

---

[45] On these instruments, see for instance European Commission, 'EU–China Comprehensive Agreement on Investment (CAI)', *News Archive*, 22 January 2021a, https://trade.ec.europa.eu/doclib/press/index.cfm?id=2237; Council of the European Union, 'A Globally Connected Europe', Council Conclusions, 12 July 2021b; European Commission, 'Connecting Europe and Asia—Building Blocks for an EU Strategy', Joint Communication JOIN(2018) 31 final, Brussels, 18 September 2018; European Parliament, 'A New EU International Procurement Instrument (IPI)', *Legislative Train*, August 2021a; and European Commission, 'EU Strengthens Protection against Economic Coercion', *Press Corner*, 8 December 2021e, https://ec.europa.eu/commission/presscorner/detail/en/ip_21_6642.

contain China, nor to systematically align with the United States, nor to maintain equidistance between the two (because of their closer commonalities with the United States on many issues). Instead, they have sought to define an autonomous position for themselves in the context of rising United States–China strategic competition.

To corroborate this argument, the country-based chapters of Part II are organized as follows. The first two sections of each chapter examine two key drivers of the country's policy towards Beijing, namely its economic interests in fostering Chinese capital inflows and its threat perceptions of China's foothold in Europe respectively. The two following sections show how these drivers have, in turn, caused their policy goals and the resulting policy instruments to change over time. Each section first provides an overview of the first two post-Cold War decades and then presents an in-depth analysis of the 2010s. Thereby, the chapters of Part II jointly shed light on how and why the 2010s witnessed a major policy shift in the Big Three's 'China policies'.

4
France and the Rise of China
From Open Door to Clear-Eyed

Introduction

France's policy towards the People's Republic of China (PRC) followed a parallel trajectory to that of its larger regional policy in the Asia-Pacific. China's increasingly muscular posture in the Indian and Pacific Oceans regions coupled with its concurrent expanding reach into Europe sparked France to harden its 'China policy'. This chapter examines how France has grappled with China's rising assertiveness on the European continent. In particular, it examines Paris's response to Chinese foreign direct investments (FDIs) into sensitive sectors and to its supply of telecommunications (or telecoms) equipment for France's digital infrastructure. It will be shown that, after two decades in which Paris mostly focused on the pursuit of economic opportunities, concerns over China's inroads into strategic sectors in France and in Europe in the 2010s—coupled with increasingly competitive bilateral economic relations—have been the main driver of change in France's 'China policy'.

Throughout the 1990s and 2000s, France displayed growing economic interests in the vast Chinese market, while French policymakers exhibited few security concerns vis-à-vis China's limited presence on the European continent. The PRC was largely perceived as an emerging power whose technological capabilities lagged far behind those of the French high-tech industry. Therefore, even its industrial espionage and cyber practices, although concerning, were not deemed to pose a major security challenge. It is in the 2010s, fuelled by China's growing foothold in the French and European high-tech industrial fabric, that French threat perceptions heightened at a time when economic relations with Beijing also became more competitive as the result of China's moving up the value-added ladder (on the concomitant rising concerns over Chinese behaviour in the Asia-Pacific, see chapter 1). Chinese FDIs increasingly targeted sensitive sectors, while Chinese corporations like Huawei became important suppliers of advanced telecommunications equipment for France's digital infrastructure. As a result of these shifting economic interests and threat assessment, France hardened the goals of its 'China policy', putting greater emphasis on security considerations, after two decades in which it had overwhelmingly prioritized deepening economic and diplomatic engagement with China. To that end, Paris strengthened its national policy instruments to better monitor and restrict both FDIs in sensitive sectors and the role of telecoms suppliers of concern like Huawei, first for 4G and subsequently for 5G technology. At the same time, France played a significant role in the development of EU policy instruments such as the EU FDI screening mechanisms and the EU Toolbox for 5G Cybersecurity.

The remainder of the chapter proceeds as follows. The first two sections delineate the two main drivers of France's policy towards the PRC, i.e. the evolving French economic interests vis-à-vis China—as its economic imprint in Europe expanded—and Paris's heightened threat perceptions of the PRC. The chapter then shows how these evolving economic interests and threat assessment, in turn, caused France to harden the goals of its 'China policy' and to bolster the policy instruments that it mobilized to achieve such goals.

Economic Interests

The Sino-French economic relationship has steadfastly deepened since the end of the Cold War, although from a low starting point and with significant imbalances. During the 1990s and 2000s, whereas China emerged as a major recipient of French exports and investments, the PRC's economic presence in France, though rising, remained fairly modest.[1] It is only in the subsequent decade that its FDIs in France substantially increased while Chinese corporations became ever more important providers of advanced telecoms equipment. As such, the PRC's presence in France noticeably expanded, although remaining smaller than in other major European powers.

Small Yet Growing Chinese Economic Presence

Chinese FDIs in France rose in the 2000s in large part as a result of Beijing's 'Go Out' policy—initiated in 1999 and intended to encourage corporations to invest overseas.[2] While between 1993 and 2003 Chinese companies had made only six investment projects in France (creating 235 jobs),[3] the stock of Chinese FDIs in

---

[1] On French investments in China and on the broader bilateral economic relationship, see Chapter 1. See also the comparative charts in Appendix B.

[2] On China's 'Go Out' policy and the rise of its FDIs in Europe, see Françoise Nicolas and Stephen Thomsen, 'The Rise of Chinese Firms in Europe: Motives, Strategies and Implications', Draft Paper for presentation at the Asia Pacific Economic Association Conference, Beijing, 13–14 December 2008, pp. 3–9.

[3] National Assembly, *Les échanges commerciaux entre la Chine et la France*, Report no. 2473. Committee on Finance, General Economics and the Plan, 13 July 2005a, p. 54. See also Senate, *L'Agence française pour les investissements internationaux (AFII)*, Report no. 453, 5 July 2006, p. 19.

France increased from $34m in 2005 to $221m in 2009, and gradually shifted from trade representative offices to also include production, manufacturing, assembly, and research and development (R&D) activities.[4]

The bulk of these investments, mostly by government-controlled enterprises, went into the chemical sector (totalling 40 per cent of all jobs created by Chinese firms) and, to a lesser extent, in the electronics and telecommunication equipment sectors, followed by the automobile industry, machinery, and mechanical equipment industry.[5] Through these investments, Chinese firms sought to increase their market shares, enable faster entry into new markets, and obtain French advanced technology.[6] France also attracted Chinese companies because of its location at the heart of the European market and because, given its post-colonial ties, it offered a springboard into the markets of French-speaking countries in West and North Africa.[7]

In the telecommunications sector, Chinese firms became increasingly active through the establishment of R&D laboratories in France. Huawei first entered the French market in 2003.[8] By the mid-to-late 2000s, it established R&D centres in Lannion and Cergy-Pontoise while ZTE set up a research, training, and maintenance centre at the Futuroscope technology park near Poitiers, and a R&D centre in Boulogne-Billancourt.[9]

Yet, throughout the decade, not only did the volume of Chinese FDIs in France remain quite low and continued to be dwarfed by French investments in the PRC, but several of these investments failed.[10] Examples include Chinese investments in the information and communications technology (ICT) and electronics sectors, such as in Alcatel Mobile, Thomson, Novel Vision, or the Société Européenne de

---

[4] Data retrieved from National Bureau of Statistics of China, *Statistical Yearbooks of China*, http://www.stats.gov.cn/english/Statisticaldata/AnnualData/ (for details, see Appendix B). On the shifting sectoral focus of Chinese FDIs, see Françoise Nicolas, 'Chinese Direct Investments in France: No French Exception, No Chinese Challenge', Chatham House, *IE Programme Paper IE PP 2010/2*, January 2010, pp. 12 and 17 (based upon figures from the Chinese Ministry of Commerce, MOFCOM), https://www.ifri.org/fr/publications/publications-ifri/articles-ifri/chinese-direct-investments-france-no-french-exception.

[5] Nicolas, 2010, p. 19.

[6] Agyenim Boateng, Wang Qian, and Yang Tianle, 'Cross-Border M&As by Chinese Firms: An Analysis of Strategic Motives and Performance', *Thunderbird International Business Review* 50, no. 4 (2008): p. 259.

[7] Ni Gao and Jan Schaaper, 'Chinese Companies Go Global: The Case of Chinese Investments in France', in *China's Global Political Economy: Managerial Perspectives*, edited by Robert Taylor and Jacques Jaussaud (London: Routledge, 2018), p. 127. See also David Appia, President of the French Agency for International Investments (AFII), 'Les investissements chinois en France et en Europe, quel impact sur l'emploi ?', Proceedings of the Conference *Rencontres économiques : Quel impact de l'expansion chinoise sur l'économie mondiale ?*, Institute for Public Management and Economic Development (IGPDE), 18 September 2012, p. 9.

[8] Brigitte Dyan and Hubert Testard, *Quand la Chine investit en France* (Paris: Agence Française pour les Investissements, 2014), p. 55.

[9] Nicolas, 2010, pp. 18–19 and 28.

[10] Nicolas, 2010, pp. 15 and 37–38.

Production d'Écrans Plats (SEPEP) which either ceased production, were subsequently acquired by other companies or were placed in compulsory liquidation.[11] Overall, France thus continued to be 'overshadowed', as one analyst puts it, by 'Germany's strength in key industrial sectors and by the UK's attractiveness', ranking third among EU destinations of Chinese investors.[12]

China's Broadening Economic Foothold

In the 2010s, however, largely because of Beijing's financial and regulatory support, investments by Chinese companies into France—and more broadly in Europe—considerably expanded and the range of targeted sectors diversified.[13] Nonetheless, the volume of China's FDIs remained relatively low in relation to its investments in other major European countries (see the comparative charts of Chinese FDIs in the Big Three in Appendix B).[14]

As Sino-French bilateral trade expanded and as China became France's fifth largest trading partner, the PRC's foothold in the French economy also increased.[15] The stock of FDIs in France grew considerably, rising from $0.2bn in 2010 to $6bn in 2019.[16] In 2019, China was the seventh largest source country of FDIs and the leading Asian investor in France.[17] In particular, these investments went into decision-making centres such as headquarters (28 per cent) and into R&D (14 per cent).[18] The main business sectors in which Chinese companies invested encompassed aerospace, naval and railway equipment, electronic and information technology equipment as well as sporting, recreative activities, and leisure.[19]

Some notable Chinese investments in France included, among others: the 2011 acquisition by the China Investment Corporation (CIC) of a 30 per cent stake in the exploration and production division of the energy company GDF Suez (subsequently renamed Engie) for €2.3bn, then expanded to 49 per cent in 2017; CIC's 2012 investment in the satellite company Eutelsat; Dongfeng's capital injection into

---

[11] Nicolas, 2010, pp. 37–38.
[12] Nicolas, 2010, p. 2. See the comparative charts of Chinese FDIs in the Big Three in Appendix B.
[13] See Thilo Hanemann and Mikko Huotari, 'Record Flows and Growing Imbalances: Chinese Investment in Europe in 2016', *MERICS Paper on China no. 3*, January 2017; Thilo Hanemann, Mikko Huotari, and Agatha Kratz, *Chinese FDI in Europe, 2018 Trends and Impact of New Screening Policies*, Report by Rhodium Group and Mercator Institute for China Studies (MERICS), March 2019, p. 7.
[14] See the comparative charts on China's FDIs in the Big Three in Appendix B.
[15] MFA, 'Fiche Pays—Repères économiques', Direction de la diplomatie économique, April 2021b, https://www.diplomatie.gouv.fr/fr/politique-etrangere-de-la-france/diplomatie-economique-et-commerce-exterieur/la-france-et-ses-partenaires-economiques-pays-par-pays/asie/article/chine.
[16] Data retrieved from National Bureau of Statistics of China, *Statistical Yearbooks of China*, http://www.stats.gov.cn/english/Statisticaldata/AnnualData/ (for details, see Appendix B).
[17] Agatha Kratz, Mikko Huotari, Thilo Hanemann, and Rebecca Arcesati, *Chinese FDI in Europe: 2019 Update—Special Topic: Research Collaborations*, Report by Rhodium Group (RHG) and the Mercator Institute for China Studies (MERICS), April 2020, p. 11; Business France, *Annual Report: Foreign Investment in France*, 2019, pp. 32–34.
[18] Business France, 2019, p. 101.
[19] Business France, 2019, p. 101.

the ailing automaker Peugeot in 2014; Fosun's investment in Club Méditerranée in 2014; the Jin Jiang Group's 2015 purchase of Louvre Hotels Group; the 2015 acquisition of a 49.99 per cent stake in the Toulouse-Blagnac Airport by China Airport Synergy Investment Limited (CASIL); or the acquisition of the French semiconductor company Linxens by Tsinghua Unigroup in 2018, among many others.[20] As further discussed in Chapter 6, China General Nuclear Power Corporation (CGN) and the French utility company Électricité de France (EDF) also signed an agreement in 2015 for the construction and operation of the Hinkley Point C nuclear power station in the United Kingdom, and for the joint development of new nuclear power stations at Sizewell and Bradwell.[21]

In the telecommunications sector, Chinese companies such as Huawei expanded their presence in France, although comparatively less so than in other major European countries. In 2014, Huawei founder Ren Zhengfei announced that the company would invest €1.5bn in France over three years, focusing on its smartphone business.[22] At the end of the decade, Huawei provided 52 per cent of SFR's 4G radio access network (RAN), 47.5 per cent of Bouygues Telecom's RAN, but only 0.7 per cent of Free's network (and none for Orange, which relied instead entirely on Nokia and Ericsson).[23]

By 2020, Huawei had six research centres in France focusing on both fundamental and applied research, e.g. wireless communications, artificial intelligence, design, image processing, and sensors.[24] The Chinese corporation also announced

---

[20] In 2020, CASIL's stake in the Toulouse-Blagnac Airport was sold to the French conglomerate Eiffage. For details on the listed investments, see: French Embassy in China, 'Investissements chinois dans le monde : perte de vitesse depuis deux ans, recentrage vers l'ASEAN et les pays des routes de la soie', Economic Section in Beijing, 29 October 2020 (shared by the MEF with the author); Zak Bentley, 'Chinese Investors End Controversial Toulouse Airport Reign with €500m Departure', *Infrastructure Investor*, 3 January 2020, https://www.infrastructureinvestor.com/chinese-investors-end-controversial-toulouse-airport-reign-with-e500m-departure/; Clara Denina and Ron Bousso, 'Neptune Nears Engie E&P Deal after CIC Ups Stake', *Reuters*, 21 April 2017; Thilo Hanemann, Cassie Gao, and Agatha Kratz, *Comparing Chinese Investment into North America and Europe*, Rhodium Group and Baker McKenzie, 13 January 2019, p. 43; Joseph Percy, 'Chinese FDI in the EU's Top 4 Economies', *China Briefing*, 8 May 2019; John Seaman, 'Chinese Investment in France: An Openly Cautious Welcome', in *Chinese Investment in Europe A Country-Level Approach*, edited by John Seaman, Mikko Huotari, and Miguel Otero-Iglesias (Paris: French Institute of International Relations, 2017), p. 57.
[21] EDF, 'Agreements in Place for Construction of Hinkley Point C Nuclear Power Station', *Press Release*, 21 October 2015, https://www.edf.fr/sites/default/files/contrib/en-en/groupe-edf/espaces-dedies/medias-data/pr/cp_20151021_hinkley_va.pdf.
[22] Romain Gueugneau, 'Huawei mise 1,5 milliard d'euros sur la France', *Les Echos*, 29 September 2014.
[23] Senate, *Rapport sur la proposition de loi, adoptée par l'Assemblée nationale après engagement de la procédure accélérée, visant à préserver les intérêts de la défense et de la sécurité nationale de la France dans le cadre de l'exploitation des réseaux radioélectriques mobiles*, Economic Affairs Committee, Report no. 579, 19 June 2019a, p. 30 (2019 figures); and Anne Morris, 'France Unlikely to Ban Huawei, But Will Encourage Operators to Steer Clear', *LightReading*, 7 June 2020.
[24] 'Huawei Opens Research Center in Paris', *XinhuaNet*, 10 October 2020; Bertrand Graré, 'Huawei ouvre un 6ème centre de R&D en France', *L'informaticien*, 12 October 2020.

its intention to build a production plant for equipment for 3G, 4G, and 5G antennas in Brumath, in northeastern France, a first of its kind outside of China.[25] As a result, according to a report carried out by Oxford Economics and commissioned by Huawei, the Chinese company now contributed to France's GDP with €1.8bn, which nonetheless amounted to less than half of its contribution to the German and British GDP (with €3.7bn and €3.6bn respectively).[26] Likewise, in its 'Roadmap for 5G', the government stressed that the deployment of 5G networks—of which Huawei was a leading supplier—would be a 'driver for the digitalisation of the whole economy' and was thus 'a priority'.[27]

Threat Perceptions

As a result of China's deepening and widening economic foothold in France—especially in sensitive sectors—and of its growing assertiveness on the European continent, French threat assessment shifted. In the first two post-Cold War decades, partly because of its light presence in Europe and its profound technological gaps, French policymakers perceived the PRC as an emerging market that posed few security challenges. However, starting in the late 2000s and increasingly in the 2010s, China's growing clout in Europe—and its expanding reach into strategic sectors—caused French threat perceptions to heighten, which, in turn, drove a recalibration in the goals of France's 'China policy'.

Low Security Concerns: China as an Emerging Country Seeking to Catch Up

As explained by a senior official in President Jacques Chirac's administration, from the end of the Cold War to the late 2000s, Paris 'did not consider Chinese foreign direct investments as a security concern'; 'these investments were seen as part of a large effort to catch up technologically with the West by equipping China with technologies that it desperately needed and lacked; this was both understandable and normal.'[28] The former High Representative for Economic Intelligence (2003–2009) in the Office of Prime Ministers Jean-Pierre Raffarin and then Dominique de

---

[25] 'Huawei Will Set up its French Factory in Brumath', *Archyde*, 21 December 2020, https://www.archyde.com/huawei-will-set-up-its-french-factory-in-brumath.

[26] Oxford Economics, *The Economic Impact of Huawei* (London: Oxford Economics, 2020), p. 14; on the methodology used to assess the direct, indirect, and induced contribution to national GDPs, see pp. 8–9.

[27] Quote from Electronic Communications, Postal and Print Media Distribution Regulatory Authority (ARCEP), *5G : Une feuille de route ambitieuse pour la France*, 16 July 2018, p. 7. On the deployment of 5G in France, see the ARCEP's 5G observatory: https://www.arcep.fr/cartes-et-donnees/nos-cartes/deploiement-5g/observatoire-du-deploiement-5g-fevrier-2021.html.

[28] Interview, 2 April 2021.

Villepin, Alain Juillet, confirms that, throughout the 2000s, 'China's foreign direct investments in France were not perceived as posing significant security risks; in fact, not only was their volume relatively modest, but the main concerns throughout the decade really revolved around US investments in French strategic sectors, rather than China'.[29] In particular, FDIs such as the investment by US companies like the Texas Pacific Group in the microchip manufacturer Gemplus in 2000, and Alcan's acquisition of Péchiney, an aluminum conglomerate, in 2003, sparked major apprehension over the future of France's technological industrial base.[30] With regards to FDIs in French strategic sectors, the United States was thus a greater source of concern than the PRC.

One area that was being closely monitored was China's increasingly active industrial espionage and its theft of advanced technologies, including through cyber-attacks, especially in the 2000s.[31] According to a former official in the Secretariat-General for National Defence and Security (SGDSN), the interministerial coordinating body in charge of political-military affairs in the Prime Minister's Office, Paris witnessed 'a clear increase in Chinese attempts at collecting information on sensitive French scientific and technological assets, both through the industry and through universities and research institutes, including in the nuclear, aerospace, and dual-use sectors'.[32] By 2008, as a MoD report stressed, 'major attacks against information systems' had become 'a rising concern'.[33]

Yet, according to the former High Representative for Economic Intelligence (2003–2009), 'although disquiet emerged over its industrial espionage and theft of advanced technologies, China was seen not only as a massive market but also as a developing country whose technological capabilities lagged far behind those of the French high-tech industry. Accordingly, these practices—although concerning—were not deemed to pose a major threat in that they would not undermine the technological edge of French companies over their Chinese counterparts'.[34] Overall, with the exception of China's industrial espionage and cyber activities (and of concerns in the nuclear domain, detailed in Chapter 1), French

---

[29] Interview, 2 April 2021.
[30] Alain Juillet, interview, 2 April 2021. See also National Assembly, *Participation de capitaux étrangers aux industries européennes de l'armement*, no. 2022, Committee on National Defence and Armed Forces, 23 March 2005b, pp. 14–17 and 29.
[31] Interviews with former diplomats, defence, and intelligence officials, January–April 2021. On Chinese cyber-attacks in France, see also Senate, *Cyberdéfense*, Report no. 449, Committee on Foreign Affairs, Defence and Armed Forces, 8 July 2008, pp. 5–11. In a high-visibility case in the mid-2000s, a Chinese student, Li Li Whuang, was convicted for industrial espionage in the French company Valeo ('Soupçonnée d'espionnage industriel, une étudiante chinoise est finalement condamnée pour "abus de confiance"', *Le Monde*, 18 December 2007).
[32] Interview, 20 April 2021.
[33] MoD, 'The French White Paper on Defence and National Security', Press Kit, 2008b, http://archives.livreblancdefenseetsecurite.gouv.fr/2008/IMG/pdf/white_paper_press_kit.pdf.
[34] Alain Juillet, interview, 2 April 2021.

policymakers largely perceived the PRC through economic lenses, with little emphasis on national security considerations.

Rising Concerns over Chinese Assertiveness in Europe

During the 2010s, however, the threat perceptions of French policymakers intensified in response to China's expanding foothold in France and in Europe (at a time when the PRC's behaviour also became more assertive in the Asia-Pacific, as discussed in Chapter 4). As stressed by one Ministry of Foreign Affairs (MFA) official, 'our threat assessment changed because China was getting closer to Europe; we witnessed a growing presence of China in our "backyard" which did not exist before. So, as the Chinese risk approached, French perceptions evolved.'[35] In particular, the main areas of concern revolved around the intertwined security, economic, and political ramifications of China's growing presence in France and on the European continent.

Security Concerns: Acquisition of Sensitive Technologies and the Cybersecurity of the Digital Infrastructure

For one thing, French policymakers grew alarmed by the national security implications of Chinese investments in, and supply of, sensitive technologies in strategic sectors. The growing volume of Chinese FDIs in France was accompanied by rising fears over the PRC's attempts at obtaining dual-use technologies, with FDIs being one vehicle for such acquisitions.[36] As a former MFA official explains, 'the government grew aware of how certain Chinese investments were targeting the acquisition of sensitive technologies. The fear was that through these investments they would obtain sensitive technologies that could be used, for instance, in weapon systems.'[37] Relatedly, according to an official in the Ministry for the Economy and Finance (MEF), a significant concern spurred by Chinese investments in the advanced technological sector was linked to China's 'civil-military fusion'; 'with China it is really hard to identify the frontier between what relates to economic applications and what relates to national security applications, notably because the frontier between public and private sectors is blurred in China.'[38] Accordingly, the MoD stressed the need 'to better identify supply chain risks', and concluded that China, 'now endowed with unprecedented capabilities',

---

[35] Interview, 18 November 2016.
[36] Seaman, 2017, p. 59.
[37] Interview, 10 March 2020.
[38] Interview, 25 March 2021. On this point, see for instance, Tai Ming Cheung and Eric Hagt, 'China's Efforts in Civil–Military Integration, its Impact on the Development of China's Acquisition System, and Implications for the United States', in *Proceedings of the 16th Annual Acquisition Research Symposium—Volume I* (Monterey, CA: Naval Postgraduate School, 2019), pp. 146–171.

was 'wielding its new economic and industrial weight' and bolstering its 'efforts relating to espionage' and 'technological appropriation'.[39]

These apprehensions went hand in hand with mounting controversies over the role of Chinese companies like Huawei in the supply of digital technology. Starting in the early 2010s, suspicions first emerged over the risks linked to Huawei's supply of core network routers for 4G infrastructures. These routers, which are used in large computer networks to manage the flow of data packets within digital networks, were deemed 'highly sensitive equipment because they have the capacity to intercept, analyse, exfiltrate, modify, or destroy any information' that passes through the network.[40] In discussing the supply of 4G technology by Huawei, a 2012 Senate report stressed how 'nothing would prevent a country producing this type of equipment from placing a vulnerability [e.g. a 'backdoor'] to monitor, intercept, or even interrupt all communication flows', adding that, in that regard, there were 'strong suspicions' that China was a major source of cyber-attacks in France 'for the purposes of economic espionage'.[41] Huawei and ZTE, in particular, were considered to 'raise serious concerns' because of 'the companies' links with the Chinese government and suspicion of computer espionage hanging over China'.[42] The Senate report therefore advocated for a full-blown prohibition of core network routers produced by Chinese companies, stressing that it was 'crucial that the European Union establish a total ban on the deployment and use of Chinese routers, or of other large equipment computers of Chinese origin', with a direct reference to Huawei and ZTE.[43]

These worries were further amplified after the French company Alcatel-Lucent—which produced, among other things, 4G core network equipment like routers—was sold to Nokia in 2015.[44] The French government soon realized that the only remaining suppliers of core network equipment were henceforth either American (e.g. Cisco) or Chinese (Huawei). As explained by the then MFA's Ambassador for Cyber Diplomacy and the Digital Economy (2015–2017) and later Ambassador for Digital Affairs (2017–2018), David Martinon, 'this dependency was perceived as a vulnerability and as a potential threat because when you supply core network equipment, at the very least this provides the capacity to map

---

[39] MoD, *Strategic Update*, January 2021, pp. 20–21 and 39.
[40] Senate, *Cyberdéfense*, Report no. 681, Committee on Foreign Affairs, Defence and Armed Forces, 18 July 2012a, p. 135.
[41] Senate, 2012a, p. 145.
[42] Senate, 2012a, p. 136.
[43] Senate, 2012a, pp. 145–146.
[44] Jussi Rosendahl and Leila Abboud, 'Nokia Buys Alcatel to Take on Ericsson in Telecom Equipment', *Reuters*, 15 April 2015; John Rath, 'Alcatel-Lucent Introduces New Core Routers', *Data Center Knowledge*, 24 May 2012, https://www.datacenterknowledge.com/archives/2012/05/24/alcatel-lucent-introduces-new-core-routers.

and monitor the digital network; this was the case for Huawei.'[45] Specifically, as he explains, the main concerns among French policymakers revolved around, 'at the very minimum, Huawei's capacity to monitor the digital network, but also potential risks of intrusion, espionage and network disruption or paralysis. Of course, we knew our American partners were also active in the cyber domain; but this was the classic problem of having to choose between the threat of Chinese espionage and concerns over a more "friendly" challenge posed by US practices. The decision was therefore taken to exclude Huawei from the market of 4G core networks equipment' (as detailed later).[46]

The emergence of 5G wireless technology—which French policymakers saw as a 'technological rupture'—further amplified the risks of cyber-espionage and disruption of France's digital infrastructure.[47] For one thing, compared to the technical characteristics of previous generations (such as 3G and 4G), fifth-generation networks displayed 'a greater surface area of vulnerability' to cyber-attacks because of their 'high capillarity', with more antennas and sensors.[48] 5G networks were thus seen as more vulnerable to cyber-attacks intended to spy over data traffic or to disrupt parts of the network for the purpose of sabotage.[49] Specifically, according to the Ministry of Interior's National Security Science and Technology Observatory (ONISTS), 'the main threats' linked to 5G networks were related to 'their confidentiality (surveillance, theft, or redirection of traffic or data), their availability (disruption of the local or global network) or their integrity (alteration or destruction of network infrastructures)'.[50] In turn, the main vulnerabilities could result, among other things, from the hardware or software (e.g. quality of product design, backdoors, quality of the network architecture, lack of physical security in the network infrastructures), from flaws in the procedures (e.g. poorly controlled remote maintenance), or from the choice of third suppliers, with the 'risk of dependence on a single unreliable supplier or on foreign suppliers subject to pressure from a

---

[45] David Martinon, interview, 5 May 2021.
[46] David Martinon, interview, 5 May 2021.
[47] Quote from ARCEP, 2018, p. 7.
[48] Éric Bothorel, Committee Rapporteur, in National Assembly, *Rapport sur La Proposition de Loi visant à préserver les intérêts de la défense et de la sécurité nationale de la France dans le cadre de l'exploitation des réseaux radioélectriques mobiles*, Economic Affairs Committee, no. 1832, 13 April 2018a, p. 8. See also Senate, 2019a, p. 16.
[49] On the vulnerability of 5G networks to cyber-attacks, see Senate, 2019a, pp. 15–24; National Assembly, 2018a, pp. 5–6. This point was confirmed in interviews with MEF officials, March and April 2021. On the link between digitization and growing cybersecurity risks, see Ministry of Interior, *État de la menace liée au numérique en 2019*, May 2019, p. 10; and Secretariat-General for National Defence and Security (SGDSN), *Revue stratégique de cyberdéfense*, 12 February 2018, p. 15. See also ANSSI, 'Cybersecurity in France', https://www.ssi.gouv.fr/en/cybersecurity-in-france.
[50] Ministry of Interior's National Security Science and Technology Observatory (ONISTS), 'Réseau 5G et Cybersécurité', https://www.gendarmerie.interieur.gouv.fr/onsts/ressources-documentaires/veille-technologique/reseau-5g-cybersecurite.

foreign state'.[51] Accordingly, the expected growth in the use of 5G networks was seen as posing a significant national security challenge.[52]

Concurrently, the 2010s witnessed the growth in both the 'sophistication and intensity' of cyber-attacks, with China being a leading source thereof.[53] Examples of Chinese cyber-attacks included the 2010–2011 intrusion in the Ministry of Economy and Finance, which stole confidential information on the preparation of the G20, or the repeated cyber-attacks against the aerospace corporation Airbus, among numerous others.[54] In 2017, the MoD stressed how cyberattacks could "inflict significant industrial damage" or "impair networks and infrastructures critical to the proper functioning of societies or states."[55] Furthermore, according to a 2020 report of the Parliamentary Delegation on Intelligence, which oversees the government on behalf of both the Senate and the National Assembly, the 'modus operandi' of Chinese cyber-attacks increasingly resorted to the 'disruption of the supply chains of their targets' and exhibited growing efforts at 'concealment in order to complicate any technical attribution'.[56]

These perceived threats linked to the technical vulnerabilities of 5G networks and to the growth in Chinese cyber-attacks coalesced with specific concerns over Chinese companies like Huawei. This tech corporation was suspected of having close ties with the Chinese state and its security services in light of its ownership structure, the large volume of subsidies it received from Beijing (allowing it to offer lower prices than those of its competitors) and the 2017 National Intelligence Law which, in the words of a French Senate report, compelled 'all Chinese companies

---

[51] ONSTS, 'Réseau 5G et Cybersécurité'. See also Légifrance, 'Loi n° 2019-810 du 1er août 2019 visant à préserver les intérêts de la défense et de la sécurité nationale de la France dans le cadre de l'exploitation des réseaux radioélectriques mobiles', 2 August 2019c, https://www.legifrance.gouv.fr/jorf/id/JORFTEXT000038864094.

[52] National Assembly, *Compte rendu no. 31*, Committee on National Defence and the Armed Forces, 2 April 2019b, pp. 2–5; and Éric Bothorel, Committee Rapporteur, in National Assembly, 2018a, p. 8.

[53] Quote from MFA, 'Garantir la cybersécurité', November 2020b, https://www.diplomatie.gouv.fr/fr/politique-etrangere-de-la-france/diplomatie-numerique/garantir-la-cybersecurite/ (accessed on 1 December 2021). On the growing cyber-threats faced by France, see Minister of Defence Jean-Yves Le Drian (2012–2017), Speech on Cyber-defence, 12 December 2016b; SGDSN 2018; National Assembly, *Cyberdéfense*, Report no. 1141, Committee on National Defence and Armed Forces, 4 July 2018b, pp. 31–38; and Senate, *La sécurité informatique des pouvoirs publics*, Report no. 82, Finance Committee, 22 October 2019c, pp. 7–8 and 11–12. On the concerns over Chinese influence operations in France, see Senate, *Les influences étatiques extra-européennes dans le monde universitaire et académique français et leurs incidences*, Report no. 873, 29 September 2021; Paul Charon and Jean-Baptiste Jeangène Vilmer, *Les opérations d'influence chinoises* (Paris: Institute for Strategic Research IRSEM, 2021).

[54] Senate, 2012a, p. 20; Antoine Izambard, 'Cyberattaques contre Airbus: pourquoi la Chine est soupçonnée', *Challenges*, 27 September 2012; Danilo D'Elia, 'La guerre économique à l'ère du cyberespace', *Hérodote 1*, no. 152–153 (2014): pp. 240–250.

[55] MoD, *Strategic Review of Defence and National Security*, 2017a, p. 33.

[56] Parliamentary Delegation on Intelligence, *L'activité de la délégation parlementaire au renseignement pour l'année 2019–2020*, 11 June 2020, p. 244.

to cooperate with the state in intelligence gathering by all means, including technical means'.[57] As a MFA official puts it, 'given the 2017 law, we know very well that the People's Liberation Army or the Chinese Minister of State Security can ask Huawei to collaborate with the intelligence services. That's a fact.'[58] In short, French policymakers feared that the use of Huawei equipment in France's digital infrastructure could enable Chinese cyber-attacks either for espionage purposes or to disrupt parts of the digital infrastructure.

Economic Concerns: Lack of Reciprocity, Unfair Trade Practices and Shrinking Technological Edge

Besides these national security considerations, Paris became increasingly vocal about economic concerns raised by China's lack of reciprocity and market openness because of 'unfair' trade practices.[59] In particular, French policymakers considered that whereas France and the European Union remained open to foreign trade and investment flows, China's discriminatory measures provided unfair advantages to Chinese companies through, for instance, large subsidies to Chinese companies operating in France and in Europe or the appropriation of intellectual property.[60]

Relatedly, growing apprehensions emerged in the French government over the shrinking technological gap between Chinese and French companies. According to one MoD official, 'as China moved up the value-added ladder, it increasingly became an economic competitor for French high-tech companies. This, coupled with heavy distortions of competition including through state subsidies and with the porosity between politics and economics in China, changed our perspective.'[61] Another government official similarly stresses how 'in the 1990s and 2000s we had the preconceived idea that China lagged so far behind that it would take a long time to catch up. But in more recent years Beijing's industrial policy—including state subsidies and forced technology transfers—coupled with its massive investments in R&D allowed China to catch up and partly close the gap.'[62] Paris thus grew wary that France's 'manufacturing industry ha[d] fallen behind its main competitors in a context of intensifying international competition and the rise of emerging countries such as China'.[63] The 'risk of a prolonged technological gap'

---

[57] Senate, 2019a, pp. 20 and 21. See also Senate, *Souveraineté numérique*, Inquiry Commission on Digital Sovereignty, Report no. 7, Vol. 1, 1 October 2019b, pp. 73–74; and Christian Cambon, Chairman of the Senate Committee on Foreign Affairs, Defence and Armed Forces (since 2017), quoted in Public Sénat, 'Huawei, le Sénat pointe des liens avec le pouvoir chinois', 11 October 2020, https://www.publicsenat.fr/article/societe/huawei-le-senat-pointe-des-liens-avec-le-pouvoir-chinois-184978.
[58] Interview, 30 March 2021.
[59] Seaman, 2017, p. 55. Interviews with MFA and MEF officials, January–June 2021.
[60] Interviews with MFA and MEF officials, March and April 2021.
[61] Interview, 10 May 2021.
[62] Interview, 22 June 2021.
[63] French Government, *Faire de la France une économie de rupture technologique. Soutenir les marchés émergents à forts enjeux de compétitivité*, Report for the Minister for the Economy and Finance and for the Minister of Education, Research and Innovation, 7 February 2020, p. 14. On the

between France and its competitors should therefore 'not be underestimated'.[64] In particular, the sectors targeted by China's *Made in China 2025* (MiC2025) were considered 'the most sensitive'.[65] The intensity of such concerns was nonetheless relatively lower than in other European major powers, most notably Germany, also because the role of the manufacturing industry in France's GDP declined from 15 per cent in 2000 to 10 per cent in 2018 while it remained over 20 per cent in Germany.[66]

Political Concerns: Exploiting Divisions to Weaken Europe
Finally, French policymakers grew increasingly alarmed by what they saw as China's use of its economic influence across Europe to exploit existing divisions and drive a wedge between EU member states. President Emmanuel Macron (since 2017) warned that 'China displays real diplomatic genius in playing with our divisions and in weakening us.'[67] In his view, 'China cannot respect a continent where some member states open every door, where it is easy to buy essential infrastructure' and where 'some European countries are much more open to Chinese interests, sometimes at the expense of a European interest.'[68]

A senior government official similarly stresses that 'China mobilizes a variety of instruments to undermine the unity of Europe and because a strong and united Europe is not always in China's interest. It is an effective strategy because some countries are more dependent on China than others, and because China leverages its investments, for instance, through the "16+1" format, a blatant example of its attempt to undermine European unity and to exert all its weight bilaterally; thereby, China has a power of coercion which can be effective in blocking a European consensus.'[69] Other instruments leveraged by Beijing to that end included the Belt and Road Initiative (BRI) which, according to the MoD, demonstrated China's desire to extend its influence globally.[70]

---

government's concerns over the loss of France's technological edge, see also MEF, *Financer la quatrième révolution industrielle : lever le verrou du financement des entreprises technologiques*, Report by Philippe Tibi for the Minister for the Economy and Finance, July 2019.

[64] French Government, 2020, p. 17.

[65] MEF official, interview, 25 March 2021. On the sectors targeted by the MiC 2025, see the Introduction of Part II and State Council of the PRC, *Made in China 2025*, 7 July 2015b, pp. 22–27, http://www.cittadellascienza.it/cina/wp-content/uploads/2017/02/IoT-ONE-Made-in-China-2025.pdf.

[66] French Government, 2020, p. 104. Likewise, the contribution of the overall industrial sector to the GDP, between 2009 and 2019, was almost 27 per cent for Germany as opposed to 17 per cent in France and the United Kingdom. Data retrieved from the World Bank, 'World Development Indicators', https://databank.worldbank.org/source/world-development-indicators. This point was confirmed in interviews with MFA and MEF officials, January–July 2021.

[67] President Emmanuel Macron, Speech at the Conference of Ambassadors, 27 August 2019, https://basedoc.diplomatie.gouv.fr/vues/Kiosque/FranceDiplomatie/kiosque.php?fichier=bafr2019-08-28.html#Chapitre6.

[68] Quoted in Laurence Benhamou and Patrick Baert, 'Macron Urges European Unity to Face Rising China', *Space Daily*, 10 January 2018.

[69] Interview, 8 February 2021. On China's use of the '16+1' format to exert influence over Europeans, see also MoD, *Strategic Update*, 2021, p. 21. The '16+1' mechanism, previously labelled '17+1', is discussed in the Introduction of Part II.

[70] MoD, *Strategic Update*, 2021, p. 21.

Policy Goals

The policy goals of France's 'China policy' evolved as a result of these changing economic interests and threat assessment. From the end of the Cold War to the late 2000s, because of rising economic interests and low threat perceptions, French policy goals largely revolved around the pursuit of greater economic and diplomatic engagement with China so as to integrate this emerging power into the international system. In the subsequent decade, however, rising threat perceptions of China's deepening foothold in France and in Europe—coupled with increasingly competitive bilateral economic relations—drove Paris to recalibrate its policy goals and to toughen its 'China policy'.

Economic Opportunities, Diplomatic Engagement, and 'Westernization'

Throughout the 1990s and 2000s, French foreign policy towards China was geared towards deepening engagement with the PRC. Specifically, Paris pursued three overarching goals. First, the central goal of France's 'China policy' was, according to a declassified diplomatic cable of the early 1990s, the pursuit of French economic interests in the vast, expanding Chinese market.[71] During a visit to Beijing, President Jacques Chirac (1995–2007) stressed how China, being 'the largest market in the world', offered 'fantastic horizons'.[72] A senior defence advisor to President Chirac confirms that the PRC 'already appeared as one of the future major powers in the world. China would become a major player and, obviously, before becoming a political power it would become a major economic power. And so it was very important for France to have greater economic relations with China. That was fundamental.'[73]

Second, France aimed to widen the areas of diplomatic cooperation with the PRC in order to encourage its integration as a 'responsible stakeholder' in the international system.[74] The declared intent was to promote the development of

---

[71] French Embassy in China to Ministry of Foreign Affairs, 'Relations bilatérales franco-chinoises', 30 January 1992a, CADN, 513PO/2004038. This point was confirmed by a former senior diplomat in office in the 1990s and 2000s, interview, 20 March 2020.

[72] French President Jacques Chirac, Speech in Beijing, 15 May 1997b. The same point is stressed in National Assembly, *Les échanges commerciaux entre la Chine et la France*, Report no. 2473, 13 July 2005a, p. 17.

[73] General Henri Bentégeat, Deputy Chief of the Personal Military Staff of Presidents François Mitterrand and Jacques Chirac (1993–2006), Chief of the Personal Military Staff of President Chirac (1999–2002) and then Chief of the Defence Staff (2002–2006), interview, 16 May 2017.

[74] Senior official in President Chirac's administration, interview, 3 April 2021. The term 'responsible stakeholder' was first coined by former US Deputy Secretary of State Robert Zoellick (2005–2006), 'Whither China? From Membership to Responsibility', Remarks to the National Committee on US–China Relations, New York City, 21 September 2005.

a multipolar world, with 'a better balance between small and large countries'.[75] The belief, shared between Paris and Beijing, that the world was 'undergoing a profound transformation', 'moving towards a multipolar order which replaces the bipolar structure inherited from the past',[76] became a core reference point for the Sino-French bilateral relationship.[77] Accordingly, integrating the PRC into the international system through diplomatic and economic engagement was deemed crucial since, for then-President Chirac, China was 'one of the essential poles of the multipolar world which [was] taking shape'.[78]

Third, by deepening its economic and diplomatic engagement with the PRC, Paris also hoped to foster domestic liberalization in China, both economically and politically.[79] According to General Henri Bentégeat, former Deputy Chief of the Personal Military Staff of Presidents François Mitterrand and Jacques Chirac (1993–2006), Chief of the Personal Military Staff of President Chirac (1999–2002), and then Chief of the Defence Staff (2002–2006), President Chirac nurtured the hope that China's economic opening to the market economy would result in a 'Westernization of China's society and in a political liberalization'.[80] Likewise, a senior official in President Nicolas Sarkozy's administration (2007–2012) stresses how a central 'idea was that China's transition towards a market economy would result in an opening of the Chinese regime to Western values. The perception was that China was going to join the rules of the game of the globalized economy and would gradually integrate into the international order created by the West. The hope was that—in an almost mechanical way—China's economic opening would, naturally and inevitably, lead to an increase in those individual political freedoms without which the market cannot work.'[81]

Rebalancing the Policy Goals of France's 'China Policy'

By the 2010s, however, increasingly competitive economic relations and, crucially, heightened threat perceptions drove Paris to revise the goals of its 'China policy' so as to better confront the multipronged challenge posed by the PRC. Specifically, French policymakers sought to rebalance the bilateral relationship with Beijing by putting greater emphasis on security considerations, to foster greater political unity within the European Union in order to augment its negotiating leverage

---

[75] French Government, 'Déclaration conjointe franco-chinoise pour un partenariat global', signed by Jacques Chirac and Jiang Zemin, Beijing, 16 May 1997.
[76] French Government, 1997.
[77] Former senior diplomat in office in the 1990s and 2000s, interview, 13 March 2020.
[78] President Jacques Chirac, Speech in Beijing, 15 May 1997b.
[79] Interviews with former MFA and MoD officials and with former advisers to President Chirac, March–December 2020 and March 2021.
[80] Interview, 20 March 2020.
[81] Senior official in President Sarkozy's administration, interview, 3 April 2021.

vis-à-vis Beijing, and to forge an autonomous EU position in the context of the rising US-China strategic competition.

For one, in line with the relabelling of the PRC by the European Commission and the European External Action Service (EEAS),[82] Paris recalibrated its policy goals from a relatively open-door approach towards a more clear-eyed stance, now dealing with 'China as a partner, a competitor, and a systemic rival, at the same time.'[83] As one official puts it, 'we have moved away from a form of naivety that characterized previous decades; we have now become increasingly aware of all the distortions, imbalances, unfair practices, and the asymmetry in the Euro-Chinese relationship and in the different bilateral relations between China and the members states of EU. When Chinese policymakers talk about "win-win", what they really mean is that they want China to win twice. We have therefore rebalanced our relationship with the PRC in areas such as foreign direct investments and the overall investment relationship, restrictions on Chinese vendors of digital technology, as well as human rights and forced labour, among others.'[84] A MoD official delineates this recalibration as follows: 'the overarching goal is reciprocity: reciprocity in market access, in the protection of intellectual property, etc. Until the late 2000s, there was a desire to avoid entering in a power relationship, to avoid displaying force in our relationship with the PRC. This has changed. We have now realized that the competitive dimension is key to the relationship with Beijing. So when reciprocity is not respected by Beijing, we are now willing to push back.'[85]

A second, related goal of this policy was, according to the Ministry of Foreign Affairs, 'to strengthen European unity and cohesion' so as to gain leverage vis-à-vis Beijing.[86] An official in charge of China in the General Secretariat for European Affairs (SGAE) in the Prime Minister's Office (since 2017) explains that 'China has a strategy of "divide and rule" in Europe. We must therefore be vigilant; we must defend the European Union's unity vis-à-vis China. European unity is crucial in the relations between France and China, and between the EU and China.'[87] Fostering greater intra-European cohesion would rebalance the Euro-Chinese relationship and achieve greater reciprocity, while reducing the vulnerability of individual EU member states to pressures (or retaliatory threats) from China as well as from the

---

[82] European Commission and High Representative of the Union for Foreign Affairs and Security Policy (HR/VP), *EU–China: A Strategic Outlook*, 12 March 2019, p. 1.

[83] President Emmanuel Macron, Interview with the Atlantic Council, 5 February 2021, https://www.elysee.fr/en/emmanuel-macron/2021/02/05/emmanuel-macron-president-of-the-french-republic-gave-an-interview-to-the-american-think-tank-atlantic-council. See also MoD, *Strategic Update*, 2021, p. 21.

[84] Interview, 22 June 2021.

[85] Interview, 10 May 2021.

[86] Quote from MFA, 'Union européenne—Chine, Questions et réponses', Press Briefing, 27 May 2020a, https://www.diplomatie.gouv.fr/fr/dossiers-pays/chine/evenements/article/union-europeenne-chine-q-r-extrait-du-point-de-presse-27-05-20.

[87] Agnès Menet, Deputy to the Head of the SGAE's Bureau for Trade and Development Aid (since 2017), interview, 12 April 2021.

United States.[88] As President Macron put it, 'for many years we had an uncoordinated approach and China took advantage of our divisions, an awakening was necessary';[89] 'if we want to be respected by China we must first have a European approach, this is essential.'[90] This point is further confirmed by a MFA official for whom 'the Franco-Chinese bilateral relationship is now inseparable from the European Union-China one. There is a perpetual coordination effort. The European level has become key.'[91]

Finally, promoting a more coordinated EU policy was also meant to develop a distinct and autonomous role for France and the European Union in a world increasingly 'structured around two great poles: the United States and China'.[92] France had indeed come to perceive the global competition between the United States and the PRC as 'an established strategic fact, one that structures, and from now on will structure, all international relations'.[93] In this context, Paris decided that it would neither seek to contain China nor to accommodate Beijing from a position of equidistance.[94] The head of the MFA's East Asia Department Louis Riquet, (since 2020) stresses that 'France and the European Union therefore developed a threefold approach towards China, which is simultaneously considered a partner, a competitor, and a systemic rival; this is not the case at all with the United States, which is not a systemic rival. Our goal is not equidistance between the United States and China, but neither is it systematic alignment with the United States; we do not necessarily agree on every single issue, nor do we always have converging interests across the board with Washington.'[95] A MoD official confirms that Paris viewed 'the Sino-American strategic rivalry as a structural feature of international politics in the years to come. It will, in some sense, define the geostrategic compass for countries like France. This said, we are clearly not looking for a middle position between the United States and China. China is a diplomatic and economic partner. The United States is an ally. Diplomatically we can have different positions with Washington, but the structure of the underlying military alliance is rock solid. So our policy is not and cannot be equidistance but nor is it systematic alignment with

---

[88] Interviews with French MFA and MEF officials as well as with EU officials, January–May 2021. On reciprocity, see MFA, 2020a.

[89] Quoted in Françoise Nicolas, 'France and China's Belt and Road Initiative', Italian Institute for International Political Studies, *ISPI Commentary*, 8 April 2019, https://www.ispionline.it/en/pubblicazione/france-and-chinas-belt-and-road-initiative-22787.

[90] President Emmanuel Macron, 2019.

[91] Interview, 8 February 2021.

[92] President Emmanuel Macron, 2019.

[93] President Emmanuel Macron (since 2017), Speech on the Defence and Deterrence Strategy, 7 February 2020, https://www.elysee.fr/en/emmanuel-macron/2020/02/07/speech-of-the-president-of-the-republic-on-the-defense-and-deterrence-strategy.

[94] President Emmanuel Macron, 2021.

[95] Louis Riquet, interview, 8 February 2021. President Macron made a similar point in an interview with the Atlantic Council, President Emmanuel Macron, 2021.

the United States.'[96] In fact, for President Macron, France had 'only one credible European response: that of our strategic autonomy'.[97]

Policy Instruments

This evolution in the policy goals of French foreign policy towards China drove an adaptation of the policy instruments mobilized to achieve such goals. During the 1990s and 2000s, in light of its overarching objective of deepening Sino-French economic and diplomatic ties, Paris imposed few restrictions on Chinese investments in France and eagerly welcomed the entry of Chinese companies into its markets. By the 2010s, however, as France recalibrated the goals of its 'China policy', it sought to develop more stringent policy instruments—both at the national and EU levels—to better monitor (and, if needed, veto) Chinese FDIs and to bolster the resilience of its digital infrastructure vis-à-vis suppliers of concern like Huawei.

An Open Investment Regime

The first two post-Cold War decades were characterized by France's efforts to attract Chinese investments. Accordingly, Paris maintained an open investment policy vis-à-vis China at the same time as it strengthened its investment screening mechanisms in order to monitor FDIs from the United States into strategic sectors.

In light of the historically significant role of the French state in regulating the economy,[98] Paris had first introduced a FDI screening mechanism (in peacetime) in the mid-1960s.[99] After partly loosening some restrictions on foreign investments in the 1980s, France liberalized its FDI screening mechanism to bring it in line with the European Community regulation in 1996.[100] Henceforth, FDIs

---

[96] Interview, 10 May 2021.

[97] President Emmanuel Macron, Speech at the Conference of Ambassadors, 27 August 2018 https://www.elysee.fr/emmanuel-macron/2018/08/27/discours-du-president-de-la-republique-a-la-conference-des-ambassadeurs.

[98] See for instance Peter A. Hall, *Governing the Economy: The Politics of State Intervention in Britain and France* (Oxford: Oxford University Press, 1986); John Zysman, 'The French State in the International Economy', *International Organization 31*, no. 4 (Autumn, 1977): pp. 839–877; and Vivien A. Schmidt, 'Varieties of Capitalism: A Distinct French Model?', in *Oxford Handbook of French Politics*, edited by Robert Elgie, Amy Mazur, Emiliano Grossman, and Andrew Appleton (Oxford: Oxford University Press, 2016), pp. 606–635.

[99] The 1966 law established a systematic case-by-case screening for the entry of foreign enterprises which, 'in order to assure the protection of the national interest', required foreign investors to obtain an authorization from the Ministry of Finance before making a direct investment in France (Légifrance, 'Loi n° 66-1008 du 28 décembre 1966 relative aux relations financières avec l'étranger', 29 December 1966, https://www.legifrance.gouv.fr/loda/id/LEGITEXT000006068265/.)

[100] Légifrance, 'Loi n° 96-109 du 14 février 1996 relative aux relations financières avec l'étranger en ce qui concerne les investissements étrangers en France', 15 February 1996, https://www.legifrance.gouv.

would no longer be subject to prior authorization, with the exception of those in 'sensitive sectors'.[101] Specifically, FDIs that could 'jeopardize public order, public health or public security' or that targeted sectors such as 'research, production or trade in arms' would still require a prior authorization and potentially be denied.[102]

In 2003, the law was amended to include 'national defence' among the list of criteria for a prior authorization so as to also encompass dual-use technologies and 'sensitive elements in the production chain of strategic equipment'.[103] That same year, the Prime Minister tasked the Secretariat-General for National Defence (SGDN, later relabelled Secretariat-General for National Defence and Security, SGDSN) to provide an assessment of the risks linked to takeovers by foreign corporations of French companies in sectors tied to national defence and security and that could threaten France's defence industrial autonomy; it also created the position of High Representative for Economic Intelligence in the Office of the Prime Minister for that purpose.[104] According to Alain Juillet, who occupied that position from 2003 to 2009, the main driver behind this initiative was the mounting concern over the vulnerability of French companies operating in strategic sectors to non-European investments, especially after the takeover of Gemplus and Péchiney by US companies (discussed earlier).[105] As a 2005 parliamentary report put it, foreign investments in French and European strategic sectors were 'predominantly made by American investors, although we cannot rule out a significant increase in the medium term of investments from groups or funds of other nationalities', 'coming from China' for instance.[106] Using the leeway provided by the European Community (EC) Treaty in the area of national security, the French government thus issued a decree in 2005 that identified eleven sectors in which the state would now require a prior authorization for (and could also veto) FDIs by non-EU entities.[107] These sectors included, among others, activities linked to

---

fr/loda/id/JORFTEXT000000376141/. For a detailed analysis of the evolution of French FDI screening mechanisms from the 1960s to the late 1990s, see Cynthia Day Wallace, *The Multinational Enterprise and Legal Control: Host State Sovereignty in an Era of Economic Globalization* (The Hague: Martinus Nijhoff Publishers, 2002), pp. 224–235.

[101] Wallace, 2002, pp. 231–232.
[102] Légifrance, 1996. See also Wallace, 2002, p. 233.
[103] National Assembly, *Stratégie de sécurité économique*, Committee on Finance, General Economy and the Plan, 9 June 2004, p. 13. See also Légifrance, 'Loi n° 2003-706 du 1er août 2003 de sécurité financière', 2 August 2003, https://www.legifrance.gouv.fr/jorf/id/JORFTEXT000000428977 (article 28).
[104] Alain Juillet, interview, 2 April 2021. On this point, see also National Assembly, 2004, p. 14. The SGDN, later relabelled SGDSN, is the interministerial coordinating body in charge of political-military affairs under the authority of the Prime Minister.
[105] Alain Juillet, interview, 2 April 2021. See also National Assembly, 2004, p. 11; and National Assembly, 2005b.
[106] National Assembly, 2005b, p. 16.
[107] Under the EC Treaty, member states were required to allow the free movement of capital but retained the right to impose restrictions thereupon based on public security considerations. See US

communication interception equipment, computer security when used to protect critical infrastructures, certain dual-use technologies, encryption, and research, production, or supply of arms and munitions.[108]

Yet, despite the development of these new policy instruments to restrict FDI inflows, Paris continued to encourage Chinese investments in France. These regulatory changes had been spurred by concerns over US acquisitions of strategic sectors, rather than over China. Overall, as stressed by the then High Representative for Economic Intelligence, 'France sought to maintain an open investment regime so as to maximize investment flows from the PRC and to welcome Chinese companies such as Huawei into the French market.'[109]

Strengthening France's Policy Instruments

As it hardened the policy goals of its 'China policy' in the 2010s, however, France devised new policy instruments to concretize such goals. It enacted regulatory measures at the national level while also promoting the creation of EU policy instruments to better confront the multifaceted challenges posed by China's growing clout in Europe.

National Instruments: Restricting Foreign Investments and Telecoms Suppliers
Through a number of subsequent changes to its regulations, France strengthened its national FDI screening mechanism while widening the scope of sanctions in case of violations. It also imposed restrictions on telecoms suppliers of concern such as Huawei's equipment, first on 4G then on 5G technology, so as to better protect its digital infrastructure.

Screening Foreign Direct Investments
In 2014, the government extended the range of sensitive sectors for which FDIs required a prior authorization by the government to include energy, water, transport, public health, and telecommunications.[110] This revision was primarily triggered by the American company General Electrics' acquisition of Alstom, a 'crown

---

Government Accountability Office (GAO), *Foreign Investment: Laws and Policies Regulating Foreign Investment in 10 Countries*, GAO-08-320, February 2008, p. 53.

[108] Légifrance, 'Décret n° 2005-1739 du 30 décembre 2005 réglementant les relations financières avec l'étranger et portant application de l'article L. 151–3 du code monétaire et financier', 31 December 2005, https://www.legifrance.gouv.fr/loda/id/JORFTEXT000000268021/; see also Winston Maxwell, 'France Criticized for New Foreign Investment Rules', *International Financial Law Review*, 1 March 2006, p. 1.

[109] Alain Juillet, interview, 2 April 2021.

[110] Légifrance, 'Décret n° 2014-479 du 14 mai 2014 relatif aux investissements étrangers soumis à autorisation préalable', 16 May 2014, https://www.legifrance.gouv.fr/loda/id/JORFTEXT000028933611.

jewel' of French high technology, rather than concerns about China.[111] Yet, in 2017, it was out of concern over China's potential access to sensitive technology that Paris decided to temporarily nationalize the French shipbuilder STX France.[112] Italian Fincantieri intended to acquire STX France and had a joint venture with the China State Shipbuilding Corporation, thus raising the possibility of technology leakage to the PRC.[113]

Then, in November 2018, the government broadened the list of sensitive sectors subject to prior authorization by the Ministry for the Economy and Finance (MEF) to include interception or detection of correspondences and conversations, capture of computer data, security of information systems, space operations, and electronic systems used in public security missions.[114] It also expanded the scope of review to R&D activities in cybersecurity, artificial intelligence, robotics, additive manufacturing, semiconductors, certain dual-use goods and technologies, and sensitive data storage.[115] These technologies echoed the sectors listed in the *Made in China 2025* plan. One year later, as part of the Action Plan for Business Growth and Transformation (PACTE, which came into effect in 2020), Paris widened the range of possible sanctions in case of infringement and bolstered its enforcement powers.[116] It then introduced a decree that lowered the ownership threshold above which FDIs were subject to control from 33.33 per cent to 25 per cent of voting

---

See also Didier Théophile, Olivia Chriqui-Guiot, and Guillaume Griffart, 'France', in *Foreign Investment Regulation Review*, 8th edition, edited by Calvin S. Goldman and Michael Koch (London: The Law Reviews, 2017), p. 58.

[111] Erik Brattberg and Etienne Soula, 'Is Europe Finally Pushing Back on Chinese Investments?', *Carnegie Endowment for International Peace*, 14 September 2018, https://carnegieendowment.org/2018/09/14/is-europe-finally-pushing-back-on-chinese-investments-pub-77259.

[112] Brattberg and Soula, 2018; and Leigh Thomas, 'France to Nationalize STX Shipyard If Italy Snubs Ownership Deal', *Reuters*, 26 July 2017.

[113] France and Italy subsequently agreed to split STX's capital equally, although France lent 1 per cent of the capital to Fincantieri. See National Assembly, *Défense : préparation de l'avenir (Annexe no. 13)*, Report no. 2301, 21 January 2021, Committee on Finance, General Economy and Budgetary Control, p. 158. See also Denis Cosnard, 'Le montage subtil de l'Elysée pour céder le contrôle des chantiers STX à Fincantieri', *Le Monde*, 27 September 2017.

[114] Légifrance, 'Décret n° 2018-1057 du 29 novembre 2018 relatif aux investissements étrangers soumis à autorisation préalable', 2 December 2018, https://www.legifrance.gouv.fr/loda/id/JORFTEXT000037674063/; and Nathalie Nègre-Eveillard and Orion Berg, 'Foreign Investments in France: New Legislation Expands and Strengthens the National Security Review Mechanism', *White & Case*, Client Alert, 22 July 2019, p. 1.

[115] In the context of the Covid-19 pandemic, biotechnologies were subsequently added to the list of sectors. Nègre-Eveillard and Berg, 2019, p. 1; Légifrance, 'Arrêté du 27 avril 2020 relatif aux investissements étrangers en France', 30 April 2020, https://www.legifrance.gouv.fr/jorf/id/JORFTEXT000041835304.

[116] For instance, if the protection of public order, public security, or national defence was compromised or was likely to be compromised by an investment, the government could now suspend the investor's voting rights in the target company or temporarily restrict or prohibit the free disposal of the assets related to the sensitive activities carried out by the investor. Nègre-Eveillard and Berg, 2019, p. 1.

rights and capital.[117] Through these subsequent regulatory revisions, the French FDI screening mechanism was thus 'strengthened and expanded in order to better protect strategic sectors'.[118] The reform also compelled investors to disclose their links with foreign states or public entities.[119]

In explaining the rationale for such reforms, the Minister of the Economy and Finance Bruno Le Maire (since 2017) stressed that 'there are certain investments in strategic sectors that we must be able to protect';[120] in a reference to Chinese FDIs in France, he stated: 'China no longer wants to imitate Western nations, it wants to overtake them'; economic openness should 'not mean plundering our technologies, our skills, our know-how. Foreign investors [...] should simply know that these investments will henceforth obey clear rules.'[121]

Restricting Suppliers of Concern: 4G and 5G Technology
Paris also devised new instruments to tackle the security challenges posed by the PRC in the digital domain, such as tightening the restrictions on telecoms suppliers of concern like Huawei. In light of its mounting disquiet over China's provision of 4G core network equipment (e.g. routers), France introduced a series of measures which compelled telecoms companies to submit a formal authorization request to the French national cybersecurity agency (ANSSI) for the supply or procurement of 4G core network equipment.[122] In particular, in 2012, the government introduced revisions to Article 226–3 of the Penal Code which established

---

[117] In response to the Covid crisis, the government also temporarily lowered the voting rights threshold from 25 per cent to 10 per cent until the end of 2021. Légifrance, 'Décret n° 2019-1590 du 31 décembre 2019 relatif aux investissements étrangers en France', 31 December 2019b, https://www.legifrance.gouv.fr/jorf/id/JORFTEXT000039727443/; Sébastien Crepy and Nicolas Lovas, 'Foreign Investment Control in France: New Derogatory Regime Applicable to Foreign Investment in French Public Companies', *Paul Hastings—Client Alerts*, 24 July 2020, https://www.paulhastings.com/insights/client-alerts/foreign-investment-control-in-france-new-derogatory-regime-applicable-to-foreign-investment-in-french-public-companies; MEF, 'Bruno Le Maire annonce la prorogation jusqu'au 31 décembre 2021 des mesures d'adaptation du contrôle des investissements étrangers en France pendant la crise sanitaire', *Press Release*, 18 December 2020b, https://www.tresor.economie.gouv.fr/Articles/2020/12/18/prorogation-jusqu-au-31-decembre-2021-des-mesures-d-adaptation-du-controle-des-investissements-etrangers-en-france-pendant-la-crise-sanitaire.

[118] Government, 'PACTE, the Action Plan for Business Growth and Transformation', 2021, https://www.gouvernement.fr/en/pacte-the-action-plan-for-business-growth-and-transformation.

[119] MEF, 'Publication du décret et de l'arrêté relatifs aux investissements étrangers en France : une procédure plus simple, claire et rapide', *Press Release*, 2 January 2020a, https://www.tresor.economie.gouv.fr/Articles/2020/01/02/publication-du-decret-et-de-l-arrete-relatifs-aux-investissements-etrangers-en-france-une-procedure-plus-simple-claire-et-rapide.

[120] MEF, 'Interview de M. Bruno Le Maire, ministre de l'économie, des finances et de la relance, à BFM Business', 20 January 2021, https://www.vie-publique.fr/discours/278213-bruno-le-maire-20012021-politique-economique.

[121] Minister for the Economy and Finance (since 2017), Bruno Le Maire, Speech, 15 January 2018, https://www.vie-publique.fr/discours/204733-declaration-de-m-bruno-le-maire-ministre-de-leconomie-et-des-finances.

[122] On the evolution of the French regulatory framework for 4G and 5G technology, see Franck Laurent and Pascal Nourry, 'Contexte réglementaire pour les opérateurs 5G', Paper presented at the Computer & Electronics Security Applications Rendez-vous (C&ESAR) on Virtualization and Cybersecurity, Rennes, 19 November 2019, p. 5.

a prior authorization for the supply of network equipment that was designed to intercept electronic correspondence; it provided a list of telecoms equipment that required such authorization and, in particular, those whose functionalities enabled 'the interception, eavesdropping, analysis, transfer, recording, or processing' of telecommunications.[123] Building upon Article 226–3, the 2013 Military Programming Law for 2014–2019 (Article 23) then reinforced this regulatory framework by extending the prior authorization to devices that, even if not specifically designed to allow interception of communications, could be used for that purpose.[124] A 2016 decree thus extended the list of such equipment to include 'devices which allow electronic communication operators to connect their customers' equipment to the core of their mobile radio network', such as the base stations of telephone networks located on the network's edge, if their characteristics were such as to allow the interception of communications.[125] As a result of these subsequent regulatory provisions, by the end of the 2010s no Huawei equipment was included in French core networks.[126]

But the emergence of 5G technology, as discussed above, posed new, additional security challenges compared to 4G networks. France therefore passed a law in 2019 that imposed greater constraints on the supply of 5G equipment but without establishing a full-blown ban.[127] The network security law, also referred to as 'the 5G law', required that operators wishing to exploit 'hardware or software devices

---

[123] Légifrance, 'Arrêté du 4 juillet 2012 fixant la liste d'appareils et de dispositifs techniques prévue par l'article 226-3 du code pénal', 1 August 2012, https://www.legifrance.gouv.fr/loda/article_lc/LEGIARTI000033064189/2021-10-01/.

[124] Légifrance, 'Loi n° 2013-1168 du 18 décembre 2013 relative à la programmation militaire pour les années 2014 à 2019 et portant diverses dispositions concernant la défense et la sécurité nationale', 19 December 2013a, https://www.legifrance.gouv.fr/jorf/id/JORFARTI000028338919.

[125] This new measure would enter into force after a period of five years (in 2021) so that telecoms manufacturers and operators could incorporate 'the future generations of equipment and networks'. ANSSI, 'Publication de l'arrêté du 11 août 2016 modifiant celui du 4 juillet 2012 fixant la liste d'appareils et de dispositifs techniques prévue par l'article 226-3 du code pénal', https://www.ssi.gouv.fr/actualite/publication-de-larrete-du-11-aout-2016-modifiant-celui-du-4-juillet-2012-fixant-la-liste-dappareils-et-de-dispositifs-techniques-prevue-par-larticle-226-3-du-code-penal/. See also Légifrance, 'Arrêté du 11 août 2016 modifiant l'arrêté du 4 juillet 2012 fixant la liste d'appareils et de dispositifs techniques prévue par l'article 226-3 du code pénal', 25 August 2016, https://www.legifrance.gouv.fr/loda/id/JORFTEXT000033063311/.

[126] Senate, 2019a, p. 20. Throughout the 2010s, France also introduced broader measures to strengthen the cybersecurity of its critical infrastructure (i.e. what the French government refers to as 'operators of critical—or vital—importance' and 'operators of essential services') as well as to bolster the protection of its scientific and technological industrial base. See, among others, ANSSI, 'Protection des OIV en France', https://www.ssi.gouv.fr/entreprise/protection-des-oiv/protection-des-oiv-en-france; ANSSI, 'NIS Directive: ANSSI Supports the First Operators of Essential Services', News, https://www.ssi.gouv.fr/en/actualite/nis-directive-anssi-supports-the-first-operators-of-essential-services/; ANSSI, Information Systems Defence and Security: France's Strategy, 2011, p. 7, https://www.ssi.gouv.fr/uploads/IMG/pdf/2011-02-15_Information_system_defence_and_security_-_France_s_strategy.pdf; MoD, French White Paper on Defence and National Security, 2013, pp. 100–102; Senate, 2019b, pp. 109–110; SGDSN, 'Le dispositif de protection du potentiel scientifique et technique de la nation', www.sgdsn.gouv.fr/missions/protection-du-potentiel-scientifique-et-technique-de-la-nation/le-dispositif-de-protection-du-potentiel-scientifique-et-technique-de-la-nation-faq/.

[127] Légifrance, 2019c. See also Légifrance, 'Décret n° 2019-1300 du 6 décembre 2019 relatif aux modalités de l'autorisation préalable de l'exploitation des équipements de réseaux radioélectriques

that would enable end-users' terminals to be connected to the mobile radio network' should obtain a prior authorization from the Prime Minister.[128] This prior authorization would be granted for a period ranging from three to eight years (and could potentially be renewed). The Prime Minister could deny the authorization if the equipment was deemed to harm French defence and national security in relation to the confidentiality, integrity, and availability of telecoms networks.[129] In assessing such risk, the Prime Minister would take into account both technical and political considerations. The former included the level of security of the devices and their modalities of deployment and exploitation by the operator. The political considerations related to whether the supplier was 'under the control or subject to acts of interference by a State which is not a member of the European Union', in a clear yet implicit reference to China's 2017 national intelligence law.[130] Thereby, Paris sought to confront the risk 'of interference by a State having coercive leverage' over telecoms companies.[131]

While these restrictions did not impose an ad hoc ban on Huawei, they amounted to a de facto phasing out of Huawei's equipment from France's digital networks. As stressed by ANSSI's Director General Guillaume Poupard (since 2014), whereas there would 'be no total ban of Huawei', 'for operators that are not currently using Huawei, we are inciting them not to go for it'; and those who already used Huawei equipment would be issued three-to-eight years authorizations; the underlying logic, he added, was 'that all operators do not start on the same bases: some will have to dismantle equipment, others won't; therefore they cannot all be treated the same.'[132] In fact, the 2019 law affected Huawei equipment much more substantially than it did other 5G suppliers. In 2020, the four French telecoms operators had filed 157 authorization requests to ANSSI, involving a total of nearly 65,000 pieces of equipment.[133] Out of the 157 authorizations, eighty-two were granted for the maximum duration of eight years, fifty-three were granted for a shorter duration and twenty-two were rejected.[134] While most authorizations for the maximum duration were delivered for Ericsson or Nokia equipment, all

prévue à l'article L. 34–11 du code des postes et des communications électroniques', 7 December 2019a, https://www.legifrance.gouv.fr/loda/id/JORFTEXT000039455649.
[128] Légifrance, 2019c.
[129] Légifrance, 2019a, 2019c.
[130] Légifrance, 2019c.
[131] Government's position as cited in Senate, 2019a, p. 56. Furthermore, the government could impose sanctions on the supplier (e.g. five years imprisonment and financial fines) if it operated 5G equipment without prior authorization or without respecting the conditions set by the authorization (Senate, 2019a, p. 56).
[132] Quoted in Florian Dèbes and Fabienne Schmitt, "'Il n'y aura pas un bannissement total de Huawei", affirme le patron de l'Anssi', Les Echos, 6 July 2020.
[133] Senate, Direction de l'action du gouvernement, Report no. 140, Committee on Foreign Affairs, Defence and Armed Forces, 19 November 2020b, p. 13.
[134] Senate, 2020b, p. 13.

refusal decisions and all authorizations for short periods concerned Huawei equipment.[135] As a senior MEF official puts it, 'when an operator wants to deploy 5G technology and cannot do it with Huawei's equipment', because the government has denied an authorization, for instance, 'in order to shift to another 5G supplier it must remove all the previous generations antennas (4G, 3G, etc.) in its network; given this "historical path dependency" of telecommunications networks, this is what "phasing out" entails.'[136]

The 2019 law thus tightened the restrictions over the supply of 5G equipment for its digital networks but fell short of imposing an ad hoc ban on Huawei, while prompting French operators to gradually phase out its equipment in favour of other suppliers. This decision was the result of a delicate balancing act by the French government between national security considerations linked to telecoms suppliers of concern like Huawei, the economic health of French telecoms operators, and foreign policy considerations vis-à-vis Washington and Beijing.

From a national security standpoint, a central goal of the French government was to ensure the secure exploitation of digital networks.[137] As stressed by the Constitutional Council, the highest constitutional authority in France, this law sought 'to preserve defence and national security interests' by protecting 'mobile radio networks from the risks of espionage, hacking, and sabotage which may result from the new functionalities' of 5G wireless technology, especially by suppliers under the political influence of a foreign state.[138]

From an economic perspective, as explained by the Director General of the ANSSI, one of the considerations for not imposing a full ban on Huawei was the need to take into account the 'economic constraints' of French telecoms operators.[139] According to the companies' own estimates, the cost of replacing Huawei's antennas would be €1.1bn for SFR and €900m for Bouygues, with 8,000 and 3,000 antennas respectively (whereas Orange and Free did not include Huawei's equipment in their network and had turned to other suppliers such as Nokia and Ericsson).[140] Furthermore, according to a MFA official, 'replacing existing equipment would not only require time and financial resources, but it would also entail

---

[135] Some authorizations for the maximum duration were nonetheless also issued for Huawei equipment. See Senate 2020b, p. 13; and Mathieu Rosemain and Gwénaëlle Barzic, 'Exclusive: French Limits on Huawei 5G Equipment Amount to De Facto Ban by 2028', *Reuters*, 22 July 2020.

[136] Interview, 20 May 2021.

[137] Senate, 2019a, p. 7.

[138] Constitutional Court, 'Décision n° 2020-882 QPC du 5 février 2021', *Press Release*, 5 February 2021, https://www.conseil-constitutionnel.fr/actualites/communique/decision-n-2020-882-qpc-du-5-fevrier-2021-communique-de-presse.

[139] Quoted in Dèbes and Schmitt, 2020. On this point, see also Senate, '"Loi 5G": mission accomplie pour la commission des affaires étrangères et de la défense du Sénat, l'application de la "loi 5G" remplit bien son objectif : réduire l'exposition des réseaux 5G au risque de sécurité', *Press Release*, 19 November 2020a, https://www.senat.fr/presse/cp20201119b.html.

[140] See Mickaël Bazoge, 'Interdiction des équipements Huawei : SFR et Bouygues Telecom réclament 2 milliards d'euros à l'État', *iGeneration*, 30 November 2020; and Julien Lausson, '5G : la France s'organise pour écarter Huawei des réseaux télécoms', *Numerama*, 6 July 2020.

possible consequences on jobs and would have repercussions on other sectors as well, given that Huawei is a major equipment manufacturer, but behind it there is a whole series of subcontractors. The two main reasons why we have not established an anti-Huawei ban are these economic considerations and, diplomatically, the fact that we do not want to adopt an excessively confrontational posture towards China which would not be in our interest.'[141]

Finally, and relatedly, French policymakers needed to balance the consequences of any decision on Huawei for Paris's diplomatic and economic ties with both Washington and Beijing, at a time of rising Sino-American competition. On the one hand, the United States pressured France during bilateral encounters to ban Huawei's 5G equipment from its network.[142] A former senior official in the Trump administration explains that 'the main purpose of our conversations on 5G and Huawei with our European friends and allies such as France, Germany, and the United Kingdom was to raise their awareness to what we understood to be China's intentions with regard to taking over 5G networks with Huawei. We stressed that it would be disastrous for countries to trust Huawei with secure communications, and we really tried to help the European governments understand that if you gave any access to Huawei into your 5G network, it meant you were compromised across the board, and you really could not trust your networks any longer. But our colleagues in European capitals were reluctant to come on board to our point of view wholesale.'[143] Likewise, Washington sought to persuade France to clarify whether it would be part of US initiatives such as the 5G Clean Path Initiative and the Clean Network Program.[144] While the 5G Clean Path Initiative required that all mobile data traffic entering American diplomatic systems be subject to new stringent requirements if it had transited Huawei equipment,[145] the Clean Network Program was intended to protect citizens' privacy and companies' most sensitive information 'from aggressive intrusions by malign actors, such as the Chinese Communist Party'.[146] At the same time, Beijing also exerted pressures on Paris, requiring a fair treatment for its companies in the French market and seeking to link France's position on Huawei to other economic items on the bilateral agenda.[147] For instance, the Chinese Embassy in France warned Paris not to take 'discriminatory measures' against Huawei's 5G equipment, adding 'we do not wish to see the development of European companies in the Chinese market affected

---

[141] Interview, 30 March 2021.
[142] Interviews with MFA officials, January–March 2021.
[143] Interview, 30 April 2021.
[144] Interviews with MFA officials, March 2021.
[145] US Secretary of State Michael R. Pompeo, Remarks to the Press, Press Briefing Room, Washington, DC, 29 April 2020b.
[146] US Department of State, 'The Clean Network', https://2017-2021.state.gov/the-clean-network/index.html.
[147] Interviews with MFA officials, January–March 2021.

because of the discrimination and protectionism of France and other European countries towards Huawei.'[148]

Accordingly, the decision to impose greater restrictions short of a full ban on Huawei was, in the words of the head of ANSSI, the result of 'a compromise' which required 'a delicate equilibrium' between these various security, economic, and diplomatic considerations.[149] A MoD official confirms that France sought 'to achieve this balanced position between, on the one hand, Beijing's retaliatory threats and Huawei's lobbying campaign and, on the other, the heavy pressures from the United States. We defined a middle ground, autonomous position: scaling down Huawei's equipment without imposing a full-blown ban.'[150]

Forging New EU Policy Instruments

In conjunction with these national initiatives, France worked with other EU member states to develop common EU instruments intended to bolster the Union's capacity to confront the security challenges posed by Chinese inroads into Europe's strategic sectors. These included the creation of an EU screening mechanism for FDIs and of the EU Toolbox for 5G Cybersecurity.

Developing an EU Investment Screening Framework
Working with other EU member states, France promoted the development of an EU mechanism to screen foreign direct investments.[151] In February 2017, together with Germany and Italy, Paris sent a joint letter to then European Commissioner for Trade Cecilia Malmström (2014–2019) on unfair foreign practices in areas such as FDIs.[152] Given that the instruments then available to EU member states were deemed insufficient to guarantee protection from state-led 'strategic direct investment made by foreign buyers in areas sensitive to security or industrial policy', they advocated for the establishment of a common EU FDI screening mechanism.[153] In a subsequent July 2017 non-paper, they detailed such proposal, stressing that whereas the European Commission's 'opinion would remain consultative', any intervention, including a veto, 'should ultimately occur at the discretion of the member state'.[154] One month later, in his State of the Union Address,

---

[148] Chinese Embassy in France, 'Déclaration du Porte-parole de l'Ambassade de Chine en France sur la question de Huawei et de la 5G', 9 February 2020, www.amb-chine.fr/fra/zfzj/t1742545.htm.
[149] Quoted in Dèbes and Schmitt, 2020.
[150] Interview, 10 May 2021.
[151] Interviews with MFA and MEF officials, January–May 2021.
[152] French, German, and Italian Ministers for Economic Affairs, Letter to the EU Commissioner for Trade Cecilia Malmström, February 2017.
[153] 'Proposals for Ensuring an Improved Level Playing Field in Trade and Investment' attached to French, German, and Italian Ministers for Economic Affairs' Letter to the EU Commissioner for Trade Cecilia Malmström, 2017, p. 1.
[154] French, German, and Italian Ministers for Economic Affairs, 2017.

then-President of the European Commission Jean-Claude Juncker (2014–2019) announced that the European Commission would introduce a new EU investment screening framework to scrutinize foreign state-directed FDIs in the European Union.[155]

The new EU regulation on FDI screening mechanisms (approved in 2018 and fully operational since 2020) established an EU-wide cooperation mechanism between the member states and the European Commission to inform each other of FDIs that may threaten security or public order, and to exchange information related to such investments.[156] The Commission could issue non-binding opinions related to the FDI, but member states retained the last word on whether or not a specific investment operation should be allowed in their territory.[157] In particular, in assessing whether a FDI was likely to affect security or public order, member states and the Commission would now take into account, among other considerations, whether the foreign investor was directly or indirectly controlled by the government and whether the FDI involved: (i) critical infrastructures such as energy, transport, water, health, communications, media, and data processing or storage, aerospace, defence, electoral or financial infrastructure; (ii) critical technologies and dual-use items such as artificial intelligence, robotics, semiconductors, cybersecurity, aerospace, defence, energy storage, quantum and nuclear technologies as well as nanotechnologies and biotechnologies; or (iii) the supply of critical inputs, including energy or raw materials.[158] The Commission could also issue an opinion when an investment may undermine a project or programme of interest to the whole European Union, such as the Horizon 2020 Research Innovation Programme.[159]

Concerns over China played a significant role in France's promotion of the EU FDI screening mechanism. As explained by Jonas Roule, an official in charge of FDIs in the General Secretariat for European Affairs (SGAE) in the Prime Minister's Office (since 2020), 'the EU FDI screening mechanism does not target nor discriminate against any country. At the same time, the monitoring mechanism put in place by the new investment screening regulation has given the

---

[155] President of the European Commission Jean-Claude Juncker, State of the Union Address, 13 September 2017. See also European Commission, 'Regulation of the European Parliament and of the Council Establishing a Framework for Screening of Foreign Direct Investments into the European Union', COM(2017) 487 Final, Brussels, 13 September 2017; and European Commission, 'A New Industrial Strategy for Europe', Communication COM(2020) 102 Final, Brussels, 10 March 2020b.

[156] Official Journal of the European Union, 'Regulation (EU) 2019/452 of the European Parliament and of the Council Establishing a Framework for the Screening of Foreign Direct Investments into the Union', 19 March 2019b.

[157] European Commission, 'Screening of Foreign Direct Investment', News Archive, 24 November 2020e.

[158] Official Journal of the European Union, 2019b.

[159] European Commission, 'EU Foreign Investment Screening Mechanism Becomes Fully Operational', Press Release, 9 October 2020d.

EU a clearer view of foreign investment strategies in EU strategic sectors, especially with regards to major players such as China or Russia.'[160] Likewise, for another government official, 'foreign investments are welcome as long as they do not threaten our strategic autonomy; we need to make sure that—through their investments—certain actors, such as China but also others cannot influence or coerce our policy choices. It is really a question of freedom of manoeuvre for France and the European Union, which is why investments in certain areas such as critical infrastructure and other sensitive sectors can now be restricted.'[161]

Protecting Europe's Digital Infrastructure
Coupled with the establishment of this EU FDI framework, Paris contributed to the development of a common EU approach to 5G technology in order to better protect the European digital infrastructure from vendors of concern such as Huawei. Between 2018 and January 2020, France and other EU member states worked through 5G Cybersecurity Work Stream, a subgroup of the Network and Information Systems (NIS) Cooperation Group, to develop what became the EU Toolbox for 5G Cybersecurity. The NIS Cooperation Group had been created 'to ensure cooperation and information exchange among Member States' and 'to achieve a high common level of security for network and information systems in the European Union'.[162] Within it, the subgroup 5G Cybersecurity Work Stream was formed to facilitate coordination between member states in the areas of 5G standardization, avoid duplication of national approaches, and promote more secure products and processes, with the support of the European Commission and the EU Agency for Cybersecurity (ENISA).[163] This subgroup was formally co-led by several member states, including France, the Czech Republic, Italy, and Sweden, but also included other member states.[164] As explained by an EU official, 'France took a role as co-leader of the working group.'[165] The United Kingdom participated actively in the subgroup although it had no formal leading position (largely because it was in the process of leaving the Union after Brexit); and for its part,

---

[160] Jonas Roule, Deputy to the Head of the SGAE's Bureau for Trade and Development Aid (2020-present), interview, 12 April 2021.
[161] Interview, 22 June 2021.
[162] European Commission, 'NIS Cooperation Group', 26 March 2021b, https://digital-strategy.ec.europa.eu/en/policies/nis-cooperation-group.
[163] European Commission, 'FAQ—Report on the Impacts of the Commission Recommendation of 26 March 2019 on the Cybersecurity of 5G Networks', 15 December 2020l, https://ec.europa.eu/digital-single-market/en/faq/faq-report-impacts-commission-recommendation-26-march-2019-cybersecurity-5g-networks (accessed 1 December 2021).
[164] Interviews with French and EU officials, January–May 2021.
[165] Interview, 7 April 2021. The Work Stream met fourteen times between April 2019 and November 2020. European Commission, *Report on the Impacts of the Commission Recommendation of 26 March 2019 on the Cybersecurity of 5G Networks 2020*, Commission Staff Working Document, SWD(2020) 357 final, Brussels, 16 December 2020k, p. 5.

Germany, who also did not have a formal leading position, took a slightly less proactive role in the subgroup.[166]

An overarching goal of the French government was, as one MFA official explains, to achieve 'a balanced European approach on the question of 5G. We did not want the debate to crystallize around either pro-Huawei or anti-Huawei positions; that would not be a good solution for Europe.'[167] Specifically, two central considerations drove the French government to promote the development of the 5G Toolbox. One was to raise awareness among member states of the need to bolster the protection of their networks from suppliers of concern and to strengthen the capacity of EU member states to monitor and ensure the security of 5G networks. Secondly, Paris sought to overcome political fragmentation within the European Union on the question of 5G and Huawei and to foster greater political unity on this issue, thereby also reducing the vulnerability of EU member states to pressures from either Beijing or Washington.[168] In the words of another MFA official: 'in the triangle formed by Europe, China, and the United States on digital issues, we are of course much closer to the Americans than to the Chinese, but we do not want Europe to serve as a playground for the US–China confrontation on digital issues. So we want to have our own decision-making autonomy.'[169] Sir Julian King, the former EU Commissioner for the Security Union (2016–2019), further expounds this point: 'all the member states, even the large ones, took comfort in developing a collective policy instrument, the EU 5G Toolbox, because it meant that they would not be individually subject to pressures from either China or the United States, and so there was a kind of mutual benefit in doing it, to reduce vulnerability. The issue of Huawei was a difficult debate internally in some countries and therefore the best way to manage it was to manage it together.'[170]

The 5G Cybersecurity Work Stream proceeded in three steps: (i) its members completed national risk assessments on the key cybersecurity threats affecting their 5G networks (completed in July 2019); (ii) they jointly developed a coordinated EU risk assessment that built on their national risk assessments (published in October 2019); and (iii) they identified a set of common measures to be taken to mitigate the cybersecurity risks related to 5G networks, what became the EU Toolbox for 5G Cybersecurity (published in January 2020).[171]

---

[166] For a detailed analysis of the British and German positions, see Chapters 5 and 6.
[167] Interview, 30 March 2021.
[168] Interviews with French MFA and MEF officials as well as with EU officials, January–May 2021.
[169] Interview, 30 March 2021.
[170] Sir Julian King, interview, 28 May 2021.
[171] See Network and Information Systems (NIS) Cooperation Group, *EU Coordinated Risk Assessment of the Cybersecurity of 5G Networks*, Report, 9 October 2019; and European Commission, *Secure 5G Deployment in the EU—Implementing the EU Toolbox*, Communication COM(2020) 50 final, 29 January 2020i. For a description of the three steps, see European Commission, 'Recommendation 2019/534 of 26 March 2019: Cybersecurity of 5G Networks', C(2019)2335 final, 26 March 2019a; and European Commission, 2020k.

The third step proved to be the most challenging. While the members of the subgroup agreed on a set of 'technical measures' 'to strengthen the security of 5G networks and equipment by addressing the risks arising from technologies, processes, human and physical factors',[172] the definition of 'non-technical' (also referred to as 'strategic' or 'political') criteria in the identification of high-risk vendors—and the related measures to be implemented—were slightly more contentious. France sought to replicate at the EU level the two-fold criteria adopted in its national measures, namely technical and political criteria.[173] In particular, it sought to develop an objective risk assessment and policy instruments that would take into account both technical factors (i.e. the technical vulnerabilities of the equipment) and non-technical factors, including the degree of political influence of a third state on the 5G supplier.[174] Paris's approach was 'risk-based rather than company-based'; it did not want to discriminate against individual firms but rather aimed to adopt the same evaluation criteria for all firms, reserving the right to restrict certain equipment.[175] As detailed in Chapters 5 and 6, the United Kingdom and Germany initially pursued partly different approaches: London publicly identified Huawei as a company deemed to be a 'high-risk vendor'; Berlin, by contrast, initially sought to include in its national framework criteria only technical measures while eschewing political/strategic measures.

The members of the 5G Cybersecurity Work Stream finally agreed to implement a set of both technical and strategic measures that would, however, be 'company-agnostic' (or 'company-neutral'), i.e. not directed at one specific corporation or country. The final EU Toolbox for 5G Cybersecurity required member states to take measures such as strengthening security requirements for mobile network operators, assessing the risk profile of suppliers such as 'the risk of interference from non-EU state or state-backed actors through the 5G supply chain', applying restrictions for suppliers considered as high risk, including their exclusions for key assets, and developing a multi-vendor strategy to avoid dependency on a single supplier (especially for high-risk suppliers).[176] Ultimately, Chinese companies like Huawei were thus not explicitly targeted by the EU Toolbox. Yet, as explained by an EU official, 'the whole process around the EU 5G Toolbox was prompted to a large extent by the concerns linked to the Chinese national intelligence law in a context marked by very strong tensions between—and pressure by—the United States and China.'[177]

---

[172] European Commission, 2020i, p. 5.
[173] MFA official, interview, 30 March 2021.
[174] MFA official, interview, 30 March 2021.
[175] MFA official, interview, 30 March 2021.
[176] European Commission, 2020i, pp. 5–6.
[177] Interview, 7 April 2021. This process was first proposed by the Commission and the HRVP in the 2019 document *EU-China—A Strategic Outlook* (European Commission and HR/VP, 2019, p. 1).

Conclusion

France's 'China policy' has followed a similar path to its broader Asia-Pacific policy. After two decades in which French foreign policy mostly revolved around the pursuit of economic opportunities, China's rising assertiveness in Europe in the 2010s has, gradually and cumulatively, driven a major policy shift. Because of heightened threat perceptions of the PRC—combined with increasingly competitive economic relations with Beijing—France has rebalanced and hardened its 'China policy', putting greater emphasis on security considerations. These revised policy goals have been concretized in France's development, both nationally and at the EU level, of more stringent policy instruments to monitor and, if necessary, veto Chinese FDIs in sensitive sectors and to restrict the supply of advanced digital equipment by vendors with close links to the Chinese state, like Huawei. By doing so, Paris has promoted the development of an autonomous position for itself and for the European Union in the context of the mounting US-China strategic competition; one that would neither seek to contain the PRC, nor to maintain equidistance between the United States and China nor to pursue systematic alignment with Washington.

5
Germany's 'China Policy'
Engagement, Resilience, Leverage

Introduction

In light of its economic and political weight in Europe, Germany has long been the key trading partner for Beijing on the European continent. Yet, as China's capabilities and ambitions expanded, and as its companies became increasingly entrenched in Europe's industrial fabric, German policymakers have grown alarmed by the PRC's inroads into Europe's most sensitive high-tech sectors and by its rising economic and political clout across the region. These heightened threat perceptions, coupled with mounting Sino-German economic competition, have prompted Berlin to forge a comprehensive, cross-sectoral 'China policy' and to strive for greater intra-European coordination to better confront Chinese assertiveness in Europe.

While for the first two decades of the post-Cold War period German policymakers viewed the PRC primarily as an economic opportunity, by the 2010s they became increasingly wary of the political, security, and economic ramifications of Beijing's growing influence in Germany and, more broadly, in Europe (while simultaneously displaying mounting disquiet over Beijing's behaviour in the Asia-Pacific, as discussed in Chapter 2). Their core concerns revolved around the growing capacity of the PRC, through state-guided investors and suppliers, to siphon advanced technology with potential military applications and to endanger the integrity of the Germany's digital infrastructure; the mounting competition between Chinese and German firms which risked undermining Germany's technological edge because of discriminatory practices and the lack of reciprocity; and Beijing's use of its economic and political ties across Europe to drive a wedge between EU member states and exploit intra-EU fragmentation.

As a result, Berlin formulated a new 'China policy' that aimed to balance continued political and economic engagement vis-à-vis Beijing with a hardened stance across these various areas of concern. In cooperation with other European powers, Germany also promoted greater EU coordination in order to strengthen the collective leverage of the Union and of its member states vis-à-vis China, whilst carving a middle path for itself and the European Union amidst the mounting strategic rivalry between China and the United States. To achieve these goals, Berlin developed more stringent policy instruments at the national level to better control FDI inflows and to restrict 5G suppliers of concern like Huawei, while also fostering the creation of EU tools such as the EU FDI screening mechanism and the EU 5G Toolbox for Cybersecurity.

To substantiate this argument, this chapter proceeds as follows. The first two sections analyse the evolution of China's growing economic presence in the German high-tech industrial landscape and Berlin's heightened threat assessment of the PRC, two key factors influencing the making of Germany's 'China policy'. The subsequent two sections delineate how these evolving economic interests and threat perceptions have, in turn, led Germany to revise its policy goals and the policy instruments leveraged to achieve such goals.

Economic Interests

From the German reunification onward, the overall Sino-German economic relationship considerably deepened and broadened, but gradually also became more competitive. During the first two decades after the Cold War, Germany pursued major trade and investment opportunities in this large, emerging market, whereas Chinese FDIs in Germany—and, more broadly, its economic foothold on the continent—remained minimal. Yet, as China gradually transitioned towards value-added high-tech manufacturing in the 2010s, the two countries increasingly became economic competitors, thereby causing mounting frictions in the bilateral relationship.

China: An Emerging, Faraway Market

After reunification, as Germany's growth model came to rely ever more on foreign demand,[1] its exports to the PRC soared from $2.5bn to $52bn between 1991 and 2009,[2] making Germany by far China's largest trading partner in the European Union.[3] The two economies became largely complementary. Whereas China specialized in labour-intensive manufacturing, providing a large market and a cheap labour force, the German industry—skilled in high value-added capital

---

[1] Stephan Danninger and Fred Joutz, 'What Explains Germany's Rebounding Export Market Share', *IMF Working Paper*, WP/07/24, 2007. See also Chapter 2.
[2] UN Comtrade—International Trade Statistics Database, https://comtrade.un.org.
[3] Gudrun Wacker, 'Changes and Continuities in EU–China Relations: A German Perspective', in *US–China–EU Relations: Managing the New World Order*, edited by Robert S. Ross, Øystein Tunsjø, and Zhang Tuosheng (New York: Routledge, 2010), pp. 78–79. For more details on Sino-German trade relations, see Chapter 2 and the comparative charts in Appendix B.

goods—brought high-tech capital equipment.[4] For Heinrich Kreft, in charge of the Asia-Pacific in the Policy Planning Staff of the Federal Foreign Office (FFO, 1996–2001) and later Deputy Head of the FFO Policy Planning Staff (2004–2006), the 'unwritten deal was market entry and market shares in China in exchange for German know-how.'[5]

In this context, Chinese direct investments in Germany remained very limited. As detailed in a report of the Deutsche Bundesbank they totalled a value of merely €0.5bn between 1995 and 2004.[6] Furthermore, most of Chinese acquisitions revolved around 'pilot projects', several of which failed.[7] Examples include Chinese investments in the Northern German Pencil Factory (Norddeutsche Bleistiftfabrik), Hirschfelder Leinen und Textil GmbH, or Fairchild Dornier, which all subsequently declared bankruptcy and dissolved.[8] In the telecommunications sector, the Chinese company Huawei first entered the German market in the early 2000s. In 2003, it established a joint venture with Siemens to develop the Chinese 3G mobile communications standard (TD-SCDMA), subsequently supplying also 4G telecoms equipment in Germany.[9] By the late 2000s, Huawei had eight subsidiaries in Germany and a workforce of over five hundred employees.[10]

Overall, whereas the PRC gradually became a major destination for German exports and investments, until the late 2000s the volume of Chinese FDIs in Germany remained inconsequential, largely revolving around unsuccessful projects. The PRC's economic reach in Germany was thus marginal.

China Comes to Germany

It is only in the 2010s that the pace of China's FDIs in Germany soared as a result of Beijing's policies aimed at fostering China's technological development and

---

[4] On Sino-German economic ties in the 1990s and early 2000s, see Markus Taube, 'Economic Relations between Germany and Mainland China, 1979–2000', *Duisburg Working Papers on East Asian Economic Studies*, no. 59 (2001): pp. 1–24; and Hans Kundnani and Jonas Parello-Plesner, 'China and Germany: Why the Emerging Special Relationship Matters for Europe', European Council on Foreign Relations, *Policy Brief*, 2012, pp. 1–24; Wacker, 2010.

[5] Interview, 6 December 2020. This point was confirmed by a former representative of the Federation of German Industries (BDI), interview, 17 December 2020.

[6] Deutsche Bundesbank. 'Germany's External Relations with the People's Republic of China', *Monthly Report*, July 2005, p. 49.

[7] Shuwen Bian and Oliver Emons, 'Chinese Investments in Germany: Increasing in Line with Chinese Industrial Policy', in *Chinese Investments in Europe: Corporate Strategies and Labour Relations*, edited by Jan Drahokoupil (Brussels: Europe Trade Union Institute, 2017), pp. 157–158.

[8] Bian and Emons, 2017.

[9] TD-SCDMA refers to Time Division Synchronous Code Division Multiple Access. See Mario Glowik, 'Market Entry Strategies of Huawei in Germany and the Russian Federation from a Network Theory Perspective' in *Huawei Goes Global, Vol. II: Regional, Geopolitical Perspectives and Crisis Management*, edited by Wenxian Zhang, Ilan Alon, and Christoph Lattemann (Cham, Switzerland: Palgrave Macmillan, 2020), p. 15.

[10] Stefanie Sohm, Bernd Michael Linke, and Andreas Klossek, *Chinese Companies in Germany: Chances and Challenges* (Gütersloh: Deloitte/Bertelsmann Stiftung, 2009), p. 31.

FDI outflows.[11] The gradual transformation of China from an FDI import country to an FDI export country, coupled with the attractiveness of Germany for Chinese companies, drove a considerable expansion in China's economic presence in Germany.

Not only did the PRC become Germany's first trading partner in the world,[12] but its presence in the German industrial landscape very substantially increased. Chinese FDIs in Germany rose from $1.5bn to $14bn between 2010 and 2019 (in stock), making it the second-largest European destination for Chinese investments after the United Kingdom (see the comparative charts on the Big Three's investment ties with China in Appendix B).[13] These investments largely targeted advanced manufacturing capabilities such as automotive and industrial equipment (which accounted for more than 65 per cent of all Chinese FDIs in Germany), thus reflecting the PRC's interest in high-end manufacturing capabilities.[14] However, they also focused on sectors such as finance, business services, and information technology, among others.[15]

Some of the major Chinese FDIs in Germany included, among others: Lenovo's investment in Medion (consumer electronics, 2011), Weichai Power's acquisition of the Kion Group (industrial machinery and equipment, 2012), the Aviation Industry Corporation of China (AVIC)'s purchase of the aircraft engine maker Thielert (2013), Beijing Enterprises' investment in EEW Energy from Waste (utilities, 2016) or Luxshare's takeover of ZF Friedrichshafen (automotive, 2017).[16] But the largest and, as detailed later, most controversial deal was Midea's takeover of the leading robot manufacturer Kuka, in 2016, for $5bn.[17]

---

[11] These policies are discussed in the Introduction of Part II. On China's growing FDIs in Germany, see Thilo Hanemann and Mikko Huotari, 'Preparing for a New Era of Chinese Capital: Chinese FDI in Europe and Germany', *MERICS Papers on China*, June 2015, p. 5; Bian and Emons, 2017, pp. 163–168.

[12] FFO, 'China: Land with Many Faces', at https://www.auswaertiges-amt.de/en/aussenpolitik/regionaleschwerpunkte/asien/-/231348. See also Chapter 2 and the comparative charts on the Big Three's trade relations with China in Appendix B.

[13] National Bureau of Statistics of China, *Statistical Yearbooks of China*, http://www.stats.gov.cn/english/Statisticaldata/AnnualData/ (see Appendix B for details on the data). See also Hanemann and Huotari, 2015, p. 5; Rhodium Group, 'People's Republic of China/European Union Direct Investment', *Cross Border Monitor*, 16 January 2019, p. 12; Thilo Hanemann, Mikko Huotari, and Agatha Kratz, *Chinese FDI in Europe, 2018 Trends and Impact of New Screening Policies*, Report by Rhodium Group (RHG) and Mercator Institute for China Studies (MERICS), March 2019, p. 7.

[14] Hanemann and Huotari, 2015, p. 5.

[15] Hanemann and Huotari, 2015, p. 5.

[16] Mikko Huotari, 'Germany's Changing Take on Chinese Direct Investment: Balancing Openness with Greater Scrutiny', in *Chinese Investment in Europe: A Country-Level Approach*, edited by John Seaman, Mikko Huotari, and Miguel Otero-Iglesias (Paris: French Institute of International Relations, 2017), p. 63; and Christoph Schnellbach and Joyce Man, 'Germany and China: Embracing a Different Kind of Partnership?', Center for Applied Policy Research, *CAP Working Paper*, September 2015, p. 15; Hanemann and Huotari, 2015, pp. 16 et seq.

[17] Hanemann and Huotari, 2015, p. 16; Thilo Hanemann and Mikko Huotari, 'Record Flows and Growing Imbalances: Chinese Investment in Europe in 2016', *MERICS Papers on China no. 3*, January 2017, p. 5.

Chinese companies also became increasingly involved in the digitization of the German economy, referred to as Industry 4.0.[18] Huawei, in particular, substantially increased its presence in Germany first with the supply of 4G and then also of 5G technology.[19] By the late 2010s, as Berlin aimed to support the deployment of 5G networks and to make Germany 'a lead market for 5G applications',[20] it became the largest European recipient of Chinese capital in the information technology (IT) sector, receiving twice as much investment as France and the United Kingdom in this sector.[21] The majority of 5G trials in Germany (nine out of fifteen) were built by Huawei.[22] In 2018, Huawei signed a memorandum of understanding (MoU) with the city of Düsseldorf to deploy 'Smart City' services through the development of their 5G infrastructure.[23] The Chinese company also established a variety of collaborative research and development (R&D) activities with German universities and research institutes such as the Technical University of Munich and RWTH Aachen University while also founding the Huawei European Research Center (ERC), in Munich, which focused on advanced technology R&D, architecture evolution as well as design and strategic technical planning.[24] According to a report commissioned by Huawei and carried out by Oxford Economics, this high-tech company reportedly contributed to Germany's gross domestic product (GDP) more than to that of the United Kingdom and France (€3.7bn versus €3.6bn and €1.8bn respectively).[25]

As Sino-German economic relationship deepened, however, it also became increasingly competitive. With the PRC gradually transitioning from labour-intensive manufacturing to higher value-added capital goods manufacturing, the

---

[18] Industry 4.0 is an initiative of the German government that aims to spur digital manufacturing by increasing digitization and the interconnection of products, value chains and business models, focusing on the concepts of smart factory and cyber-physical systems (CPS) which integrate advanced technologies such as automation, data exchange in manufacturing technology, 3D printing, cloud computing, and the Internet of Things. See Heiner Lasi, Peter Fettke, Hans-Georg Kemper, Thomas Feld, and Michael Hoffmann, 'Industry 4.0', *Business and Information Systems Engineering* 6, no. 4 (2014): pp. 239–242; Ling Li, 'China's Manufacturing Locus in 2025: With a Comparison of "Made-in-China"', *Technological Forecasting & Social Change* 135 (2018): pp. 66–74. See also Federal Minister of State for Cultural and Educational Relations, Maria Böhmer, Speech at the second Business Forum on Digital Innovation, IT and Communications Technology', *Newsroom*, 30 September 2016.
[19] See for instance, Glowik, 2020; and Huawei Investment & Holding Co., *2015 Annual Report: Building a Better Connected World*, 2016, p. 7.
[20] Federal Ministry of Transport and Digital Infrastructure, *5G Strategy for Germany*, July 2017, p. 2.
[21] Hanemann and Huotari, 2015, p. 20.
[22] In 2019, nine 5G trials were built by Huawei, four by Ericsson and one by Nokia (and two by other companies). European 5G Observatory, 'Germany', https://5gobservatory.eu/5g-trial/major-european-5g-trials-and-pilots.
[23] Huawei, 'Duisburg Germany and Huawei Sign MoU to Build a Smart City', *News and Events*, 12 January 2018.
[24] Ingo Liefnera, Yue-fang Sib, and Kerstin Schäfera, 'A Latecomer Firm's R&D Collaboration with Advanced Country Universities and Research Institutes: The Case of Huawei in Germany', *Technovation* 86–87 (2019): pp. 3–14.
[25] Oxford Economics, *The Economic Impact of Huawei* (London: Oxford Economics, 2020), p. 14. On the methodology used to assess the direct, indirect, and induced contribution to national GDPs, see pp. 8–9.

2010s witnessed growing concerns in Berlin over the increasingly direct competition between German and Chinese companies—a trend aggravated by the PRC's extensive subsidizing of Chinese companies and by the continued regulatory restrictions on German investments in China.[26] With China becoming technologically more advanced, the PRC developed into an economic competitor, and the bilateral economic relationship grew increasingly strained.[27]

Threat Perceptions

As China's reach into Europe expanded and as Sino-German economic relations gradually became more competitive, Berlin's threat assessment of the PRC evolved accordingly. From the early 1990s to the late 2000s, Germany looked at China as a lucrative market that posed few security challenges. It is only in the subsequent decade that China's growing clout in Germany and across Europe caused German policymakers' threat perceptions to intensify. These heightened political, security, and economic concerns, in turn, drove Berlin to revise and harden its 'China policy'.

China: Minute Economic Foothold, Few Security Concerns

From the end of the Cold War to the late 2000s, the rise of China was not a source of apprehension in Berlin. The PRC's very limited presence in Germany and in Europe caused no significant concern among German policymakers from either an economic or a security perspective.[28]

This was not only because very few Chinese companies were active in Germany but also because, as previously noted, the few takeovers by Chinese companies had mostly resulted in failures.[29] Accordingly, in the words of an official in the Federal Ministry of Economic Affairs (FMEA), 'at that time, foreign direct Chinese investment didn't play any significant role; it was rather the other way around', with German companies being increasingly involved in the Chinese market.[30]

As explained by the former German Ambassador to the PRC Volker Stanzel (2004–2007), Berlin looked at the rise of China 'through the lens of our economic

---

[26] See, e.g. the report by the BDI, 'Systemic Competitor – How Do We Deal with China's State-Controlled Economy?', *BDI Policy Paper*, January 2019, pp. 3 and 7. See also Thilo Hanemann and Mikko Huotari, 'Preparing for New Era of Chinese Capital: Chinese FDI in Europe and Germany', *MERICS Papers on China*, June 2015, p. 35.
[27] Interviews with officials in the Federal Ministry of Economic Affairs (FMEA) and FFO, September–December 2020. See also the previous foonote.
[28] Interviews with former officials in the FFO, MoD, and the Federal Chancellery, January–December 2020.
[29] Interviews with FFO officials working in the 2000s, December 2020.
[30] Interview, 9 December 2020.

interests and not through the lens of security'.[31] A former official in the Chancellery confirms that 'there was little to no concern; China was perceived as such an interesting market that all other considerations were deemed secondary'.[32]

The main if not only area of apprehension in the bilateral relationship was China's theft of technology through industrial espionage, including cyber-espionage.[33] Yet, German innovation capabilities were considered sufficiently advanced to maintain a technological edge despite China's illicit acquisition of German technologies and know-how.[34] A widespread belief was, as explained by a former representative of the BDI, that 'because we had one of the most innovative industries of the world, we didn't have to be afraid of the competition with China.'[35] Likewise, in the words of a former FFO official, 'we worried about this issue, but it was a nuisance rather than a big strategic problem.'[36]

Heightened Concerns over China's Inroads into Europe

Beginning in the 2010s and accelerating after the middle of the decade, however, Berlin grew increasingly concerned by the mounting Sino-German economic competition and by China's expanding reach and influence in Germany and Europe (while it concurrently grew wary of Chinese assertiveness in the Asia-Pacific, as discussed in Chapter 2). Specifically, the core concerns of German officials revolved around what they saw as a three-fold—economic, security, and political—challenge posed by the PRC.

Economic Competition, Reciprocity, and Technological Edge

For one, policymakers and the business community shared rising apprehension over the intensifying economic competition between German and Chinese companies as well as over the lack of economic reciprocity.[37] They considered that whereas growing bilateral economic exchanges benefitted the PRC by upgrading and modernizing its industrial base—thus also partly fuelling Sino-German economic competition—China's industrial policies were unfairly putting the German industry at a comparative disadvantage through various discriminatory measures on market access and investments.[38] These measures included: restrictions on German FDIs in the PRC such as investment caps or the obligation to establish

---

[31] Interview, 12 November 2020.
[32] Interview, 4 December 2020.
[33] Interviews with FFO and MFEA officials working in the 2000s, September–December 2020.
[34] Interviews with former FFO officials, September–December 2020.
[35] Interview, 17 December 2020.
[36] Interview, 17 November 2020.
[37] Interviews with officials in the FFO and MFEA as well as with representatives of the BDI, September-December 2020. See also BDI, 2019, p. 7.
[38] Interviews with officials in the FFO and MFEA as well as with representatives of the BDI, September–December 2020.

joint ventures, forced technology transfers and the appropriation of intellectual property, the distortion of markets and prices through direct and indirect state subsidies, and state-guided takeovers of German high-tech companies while protecting Chinese industry against FDIs.[39] These concerns were particularly intense in Germany, as compared to France and the United Kingdom, partly because of the relatively greater size of the industrial sector, and of manufacturing in particular, in the German economy.[40]

Through these practices, Beijing was seen as supporting its ambition to become a global technological power by favouring its industry at the expense of German companies.[41] As a senior diplomat puts it, 'the fear is that, because of China's investments and its acquisitions of German technology, we will end up losing our edge over China in key industrial sectors, especially those identified in the *Made in China 2025* (MiC25) development plan.'[42]

Most notably, the acquisition by the Chinese group Midea of the German robotics company Kuka constituted, in the word of a FFO official, 'an eye opener.'[43] Robotics was one of the key sectors targeted by the MiC25 plan and Beijing had manifested its ambition to expand the global market share of Chinese-made robots from 31 per cent in 2016 to over 50 per cent by 2020.[44] The acquisition by China of such a cutting-edge high-tech manufacturing company constituted a critical moment which brought to the fore the issue of Chinese access to German advanced technology manufacturing and the question of investment screening and protection.[45]

---

[39] Interviews with officials in the FFO and MFEA as well as with representatives of the BDI, September–December 2020. See also Federal Minister of Defence Annegret Kramp-Karrenbauer (since 2019), Speech at the Presentation of the Steuben Schurz Media Award, 23 October 2020; Federal Minister for Economic Affairs and Energy Sigmar Gabriel (2013–2017) quoted in Michael Nienaber, 'German Minister Ups Rhetoric against Takeovers ahead of China Trip', *Reuters*, 29 October 2016; BDI, 2019, pp. 3 and 7.

[40] Between 2009 and 2019, the contribution of the industrial sector to the German GDP was almost 27 per cent as opposed to 17 per cent in the United Kingdom and in France. Similarly, the value added by the manufacturing sector (as a per cent of GDP) in 2019 was 19 per cent for Germany but only 8.6 per cent for the United Kingdom and for France. Data retrieved from the World Bank 'World Development Indicators', https://databank.worldbank.org/source/world-development-indicators.

[41] Interviews with FFO and MFEA officials, September–December 2020. See also French, German, and Italian Ministers for Economic Affairs, Letter to the EU Commissioner for Trade Cecilia Malmström, February 2017, p. 1.

[42] Interview, 2 December 2020. The ten sectors identified by the MiC2025 are: new generation information technology, automated machine tools and robotics, space and aviation equipment, maritime equipment and high-tech shipping, modern rail transportation equipment, new energy vehicles and equipment, power generation equipment, agricultural equipment, new materials, and biopharma and advanced medical products. State Council of the PRC, *Made in China 2025*, 7 July 2015b, pp. 22–27, http://www.cittadellascienza.it/cina/wp-content/uploads/2017/02/IoT-ONE-Made-in-China-2025.pdf. For a discussion, see the Introduction of Part II.

[43] Interview, 6 November 2020.

[44] See State Council of the PRC, 2015b; and Meia Nouwens and Helena Legarda, 'China's Pursuit of Advanced Dual-Use Technologies', *IISS Research Papers*, 18 December 2018, https://www.iiss.org/blogs/research-paper/2018/12/emerging-technology-dominance.

[45] Interviews with officials in the FFO, MFEA, the Chancellery, and the Office of the President, January–December 2020 and January 2021.

Security Concerns: Advanced Dual-Use Technology, Cybersecurity, and Critical Infrastructure

Relatedly, Berlin also displayed rising concerns over the security ramifications of China's investments in, and supply of, certain advanced technologies in Europe. The PRC's acquisitions in strategic sectors spurred rising fears not only over China's growing technological capabilities and economic competition with German companies but also over its capacity to siphon advanced dual-use technology (i.e. with both civilian and military applications).[46]

Against the background of China's 'civil-military fusion' and of its MiC2025 plan, the main concerns of German policymakers revolved around dual-use technology transfers in those sensitive sectors that received greater volumes of Chinese investments in Germany, such as the semiconductor industry (including sensors, optics, radar, information and communications technology (ICT), and aerospace insofar as they involved semiconductor technology) and emerging technologies (e.g. artificial intelligence).[47] For instance, as further discussed below, German officials grew wary over the attempted acquisition by China's Vital Materials of PPM Pure Metals, a supplier of metals used in semiconductors and in infrared detectors with military applications; and over the bid by a subsidiary of the state-controlled missile producer China Aerospace and Industry Group (CASIC) to take over a German company (IMST) specialized in satellite and radar systems and in technologies used for critical infrastructure.[48] In particular, they worried about the transfer of sensitive know-how to companies with ties to the Chinese military and security services and about the possible disruption of the security of supply for German armed forces.[49]

The growing role of Huawei in the provision of 5G equipment fuelled further concerns over the ensuing risks of cyber-espionage and disruption of Germany's digital infrastructure. Policymakers in Berlin feared that Germany's excessive dependence on Huawei for the provision of such networks could hinder the security of supply for its critical infrastructure. Furthermore, given the suspected ties of Huawei with Chinese intelligence services and the growing sophistication of

---

[46] Interviews with officials in the FFO, MFEA, the Chancellery, and the Office of the President, January–December 2020 and January 2021.

[47] For a sectoral analysis of Chinese investments in Germany, see for instance Wan-Hsin Liu and Xinming Xia, 'China's Investments in Germany and the Impact of the COVID-19 Pandemic', *Intereconomics* 56, no. 2 (2021): pp. 113–119; Emily de La Bruyère and Nathan Picarsic, *Made in Germany: Co-opted by China* (Washington, DC: Foundation for Defense of Democracies, 2020), p. 13; and Cora Jongbluth, *Is China Systematically Buying Up Key Technologies? Chinese M&A Transactions in Germany in the Context of 'Made in China 2025'* (Gütersloh: Bertelsmann Stiftung, 2018), p. 19.

[48] Zandi Shabalala and Tom Daly, 'Germany Blocked Chinese Metals Takeover on Military Concerns—-Sources', *Reuters*, 14 August 2020; Falk Schöning et al., 'This Time's for Real: German Government Prohibits Acquisition of a Tech Company by a Chinese Acquirer', *Hogan Lovells*, 4 December 2020.

[49] Interviews with officials in the FMoD, BMI, FFO, and FMEA, December 2020 and January 2021.

Chinese cyberattacks on the German government and high-tech industry, this dependence raised the possibility of attacks aimed at spying over the data traffic flowing in the network therein or at disrupting parts of the digital infrastructure.[50]

A senior intelligence official details Berlin's threat assessment as follows. The former Vice President of the German cybersecurity agency, the Federal Office for Information Security (BSI, in the German acronym, 2013–2016), and later Director General for Cyber and Information Security at the Federal Ministry of the Interior (BMI in the German acronym, since 2018), Andreas Könen, stresses that the BMI and BSI saw evidence that 'the threat had shifted: it had broadened from an exclusive concern over "confidentiality"—namely external actors entering the telecommunications network to spy over data flows—to a concern also over "availability", with external actors inserting malware to take control of the network or disrupt the supply chain of key components for the critical digital infrastructure.'[51] This concern over the integrity of critical supply chains, he adds, had become 'much more prominent' than in the previous decade.[52] These threats were, in turn, heightened by two concerns linked specifically to Huawei:

> The clear, key concern is that Huawei is not really a private company. It is, de facto, a state-owned company. In the end, if you look carefully into it, the final decisions are taken only by a small number of people and they are under a strong influence of the Chinese government. And so the basic fear is that the influence of the Communist Party and of the intelligence services goes deeply into the company and influences the management level and how this company behaves. That is the basic concern. A second concern is the question of how Huawei's products are designed, namely whether Huawei is required to build backdoors and to open up a product so that Chinese intelligence services can look into it remotely—which is linked to the concerns over both confidentiality and availability.[53]

---

[50] Interviews with officials in the FMoD, BMI, FFO, and FMEA, December 2020 and January 2021. See also Federal Minister for Foreign Affairs Heiko Maas, 'European Digital Sovereignty Is Long Overdue: FM Maas Talks to *Die Zeit* Weekly Newspaper', 12 April 2019c; FFO Commissioner for International Cyber Policy Norbert Riedel, 'Cyber Security as a Dimension of Security Policy', Speech at Chatham House, London, 18 May 2015; Secretary of State at the Federal Foreign Office Antje Leendertse, Inaugural Address to the Cyber Security Summit, Berlin, 26 November 2019; Federal Minister for Foreign Affairs Heiko Maas, Speech at the Ambassadors Conference of the French Republic, 31 August 2020e; Federal Minister for Foreign Affairs Heiko Maas, 'An Agenda for Peace and Security? Priorities for a Social Democratic Foreign Policy for the European Union and the United Nations', Speech at the Friedrich-Ebert-Stiftung's Tiergarten Conference, 28 November 2019b; Federal Minister of State for Europe Michael Roth, 'The Security of our Citizens Is at Stake', published in *Der Spiegel*, 2 August 2020. See also Reuters Staff, 'German Security Office Warned German Firms about Chinese Hacking: Report', *Reuters*, 19 December 2019; Tom Jowitt, 'German Industrial Giants Attacked by Chinese Hackers—-Report', *Silicon.co.uk*, 24 July 2019.
[51] Andreas Könen, interview, 6 January 2021.
[52] Andreas Könen, interview, 6 January 2021.
[53] Andreas Könen, interview, 6 January 2021.

Furthermore, the research partnerships between Chinese companies like Huawei and German universities and research institutes provoked additional concerns because, as explained by one government official, the latter often ignored the companies' ties with the Chinese intelligence services and the ensuing risks of interference and espionage.[54] Thomas Bagger, the Director of Foreign Policy in the Office of President Steinmeier (since 2017), emphasizes the growing disquiet over certain cooperation channels established by Chinese universities and companies with German universities and research institutes; notably, 'the question of infiltration, manipulation all the way to intellectual property theft and of Chinese attempts at infiltrating these institutes and recruit people is becoming more and more prominent.'[55] The President of the Federal Intelligence Service (BND in the German acronym), Germany's foreign intelligence agency, therefore warned against integrating Huawei into the country's 5G network given that the company 'cannot be trusted fully' because of its ties with the Chinese state and the Communist Party.[56]

China's Political Influence in Europe: A Wedge Strategy

Finally, Berlin grew increasingly wary of how the PRC was leveraging its growing economic ties in Germany and across Europe to gain political influence over the European Union and its member states as part of a strategy, in the words of a senior foreign policy advisor to the German President, of 'divide and rule in Europe.'[57] Specifically, a core concern was that through a combination of economic incentives and coercion, coupled with domestic political interference, Beijing sought to influence national policies and to drive a wedge between EU members—thereby exploiting existing intra-European divisions to weaken the European Union in its dealings with the PRC.[58] Former Foreign Minister Sigmar Gabriel (2017–2018) bluntly stated that China was 'constantly trying to test and undermine the unity of the European Union'; 'individual states or groups are tested with sticks and carrots to see whether they want to remain in the community that is the European Union or whether they can be detached from it.'[59] Likewise, as the Minister of State for Europe Michael Roth (2013–2021) put it, China's 'authoritarian, one-party state passes up no opportunity to drive a wedge between the

---

[54] Interview, 17 December 2020.
[55] Thomas Bagger, interview, 20 January 2021.
[56] Bruno Kahl quoted in Patrick Donahue, 'German Spy Chief Says Huawei Can't Be "Fully Trusted" in 5G', *Bloomberg*, 29 October 2019.
[57] Thomas Bagger, the former Head of Policy Planning at the FFO (2011–2017) and then Director of Foreign Policy in the Office of the President (since 2017), interview, 6 May 2020.
[58] Interviews with current and former FFO officials, January–December 2020.
[59] Federal Minister for Foreign Affairs Sigmar Gabriel (2017–2018), Speech at the Munich Security Conference, 17 February 2018.

EU member states and weaken them'—a point also stressed by several German diplomats.[60]

For instance, the development of China's political and economic ties with smaller European countries through the '16+1' mechanism (previously labelled '17+1') or its infrastructure investments as part of its Belt and Road Initiative (BRI) were viewed, as one diplomat puts it, as 'directed towards weakening EU unity; that is a very serious issue for us that also has obvious security implications'[61]—which is also why Germany refused to join the BRI.[62] In the words of one official, 'the Belt and Road Initiative is more than an economic initiative, it is a strategic and geopolitical initiative.'[63]

Policy Goals

As a result of these shifting economic interests and changing threat assessment, the goals of Berlin's 'China policy' evolved accordingly. In the first two decades after the Cold War, because of low threat perceptions and complementary economic models, Germany's policy towards Beijing was geared towards further deepening its bilateral economic and political ties while seeking to integrate the PRC in the international system. However, by the 2010s, heightened threat perceptions of China's growing clout in Germany and Europe—coupled with concerns over the increasingly competitive character of their economic relationship—drove Berlin to revise the goals of its 'China policy' and to harden its stance vis-à-vis Beijing.

An Exclusive Economic Lens

The overwhelming focus of Berlin's 'China policy' in the 1990s and 2000s was economic, with little if any emphasis on national security considerations. In particular, as detailed in Chapter 2, Germany pursued three intertwined policy goals. First, it aimed to expand its trade and investments opportunities in this major,

---

[60] Federal Minister of State for Europe Michael Roth, 2020. In the words of one diplomat, 'we see this as an attempt to divide the unity of the EU member states. [...] This is something we find very worrying.' Joern Beissert, then Counselor for Asia and Security Policy at the German Embassy in the United States (2017–2019) and later Head of the FFO's China Division (since 2019), 'The China Challenge', Speech at the University of North Carolina at Chapel Hill, 20 September 2018, https://www.youtube.com/watch?v=Lz5RqjkHzmQ&list=PUPssYbwV8FFSw_ZbhBV5X3Q&index=83.

[61] Interview, 14 March 2020. On Berlin's scepticism over the then '17+1' mechanisms and the BRI, see also Federal Minister of State Niels Annen, Opening Remarks at the SWP Conference on U.S. Foreign Policy under the Trump Administration, 19 February 2019. On the transition from '17+1' to '16+1', see Stuart Lau, 'Lithuania Pulls out of China's "17+1" Bloc in Eastern Europe', *Politico EU*, 21 May 2021.

[62] 'Germany Demands More Free Trade Guarantees on China Silk Road Plan: Minister', *Reuters*, 14 May 2017.

[63] Interview, 9 December 2020.

emerging market.⁶⁴ A former senior foreign policy official explains that the PRC was 'mostly seen through economic and business lenses with great, great potential for further development'.⁶⁵ A former Asia-hand in the FFO confirms that, in these decades, 'the German angle on China was essentially an economic one'; the PRC 'was largely perceived as an economic opportunity; and Germany prided itself on having seized the opportunity of trade and investment with China and that, for a very long time, we probably did it better than anybody else'.⁶⁶ Additionally, German policymakers sought to broaden the areas of diplomatic and economic cooperation in order to entice China to become a 'responsible stakeholder' in the international system.⁶⁷ Finally, in line with its so-called 'change through trade' policy, Berlin hoped that greater bilateral and multilateral engagement with the PRC might encourage Beijing to implement domestic reforms and foster its convergence towards a Western open market, liberal democracy.⁶⁸

The former Consul General in Chengdu (2004–2006) and then Deputy Head of the FFO's East Asia Division (2006–2008), Thomas Gerberich, summarizes these goals as follows: 'In the relationship between Germany and China, our main focus was on economic relations and economic goals; we created a bilateral relationship based on mutual trust and cooperation in a variety of areas with the goal of binding China into a system of multilateral institutions; and the hope, at that time, was that China would change, that economic and social change would advance rapidly.'⁶⁹

'China Policy' Revisited: Engagement, Resilience, and Leverage

It is only in the 2010s, because of rising threat perceptions of the PRC and of growing Sino-German economic competition, that Berlin recalibrated the goals of its 'China policy' to better confront the multipronged challenge posed by China's growing foothold in Europe.

On the one hand, Germany continued to seek deeper economic ties with China and to enable its integration in the international system as a 'responsible global player'.⁷⁰ On the other hand, however, it revised its policy in order to take into greater account the increasingly competitive dimensions of its relationship with

---

⁶⁴ For more details, see the section 'Trade, Integration and Convergence' in Chapter 2.
⁶⁵ Interview, 17 November 2020.
⁶⁶ Interview, 2 December 2020.
⁶⁷ See the section 'Trade, Integration and Convergence' in Chapter 2.
⁶⁸ See the section 'Trade, Integration and Convergence' in Chapter 2.
⁶⁹ Interview, 15 October 2020.
⁷⁰ Federal Minister for Foreign Affairs Guido Westerwelle (2009–2013), Article to Mark the 40th Anniversary of the Establishment of Diplomatic Relations with the People's Republic of China, *Frankfurter Allgemeine Zeitung*, 11 October 2012b. See also Federal Minister for Foreign Affairs Frank-Walter Steinmeier (2013–2017), Interview with the *Global Times Beijing*, 17 April 2014; and FFO, 'Maas: "Solutions to Many of the World's Problems Can Only Be Found by Working with China"', 12 November 2018, https://www.auswaertiges-amt.de/en/aussenpolitik/laenderinformationen/china-node/maas-visits-china/2161122.

Beijing. Consistently with the relabelling of the PRC by the European Commission and the EEAS as a 'partner', 'competitor', and 'systemic rival',[71] Berlin sought to deal with the PRC as a partner on a variety of bilateral, regional, and global issues, but also as a competitor and a systemic rival on other issues.[72] As explained by the former Head of Policy Planning at the FFO (2011–2017) and then Director of Foreign Policy in the Office of President Frank-Walter Steinmeier (since 2017), Thomas Bagger, 'the assumption of China's gradual convergence with the West, which had characterized previous decades, gradually faded away and was replaced by a more realistic, more sceptical perspective of China's rise'; Berlin now aimed to 'maintain a co-operative approach wherever possible, but acknowledged that there are parts of the relationship that are more competitive and some that are more adversarial; we therefore seek to promote cooperation wherever possible and to push back—or establish countermeasures—where necessary.'[73]

Germany pursued these goals also by prompting greater intra-European cohesion and unity in order to more effectively tackle the concerns posed by China's rise. 'If we do not succeed in developing a single [EU] strategy towards China,' as former Foreign Minister Sigmar Gabriel stated, 'then China will succeed in dividing Europe.'[74] Likewise, in the words of former Chancellor Merkel (2005–2021), 'one of the greatest dangers [is] that every member state in Europe makes its own China policy and that we end up sending quite different signals'; that 'would be disastrous for us in Europe.'[75] German policymakers therefore considered that only through a united and coherent approach could the European Union and its member states better protect and enforce their interests vis-à-vis China.[76] In the words

---

[71] European Commission and High Representative of the Union for Foreign Affairs and Security Policy (HR/VP), *EU-China: A Strategic Outlook*, 12 March 2019, p. 1.

[72] Interviews with FFO officials, January–June 2020. See also Federal Minister for Foreign Affairs Heiko Maas (since 2018), 'China ist Partner, Wettbewerber und Rivale', Interview with *Redaktionsnetzwerk Deutschland*, 12 July 2020b; and State Secretary at the FFO Andreas Michaelis, 'Keynote Speech "EU Retreat on China: A Strategic Approach for Dealing with China"', FFO News Room, 2 March 2020.

[73] Thomas Bagger, interview, 6 May 2020. On this point see also Secretary of State at the FFO Andreas Michaelis, 2020.

[74] Quoted in Lucrezia Poggetti, 'One China—One Europe? German Foreign Minister's Remarks Irk Beijing', *The Diplomat*, 9 September 2017.

[75] Quoted in Federal Government, 'Rede von Bundeskanzlerin Merkel im Deutschen Bundestag', 27 November 2019b, https://www.bundesregierung.de/breg-de/suche/rede-von-bundeskanzlerin-merkel-im-deutschen-bundestag-1699682. See also 'German Chancellor Angela Merkel Urges Europe to Stick Together in China Dealings', *The Straits Times*, 27 November 2019.

[76] Federal Government, *Policy Guidelines for the Indo-Pacific: Germany—Europe—Asia. Shaping the 21st Century Together*, 2020a, p. 11. On the need for greater unity in EU policy toward the PRC, see also Federal Minister for Foreign Affairs Sigmar Gabriel, 'Europe Needs Vision, Not Technocrats', published in French in *Le Monde*, 19 October 2017; Federal Government, 'Regierungserklärung von Bundeskanzlerin Merkel', 17 October 2019c, https://www.bundesregierung.de/breg-de/suche/regierungserklaerung-von-bundeskanzlerin-merkel-1682852; Federal Minister for Foreign Affairs Heiko Maas, Opening Address at the Virtual Annual Council Meeting of the European Council for Foreign Relations (ECFR), 29 June 2020a; Office of the Federal Chancellor, 'Driving Europe Forward as a trio', News, 23 June 2020a; Federal Minister of State for Europe Michael Roth, 2020;

of Foreign Minister Heiko Maas, it was 'indispensable for Europe to speak with a single voice to China'.[77]

But intra-European unity was not an end in itself; because 'not a single country in Europe is capable of permanently standing up for its interests and values vis-à-vis China on its own',[78] greater cohesion was seen as a necessary condition for the European Union to strengthen both its resilience and leverage vis-à-vis China. According to a FFO official, 'the idea was that this would provide leverage to create greater reciprocity'.[79] A high-ranking diplomat similarly stresses that, 'if you want to have clout vis-à-vis the Chinese, you need to act within the European Union, full stop.'[80]

Besides exerting leverage vis-à-vis the PRC, forging a common EU 'China policy' was also meant to reduce the vulnerability of EU member states to Chinese or American pressures and to enable the Union to create a distinct role for itself in the context of the rising Sino-American competition—one that would eschew taking sides between China and the United States.[81] As one FFO official puts it, the growing rivalry between Washington and Beijing 'puts pressure on us, on all Europeans, to position ourselves, which is something that on all China-related issues we are trying to avoid. We do not want to choose between our security guarantor and our biggest economic partner.'[82] Germany thus hoped that through a coordinated EU position it could confront the multipronged challenge posed by China's rising assertiveness in Europe while maintaining open and extensive political and economic ties with Beijing without having to choose sides between the United States and China. Berlin's position thus entailed neither containment of the PRC, nor equidistance between the two great powers, nor systematic alignment with the United States.[83]

Policy Instruments

As it revised the goals of its 'China policy', Germany forged new policy instruments that could be leveraged to achieve such objectives. In the first two post-Cold War decades, Berlin's overarching objective of fostering greater economic engagement and exchanges with the PRC resulted in the imposition of very few restrictions on China's economic engagement with Germany and the European Union. By contrast, in the 2010s Berlin developed new policy instruments, both at the national and European level, to concretize the revised goals of its 'China policy', e.g. FDI screening mechanisms and measures to protect its digital infrastructure.

---

[77] Federal Minister for Foreign Affairs Heiko Maas, 2020a.
[78] Federal Minister of State for Europe Michael Roth, 2020.
[79] Interview, 14 March 2020.
[80] Interview, 6 November 2020.
[81] Secretary of State Andreas Michaelis, 2020. For more details, see Chapter 2.
[82] Interview, 25 March 2020.
[83] Thomas Bagger, Director of Foreign Policy in the Office of the President (since 2017), interview, 6 May 2020. On this point, see also Chapter 2.

An Open Door: Market Forces and Economic Openness

Throughout the 1990s and 2000s, Germany prioritized relying on market mechanisms to remain an open and attractive destination for foreign investments. Accordingly, although a new FDI screening mechanism was introduced, Berlin maintained loose restrictions in order to maximize the volumes of Chinese FDI inflows.

In 2004, the German government amended its German Foreign Trade and Payments Act to introduce, for the first time, a foreign investment screening mechanism. Specifically, it established exceptions to the free movement of foreign investment into Germany for the protection of 'public order and security'.[84] The revised framework identified a number of sectors in which the direct or indirect acquisition of at least 25 per cent of the voting rights in a company would trigger the review mechanism, i.e. investments in German companies that produced or developed weapon systems and other military equipment or cryptographic systems for the transmission of classified information.[85]

In April 2009, Germany further revised the FDI screening system. In particular, it broadened the review mechanism—previously limited to the defence and encryption sectors (the so-called sectoral review)—to also include a 'cross-sectoral' review for all the other sectors of the economy in which the acquisition by a non-EU resident of a direct or indirect stake of at least 25 per cent in a German company would threaten public security or public order.[86]

Yet, although Berlin did dispose of instruments to restrict FDI inflows, in its relationship with Beijing it focused upon attracting Chinese investments in Germany. For one, the main trigger for the 2004 measure had been the acquisition of a majority stake in a German submarine manufacturer by a US company in 2003.[87] Concerns over China played no role in these regulatory changes. As explained by a FMEA official, 'there was no perceived challenge from China at the time; the priority was to keep markets open, not to build up the restrictions and to avoid protectionist measures'; 'the approach to the whole issue of foreign direct investments was a political decision to introduce a rather weak FDI screening mechanism; we wanted to attract foreign direct investments and so we should keep few restrictions.'[88]

---

[84] US Government Accountability Office (GAO), *Foreign Investment: Laws and Policies Regulating Foreign Investment in 10 Countries*, GAO-08-320, February 2008, pp. 60–61.
[85] GAO, 2008, p. 61.
[86] Organisation for Economic Co-operation and Development (OECD), 'Freedom of Investment Process', Note by the Secretariat, DAF/INV/WD(2009)14, 3 November 2009, p. 4; Dirk Uwer and Bera Jungkind, 'Reform of Foreign Investment Control in Germany', *Hengeler Mueller Newsletter*, July 2017.
[87] GAO, 2008, p. 61.
[88] MFEA official, interview, 6 December 2020.

Gearing up to Confront China: Investment Screening and 5G Restrictions

It is only in the 2010s that Berlin developed new policy instruments to implement its revised 'China policy' and its hardened stance towards Beijing. In particular, Germany leveraged a combination of national measures with the promotion of EU sectoral instruments tailored to address the range of sectors in which Chinese practices alarmed the government, including the EU FDI screening mechanism and the EU 5G Toolbox for Cybersecurity.

National Instruments

At the national level, Germany strengthened and widened its FDI screening mechanisms in order to be better able to monitor and block Chinese investments in Germany's high-tech industry. Berlin also imposed greater restrictions on suppliers of potential concern, like Huawei, to protect its digital infrastructure.

Screening Foreign Direct Investments
Following the acquisition of the robotics manufacturer Kuka by Chinese company Midea in 2016 (discussed earlier), the belief that Germany lacked the policy instruments required to veto this type of transaction led to a first revision of the foreign investment rules in 2017.[89] Through this revised regulation, investments in 'critical infrastructure' were now included among the potential threats to public order and security that would trigger the FDI review mechanism; the timeline for the review was also significantly expanded although the threshold that triggered the review (the acquisition of 25 per cent of the voting rights) remained unaltered.[90] In particular, the sensitive sectors identified by the new regulation included, among others, energy, information technology, telecommunications, transport and traffic, health, water supply, food, finance, and insurance.[91] Germany thereby tightened its rules on inbound FDI in response to the perceived threats from foreign investors like China.

In the summer of 2018, two events convinced German policymakers that the FDI screening mechanism should be further tightened. When China's State Grid Corporation sought to acquire a 20 per cent stake in 50Hertz, an electricity

---

[89] Interviews with FFO and MFEA officials, September–December 2020.
[90] The MFEA could now open *ex officio* investigations within three months after becoming aware of the signing (execution) of a purchase agreement. See Uwer and Jungkind, 2017.
[91] Uwer and Jungkind, 2017.

transmission system operator, Berlin lacked the policy instruments to veto the acquisition because existing regulation applied only to a 25 per cent threshold of voting rights. Accordingly, the government directed the state development bank Kreditanstalt für Wiederaufbau (KfW) to acquire this stake to prevent the takeover of 50Hertz by the Chinese state-owned company and, thereby, to protect Germany's critical energy infrastructure.[92] Likewise, when the Chinese Yantai Taihai Corporation decided to purchase Leifeld Metal Spinning, which produced among other things advanced material for the aerospace, energy, automotive, and civilian nuclear industries, for the first time the German government moved to veto a FDI. Before the implementation of the veto, however, the Chinese company pre-emptively withdrew its bid.[93]

In reaction to the concerns raised by the 50Hertz affair, Berlin further tightened its FDI screening rules in 2018. It lowered the threshold from 25 per cent to 10 per cent for the direct or indirect acquisition of enterprises that develop or manufacture weapons systems, produce certain products with IT security functions to process classified information, or certain goods subject to export controls, e.g. in the fields of sensor systems or electronic warfare, among others.[94] In 2020, the FDI screening mechanism rules were further amended twice and tightened in application of the newly established EU FDI Screening Regulation (discussed later). The level of threat to public order or security that could trigger restrictions on FDIs was lowered from the previously required 'actual and serious threat' to an 'expected impairment' of public order or security. Furthermore, the reach of the review mechanisms was expanded by requiring the government to consider whether an investment would affect public order and security not only in Germany but also in other EU member states or in relation to joint EU projects (e.g. the Galileo satellite navigation system or the European Defence Industrial Development Programme) while requiring the suspension of any FDI subject to notification for the duration of the review.[95]

That same year, Berlin made use twice of its revised screening mechanism to block Chinese FDIs in Germany. As mentioned above, the government rejected a bid by China's Vital Materials to acquire PPM Pure Metals, a supplier of high-purity minor metals used in semiconductors and in infrared detectors, due to

---

[92] Victoria Bryan and Gernot Heller, 'Germany Moves to Protect Key Companies from Chinese Investors', *Reuters*, 27 July 2018; Oliver Schröder and Stephanie Birmanns, 'Germany', in *The Foreign Investment Regulation Review*, 8th edition, edited by Calvin S. Goldman and Michael Koch (London: Law Business Research, 2020), p. 68.

[93] Maria Brakalova, 'Foreign Direct Investments in Germany—Germany Significantly Lowers Threshold to Veto Deals; FDI Screening Mechanism at European Level Is Coming Soon', *JDSupra*, 20 December 2018.

[94] Anahita Thoms, 'Germany Widens the Scope of its Foreign Investment Review Regime', Baker McKenzie, *Insight*, January 2019.

[95] Maria Brakalova, 'Update on Foreign Direct Investments in Germany', *Denton*, 18 February 2020; Markus Nauheim et al., 'Update on German Foreign Investment Control: New EU Cooperation Mechanism and Overview of Recent Changes', *Gibson Dunn*, 11 November 2020.

concerns that PPM sold various products to the German military.[96] A few months later, Berlin blocked the takeover by a subsidiary of the state-controlled CASIC of the German firm IMST.[97] IMST was a provider of satellite and radar technology with expertise also relevant to the future construction of critical infrastructure (such as 5G networks); it also developed a key component for the German earth observation satellite TerraSAR-X whose data were used by the German FMoD to calculate a highly accurate 3D-elevation model for military purposes.[98] The core national security concerns at the root of the decision included, as previously discussed, the ties of the company with the PLA and the security services, the related risk of transferring IMST's know-how in the field of satellite/radar communication to a Chinese state-owned company as well as the dangers that such an acquisition might pose to the security of supply of the Bundeswehr.[99]

National Restrictions on 5G Suppliers of Concern
In the digital domain, the government introduced the IT Security Act 2.0 to bolster the protection of its critical infrastructure vis-à-vis suppliers of concern such as Huawei (the draft law was proposed in December 2020 and became effective in 2021). The new law required that suppliers of 5G equipment inform the authorities about the critical components that they planned to deploy in their infrastructure; and the German government could then prohibit their use if it conflicted with 'the overriding public interest, in particular security policy concerns'.[100] The vendors would also now have to submit a 'guarantee' as to their trustworthiness, ensuring that their equipment could not be used for the purposes of sabotage, espionage, or terrorism.[101]

A two-stage procedure was introduced to review bids through a 'technical test' on the reliability of the components to be used in the 5G infrastructure, coupled with a 'political assessment' of the trustworthiness of the manufacturer.[102] If the newly established review committee—composed of representatives from the Chancellery, FFO, MFEA, and BMI—concluded that the provider violated the written guarantee or failed to report or address vulnerabilities in its critical components, it could ban either those components or, after multiple breaches, the

---

[96] Shabalala and Daly, 2020.
[97] Michael Nienaber, 'Germany Blocks Chinese Takeover of Satellite Firm on Security Concerns: Document', *Reuters*, 8 December 2020.
[98] Schöning et al., 2020.
[99] Interviews with BMI and FMoD officials, December 2020 and January 2021. See also Schöning et al., 2020.
[100] The text of the law, as quoted in Guy Chazan, 'Germany Sets High Hurdle for Huawei', *Financial Times*, 16 December 2020.
[101] Chazan, 2020.
[102] Samuel Stolton, 'US Praises German Moves to Sideline Huawei from 5G Networks', *EurActiv*, 30 September 2020; Andreas Rinke, 'German Draft IT Security Law Strives for Consensus on Telecoms Vendor Risks', *Reuters*, 20 November 2020.

supplier.¹⁰³ The original driver for the establishment of this two-pronged system was the concern linked to Huawei.¹⁰⁴

Germany thus tightened the controls over the supply of 5G technology while falling short of singling out Huawei with a targeted ban.¹⁰⁵ In devising this measure, the government took into account national security concerns, economic and legal considerations, as well as foreign policy objectives.

First, Berlin evaluated the security risks related to the inclusion of Huawei's 5G technology into its digital infrastructure. Even though it found no 'smoking gun', i.e. no evidence that actors linked to the Chinese secret services had already penetrated 5G networks to disrupt them or spy over the data traffic, German policymakers intended to prevent that such a risk could materialize in the future while also minimizing dependence on suppliers of concern.¹⁰⁶ Secondly, given that a high percentage of Huawei equipment was already used in Germany's 3G and 4G networks, 'it became clear very rapidly that' from an economic perspective, according to one official, 'removing all Chinese components from the German network was nearly impossible for us' because it would require enormous financial resources and considerable time.¹⁰⁷ According to a senior government official, conservative estimates forecasted that doing so would require approximately €5bn; removing only critical components from the network would take between two and three years, and removing Huawei's equipment from the access networks would take up to five years.¹⁰⁸ Furthermore, German policymakers considered whether a full ban on Huawei might violate its international trade policy obligations, especially at the World Trade Organization, or European Union laws and regulations, such as EU competition laws.¹⁰⁹

Finally, Berlin also took into account the likely foreign policy consequences of any decision on Huawei for its relationships with both Washington and Beijing. The United States pressed Germany to impose a full ban on Huawei, whereas Beijing forcefully stressed the adverse repercussions of such a choice for Sino-German bilateral ties, raising fears of retaliation.¹¹⁰ Berlin found itself caught between a

---

¹⁰³ Rinke, 2020; and 'German Ministers Agree Security Law with High Hurdles for Suppliers', *Reuters*, 16 December 2020.

¹⁰⁴ Yet, this two-pronged measure also responded to potential concerns over US telecommunications equipment, especially in the aftermath of the revelations by the former contractor at the National Security Agency (NSA), Edward Snowden, over the NSA's eavesdropping in Germany. Government official, interview, 6 January 2021. On the latter point, see 'German Prosecutors Close Case on NSA Spying Scandal', *DW*, 5 October 2017.

¹⁰⁵ On this point, see for instance Federal Government, 'Antwort der Bundesregierung auf die Kleine Anfrage der Abgeordneten Uwe Schulz, Joana Cotar, Dr. Michael Espendiller und der Fraktion der AfD', 10 September 2020c, https://dserver.bundestag.de/btd/19/223/1922310.pdf.

¹⁰⁶ Interviews with government officials, December 2020–January 2021.

¹⁰⁷ Government official, interview, January 2021.

¹⁰⁸ Government official, interview, January 2021.

¹⁰⁹ Interviews with government officials, September–December 2020 and January 2021.

¹¹⁰ Interviews with government officials, January 2021, September–December 2020, and January 2021.

rock and a hard place. In the words of a government official, 'it is a discussion that has been imposed from the outside, under strong pressure, and we are forced to position ourselves.'[111] As stressed by another official: 'there is a great power struggle at the moment between China and the United States and we are in the middle of it, so how do we position ourselves between those two great powers?'[112]

The decision taken by Berlin—one entailing a greater capacity to monitor and restrict potential suppliers of concern but no ad hoc ban of Huawei—was the result of a delicate balancing act: to protect its national security interests and to minimize the potentially adverse economic consequences while assuaging Washington's diplomatic pressures without alienating a crucial economic and political partner like Beijing.[113]

Forging EU Policy Instruments

As a complement to these national initiatives, Germany promoted the development of new EU policy instruments intended to reinforce the European Union's collective capacity to confront the multifaceted challenge posed by China.

An EU Foreign Direct Investment Screening Framework

Together with other EU member states, Berlin pushed for the establishment of an EU-wide FDI screening mechanism, largely in reaction to the security concerns sparked by Chinese investments in strategic sectors. In 2017, together with France and Italy, Germany sent a joint letter to then European Commissioner for Trade Cecilia Malmström (2014–2019) in which they advocated for the creation of a common FDI screening mechanism, that was then detailed in a subsequent non-paper (as discussed in Chapter 4).[114] Concerns over China played a central role in this effort. According to one official, 'the reason why Germany took the initiative—together with France and Italy—to address the issue at the European level was the acquisition of Kuka by the Chinese company Midea, when we understood that our investment screening tool was too limited in scope.'[115] The German Minister for Economic Affairs Brigitte Zypries (2017–2018) then sent a second letter, in August 2017, to the President of the European Commission Jean-Claude Juncker (2014–2019) to further highlight the urgent need for such a reform.[116] As she put it, 'open

---

[111] Interview, 9 December 2020.
[112] Interview, 17 December 2020.
[113] Interviews with government officials, September–December 2020.
[114] French, German, and Italian Ministers for Economic Affairs, Letter to the EU Commissioner for Trade Cecilia Malmström, February 2017 (see the 'Proposals for Ensuring an Improved Level Playing Field in Trade and Investment' attached to German, French, and Italian Ministers for Economic Affairs' letter).
[115] Government official, interview, 10 June 2021.
[116] Federal Minister for Economic Affairs and Energy Brigitte Zypries, Letter to the President of the European Commission Jean-Claude Juncker, August 2017.

markets cannot be a one-way street.'[117] These moves prompted the introduction of the new EU investment screening framework to scrutinize foreign state-directed FDIs in the Union.[118] The proposal was welcomed by Zypries as a 'very important signal for Europe'.[119]

Berlin thereby aimed to ensure that the European Union as a whole would now have the instruments to monitor and, if needed, veto FDIs from China (and from other investors); that member states (and itself in particular) would be protected by this common EU framework from Beijing's retaliation in the event that Germany blocked a Chinese investment; and that other member states could not unfairly take advantage of discrepant national regulations by seeking to attract an investment that might have been rejected by another member state.[120] Coupled with the completion of the European Union–China Comprehensive Agreement on Investment (CAI)—an economic priority of the German EU Presidency in 2020—this initiative was also intended to rebalance the overall investment relationship with the PRC (although the CAI was subsequently frozen in 2021).[121]

Bolstering the Resilience of Europe's Digital Infrastructure
Besides the establishment of this EU FDI framework, Germany also pushed for the achievement of an EU 'digital sovereignty',[122] a 'third path for technological sovereignty' in the context of the mounting rivalry between the United States

---

[117] Federal Minister for Economic Affairs and Energy Brigitte Zypries, 2017.

[118] President of the European Commission Jean-Claude Juncker, State of the Union Address, 13 September 2017. See also European Commission, 'Regulation of the European Parliament and of the Council Establishing a Framework for Screening of Foreign Direct Investments into the European Union', COM(2017) 487 Final, Brussels, 13 September 2017; European Commission, 'A New Industrial Strategy for Europe', Communication COM(2020) 102 Final, Brussels, 10 March 2020b.

[119] FMEA, 'Minister Zypries: President Juncker's Proposal for a European Industrial Policy Strategy is an Important Signal for Europe as an Industrial Base', Press Release, 13 September 2017.

[120] Interviews with FFO and MFEA officials as well as with EU officials, March and December 2020.

[121] In 2021, the European Parliament passed a resolution that froze the ratification of the European Union–China CAI in response to Chinese sanctions on European human rights advocates. See European Commission, 'Key Elements of the EU–China Comprehensive Agreement on Investment', *Press Release*, 30 December 2020j; and Theresa Fallon, 'The Strategic Implications of the China–EU Investment Deal', *The Diplomat*, 4 January 2021. For an analysis of national European positions on the CAI, see Axel Berger, 'The China–EU Investment Agreement: Negotiations, Rationale, Motivations, and Contentious Issues', in *China, the EU, and International Investment Law: Reforming Investor-State Dispute Settlement*, edited by Yuwen Li, Tong Qi, and Cheng Bian (New York: Routledge, 2019), pp. 11–25; and EU, 'EU Imposes Further Sanctions over Serious Violations of Human Rights around the World', Press Release, 22 March 2021a, https://www.consilium.europa.eu/en/press/press-releases/2021/03/22/euimposes-further-sanctions-over-serious-violations-of-human-rights-around-the-world/.

[122] Minister of State for Europe Michael Roth, 2020. See also Federal Government, *Together for Europe's Recovery—Programme for German's Presidency of the Council of the European Union*, 2020b, p. 8; Federal Minister for Foreign Affairs Heiko Maas, 'An Agenda for Peace and Security? Priorities for a Social Democratic Foreign Policy for the European Union and the United Nations', Speech at the Friedrich-Ebert-Stiftung's Tiergarten Conference, 28 November 2019b; and Secretary of State at the Federal Foreign Office Antje Leendertse, Inaugural Address to the Cyber Security Summit, Berlin, 26 November 2019.

and China.¹²³ Because of the deep interdependencies between EU member states, Berlin considered that strengthening the resilience of its national critical infrastructure should be achieved through a joint, coordinated effort by the whole Union.¹²⁴ This entailed developing indigenous digital capabilities, revising the existing regulations, and reducing dependence on untrustworthy suppliers from third countries, such as China, so as to protect German and European critical infrastructure from espionage, cyber-attacks and or/disruption that could 'endanger our industrial base'.¹²⁵ Ensuring the confidentiality, integrity, and availability of the European digital infrastructure was thus seen as the central goal.¹²⁶

To that end, between 2018 and January 2020, Germany worked together with France, the United Kingdom, and other EU member states through the 5G Cybersecurity Work Stream, one of several work streams of activities inside the Network and Information Systems (NIS) Cooperation group, to foster greater coordination on 5G technology and to establish what became the EU Toolbox on 5G Cybersecurity (or 'EU 5G Toolbox').¹²⁷ One government official explains the rationale behind this endeavour as follows:

> The member states identified 5G very early on as an important topic. There was no legislation at the EU level regarding 5G because everything concerning the security of telecommunications is within the responsibility of the member states, so every member state has its own telecommunication laws and regulations, and these national laws and regulations are very different from one another. So there was no unified answer in the 5G domain. That is why we created the Toolbox.

---

[123] Federal Minister for Foreign Affairs Heiko Maas, 2020e. See also Federal Minister for Foreign Affairs Heiko Maas, 2019b; Federal Minister for Foreign Affairs Heiko Maas, Speech at the Opening of the Conference on Europe at the Federal Foreign Office, 2 March 2020c; Federal Minister for Foreign Affairs Heiko Maas, Speech on European Digital Sovereignty on the Occasion of the Opening of the Smart Country Convention of the German Association for Information Technology, Telecommunications, and New Media (Bitkom), 27 October 2020d; FFO, 'EU Cyber Diplomacy—Working Together for a Free and Secure Cyberspace', 19 November 2020d.
[124] Secretary of State Antje Leendertse, 2019. See also Federal Government, 2020c. On the EU's role in protecting the integrity and resilience of the European digital infrastructure, see also European Commission, 'Cybersecurity: Shaping Europe's Digital Future', 25 August 2020c, https://ec.europa.eu/digital-single-market/en/policies/cybersecurity.
[125] Federal Minister for Foreign Affairs Heiko Maas, 2020e. See also Federal Chancellor Angela Merkel. Speech on the German Presidency of the Council of the EU 2020, European Parliament, Brussels, 8 July 2020; Office of the Federal Chancellor, 'We Want to See Digital Sovereignty in the EU', News, 2 October 2020b; Federal Minister for Foreign Affairs Heiko Maas, 2020d; FFO, 'In Dialogue with China', Bilateral Relations and German Missions—China, 24 July 2020f; Minister of State for Europe Michael Roth, 2020.
[126] Federal Ministry of Transport and Digital Infrastructure, 5G Strategy for Germany, July 2017, p. 12.
[127] Interviews with German and EU officials, January 2020–May 2021. Berlin also used its Presidency of the Council of the European Union (1 July-31 December 2020) to develop and put forward proposals to strengthen EU 'cyber diplomacy' and to promote the creation of a European critical infrastructure, including broadband and 5G networks. German Presidency of the European Union, 'Driving Prosperity with Competition', https://www.eu2020.de/eu2020-en/competitiveness-eu-prosperity-mobility/2352830; FFO, 2020d.

It did not target specific companies or countries. The Toolbox aimed to address security risks that can come from all the vectors of attack. But China was the elephant in the room, we were not talking about Iceland or something.[128]

Germany nonetheless assumed a less proactive role than France and the United Kingdom in developing the EU 5G Toolbox in part because, according to one EU official, it 'was still in the process of defining its national approach and had no formal leading position' within the 5G Cybersecurity Work Stream (as discussed earlier, the German draft law that established national restrictions of 5G suppliers was introduced only at the end of 2020).[129] As further detailed in Chapter 4, the 5G Cybersecurity Work Stream proceeded in three steps: the completion of national risk assessments of the cybersecurity threats to their 5G networks, the development of a joint EU risk assessment which built on the national threat assessments, and the identification of a set of common measures to be taken to mitigate the cybersecurity risks to 5G networks, i.e. what became the EU 5G Toolbox, which included both 'technical' and 'non-technical' (i.e. strategic/political) measures.[130]

One official involved in these discussions explains that whereas Germany 'had no problem' with the definition of the technical measures developed to strengthen the security of 5G networks, it did initially adopt a different approach to the strategic criteria to be used in the identification of high-risk vendors.[131] In his words, 'we were not willing to characterize a specific company as a high-risk vendor; that is not our approach.'[132] As an EU official involved in these discussions puts it, Germany 'kept a very neutral stance when it came to the non-technical criteria used to define high-risk vendors'.[133] According to the German official, Berlin would 'have preferred a different way to proceed', and to focus exclusively upon technical measures; but several other member states—such as France and the United Kingdom—and the European Commission put forward a broader approach that covered also non-technical (i.e. political or strategic) criteria; as a result, 'there were strong discussions on how these high-risk vendors should be defined and how this should be implemented in the 5G Toolbox.'[134] The broader debate underlying the issue of the 'non-technical' measures revolved around China. The then EU Commissioner for the Security Union (2016–2019), Sir Julian King, elucidates this point as follows:

---

[128] Government official, interview, 29 January 2021.
[129] EU official, interview, 7 April 2021.
[130] European Commission, 'The EU Toolbox for 5G Security', *Factsheet*, 29 January 2020g; European Network and Information Security Agency (ENISA), 'The EU Agency for Cybersecurity endorses the EU Toolbox for 5G Security', 30 January 2020, https://www.enisa.europa.eu/news/enisa-news/5g. For more details on the decision-making process within the 5G Cybersecurity Work Stream, see Chapter 4.
[131] Government official, interview, 29 January 2021.
[132] Government official, interview, 29 January 2021.
[133] EU official, interview, 7 April 2021.
[134] Government official, interview, 29 January 2021.

Once you actually start talking about so-called 'non-technical' issues, it becomes a little more contentious because you are talking about the nature of suppliers and their relationships with states. Some of it was linked to a sort of political sensitivity about, essentially, how outspoken each member state was about China; because we were not doing this in a vacuum: although this was all about 'country-neutral' criteria and although we were strictly 'supplier-neutral', we were doing it at a time when there was a raging political debate about Huawei and thus about China, so the member states needed to find a way of being comfortable with the development of these criteria. We took a 'country-neutral' approach quite deliberately in order to make it possible to get further in the discussion. If we had said that we were creating a set of strategic criteria that targeted China and Huawei, the discussion would not have gone far.[135]

What became the EU 5G Toolbox ultimately indicated both the main technical and non-technical factors to be taken into account in evaluating a supplier's risk profile but it gave member states the leeway to define the specific, national measures to be implemented through domestic laws or regulations.[136] The German IT Security Act 2.0 that introduced restrictions on 5G suppliers of concern included, as mentioned above, a 'technical assessment' as well as a 'political assessment' of the trustworthiness of the manufacturer which revolved around 'the concrete influence of the state into the structures of the company'.[137] Furthermore, according to EU officials, Berlin finally came onboard with the inclusion of both technical and strategic/political measures also because a joint, EU-wide policy instrument would reduce the exposure of Germany, and of other member states, to the potential pressures from either Beijing or Washington.[138]

Conclusion

In combination with mounting apprehensions over Chinese assertiveness in the Asia-Pacific, the concerns over China's rising clout in Germany and Europe—especially in strategic sectors—have been the main driver of change in Berlin's 'China policy'. Since the 2010s, Germany has responded to Beijing's rising assertiveness in Europe by hardening its 'China policy' and by promoting the formulation of a common EU policy towards Beijing. To that end, it has developed a variety of national measures and supported the establishment of EU instruments

---

[135] Sir Julian King, interview, 28 May 2021. See also Julian King, 'Europe's 5G Network Will be Secure—If We Work Together', *The Guardian*, 28 October 2019.
[136] Network and Information Systems (NIS) Cooperation Group, *Cybersecurity of 5G Networks EU Toolbox of Risk Mitigating Measures*, Report for the European Commission, January 2020, p. 11.
[137] Government official, interview, 13 April 2021. See also Stolton, 2020; Rinke, 2020.
[138] Interviews with EU officials, 7 April 2021 and 29 May 2021.

such as FDI screening mechanisms and the EU 5G Toolbox. To be sure, the combination of Germany's economic interests in China—with its resulting vulnerability to potential Chinese retaliation—and of US pressures have forced Berlin to walk a tightrope. In devising new policy instruments, Germany has had to balance national security, economic, and foreign policy considerations. Yet, in part to address such challenges, Berlin has sought to forge a comprehensive, cross-sectoral 'China policy' and has encouraged greater intra-European coordination in the pursuit of an autonomous EU policy towards the PRC, seeking to carve out a distinct role for itself—and for the European Union—amidst rising Sino-American strategic competition.

6
The China Challenge
Rebalancing Economics and National Security in UK Foreign Policy

Introduction

The balance between national security and economic interests at play in the United Kingdom's 'China policy' has significantly evolved in the post-Cold War era. As the first recipient of Chinese FDIs in Europe but also a close ally of the United States, the United Kingdom has faced difficult trade-offs in formulating its policy towards the People's Republic of China (PRC). This chapter investigates how London has responded to China's growing foothold in the United Kingdom through increased FDIs and the supply of advanced telecoms equipment for its digital infrastructure. It will be shown that Chinese inroads into these strategic sectors in the 2010s—and British policymakers' perception thereof—have been a key driver of change in United Kingdom's 'China policy'. In particular, rising threat perceptions, coupled with increasingly competitive economic relations with the PRC, have caused the United Kingdom to recalibrate the national security and economic interests at stake in its 'China policy' and to harden its stance towards Beijing.

During the first two decades after the Cold War, policymakers in London viewed the PRC as a source of major economic opportunities for British companies, whereas China's minute presence in the United Kingdom's economy provoked few security concerns. Accordingly, especially after the retrocession of Hong Kong to the PRC in 1997, London's policy goals overwhelmingly revolved around bolstering bilateral economic ties with scarce emphasis on national security considerations. But starting in the early 2010s and increasingly so in the latter part of the decade, the ever-expanding Chinese involvement in the United Kingdom's industrial fabric—and specifically in its most strategic sectors—sparked rising threat perceptions among British policymakers (at a time when Beijing came to be seen as increasingly assertive also in the Asia-Pacific, as discussed in Chapter 3). This, in turn, caused London to toughen its approach towards the PRC. While it had previously strongly encouraged Chinese FDIs with one of the least restrictive investment environments in Europe, it now strengthened its FDI screening mechanism to be able to monitor and, if needed, veto Chinese investments in sensitive sectors. Likewise, while London had openly welcomed Huawei's entry into the British telecommunications market in the 2000s, it began gradually imposing ever more stringent restrictions on Chinese telecoms company, like Huawei, climaxing in a full-blown ban. At the same time, the United Kingdom remained more sceptical of the development of EU-level instruments than the other major European powers, especially as it concurrently began negotiating its exit from the Union.

To corroborate this argument, the chapter is organized as follows. The first two sections examine two key drivers of the United Kingdom's 'China policy', namely British economic interest—including in China's involvement in the critical national infrastructure and in the telecoms sector—and London's heightened threat assessment of the PRC. The subsequent two sections show how shifting economic interests and threat perceptions have, in turn, caused the United Kingdom to recalibrate its policy goals and to strengthen the policy instruments leveraged to achieve such goals.

Economic Interests

The United Kingdom and the PRC developed very substantial economic ties throughout the post-Cold War era, although from an asymmetric basis. Between the early 1990s and the late 2000s, whereas the growth potential of the Chinese market attracted major British exports and investments, China's economic involvement within the United Kingdom—while increasing in the 2000s—remained modest. It is in the 2010s that the PRC's economic foothold in the United Kingdom substantially grew and spiked, with a surge in Chinese investments and with leading Chinese companies like Huawei acquiring a central role in the supply of key technologies for the British digital infrastructure. Over time, as China moved up the value-added ladder and its technological capabilities increased, the PRC gradually entrenched its footprint in the United Kingdom's industrial landscape which, in turn, raised concerns over mounting economic competition by Chinese high-tech companies.

Rising, Yet Modest Chinese Investments in the United Kingdom

In the two decades that followed the end of the Cold War, London saw China as a major emerging market for British companies with a great potential for further expansion.[1] Conversely, China only maintained a thin economic presence in

---

[1] On the UK trade, investment and financial interests in China, see Chapter 3.

the United Kingdom. During the 1990s, although the United Kingdom was home to major FDIs from Hong Kong, the volume of investments in the UK by companies based in mainland China remained marginal.² After the retrocession of Hong Kong to Beijing in 1997 (discussed in Chapter 3), however, Chinese FDIs into the United Kingdom began to gradually increase, largely as a result of Beijing's 'Go Out' policy.³ The liberalization of China's investment regime enabled a growing number of state-owned enterprises (SOEs) to expand their operations in the United Kingdom in search of new markets and consumers.⁴

The value of FDI transactions from mainland China (excluding Hong Kong) in the United Kingdom rose from virtually zero in 2000 to €1.14bn in 2009.⁵ The UK became the largest European recipient of Chinese FDIs, with 41 per cent of all Chinese investments into Europe, far ahead of Germany and France with 15 per cent and 10 per cent respectively (see also the comparative charts on Chinese FDIs in the Big Three in Appendix B).⁶ These investments largely focused on the manufacturing sector (63 per cent), most notably in electronics, but also on financial and business services (17 per cent).⁷ Through these FDIs, Chinese companies sought to develop their innovation capacity and to gain access to one of the world's most favourable regulatory environments, which was also a key launchpad into the major markets of Europe and North America.⁸

The biggest investment by a Chinese company in the United Kingdom (measured in workforce size) was by Huawei Technologies in 2004 when it opened its European headquarters (HQ) in Basingstoke, in Southeast England.⁹ The year before, the British telecommunications company BT had informed the government that Huawei had expressed interest in BT's tender for the so-called '21st Century Network' contract (21CN).¹⁰ This contract covered a £10bn project to upgrade

---

² Between 1992 and 1994, Hong Kong was the most important investor among the Asian developing economies in the European Union, and 40 per cent of the entire FDI stock from the Asia-Pacific to the European Union went to the United Kingdom. See The National Archives (United Kingdom), 'UK Leads in Asia Rush to Europe', 29 January 1999, https://webarchive.nationalarchives.gov.uk/19990129040048/http://www.dti.gov.uk:80/IBB/GB/1997-02-031.html; and Tim Summers, 'Chinese Investment in the UK: Growing Flows or Growing Controversy?', in *Chinese Investment in Europe: A Country-Level Approach*, edited by John Seaman, Mikko Huotari, and Miguel Otero-Iglesias (Paris: French Institute of International Relations, 2017), p. 160.

³ Nora Burghart and Vanessa Rossi, 'China's Overseas Direct Investment in the UK', Chatham House, Programme Paper IE PP 2009/06, December 2009, p. 4. On the 'Go Out' policy, see the Introduction of Part II.

⁴ Burghart and Rossi 2009.

⁵ Summers, 2017, p. 161. On the methodological challenges of gathering data on UK–PRC investment ties, and the role of Hong Kong therein, see Appendix B.

⁶ Burghart and Rossi, 2009, p. 4 (data for the 1997–2007 period).

⁷ Burghart and Rossi, 2009, p. 12.

⁸ See Kerry Brown, *Erase and Rewind: Britain's Relations with China* (Sydney: The Australia-China Relations Institute, 2015), p. 7; and Burghart and Rossi, 2009, p. 22. See also Organisation for Economic Co-operation and Development (OECD), 'FDI Regulatory Restrictiveness Index', https://www.oecd.org/investment/fdiindex.htm.

⁹ Burghart and Rossi, 2009, p. 15.

¹⁰ Intelligence and Security Committee (ISC), *Foreign Involvement in the Critical National Infrastructure: The Implications for National Security*, Report Presented to Parliament by the Prime

BT's communications network over the subsequent decade which would allow all of BT's traffic to be carried over fibre-optic cables, rather than copper wires, and to be transmitted using Internet Protocol technology.[11] In 2005, BT signed a contract with Huawei for the supply of some of the transmission and access equipment, including routers, and the two companies established a R&D partnership in Ipswich to develop the optical transmission network.[12]

Overall, however, China's economic involvement in the United Kingdom remained quite limited. Although investments from China into the United Kingdom increased in the 2000s, their volume continued to be relatively small in terms of both overall inward investment and relative project size.[13]

China Widens its Economic Foothold in the United Kingdom

By the 2010s, however, the PRC's FDIs in Europe in general, and in the United Kingdom in particular, grew considerably thanks to Beijing's regulatory and financial incentives.[14] Chinese state-owned and private companies expanded and diversified their operations in the United Kingdom across investment sectors and infrastructure projects, while also emerging as leading providers of telecommunications equipment.

Chinese investments in the United Kingdom soared from $1.3bn to almost $17bn between 2010 and 2019 (in stock).[15] Great Britain thereby further amplified its lead as the first recipient of Chinese investments in Europe before Germany and France (with $14bn and $6bn respectively in 2019).[16] The UK Department for International Trade (DIT) estimated that, between 2016 and 2019, over nine thousand jobs had been either created or safeguarded by Chinese FDIs in UK projects.[17] London and Beijing also deepened their ties in the field of infrastructure projects. The United Kingdom was the first major Western economy to join the China-instigated Asia Infrastructure Investment Bank (AIIB), in 2015,[18] and

---

Minister on behalf of Her Majesty, June 2013, Annex A: 'Huawei's Involvement in the Critical National Infrastructure: A Chronology', p. 22.

[11] ISC, 2013, p. 22.

[12] ISC, 2013, p. 4; Burghart and Rossi, 2009, p. 15.

[13] Burghart and Rossi, 2009, p. 7. See also the comparative charts on China's investments in the Big Three in Appendix B.

[14] On the increase in China's global outward FDI flows, see the Introduction of Part II as well as EY, 'How Will Chinese Enterprises Navigate New Challenges when "Going Abroad" under the New Global Trade Landscape?', *ChinaGoAbroad*, no. 9, October 2019, pp. 4 and 6.

[15] National Bureau of Statistics of China, *Statistical Yearbooks of China*, http://www.stats.gov.cn/english/Statisticaldata/AnnualData/.

[16] National Bureau of Statistics of China, *Statistical Yearbooks of China*, http://www.stats.gov.cn/english/Statisticaldata/AnnualData/. See also the comparative charts in Appendix B.

[17] Data cited in China–Britain Business Council, *UK Jobs Dependent on Links to China* (Cambridge, UK: Cambridge Econometrics, 2020), p. 7.

[18] See Her Majesty's Treasury, 'Asian Infrastructure Investment Bank (AIIB) Special Fund', *Guidance*, 30 September 2019a; and Her Majesty's Treasury, *AIIB Special Fund Business Case*, 30 September 2019b.

it also endorsed China's Belt and Road Initiative (BRI), without formally joining it, which opened new opportunities for British companies to participate in infrastructure development projects.[19]

Likewise, Chinese corporations became involved in a growing number of major UK infrastructure assets, such as: the Hinkley Point C, Sizewell C, and Bradwell nuclear power projects; Heathrow Airport; Thames Water; the National Grid; key North Sea oilfields; British Steel; South Western Trains; and Crossrail.[20] In particular, as detailed below, the investments by China General Nuclear Power Group in the construction of British nuclear power plants spurred controversy because of the influence that this deal would give to a Chinese SOE in the United Kingdom's critical energy infrastructure.[21]

Notably, the presence of Chinese companies—such as Huawei—in the United Kingdom's telecommunications sector significantly expanded during the 2010s. In 2012, then Prime Minister (PM) David Cameron and Huawei's founder Ren Zhengfei agreed that the latter would invest £1.3bn in Britain, between 2013 and 2017, including in R&D.[22] Throughout the decade, the Chinese corporation developed research centres in Edinburgh, Bristol, Cambridge, and Ipswich, including a £1bn research centre at Sawston. Moreover, it forged partnerships with several universities, such as the University of Cambridge, the University of Surrey (where it opened the 5G Innovation Centre), the University of Southampton, and Imperial College London.[23] By 2019, according to a study commissioned by Huawei, the Chinese company contributed to the United Kingdom's GDP with €3.6bn.[24]

Huawei thereby became the dominant player in the already highly concentrated British telecommunications market, with only two other suppliers, namely Ericsson and Nokia. In 2019, it was the leader in the United Kingdom's 4G mobile access market (with 35 per cent market share) and also in fixed access with a 45 per cent

---

[19] In 2017, together with another twenty-six countries, London endorsed 'Guiding Principles on Financing the Development of the Belt and Road' while refusing, in 2018, to sign an MoU endorsing the BRI as a whole because of concerns over transparency in financing and tendering processes, and the adherence to social standards such as labour rights, environmental standards, and debt sustainability. See FCO, 'Written Evidence from the Foreign and Commonwealth Office (CIR0018)', in response to House of Commons (HoC), 2019a. See also HoC, 'Belt and Road Initiative: China', Question for Department for International Trade, 24 June 2019b, https://questions-statements.parliament.uk/written-questions/detail/2019-06-24/268527; HoC, *Oral Evidence: China and the International Rules-Based System*, Foreign Affairs Committee, HC 612, 15 January 2019a, pp. 14–18; and Chancellor of the Exchequer Philip Hammond (2016–2019), Speech at the Belt and Road Forum, 26 April 2019.
[20] Jon Lunn and John Curtis, 'The UK–China Relationship', House of Commons Library, *Briefing Paper 9004*, 14 September 2020, p. 4.
[21] Felix Ruechardt, *Non-Proliferation and Foreign Direct Investment Reviews: Implications for Reform in the UK*, Report prepared by Project Alpha at the Centre for Science and Security Studies (CSSS), King's College London, 16 April 2018, p. 6, fn. 2.
[22] Thomas Brewster, 'Huawei to Invest £1.3bn in UK', *Silicon.co.uk*, 12 September 2012.
[23] See HoC, *The Security of 5G*, Defence Committee, 22 September 2020a, p. 49; and William Xu, 'How Huawei Collaborates with Universities', Huawei Blog, 17 December 2019, https://blog.huawei.com/2019/12/17/how-huawei-collaborates-with-universities.
[24] Oxford Economics, *The Economic Impact of Huawei* (London: Oxford Economics, 2020), p. 14.

market share in full fibre (FTTP broadband).[25] Furthermore, as the British government set the goal to provide the majority of the population with 5G networks by 2027, Huawei was projected to become a key supplier of 5G wireless technology.[26] BT reportedly expected to use Huawei equipment in around two-thirds of its networks, Vodafone in a significant portion of its network, and Three had opted to procure its radio access network (RAN) from Huawei only.[27]

In short, China's economic presence in the United Kingdom had both deepened and widened and it had now established itself in the UK industrial fabric as both a major investor and a key supplier of advanced telecoms equipment. In this process, some concerns emerged over the growing competition from Chinese high-tech companies for UK businesses. According to Sir Sherard Cowper-Coles, the Chair of the China-Britain Business Council (CBBC, since 2019), 'in recent years it has become increasingly obvious that in many of the technologies of tomorrow, whether it is high-speed rail, battery technology, artificial intelligence, autonomous mobility or biometric recognition, China has overtaken the West; the worries that we used to have about China stealing our technology are therefore almost out of date.'[28] TechUK, a British technology trade association, similarly stressed that, while the Chinese market offered 'huge potential', British companies faced 'some major barriers and concerns' because of the Chinese government's 'push towards making China a global leader in science and technology' and 'a leading global technological superpower' through state subsidies and investments in R&D.[29] In particular, London grew wary of how UK businesses were increasingly competing against harmful industrial subsidies, opaque SOEs, forced technology transfers, as well as intellectual property violations that put them at a comparative disadvantage.[30] These worries, however, were less acute than in other major

---

[25] Department for Digital, Culture, Media and Sport (DCMS), *UK Telecoms Supply Chain Review Report*, July 2019, pp. 29–30.
[26] The timeline for the complete 5G coverage in the United Kingdom was presented in DCMS, *Future Telecoms Infrastructure Review*, 23 July 2018, p. 3.
[27] HoC, 2020a, p. 18.
[28] Interview, 25 June 2021.
[29] TechUK, 'China's Tech Landscape', 22 January 2021, https://www.techuk.org/resource/china-s-tech-landscape.html.
[30] See Parliamentary Under-Secretary of State (Minister for Exports), Department for International Trade, Graham Stuart (since 2018), in House of Lords, *Oral Evidence: The UK's Security and Trade Relationship with China*, International Relations and Defence Committee, 9 June 2021, https://committees.parliament.uk/oralevidence/2329/html/; Minister of State for Asia at FCO, Nigel Adams (since 2020), in House of Lords, *Oral Evidence: The UK's Security and Trade Relationship with China*, International Relations and Defence Committee, 9 June 2021, https://committees.parliament.uk/oralevidence/2329/html/; and the Secretary of State for International Trade Liz Truss (2019–2021), quoted in Graham Lanktree and Anna Isaac, 'Trade Secretary Liz Truss: UK Must Not Become Dependent on China', *Politico EU*, 26 May 2021. Likewise, the 2021 Integrated Review identified China as 'the biggest state-based threat to the UK's economic security' (Her Majesty's Government (HMG), *Global Britain in a Competitive Age: The Integrated Review of Security, Defence, Development and Foreign Policy*, Presented to Parliament by the Prime Minister, March 2021, p. 62). See also British Chamber of Commerce in China, *British Business in China: Position Paper*, 2020. This point was further confirmed in interviews with officials in the Department of International Trade, June 2021.

European powers, most notably Germany, given the lesser contribution of the industrial sector—and of manufacturing in particular—to the British GDP.[31] In the words of the Chair of the CBBC, 'there have been some growing concerns over Chinese economic competition in specific high-tech sectors in the United Kingdom but, overall, these concerns have been less pronounced than in Germany because manufacturing is much less important'[32]—a point also confirmed by Richard Burn, the former Director-General for Trade and Investment for China in the Department for International Trade (DIT, 2017–2018) and then Trade Commissioner for China (2018–2020).[33] Likewise, the Chair of the British Chamber of Commerce in China Julian MacCormac (since 2021) emphasizes that a key factor explaining these differentiated levels of concern is that 'the structure of the British economy is very different from that of the German economy in that services are much more prominent than manufacturing. Accordingly, a significant proportion of very important companies in the United Kingdom just have not had the same areas of concern as German companies when it comes to China.'[34]

Threat Perceptions

As the depth and breadth of China's economic imprint in the United Kingdom expanded, the threat assessment of British policymakers changed. From the 1990s to the late 2000s, London perceived the PRC as a highly profitable market and its minute presence in the United Kingdom generated few if any national security concerns. In the subsequent decade, however, China's growing foothold in the United Kingdom's strategic sectors caused London to gradually revise its threat assessment (at a time when Chinese assertiveness in the Asia-Pacific also sparked mounting apprehensions, as discussed in Chapter 3). This, in turn, drove a recalibration of the goals of its 'China policy' and a hardened posture vis-à-vis Beijing.

China's Rise: A Low Priority Country Posing Few Security Concerns

During the first two decades after the Cold War, given that the PRC's economic presence in the United Kingdom remained modest (though growing) and that its

---

[31] The contribution of the industrial sector to GDP between 2009 and 2019 was almost 27 per cent for Germany as opposed to 17 per cent in the United Kingdom (and in France). Similarly, the value added by the manufacturing sector (as a percent of GDP) in 2019 was 8.6 per cent for the United Kingdom (and for France) but 19 per cent for Germany. Data retrieved from the World Bank, 'World Development Indicators', https://databank.worldbank.org/source/world-development-indicators.
[32] Sir Sherard Cowper-Coles, interview, 25 June 2021.
[33] Richard Burn, interview, 13 July 2021.
[34] Interview, 28 July 2021.

investments did not target 'areas of obvious national security interest', a former senior intelligence official explains that 'there were no security concerns linked to Chinese foreign direct investments'.[35] Similarly, according to the former MoD's Policy Director Simon Webb (2001–2004), these FDIs were 'not perceived as particularly threatening because these investments were seen as part of a wider general effort by China to broaden its high-tech manufacturing base for predominantly commercial use'.[36]

One area in which the PRC was deemed to pose a growing security challenge was its programme of theft of Western intellectual property and its efforts to secure technological advances through espionage, including cyber-espionage, especially from the latter half of the 2000s.[37] During the 1990s and early 2000s the intelligence community, in the words of one official, 'did not see China as posing a high security risk' in cyber-space; with little evidence of Chinese state-directed cyber espionage, they maintained 'a fairly low risk assessment'.[38] Concurrently, in these years, as detailed below, the British government considered that the security risk posed by Huawei's entry in the UK telecoms network was manageable and it thus allowed the Chinese company to supply equipment for BT's network.

It was mostly in the latter half of the 2000s, as explained by a former senior intelligence official, that the government uncovered 'growing evidence of large-scale cyber-espionage that was targeted against private-sector corporations, but with significant national security and national prosperity implications'.[39] Likewise, a study on the cyber-threat faced by the United Kingdom concluded that an increasing number of electronic intrusions were reported to originate in China, including the 2007 'Titan Rain' cyber-attack that also targeted Whitehall and the House of Commons.[40] By the end of the decade, the Government Communications Headquarters (GCHQ), Britain's signal-intelligence agency, assessed that the 'greatest threat of electronic attack to the UK' came from state actors, with China and Russia posing 'the greatest threat'.[41]

As the perceived cyber-threat from China increased in the second half of the decade, several intelligence officials voiced their concerns over the security risks linked to Huawei's presence in the British telecoms network. In 2008, the Security

---

[35] Interview, 4 June 2020.
[36] Simon Webb, interview, 25 January 2021.
[37] Interviews with former FCO, MoD, and intelligence officials in office during the 1990s and 2000s, January–June 2020 and January 2021.
[38] Former senior defence official, interview, 25 January 2021. This point was confirmed in interviews with former MoD and intelligence officials, December 2020 and January 2021.
[39] Former senior intelligence official, interview, 4 June 2020.
[40] Paul Cornish, Rex Hughes, and David Livingstone, 'Cyberspace and the National Security of the United Kingdom: Threats and Responses', Chatham House, March 2009, p. 4; and Richard Norton-Taylor, 'Titan Rain—How Chinese Hackers Targeted Whitehall', *The Guardian*, 5 September 2007.
[41] Quoted in ISC, *Annual Report 2009-2010*, March 2010, p. 16. See also ISC, *Annual Report 2007-2008*, March 2009, p. 18.

Service (or MI5) told the Joint Intelligence Committee (JIC), the interagency body responsible for intelligence assessment, coordination, and oversight, that 'the Chinese State may be able to exploit any vulnerabilities in Huawei's equipment in order to gain some access to the BT network, which would provide them with an attractive espionage opportunity.'[42] Likewise, in 2009, the JIC chairman Alex Allan (2007–2011) told then Home Secretary Jacqui Smith (2007–2009) that if a hostile actor were to exploit vulnerabilities in Huawei's equipment, an attack 'would be very difficult to detect or prevent and could enable the Chinese to intercept covertly or disrupt traffic passing through Huawei supplied networks'.[43]

Yet, in the 2000s, not only were the cyber-security concerns linked to Huawei's entry in the United Kingdom's telecoms market largely confined to the intelligence agencies but, according to a former senior intelligence official, even within the intelligence agencies 'China and the Asia-Pacific were not a priority; the overarching focus was on counterterrorism and the involvement in Iraq and Afghanistan, so not that many resources were being devoted to China.'[44]

The Challenge of an Increasingly Assertive China

It is only in the subsequent decade that London's threat assessment of the PRC heightened. Beginning in the early 2010s, rising security concerns over the PRC gradually and cumulatively developed within Whitehall in a process that culminated, in the latter half of the decade, in an overall shift in London's threat perceptions of China.

Until the mid-2010s, the British government—and the National Security Council in particular—was divided in two main camps. On the one hand, as explained by the former Chief of the Defence Staff General Lord Nick Houghton (2013–2016), Her Majesty's Treasury and the DIT considered that the PRC 'did not represent, in any imminent respect, a hard security challenge'; instead, they focused primarily on accommodating China's economic expansion and 'on the benefits of engaging China in areas like energy, trade, inward investments, banks, and technology'.[45] This was the so-called 'Golden Era' of Sino-UK economic relations promoted by George Osborne, then Chancellor of the Exchequer (2010–2016), and it was largely

---

[42] ISC, 2013, p. 11.
[43] Quoted in ISC, 2013. See also Tamlin Magee, 'Huawei Controversies Timeline', *Computerworld*, 24 April 2019.
[44] Interview, 4 June 2020.
[45] General Lord Nick Houghton, interview, 9 June 2020. This point was confirmed in interviews with Lord Peter Ricketts, former National Security Adviser (2010–2012), 3 June 2020; General Lord David Richards, former Chief of the Defence Staff (2010–2013), 3 June 2020; a senior former MoD official, interview, 3 July 2020; and a senior official, 26 June 2020.

in continuity with the assessment of Chinese intentions and capabilities that had characterized the previous decades.[46]

On the other hand, however, the FCO, the MoD, and the intelligence agencies grew increasingly alarmed by China's aggressive inroads into the United Kingdom's critical national infrastructure and its cyber and industrial espionage practices.[47] Yet, as explained by former high-ranking officials, until the mid-2010s the economically oriented agencies of the government advocating for engagement with China remained more influential than those stressing national security concerns.[48]

It is after 2016 that the overall thrust within Whitehall shifted towards a greater emphasis on the national security implications of China's growing capabilities and ambitions. According to a senior MoD official, with the incoming Theresa May's government (2016–2019), the United Kingdom's 'China policy' started to shift from an approach overwhelmingly focused on economic considerations to one that was more driven by security concerns. Whereas the PRC had previously been seen as a 'distant' emerging power, London now witnessed 'more and more Chinese activity, including in Europe'.[49] As a House of Lords' report on United Kingdom–China relations puts it, 'the mid-2010s precipitated a shift in the UK's approach to China.'[50] The security concerns over China's rise continued to intensify in the latter half of the 2010s and, by 2021, the British government considered that 'the scale and reach of China's economy, size of its population, technological advancement and increasing ambition to project its influence on the global stage' had fuelled the PRC's growing 'power and assertiveness internationally'. This, in turn, posed a 'systemic challenge' to UK 'security, prosperity and values'.[51] China was now seen as a 'systemic competitor' of the United Kingdom.[52]

Specifically, the main areas of concern revolved around China's inroads into the United Kingdom's critical infrastructure and in defence-related sectors through targeted investments, and its increasingly aggressive cyber practices which were further enabled by the central role that Chinese companies like Huawei had

---

[46] On the 'Golden Era' see, e.g. FCO, 'Chancellor: "Let's Create a Golden Decade for the UK–China Relationship"', *Speech*, 22 September 2015; and FCO, 'UK–China Joint Statement on Building a Global Comprehensive Strategic Partnership for the 21st Century', 22 October 2015a.
[47] Interviews with Lord Peter Ricketts, former National Security Adviser (2010–2012), 3 June 2020; General Lord David Richards, former Chief of the Defence Staff (2010–2013), 3 June 2020; General Lord Nick Houghton, former Chief of the Defence Staff (2013–2016), 9 June 2020; a senior former MoD official, interview, 3 July 2020; and a senior official, 26 June 2020.
[48] Interviews with Lord Peter Ricketts, former National Security Adviser (2010–2012), 3 June 2020; General Lord David Richards, former Chief of the Defence Staff (2010–2013), 3 June 2020; General Lord Nick Houghton, former Chief of the Defence Staff (2013–2016), 9 June 2020; a senior former MoD official, interview, 3 July 2020; and a senior official, 26 June 2020.
[49] Senior MoD official, interview, 3 July 2020.
[50] House of Lords, *The UK and China's Security and Trade Relationship: A Strategic Void*, International Relations and Defence Committee, 10 September 2021, p. 15.
[51] HMG, 2021, pp. 22, 24, and 26.
[52] HMG, 2021, p. 26.

gained in the supply of advanced equipment for the United Kingdom's digital networks.

Chinese Investments in Strategic Sectors

'As Chinese investments grew in Europe,' in the words of a senior official, 'there has been a growing awareness of the national security concerns over foreign direct investments in strategic assets and of the need for stronger investment screening mechanisms.'[53] A controversy over China's involvement in the British critical infrastructure first arose in 2015 when the state-owned China General Nuclear Power Group (CGN) signed an agreement with the French energy company Électricité de France (EDF) which would allow CGN's 'progressive entry' in the UK nuclear power sector.[54] In particular, in partnership with EDF, CGN would acquire a 33.5 per cent stake in the Hinkley Point C nuclear power plant.[55] Through consortia, China's CGN and France's EDF also jointly proposed to construct and operate nuclear power plants at the Sizewell C site, in Suffolk, and at the Bradwell B site, in Essex.[56] Whereas at Sizewell EFD would have the largest share (80 per cent v. 20 per cent for CGN), at Bradwell the Chinese state-owned corporation would have the lead (with 66.5 per cent share v. 33.5 per cent for EDF).[57]

After a first review of the security implications of this investment, the David Cameron government (2010–2016) agreed to it.[58] As a FCO official puts it, 'this decision exemplified the Chancellor of the Exchequer George Osborne's approach to China', namely an overarching focus on bolstering trade and investment ties with the PRC.[59] In his words, 'Osborne had a very clear view that, as China would continue to develop, it would offer huge benefits for the United Kingdom both in terms of the opportunities for partnership in China and of Chinese investments in the United Kingdom; and it was therefore a race between Western countries to enjoy these benefits, and we should therefore move quickly' in welcoming Chinese investments into the United Kingdom.[60]

---

[53] Interview, 17 June 2020.
[54] EDF, 'Agreements in Place for Construction of Hinkley Point C Nuclear Power Station', *Press Release*, 21 October 2015, https://www.edf.fr/en/edf/agreements-in-place-for-construction-of-hinkley-point-c-nuclear-power-station; see also Sizewell C Supply Chain, 'New Nuclear Update', September 2017, p. 11, https://www.sizewellcsupplychain.co.uk/wp-content/uploads/2017/09/SZC_New-Nuclear-Update-Sep-17-VL.pdf; and Jonathan Ford, 'UK's Reliance on China's Nuclear Tech Poses Test for Policymakers', *Financial Times*, 14 February 2019.
[55] See Sizewell C Supply Chain, 2017, p. 11, and Ford, 2019.
[56] UK Environment Agency, 'Consultation Launched on New Nuclear Power Station Design Proposed for UK', *Press Release*, 11 January 2021.
[57] Sizewell C Supply Chain, 2017, p. 11.
[58] On the government's rationale for allowing this deal, see HoC, 'The Government's Decision to Support Hinkley Point C', Public Accounts Committee, 20 November 2017, https://publications.parliament.uk/pa/cm201719/cmselect/cmpubacc/393/39306.htm.
[59] Interview, 12 June 2020.
[60] Interview, 12 June 2020.

When entering office in 2016, however, Prime Minister Theresa May decided to delay the final decision in order to undertake a second vetting of the project to assess its national security ramifications. According to her Chief of Staff Nick Timothy (2016–2017), one of the drivers behind this second review was 'the concern over the penetration into the UK critical infrastructure by investors from hostile states or states about which we would have a concern, and whether China wanted to make Britain dependent through the reliance on foreign direct investments, in particular into big infrastructure, so that they would have greater diplomatic leverage over the UK.'[61] The decision to conduct a second review of the Hinkley Point project indicated, according to a FCO official, 'that there was a degree of caution, maybe a degree of concern even, about how far the relationship with China had developed and a need to look more carefully into it, and to be more careful about due diligence'; during this review, he adds, 'there were those who were instinctively concerned about letting China into such a critical area of the national infrastructure; but a careful assessment was made that allowed us to be clear and confident that there would not be a security risk.'[62]

After the second vetting process, the deal was allowed to move ahead.[63] According to Prime Minister May's then Chief of Staff, the rationale for such decision was threefold: first, significant economic interests were involved in the revitalization of the United Kingdom's nuclear power sector; second, the security concerns linked to such investment were deemed to be manageable; and, finally, blocking the investment might have adverse diplomatic ramifications for United Kingdom's relations with China as well as with France.[64]

The Hinkley Point decision stirred significant domestic political controversies and laid the ground for the subsequent rise in security concerns over Chinese FDIs into the United Kingdom's critical infrastructure. Various Members of Parliament (MP) voiced their disquiet over the national security implications of allowing Chinese SOEs within the United Kingdom's critical energy infrastructure.[65] As one MP puts it, China's presence in UK nuclear power plants 'caused a lot of concern'.[66] Overall, according to a former MoD official, the debate over Hinkley Point within Whitehall 'first crystallized' the mounting apprehension over Chinese investments into the critical national infrastructure, sparking a 'recognition of the need to

---

[61] Interview, 18 May 2021. Before entering government, Timothy had accused the former Chancellor of the Exchequer Osborne of 'selling our national security to China' by allowing Chinese companies into the British critical energy infrastructure. Nick Timothy, 'The Government Is Selling Our National Security to China', *Conservative Home*, 20 October 2015.
[62] Interview, 12 June 2020.
[63] Sara Stefanini, 'Theresa May Gives Hinkley the Green Light', *Politico EU*, 15 September 2016.
[64] Nick Timothy, interview, 18 May 2021.
[65] See, for instance, Andrew Woodcock, 'Senior MP Calls for Safeguards over Proposed Chinese-Built Nuclear Power Station', *The Independent*, 14 July 2020. The growing anxieties over the PRC within Parliament were subsequently reflected in the creation, in 2020, of the 'China Research Group' (CRG), a group of Conservative MPs seeking to promote debate about how Britain should respond to the rise of China. For more details, see China Research Group (CRG), https://chinaresearchgroup.org/about.
[66] Interview, 10 June 2020.

be more careful across the board'.⁶⁷ As a testament of such growing disquiet, the government subsequently decided, as detailed later, to change the funding model of British nuclear power plants which would result, among other things, in the removal of China's CGN from the Sizewell C nuclear power.

Additional worries emerged over Chinese FDIs when the MoD became aware, in 2018, of activities by Chinese-owned investment vehicles that sought to acquire companies in the United Kingdom's defence supply chains (e.g. in the third or fourth tiers), concealing that they were Chinese-owned companies through a variety of investment vehicles.⁶⁸ For instance, the MoD investigated the acquisition by China's Gardner Aerospace of Northern Aerospace, a UK company producing components for both civilian and military aircraft.⁶⁹ The fear was that, through such investments, Chinese companies would seek to establish themselves in the supply chains for key defence equipment.⁷⁰

China in the United Kingdom's Digital Infrastructure: Cyber-Espionage and Disruption

These concerns went hand in hand with mounting alarm over the rise in cyber-attacks against the British government, the United Kingdom's critical national infrastructure, and UK businesses.⁷¹ Considering cyber-attacks as a major source of threat,⁷² British policymakers grew wary over how state actors like China had both the intent and capability 'to carry out espionage, sabotage and destructive or disruptive cyber-attacks, including through access to the telecoms supply chain'.⁷³ One notable example was when London accused a group known as APT10, acting on behalf of the Chinese Ministry of State Security, of having carried out 'one of the most significant and widespread cyber intrusions against the UK' through a malicious cyber-campaign that managed to compromise several providers to the UK telecoms sector.⁷⁴

---

⁶⁷ Interview, 25 January 2021.
⁶⁸ Former senior MoD official, interview, 3 July 2020.
⁶⁹ After an in-depth analysis of the two companies' profiles and supply chains, however, the government concluded that they operated almost entirely in the civil sector and that the investment posed no national security concerns; it therefore allowed the deal to be finalized (former senior MoD official, interview, 3 July 2020). For details, see Competition and Markets Authority, 'Gardner Aerospace Holdings/Northern Aerospace Merger Inquiry', 20 July 2018, https://www.gov.uk/cma-cases/gardner-aerospace-holdings-northern-aerospace-merger-inquiry. See also Rob Davies, 'Government Criticised as Chinese Bid for Northern Aerospace Is Derailed', *The Guardian*, 9 July 2018.
⁷⁰ Former senior MoD official, interview, 3 July 2020.
⁷¹ ISC, *Annual Report 2018-2019*, 21 July 2020, p. 9.
⁷² See, e.g., HMG Government, *National Security Strategy and Strategic Defence and Security Review*, 2015, Annex A—Summary of the National Security Risk Assessment 2015, p. 85; and HMG, 2021, pp. 15 and 28-29.
⁷³ DCMS, 2019, p. 4. On Chinese cyber-threats, see also HoC, 2020a, pp. 34-36.
⁷⁴ Quoted in FCO, 'UK and Allies Reveal Global Scale of Chinese Cyber Campaign', *Press Release*, 20 December 2018e. See also Department for Digital, Culture, Media and Sport, and Ministry of Defence, 'Written Evidence (SFG0026)' submitted to the House of Commons, The Security of 5G, Defence Committee, 22 September 2020, p. 15; National Cyber Security Center, 'APT10 Continuing to Target

In this context, the emergence of Huawei as the market leader in the United Kingdom's 4G telecommunications market and its central role in the supply of 5G wireless technology fuelled growing disquiet within the British government over the likely implications thereof in the cyber-domain and for the British critical infrastructure. For one, according to the National Cyber Security Centre (NCSC), the United Kingdom's technical authority confronting cyber threats within GCHQ, the 'main class of risk' associated with Huawei was the insertion of 'backdoors' in its equipment.[75] Backdoors refer to the embedding of malicious functionality into the equipment either intentionally by the vendor or covertly by a hostile actor who has access to the vendor's hardware or software.[76] This threat was particularly salient because Huawei was believed to have close ties with China's security services, as evidenced by the opacity of its ownership structure, the volume of state subsidies that it received, and its 'willingness to support China's intelligence agencies and China's 2017 National Intelligence Law'.[77] A report by the House of Commons' Defence Committee concluded that the 'concern about Huawei' was 'based on clear evidence of collusion between the company and the Chinese Communist Party apparatus'.[78]

A second, related security concern was, according to a comprehensive review of the UK telecoms supply chain, that the over-concentration of the British telecoms sector created the possibility of national dependence on single suppliers which, in turn, endangered the security and resilience of UK digital infrastructure.[79] In particular, over-dependence on few suppliers—especially on 'high risk vendors' like Huawei—considerably increased the impact of any systemic failures or hostile exploitations, while also potentially giving 'inappropriate strategic economic leverage' to a foreign company or state.[80] Overall, as the Intelligence and Security Committee put it, with the 5G 'technology sector now monopolised by such a few key players, we are over-reliant on Chinese technology'.[81]

Third, the technical vulnerabilities of Huawei's equipment opened the door to Chinese cyber-attacks. Low product quality which may stem from legacy equipment, poor software development processes, or poor vulnerability management could result either in a systemic failure of the network or in the equipment

---

UK Organisations', *Alert*, 20 December 2018; and Bryce Boland, 'The G20 and the New Reality of Cyber Espionage', *FireEye*, 4 November 2014.

[75] As reported in HoC, 2020a, p. 38.
[76] DCMS, 2019, p. 25.
[77] HoC, 2020a, p. 5. See also NCSC, 'NCSC Advice on the Use of Equipment from High-Risk Vendors in UK Telecoms Networks', *Guidance*, 28 January 2020a, p. 4. On the 2017 Chinese National Intelligence Law, see the Introduction of Part II.
[78] HoC, 2020a, p. 5. For a similar assessment, see ISC, 2013, p. 5.
[79] DCMS, 2019, July, p. 5.
[80] DCMS, 2019, pp. 5 and 24.
[81] ISC, 'Statement on 5G Suppliers', *News Archive*, 19 July 2019, p. 3, https://isc.independent.gov.uk/wp-content/uploads/2021/01/20190719_ISC_Statement_5GSuppliers_Web.pdf.

vulnerability being exploited by an attacker.[82] The Head of the NCSC Ciaran Martin (2016–2020) assessed that Huawei's poor software engineering and cyber-security processes—'objectively lower' than those of their main competitors—created vulnerabilities that, even without 'direct evidence of deliberate insertion', could be exploited by external actors.[83] In his own words, 'a concern was that these vulnerabilities in Huawei's equipment could have been exploited by outside actors. That is what people were worried about: China introducing certain backdoors into Huawei's equipment. We were pretty confident that we could prevent that, but the main problem was that most cyber-attacks result from poor security. Huawei was doing such poor-quality work that they were leaving us vulnerable to a range of possible attacks.'[84] Likewise, as stressed in various reports by the Oversight Board of the Huawei Cyber Security Evaluation Centre (HCSEC),[85] if an attacker had knowledge of these vulnerabilities and sufficient access to exploit them, it 'may be able to affect the operation of the network, in some cases causing it to cease operating correctly.'[86]

In short, British policymakers grew alarmed by how the supply of key technologies for the UK critical national infrastructure had become overly dependent on a company with close ties to the CCP and security services; furthermore, Huawei's products displayed vulnerabilities that could be exploited by the PRC to conduct cyber-attacks for espionage purposes or to disrupt the United Kingdom's digital infrastructure. As such, for the House of Common's Defence Committee, 'the presence of Huawei in the United Kingdom's 5G networks posed a significant security risk.'[87]

Policy Goals

The goals of the United Kingdom's 'China policy' evolved as a result of China's growing foothold in the British economy and of London's rising threat perceptions of the PRC. If the retrocession of Hong Kong had dominated the United Kingdom–China bilateral agenda before 1997, thereafter and until the late 2000s London's foreign policy priority revolved almost exclusively around furthering economic opportunities in the Chinese market with little emphasis on national

---

[82] DCMS, 2019, p. 4.
[83] Ciaran Martin, CEO of the NCSC (2016–2020) in HoC, *Oral Evidence: The Security of 5G*, 30 June 2020, Q222.
[84] Ciaran Martin, head of GCHQ's NCSC (2016–2020), interview, 22 February 2021.
[85] As detailed below, the task of the HCSEC Oversight Board is to oversee the effectiveness of the mitigation strategy put in place to manage the risks presented by Huawei's presence in parts of the United Kingdom's critical national infrastructure. It is chaired by the CEO of the NCSC, and also includes an executive member of GCHQ's Board with responsibility for cyber security and a senior executive from Huawei as Deputy Chair. HCSEC, *Annual Report*, March 2019, pp. 7–8.
[86] HCSEC, 2019, p. 20. See also HCSEC, *Annual Report*, July 2020, pp. 4, 10, 16 et seg.
[87] HoC, 2020a, p. 4.

security considerations. It is only in the 2010s (and especially in the second half of the decade) that a hightened threat assessment of the PRC and increasingly competitive bilateral economic relations caused the United Kingdom to gradually recalibrate its policy goals vis-à-vis Beijing.

Economic Engagement

After the handover of Hong Kong to the PRC in 1997, the Blair government established the policy of 'engagement' with China—then de facto continued by his successor Gordon Brown (2007–2010)—that revolved around three main goals.[88]

First, London sought to expand trade, investment, and financial opportunities in China for UK companies. A report of the House of Commons' Foreign Affairs Committee stressed that 'the heart of the Government's new China policy' was a 'focus on promoting the United Kingdom's commercial interest'.[89] The second goal was to broaden the areas of bilateral cooperation so as to encourage and enable China's integration into the international system 'as a friendly and responsible partner in dealing with global and regional issues'.[90] Third, and relatedly, the 'underlying strategic hope' was, in the words of Lord Peter Ricketts, the former FCO's Permanent Secretary (2006–2010), that 'increasing economic integration would lead over time to political liberalization, that there would be a new middle class, and that this would bring about political liberalization'.[91]

In short, as summarized by the former British Ambassador to the PRC Christopher Hum (2002–2005), the United Kingdom aimed to foster bilateral economic ties and to emphasize that it was 'the country in Europe most favourably disposed towards Chinese investments'; at the same time, London sought to 'establish the widest possible range of dialogues and consultations with Beijing so as to integrate China into the existing multilateral rules-based system of global governance'; and,

---

[88] On the United Kingdom's 'China policy' in the 2000s, see among others Shaun Breslin, 'Beyond Diplomacy? UK Relations with China since 1997', *The British Journal of Politics and International Relations* 6, no. 3 (2004): pp. 409–425; and Peter Ferdinand, 'UK Policy towards China', in *Europe, China and the Two SARs: Towards a New Era*, edited by Miguel Santos Neves and Brian Bridges (Basingstoke: Palgrave Macmillan, 2000), pp. 29–62.

[89] HoC, *Tenth Report: China*, Foreign Affairs Committee, 22 November 2000, Section 'Advancing British Commercial Interests', https://publications.parliament.uk/pa/cm199900/cmselect/cmfaff/574/57402.htm. See also FCO, *The UK and China: A Framework for Engagement*, 2009, p. 5.

[90] Foreign and Commonwealth Office, Memorandum Submitted to the House of Commons Select Committee on Foreign Affairs Memoranda, 30 October 2000b, https://publications.parliament.uk/pa/cm199900/cmselect/cmfaff/uc574iv/574m01.htm. See also FCO, 'Written Evidence Submitted by the Foreign and Commonwealth Office', in HoC, *East Asia*, Foreign Affairs Committee, Vol. II, 2006, Ev. 113.

[91] Interview, 3 June 2020. On this point, see also HoC, 2000; FCO, 2009, pp. 6, 14, and 18; and Kerry Brown, *The Future of UK–China Relations: The Search for a New Model* (London: Agenda Publishing, 2019), ch. 3.

by doing so, it hoped to 'encourage the possibility of domestic reforms in China, including tentative experiments with local elections'.[92]

Recalibrating National Security and Economic Interests in the United Kingdom's 'China Policy'

By the 2010s, however, rising threat perceptions of the PRC—coupled with increasingly competitive bilateral economic relations—drove London to gradually revise the goals of its 'China policy' in order to better confront the multipronged challenge posed by China's inroads into the United Kingdom.

On the one hand, London continued to pursue the expansion of Sino-British economic and diplomatic ties, and to integrate the PRC into the international system so as 'to encourage and support China's greater cooperation in helping resolve global challenges'.[93] To that end, the two countries established a 'global comprehensive strategic partnership', in 2015, which expanded high-level bilateral exchanges on foreign policy, economic, and financial issues.[94] On the other hand, the gradual accretion of security concerns that began in the early 2010s culminated in the second half of the decade into a heightened threat assessment of the PRC (described above), thereby driving a recalibration of London's 'China policy'. As explained by the former Chief of the Defence Staff General Lord Nick Houghton (2013–2016), Whitehall developed a more 'pragmatic engagement' policy towards the PRC, one that was 'more balanced and realistic in terms of how it saw the implications of China's rise'.[95]

In the mid-to-late 2010s, the government came to consider that the previous balance between the economic imperatives of the so-called 'Golden Era' of United Kingdom–China relations and the national security concerns linked to China's growing clout should be re-evaluated and that greater prominence should be given to the latter.[96] And, by 2021, London's policy towards China aimed 'to pursue a positive economic relationship' with China, 'including deeper trade links and

---

[92] Interview, 15 June 2020.
[93] FCO, 'Appendix: Memorandum from the Foreign and Commonwealth Office', in HoC, *Global Britain*, Foreign Affairs Committee, HC 780, 6 March 2018a, p. 23. See also HoC, 2019a, pp. 3, 12, and 52; FCO, 2015a; and Kerry Brown, 2019, ch. 3. The third goal of the previous engagement policy, i.e. China's political and economic liberalization, gradually faded away as London's threat perceptions of the PRC intensified.
[94] FCO, 2015a; FCO, 'Written Evidence from the Foreign and Commonwealth Office (CIR0018)', in response to HoC, 2019a. On the United Kingdom's 'China policy', see also Brown, 2019; and Paul Irwin Crookes and John Farnell, 'The UK's Strategic Partnership with China beyond Brexit: Economic Opportunities Facing Political Constraints', *Journal of Current Chinese Affairs* 48, no. 1 (2019): pp. 1–16.
[95] Interview, 9 June 2020.
[96] See among others National Security Adviser, Sir Mark Sedwill, in Joint Committee on the National Security Strategy, *Oral Evidence: Work of the National Security Adviser*, HC 625, 28 January 2019, Q56; FCO, 'Written Evidence from the Foreign and Commonwealth Office (CIR0031)', in response to HoC,

more Chinese investment in the UK', while at the same time 'increase protection of our CNI [critical national infrastructure], institutions and sensitive technology, and strengthen the resilience of our critical supply chains'.[97] Overall, as a former senior MoD official succinctly puts it, 'the balance has changed', 'we have gone from a situation in which economic considerations were dominant to one in which security considerations became stronger.'[98]

Policy Instruments

The recalibration of the goals of the United Kingdom's 'China policy' prompted the creation of new policy instruments to concretize these goals. In the first two post-Cold War decades, consistently with its economically driven foreign policy towards China, London maintained no restrictions on Chinese FDI inflows, aiming to remain the leading destination for Chinese investments in Europe. Likewise, it welcomed Chinese companies such as Huawei to supply equipment for its telecoms network. It is in the 2010s, as it gradually reassessed the national security implications of China's rise, that London forged more stringent national policy instruments, such as FDI screening mechanisms and greater restrictions on Huawei. At the same time, prior to its exit from the European Union, it remained more ambivalent towards the development of robust EU policy instruments to restrict Chinese presence in sensitive sectors.

Unrestricted: Attracting Chinese Investments and Telecoms Vendors

Throughout the 1990s and 2000s, although London disposed of policy instruments to restrict FDI inflows, its overarching priority remained to attract Chinese FDIs into the United Kingdom. Accordingly, as the then world's second largest recipient of inbound foreign investment after the United States, the British government maintained a highly liberal investment policy while also welcoming Huawei's entry into the UK telecoms market.[99]

The 2002 Enterprise Act (EA2002) had introduced a legal framework for state interventions in mergers and acquisitions (M&A) deals.[100] This law enabled the

---

China and the International Rules-Based System, Foreign Affairs Committee, HC 612, February 2019d; and House of Lords, 2021, pp. 15–16.

[97] HMG, 2021, pp. 17, 22, and 62–63.

[98] Interview, 1 February 2021. The same point was stressed by a senior diplomat, interview, 3 March 2021.

[99] On the United Kingdom being the world's second-largest FDI recipient, see US Government Accountability Office (GAO), *Foreign Investment: Laws and Policies Regulating Foreign Investment in 10 Countries*, GAO-08-320, February 2008, p. 99 (data for the 2000–2006 period).

[100] In order to restrict foreign investments in specific companies that it deemed key to national security, the British government could also leverage 'golden shares', i.e. restrictions on ownership shares

government to intervene to block or place conditions on the approval of M&As in cases where a clear public interest was considered to be at stake, that is, in relation to national security, media plurality, or financial stability.[101] Specifically, the government could intervene on national security grounds if the total turnover of the company resulting from the M&As was higher than £70m or if the share of the target company exceeded 25 per cent.[102]

Nonetheless, during this timeframe, not only did the British government never leverage the existing instruments to restrict Chinese FDIs, but on the contrary it proactively encouraged China to expand its investments into the United Kingdom, priding itself to be one of the least restrictive destinations in Europe for FDIs.[103] According to a FCO policy paper, 'China's sovereign wealth funds, and even more so its corporations', were 'a potential source of very large flows of inward investment to the UK'.[104] London was therefore 'quite keen to attract Chinese direct investments' and to ensure that the United Kingdom would remain, as a former FCO official puts it, 'open to unrestricted investments'.[105] The former Permanent UK Representative to NATO (2003–2006) and then FCO's Permanent Secretary (2006–2010), Lord Peter Ricketts, confirms that 'the attitude was that Chinese investments, in infrastructure for example, would be subject to the same regulation as any other investment, whatever the sector. The British government took a pretty relaxed view of Chinese investments.'[106]

Similarly, in the telecommunications sector, London welcomed Huawei's entry into the British telecoms market. After BT had informed the government of Huawei's interest in providing their equipment as part of BT's network upgrading plans, an informal cross-departmental working group was set up in 2003 by Sir David Omand, Cabinet Office Intelligence and Security Coordinator (2002–2005), to consider what advice should be given to BT.[107]

Omand explains that the working group concluded that BT be advised that government subsidy (which would have likely been requested by BT if the deal had been blocked) was very unlikely to be possible; and that, based on the available information on existing legal authorities, Ministers could not be advised to use

---

that could be used to control the percentages of foreign-owned shares or to approve the requirements for the dissolution or disposal of any strategic assets. US GAO, 2008, pp. 101–102.

[101] Parliamentary Under-Secretary of State for Trade and Industry, Melanie Johnson (2001–2003), in HoC, *Draft Enterprise Act 2002 (Protection of Legitimate Interests) Order 2003 and Draft Enterprise Act 2002 (Anticipated Mergers) Order 2003*, Third Standing Committee on Delegated Legislation, 21 May 2003. For more details, see Department for Trade and Industry, 'Explanatory Notes' on the 2002 Enterprise Act, 2002, https://www.legislation.gov.uk/ukpga/2002/40/notes/contents.

[102] Ruechardt, 2018, p. 24.
[103] Brown, 2015, p. 20.
[104] FCO, 2009, p. 9.
[105] Rod Wye, FCO's Head of the Asia Research Group (2002–2010), interview, 1 June 2020.
[106] Interview, 3 June 2020.
[107] ISC, 2013, Annex A: 'Huawei's Involvement in the Critical National Infrastructure: A Chronology', p. 22.

existing powers to direct BT.[108] BT should thus be encouraged to continue to work with national cyber-security authorities to explore how any potential risk could be minimized in the design of the network (and the redundancy built into the network) and in the choice of where Cisco, a US company, rather than Huawei equipment was used, such as in the central core.[109] The hope was that any future risk that the Chinese authorities might try to exploit the position of Huawei in the British digital infrastructure could thus be managed, both in terms of any potential use for electronic espionage and of vulnerability to Chinese withdrawal of support (such as suspending regular code upgrades in the event of a major crisis in relations with China).[110]

Furthermore, for the United Kingdom to seek a ban on such a high-profile deal would have had serious diplomatic and trade implications, and possibly major ramifications for the larger United Kingdom–China relationship at a time, as detailed above, when London sought to strengthen and broaden its diplomatic and economic engagement with the PRC.[111]

Tightening the Grip on China

It is only in the 2010s—and especially in the latter part of the decade—that London established more stringent national restrictions both on Chinese FDIs in the United Kingdom and on Huawei's supply of advanced telecommunications equipment for its digital infrastructure, in line with the hardened policy goals of its 'China policy'. By contrast, it remained ambivalent towards the development of EU instruments, especially as it concurrently engaged in protracted negotiations over its exit from the European Union.

National Instruments: FDI Screening Mechanisms and Restrictions on Huawei

The gradual accretion of security concerns over the PRC within Whitehall that started in the early 2010s—and then drove a shift in the goals of London's 'China policy' in the second half of the decade—was reflected in the establishment of new policy instruments to monitor and check both Chinese FDIs and the supply of equipment for the British digital infrastructure.

---

[108] David Omand, interview, 15 January 2021.
[109] David Omand, interview, 15 January 2021.
[110] David Omand, interview, 15 January 2021.
[111] Written evidence provided by the Cabinet Office to the ISC, quoted in ISC, 2013, p. 10.

Screening Foreign Direct Investments

The government launched a sweeping review of the existing FDI screening mechanisms which resulted in the publication of the 2017 Green Paper *National Security Infrastructure Investment Review* and of a subsequent *National Security and Investment White Paper*.[112] Based upon this review, the government came to the conclusion that, with the existing FDI screening framework (the EA2002), it '[did] not have the necessary powers to ensure the national security of the UK'.[113] It therefore took a series of 'short-term' and 'long-term' measures intended to bolster its capacity to scrutinize investments and to address the risks linked to 'hostile parties acquiring ownership of, or control over, businesses or other entities and assets that have national security implications'.[114]

The 'short-term' measures focused on amending the existing legislation, in 2018, with the purpose of lowering the threshold for state intervention in a FDI transaction.[115] The government could now intervene in an investment deemed concerning for national security if the target's turnover exceeded £1m (much lower than the previous £70m threshold) or if the target had a 25 per cent share of the supply of any goods or services in the following sectors: military or dual-use items, computer hardware, or quantum technology.[116] These sectors were later expanded to include artificial intelligence, cryptographic authentication technology, and advanced material.[117] According to a former senior MoD official, these were areas deemed critical for the future development of advanced technological capabilities.[118]

Then, in 2020, London also introduced a 'long-term' measure, namely an entirely new, standalone legislative framework to scrutinize FDIs, the *National Security and Investment Bill* (NSI Bill), that replaced the previous FDI regime. To that end, it created a hybrid system of both mandatory and voluntary notifications.[119] With the mandatory requirement, the investors were now compelled to notify and receive approval from the government if they gained control of the target company or if they acquired 15 per cent or more of the votes (or shares) in the target company in seventeen key sectors deemed to pose the greatest potential

---

[112] Department for Business, Energy and Industrial Strategy (BEIS), *National Security and Infrastructure Investment Review*, 15 March 2018a; BEIS, *National Security and Investment White Paper*, November 2020b.
[113] BEIS, 2018a, p. 5.
[114] BEIS, 'Government Upgrades National Security Investment Powers', *News Story*, 24 July 2018b.
[115] For a detailed analysis of these changes, see BEIS, *Enterprise Act 2002: Changes to the Turnover and Share of Supply Tests for Mergers: Guidance 2020*, June 2020a.
[116] HoC, 'DIT Screening of Foreign Direct Investment', *European Scrutiny Committee*, 29 January 2019d, https://publications.parliament.uk/pa/cm201719/cmselect/cmeuleg/301-li/30109.htm.
[117] BEIS, 2020a, pp. 22–26.
[118] Interview, 25 January 2021.
[119] Steve Browning and Oliver Bennett, 'National Security and Investment Bill 2019–2021', House of Commons Library, *Briefing Paper*, 16 November 2020.

risks.[120] These sectors included among others: military or dual-use technologies, satellite and space technologies, civil nuclear, communications, autonomous robotics, artificial intelligence, as well as critical suppliers to the government.[121] The voluntary notification system would allow companies to notify the government (and, specifically, the new established Investment Security Unit), of 'trigger events', i.e. when there was 'a risk to national security' as a result of the acquisition of control'.[122] Through these measures, the NSI Bill substantially widened the range of potential intervention by the state to monitor or block FDIs in the United Kingdom.[123] Then, in October 2021, the government also introduced a bill to reduce the United Kingdom's reliance on overseas developers for financing new nuclear projects while attracting a wider range of private investment into new nuclear power projects; an intended result of this decision was to remove CGN from the Sizewell C nuclear power and, thereby, to reduce the United Kingdom's reliance on China for its critical national infrastructure.[124]

Prime Minister Boris Johnson (since 2019) explained that the overarching goal of these reforms was to strike a 'balance' between 'continuing to be open to investment from China' and making sure the United Kingdom would do nothing 'that prejudices our critical national infrastructure, our security, or not do anything that would compromise our ability to cooperate with Five-Eyes security partners'.[125] Foreign Secretary of State Liz Truss (since 2021) similarly emphasized that it was 'very important that we do not become strategically dependent' on China, 'particularly in areas of critical national infrastructure'.[126] As one analyst summarizes it:

---

[120] See Debevoise & Plimpton, 'UK National Security and Investment Bill', *Debevoise Update*, 23 November 2020, p. 2.

[121] Debevoise & Plimpton, 2020, p. 20. The seventeen sectors are: advanced materials, advanced robotics, artificial intelligence, civil nuclear, communications, computing hardware, critical suppliers to government, critical suppliers to the emergency services, cryptographic authentication, data infrastructure, defence, energy, military and dual-use, quantum technologies, satellite and space technologies, synthetic biology, and transport. https://assets.publishing.service.gov.uk/government/uploads/system/uploads/attachment_data/file/965784/nsi-scope-of-mandatory-regime-gov-response.pdf.

[122] BEIS, 'National Security and Investment Bill: Statement of Policy Intent', *Policy Paper*, 2 November 2020c, https://www.gov.uk/government/publications/national-security-and-investment-bill-2020/statement-of-policy-intent.

[123] Prime Minister's Office (PMO), 'The Queen's Speech 2019: Background Briefing Notes', 19 December 2019, p. 105; Debevoise & Plimpton, 2020, p. 3. On the Five Eyes arrangement, see chapter 3.

[124] BEIS, 'New Finance Model to Cut Cost of New Nuclear Power Stations', *Press Release*, 26 October 2021a, https://www.gov.uk/government/news/new-finance-model-to-cut-cost-of-new-nuclear-power-stations. See also George Parker and David Sheppard, 'UK to Shut out China with Revamped Nuclear Funding Model', *Financial Times*, 26 October 2021; and John Collingridge and Jillian Ambrose, 'Ministers Close to Deal that Could end China's Role in UK Nuclear Power Station', *The Guardian*, 25 September 2021.

[125] Quoted in Greg Ritchie, 'Police Shoot Man Dead after London Terrorist Attack', *Bloomberg*, 29 November 2019. On this point, see also PMO, 2019, p. 105.

[126] Quoted in Ben Riley-Smith, 'Liz Truss: "Thatcher's Devotion to Democracy Inspires Me to Tackle Today's Global Challenges"', *The Telegraph*, 22 October 2021.

'fear over Chinese influence as well as the loss of technological superiority in key sectors can be understood as the main drivers of this development.'[127]

London's Shifting Position on Huawei: From Mitigation to Full Ban

A similar trajectory characterized the United Kingdom's position on Huawei. Whereas in the previous decade the Chinese company had been allowed to enter the British market, in the 2010s London took a series of measures that gradually bolstered its oversight of, and restrictions on, Huawei which culminated in the establishment of a full-blown ban on the Chinese company in 2020.

London first created the HCSEC (also known as the 'Cell') in 2010. In this facility jointly run by the British government and Huawei, GCHQ would evaluate Huawei's products and test its updates so as to 'mitigate any perceived risks arising from the involvement of Huawei in parts of the United Kingdom's critical national infrastructure'.[128] In 2014, London then further strengthened the capacity of GCHQ to monitor the Cell by establishing an HCSEC Oversight Board, chaired by the GCHQ's Director General for Cyber Security (subsequently replaced by the NCSC's CEO) and tasked with overseeing the effectiveness of the United Kingdom's mitigation strategy and to advise the National Security Adviser on that basis.[129]

In January 2020, based upon the recommendations of a far-reaching inquiry into the supply arrangements for the UK telecoms critical national infrastructure (the *Telecoms Supply Chain Review*), the government adopted new measures to better confront 'high-risk vendors' (HRVs) like Huawei and ZTE, namely those that posed 'greater security and resilience risks to UK telecoms networks'.[130] For one, new telecoms security requirements (TSR) would be established to ensure higher standards and practices of cyber security.[131] Furthermore, in order to reduce the risk of dependency on individual vendors, the government decided to encourage greater competition, innovation, and diversification within the telecoms supply chain, while attracting foreign vendors like South Korean Samsung

---

[127] Ruechard, 2018, p. 33.

[128] HCSEC, 2019, p. 2. Located in Banbury, Oxfordshire, HCSEC is funded entirely by Huawei, staffed by security-cleared UK personnel, and its Director was initially an ex-GCHQ Deputy Director, later replaced by the NCSC's CEO. HCSEC, 2020, pp. 3, 10–15. For more details, see European Network and Information Security Agency (ENISA), *Technologies with Potential to Improve the Resilience of the Internet Infrastructure*, December 2011, pp. 56–57.

[129] The Board also comprised senior executives from Huawei as well as senior representatives from across British government and telecommunications sector. See HCSEC, *Annual Report*, March 2015, p. 2; and HCSEC, 2020, pp. 3 and 9.

[130] On the criteria used to define HRV, see NCSC, 2020a, p. 4; and Secretary of State for DCMS, Oliver Dowden, Statement on Telecoms to the House of Commons, 14 July 2020, https://www.gov.uk/government/speeches/digital-culture-media-and-sport-secretarys-statement-on-telecoms.

[131] These TSR covered a range of areas including, among others, business and governance processes, the building of telecoms networks, and the secure management of networks. DCMS, 2019, p. 36.

and the Japanese NEC and Fujitsu.[132] Finally, London tightened the restrictions on the use of equipment supplied by HRVs without, however, imposing a full-blown ban. Henceforth, HRVs' equipment would be excluded from the critical core functions of the United Kingdom's telecoms networks, excluded from sensitive geographic locations, and limited to a minority presence of no more than 35 per cent on the edge of the network (corresponding to Huawei's existing UK market share in the 4G mobile access network).[133] The government considered that this mitigation strategy was the best way to manage the security risks posed by the presence of Huawei and other HRVs in the UK telecoms infrastructure, and that it was more effective than a full-blown ban.[134] Specifically, this decision was the result of a delicate balancing act between national security, economic, and foreign policy considerations.

From a national security and technical standpoint, London assessed that Huawei's presence in the United Kingdom's 5G network did not endanger the sharing of classified information either within the government or with its allies, whereas banning Huawei would have increased the United Kingdom's overdependence on even fewer suppliers and thus amplified potential security and resilience risks.

The ministries of defence and of digital affairs, GCHQ, MI5, as well as the House of Common's Defence Committee and the Science and Technology Committee considered that maintaining Huawei's 5G equipment (with the new restrictions) did 'not affect our ability to share sensitive intelligence data over highly secure networks both within the United Kingdom and with our partners, including the Five Eyes'.[135] The NCSC's CEO explained that telecoms systems were 'very layered', 'depending on risk', going from networks for sharing classified and encrypted data within the government and with allies (with no non-UK parts in their supply

---

[132] DCMS, 2019, p. 7; DCMS, '5G Supply Chain Diversification Strategy', *Guidance*, 7 December 2020; Secretary of State for Digital, Culture, Media and Sport, Baroness Nicky Morgan, Oral Statement to Parliament on UK Telecommunications, 28 January 2020, https://www.gov.uk/government/speeches/baroness-morgans-oral-statement-on-uk-telecommunications.

[133] Furthermore, such equipment would be excluded from all safety related and safety critical networks in wider critical national infrastructure, and only permitted into the UK market in accordance with a vendor specific mitigation strategy. Department for Digital, Culture, Media and Sport, and Ministry of Defence, 'Written Evidence (SFG0026)' submitted to the House of Commons, *The Security of 5G*, Defence Committee, 22 September 2020, pp. 16–17; NCSC Technical Director, Ian Levy, 'The Future of Telecoms in the UK', *Blog Post*, 28 January 2020.

[134] On this mitigation strategy, see, e.g., NCSC, 2020a; and NCSC, 'Summary of the NCSC Analysis of May 2020 US Sanction', *Report*, 14 July 2020b.

[135] DCMS and MoD, 2020, p. 7. See also CEO of the NCSC (2016–2020), Ciaran Martin, in HoC, *Oral Evidence: The Security of 5G*, 30 June 2020, Q222; Secretary of State for Defence, the Rt Hon Ben Wallace MP, in HoC, *Oral Evidence: The Security of 5G*, 30 June 2020, Q186; Chair of the HoC's Science and Technology Commitee Norman Lamb, Letter to the Secretary of State for Digital, Culture, Media and Sport Jeremy Wright, 10 July 2019, https://www.parliament.uk/globalassets/documents/commons-committees/science-technology/correspondence/190710-chair-to-jeremy-wright-re-huawei.pdf; HoC, 2020a, pp. 42–43; Lionel Barber, 'MI5 Head Shrugs off Risk to Intelligence Sharing from Huawei Links', *Financial Times*, 12 January 2020.

chain) to public networks for ordinary and business communications.¹³⁶ GCHQ 'confirmed categorically that how we construct our 5G and full-fibre public telecoms networks has nothing to do with how we share classified data'.¹³⁷ As a former senior defence official puts it, 'people do not pass their most precious secrets on 5G networks.'¹³⁸

Moreover, removing Huawei's equipment from the United Kingdom's telecoms networks would, in fact, further consolidate the UK telecoms market to only two players, namely Nokia and Ericsson, and thereby reduce competition and increase over-dependence. The GCHQ's NCSC concluded that a full ban on Huawei would 'present substantial resilience and security risks for the UK, and that these far outweighed the risk of retaining [Huawei's] equipment within UK networks.'¹³⁹

From an economic perspective, entirely removing Huawei—the leading player in the United Kingdom's telecoms market—would have significant consequences.¹⁴⁰ The Head of the NCSC Ciaran Martin (2016–2020) explains that the estimated cost of a full ban on the Chinese company's equipment ranged from £2bn to £3bn over three years.¹⁴¹ By contrast, BT expected that limiting Huawei to a presence of no more than 35 per cent in the network would cost approximately £500m over a five-year period.¹⁴²

Coupled with these national security/technical and economic considerations, London also needed to grapple with the foreign policy ramifications of its stance on Huawei for its relations with both the United States and China. On the one hand, Washington exerted substantial pressures on the United Kingdom to impose a full-blown ban, such as the one it (and Australia) had done.¹⁴³ In the words of a former senior defence official, 'it was a geopolitical concern wrapped into a security argument'; the geopolitical concern was that 'the US saw China as a challenger to American hegemony and considered that, by eschewing a full ban on Huawei, the United Kingdom was surrendering an element of economic and technological sovereignty to China to the detriment of the United States' geopolitical position.'¹⁴⁴

---

¹³⁶ NCSC's CEO Ciaran Martin in HoC, *Oral Evidence: The Security of 5G*, 30 June 2020, Q193.
¹³⁷ Cited in DCMS and MoD, 2020, p. 7.
¹³⁸ Chief of the Defence Staff General Lord Nick Houghton (2013–2016), interview, June 2020.
¹³⁹ NCSC, 2020b, p. 13. This point is confirmed by ISC, 2019, p. 2; and Chair of the HoC's Science and Technology Committee Norman Lamb, 2019, p. 1; and HoC, 2020a, p. 4.
¹⁴⁰ ISC, 2019.
¹⁴¹ Ciaran Martin, interview, 22 February 2021.
¹⁴² BT Group, Written Evidence Submitted to HoC, *Oral Evidence: The Security of 5G*, 28 July 2020, Q269.
¹⁴³ The White House, 'Executive Order on Securing the Information and Communications Technology and Services Supply Chain', 15 May 2019; Australian Acting Minister for Home Affairs and the Minister for Communications and the Arts, 'Government Provides 5G Security Guidance to Australian Carriers', *Joint Media Release*, 23 August 2018. On US pressures on the United Kingdom, see ISC, 2019, p. 2; and HoC, 2020a, p. 48.
¹⁴⁴ Interview, 9 June 2020.

On the other hand, the PRC warned the United Kingdom not to ban Huawei from its digital infrastructure. The Chinese government threatened to withdraw from some areas of the United Kingdom's economy, including its critical energy infrastructure (e.g. nuclear power plants) and from other projects such as the HS2 high-speed rail network.[145] The then Chinese Ambassador to the United Kingdom Liu Xiaoming (2010–2021) hinted that such a decision could also jeopardize the overall United Kingdom–China trade relationship.[146] An editorial in the CCP-run *China Daily* similarly warned that the United Kingdom would 'pay price' if it carried out its decision to exclude Huawei from its telecoms network.[147] And HSBC, the British banking and financial services institution, reportedly informed the government that it could face reprisals by China if Huawei was banned from the United Kingdom's 5G network.[148] Yet, according to the then-Head of GCHQ's NCSC, 'US pressures were huge; the US lobbying was far more heated than any Chinese lobbying in the other direction.'[149]

Ultimately, the United Kingdom's decision to opt for a mitigation strategy rather than a full-blown ban of Huawei therefore rested upon this complex mixture of national security, economic, and foreign policy considerations. Soon thereafter, however, London was forced to reconsider its position both because of the establishment of new American export controls on Huawei and because of major political pressures, both domestically and from Washington.

In May 2020, the US Department of Commerce imposed new export controls on Huawei's equipment. With these restrictions, Washington intended to curtail Huawei's ability to use US technology and software to design and manufacture its semiconductors outside the United States.[150] The establishment of these new American export controls marked a turning point in that it instantly altered the British threat assessment of Huawei's equipment, causing it to shift away from a mitigation strategy and to establish a full ban on the Chinese company. This is because London considered that these American export controls had, for the first time, 'potentially severe impacts on Huawei's ability to supply new equipment' to the United Kingdom.[151] The Chinese company now faced two main options. It could start designing and building new equipment independent of US technology; this was, however, deemed largely unrealistic (a 'Herculean task') because Huawei

---

[145] HoC, 2020a, p. 54.

[146] Catherine Philp, Lucy Fisher, and Francis Elliott, 'Ditch Huawei and Trade Will Suffer, Warns China', *The Times*, 7 July 2020.

[147] 'UK Will Pay Price If It Carries out Decision to Exclude Huawei: China Daily Editorial', *China Daily*, 25 May 2020.

[148] Steven Swinford, Lucy Fisher, and Didi Tang, 'China Threatens to Make British Companies Pay for Huawei Ban', *The Times*, 15 July 2020.

[149] Ciaran Martin, CEO of the NCSC (2016–2020), interview, 22 February 2021.

[150] US Department of Commerce, 'Export Administration Regulations: Amendments to General Prohibition Three (Foreign-Produced Direct Product Rule) and the Entity List', *Federal Register*, 19 May 2020a; US Department of Commerce, 'Commerce Addresses Huawei's Efforts to Undermine Entity List, Restricts Products Designed and Produced with U.S. Technologies', *Press Release*, 15 May 2020b.

[151] Secretary of State for DCMS, Oliver Dowden, 2020.

would need to recreate in a very short time some of the world's most advanced and complex technologies which had required US companies decades of research.[152] Alternatively, Huawei could switch to non-US providers, which would introduce new security and reliability risks into the equipment because it could no longer 'source its chips from reputable manufacturers or use reputable equipment in its manufacturing processes'.[153] As a result, the NCSC's threat assessment of Huawei's presence in UK telecoms network 'significantly changed', now concluding that the resulting security risks could no longer be effectively mitigated.[154]

Concurrently, a major Conservative backbench rebellion developed in Parliament, with amendments being proposed to ban Huawei.[155] These domestic pressures were supported by the United States, who used them to exert pressure on the British government; it was obvious to UK government officials that the Americans were in contact with Conservative backbenchers.[156] Yet, according to Ciaran Martin, the then-NCSC's head, 'even if there had been no American pressure, we would still have had to ban Huawei in light of the 2020 US export controls.'[157]

Based upon the NCSC's revised assessment and because of these enhanced domestic and US political pressures, the government abandoned its previous mitigation strategy, decided to entirely ban the purchase of new Huawei 5G equipment after the end of 2020 and ordered the removal of all existing Huawei equipment by the end of 2027.[158] The United Kingdom was now the only major European power—and one of the very few European countries—to impose a full-blown ban on the Chinese company.[159]

An Ambivalent Stance on EU Policy Instruments

If the United Kingdom considerably tightened its national restrictions both on Chinese FDIs and on Huawei, it maintained an ambivalent position towards the development of EU policy instruments, most notably the EU screening framework for FDIs.

The EU FDI Screening Framework: The United Kingdom's Reluctant Stance

The proposal to establish an EU FDI screening framework—which, as discussed in Chapters 4 and 5, largely resulted from a joint Franco-German initiative—was

---

[152] NCSC, 2020b. See also NCSC, 'A Different Future for Telecoms in the UK', *Blog Post*, 14 July 2020c.
[153] HoC, 2020a, p. 41.
[154] NCSC, 2020b, 2020c.
[155] See for instance Dan Sabbagh, 'Rebel Tory MPs Put down Amendment to Bar Huawei Technology', *The Guardian*, 6 March 2020.
[156] Interview with former senior officials, January–March 2021.
[157] Ciaran Martin, CEO of the NCSC (2016–2020), interview, 22 February 2021.
[158] Secretary of State for DCMS, Oliver Dowden, 2020.
[159] In 2020, Sweden had also imposed a ban on Huawei. Supantha Mukherjee and Helena Soderpalm, 'Sweden Bans Huawei, ZTE from Upcoming 5G Networks', *Reuters*, 20 October 2020.

met with considerable scepticism, if not hostility, in London.[160] According to an explanatory memorandum sent by the DIT to the European Commission, the rationale for this position was threefold.[161]

For one, Brussels's proposal for an EU FDI screening mechanism was announced at the same time as the British government was moving forward with its own proposals for an enhanced investment screening regime; the concern was thus that an EU screening mechanism could 'add additional process' to the United Kingdom's national investment screening activity before its exit from the European Union, thereby 'constraining the ability of the United Kingdom to act swiftly in cases of genuine national security concern'.[162] Secondly, while the United Kingdom already shared information on security risks with other member states through 'appropriate channels on a voluntary basis', the compulsory sharing of information that the EU regulation required was 'likely to be highly sensitive both for security and commercial reasons', and would thus 'not be acceptable to the UK'.[163] Finally, allowing the European Commission 'to encroach upon Member States' ability to act on a national basis to protect their security interests' was deemed to set a dangerous precedent both in relation to security matters and in respect of other areas of member state competence and, if allowed, could 'be taken as precedent to expand further in future'.[164] And not only did London oppose this regulation whilst still a member of the European Union, but it also feared that, after its exit from the Union, as a third country, it could potentially still be subject to these provisions depending on the future outcome of the negotiations over the Framework for the UK-EU Economic Partnership.[165]

Based upon these considerations, as detailed in a DIT letter to the House of Commons, the government decided to abstain from voting on the EU regulation at the December 2018 Committee of Permanent Representatives (COREPER).[166] The Regulation was passed by qualified majority vote and, having been approved by the European Parliament Committee on International Trade, it would then go to European Parliament for a plenary decision and to the Council for final approval.[167]

---

[160] Ruechard, 2018, p. 31–32.
[161] Minister of State for Trade Policy Greg Hands (2016–2018), Explanatory Memorandum–Communication from the Commission 'Welcoming Foreign Direct Investment While Protecting Essential Interests', 5 October 2017, https://www.parliament.uk/documents/lords-committees/eu-external-affairs-subcommittee/foreign-direct-investment/EM-foreign-direct-investment.pdf.
[162] Minister of State for Trade Policy Greg Hands, 2017, p. 5.
[163] Minister of State for Trade Policy Greg Hands, 2017, p. 5.
[164] Minister of State for Trade Policy Greg Hands, 2017, p. 5.
[165] Minister of State for Trade Policy Greg Hands, 2017, p. 5. See also Annex A to this Memorandum ('Agreed Regulation Implications for the UK'), p. 2. On the Framework, see Department for Exiting the European Union, 'Framework for the UK–EU Economic Partnership', 24 May 2018, https://www.gov.uk/government/publications/framework-for-the-uk-eu-economic-partnership.
[166] Minister of State for Trade Policy George Hollingbery (2018–2019), 'EU Investment Screening Regulation', Letter to the Chair of the European Scrutiny Committee, 19 December 2018, p. 2.
[167] Minister of State for Trade Policy George Hollingbery, 2018, p. 2

EU Instruments in the Digital Domain

While London adopted a reluctant stance towards the development of the EU FDI screening mechanism, it played a more prominent role in the creation of a new EU instrument intended to restrict 5G suppliers of concern like Huawei, the EU Toolbox for 5G Cybersecurity. The United Kingdom worked with France, Germany, and other EU members in the 5G Cybersecurity Work Stream, the dedicated subgroup of the NIS Cooperation Group, between 2018 and January 2020 (the key steps in the subgroup's decision-making process are detailed in Chapter 4). France had a formal leading role in this subgroup, while Germany was still in the process of defining its national approach and had thus no formal leading position.[168] For its part, according to an EU official involved in these discussions, 'even though the UK had no formal leading position—because it was in the process of leaving the Union after Brexit—it participated actively in the subgroup.'[169] Specifically, Sir Julian King, the then EU Commissioner for the Security Union (2016-2019)—and the last British EU Commissioner before Brexit—explains that the British government 'was interested in being quite actively engaged in EU policy work in several areas, and a number of those related to security because, under Prime Minister Theresa May (2016-2019), it was still envisaged that if and when there would be a deal, the future EU-UK relationship would involve cooperation on security; and one of the areas within security where, during the May era, the British government was interested in fostering cooperation was on cyber.'[170]

Building upon its experience with the HCSEC, the United Kingdom's national approach was to publicly designate high-risk vendors—unlike France and Germany. The NCSC identified HRVs based upon their strategic position and scale in the United Kingdom and other telecoms markets, the quality and transparency of their engineering, and factors relating to the ownership and operating location of the vendor, such as domestic security laws.[171] On these grounds, the government had publicly identified Huawei and ZTE as HRVs.[172] The discussion conducted within the 5G Cybersecurity Work Stream, however, as discussed in chapters 4 and 5, coalesced around a different, 'company-neutral' approach; one that would not be targeted at one specific corporation or country. The members of the subgroup finally agreed on a set of both technical and 'non-technical' (or strategic/political) measures, including strengthening security requirements for mobile network operators, assessing the risk profile of suppliers, applying restrictions for high-risk suppliers (and potentially excluding them from the networks), and developing a multi-vendor strategy to reduce dependency on a single supplier (especially if

---

[168] See Chapters 4 and 5.
[169] Interview, 7 April 2021.
[170] Sir Julian King, interview, 28 May 2021.
[171] NCSC, 2020a, p. 4.
[172] Secretary of State for DCMS, Oliver Dowden, 2020.

high-risk suppliers).¹⁷³ By working on the establishment of the EU 5G Toolbox, the United Kingdom and the other member states aimed, according to the then EU Commissioner for the Security Union, to develop 'a European approach to managing the issue of 5G and Huawei, one that was not going to be the Chinese approach, but nor was it going to be a full ban as the US did. And the UK pursued this goal until its exit from the European Union.'¹⁷⁴

Overall, even though the United Kingdom was concurrently in the process of withdrawing from the Union, it thus played a significant role—prior to Brexit—in the development of an EU instrument intended to restrict 5G suppliers of concern like Huawei.¹⁷⁵ The EU 5G Toolbox on Cybersecurity was published the same month as the United Kingdom's announcement of the initial restrictions imposed on HRVs like Huawei in January 2020, when London excluded HRVs from the critical core functions of the British telecoms networks and limited their presence to no more than 35 per cent on the edge of the network (as discussed earlier).¹⁷⁶ At the end of the month (31 January), however, the United Kingdom formally exited the European Union and, in May of the same year, Prime Minister Boris Johnson (since 2019) changed the British policy, imposing a full-blown ban on Huawei. The United Kingdom's approach to Huawei had come full circle.

Conclusion

The overall balance between national security and economic considerations at play in United Kingdom's 'China policy' has substantially shifted. In the first two post-Cold War decades London looked at the PRC mostly through an economic prism. Since the 2010s, however, China's growing foothold in strategic sectors in the United Kingdom has caused the threat perceptions of British policymakers to heighten, at a time when Chinese assertiveness in the Asia-Pacific also spurred growing concerns. This changing threat assessment, coupled with increasingly competitive economic relations with the PRC, drove a hardening of United Kingdom's 'China policy'. The Director General for Security Policy (2014-17) and Director General for Strategy and International (2017-18) in the UK Ministry of Defence, Peter Watkins, subsequently summarized this evolution as follows:

---

¹⁷³ European Commission, *Secure 5G Deployment in the EU—Implementing the EU Toolbox*, Communication COM(2020) 50 final, 29 January 2020i, pp. 5–6.

¹⁷⁴ Sir Julian King, interview, 28 May 2021.

¹⁷⁵ After its exit from the European Union, the United Kingdom affirmed its intention to continue cyber-cooperation with the European Union and its member states through a newly established UK–EU strategic dialogue of cybersecurity, to share information on cyber threats, and to further collaboration between the United Kingdom and the NIS Cooperation Group, the Computer Security Incident Response Team (CSIRT) Network, and the European Union Agency for Network and Information Security (ENISA). HMG, *The Future Relationship between the United Kingdom and the European Union*, July 2018d, pp. 166 and 170.

¹⁷⁶ DCMS and MoD, 2020, pp. 16–17; NCSC Technical Director, Ian Levy, 2020.

'China has gone from being rather peripheral to the UK debate on international policy and security to being increasingly central. In the same period, it has gone from being seen primarily as an economic opportunity to a growing challenge to our security.'[177] As a result, London has taken a variety of national measures to strengthen its capacity to monitor and restrict Chinese investments in sensitive sectors in the United Kingdom, and it has imposed a full ban on Huawei's equipment in its 5G networks—thus taking the harshest position among the three major European powers on this issue. However, it has exhibited more ambivalence than the other major European powers vis-à-vis EU policy instruments after the Brexit referendum. While it advocated for the development of EU tools in the digital domain, it remained more sceptical about the establishment of an EU FDI screening mechanism, perceiving it as an infringement upon its national prerogatives in a sensitive national security area. With its exit from the Union, London pulled out of these EU instruments. It now remains to be seen whether, to what extent, and through what channels, the United Kingdom will cooperate with the European Union and/or individual European countries in formulating a common stance towards the PRC, or instead pursue increasingly antagonistic policies.

---

[177] Peter Watkins, 'China and the "Integrated Review"', *Chatham House*, 23 November 2020, https://americas.chathamhouse.org/article/china-and-the-integrated-review/.

Conclusions

Europe in the Midst of the United States–China Rivalry

Through a unique cross-regional comparison, *Awakening to China's Rise* has delivered the most comprehensive analysis to date of how Europe's major powers have responded to the re-emergence of China as a great power in world politics since the end of the Cold War. A longstanding assumption in the IR literature has been that European foreign policies towards the PRC have been driven by a 'naïve' and self-interested focus on the economic opportunities presented by such vast market, overlooking security considerations. This book challenges such common belief. Its central argument is that, whereas this assessment aptly characterized the first two post-Cold War decades, Beijing's growing assertiveness in the 2010s caused the three major European powers to awaken to the security implications of China's rise. China's shifting foreign policy behaviour, as an exogenous driver, has altered their national threat assessments and economic interests which, in turn, has impacted the policy goals and the policy instruments mobilized to achieve such goals. This finding has major implications at a time when the European Union and NATO have been revising their approaches towards Beijing amidst mounting United States–China strategic competition and when China's rise is bound to become a, if not the, defining issue for transatlantic relations in the years to come. This concluding chapter first summarizes and compares the book's core findings on the policies of the three major European powers towards China—across both the Asia-Pacific and Europe—and then, building thereupon, outlines new important avenues for future research.

Core Findings

The post-Cold War trajectories of French, British, and German policies towards the PRC, both in the Asia-Pacific and in Europe, reveal significant similarities. Throughout the 1990s and the 2000s, Europe's three major powers eagerly expanded their exports and investments in the vast, emerging Chinese market and developed significant economic interests across the Asia-Pacific, with a focus on trade, investments, and arms sales—although to varying degrees. France also maintained significant interests in its exclusive economic zone (EEZ) in the Indian and Pacific Oceans while the United Kingdom gradually developed substantial financial ties with the PRC.

At the same time, policymakers in Paris, Berlin, and London exhibited low threat perceptions of China. They considered that the Beijing's foreign policy abided by Deng Xiaoping's guidelines of maintaining a low profile and refraining from claiming leadership. The PRC was seen as a peaceful rising power that largely focused on domestic priorities such as internal stability and economic growth. And even though they monitored China's military modernization, British, French, and German policymakers viewed the PLA's capabilities as being largely outdated and as posing few security concerns. One exception was, for France, the growing range of the PLA's intercontinental ballistic missiles. Likewise, Chinese espionage and technology theft, including through cyber means, did provoke some disquiet among the Big Three, but the technological gap between European and Chinese industrial and technological capabilities was deemed so profound that these practices were not perceived as posing a major security challenge.

In light of these rising economic interests and low threat perceptions, their foreign policy goals vis-à-vis China and the Asia-Pacific overwhelmingly revolved around the pursuit of economic opportunities. One specificity which differentiated the United Kingdom's 'China policy' from those of France and Germany prior to 1997 was the utmost centrality of the negotiations over the future status of Hong Kong in the United Kingdom–PRC relationship. The handover of the former British colony to the PRC in 1997, however, removed a major source of friction and enabled the subsequent thickening of Sino-British economic and political ties. Thereafter, the 'China policies' of Europe's major powers converged around three policy goals: to broaden their economic and diplomatic engagement with Beijing; to integrate China in the international system; and to thereby encourage a gradual economic and political liberalization within the PRC. Except for this overarching focus on deepening ties with China, the foreign policies of the Big Three in the Asia-Pacific region remained piecemeal and lacked a clearly defined policy framework, receiving little prioritization in their overall foreign policy.

Their engagement in the region mostly consisted of patchworks of loosely coordinated diplomatic and economic endeavours with little emphasis on the security dimension. They all focused on deepening their economic and diplomatic relations especially with China and, to a lesser extent, with a few selected emerging regional powers through bilateral and multilateral initiatives, with little centralized coordination. Likewise, in Europe, these policy goals translated into very open investments regimes, with the three countries eagerly encouraging Chinese firms to establish a presence in Europe and imposing few, if any, restrictions on Chinese

FDIs. In fact, the Big Three competed for which country would become Beijing's main economic and political partner in Europe. Consistently with these largely economically oriented goals, they also initially jointly pushed for lifting the EU arms embargo on China in the early 2000s. However, London and Berlin's positions thereafter shifted, and they subsequently decided to oppose such move. The combination of US forceful pressure on EU member states, China's adoption of the 2005 Anti-Secession Law, and persistent intra-European fragmentation on this issue—which was further reinforced by the British and German policy shift—resulted in the issue of the EU arms embargo on China being de facto shelved.

It is only during the 2010s that the Big Three reassessed the potential security implications of China's rise because of the PRC's growing assertiveness both in the Asia-Pacific and in Europe, at a time when their economic relations with Beijing also became more competitive.

As the importance of the Asia-Pacific in the world's economy continued to grow, their economic interests therein expanded. Most notably, the three countries became ever more dependent upon trade flows passing through the Indian and Pacific Oceans and, therefore, upon the stability of the regional sea lines of communication (SLOCs). Concurrently, China became an increasingly important trade and investment partner. By the end of the decade, China was Germany's first trading partner and the third and fifth for the United Kingdom and France respectively. Germany also became the largest EU investor in the PRC and the United Kingdom the largest recipient of Chinese FDIs in Europe. Yet, as the Chinese economy transitioned towards value-added high-tech manufacturing, and as the economic presence of Chinese corporations in Europe deepened through FDIs and the supply of advanced technology equipment, Chinese and European high-tech industries increasingly became economic competitors. This trend was nonetheless markedly more prevalent in Germany, partly because, among the Big Three, its industrial sector—and the manufacturing industry in particular—represented the largest share of its gross domestic product (GDP).[1]

Concurrently, spurred by growing economic, military, and technological capabilities, China became increasingly assertive on both continents—although with different means—thereby causing the threat assessments of the Big Three to heighten (with slightly differing timings in each country).[2] In the Asia-Pacific, the

---

[1] Between 2009 and 2019, the contribution of the industrial sector to the GDP was almost 27 per cent for Germany as opposed to 17 per cent in France and the United Kingdom. Likewise, the value added by the manufacturing sector (as a percent of GDP) in 2019 was 19 per cent for Germany, but only 9.8 per cent and 8.6 per cent for France and the United Kingdom respectively. Data retrieved from the World Bank, 'World Development Indicators', https://databank.worldbank.org/source/world-development-indicators.

[2] The exact timing of this shift slightly differed across countries by a few years, largely because of domestic politics and bureaucratic disagreements between different ministries (e.g., between Ministries of Foreign Affairs, Defence, Economy, Interior etc.). French threat perceptions of China markedly shifted

PRC displayed a more muscular foreign policy geared to the establishment of a Sino-centric regional order. Coupled with its military modernization programme, Chinese regional behaviour, including its land reclamation practices, its contestation of international law, and its growing tensions with Asian neighbours, sparked rising concerns. In particular, while the three major European powers did not consider that China posed a direct military threat, they came to see Beijing's regional posture—in a context of mounting Sino-American strategic rivalry—as potentially threatening regional stability (fuelling risks of unintended escalation and conflict), foundational norms of the rules-based order (freedom of navigation and peaceful resolution of disputes), as well as vital SLOCs upon which their prosperity relied. France, in contrast to the United Kingdom and Germany, also emphasized the protection of sovereignty over its overseas territories and EEZ in the Indian and Pacific Oceans. And both France and the UK worried about the potential implications of a regional crisis or conflict not only for their security partnerships in the region but also in light of their role as permanent members of the UN Security Council.

In Europe, China's deepening foothold in sensitive industrial sectors also generated mounting disquiet. France, Germany, and the United Kingdom grew increasingly wary over how Chinese state-owned and private companies could siphon advanced technologies with military applications, gain control over strategic assets in Europe's critical infrastructure, and endanger their high-tech industrial base as well as the security of supply in dual-use sectors. Likewise, they assessed that acquiring technology for their digital infrastructure from companies linked to the Chinese state, such as Huawei, could enable Chinese cyber-attacks intended to spy on data traffic or to disrupt digital networks. They also feared that Beijing could mobilize its growing economic influence to exploit the existing divisions among Europeans in order to politically weaken the European Union in its dealings with China (although, after the Brexit referendum, this concern faded away in the United Kingdom).

As a result of these shifting economic interests and heightened threat perceptions, the three countries gradually and cumulatively recalibrated their policy goals. At the national level, they formulated more comprehensive and cohesive regional policy frameworks and hardened their 'China policies' in order to better confront Beijing's rising assertiveness. The Big Three all broadened the scope of their Asian-Pacific policy to the larger 'Indo-Pacific' region, encompassing both

---

after 2009 and then continued to intensify throughout the rest of the decade. In Germany and the UK, threat perceptions also began to gradually heighten after 2009 and increased in the early 2010s. It is nonetheless in the second half of the decade, and specifically after 2016, that in both countries the overall threat assessment of China displayed a fundamental shift. Overall, by the latter half of the decade, the three major European powers all shared mounting apprehensions of China's rising assertiveness both in the Asia-Pacific and in Europe.

the Indian and Pacific regions.³ Their policy goals in the Indo-Pacific now specifically revolved around upholding regional stability and preventing unintended escalations to conflict, defending foundational norms of the rules-based order (most notably freedom of navigation and the peaceful resolution of disputes), while furthering their economic interests in the region. Concomitantly, whilst continuing to engage China diplomatically and economically, the Big Three hardened their national stance towards Beijing giving greater prominence to security considerations. At the same time, they promoted greater EU political cohesion vis-à-vis China and in the Indo-Pacific, in part to reduce their exposure to potential Chinese and US pressures and to increase their collective negotiating leverage vis-à-vis Beijing—although after Brexit the United Kingdom abandoned such an objective. Thereafter, in line with a common decision taken at the EU level, France and Germany relabelled China a partner, a competitor, and a systemic rival. For its part, while London continued to pursue a positive trade and investment relationship with Beijing, it now identified the PRC's rising assertiveness as a systemic challenge to its security and prosperity.

Overall, through their 'China policies', the three major European powers have all sought to combine continued engagement and cooperation with the PRC in areas of common interests, with a toughened stance—and the willingness to now push back—against Beijing where their interests collided. Likewise, their overarching ambition in the Indo-Pacific has not been to balance China, an unviable goal given their capability shortfalls, the tyranny of distance, and their continued engagement with the PRC. Rather, they have pursued the 'milieu goal' of seeking to shape the regional environment in which China's rise unfolded while forging a distinct position for themselves in the context of the mounting United States–China rivalry.

To concretize these new policy frameworks, the Big Three revised and strengthened the instruments leveraged to achieve such goals. For one, they moved beyond their previous 'China-centric' approaches by diversifying their networks of bilateral diplomatic and security arrangements with greater emphasis now also on South East Asia and into the larger Indo-Pacific. Likewise, they deepened their engagement with minilateral and/or multilateral regional security fora and fostered greater multinational security cooperation with the United States and other European states—although, largely because of capability constraints, Germany privileged the latter over the former. Paris and London also expanded their naval deployments in the Indo-Pacific, while Berlin decided to deploy a frigate to the region. Although Brexit removed the United Kingdom from formal EU channels, the Big Three continued their consultations on regional security in bilateral interactions and through minilateral groupings such as the E3, the Quad, and the

---

³ The 'Indo-Pacific' label was formally adopted in 2018 by France, in 2020 by Germany, and in 2021 by the United Kingdom.

Quint, outside the European Union's formal structures. For their part, France and Germany (together with the Netherlands and other member states) promoted—after Brexit—the development of an EU strategy for the Indo-Pacific intended to promote the 'stability, security and prosperity' of the region, while thereby also 'enhancing [the European Union's] strategic autonomy'.[4]

To confront the PRC's inroads into Europe, the Big Three strengthened their national instruments to better monitor and, if needed, veto foreign investments deemed to be harmful to their security interests, and to restrict 5G suppliers of concern like Huawei. Initially, the three countries all opted for tighter national restrictions on 5G suppliers while eschewing a full-blown ban on Huawei. The specifics of their national measures partly differed because of the relative importance of their economic interests in China, their degree of reliance on Huawei, and the intensity of US pressure. The decision to tighten restrictions on 5G vendors was, in each country, the result of a careful balancing act between national security, economic, and diplomatic considerations. In 2020, however, because of new US export controls on Huawei coupled with substantial political pressures, both domestically and from Washington, the United Kingdom revised its policy and decided to ban the Chinese corporation from its 5G networks. Thereby, it became the only one of the three major European powers to impose a full-blown ban on the Chinese company. Prior the United Kingdom's exit from the European Union, the Big Three also cooperated among themselves and with other EU member states to create new EU policy instruments, such as the EU FDI screening mechanism and the EU 5G Toolbox for Cybersecurity. Yet, as the United Kingdom began the process of exiting from the Union, it adopted an increasingly ambivalent position vis-à-vis such instruments, most notably on the EU controls over FDI inflows.

In sum, what emerges from this analysis is that China's rising assertiveness has been the key driver of change in the hardening of the Big Three's policies towards the PRC, both in Europe and in the Asia-Pacific. Whereas growing economic interests have provided the underlying impetus for the three countries' growing attention to the PRC and the Asia-Pacific, their threat perceptions of China—coupled with increasingly competitive bilateral economic relations—have been the main driver of change in their policies towards Beijing. These findings lay the foundations for at least two important avenues of future research on key dimensions of Europe's role amidst rising United States–China strategic competition.

The European Union and China

The first one focuses on the broader trends of convergence (or divergence) in how the member states of the European Union, beyond those examined in this book,

---

[4] Council of the European Union, 'EU Strategy for Cooperation in the Indo-Pacific', Council Conclusions, 16 April 2021c, pp. 2 and 3.

have grappled with the security ramifications of China's rise, and on the impact of Brexit thereupon.[5]

On the one hand, the main pattern identified by this book in the 'China policies' of the three major European powers appears to be partly reflected at the European Union level, with a hardened stance vis-à-vis Beijing. As a senior EU official puts it, in the 2010s 'Chinese assertiveness in the Asia-Pacific but also globally—including closer to Europe—became ever more manifest and, as a result, there has been a greater convergence around the need for a more robust and hard-nosed approach vis-à-vis China.'[6] Largely as a result of French, German, and Dutch advocacy and initiatives, the European Union has adopted a common strategy for the Indo-Pacific and increasingly emphasized as its core regional policy goals the preservation of regional stability and of the central norms of the rules-based order.[7] This strategy partly differed, however, from that of the United States and of regional powers such as, for instance, Japan or Australia, with less emphasis on the military component. As stressed by Gunnar Wiegand, the Managing Director for Asia and the Pacific in the EU's diplomatic service, the European External Action Service (EEAS, since 2016):

> We do not want to design a strategy for confrontation in the Indo-Pacific, but one of cooperation. Europe has been the theatre of so many wars and of the long Cold War period, and then overcame the division caused by this Cold War and now is the place not only of alliances and of the world's most successful regional integration, the EU, but also of cooperative security structures. The EU therefore wants to make a distinct European contribution to cooperation in the region and considers that its Indo-Pacific strategy should be inclusive and not exclusive.

---

[5] This section builds upon Hugo Meijer, 'The European Union's "China Policy": Convergences or Divergences?', European University Institute, *Policy Brief*, 2021b, https://cadmus.eui.eu/bitstream/handle/1814/72201/QM-AX-21-032-EN-N.pdf?sequence=1&isAllowed=y.

[6] Interview, 6 March 2020. On this point, see also European Commission and High Representative of the Union for Foreign Affairs and Security Policy (HR/VP), *EU-China: A Strategic Outlook*, 12 March 2019, p. 1; Council of the European Union, 2021c, p. 2; European Commission, 'The EU Strategy for Cooperation in the Indo-Pacific', Joint Communication JOIN(2021) 24 final, 16 September 2021c, p. 2.

[7] European Commission, 2021c; Council of the European Union, 2021c; EEAS, 'EU Strategy for Cooperation in the Indo-Pacific', *Factsheet*, 19 April 2021a; and EEAS, 'Indo-Pacific: Remarks by the High Representative/Vice-President at the Press Conference on the Joint Communication', 16 September 2021b, https://eeas.europa.eu/headquarters/headquarters-homepage_en/104215/Indo-Pacific:%20Remarks%20by%20the%20High%20Representative/Vice-President%20at%20the%20press%20conference%20on%20the%20Joint%20Communication. On the evolution of the European Union's policy goals in the region, see also Council of the European Union, 'Guidelines on the EU's Foreign and Security Policy in East Asia', Brussels, 15 June 2012; Council of the European Union, 'EU Strategy on China', Council Conclusions, 18 July 2016a, p. 6; Council of the European Union, 'Enhanced EU Security Cooperation in and with Asia', Council Conclusions, 28 May 2018b, p. 4; European Parliament, *Report on the State of EU-China Relations*, Committee on Foreign Affairs, 7 October 2018, p. 21; and European Parliament, *Challenges to Freedom of the Seas and Maritime Rivalry in Asia*, Directorate-General for External Policies Department, March 2017; Josep Borrell, 'The EU Needs a Strategic Approach for the Indo-Pacific', Blog by HR/VP Josep Borrell 'A Window on the World', 12 March 2021a, https://eeas.europa.eu/headquarters/headquarters-homepage/94,898/eu-needs-strategic-approach-indo-pacific_en; and Josep Borrell, 'What the EU Can Do in and with the Indo-Pacific', *Groupe d'études géopolitiques*, 2021b, https://geopolitique.eu/en/2021/06/22/what-the-eu-can-do-in-and-with-the-indo-pacific/.

So, there is certainly a nuance in our approach which in its essence is about the very same—namely a free and open Indo-Pacific—but in method and emphasis somehow different from the strategies of some other partners.[8]

In its bilateral relationship with Beijing, the European Union has aimed to bilaterally engage China to foster cooperation on issues of common interest while, at the same time, working with international partners who shared similar concerns 'to protect its essential interests', 'pushing back where fundamental disagreements exist[ed] with China'.[9] Specifically, as previously noted, the European Union developed a threefold policy which looked at China as a partner, a competitor, and a systemic rival.[10] It thereby sought to develop an autonomous position amidst rising United States–China competition, one that would neither aim at containing China, nor at systematic alignment with the United States, nor at equidistance between Washington and Beijing given its closer position to the United States on many issues.

In the words of the EU High Representative for Foreign Affairs and Security Policy and Vice-President of the European Commission Josep Borrell (HR/VP, since 2019), 'this US-China strategic rivalry will probably be the dominant organising principle for global politics' and, in this context, the European Union should frame its own approach; 'we must follow our own path', which 'does not mean we should be equidistant from the two protagonists'.[11] In essence, according to a senior advisor to HR/VP Borrell, the European Union has aimed to pragmatically position itself within this mounting Sino-American strategic competition depending on the issue area, e.g. trade, investments, digital technologies/5G, human rights, Indo-Pacific security, etc.[12]

To that end, supported by member states' initiatives, it has developed new policy instruments such as, among others, the EU FDI screening mechanism and the EU 5G Toolbox, discussed in this book, as well as instruments against Chinese economic coercion and sanctions on Beijing's human rights violation, while simultaneously seeking to rebalance the overall investment relationship through the proposed European Union–China Comprehensive Agreement on Investment (subsequently frozen in 2021).[13] Likewise, the European Union has aimed to

---

[8] Gunnar Wiegand, interview, 5 November 2021.
[9] European Commission, 2021c, p. 4.
[10] European Commission and HR/VP, 2019, p. 1.
[11] Josep Borrell, 'China, the United States and Us'. *Blog by HR/VP Josep Borrell 'A Window on the World'*, 31 July 2020, https://eeas.europa.eu/headquarters/headquarters-homepage/83644/china-united-states-and-us_en.
[12] Zaki Laïdi, Senior adviser to the HR/VP Josep Borrell (since 2020) interview, 29 March 2021.
[13] The European Parliament subsequently passed a resolution, in May 2021, to freeze ratification of the European Union–China CAI in response to Chinese sanctions on European human rights advocates, stating that it would not consider the agreement until Chinese countersanctions were lifted. On the Comprehensive Agreement on Investment (CAI), see European Commission, 'EU-China Comprehensive Agreement on Investment (CAI)', *News Archive*, 22

expand its security ties with Indo-Pacific partners through 'tailor-made cooperation with an initial set of five pilot countries' (i.e. India, Indonesia, Japan, Republic of Korea, and Vietnam) in areas such as maritime security, crisis management and cybersecurity, although with a meagre budget of €8.5m.[14] Venues that have been explored to develop an EU naval presence in critical waterways, including in the Indo-Pacific, comprised the EU CRIMARIO II, the so-called Coordinated Maritime Presences (CMP), and operation NAVFOR/Atalanta.[15] At the multilateral level, the European Union upgraded its relations with ASEAN to the level of a 'strategic partnership', bolstered cooperation with the Indian Ocean Rim Association (IORA), applied for observer status in working groups of the ASEAN Defence Ministers Meeting Plus (ADMM+), and sought membership in the East Asia Summit (EAS).[16] With the United States, the European Union first proposed and then launched, in 2020, the EU–US China Dialogue between the US Secretary of State and the EU HR/VP as a mechanism for discussing the security concerns

---

January 2021a, https://trade.ec.europa.eu/doclib/press/index.cfm?id=2237; and European Parliament, 'MEPs Refuse Any Agreement with China Whilst Sanctions Are in Place', *News*, 20 May 2021b, https://www.europarl.europa.eu/news/en/press-room/20210517IPR04123/meps-refuse-any-agreement-with-china-whilst-sanctions-are-in-place. On US-EU sanctions on China for large-scale arbitrary detentions of, in particular, Uyghurs in Xinjiang, see Council of the EU, 'EU Imposes Further Sanctions over Serious Violations of Human Rights around the World', *Press Release*, 22 March 2021a, https://www.consilium.europa.eu/en/press/press-releases/2021/03/22/eu-imposes-further-sanctions-over-serious-violations-of-human-rights-around-the-world/. On the EU's 'anti-coercive' instruments, see European Commission, 'EU Strengthens Protection against Economic Coercion', *Press Corner*, 8 December 2021e, https://ec.europa.eu/commission/presscorner/detail/en/ip_21_6642.

[14] The initiative was intended to be subsequently expanded to a wider range of partners, including Australia, New Zealand, Singapore, and Malaysia, among others, in one or more of these issue areas (European Commission, 'Implementing Decision on the Financing of the 2019 Partnership Instrument Annual Action Programme', C(2019) 3277 final, 6 May 2019c, 'Annex 3: Action Document for "Security Cooperation in and with Asia"', p. 5). On the strengthening of EU political and security ties with partners in the Asia-Pacific, see also Council of the European Union, 2018b; European Commission, 'Service for Foreign Policy Instruments (FPI)', 2019b, https://ec.europa.eu/fpi/content/partnership-instrument-annual-action-programme-2019_en ('Annex 12: EU-Malaysia and EU-Singapore Partnership Facility' and 'Annex 9: Policy Dialogue Support Facility India'); EEAS, 'The Republic of Korea and the EU', Updated 10 May 2016, https://eeas.europa.eu/delegations/south-korea_en/8789/; EEAS, 'Australia and the EU', Updated 17 July 2018, https://eeas.europa.eu/delegations/australia/610/australia-and-eu_en; and Sunghoon Park and Jae-Seung Lee, 'EU's Strategic Partnerships with Asian Countries', *Asia-Europe Journal 17*, no. 3 (2019), Special Issue.

[15] These initiatives are discussed in Chapter 1.

[16] With ASEAN, the European Union also ran the high-level dialogues on maritime security and co-chaired the Intersessional Meetings on Maritime Security in the ASEAN Regional Forum (ARF). On these various initiatives, see European Commission, 'Service for Foreign Policy Instruments (FPI)', 2019b, Annex 3: Action Document for 'Security Cooperation in and with Asia', p. 3, https://ec.europa.eu/fpi/content/partnership-instrument-annual-action-programme-2019_en; ASEAN, 'ASEAN–EU Plan of Action 2018–2022', 6 August 2017; European Commission, 'The EU and ASEAN: A Partnership with a Strategic Purpose', Joint Communication JOIN(2015) 22 final, 18 May 2015; Council of the European Union, 'Joint Statement of the 22nd EU–ASEAN Ministerial Meeting', *Press Release*, 21 January 2019; and European Commission, 'Implementing Decision on the Financing of the 2020 Partnership Instrument Annual Action Programme', C(2020) 2779 final, 5 May 2020h, 'Annex 12: Action Document for Enhancing EU's Role in Multilateral Fora in Asia'. See also Park and Lee, 2019.

over China on both sides of the Atlantic.[17] One year later, Brussels and Washington inaugurated the EU-US Trade and Technology Council to foster exchanges and cooperation in areas such as technology standards cooperation, secure supply chains, and investment screening mechanisms, while also launching EU-US consultations on the Indo-Pacific.[18] Overall, this book's findings on the Big Three's awakening to China's rise thus appear to extend to the broader European Union.

On the other hand, the European Union has faced two interrelated challenges in the formulation of a common policy towards Beijing and in the Indo-Pacific: the profound shortfalls and discrepancies in defence capabilities across the European Union, which have been further amplified by Brexit; and persistently differing priorities vis-à-vis China among EU member states. In combination these two constraints, which mutually feed one another, raise questions about the capacity of the European Union to forge a cohesive 'China policy'.[19]

For one, the power projection capabilities of EU member states in the Indo-Pacific have been hindered by severe shortfalls and asymmetries. This applies to major powers but even more so to medium and smaller powers. What emerges from this book is that, while the European Union has played a relatively larger role in responding to China's inroads into Europe's industrial fabric (because several relevant competences, e.g. on investments, are located at the EU level), the bulk of the European Union's political-military engagement in the Asia-Pacific has been conducted nationally by few major powers—most notably by France and, prior to Brexit, the United Kingdom—with little operational cooperation among EU member states. But these major powers have all faced major capability constraints. Building upon different colonial and post-colonial trajectories in the region, the Big Three have displayed profoundly discrepant defence capacities, with France maintaining the largest military footprint in the Indo-Pacific, followed by the United Kingdom (with around 7,000 and 1,600 defence personnel in the region respectively), while Germany lacks any direct presence in the region. And, after Brexit, France remains the only EU country with a permanent military

---

[17] Borrell, 2020; US Secretary of State Mike Pompeo, 'A New Transatlantic Dialogue', Speech at the German Marshall Fund's Brussels Forum, Washington, DC, 25 June 2020a.

[18] See EEAS, 'EU–US Trade and Technology Council Inaugural Joint Statement', 29 September 2021d, https://ec.europa.eu/commission/presscorner/detail/en/STATEMENT_21_4951; European Commission, 'EU–US Relations: EU-US Trade and Technology Council', September 2021d, https://trade.ec.europa.eu/doclib/html/159642.htm; and EEAS, 'United States: High Representative/Vice-President Josep Borrell met with Secretary of State Antony Blinken', 14 October 2021e, https://eeas.europa.eu/headquarters/headquarters-homepage/105674/united-states-high-representativevice-president-josep-borrell-met-secretary-state-antony_en.

[19] Profound capability gaps and diverging strategic priorities similarly hamper Europeans' broader defence capacity. See Hugo Meijer and Stephen G. Brooks, 'Illusions of Autonomy: Why Europe Cannot Provide for its Security If the United States Pulls Back', *International Security* 45, no. 4 (Spring 2021): pp. 7–43.

presence in the Indo-Pacific region. These imbalances have been further exacerbated by the post-Cold War sharp decline in their overall defence capabilities and by persistent capability gaps, most markedly in Germany but also in France and the United Kingdom. Competing regional priorities imposed additional constraints. The diplomatic and defence means devoted to contingencies closer to the European continent, e.g. Libya, Syria, and Ukraine (as well as Afghanistan), compelled the three countries to engage in difficult trade-offs in regional prioritization and, crucially, in the allocation of scarce resources. Overall, the capabilities that the three major European powers have been able to deploy in the region, most notably in the naval domain, have been very limited (see the comparative chart on their naval power-projection units capable of deployment in the region in Annex A). But the defence capabilities of medium and small EU member states are even more constrained. For instance, very few have the naval capabilities—not to mention the political will—to conduct naval deployments in the Indo-Pacific. And the exit of the United Kingdom from the European Union deprived the European Union of the country with the largest defence budget in Europe and one of the two largest defence R&D spenders, along with France.[20] Brexit has thereby further curtailed the political and defence capabilities that the European Union could leverage vis-à-vis China and in the Indo-Pacific. As a result, a major challenge to the development of an EU policy in the region, as explained by an EU official, is how 'to marshal resources which are very much in short supply, particularly in the hard security domain'.[21]

Persistently differing priorities among EU member states constitute the second challenge. Because of their strong economic ties with the PRC and of disagreements on how to prioritize the key regions of strategic interest, which often revolve around Russia or the Mediterranean region rather than the Indo-Pacific, many countries in Europe have been disinclined to support policies that could alienate Beijing, such as an enhanced military and naval presence in the Indo-Pacific (this is also partly why, in addition to capability shortfalls, the European Union's role in the region has largely revolved around 'non-traditional' security challenges, e.g. humanitarian assistance and disaster relief or climate change).[22] Furthermore,

---

[20] On the implications of Brexit for EU defence capabilities, see Bastian Giegerich and Christian Mölling, 'The United Kingdom's Contribution to European Security and Defence', IISS/DGAP (February 2018), pp. 7–8.

[21] Interview, 6 March 2020.

[22] Thomas Christiansen, Emil Kirchner, and See Seng Tan, eds. *The European Union's Security Relations with Asian Partners* (London: Palgrave Macmillan, 2021); Thomas Christiansen, Emil Kirchner, and See Seng Tan, 'EU–Asia Security Relations—Cooperation against the Odds?', Paper presented at the 16th Biennial Conference of EUSA, Denver, May 2019; May-Britt Stumbaum, 'Impact of the Rebalance on Europe's Interest in East Asia: Consequences for Europe in Economic, Diplomatic, and Military/Security Dimensions', in *Origins and Evolution of the US Rebalance toward Asia: Diplomatic, Military, and Economic Dimensions*, edited by Hugo Meijer (New York: Palgrave Macmillan, 2015), pp. 223–251.

the PRC has sought to leverage its economic ties with these countries so as to influence their policy positions (largely through bilateral channels), inhibit intra-European coordination, and discourage the formulation of common EU policies that would antagonize Chinese interests.[23] One notable instance of the capacity of Beijing's wedge strategy to exploit existing fragmentation within Europe was when the EU member states negotiated a common reaction to the 2016 Arbitral Tribunal ruling on the Philippines' case against China. Because of Beijing's economic and political leverage over Hungary, Greece, and Croatia, these three countries opposed any strong language (e.g. 'support' or 'welcome' the tribunal's decision).[24] As a result, the final EU statement was considerably diluted and merely 'acknowledged' the Tribunal's ruling.[25]

These divergences are well recognized by policymakers. As one senior EU official puts it, 'the differing perspectives within the European Union on China and the Indo-Pacific can be categorized along two axes: countries that give more prominence to security interests or to economic interests; and countries that have a more regional outlook versus countries with a globalist outlook. With Brexit, the European Union lost a globalist, security-oriented member state, and there are not many.'[26] A senior foreign policy adviser to the German President similarly stresses that the misalignment of positions on China in the European Union is rooted in different threat perceptions and levels of economic exposure vis-à-vis China:[27] on the economic side, 'the short-term gain of having positive economic relations

---

[23] Although some countries have displayed disappointment with regard to the opportunities initially expected from the '16+1' mechanism (previously called '17+1'), China's economic influence in Central and Eastern European countries nonetheless remains important. See among others Sophie Meunier, 'Divide and Conquer? China and the Cacophony of Foreign Investment Rules in the EU', *Journal of European Public Policy 21*, no. 7 (2014): pp. 996–1016; Thomas Christiansen, Emil Kirchner and Uwe Wissenbach, *The European Union and China* (London: Red Globe Press, 2019), p. 139; François Godement and Abigaël Vasselier, *China at the Gates: A New Power Audit of EU-China Relations* (London: European Council on Foreign Relations, 2017), pp. 64–74; James Reilly, *Orchestration: China's Economic Statecraft across Asia and Europe* (New York: Oxford University Press, 2021); Philippe Le Corre and Alain Sepulchre, *China's Offensive in Europe* (Washington, DC: Brookings Institution Press, 2016); Nicola Casarini, 'When All Roads Lead to Beijing: Assessing China's New Silk Road and its Implications for Europe', *The International Spectator 51*, no. 4 (2016): pp. 95–108; Ramon Pacheco Pardo, 'Europe's Financial Security and Chinese Economic Statecraft: The Case of the Belt and Road Initiative', *Asia-Europe Journal 16*, no. 3 (2018): pp. 237–250; and Andrea Kendall-Taylor, Statement Prepared for the Hearing 'China's Expanding Influence in Europe and Eurasia', US House Subcommittee on Europe, Eurasia, Energy, and the Environment, 9 May 2019. On the disillusionment with regards to the '16+1' mechanism, see Grzegorz Stec, 'Central and Eastern Europe and Joint European China Policy: Threat or Opportunity?', *MERICS Short Analysis*, 1 October 2020.
[24] Theresa Fallon, 'The EU, the South China Sea and China's Successful Wedge Strategy', *Asia Maritime Transparency Initiative*, 15 October 2016; Philippe Le Corre, 'On China's Expanding Influence in Europe and Eurasia', Testimony before the House of Representatives, Foreign Affairs Committee, 9 May 2019.
[25] Council of the European Union, 'Declaration on the Award Rendered in the Arbitration between the Philippines and China', *Press Release*, 15 July 2016b.
[26] Interview, 8 January 2021.
[27] Thomas Bagger, former Head of Policy Planning at the German Federal Foreign Office (2011–2017) and then Director of Foreign Policy in the Office of President Frank-Walter Steinmeier (since 2017), interview, 20 January 2021.

with China bilaterally can create a long-term damage to the unity of the European Union'; and on the security side, 'the countries in the European Union have different regional priorities, they care about the wider world to very different degrees. Some smaller countries may look at their foreign policy challenges through the prism of Europe or of their immediate neighbourhood, and may be less directly interested in China or in an Indo-Pacific strategy. Eastern European countries may focus more on Russia than on China. And some larger countries may have more pronounced security policy interests and postures across the globe, and may care more about China and the Indo-Pacific.'[28] As a result, 'the combination of economic and security considerations that shape how countries define their China policy is naturally very different from country to country. You cannot and you will not completely align national perspectives.'[29] Likewise, according to a French diplomat, the central strategic priorities of many countries in Northern, Eastern, and Southern Europe are not China or the Indo-Pacific, but rather the Baltic region, the Black Sea, or the Eastern Mediterranean; and, given their close economic ties with the PRC, they tend to be reluctant to any diplomatic or defence initiative that may irritate Beijing and hinder their relationship with China.[30] Furthermore, given these existing divergences, it remains to be seen whether, in light of Russia's invasion of Ukraine in 2022, Europeans will be able to manage the enhanced security challenge from Russia whilst maintaining the thrust of their policies in the Indo-Pacific.

Building upon these insights, future research should broaden the comparative analysis put forward in this book to encompass also the 'China policies' of medium and smaller European powers. Complementing the findings of this book, such comparisons would shed light on the larger trends of convergence (or fragmentation) in the national responses to China's rise across the whole European Union, and thereby gauge the extent to which the European Union has been able to match its ambition to 'project a strong, clear and unified voice in its approach to China'.[31] Relatedly, scholars could explore the shifting interactions between the United Kingdom, the European Union, and its member states in coping with China and in the Indo-Pacific prior to and after Brexit. As shown in this book, the United Kingdom did engage with other European powers in areas such as, among others, diplomatic consultations over China and some operational cooperation in the Indo-Pacific region (especially with France). At times, however, the United Kingdom has also competed with other European powers for influence and contracts in the region, pursuing competing endeavours. This was the case, for instance, of the United Kingdom's trilateral partnership with the United States and Australia

---

[28] Thomas Bagger, interview, 20 January 2021.
[29] He adds that 'the key to forge a unified approach is therefore really to strengthen the awareness of the costs of non-Europe' (interview, 20 January 2021).
[30] MFA official, interview, 3 October 2021.
[31] European Council, 'EU Strategy on China', Council Conclusions, 18 July 2016, p. 8.

(AUKUS) that scrapped the previous French-Australian agreement for the delivery of submarines to Canberra. Future research could explore the shifting patterns of cooperation and competition between the United Kingdom, the European Union, and its member states, prior to and after Brexit, in responding to China's rise.

American Views on Transatlantic Cooperation on China

A second avenue of future research that stems from the findings of this book is the evolving US perspective on the potential role of Europeans in confronting China. For years, the United States has shown only desultory interest in fostering greater transatlantic cooperation and coordination vis-à-vis Beijing and in the Indo-Pacific. As described in Part I, since the end of the Cold War cooperation between the United States and Europe's major powers in the Asia-Pacific, subsequently reframed around the larger Indo-Pacific, has remained limited to few areas of diplomatic consultations, operational military cooperation, and intelligence-sharing, mostly with France and the United Kingdom. Ultimately, as stressed by Kurt Campbell, the former Assistant Secretary of State for East Asian and Pacific Affairs (2009–2013) in the Barack Obama administration and later coordinator for Indo-Pacific affairs on the National Security Council (since 2021) in the Joe Biden administration, for years the United States has 'done a poor job of really engaging strategically Europe on [Indo]-Pacific security issues'.[32] In fact, at times, the relations between the United States and its European counterparts have been dented by significant frictions over China. This was the case, for instance, when a major transatlantic dispute emerged in the early 2000s over European attempts at lifting the EU arms embargo on China or when the Trump administration exerted substantial pressure on the Europeans to persuade them to toughen their restrictions on Huawei's supply of 5G technology.

Yet, having long neglected the potential role of the 'old continent' in confronting Chinese assertiveness, the United States appears to have gradually come to consider Europeans as increasingly important partners vis-à-vis China and in the Indian and Pacific Oceans regions. In fact, greater convergence seems to be emerging in how the two sides of the Atlantic evaluate the rise of China.[33] For example, US Secretary of State Antony Blinken and the EU HR/VP Josep Borrell

---

[32] Interview, 17 May 2017. On the Trump administration's emphasis on the need to foster transatlantic cooperation in the Asia-Pacific, see for instance US Assistant Secretary of Defence for Asian and Pacific Security, Randall Schriver, Testimony before the Senate Foreign Relations Committee, 15 May 2018, p. 4; and US DoD, *Indo-Pacific Strategy Report*, 1 June 2019, p. 21.

[33] See for instance US Department of State, 'Secretary Antony J. Blinken and High Representative for Foreign Affairs Josep Borrell after their Meeting', Remarks to the Press, 24 March 2021, https://www.state.gov/secretary-antony-j-blinken-and-high-representative-for-foreign-affairs-josep-borrell-after-their-meeting/; and US Secretary of State Antony Blinken, 'Reaffirming and Reimagining America's Alliances', Speech at NATO Headquarters Agora, Brussels, 24 March 2021.

stressed that the United States and the European Union 'share an assessment of China's role as a partner, as a competitor, and a systemic rival'.[34] The potential venues of enhanced transatlantic cooperation include bilateral channels with individual EU member states and/or the United Kingdom; minilateral groupings like the E3 (i.e. the Big Three) or the Quad, which includes the Big Three and the United States; and/or EU channels, including the EU-US dialogue on China. The security implications of China's rise have also become an increasingly important topic of consultations within NATO by the late 2010s. The Alliance has stressed how 'China's growing influence and international policies present both opportunities and challenge' that NATO members should 'address together'.[35] It has therefore developed a variety of work strands to address such challenges and opportunities, namely: political cooperation to uphold the international rules-based order, including with like-minded partners in the Indo-Pacific; bolstering its resilience agenda in critical infrastructures including telecommunication (e.g. 5G) or transportation; maintaining the technology edge; assessing China's defence modernization; and engaging China through regular dialogue and exchanges.[36] Nonetheless, the competences for tackling the security challenges posed by China in many of these areas remain the purview of European nation-states and/or of the European Union rather than of NATO.[37] Accordingly, in several areas, NATO's remit is limited to providing guidelines and sharing best practices.[38] Furthermore, although NATO has developed several partnerships in the Indo-Pacific since the war in Afghanistan, the Alliance is unlikely to provide a viable venue for greater transatlantic cooperation in the region.[39] As a NATO official puts it, the Alliance 'is not intended to have a role' in the Indo-Pacific; 'its role remains in the Euro-Atlantic area and there is no consensus today to extend that mandate beyond the Euro-Atlantic area'.[40] Future research should investigate Washington's evolving

---

[34] Quote by Borrell in US Department of State, 2021.
[35] NATO, 'London Declaration', 4 December 2019, https://www.nato.int/cps/en/natohq/official_texts_171584.htm. See also NATO, *NATO 2030: United for a New Era: Analysis and Recommendations of the Reflection Group Appointed by the NATO Secretary General*, 25 November 2020, pp. 12, 16–19, and 27–28, https://www.nato.int/nato_static_fl2014/assets/pdf/2020/12/pdf/201201-Reflection-Group-Final-Report-Uni.pdf; Meia Nouwens and Helena Legarda, 'China's Rise as a Global Security Actor: Implications for NATO', IISS and MERICS, *China Security Project Briefing*, December 2020; and François Heisbourg, 'NATO 4.0: The Atlantic Alliance and the Rise of China', *Survival 62*, no. 2 (2020); pp. 83–102.
[36] NATO official, interview, 1 April 2021.
[37] NATO official, interview, 1 April 2021.
[38] NATO official, interview, 1 April 2021.
[39] NATO developed partnership agreements with Australia, Japan, the Republic of Korea, New Zealand, and Mongolia as well as, in South Asia, Afghanistan and Pakistan. See Joe Burton, 'NATO's "Global Partners" in Asia: Shifting Strategic Narratives', *Asian Security 14*, no. 1 (2017): pp. 1–16; and Alexander Moens and Brooke Smith-Windsor , eds, *NATO and Asia-Pacific* (Rome: NATO Defense College, 2016). See also NATO, 'Relations with Partners across the Globe', https://www.nato.int/cps/en/natolive/topics_49188.htm.
[40] Interview, 21 June 2017. See also Mark Webber, 'The Perils of a NATO Rebalance to Asia-Pacific', in *NATO and Asia-Pacific*, edited by Alexander Moens and Brooke Smith-Windsor (Rome: NATO Defense College, 2016), pp. 83–100.

perspective on the role of Europeans in facing China's rise as well as the main venues through which such cooperation unfolds.

***

In the decades ahead, a central question for the states of Europe will be how to position themselves with regard to the intensifying great power competition between the United States and China. How they manage to bolster their support to their American and Asian allies and partners in confronting Chinese assertiveness, to maintain areas of diplomatic and economic engagement with the PRC, while preserving an autonomous position between Washington and Beijing will be crucial for defining their role in world politics. Only the future will tell if Europeans can come together and develop a credible role on the world stage that can tame the destabilizing consequences of mounting United States–China rivalry and help prevent the ensuing possibility of a great power war.

APPENDICES

APPENDIX A

Data, Sources, and Chart on France and the United Kingdom's Naval Deployments in the Asia-Pacific

This Appendix first explains the data and sources on British and French naval deployments in the Asia-Pacific that were used in this book. It then provides an assessment of the number and types of British and French power-projection units capable of deployment in the Asia-Pacific (Figure A.1).

France's Naval Deployments

The source used to gather data on French naval deployments in the Indian and Pacific Oceans (Figure 1.1 and Table 1.1) is the French Navy magazine *Cols Bleus*. Given the lack of publicly available, detailed information on French naval deployments in the region, *Cols Bleus* provides the most systematic and reliable source. Data were gathered for the 2012–2019 (both included) period. Prior to 2012, data were not included because the magazine listed missions differently (e.g. with a focus on some major missions and the exclusion of smaller and middle-sized missions), which would have prevented comparability over time. The data were organized along the following categories:

- *Mission Statement.* The name of the mission as used in a given issue of the magazine is indicated. Each issue of *Cols Bleus* lists so-called 'generic' and 'non-generic' missions. Generic missions take place on a regular basis and always under the same mission statement, such as 'Maritime Surveillance' or 'Fisheries Policing'. Non-generic missions are singular missions that take place either only once or on a six-month, annual, or biannual basis, such as the missions 'Jeanne d'Arc' or 'Bois Belleau' (discussed in Chapter 1), for example. For those missions, complementary information on the respective deployment was found on the website of the French MoD (https://www.defense.gouv.fr) when searching for the mission statement in combination with the year in which it took place.
- *Type of Ship* involved in a specific mission. Figure 1.1 does not visualize all French deployments in the region but only those of the French Navy's capital ships listed in Table 1.1. This allows us to focus on major deployments and to set aside minor deployments, e.g. for hydrographic missions.
- *Name of Ship* as indicated in *Cols Bleus*.
- *End Date of Mission.* In Figure 1.1, missions are listed based on their end date (rather than their starting date). This was done because some missions start at the end of the year (e.g. November/December) and continue into the following year. In order to avoid listing missions twice, the end date of a mission was therefore used.

- *Nationality of Deployment.* For vessels from other European countries and the United States which conducted deployments with the French Navy in the Indian and Pacific Oceans, their nationality was coded based upon the Correlates of War country codes (https://correlatesofwar.org/data-sets/cow-country-codes).
- *Indian and Pacific Oceans.* The location of the mission as shown in the *Cols Bleus* is indicated, i.e. whether each ship transits through the Indian and/or Pacific Ocean.

The United Kingdom's Naval Deployments

This section describes primary and secondary sources used to gather data on British naval deployments in the Asia-Pacific for the 2009–2019 period (Figure 3.1 and Table 3.1). It first delineates the categories along which the data were organized and then explains the sources used to compile such data.

The data were organized along the following categories:

- *Mission Statement.* The name of the mission as used in the source is indicated. Mission names that appeared in non-official publications (such as news articles) were cross-checked with the websites of the Ministry of Defence and the House of Commons Library in order to ensure that only the official name of the mission is listed.
- *Type of Ship* involved in a specific mission. Ships were categorized into five types: aircraft carrier, frigate, destroyer, amphibious assault ship, auxiliary support ship.
- *Name of Ship* as indicated in the source.
- *End Date of Mission.* The date as indicated in the source was used to list the end date of the mission.
- *Nationality of Joint Deployment.* For vessels from European countries and the United States which have conducted deployments with the UK Navy in the Indian and Pacific Oceans, their nationality is indicated based upon the Correlates of War country codes (https://correlatesofwar.org/data-sets/cow-country-codes).
- *Indian and Pacific Oceans.* The location of the mission is indicated. If a mission traverses both oceans, both oceans are indicated in the database.

The sources used to gather data on British naval deployments to and in the Indian and Pacific Oceans are the websites of the UK Ministry of Defence and of the House of Commons Library (https://www.parliament.uk/mps-lords-and-offices/offices/commons/commonslibrary/), scholarly books, research articles on British military engagement in the world, written questions from British Parliamentarians to the defence ministry, as well as various online news media. More specifically, the following sources were used to gather the data:

Air & Cosmos International. 'RAF Typhoons Land in Japan for Bilateral Exercise', 24 October 2016, https://www.aircosmosinternational.com/article/raf-typhoons-land-in-japan-for-bilateral-exercise-1998.

Asia-Pacific Defence Reporter. 'Exercise Bersama Lima 2013—Boosting Regional Security', 11 August 2013, https://asiapacificdefencereporter.com/exercise-bersama-lima-2013-boosting-regional-security/.

Ballantyne, Iain. *Strike from the Sea: The Royal Navy and US Navy at War in the Middle East* (Barnsley, UK: Pen & Sword Maritime, 2004).

Benbow, Tim. 'British Uses of Aircraft Carriers and Amphibious Ships: 1945–2010'. *Corbett Paper 9*, no. 1 (2012), https://www.kcl.ac.uk/dsd/assets/corbettpaper9.pdf.

Brooke-Holland, Louisa. 'Royal Navy: A Return to the Far East?'. House of Commons Library, 24 May 2018, https://commonslibrary.parliament.uk/royal-navy-a-return-to-the-far-east/.

Brooke-Holland, Louisa. 'Integrated Review: The Defence Tilt to the Indo-Pacific'. House of Commons Library, Briefing Paper no. 09217, 11 May 2021.

Caputo, Victor J. 'US, UK, South Korean Air Forces Conduct Strategic Exercise'. US Air Force, 51st Fighter Wing Public Affairs, 8 November 2016, https://www.af.mil/News/Article-Display/Article/999,020/us-uk-south-korean-air-forces-conduct-strategic-exercise/.

French Embassy in Australia. 'The Mission "Jeanne d'Arc 2017"', 2017, https://au.ambafrance.org/The-mission-Jeanne-d-Arc-2017 (accessed on 1 Decenber 2021).

French Ministry of Defence. 'Mission Arromanches: Le groupe aéronaval de retour à Toulon', 2015b, https://www.defense.gouv.fr/marine/a-la-une/mission-arromanches-le-groupe-aeronaval-de-retour-a-toulon.

French Ministry of Defence. Mission 'Jeanne d'Arc' 2017b. Press Kit, http://www.colsbleus.fr/exemplaires/9349 (accessed on 1 December 2021).

Gain, Nathan. 'UK-French Combined Staff Assumed Command of Combined Task Force 150'. *NavalNews*, 12 August 2019, https://www.navalnews.com/naval-news/2019/08/uk-french-combined-staff-assumed-command-of-combined-task-force-150/.

Government of Singapore. 'Exercise Bersama Padu', 2006, https://www.nas.gov.sg/archivesonline/data/pdfdoc/20,060,907,997.htm.

Her Majesty's Government. 'Britain's Royal Air Force in Malaysia for Exercise Bersama Lima'. *Press Release*, 4 October 2016, https://www.gov.uk/government/news/britains-royal-air-force-in-malaysia-for-exercise-bersama-lima.

House of Commons. 'Written Answers: Military Exercises 1999', 4 March 1999, vol. 326, cc 866–7W 866W, https://api.parliament.uk/historic-hansard/written-answers/1999/mar/04/military-exercises.

Jianwei, Li and Ramses Amer. 'British Naval Activities in the South China Sea: A Double-Edged Sword?'. Institute for Security and Development Policy, April 2019, https://isdp.eu/publication/british-navy-south-china-sea/.

Kelly, Tim. 'British Navy Warship Sails near South China Sea Islands, Angering Beijing'. *Reuters*, 6 September 2018.

Lennard, Jeremy. 'UK Boosts Help for Tsunami Victims'. *The Guardian*, 31 December 2004.

Ministry of Defence. Mission 'Jeanne d'Arc' 2018d. Press Kit.

Naval Technology. 'UK Navy Completes Taurus-09 Deployment', 4 August 2009, https://www.naval-technology.com/news/news61264-html/.

Naval Today. 'HMS Montrose Heads to Bahrain after Operations in Japan', 20 March 2019, https://www.navaltoday.com/2019/03/20/hms-montrose-heads-to-bahrain-after-operations-in-japan/.

Ng, Teddy. 'British Navy Vessel Passes through Taiwan Strait'. *South China Morning Post*, 7 December 2019.

Rahn, Wesley. 'South China Sea: France and Britain Join the US to Oppose China'. *Deutsche Welle*, 27 June 2018.

Roberts, John. *Safeguarding the Nation: The Story of the Modern Royal Navy* (Barnsley, UK: Seaforth Publishing, 2009).

Royal Air Force. 'Closing Ceremony Held for Exercise Bersama Lima in Malaysia', 21 October 2019, https://www.raf.mod.uk/news/articles/closing-ceremony-held-for-exercise-bersama-lima-in-malaysia/.

Royal Navy. 'HMS Daring Welcomed Home by Philippines Officials', 28 February 2014, https://www.gov.uk/government/news/hms-daring-welcomed-home-by-philippines-officials.

Royal Navy. 'Search for MH370', 2017, https://webarchive.nationalarchives.gov.uk/+/http://www.royalnavy.mod.uk/news-and-latest-activity/operations/indian-ocean/mh370-search.

Royal Navy. 'HMS Argyll Shows Firepower on Exercise Bersama Lima', 18 October 2018, https://www.royalnavy.mod.uk/news-and-latest-activity/news/2018/october/18/181,018-argyll-firepower-ex-bersama-lima.

Royal Navy. 'HMS *Argyll*'s US Navy Link-Up in South China Sea', 16 January 2019, https://www.royalnavy.mod.uk/news-and-latest-activity/news/2019/january/16/190,116-argylls-us-link-up-south-china-sea.

Singh, Daljit and Pushpa Thambipillai. *Southeast Asian Affairs 2012* (Singapore: ISEAS Publishing, 2012).

UK Parliament. 'Joint Exercises: Questions for Ministry of Defence'. Questions and Answers, 24 March 2016, https://questions-statements.parliament.uk/written-questions/detail/2016-03-24/32484.

Wikipedia. 'Exercise RIMPAC', 2020 https://en.wikipedia.org/wiki/Exercise_RIMPAC#RIMPAC_2004 (accessed 12 September 2020)

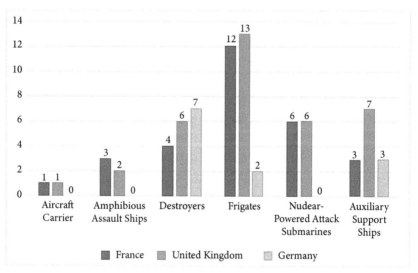

Fig. A.1 Big Three's power-projection units capable of deployments in the Asia-Pacific, 2018

Source: Data retrieved from IISS, *Asia-Pacific Regional Security Assessment* (London: IISS, 2018), ch. 'European Navies and Regional Security', pp. 123 and 126.

APPENDIX B

Data, Sources, and Charts on FDIs, Trade, and Arms Transfers

This Appendix first describes the challenges of gathering systematic and comparable foreign direct investments (FDIs) data and the criteria adopted in this book to select the data on FDIs, trade, and arms transfers. It then presents charts on trade and investment ties between the Big Three and China and between the European Union and China.

Data on FDIs

Challenges: Data gathering on FDI transactions with China is complicated by three main challenges: a lack of complete and consistent data on bilateral FDIs, data distortion, and diverging ways of measuring FDI.

1. *Availability of Data*

The first challenge concerns the availability of data on FDI transactions by partner country. There are few official FDI statistics that fulfil the criteria of (a) covering country-to-country FDIs, (b) covering a longer time-period to observe trends (1990–2020), and (c) being consistent in their annual reporting and methodologies applied to measure FDIs. Possible sources include, among others, the Organisation for Economic Co-operation and Development (OECD),[1] the European national governments and central banks,[2] and Chinese official statistics.[3] However, official data can be distorted and suffer from serious issues (as detailed later). An alternative to official FDI statistics are the data provided by private research institutes such as Datenna,[4] the Mercator Institute for China Studies (MERICS) and

---

[1] See for example OECD, *FDI by country and economic activity_BMD4 and historical BMD3 series*, https://stats.oecd.org/Index.aspx?QueryId=82888.

[2] See for example for the United Kingdom: Office for National Statistics, *Foreign Direct Investment Involving UK Companies: 2019*, 21 December 2020, https://www.ons.gov.uk/economy/nationalaccounts/balanceofpayments/bulletins/foreigndirectinvestmentinvolvingukcompanies/2019. For France: Banque de France, *Foreign Direct Investment: Annual Series*, 17 June 2020, https://www.banque-france.fr/en/statistics/balance-payments/foreign-direct-investment/statistics/foreign-direct-investment-annual-series. For Germany: Deutsche Bundesbank. *Direct Investments and Foreign Affiliates Statistics (FATS)*, https://www.bundesbank.de/en/statistics/external-sector/direct-investments.

[3] National Bureau of Statistics, *Statistical Yearbooks of China*, http://www.stats.gov.cn/english/Statisticaldata/AnnualData/.

[4] Datenna, 'China–EU FDI Radar', https://www.datenna.com/china-eu-fdi-radar/ (accessed 12 May 2021).

Rhodium Group,[5] or by the American Enterprise Institute (AEI).[6] A disadvantage of research by private institutes is that while numerous reports focus on Chinese FDIs abroad, there are significantly fewer studies that comprehensively cover the Big Three's and the European Union's bilateral investments in China. Besides this issue, the datasets that form the basis of the reports by MERICS/Rhodium Group are not always publicly available. Furthermore, many datasets developed by private research institutes rely on investment values that were publicly announced by companies or reported in the media. These projects, however, are not always fully implemented and/or the value of the direct investment may change after the announcement.[7]

2. *Differing Definitions of FDI*

Secondly, definitions and methodologies used to calculate FDI vary across sources, which sometimes leads to sharply diverging results. For example, official FDI statistics as provided by the individual countries, the OECD, the International Monetary Fund (IMF) or the United Nations Conference on Trade and Development (UNCTAD), usually publish the FDI accounts that were ultimately reported to them by companies involved in FDIs.[8] By contrast, independent research companies such as the American Enterprise Institute/Heritage Foundation or MERICS/Rhodium Group base their research on data they aggregate from media reports, commercial databases, company reports, etc.[9] Furthermore, the MERICS/Rhodium Group's studies do not account for reverse flows back to China through intra-company transactions or divestitures as recommended by the IMF's Balance of Payment Principle (BOP).[10] Another factor is that some countries also include investments that do not strictly follow the definition of a 'lasting interest' by the OECD where an investor owns either an entire branch in another country or at least 10 per cent of the voting power of the recipient enterprise.[11] As such, different sources use different definitions and methodologies to calculate FDIs.

3. *Investments through Offshore Financial Centres*

Finally, official data might be distorted by the practice of channelling investments through offshore financial centres such as Hong Kong, Luxembourg, the Cayman Islands, or the British Virgin Islands.[12] Companies can invest through their subsidies to avoid taxes, which makes it almost impossible to assess the actual amount of FDI from and to China. It is

---

[5] See for example Thilo Hanemann and Mikko Huotari, 'Preparing for a New Era of Chinese Capital: Chinese FDI in Europe and Germany', *MERICS Papers on China*, June 2015.

[6] American Enterprise Institute and Heritage Foundation, *China Global Investment Tracker*, https://www.aei.org/china-global-investment-tracker/.

[7] Andres B. Schwarzenberg, 'Tracking China's Global Economic Activities: Data Challenges and Issues for Congress', *Congressional Research Service, Report R46302*, 14 June 2020, p. 4.

[8] UNCTAD FDI data were not used as a source as they do not cover country-to-country FDIs.

[9] See for example Hanemann and Huotari, 2015, p. 52.

[10] Hanemann and Huotari, 2015, p. 52. See also International Monetary Fund, *Balance of Payments and International Investment Position Manual* (Washington, DC: IMF 2009), sixth edition. This manual is a guideline that provides a standardized framework for compiling statistics on FDI transactions and positions.

[11] OECD, *OECD Benchmark Definition of Foreign Direct Investment* (Paris: OECD 2008), 4th edition, p. 17.

[12] Jerker Hellström, *China's Acquisitions in Europe: European Perceptions of Chinese Investments and their Strategic Implications* (Stockholm: Swedish Defence Research Agency (FOI), 2016), Report FOI-R-4384-SE, p. 9.

estimated that up to three-quarters of Chinese outward FDIs are flowing through these financial centres.[13]

Data Selection: To overcome these issues, the author first gathered and compared a wide range of data from a variety of sources in order to identify, amongst all the available options, the most systematic and comprehensive data to illustrate trends in bilateral FDI transactions between the Big Three and China. These sources include:

- Reports by MERICS/Rhodium Group
- Data from the China Global Investment Tracker by the American Enterprise Institute (AEI)
- Reports and data by the European banks and governments
- Data by the OECD
- Data provided by the Chinese Ministry of Commerce (MOFCOM) and the National Bureau of Statistics of the People's Republic of China (NBS).
- This quantitative data were further complemented by information provided in official statements in speeches and non-governmental organization (NGO) reports.[14]
- To meet the offshore problem discussed above, OECD data were adjusted by also including FDI that is going to and coming from Hong Kong which had a significant effect on China–United Kingdom FDI transactions, but only a small effect on transactions from and to France and Germany.

Amongst these various sources, in light of the challenges of FDI data gathering discussed earlier, the data provided by the NBS in the *Statistical Yearbooks of China* were eventually chosen as the main source for illustrating bilateral FDI transactions, covering the timeframe from 2000 to 2019. In addition to the data provided by the NBS, this book also draws on data from the MERICS/Rhodium Group's research on Chinese FDIs in the European Union. Specifically, the data used in this book encompass the following sources:

- *For FDIs from the Big Three and the European Union into China*: the data are published in the *Statistical Yearbooks of China* as the 'value of actually utilized FDI'. This refers to the investments ultimately used by companies in China, in contrast to the values of agreed investments in contracts. The main reason for using these data is that they cover FDI transactions between the Big Three (and the European Union) and China over a longer time-period and not only for a couple of years, and because—unlike other sources—NBS is consistent in its annual reporting of FDI data. The *Statistical Yearbooks* are based on data compiled by MOFCOM. FDIs in China, as defined by the NBS, include foreign investments for establishing exclusively foreign ventures, Sino-foreign joint ventures, and cooperative enterprises, and also encompass government-approved re-investments of profits and funds that enterprises borrow from abroad.[15]

---

[13] Schwarzenberg, 2020, p. 5.
[14] Additional research on official statements was conducted to see which data are used in national policy debates. For example, the German Federal Ministry for Economic Affairs and Energy uses data on Chinese FDI positions in Germany with a value of €3.2 bn in 2018 as reported by the Deutsche Bundesbank (see, e.g. Ministry for Economic Affairs and Energy, 'China—Wirtschaftliche Beziehungen'. Available online at https://www.bmwi.de/Redaktion/DE/Artikel/Aussenwirtschaft/laendervermerk-china.html). By contrast, the value of Chinese FDI positions in Germany for the same year as reported by the NBS in the *Statistical Yearbooks* is $13.7 bn, more than three times higher.
[15] NBS, *Classification and Methods: Foreign Trade and Economic Cooperation*, 2014. Available online at http://www.stats.gov.cn/english/ClassificationsMethods/Definitions/200205/t20020517_72378.html.

- *For FDIs from China into the Big Three*: the data are published in the *Yearbook* as value of the cross-border FDIs transactions during a given year (flows) and the accumulated value of FDIs (stock). In this book, the data on FDIs in the Big Three are presented as the accumulated value of FDIs held at the end of the respective year (stock).
- *For FDIs from China into the EU*: the data are published by MERICS and Rhodium Group in the *Chinese FDI in Europe 2020 Update* (published in June 2021), and refer to the annual value of completed Chinese FDI transactions in the EU-27 and the United Kingdom from 2000–2020 which includes mergers and acquisitions (M&A) as well as greenfield investments. The data were originally published in euros (billions), but in this book they were converted to US dollars (billions) at the average exchange rate for the respective year in order to maintain consistency across chapters.

As with any other source on bilateral FDIs, the *Statistical Yearbooks* data come with a range of issues regarding their reliability.[16] First, as these statistics on FDI usage and transactions rely on the values that were reported by Chinese companies to MOFCOM, the data might be not entirely complete as MOFCOM only records FDI that were approved by the government.[17] Furthermore, the data are often reported with a significant time lag which makes real-time monitoring of transactions difficult. Thirdly, inward and outward FDIs as well as different timeframes are not equally covered in the *Statistical Yearbooks* which complicates a comparison between the Big Three's investment ties with the PRC over time. In the book's chapters, additional sources for FDIs were therefore used for those timeframes that are not covered by the *Statistical Yearbooks*. Specifically, for Germany's direct investment stocks in China from 1990–2012, the data provided by the Deutsche Bundesbank were used (in Deutsche Marks and euros).[18] For the position of France's bilateral FDIs with China, data published by the Banque de France (in euros) were used, covering the period from 2000–2019.[19] For the United Kingdom, the official data provided by the Office for National Statistics were not utilized because these data indicate that a disproportionally high amount of FDIs is coming and going to Hong Kong, while only a small amount is transferred from and to the PRC.[20] Given the aforementioned offshore problem, it is thus impossible to assess the actual amount of FDIs between the United Kingdom and China by using such data, and the book thus relied on existing secondary sources.[21]

---

[16] For more information on issues with official Chinese and European FDI statistics see Hanemann and Huotari, 2015, p. 12

[17] Schwarzenberg, 2020, p. 5.

[18] Deutsche Bank, *Unmittelbare und mittelbare deutsche Direktinvestitionen im Ausland (konsolidiert) / Summe; China, Volksrepublik*, available online at: https://www.bundesbank.de/dynamic/action/de/statistiken/zeitreihen-datenbanken/zeitreihen-datenbank/723452/723452?tsTab=0&tsId=BBK01.RJ1994&statisticType=BBK_ITS&listId=www_s201_ddi_720&id=0.

[19] Banque de France, *Foreign Direct Investment: Annual Series*, 17 June 2020. Available online at: https://www.banque-france.fr/en/statistics/balance-payments/foreign-direct-investment/statistics/foreign-direct-investment-annual-series.

[20] Office for National Statistics, 'Foreign Direct Investment Involving UK Companies: 2019', 21 December 2020, https://www.ons.gov.uk/economy/nationalaccounts/balanceofpayments/bulletins/foreigndirectinvestmentinvolvingukcompanies/2019.

[21] Tim Summers, 'Chinese Investment in the UK: Growing Flows or Growing Controversy?', in *Chinese Investment in Europe. A Country-Level Approach*, edited by John Seaman, Mikko Huotari, and Miguel Otero-Iglesias (Paris: French Institute of International Relations, 2017), pp. 159–166.

Data on Trade: Exports and Imports

The data and charts on trade with China and the Asia-Pacific were retrieved from the United Nations International Trade Statistics Database (UN Comtrade)[22] and the World Bank's World Integrated Trade Solution (WITS)[23] and refer to trade in goods. UN Comtrade gathers data that 170 countries and regions reported to the United Nations Statistics Division (UNSD) with detailed information on trade in commodities and services.[24] WITS is a trade software that bases its numbers on UN trade statistics and allows users to do specific queries, such as geographical groupings on export and import data, which was specifically useful for researching trade between the Big Three and Asia-Pacific. The book's data on trade include exports, imports, and total trade (exports + imports) with Asia-Pacific countries: American Samoa, Australia, Brunei, China, Federated States of Micronesia, Guam, Hong Kong, Indonesia, Japan, Cambodia, French Polynesia, Kiribati, Lao People's Democratic Republic, Macao, Marshall Islands, Myanmar, Mongolia, Northern Mariana Islands, Malaysia, New Caledonia, New Zealand, Philippines, Palau, Papua New Guinea, Republic of Korea, Singapore, Solomon Islands, Thailand, East Timor, Tonga, Tuvalu, Vietnam, Vanuatu, and Samoa.

Data on Arms Transfers

The data and charts on the Big Three's arms transfers are based on the *SIPRI Arms Transfers Database* produced by the Stockholm International Peace Research Institute (SIPRI).[25] SIPRI is an independent international institute researching conflict, arms control, disarmament, and armaments. The statistical data on arms transfers cover the actual deliveries of what SIPRI terms 'major conventional weapons'.[26] As a unit, SIPRI uses the so-called trend-indicator value (TIV) which is based on the production costs of weapons rather than the financial value of the arms transfer to measure the transfer of military resources instead of military expenditures.[27] The research provided by SIPRI is based on media reports, information published by the arms-producing companies, national policy reports, and documents, and the United Nations Register of Conventional Arms. For the Asia-Pacific countries, the data on arms transfers were available for Australia, Brunei, Cambodia, China, India, Indonesia, Japan, Laos, Malaysia, Myanmar, New Zealand, Papua New Guinea, Philippines, Singapore, South Korea, Taiwan, Thailand, and Vietnam. No data were available for American Samoa, Federated States of Micronesia, Guam, Hong Kong, Kiribati, Marshall Islands, Mongolia, Northern Mariana Islands, New Caledonia, Palau, East Timor, Tonga, Tuvalu, Vanuatu, and Samoa.

As mentioned in the Introduction to Part I, for analytical purposes the book distinguishes three geographical groupings. The 'Asia-Pacific' encompasses the region from Myanmar to

---

[22] United Nations, *UN Comtrade Database*. Available online at: https://comtrade.un.org/data/.
[23] World Bank, *World Integrated Trade Solution (WITS)*. Available online at: https://wits.worldbank.org.
[24] United Nations, *What Is UN Comtrade?* December 2020. Available online at: https://unstats.un.org/unsd/tradekb/knowledgebase/what-is-un-comtrade (accessed on 1 December 2021).
[25] SIPRI, *SIPRI Arms Transfers Database*. Available online at https://www.sipri.org/databases/armstransfers.
[26] These include aircraft, air defence systems, anti-submarine warfare weapons, armoured vehicles, artillery, engines, missiles, sensors, satellites, ships, and other weapons. For more information see SIPRI, *Sources and Methods*. Available online at: https://www.sipri.org/databases/armstransfers/sources-and-methods#TIV-tables.
[27] SIPRI, *Sources and Methods*.

Australia and to Japan (excluding India and Russia). 'Asia and Oceania' embraces the Asia-Pacific and South Asia (Bangladesh, India, and Pakistan). The 'Indo-Pacific' is a more recent label developed by various governments in the late 2010s; although different governments have adopted different definitions, it generally refers to a larger region which includes Asia-Oceania and the broader maritime Indian and Pacific Oceans areas. As discussed in Part I, the 'Indo-Pacific' label was adopted in 2018 by France, in 2020 by Germany, and in 2021 by the United Kingdom. The data used in the book (e.g. on trade, naval deployments, forward-deployed forces, etc.) refer to different geographical groupings because it was sometimes not possible, based upon publicly available figures, to disaggregate the data for the various (sub-)groupings.

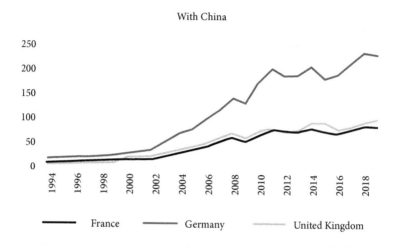

Fig. B.1 The Big Three's total trade (exports + imports) with China and the Asia-Pacific (US$ bn)

Source: United Nations Comtrade—International Trade Statistics Database, https://comtrade.un.org.

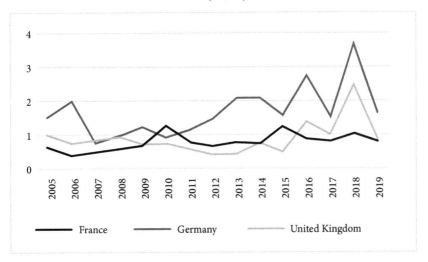

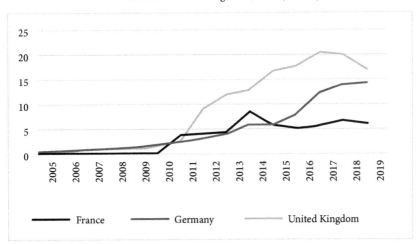

Fig. B.2 The Big Three's FDIs to and from China

Source: National Bureau of Statistics of China, *Statistical Yearbooks of China*, http://www.stats.gov.cn/english/Statisticaldata/AnnualData/.

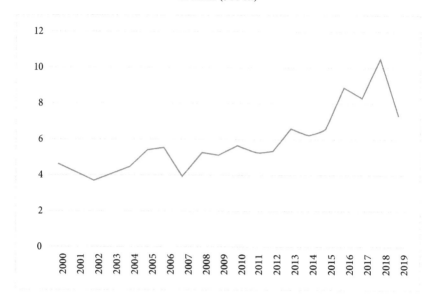

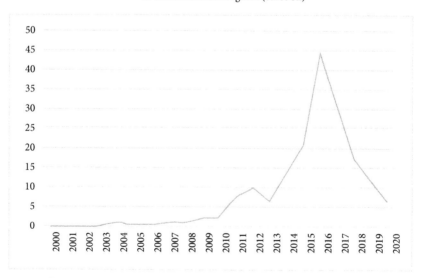

Fig. B.3 The European Union (27 + United Kingdom) FDIs to and from China

Source: Agatha Kratz, Max J. Zenglein, and Gregor Sebastian, *Chinese FDI in Europe—2020 Update*, MERICS/Rhodium Group, June 2021.

Bibliography

Content of the Bibliography

- **Primary Sources**
  - Archival Documents and Leaked Diplomatic Cables
    - France
    - United Kingdom
    - Germany
    - United States
  - Government Documents and Publications
    - Australia
    - European Union
    - France
    - Germany
    - India
    - Japan
    - Netherlands
    - People's Republic of China
    - Singapore
    - United Kingdom
    - United States
    - International and Regional Organizations
  - Parliamentary Reports
    - European Union
    - France
    - Germany
    - United Kingdom
    - United States
  - Oral Testimonies, Speeches, and Interviews
    - European Union
    - France
    - Germany
    - United Kingdom
    - United States
  - Databases
- **Secondary Sources**

Note on acronyms: for the purpose of clarity and simplicity, the book refers to the same name of a ministry even if the name changed during the 1990–2020 timeframe.

Primary Sources

Archival Documents and Leaked Diplomatic Cables

France

Ministry of Foreign Affairs to French Embassy in China. 'Relations franco-chinoises', 15 September 1989, Centre of Diplomatic Archives in Nantes, 513PO/2004038.

Ministry of Foreign Affairs to French Embassy in China. 'Situation intérieure en Chine et relations franco-chinoises', 24 April 1990, Centre of Diplomatic Archives in Nantes, 513PO/2004038.

Embassy in China to Ministry of Foreign Affairs. 'Relations bilatérales entre la France et la Chine en 1989', 4 January 1990, Centre of Diplomatic Archives in Nantes, 513PO/2004038.

Embassy in China to Ministry of Foreign Affairs. 'Relations bilatérales franco-chinoises', 30 January 1992a, Centre of Diplomatic Archives in Nantes, 513PO/2004038.

Embassy in China to Ministry of Foreign Affairs. 'La Chine de 1991 à 1992 : relations bilatérales franco-chinoises'. 30 January 1992b, Centre of Diplomatic Archives in Nantes, 513PO/2004038.

Germany

Federal Foreign Office. 'Deutschland-Besuch PM Li Peng', 6 June 1989a, Politisches Archiv des Auswärtigen Amts, B 37-ZA/161825.

Federal Foreign Office. 'Deutschland-Besuch PM Li Peng', 13 June 1989b, Politisches Archiv des Auswärtigen Amts, B 37-ZA/161825.

Federal Foreign Office. 'Deutschland-Besuch PM Li Peng', 9 June 1989c, Politisches Archiv des Auswärtigen Amts, B 37-ZA/161825.

United Kingdom

Foreign and Commonwealth Office to Private Secretary for Foreign Affairs to the Prime Minister. 'Proposed Asia-Europe Meeting', 15 May 1995, The National Archives, Prime Minister's Office Record 19/5633.

Foreign and Commonwealth Office to Private Secretary for Foreign Affairs to the Prime Minister. 'Asia–Europe Meeting, Bangkok, 1–2 March 1996', Brief No. 5, 27 February 1996a, TNA, Prime Minister's Office Record 19/5633.

Foreign and Commonwealth Office to Private Secretary for Foreign Affairs to the Prime Minister. 'Asia–Europe Meeting, Bangkok, 1–2 March 1996', Brief No. 17, 27 February 1996b, The National Archives, Prime Minister's Office Record 19/5633.

Foreign and Commonwealth Office to Private Secretary for Foreign Affairs to the Prime Minister. 'Asia–Europe Meeting, Bangkok, 1–2 March 1996', Brief No. 21, 27 February 1996c, The National Archives, Prime Minister's Office Record 19/5633.

Foreign and Commonwealth Office to Private Secretary for Foreign Affairs to the Prime Minister. 'Asia–Europe Meeting, Bangkok, 1–2 March 1996', Brief No. 26, 27 February 1996d, The National Archives, Prime Minister's Office Record 19/5633.

Foreign and Commonwealth Office to Private Secretary for Foreign Affairs to the Prime Minister. 'ASEAN Regional Forum', 23 February 1996e, The National Archives, Prime Minister's Office Record 19/5633.

Ministry of Defence to Foreign and Commonwealth Office. 'Follow-Up Meeting: UK Offer to Host?', 29 November 1995, The National Archives, Prime Minister's Office Record 19/5633.

Private Secretary for Foreign Affairs to the Prime Minister. 'Asia Manifesto', 18 January 1995, The National Archives, Prime Minister's Office Record 19/5633.
Private Secretary for Foreign Affairs to the Prime Minister. 'Asia–Europe Meeting: Interventions in First Closed Session', 29 February 1996, The National Archives, Prime Minister's Office Record, 19/5633.
Private Secretary to the Prime Minister to Foreign and Commonwealth Office. 'Asia–Europe Meeting: Round 2', 2 December 1995, The National Archives, Prime Minister's Office Record 19/5633.
Private Secretary to the Secretary of State for Trade and Industry to the Prime Minister Private Secretary. 'Prime Minister's Visit to the EU/Asia Summit, 28 February–2 March: Statistical Briefing', 23 February 1996, The National Archives, Prime Minister's Office Record 19/5633.

United States
American Institute in Taiwan. 'Taiwan Pessimistic about EU Embargo'. Confidential, Wikileaks Cablegate, 23 November 2004.
Embassy in Belgium. 'Is the EU Retreating on the China Arms Embargo?'. Confidential, Wikileaks Cablegate, 24 March 2005.
Embassy in China. 'EU Arms Embargo Unlikely to Be Lifted during the German EU Presidency'. Confidential, Wikileaks Cablegate, 9 November 2006.
Embassy in France. 'Codel Smith Meets Chirac, French Officials'. Confidential, Wikileaks Cablegate, 31 January 2005a.
Embassy in France. 'MoD Advisor Upbeat on Bilateral Relationship; Sees Rapprochement on Middle East; No Change on EU China Arms Embargo'. Confidential, Wikileaks Cablegate, 18 March 2005b.
Embassy in France. 'France/GAERC: Agreement on Most Issues Except China Embargo'. Confidential, Wikileaks/Cablegate, 8 December 2006.
Embassy in Germany. 'German Foreign Minister Steinmeier Talks UNSC Reform, Iran, ROK and East Asian Security with GOJ'. Confidential, Wikileaks Cablegate, 27 February 2006a.
Embassy in Germany. 'German Views on the December Foreign Ministers' Meeting'. Confidential, Wikileaks Cablegate, 8 December 2006b.
Embassy in Germany. 'Germany Looks Eastward: Chancellor Merkel's Trip to China, Japan'. Confidential, Wikileaks Cablegate, 8 December 2006c.
Embassy in Germany. 'German Views on the EU Arms Embargo against China and the February 22 EU Foreign Affairs Council'. Confidential, Wikileaks Cablegate, 19 February 2010.
Embassy in the United Kingdom. 'UK Views on December EU Foreign Ministers' Meeting (GAERC)'. Confidential, Wikileaks Cablegate, 8 December 2006.

Government Documents and Publications

Australia
Department of Defence. 'Inaugural Australia–France 2+2 Ministerial Consultations', 30 August 2021, https://www.foreignminister.gov.au/minister/marise-payne/media-release/inaugural-australia-france-22-ministerial-consultations.
Department of Foreign Affairs and Trade. 'Australia–United States Ministerial Consultations 2009 Joint Communiqué', 9 April 2009.

Department of Foreign Affairs and Trade. 'Joint Ministerial Media Release: Inaugural German-Australian 2+2 Ministerial Meeting in Berlin', 6 September 2016.

Department of Foreign Affairs and Trade. 'Vision Statement on the Australia–France Relationship', 2 May 2018.

Government. *Agreement between the Government of Australia and the Government of the French Republic Regarding Defence Cooperation and Status of Forces*, Paris, France, 14 December 2006 (ratified in 2009).

Government. 'Joint Statement of Enhanced Strategic Partnership between Australia and France', 19 January 2012.

Government. 'Enhanced Strategic Partnership between Australia and the Federal Republic of Germany', 10 June 2021, https://www.dfat.gov.au/about-us/publications/international-relations/enhanced-strategic-partnership-between-australia-and-federal-republic-germany.

Minister for Home Affairs (Acting) and the Minister for Communications and the Arts. 'Government Provides 5G Security Guidance to Australian Carriers'. *Joint Media Release*, 23 August 2018.

Office of the Prime Minister. 'Australia to Pursue Nuclear-Powered Submarines through New Trilateral Enhanced Security Partnership', *Media Statement*, 16 September 2021, https://www.pm.gov.au/media/australia-pursue-nuclear-powered-submarines-through-new-trilateral-enhanced-security.

European Union

Borrell, Josep. 'China, the United States and Us'. *Blog by HR/VP Josep Borrell 'A Window on the World'*, 31 July 2020, https://eeas.europa.eu/headquarters/headquarters-homepage/83644/china-united-states-and-us_en.

Borrell, Josep. 'The EU Needs a Strategic Approach for the Indo-Pacific'. *Blog by HR/VP Josep Borrell 'A Window on the World'*, 12 March 2021a, https://eeas.europa.eu/headquarters/headquarters-homepage/94898/eu-needs-strategic-approach-indo-pacific_en.

Borrell, Josep. 'What the EU can do in and with the Indo-Pacific'. *Groupe d'études géopolitiques*, 2021b, https://geopolitique.eu/en/2021/06/22/what-the-eu-can-do-in-and-with-the-indo-pacific/.

Council of the European Union. 'Guidelines on the EU's Foreign and Security Policy in East Asia', Brussels, 15 June 2012.

Council of the European Union. 'EU Strategy on China'. Council Conclusions, 18 July 2016a.

Council of the European Union. 'Declaration on the Award Rendered in the Arbitration between the Philippines and China'. *Press Release*, 15 July 2016b.

Council of the European Union. 'EU External Cyber Capacity Building Guideline'. Council Conclusions, Brussels, 26 June 2018a.

Council of the European Union. 'Enhanced EU Security Cooperation in and with Asia'. Council Conclusions, 28 May 2018b.

Council of the European Union. 'Joint Statement of the 22nd EU-ASEAN Ministerial Meeting'. *Press Release*, 21 January 2019.

Council of the European Union. 'EU Imposes Further Sanctions over Serious Violations of Human Rights around the World'. *Press Release*, 22 March 2021a, https://www.consilium.europa.eu/en/press/press-releases/2021/03/22/eu-imposes-further-sanctions-over-serious-violations-of-human-rights-around-the-world/.

Council of the European Union. 'A Globally Connected Europe'. Council Conclusions, 12 July 2021b.
Council of the European Union. 'EU Strategy for Cooperation in the Indo-Pacific'. Council Conclusions, 16 April 2021c.
Council of the European Union, 'Coordinated Maritime Presences: Council Extends Implementation in the Gulf of Guinea for Two Years and Establishes a new Maritime Area of Interest in the North-Western Indian Ocean', *Press Release*, 21 February 2022.
Critical Maritimes Route Programme, 'CRIMARIO: Indo-Pacific 2015-2024', https://criticalmaritimeroutes.eu/projects/crimario/.
Eur-Lex. 'Consolidated Version of the Treaty on European Union—Title I Common Provisions—Article 4', https://eur-lex.europa.eu/legal-content/EN/TXT/?uri=CELEX%3A12012M004.
European Commission. 'Towards a New Strategy in East Asia'. Communication C0M(94) 314, Brussels, 13 July 1994.
European Commission. 'Connecting Europe and Asia—Building Blocks for an EU Strategy'. Joint European Commission, 'Europe and Asia: A Strategic Framework for Enhanced Partnerships'. Communication COM (2001) 469, 4 September 2001.
European Commission. 'The EU and ASEAN: A Partnership with a Strategic Purpose'. Joint Communication JOIN(2015) 22 final, 18 May 2015.
European Commission. *5G for Europe: An Action Plan*. Communication COM(2016)588 final, 14 September 2016.
European Commission. 'Regulation of the European Parliament and of the Council Establishing a Framework for Screening of Foreign Direct Investments into the European Union'. COM(2017) 487 Final, Brussels, 13 September 2017.
European Commission. 'Connecting Europe and Asia—Building Blocks for an EU Strategy'. Joint Communication JOIN(2018) 31 final, Brussels, 18 September 2018.
European Commission. 'Recommendation 2019/534 of 26 March 2019: Cybersecurity of 5G Networks'. C(2019)2335 final, 26 March 2019a.
European Commission. 'Service for Foreign Policy Instruments (FPI)', 2019b, https://ec.europa.eu/fpi/content/partnership-instrument-annual-action-programme-2019_en.
European Commission. 'Implementing Decision on the Financing of the 2019 Partnership Instrument Annual Action Programme'. C(2019) 3277 final, 6 May 2019c.
European Commission. 'Countries and Regions—China', Updated on 28 July 2020a, https://ec.europa.eu/trade/policy/countries-and-regions/countries/china/.
European Commission. 'A New Industrial Strategy for Europe'. Communication COM(2020) 102 Final, Brussels, 10 March 2020b.
European Commission. 'Cybersecurity: Shaping Europe's Digital Future', 25 August 2020c, https://ec.europa.eu/info/sites/default/files/communication-shaping-europes-digital-future-feb2020_en_4.pdf.
European Commission. 'EU Foreign Investment Screening Mechanism Becomes Fully Operational'. *Press Release*, 9 October 2020d.
European Commission. 'Screening of Foreign Direct Investment'. *News Archive*, 24 November 2020e.
European Commission. 'Secure 5G networks: Questions and Answers on the EU Toolbox'. Questions and Answers, Brussels, 29 January 2020f.
European Commission. 'The EU Toolbox for 5G Security'. *Factsheet*, 29 January 2020g.
European Commission. 'Implementing Decision on the Financing of the 2020 Partnership Instrument Annual Action Programme'. C(2020) 2779 final, 5 May 2020h.
European Commission. *Secure 5G Deployment in the EU—Implementing the EU Toolbox*. Communication COM(2020) 50 final, 29 January 2020i.

European Commission. 'Key Elements of the EU–China Comprehensive Agreement on Investment'. *Press Release*, 30 December 2020j.
European Commission. *Report on the Impacts of the Commission Recommendation of 26 March 2019 on the Cybersecurity of 5G Networks*. Commission Staff Working Document, SWD(2020) 357 final, Brussels, 16 December 2020k.
European Commission. 'FAQ—Report on the Impacts of the Commission Recommendation of 26 March 2019 on the Cybersecurity of 5G Networks', 15 December 2020l, https://ec.europa.eu/digital-single-market/en/faq/faq-report-impacts-commission-recommendation-26-march-2019-cybersecurity-5g-networks (accessed on 1 December 2021).
European Commission. 'EU–China Comprehensive Agreement on Investment (CAI)'. *News Archive*, 22 January 2021a, https://trade.ec.europa.eu/doclib/press/index.cfm?id=2237.
European Commission. 'NIS Cooperation Group', 26 March 2021b, https://digital-strategy.ec.europa.eu/en/policies/nis-cooperation-group.
European Commission. 'The EU Strategy for Cooperation in the Indo-Pacific'. Joint Communication JOIN(2021) 24 final, 16 September 2021c.
European Commission. 'EU–US Relations: EU–US Trade and Technology Council', September 2021d, https://trade.ec.europa.eu/doclib/html/159642.htm.
European Commission. 'EU Strengthens Protection against Economic Coercion'. *Press Corner*, 8 December 2021e, https://ec.europa.eu/commission/presscorner/detail/en/ip_21_6642.
European Commission and the High Representative of the Union for Foreign Affairs and Security Policy (HR/VP). *EU–China: A Strategic Outlook*, 12 March 2019.
European Commission and the High Representative of the Union for Foreign Affairs and Security Policy (HR/VP). *A New EU-US Agenda for Global Change*, Brussels, JOIN(2020) 22 final, 2 December 2020.
European Council. Presidency Conclusions, Madrid, 26 and 27 June 1989.
European Council. 'Guidelines on the EU's Foreign and Security Policy in East Asia', 2007.
European Council. 'EU Strategy on China'. Council Conclusions, 18 July 2016.
European Council. 'European Council Meeting'. Conclusions, Brussels, 22 March 2019.
European Council. 'Special Meeting of the European Council'. Conclusions, Brussels, 2 October 2020.
European Court of Auditors. *The EU's Response to China's State-Driven Investment Strategy*. Review no. 3, 2020.
European External Action Service (EEAS). 'The Republic of Korea and the EU', Updated 10 May 2016, https://eeas.europa.eu/delegations/south-korea_en/8789/.
European External Action Service (EEAS). 'Australia and the EU', Updated 17 July 2018, https://eeas.europa.eu/delegations/australia/610/australia-and-eu_en.
European External Action Service (EEAS). 'EU Strategy for Cooperation in the Indo-Pacific'. *Factsheet*, 19 April 2021a.
European External Action Service (EEAS). 'Indo-Pacific: Remarks by the High Representative/Vice-President at the Press Conference on the Joint Communication', 16 September 2021b, https://eeas.europa.eu/headquarters/headquarters-homepage_en/104215/Indo-Pacific:%20Remarks%20by%20the%20High%20Representative/Vice-President%20at%20the%20press%20conference%20on%20the%20Joint%20Communication.

European External Action Service (EEAS). 'Coordinated Maritime Presences'. Factsheets, 25 January 2021c, http://eeas.europa.eu/sites/default/files/coordinated_maritime_presences.pdf.
European External Action Service (EEAS). 'EU-US Trade and Technology Council Inaugural Joint Statement', 29 September 2021d, https://ec.europa.eu/commission/presscorner/detail/en/STATEMENT_21_4951.
European External Action Service (EEAS). 'United States: High Representative/Vice-President Josep Borrell met with Secretary of State Antony Blinken', 14 October 2021e, https://eeas.europa.eu/headquarters/headquarters-homepage/105674/united-states-high-representativevice-president-josep-borrell-met-secretary-state-antony_en.
European Network and Information Security Agency (ENISA). *Technologies with Potential to Improve the Resilience of the Internet Infrastructure*, December 2011.
European Network and Information Security Agency (ENISA). 'The EU Agency for Cybersecurity Endorses the EU Toolbox for 5G Security', 30 January 2020, https://www.enisa.europa.eu/news/enisa-news/5g.
European Union Naval Force Somalia. 'EU NAVFOR Force Commander Thanks German Maritime Air Patrol Team for Invaluable Contribution to Operation Atalanta off Coast of Somalia', 14 June 2017, at https://eunavfor.eu/.
French, German, and Italian Ministers for Economic Affairs. Letter to the EU Commissioner for Trade Cecilia Malmström, February 2017.
Network and Information Systems (NIS) Cooperation Group. *EU Coordinated Risk Assessment of the Cybersecurity of 5G Networks*. Report, 9 October 2019.
Network and Information Systems (NIS) Cooperation Group. *Cybersecurity of 5G Networks EU Toolbox of Risk Mitigating Measures*. Report for the European Commission, January 2020.
Official Journal of the European Union. 'Commission Recommendation (EU) 2019/534: Cybersercurity of 5G Networks'. L. 88/45, 26 March 2019a.
Official Journal of the European Union. 'Regulation (EU) 2019/452 of the European Parliament and of the Council Establishing a Framework for the Screening of Foreign Direct Investments into the Union', 19 March 2019b.
Official Journal of the European Union. *Regulation (EU) 2019/881 on ENISA (the European Union Agency for Cybersecurity) and on Information and Communications Technology Cybersecurity Certification and Repealing Regulation (EU) No 526/2013 (Cybersecurity Act)*, 17 April 2019c.

France

Constitutional Court. 'Décision n° 2020-882 QPC du 5 février 2021'. *Press Release*, 5 February 2021, https://www.conseil-constitutionnel.fr/actualites/communique/decision-n-2020-882-qpc-du-5-fevrier-2021-communique-de-presse.
Electronic Communications, Postal and Print Media Distribution Regulatory Authority (ARCEP). *5G : Une feuille de route ambitieuse pour la France*, 16 July 2018.
Electronic Communications, Postal and Print Media Distribution Regulatory Authority (ARCEP). 5G Observatory: https://www.arcep.fr/cartes-et-donnees/nos-cartes/deploiement-5g/observatoire-du-deploiement-5g-fevrier-2021.html (accessed 1 June 2021).
Embassy in Australia. 'The Mission "Jeanne d'Arc 2017"', 2017, https://au.ambafrance.org/The-mission-Jeanne-d-Arc-2017 (accessed on 1 December 2021).
Embassy in China. 'Investissements chinois dans le monde : perte de vitesse depuis deux ans, recentrage vers l'ASEAN et les pays des routes de la soie'. Economic Section in Beijing, 29 October 2020.

Embassy in India. 'Coopération spatiale'. *Factshee*t, 14 July 2018, https://in.ambafrance.org/Cooperation-spatiale.
Embassy in India. 'Relations franco-indiennes', 18 September 2019, https://in.ambafrance.org/-Relations-franco-indiennes (accessed on 1 December 2021).
Government. 'Déclaration conjointe franco-chinoise pour un partenariat global', signed by Jacques Chirac and Jiang Zemin, Beijing, 16 May 1997.
Government. *Faire de la France une économie de rupture technologique : Soutenir les marchés émergents à forts enjeux de compétitivité*. Report for the Minister for the Economy and Finance and for the Minister of Education, Research and Innovation, 7 February 2020.
Government. 'PACTE, the Action Plan for Business Growth and Transformation', 2021, https://www.gouvernement.fr/en/pacte-the-action-plan-for-business-growth-and-transformation.
Légifrance. 'Loi n° 66-1008 du 28 décembre 1966 relative aux relations financières avec l'étranger', 29 December 1966, https://www.legifrance.gouv.fr/loda/id/LEGITEXT000006068265/.
Légifrance. 'Loi n° 96-109 du 14 février 1996 relative aux relations financières avec l'étranger en ce qui concerne les investissements étrangers en France', 15 February 1996, https://www.legifrance.gouv.fr/loda/id/JORFTEXT000000376141/.
Légifrance. 'Loi n° 2003-706 du 1er août 2003 de sécurité financière', 2 August 2003, https://www.legifrance.gouv.fr/jorf/id/JORFTEXT000000428977 (article 28).
Légifrance. 'Décret n° 2005-1739 du 30 décembre 2005 réglementant les relations financières avec l'étranger et portant application de l'article L. 151-3 du code monétaire et financier', 31 December 2005, https://www.legifrance.gouv.fr/loda/id/JORFTEXT000000268021/.
Légifrance. 'Arrêté du 4 juillet 2012 fixant la liste d'appareils et de dispositifs techniques prévue par l'article 226-3 du code pénal', 1 August 2012, https://www.legifrance.gouv.fr/loda/article_lc/LEGIARTI000033064189/2021-10-01/.
Légifrance. 'Loi n° 2013-1168 du 18 décembre 2013 relative à la programmation militaire pour les années 2014 à 2019 et portant diverses dispositions concernant la défense et la sécurité nationale', 19 December 2013a, https://www.legifrance.gouv.fr/jorf/id/JORFARTI000028338919.
Légifrance. 'Arrêté du 2 janvier 2013 relatif aux formations et aux unités relevant du ministère de la défense pouvant bénéficier de l'avance de trésorerie pour l'activité des forces', 18 January 2013b, https://www.legifrance.gouv.fr/loda/id/LEGIARTI000026953778/2013-01-19/.
Légifrance. 'Décret n° 2014-479 du 14 mai 2014 relatif aux investissements étrangers soumis à autorisation préalable', 16 May 2014, https://www.legifrance.gouv.fr/loda/id/JORFTEXT000028933611.
Légifrance. 'Arrêté du 11 août 2016 modifiant l'arrêté du 4 juillet 2012 fixant la liste d'appareils et de dispositifs techniques prévue par l'article 226-3 du code pénal', 25 August 2016, https://www.legifrance.gouv.fr/loda/id/JORFTEXT000033063311/.
Légifrance. 'Décret n° 2018-1057 du 29 novembre 2018 relatif aux investissements étrangers soumis à autorisation préalable', 2 December 2018, https://www.legifrance.gouv.fr/loda/id/JORFTEXT000037674063/.
Légifrance. 'Décret n° 2019-1300 du 6 décembre 2019 relatif aux modalités de l'autorisation préalable de l'exploitation des équipements de réseaux radioélectriques prévue à l'article L. 34-11 du code des postes et des communications électroniques', 7 December 2019a, https://www.legifrance.gouv.fr/loda/id/JORFTEXT000039455649/.

Légifrance. 'Décret n° 2019-1590 du 31 décembre 2019 relatif aux investissements étrangers en France', 31 December 2019b, https://www.legifrance.gouv.fr/jorf/id/JORFTEXT000039727443/.

Légifrance. 'Loi n° 2019-810 du 1er août 2019 visant à préserver les intérêts de la défense et de la sécurité nationale de la France dans le cadre de l'exploitation des réseaux radioélectriques mobiles', 2 August 2019c, https://www.legifrance.gouv.fr/jorf/id/JORFTEXT000038864094.

Légifrance. 'Arrêté du 27 avril 2020 relatif aux investissements étrangers en France', 30 April 2020, https://www.legifrance.gouv.fr/jorf/id/JORFTEXT000041835304.

Ministry of Defence. *Livre Blanc sur la défense*, 1994.

Ministry of Defence. *French White Paper on Defence and National Security*, 2008.

Ministry of Defence. 'The French White Paper on Defence and National Security'. Press Kit, 2008b, http://archives.livreblancdefenseetsecurite.gouv.fr/2008/IMG/pdf/white_paper_press_kit.pdf.

Ministry of Defence. *French White Paper on Defence and National Security*, 2013.

Ministry of Defence. *France and Security in the Asia-Pacific*, 2014.

Ministry of Defence. 'Mission Jeanne d'Arc : des manœuvres amphibies encore jamais réalisées', 1 June 2015a. http://www.defense.gouv.fr/english/marine/a-la-une/mission-jeanne-d-arc-des-manoeuvres-amphibies-encore-jamais-realisees.

Ministry of Defence. 'Mission Arromanches : Le groupe aéronaval de retour à Toulon', May 2015b, https://www.defense.gouv.fr/marine/a-la-une/mission-arromanches-le-groupe-aeronaval-de-retour-a-toulon.

Ministry of Defence. *France and Security in the Asia-Pacific*, 2016.

Ministry of Defence. *Strategic Review of Defence and National Security*, 2017a.

Ministry of Defence. *Mission 'Jeanne d'Arc' 2017*. Press Kit, http://www.colsbleus.fr/exemplaires/9349 (accessed on 1 December 2021)

Ministry of Defence. *France's Defence Strategy in the Indo-Pacific*, 2018a.

Ministry of Defence. 'FANC : bilan de l'exercice Croix du Sud', 25 May 2018b.

Ministry of Defence. *France and Security in the Indo-Pacific*, 2018c.

Ministry of Defence. Mission 'Jeanne d'Arc' 2018d. Press Kit

Ministry of Defence. *France's Defence Strategy in the Indo-Pacific*, 2019a.

Ministry of Defence. *France and Security in the Indo-Pacific*, 2019b.

Ministry of Defence. Opération Clémenceau. Press Kit, 5 March 2019c, https://www.defense.gouv.fr/content/download/554047/9619146/DP_MinARM_d%C3%A9part%20Clemenceau_GAN%2019.pdf.

Ministry of Defence. *Strategic Update*, January 2021.

Ministry for the Economy and Finance. *Financer la quatrième révolution industrielle : lever le verrou du financement des entreprises technologiques*. Report by Philippe Tibi for the Minister for the Economy and Finance, July 2019.

Ministry for the Economy and Finance. 'Publication du décret et de l'arrêté relatifs aux investissements étrangers en France : une procédure plus simple, claire et rapide'. *Press Release*, 2 January 2020a, https://www.tresor.economie.gouv.fr/Articles/2020/01/02/publication-du-decret-et-de-l-arrete-relatifs-aux-investissements-etrangers-en-france-une-procedure-plus-simple-claire-et-rapide.

Ministry for the Economy and Finance. 'Bruno Le Maire annonce la prorogation jusqu'au 31 décembre 2021 des mesures d'adaptation du contrôle des investissements étrangers en France pendant la crise sanitaire'. *Press Release*, 18 December 2020b, https://www.tresor.economie.gouv.fr/Articles/2020/12/18/prorogation-jusqu-au-31-decembre-2021-des-

mesures-d-adaptation-du-controle-des-investissements-etrangers-en-france-pendant-la-crise-sanitaire.
Ministry for the Economy and Finance. 'Interview de M. Bruno Le Maire, ministre de l'économie, des finances et de la relance, à BFM Business', 20 January 2021, https://www.vie-publique.fr/discours/278213-bruno-le-maire-20012021-politique-economique.
Ministry of Foreign Affairs. 'Communiqué conjoint franco-chinois sur le rétablissement de relations de coopération entre la France et la Chine', 12 January 1994, https://www.vie-publique.fr/discours/133004-communique-conjoint-franco-chinois-en-date-du-12-janvier-1994-sur-le-r.
Ministry of Foreign Affairs. 'Indo-French Dialogue on Maritime Cooperation and Signing of White Shipping Agreement'. French Embassy in Delhi, New Delhi, 19 January 2017a.
Ministry of Foreign Affairs. 'Joint Statement of Enhanced Strategic Partnership between Australia and France', 3 March 2017b.
Ministry of Foreign Affairs. *White Paper—2030 French Strategy in Asia-Oceania: Towards an Inclusive Asian Indo-Pacific Region*, 2018a.
Ministry of Foreign Affairs. 'Les relations économiques entre la France et la région Asie-Océanie'. *Country Factsheet*, June 2018b.
Ministry of Foreign Affairs. 'Présentation de la Mission de Défense'. French Embassy in Hanoi, 4 October 2018c.
Ministry of Foreign Affairs. *The French Strategy in the Indo-Pacific*, 2019a.
Ministry of Foreign Affairs. 'The Indo-Pacific Region: A Priority for France'. *Country Files*, August 2019b.
Ministry of Foreign Affairs. 'Indonésie—Relations bilatérales'. *Country Factsheet*, August 2019c.
Ministry of Foreign Affairs. 'Conseil des ministres franco-allemand : Feuille de route ministérielle "Affaires étrangères"', 16 October 2019d.
Ministry of Foreign Affairs. 'Déclaration conjointe de la France, de l'Allemagne et du Royaume-Uni—Situation en mer de Chine méridionale', 30 August 2019e, https://www.diplomatie.gouv.fr/fr/dossiers-pays/asie-oceanie/evenements/article/declaration-conjointe-de-la-france-de-l-allemagne-et-du-royaume-uni-situation.
Ministry of Foreign Affairs. 'Relations bilatérales—China'. *Country Factsheet*, 28 June 2019f, https://www.diplomatie.gouv.fr/fr/dossiers-pays/chine/relations-bilaterales/.
Ministry of Foreign Affairs. 'Union européenne—Chine, Questions et réponses'. Press Briefing, 27 May 2020a, https://www.diplomatie.gouv.fr/fr/dossiers-pays/chine/evenements/article/union-europeenne-chine-q-r-extrait-du-point-de-presse-27-05-20.
Ministry of Foreign Affairs. 'Garantir la cybersécurité', November 2020b, https://www.diplomatie.gouv.fr/fr/politique-etrangere-de-la-france/diplomatie-numerique/garantir-la-cybersecurite/ (accessed on 1 December 2021).
Ministry of Foreign Affairs. 'The Indo-Pacific: A Priority for France, April 2021a, https://www.diplomatie.gouv.fr/en/country-files/asia-and-oceania/the-indo-pacific-region-a-priority-for-france/ (accessed on 1 December 2021).
Ministry of Foreign Affairs. 'Fiche Pays—Repères économiques'. Direction de la diplomatie économique, April 2021b, https://www.diplomatie.gouv.fr/fr/politique-etrangere-de-la-france/diplomatie-economique-et-commerce-exterieur/la-france-et-ses-partenaires-economiques-pays-par-pays/asie/article/chine.
Ministry of Foreign Affairs. *France's Partnerships in the Indo-Pacific*, 2021c, https://www.diplomatie.gouv.fr/IMG/pdf/en_a4_indopacifique_16p_2021_v4_cle4b8b46.pdf.
Ministry of Foreign Affairs. 'India-France-Australia Joint Statement on the Occasion of the Trilateral Ministerial Dialogue'. *News*, 4 May 2021d, https://www.diplomatie.gouv.fr/

en/country-files/asia-and-oceania/news/article/india-france-australia-joint-statement-on-the-occasion-of-the-trilateral.

Ministry of Foreign Affairs. *France's Indo-Pacific Strategy*, July 2021e, https://www.diplomatie.gouv.fr/IMG/pdf/en_a4_indopacifique_v2_rvb_cle432726.pdf.

Ministry of Interior. *État de la menace liée au numérique en 2019*, May 2019.

Ministry of Interior's National Security Science and Technology Observatory (ONISTS). 'Réseau 5G et Cybersécurité', https://www.gendarmerie.interieur.gouv.fr/onists/ressources-documentaires/veille-technologique/reseau-5g-cybersecurite (accessed 1 June 2021).

National Cybersecurity Agency (ANSSI). 'Cybersecurity in France', https://www.ssi.gouv.fr/en/cybersecurity-in-france (accessed 1 June 2021).

National Cybersecurity Agency (ANSSI). 'NIS Directive: ANSSI Supports the First Operators of Essential Services'. *News*, https://www.ssi.gouv.fr/en/actualite/nis-directive-anssi-supports-the-first-operators-of-essential-services/ (accessed 1 June 2021).

National Cybersecurity Agency (ANSSI). 'Protection des OIV en France', https://www.ssi.gouv.fr/entreprise/protection-des-oiv/protection-des-oiv-en-france (accessed 1 June 2021).

National Cybersecurity Agency (ANSSI). *Information Systems Defence and Security: France's Strategy*, 2011, https://www.ssi.gouv.fr/uploads/IMG/pdf/2011-02-15_Information_system_defence_and_security_-_France_s_strategy.pdf.

National Cybersecurity Agency (ANSSI). 'Publication de l'arrêté du 11 août 2016 modifiant celui du 4 juillet 2012 fixant la liste d'appareils et de dispositifs techniques prévue par l'article 226-3 du code pénal', https://www.ssi.gouv.fr/actualite/publication-de-larrete-du-11-aout-2016-modifiant-celui-du-4-juillet-2012-fixant-la-liste-dappareils-et-de-dispositifs-techniques-prevue-par-larticle-226-3-du-code-penal/.

Office of the Prime Minister. *National Strategy for the Security of Maritime Areas*, 2015.

Permanent Mission of France to the United Nations. 'Note verbale' to the Commission on the Limits of the Continental Shelf, no. BF N° 2020–0343647, New York, 16 September 2020.

Presidency's Office. 'Déclaration conjointe Chine–France', 27 January 2004.

Presidency's Office. 'Déclaration commune publiée à l'occasion du Sommet franco-indien', 30 September 2008.

Presidency's Office. 'Déclaration conjointe du Président de la République française et du Président de la République populaire de Chine', 10 January 2018.

Secretariat-General for National Defence and Security. *Revue stratégique de cyberdéfense*, 12 February 2018.

Secretariat-General for National Defence and Security. 'Le dispositif de protection du potentiel scientifique et technique de la nation', www.sgdsn.gouv.fr/missions/protection-du-potentiel-scientifique-et-technique-de-la-nation/le-dispositif-de-protection-du-potentiel-scientifique-et-technique-de-la-nation-faq/ (accessed 1 June 2021).

Germany

Federal Foreign Minister Sigmar Gabriel. 'Europe Needs Vision, Not Technocrats', published in French in *Le Monde* on 19 October 2017.

Federal Foreign Office. 'China: A Land with Many Faces', https://www.auswaertiges-amt.de/en/aussenpolitik/regionaleschwerpunkte/asien/-/231348 (accessed 1 June 2021).

Federal Foreign Office. 'Asia in German Foreign Policy', https://www.auswaertiges-amt.de/en/aussenpolitik/regionaleschwerpunkte/asien/-/231344 (accessed 1 June 2021).

Federal Foreign Office. 'Agenda for the Indo-German Partnership in the 21st Century', 18 May 2000.
Federal Foreign Office. *Tasks of German Foreign Policy: East Asia*, 2002a.
Federal Foreign Office. *Tasks of German Foreign Policy: Southeast Asia, Australia, New Zealand and Pacific Islands*, 2002b.
Federal Foreign Office. 'Germany and ASEAN to Cooperate on Strengthening ASEAN Institutions', 27 February 2008.
Federal Foreign Office. 'German Government Accredits First Ambassador to the ASEAN', 12 February 2009.
Federal Foreign Office. *Globalisierung gestalten—Partnerschaften ausbauen—Verantwortung teilen. Konzept der Bundesregierung*, 2012a.
Federal Foreign Office. 'Antwort der Bundesregierung zur sicherheitspolitischen Lage in Ost- und Südostasien'. *German Parliament*, 8 February 2012b.
Federal Foreign Office. 'Berlin–Canberra Declaration of Intent on a Strategic Partnership', 28 January 2013.
Federal Foreign Office. 'Joint Declaration: Establishment of a Comprehensive Strategic Partnership between Germany and China', 28 March 2014.
Federal Foreign Office. 'Germany and China: Fostering Fairness in Business and Politics', 24 November 2016a.
Federal Foreign Office. 'Joint Statement on U.S.–Germany Cyber Bilateral Meeting'. *Press Release*, 24 March 2016b.
Federal Foreign Office. 'Joint Declaration by the Minister for Foreign Affairs of the Republic of Singapore Balakrishnan and the Minister for Foreign Affairs of the Federal Republic of Germany Heiko Maas', 28 September 2018.
Federal Foreign Office. 'Treaty between the Federal Republic of Germany and the French Republic on Franco-German Cooperation and Integration', 22 January 2019a.
Federal Foreign Office. 'Erklärung der Außenminister anlässlich des Deutsch-Französischen Ministerrats', 16 October 2019b.
Federal Foreign Office. 'Non-Paper on EU Cyber Diplomacy by Estonia, France, Germany, Poland, Portugal and Slovenia', 2020a, https://www.auswaertiges-amt.de/blob/2418986/206b3bf9aa4ef45a2887399231840d23/201119-non-paper-pdf-data.pdf.
Federal Foreign Office. 'Foreign Minister Maas on the Adoption of the German Government Policy Guidelines on the Indo-Pacific Region'. *Press Release*, 2 September 2020b.
Federal Foreign Office. 'Germany and China: Bilateral Relations China', 17 August 2020c.
Federal Foreign Office. 'EU Cyber Diplomacy—Working Together for a Free and Secure Cyberspace', 19 November 2020d.
Federal Foreign Office. '*Germany–Europe–Asia: Shaping the 21st Century Together*': The German Government Adopts Policy Guidelines on the Indo-Pacific Region, 1 September 2020e, https://www.auswaertiges-amt.de/en/aussenpolitik/regionaleschwerpunkte/asien/german-government-policy-guidelines-indo-pacific/2380510.
Federal Foreign Office. 'In Dialogue with China'. *Bilateral Relations and German Missions—China*, 24 July 2020f.
Federal Foreign Office. 'Sign of Mutual Trust: Japan and Germany Sign Agreement on the Security of Information', 22 March 2021, https://www.auswaertiges-amt.de/en/aussenpolitik/laenderinformationen/japan-node/japan-agreement-security-information/2449392.
Federal Government. *The Federal Government's Concept on Asia*, 22 September 1993, https://www.asienhaus.de/public/archiv/brdasia.htm.

Federal Government. 'Angela Merkel in Japan: Long-Standing Friendship is an "Incentive to Cooperate More Closely"', 5 February 2019a, https://www.bundesregierung.de/breg-en/search/long-standing-friendship-is-an-incentive-to-cooperate-more-closely--1577310.
Federal Government. 'Rede von Bundeskanzlerin Merkel im Deutschen Bundestag', 27 November 2019b, https://www.bundesregierung.de/breg-de/suche/rede-von-bundeskanzlerin-merkel-im-deutschen-bundestag-1699682.
Federal Government. 'Regierungserklärung von Bundeskanzlerin Merkel', 17 October 2019c, https://www.bundesregierung.de/breg-de/suche/regierungserklaerung-von-bundeskanzlerin-merkel-1682852.
Federal Government. *Policy Guidelines for the Indo-Pacific: Germany–Europe–Asia. Shaping the 21st Century Together*, 2020a.
Federal Government. *Together for Europe's Recovery—Programme for German's Presidency of the Council of the European Union*, 2020b.
Federal Government. 'Antwort der Bundesregierung auf die Kleine Anfrage der Abgeordneten Uwe Schulz, Joana Cotar, Dr. Michael Espendiller und der Fraktion der AfD', 10 September 2020c, https://dserver.bundestag.de/btd/19/223/1922310.pdf.
Federal Government. *Progress Report on the Implementation of the German Government Policy Guidelines on the Indo-Pacific Region*, 13 September 2021.
Federal Ministry of Defence. *White Paper on the Security of the Federal Republic of Germany and the Situation of the Future Bundeswehr*, 4 May 1994.
Federal Ministry of Defence. *White Paper on German Security Policy and the Future of the Bundeswehr*, 2006.
Federal Ministry of Defence. *White Paper on German Security Policy and the Future of the Bundeswehr*, 2016.
Federal Ministry of Defence. 'Ministerin betont enge Kooperation mit australischen Streitkräften', 24 October 2018.
Federal Ministry of Defence. *Bericht zur Materiellen Einsatzbereitschaft der Hauptwaffensysteme der Bundeswehr*, 2019.
Federal Ministry of Defence. 'For Stability, Prosperity and a Rules-Based Order in the Indo-Pacific Region'. *News*, 9 December 2020.
Federal Minister for Economic Affairs, French Minister for Economic Affairs and Italian Minister for Economic Affairs. Letter to the EU Commissioner for Trade Cecilia Malmström, February 2017.
Federal Minister for Economic Affairs, Brigitte Zypries. Letter to the President of the European Commission Jean-Claude Juncker, August 2017.
Federal Ministry for Economic Affairs. *Report of the Government of the Federal Republic of Germany on its Policy on Exports of Conventional Military Equipment*, 2010–2019, https://www.bmwi.de/Navigation/EN/Topic/topic.html?cl2Categories_LeadKeyword=ruestungsexportkontrolle.
Federal Ministry for Economic Affairs and Japanese MEA. 'Joint Statement on Cooperation', 6 November 2019a.
Federal Ministry for Economic Affairs. 'Facts about German Foreign Trade', 30 September 2019b, https://www.bmwi.de/Redaktion/EN/Publikationen/facts-about-german-foreign-trade.html.
Federal Ministry for Economic Affairs and Energy. 'China—Wirtschaftliche Beziehungen', 2021, https://www.bmwi.de/Redaktion/DE/Artikel/Aussenwirtschaft/laendervermerk-china.html.
Federal Ministry of Transport and Digital Infrastructure. *5G Strategy for Germany*, July 2017.

Federal Statistical Office. 'Ranking of Germany's Trading Partners in Foreign Trade—2019', 17 August 2020.
Office of the Federal Chancellor. 'Germany and China: Strategic Partnership in Global Responsibility', 22 May 2006.
Office of the Federal Chancellor. 'Chancellor Visits the Far East: China and Japan', 26 August 2007, https://www.bundeskanzlerin.de/bkin-en/news/chancellor-visits-the-far-east-china-and-japan-607408.
Office of the Federal Chancellor. 'Driving Europe forward as a trio'. *News*, 23 June 2020a.
Office of the Federal Chancellor. 'Digital Sovereignty in the EU'. *News*, 2 October 2020b.
Permanent Mission of the Federal Republic of Germany to the United Nations. 'Note verbale' to the Commission on the Limits of the Continental Shelf, no. 324/2020, New York, 16 September 2020.
Presidency of the European Union. 'Driving Prosperity with Competition', https://www.eu2020.de/eu2020-en/competitiveness-eu-prosperity-mobility/2352830.

India

Embassy in Germany. 'India–Germany Relations', 30 March 2020, https://indianembassyberlin.gov.in/pages?id=eyJpdiI6ImZrK2Fvc0JDNXNBZ1YxSWdCQX NRYXc9PSIsInZhbHVlIjoic0xsaFY5eTcwZXhjUDQ5dk1ISVF5Zz09IiwibWFjIjoi OTgwYzc2YjI1NjkxOTA3YmM3MjU2ZDY5YTM2ZmVhZDkyZWE0NzA5ZDk2Z WY2NDhmMzg1NTBmNThiZjU5NmNlOCJ9 (accessed on 1 December 2021).
Ministry of Foreign Affairs. 'India–Germany Relations', August 2013, http://mea.gov.in/portal/foreignrelation/india-germany_relations.pdf.
Ministry of Foreign Affairs. 'Joint Statement—Third India–Germany Inter-Governmental Consultations', 5 October 2015, https://www.mea.gov.in/bilateral-documents.htm?dtl/25887/Joint_Statement__Third_India_Germany_InterGovernmental_Consultations_IGC_in_New_Delhi_October_05_2015.
Ministry of Foreign Affairs. 'India–Germany Joint Statement during the Visit of Prime Minister to Germany', 30 May 2017, https://www.mea.gov.in/bilateral-documents.htm?dtl/28496/IndiaGermany.
Ministry of Foreign Affairs. 'India–France Bilateral Relations'. Indian Embassy in Paris, April 2018a.
Ministry of Foreign Affairs. 'India–Germany Relations', 5 January 2018b.
Ministry of Foreign Affairs. Joint Statement 'Strategic Partnership for Sustainable Growth and a Reliable International Order', 1 November 2019.

Japan

Embassy in Germany. 'Premierminister Abe besucht Deutschland', 5 May 2016, https://www.de.emb-japan.go.jp/presse/pm_160505.html.
Embassy in Germany. 'Japanisch-Deutsches Gipfeltreffen', 4 February 2019, https://www.de.emb-japan.go.jp/presse/pm_190204.html.
Ministry of Defence. *White Paper: Defense of Japan*, 2014.
Ministry of Defence. *White Paper: Defense of Japan*, 2018.
Ministry of Defence. *White Paper: Defense of Japan*, 2020.
Ministry of Foreign Affairs. 'Japan–France Relations (Archives)', https://www.mofa.go.jp/region/europe/france/archives.html.
Ministry of Foreign Affairs. 'UK/Japan Action Agenda: Special Partnership around the World', 2 September 1996.
Ministry of Foreign Affairs. 'Action Agenda 21: The UK and Japan in the 21st Century', 1999.

Ministry of Foreign Affairs. 'Japan and Germany in the 21st Century: Seven Pillars of Cooperation', 30 October 2000.
Ministry of Foreign Affairs. 'Japanese-German Science, Technology and Academic Cooperation and Exchanges', 9 December 2004.
Ministry of Foreign Affairs. 'Japan–UK Joint Statement: A Framework for the Future', 9 January 2007, https://www.mofa.go.jp/region/europe/uk/joint0701.html.
Ministry of Foreign Affairs. 'Japan–Germany Summit Meeting', 4 February 2019.

Netherlands

Government of the Netherlands. *Indo-Pacific: Een Leidraad voor Versterking van de Nederlandse en EU-Samenwerking met Partners in Azië*, 13 November 2020, https://open.overheid.nl/repository/ronl-84107ff4-e66b-4aa2-a7a9-07fec3e3601b/1/pdf/indo-pacific-een-leidraad-voor-versterking-van-de-nederlandse-en-eu-samenwerking-met-partners-in-azie.pdf.
Government of the Netherlands. *Jaarverslag en slotwet Ministerie van Buitenlandse Zaken 2020*, 35830-V-1, 22 June 2021, https://www.rijksoverheid.nl/binaries/rijksoverheid/documenten/jaarverslagen/2021/05/19/buitenlandse-zaken-2020/V%20Buitenlandse%20Zaken.pdf.
Ministry of Foreign Affairs. *The Netherlands and China: A New Balance*, 14 May 2019a, https://www.government.nl/documents/policy-notes/2019/05/15/china-strategy-the-netherlands--china-a-new-balance.
Ministry of Foreign Affairs. 'Kabinetsreactie Op Advies "China en de Strategische Opdracht voor Nederland in Europa"', 9 September 2019b, https://www.rijksoverheid.nl/binaries/rijksoverheid/documenten/kamerstukken/2019/09/09/kamerbrief-kabinetsreactie-op-advies-china-en-de-strategische-opdracht-voor-nederland-in-europa/kamerbrief-kabinetsreactie-op-advies-china-en-de-strategische-opdracht-voor-nederland-in-europa.pdf

People's Republic of China

'Communiqué of the Third Plenary Session of the 18th Central Committee of the Communist Party of China', 12 November 2013, www.china.org.cn/china/third_plenary_session/2014-01/15/content_31203056.htm (accessed on 1 December 2021).
Embassy in France. 'Déclaration du Porte-parole de l'Ambassade de Chine en France sur la question de Huawei et de la 5G', 9 February 2020, www.amb-chine.fr/fra/zfzj/t1742545.htm.
'Full Text of China's Anti-Secession Law'. *People's Daily Online*, 14 March 2005, http://en.people.cn/200503/14/eng20050314_176746.html.
'Full Text: China's Peaceful Development Road'. *The People's Daily*, 22 December 2005, http://en.people.cn/200512/22/eng20051222_230059.html.
'Full Text of Xi Jinping's Report at 19th CPC National Congress'. *China Daily*, 18 October 2017, https://www.chinadaily.com.cn/china/19thcpcnationalcongress/2017-11/04/content_34115212.htm.
'Full Text: China's International Development Cooperation in the New Era'. *XinhuaNet*, 10 January 2021, www.xinhuanet.com/english/2021-01/10/c_139655400.htm.
Ministry of Commerce. German Investment in China: Changing Opportunities and Trends. China International Investment Promotion Agency—Germany (CIIPAG), 2019.
Ministry of Science and Technology (MOST). 'The "13th Five-Year" Special Plan for S&T Military-Civil Fusion Development' (translated in English), 26 September 2017,

https://cset.georgetown.edu/research/the-13th-five-year-special-plan-for-st-military-civil-fusion-development.
National Bureau of Statistics of China. *Classification and Methods: Foreign Trade and Economic Cooperation*, http://www.stats.gov.cn/english/ClassificationsMethods/Definitions/200205/t20020517_72378.html.
Standing Committee of the National People's Congress. 'National Intelligence Law of the People's Republic of China (2018 Amendment)', 2018, http://en.pkulaw.cn/display.aspx?cgid=313975&lib=law.
State Council of the People's Republic of China. 'China Unveils Internet Plus Action Plan to Fuel Growth', 4 July 2015a, http://english.www.gov.cn/policies/latest_releases/2015/07/04/content_281475140165588.htm.
State Council of the People's Republic of China. *Made in China 2025*, 7 July 2015b, http://www.cittadellascienza.it/cina/wp-content/uploads/2017/02/IoT-ONE-Made-in-China-2025.pdf.
State Council of the People's Republic of China. 'Full Text: Action Plan on the Belt and Road Initiative', 30 March 2015, english.www.gov.cn/archive/publications/2015/03/30/content_281475080249035.htm.

Singapore

Government of Singapore. 'Exercise Bersama Padu 2006', https://www.nas.gov.sg/archivesonline/data/pdfdoc/20060907997.htm.
Ministry of Defence. '2nd FPDA's Defence Ministers' Informal Meeting'. *News Release*, 7 June 2004.
Ministry of Defence. 'Joint Communique of the 10th Singapore–Australia Joint Ministerial Committee, Singapore, 22 August 2017, https://www.minister.defence.gov.au/minister/marise-payne/statements/joint-communique-10th-singapore-australia-joint-ministerial.
Ministry of Defence. 'Singapore and UK Strengthen Long-Standing Defence Ties for Next Bound', 2 June 2018a, https://www.mindef.gov.sg/web/portal/mindef/news-and-events/latest-releases/article-detail/2018/june/02june18_nr5.
Ministry of Defence. 'Singapore and the UK Affirm Long-Standing Defence Technology Relations with Renewal of MoU on Cooperative Defence Research', 28 June 2018b, https://www.mindef.gov.sg/web/portal/mindef/news-and-events/latest-releases/article-detail/2018/june/28jun18_nr.
Ministry of Defence. 'Singapore and France Strengthen Defence Relations through 18th Defence Policy Dialogue'. *News Releases*, 1 February 2019.
Ministry of Foreign Affairs. 'Joint Declaration on the Sidelines of the UN General Assembly', 28 September 2018.

United Kingdom

British High Commission Singapore. 'Joint Statement by UK and Singapore at the Launch of Singapore–UK "Partnership for the Future"', 4 January 2020.
BT Group. Written Evidence Submitted to House of Commons. *Oral Evidence: The Security of 5G*, 28 July 2020.
Chair of the House of Commons' Science and Technology Comittee Norman Lamb. Letter to the Secretary of State for Digital, Culture, Media and Sport Jeremy Wright, 10 July 2019, https://www.parliament.uk/globalassets/documents/commons-committees/science-technology/correspondence/190710-chair-to-jeremy-wright-re-huawei.pdf.

Competition and Markets Authority. 'Gardner Aerospace Holdings/Northern Aerospace Merger Inquiry', 20 July 2018, https://www.gov.uk/cma-cases/gardner-aerospace-holdings-northern-aerospace-merger-inquiry.

Department for Business, Energy and Industrial Strategy (BEIS). *National Security and Infrastructure Investment Review*, 15 March 2018a.

Department for Business, Energy and Industrial Strategy (BEIS). 'Government Upgrades National Security Investment Powers'. *News Story*, 24 July 2018b.

Department for Business, Energy and Industrial Strategy (BEIS). *Enterprise Act 2002: Changes to the Turnover and Share of Supply Tests for Mergers: Guidance 2020*, June 2020a.

Department for Business, Energy and Industrial Strategy (BEIS). *National Security and Investment White Paper*, November 2020b.

Department for Business, Energy and Industrial Strategy (BEIS). 'National Security and Investment Bill: Statement of Policy Intent'. *Policy Paper*, 2 November 2020c, https://www.gov.uk/government/publications/national-security-and-investment-bill-2020/statement-of-policy-intent.

Department for Business, Energy and Industrial Strategy (BEIS). 'New Finance Model to Cut Cost of New Nuclear Power Stations'. *Press Release*, 26 October 2021a, https://www.gov.uk/government/news/new-finance-model-to-cut-cost-of-new-nuclear-power-stations.

Department for Business, Energy and Industrial Strategy (BEIS). 'National Security and Investment Act 2021: Statement on the Use of the Power to Call in Acquisitions', 2 November 2021b, https://www.gov.uk/government/consultations/national-security-and-investment-act-2021-statement-on-the-use-of-the-power-to-call-in-acquisitions.

Department for Digital, Culture, Media and Sport (DCMS). *Future Telecoms Infrastructure Review*, 23 July 2018.

Department for Digital, Culture, Media and Sport (DCMS). *UK Telecoms Supply Chain Review Report*, July 2019.

Department for Digital, Culture, Media and Sport (DCMS). '5G Supply Chain Diversification Strategy'. *Guidance*, 7 December 2020, https://www.gov.uk/government/publications/5g-supply-chain-diversification-strategy/5g-supply-chain-diversification-strategy.

Department for Digital, Culture, Media and Sport, and Ministry of Defence. 'Written Evidence (SFG0026)' submitted to the House of Commons, *The Security of 5G*. Defence Committee, 22 September 2020.

Department for Exiting the European Union. 'Framework for the UK–EU Economic Partnership', 24 May 2018, https://www.gov.uk/government/publications/framework-for-the-uk-eu-economic-partnership.

Department for International Trade. *UK Defence and Security Export Statistics for 2018*, 30 July 2019.

Department for International Trade. 'Trade and Investment Factsheets: China', 18 June 2021, https://assets.publishing.service.gov.uk/government/uploads/system/uploads/attachment_data/file/993589/china-trade-and-investment-factsheet-2021-06-18.pdf (accessed on 1 December 2021).

Department for Trade and Industry. 'Explanatory Notes' on the 2002 Enterprise Act, 2002, https://www.legislation.gov.uk/ukpga/2002/40/notes/contents.

Embassy in Tokyo. 'UK Carrier Strike Group Flagship HMS Queen Elizabeth to Arrive in Japan', 3 September 2021, https://www.gov.uk/government/news/uk-carrier-strike-group-flagship-hms-queen-elizabeth-to-arrive-in-japan.

Foreign and Commonwealth Office. '1998 UK–China Joint Statement', in House of Commons, *Tenth Report: China*, Foreign Affairs Committee, 22 November 2000a, https://publications.parliament.uk/pa/cm199900/cmselect/cmfaff/574/57402.htm.
Foreign and Commonwealth Office. Memorandum Submitted to the House of Commons Select Committee on Foreign Affairs Memoranda, 30 October 2000b, https://publications.parliament.uk/pa/cm199900/cmselect/cmfaff/uc574iv/574m01.htm.
Foreign and Commonwealth Office. 'Written Evidence Submitted by the Foreign and Commonwealth Office', in House of Commons, *East Asia*, Foreign Affairs Committee, Vol. II, 2006.
Foreign and Commonwealth Office. 'Submission from the Foreign and Commonwealth Office', in House of Commons, *Global Security: Japan and South Korea*, Foreign Affairs Committee, HC 449, 12 November 2008.
Foreign and Commonwealth Office. *The UK and China: A Framework for Engagement*, 2009.
Foreign and Commonwealth Office. 'Agreement between the Government of the United Kingdom of Great Britain and Northern Ireland and the Government of Japan on the Security of Information', London, 4 July 2013a.
Foreign and Commonwealth Office. 'Treaty between the Government of the United Kingdom of Great Britain and Northern Ireland and the Government of Australia for Defence and Security Cooperation', Perth, 18 January 2013b.
Foreign and Commonwealth Office. 'UK–China Joint Statement on Building a Global Comprehensive Strategic Partnership for the 21st Century', 22 October 2015a.
Foreign and Commonwealth Office. 'Appendix: Memorandum from the Foreign and Commonwealth Office', in House of Commons, *Global Britain*, Foreign Affairs Committee, HC 780, 6 March 2018a.
Foreign and Commonwealth Office. 'The UK and Australia: A Dynamic Partnership for the 21st Century', 20 July 2018b.
Foreign and Commonwealth Office. 'UK–India Joint Statement: Shared Values, Global Capability', 18 April 2018c.
Foreign and Commonwealth Office. 'Written Evidence—Foreign and Commonwealth Office (FPW0027)', 28 February 2018d, data.parliament.uk/writtenevidence/committeeevidence.svc/evidencedocument/international-relations-committee/foreign-policy-in-changed-world-conditions/written/79900.html.
Foreign and Commonwealth Office. 'UK and Allies Reveal Global Scale of Chinese Cyber Campaign'. *Press Release*, 20 December 2018e.
Foreign and Commonwealth Office. 'Written Evidence from the Foreign and Commonwealth Office (CIR0018)', in response to House of Commons, *China and the International Rules-Based System*, Foreign Affairs Committee, HC 612, 15 January 2019a.
Foreign and Commonwealth Office. 'Written Evidence', in House of Commons, *Global Britain and India*, Foreign Affairs Committee, HC 1465, 19 March 2019b.
Foreign and Commonwealth Office. 'E3 Joint Statement on the Situation in the South China Sea'. *Press Release*, 29 August 2019c.
Foreign and Commonwealth Office. 'Written Evidence from the Foreign and Commonwealth Office (CIR0031)', in response to House of Commons, *China and the International Rules-Based System*, Foreign Affairs Committee, HC 612, February 2019d.
Foreign and Commonwealth Office. 'UK–ASEAN Factsheet', 6 January 2020, https://www.gov.uk/government/publications/uk-asean-factsheet.
Foreign and Commonwealth Office, Ministry of Defence, and Prime Minister's Office. 'UK–India Defence and International Security Partnership', 12 November 2015b, https://www.gov.uk/government/news/uk-india-defence-and-international-security-partnership.

Foreign and Commonwealth Office and Department of International Trade. 'Building Prosperity and Supporting Security in South East Asia', 8 January 2016.

Her Majesty's Government. *The UK National Strategy for Maritime Security*, 2014.

Her Majesty's Government. *National Security Strategy and Strategic Defence and Security Review*, 2015.

Her Majesty's Government. 'Britain's Royal Air Force in Malaysia for Exercise Bersama Lima'. *Press Release*, 4 October 2016, https://www.gov.uk/government/news/britains-royal-air-force-in-malaysia-for-exercise-bersama-lima.

Her Majesty's Government. *National Security Capability Review*, March 2018a.

Her Majesty's Government. 'Appendix: Memorandum from the Foreign and Commonwealth Office', in House of Commons, *Global Britain*, Foreign Affairs Committee, HC 780, 6 March 2018b.

Her Majesty's Government. 'UK Foreign Policy in a Shifting World Order', Government Response to the House of Lords Select Committee on International Relations, 2018c.

Her Majesty's Government. *The Future Relationship between the United Kingdom and the European Union*, July 2018d.

Her Majesty's Government. 'FPDA Defence Ministers' Joint Statement', *Press Release*, 27 November 2020, https://www.gov.uk/government/news/fpda-defence-ministers-joint-statement.

Her Majesty's Government. *Global Britain in a Competitive Age: The Integrated Review of Security, Defence, Development and Foreign Policy*, Presented to Parliament by the Prime Minister, March 2021.

Her Majesty's Treasury. 'Asian Infrastructure Investment Bank (AIIB) Special Fund'. *Guidance*, 30 September 2019a.

Her Majesty's Treasury. *AIIB Special Fund Business Case*, 30 September 2019b.

Huawei Cyber Security Evaluation Centre (HCSEC). *Annual Report*, March 2015.

Huawei Cyber Security Evaluation Centre (HCSEC). *Annual Report*, March 2019.

Huawei Cyber Security Evaluation Centre (HCSEC). *Annual Report*, July 2020.

Minister of State for Trade Policy, Greg Hands. Explanatory Memorandum-Communication from the Commission. 'Welcoming Foreign Direct Investment While Protecting Essential Interests', 5 October 2017, p. 5, https://www.parliament.uk/documents/lords-committees/eu-external-affairs-subcommittee/foreign-direct-investment/EM-foreign-direct-investment.pdf.

Minister of State for Trade Policy, George Hollingbery. 'EU Investment Screening Regulation'. Letter to the Chair of the European Scrutiny Committee, 19 December 2018.

Ministry of Defence. *Annual Location Statistics for UK Regular Service and Civilian Personnel*, https://assets.publishing.service.gov.uk/government/uploads/system/uploads/attachment_data/file/998488/Annual_location_statistics_1_April_2021.xlsx (accessed 1 November 2021).

Ministry of Defence. 'Joint Exercises: Written Question—32484'. House of Commons, 2016a, https://www.parliament.uk/business/publications/written-questions-answers-statements/written-question/Commons/2016-03-24/32484.

Ministry of Defence. 'Britain Extends Global Defence Reach', 12 December 2016b, https://www.gov.uk/government/news/britain-extends-global-defence-reach.

Ministry of Defence. 'Joint Statement: India–UK Defence Partnership', 13 April 2017a.

Ministry of Defence. 'New Level of Australia–United Kingdom Defence Industry Partnership', 28 July 2017b, https://www.minister.defence.gov.au/minister/christopher-pyne/media-releases/new-level-australia-united-kingdom-defence-industry.

Ministry of Defence. *Global Strategic Trends: The Future Starts Today*, 2018.

Ministry of Defence. 'Written Evidence Submitted to the House of Commons', in response to House of Commons, *UK Defence and the Far East*, Defence Committee, HC 2035, 13 June 2019a.
Ministry of Defence. *Annual Report and Accounts, 2018–2019*, 31 March 2019b.
Ministry of Defence. 'Five Eyes Defence Ministers' Meeting'. *News Story*, 23 June 2020.
Ministry of Defence. *Defence in a Competitive Age*, Presented to Parliament by the Secretary of State for Defence, March 2021.
National Audit Office. *The Equipment Plan 2019 to 2029*, 27 February 2020a.
National Audit Office. *Defence Capabilities: Delivering What Was Promised*, 18 March 2020b.
National Cyber Security Centre. 'APT10 Continuing to Target UK Organisations'. *Alert*, 20 December 2018.
National Cyber Security Centre. 'NCSC Advice on the Use of Equipment from High-Risk Vendors in UK Telecoms Networks'. *Guidance*, 28 January 2020a.
National Cyber Security Centre. 'Summary of the NCSC Analysis of May 2020 US Sanction'. *Report*, 14 July 2020b.
National Cyber Security Centre. 'A Different Future for Telecoms in the UK'. *Blog Post*, 14 July 2020c.
National Cyber Security Centre's Technical Director, Ian Levy. 'The Future of Telecoms in the UK'. *Blog Post*, 28 January 2020.
National Security Adviser, Sir Mark Sedwill, in Joint Committee on the National Security Strategy. *Oral Evidence: Work of the National Security Adviser*, HC 625, 28 January 2019.
Office for National Statistics. 'Foreign Direct Investment Involving UK Companies: 2019', 21 December 2020, https://www.ons.gov.uk/economy/nationalaccounts/balanceofpayments/bulletins/foreigndirectinvestmentinvolvingukcompanies/2019.
Parliament. 'Joint Exercises: Question for Ministry of Defence'. Questions and Answers, 24 March 2016, https://questions-statements.parliament.uk/written-questions/detail/2016-03-24/32484.
Permanent Mission of the UK to the United Nations. 'Note verbale' No. 162/20 to the UN Commission on the Limits of the Continental Shelf, New York, 16 September 2020.
Prime Minister's Office. 'Japan–UK Joint Declaration on Security Cooperation', 31 August 2017, https://www.gov.uk/government/publications/japan-uk-joint-declaration-on-security-cooperation.
Prime Minister's Office. 'UK–France Summit Communiqué'. Royal Military Academy Sandhurst, 18 January 2018.
Prime Minister's Office. 'The Queen's Speech 2019: Background Briefing Notes', 19 December 2019.
Prime Minister's Office. 'UK, US and Australia Launch New Security Partnership', 15 September 2021, https://www.gov.uk/government/news/uk-us-and-australia-launch-new-security-partnership.
Royal Air Force. 'Closing Ceremony Held for Exercise Bersama Lima in Malaysia', 21 October 2019, https://www.raf.mod.uk/news/articles/closing-ceremony-held-for-exercise-bersama-lima-in-malaysia/.
Royal Navy. 'HMS Daring Welcomed Home by Philippines Officials', 28 February 2014, https://www.gov.uk/government/news/hms-daring-welcomed-home-by-philippines-officials.
Royal Navy, Japan Maritime Self-Defence Force, and US Navy. '2016 Trilateral Maritime Talks', 20 October 2016.

Royal Navy. 'Search for MH370', 2017, https://webarchive.nationalarchives.gov.uk/+/ http://www.royalnavy.mod.uk/news-and-latest-activity/operations/indian-ocean/mh370-search.

Royal Navy. 'HMS Argyll Shows Firepower on Exercise Bersama Lima', 18 October 2018, https://www.royalnavy.mod.uk/news-and-latest-activity/news/2018/october/18/181018-argyll-firepower-ex-bersama-lima.

Royal Navy. 'HMS Argyll's US Navy Link-Up in South China Sea', 16 January 2019, https://www.royalnavy.mod.uk/news-and-latest-activity/news/2019/january/16/190116-argylls-us-link-up-south-china-sea.

Secretary of State for Foreign and Commonwealth Affairs Robin Cook, in House of Commons, *Examination of Witnesses—Minutes of Evidence*. Select Committee on Foreign Affairs, 7 June 2020.

UK Environment Agency. 'Consultation Launched on New Nuclear Power Station Design Proposed for UK'. *Press Release*, 11 January 2021.

UK Space Agency. 'Britain and Australia Enter into Space Agreement'. *News Story*, 3 October 2018.

UK Space Agency. 'UK Space Sector Lands in Singapore', 3 February 2020.

UK Trade and Investment (UKTI). 'Written Evidence Submitted by UKTI', in House of Commons, *East Asia*, Foreign Affairs Committee, Vol. I, 2006.

Williams, Richard. Written Evidence Submitted in Response to House of Commons, in *UK Defence and the Far East*. Defence Committee, HC 2035, 13 June 2019, http://data.parliament.uk/writtenevidence/committeeevidence.svc/evidencedocument/defence-committee/uk-defence-in-the-asiapacific-region/written/103172.html.

United States

Central Intelligence Agency. *The World Factbook 2008* (Washington, DC: US Government Printing Office, 2008).

Department of Commerce. 'Export Administration Regulations: Amendments to General Prohibition Three (Foreign-Produced Direct Product Rule) and the Entity List'. *Federal Register*, 19 May 2020a.

Department of Commerce. 'Commerce Addresses Huawei's Efforts to Undermine Entity List, Restricts Products Designed and Produced with U.S. Technologies'. *Press Release*, 15 May 2020b.

Department of Defence. 'DoD Annual Freedom of Navigation (FON) Reports', https://policy.defense.gov/ousdp-offices/fon/ (accessed 2 June 2021).

Department of Defence. *Indo-Pacific Strategy Report*, 1 June 2019.

Department of Justice. 'US Nuclear Engineer, China General Nuclear Power Company and Energy Technology International Indicted in Nuclear Power Conspiracy against the United States'. Office of Public Affairs—News, 14 April 2016.

Department of State. 'The Clean Network', https://2017-2021.state.gov/the-clean-network/index.html.

Government Accountability Office (GAO). *Foreign Investment: Laws and Policies Regulating Foreign Investment in 10 Countries*. GAO-08-320, February 2008.

US Indo-Pacific Command. 'Western Pacific Naval Symposium Nations Begin Diving Exercise in Guam', *News*, 8 June 2017, https://www.pacom.mil/Media/News/News-Article-View/Article/1208639/western-pacific-naval-symposium-nations-begin-diving-exercise-in-guam.

US Navy. 'Multinational Naval Forces Conduct Exercise La Perouse', 6 April 2021, https://www.navy.mil/Press-Office/News-Stories/Article/2562180/multinational-naval-forces-conduct-exercise-la-perouse/.

The White House. 'Executive Order on Securing the Information and Communications Technology and Services Supply Chain', 15 May 2019.

The White House. 'Remarks by President Biden, Prime Minister Morrison of Australia, and Prime Minister Johnson of the United Kingdom Announcing the Creation of AUKUS'. *Briefing Room*, 15 September 2021a, https://www.whitehouse.gov/briefing-room/speeches-remarks/2021/09/15/remarks-by-president-biden-prime-minister-morrison-of-australia-and-prime-minister-johnson-of-the-united-kingdom-announcing-the-creation-of-aukus/.

The White House. 'Background Press Call on AUKUS'. *Briefing Room*, 15 September 2021b, https://www.whitehouse.gov/briefing-room/press-briefings/2021/09/15/background-press-call-on-aukus.

The White House. 'Joint Statement on the Phone Call between President Biden and President Macron'. *Briefing Room*, 22 September 2021c, https://www.whitehouse.gov/briefing-room/statements-releases/2021/09/22/joint-statement-on-the-phone-call-between-president-biden-and-president-macron/.

International and Regional Organizations

Association of Southeast Asian Nations (ASEAN). 'ASEAN-EU Plan of Action 2018–2022', 6 August 2017.

Association of Southeast Asian Nations (ASEAN). 'Ambassador of the United Kingdom of Great Britain and Northern Ireland to ASEAN Presents Credentials', 28 November 2019, https://asean.org/ambassador-of-the-united-kingdom-of-great-britain-and-northern-ireland-to-asean-presents-credentials.

Association of Southeast Asian Nations (ASEAN). *Outlook on the Indo-Pacific*, June 2021, https://asean.org/speechandstatement/asean-outlook-on-the-indo-pacific/.

Indian Ocean Rim Association (IORA). 'Dialogue Partners', https://www.iora.int/en/about/dialogue-partners.

International Monetary Fund. *Balance of Payments and International Investment Position Manual*, 6th ed. (Washington, DC: IMF 2009).

North Atlantic Treaty Organization. 'Joint Declaration on EU-NATO Cooperation'. *Press Release*, 10 July 2018.

North Atlantic Treaty Organization. 'London Declaration', 4 December 2019, https://www.nato.int/cps/en/natohq/official_texts_171584.htm.

North Atlantic Treaty Organization. 'Relations with Partners across the Globe', https://www.nato.int/cps/en/natolive/topics_49188.htm.

North Atlantic Treaty Organization. *NATO 2030: United for a New Era: Analysis and Recommendations of the Reflection Group Appointed by the NATO Secretary General*, 25 November 2020, https://www.nato.int/nato_static_fl2014/assets/pdf/2020/12/pdf/201201-Reflection-Group-Final-Report-Uni.pdf.

Organisation for Economic Co-operation and Development (OECD). *OECD Benchmark Definition of Foreign Direct Investment* (Paris: OECD 2008), 4th edition.

Organisation for Economic Co-operation and Development (OECD). 'Freedom of Investment Process', Note by the Secretariat DAF/INV/WD (2009)14, 3 November 2009.

South Pacific Defence Ministers' Meeting (SPDMM). 'Joint Communiqué', 1 May 2015, https://png.embassy.gov.au/files/pmsb/150508%20SPDMM%20-Agreed%20Joint%20Communique.pdf.

South Pacific Defence Ministers' Meeting (SPDMM). 'Joint Communiqué', 8–10 May 2019.
United Nations. *What Is UN Comtrade?*, December 2020, https://unstats.un.org/unsd/tradekb/knowledgebase/what-is-un-comtrade (accessed on 1 December 2021).

Parliamentary Reports

European Union

European Parliament. *Challenges to Freedom of the Seas and Maritime Rivalry in Asia.* Directorate-General for External Policies Department, March 2017.
European Parliament. 'Defence: Member States' Spending'. Policy Department D for Budgetary Affairs, Briefing, May 2018.
European Parliament. *Report on the State of EU–China Relations.* Committee on Foreign Affairs, 7 October 2018.
European Parliament. 'A New EU International Procurement Instrument (IPI)'. *Legislative Train*, August 2021a.
European Parliament. 'MEPs Refuse Any Agreement with China Whilst Sanctions Are in Place'. *News*, 20 May 2021b, https://www.europarl.europa.eu/news/en/press-room/20210517IPR04123/meps-refuse-any-agreement-with-china-whilst-sanctions-are-in-place.
European Parliamentary Research Service (EPRS). 'State of Play of EU–China Relations'. *EPRS Briefing*, 2019.

France

National Assembly. *Stratégie de sécurité économique.* Committee on Finance, General Economy and the Plan, 9 June 2004.
National Assembly. *Les échanges commerciaux entre la Chine et la France.* Report no. 2473, Committee on Finance, General Economics and the Plan, 13 July 2005a.
National Assembly. *Participation de capitaux étrangers aux industries européennes de l'armement*, no. 2022. Committee on National Defence and Armed Forces, 23 March 2005b.
National Assembly. *Report by the Delegation of the France–China Friendship Group*, August 2010, https://www.assemblee-nationale.fr/13/pdf/rap-dian/dian003-2012.pdf (accessed 2 June 2010).
National Assembly. *La place de la France en Inde.* Report no. 4187, Committee on Foreign Affairs, 18 January 2012.
National Assembly. *Chine.* Report No. 1597, Committee on Foreign Affairs, 4 December 2013.
National Assembly. *Rapport sur La Proposition de Loi visant à préserver les intérêts de la défense et de la sécurité nationale de la France dans le cadre de l'exploitation des réseaux radioélectriques mobiles.* Report no. 1832, Economic Affairs Committee, 13 April 2018a.
National Assembly. *Cyberdéfense.* Report no. 1141, Committee on National Defence and Armed Forces, 4 July 2018b.
National Assembly. *Enjeux stratégiques en mer de Chine méridionale.* Report no. 1868, Committee on Foreign Affairs, 10 April 2019a.
National Assembly. *Compte rendu no. 31.* Committee on National Defence and the Armed Forces, 2 April 2019b.
National Assembly. *Défense : préparation de l'avenir (Annexe no. 13).* Report no. 2301, Committee on Finance, General Economy and Budgetary Control, 21 January 2021.

National Assembly. *L'espace indopacifique : enjeux et stratégie pour la France*, Committee on Foreign Affairs, Report no. 5041, 2022.

Parliamentary Delegation on Intelligence. *L'activité de la délégation parlementaire au renseignement pour l'année 2019–2020*, 11 June 2020.

Parliamentary Office on the Evaluation of Scientific and Technological Choices (OPECST). *Perspectives technologiques ouvertes par la 5G*. Compte rendu de l'audition publique, 8 November 2018.

Senate. *L'Agence française pour les investissements internationaux (AFII)*. Report no. 453, 5 July 2006.

Senate. *Cyberdéfense*. Report no. 449, Committee on Foreign Affairs, Defence and Armed Forces, 8 July 2008.

Senate. *Cyberdéfense*. Report no. 681, Committee on Foreign Affairs, Defence and Armed Forces, 18 July 2012a.

Senate. *Projet de loi de finances pour 2013 – Défense : équipement des forces*, 22 november 2012b, www.senat.fr/rap/a12-150-8/a12-150-812.html.

Senate. *La France face à l'émergence de l'Asie du Sud-Est*. Report no. 723, Committee on Foreign Affairs, Defence and Armed Forces, 14 July 2014a.

Senate. *Reprendre pied en Asie du Sud-Est*. Report no. 723, Committee on Foreign Affairs, Defence and Armed Forces, 2014b.

Senate. *Zones économiques exclusives ultramarines*. Report no. 430, 9 April 2014c.

Senate. *Australie : quelle place pour la France dans le Nouveau monde ?*. Report no. 222, Committee on Foreign Affairs, Defence and Armed Forces, 2016.

Senate. *Rapport sur la proposition de loi, adoptée par l'Assemblée nationale après engagement de la procédure accélérée, visant à préserver les intérêts de la défense et de la sécurité nationale de la France dans le cadre de l'exploitation des réseaux radioélectriques mobiles*. Report no. 579, Economic Affairs Committee, 19 June 2019a.

Senate. *Souveraineté numérique*. Report no. 7, Inquiry Commission on Digital Sovereignty, 1 October 2019b.

Senate. *La sécurité informatique des pouvoirs publics*, Report no. 82, Finance Committee, 22 October 2019c.

Senate. *"'Loi 5G" : mission accomplie pour la commission des affaires étrangères et de la défense du Sénat, l'application de la "loi 5G" remplit bien son objectif : réduire l'exposition des réseaux 5G au risque de sécurité'*. Press Release, 19 November 2020a, https://www.senat.fr/presse/cp20201119b.html.

Senate. *Direction de l'action du gouvernement*. Report no. 140, Committee on Foreign Affairs, Defence and Armed Forces, 19 November 2020b.

Senate. *Les influences étatiques extra-européennes dans le monde universitaire et académique français et leurs incidences*. Report no. 873, 29 September 2021

Germany

Parliamentary Commissioner for the Armed Forces. *Annual Report to the Bundestag—2017*, 20 February 2018.

Parliamentary Commissioner for the Armed Forces. *Annual Report to the Bundestag—2019*, 28 February 2020.

United Kingdom

House of Commons. *China and Hong Kong*. House of Commons Hansard, Vol. 258, 27 April 1995.

House of Commons. 'Written Answers—Ocean Wave 97', 24 February 1997, House of Commons Hansard, Vol 291, https://api.parliament.uk/historic-hansard/written-answers/1997/feb/24/ocean-wave-97.

House of Commons. 'Written Answers: Military Exercises 1999', 4 March 1999, Vol. 326, cc 866–7W 866W, https://api.parliament.uk/historic-hansard/written-answers/1999/mar/04/military-exercises.

House of Commons. *Tenth Report: China*. Foreign Affairs Committee, 22 November 2000, https://publications.parliament.uk/pa/cm199900/cmselect/cmfaff/574/57402.htm (accessed 2 June 2020).

House of Commons. *Draft Enterprise Act 2002 (Protection of Legitimate Interests) Order 2003 and Draft Enterprise Act 2002 (Anticipated Mergers) Order 2003*. Third Standing Committee on Delegated Legislation, 21 May 2003.

House of Commons. *East Asia*. Foreign Affairs Committee, Vol. I. HC 860–I, 2006a.

House of Commons. *East Asia*. Foreign Affairs Committee, Vol. II. HC 860–II, 2006b.

House of Commons. *UK/US Defence Trade Cooperation Treaty*. Defence Committee, HC107, 4 December 2007.

House of Commons. *Global Security: Japan and South Korea*. Foreign Affairs Committee, HC 449, 12 November 2008.

House of Commons. Written Answers to Questions—Column 1282W. *Daily Hansard*, 6 June 2013.

House of Commons. *Government Foreign Policy towards the United States*. Foreign Affairs Committee, 25 March 2014, https://publications.parliament.uk/pa/cm201314/cmselect/cmfaff/695/69502.htm (accessed 2 June 2021).

House of Commons. *Flexible Response? An SDSR Checklist of Potential Threats and Vulnerabilities*. Defence Committee, HC 493, 17 November 2015.

House of Commons. 'The Government's Decision to Support Hinkley Point C'. Public Accounts Committee, 20 November 2017, https://publications.parliament.uk/pa/cm201719/cmselect/cmpubacc/393/39306.htm.

House of Commons. *Global Britain*. Foreign Affairs Committee, HC 780, 6 March 2018.

House of Commons. *Oral Evidence: China and the International Rules-Based System*. Foreign Affairs Committee, HC 612, 15 January 2019a.

House of Commons. 'Belt and Road Initiative: China'. Question for Department for International Trade, 24 June 2019b, https://questions-statements.parliament.uk/written-questions/detail/2019-06-24/268527.

House of Commons. *Building Bridges: Reawakening UK–India Ties*. Foreign Affairs Committee, HC 1465, 11 June 2019c.

House of Commons and House of Lords, Joint Committee on the National Security Strategy. *Revisiting the UK's National Security Strategy: The National Security Capability Review and the Modernising Defence Programme*, 15 July 2019c.

House of Commons. 'DIT Screening of Foreign Direct Investment'. *European Scrutiny Committee*, 29 January 2019d, https://publications.parliament.uk/pa/cm201719/cmselect/cmeuleg/301-li/30109.htm.

House of Commons. *UK Defence and the Far East*. Defence Committee, HC 2035, 17 May 2019e.

House of Commons. *The Security of 5G*. Defence Committee, HC 201, 22 September 2020a.

House of Commons. *Oral Evidence: The Security of 5G*. HC 201, 30 June 2020b.

House of Commons and House of Lords. *Revisiting the UK's National Security Strategy: The National Security Capability Review and the Modernising Defence Programme*. Joint Committee on the National Security Strategy, HC 2072, 15 July 2019.

House of Lords. *Oral Evidence: The UK's Security and Trade Relationship with China.* International Relations and Defence Committee, 9 June 2021, https://committees.parliament.uk/oralevidence/2329/html/.
House of Lords. *The UK and China's Security and Trade Relationship: A Strategic Void.* International Relations and Defence Committee, 10 September 2021.
Intelligence and Security Committee (ISC). *Annual Report 2007–2008*, March 2009.
Intelligence and Security Committee (ISC). *Annual Report 2009–2010*, March 2010.
Intelligence and Security Committee (ISC). *Foreign Involvement in the Critical National Infrastructure: The Implications for National Security.* Report Presented to Parliament by the Prime Minister on behalf of Her Majesty, June 2013.
Intelligence and Security Committee (ISC). 'Statement on 5G Suppliers'. *News Archive*, 19 July 2019, https://isc.independent.gov.uk/wp-content/uploads/2021/01/20190719_ISC_Statement_5GSuppliers_Web.pdf.
Intelligence and Security Commitee (ISC). *Annual Report 2018–2019*, 21 July 2020.
Joint Committee on the National Security Strategy. *Oral Evidence: Work of the National Security Adviser.* HC 625, 28 January 2019.

United States
Senate. *Bill Authorizing the Ratification of the CTBT.* Committee on Foreign Affairs, Defence and Armed Forces, Report no. 330, 1997–1998.

Oral Testimonies, Speeches, and Interviews

European Union
European Union High Representative/Vice-President Federica Mogherini. Remarks at the Press Conference Following the Informal Meeting of EU Defence Ministers, 29 August 2019.
President of the European Commission Jean-Claude Juncker. State of the Union Address, 13 September 2017.

France
Chief of the Staff of the Navy Admiral Christophe Prazuck. Testimony before the National Assembly's Committee on National Defence and Armed Forces, 26 July 2017.
Chief of the Staff of the Navy Christophe Prazuck. Testimony before the National Assembly's Committee on National Defence and Armed Forces, 3 October 2019.
Errera, Philippe. 'Présentation de la politique de défense et de sécurité'. Speech at the Hôtel de la Marine, 10 April 2014.
Jospin, Lionel. Address to the Institute for Higher National Defence Studies, Paris, 22 October 1999.
Minister of the Armed Forces Sylvie Goulard. Speech at the Shangri-La Dialogue, Singapore, 3 June 2017.
Minister of the Armed Forces Florence Parly. Speech at the Shangri-La Dialogue, Singapore, 3 June 2018.
Minister of Defence Jean-Yves Le Drian. Speech at the Shangri-La Dialogue, Singapore, 5 June 2016a.
Minister of Defence Jean-Yves Le Drian. Speech on Cyber-defence, Bruz (Ille-et-Vilaine, France), 12 December 2016b.

Minister of Foreign Affairs Jean-Yves Le Drian. Testimony before the National Defence and Armed Forces Committee, National Assembly, 6 October 2021.
Minister for the Economy and Finance Bruno Le Maire. Speech, 15 January 2018, https://www.vie-publique.fr/discours/204733-declaration-de-m-bruno-le-maire-ministre-de-leconomie-et-des-finances.
Minister of Foreign Affairs Hervé de Charette, in Session of the Senate, 31 October 1996, https://www.senat.fr/seances/s199610/s19961031/s19961031_mono.html.
President Jacques Chirac. Speech in Singapore, 29 February 1996.
President Jacques Chirac. Interview with the New China Agency (Xinhua), 14 May 1997a.
President Jacques Chirac. Speech in Beijing, 15 May 1997b.
President's Office. 'Discours à Garden Island', Sydney, Australia, 3 May 2018.
President Emmanuel Macron. Speech at the Conference of Ambassadors, 27 August 2018 https://www.elysee.fr/emmanuel-macron/2018/08/27/discours-du-president-de-la-republique-a-la-conference-des-ambassadeurs.
President Emmanuel Macron. Speech at the Conference of Ambassadors, 27 August 2019, https://basedoc.diplomatie.gouv.fr/vues/Kiosque/FranceDiplomatie/kiosque.php?fichier=bafr2019-08-28.html#Chapitre6.
President Emmanuel Macron. Speech on the Defence and Deterrence Strategy, 7 February 2020, https://www.elysee.fr/en/emmanuel-macron/2020/02/07/speech-of-the-president-of-the-republic-on-the-defense-and-deterrence-strategy.
President Emmanuel Macron. Interview with the think tank Atlantic Council, 5 February 2021, https://www.elysee.fr/en/emmanuel-macron/2021/02/05/emmanuel-macron-president-of-the-french-republic-gave-an-interview-to-the-american-think-tank-atlantic-council.

Germany

Commissioner for Disarmament and Arms Control Friedrich Gröning. Opening Speech at the ASEAN Regional Forum Workshop on 'Confidence-Building Measures and Preventive Diplomacy in Asia and Europe', 13 March 2008.
Counsellor for Asia and Security Policy at the German Embassy in the United States Joern Beissert. 'The China Challenge'. Speech at the University of North Carolina at Chapel Hill, 20 September 2018, https://www.youtube.com/watch?v=Lz5RqjkHzmQ&list=PUPssYbwV8FFSw_ZbhBV5X3Q&index=83.
Federal Chancellor Gerhard Schröder. 'Rede vor dem Deutschen Bundestag zum Waffenembargo gegen China', Berlin, 14 April 2005.
Federal Chancellor Angela Merkel. Speech during the Event Hosted by the Newspaper *Asahi Shimbun*, Tokyo, 9 March 2015.
Federal Chancellor Angela Merkel. Speech on the German Presidency of the Council of the EU 2020. European Parliament, Brussels, 8 July 2020.
Federal Government. 'Rede von Bundeskanzlerin Merkel beim Bergedorfer Gesprächskreis', 29 October 2015.
Federal Minister of Defence Ursula von der Leyen. Speech at Shangri-La Dialogue, Singapore, 3 June 2018.
Federal Minister of Defence Annegret Kramp-Karrenbauer. Speech at the Bundeswehr University Munich, 7 November 2019.
Federal Minister of Defence (since 2019) Annegret Kramp-Karrenbauer. Speech at the Presentation of the Steuben Schurz Media Award, 23 October 2020.

Federal Ministry of Economic Affairs (MFEA). 'Minister Zypries: President Juncker's Proposal for a European Industrial Policy Strategy Is an Important Signal for Europe as an Industrial Base'. *Press Release*, 13 September 2017.
Federal Foreign Minister Frank-Walter Steinmeier. 'China: Partner for a Forward-Looking Foreign Policy'. Speech at the Hasso Plattner Institute, 19 September 2007.
Federal Foreign Minister Frank-Walter Steinmeier. Speech at the Opening of the Hamburg Summit 'China Meets Europe'. Hamburg Chamber of Commerce, 10 September 2008.
Federal Foreign Minister Frank-Walter Steinmeier. Interview with the *Global Times Beijing*, 17 April 2014.
Federal Foreign Minister Guido Westerwelle. Speech at the CDU/CSU Conference on 'Asia's New Global Players', 13 June 2012a.
Federal Foreign Minister Guido Westerwelle. Article to Mark the 40th Anniversary of the Establishment of Diplomatic Relations with the People's Republic of China. *Frankfurter Allgemeine Zeitung*, 11 October 2012b.
Federal Foreign Minister Guido Westerwelle. 'Four Decades of Dynamic Development'. Interview with the *China Daily*, 11 October 2012c.
Federal Foreign Minister Heiko Maas. Speech at the National Graduate Institute for Policy Studies, Tokyo, Japan, 25 September 2018.
Federal Foreign Minister Heiko Maas. Speech at the Luncheon Held by the American Council on Germany (ACG) on 'Germany, Europe and the United States: A Strategic Partnership Facing New Challenges?', 1 April 2019a.
Federal Foreign Minister Heiko Maas. 'An Agenda for Peace and Security? Priorities for a Social Democratic Foreign Policy for the European Union and the United Nations'. Speech at the Friedrich-Ebert-Stiftung's Tiergarten Conference, 28 November 2019b.
Federal Foreign Minister Heiko Maas. 'European Digital Sovereignty Is Long Overdue: FM Maas Talks to *Die Zeit* Weekly Newspaper', 12 April 2019c.
Federal Foreign Minister Heiko Maas. Opening Address at the Virtual Annual Council Meeting of the European Council for Foreign Relations (ECFR), 29 June 2020a.
Federal Foreign Minister Heiko Maas. 'China ist Partner, Wettbewerber und Rivale'. Interview with *Redaktionsnetzwerk Deutschland*, 12 July 2020b.
Federal Foreign Minister Heiko Maas. Speech at the Opening of the Conference on Europe at the Federal Foreign Office, 2 March 2020c.
Federal Foreign Minister Heiko Maas. Speech on European Digital Sovereignty on the Occasion of the Opening of the Smart Country Convention of the German Association for Information Technology, Telecommunications, and New Media (Bitkom), 27 October 2020d.
Federal Foreign Minister Heiko Maas. Speech at the Ambassadors' Conference of the French Republic, 31 August 2020e.
Federal Foreign Minister Sigmar Gabriel. Speech at the 97th Liebesmahl of the German Asia-Pacific Business Association. Hamburg, 3 March 2017.
Federal Foreign Minister Sigmar Gabriel (2017–2018). Speech at the Munich Security Conference, 17 February 2018.
Federal Foreign Office. 'Maas: "Solutions to Many of the World's Problems Can Only Be Found by Working with China"', 12 November 2018.
Federal Foreign Office Commissioner for International Cyber Policy Norbert Riedel. 'Cyber Security as a Dimension of Security Policy'. Speech at Chatham House, London, 18 May 2015.
Federal Minister of State for Cultural and Educational Relations Maria Böhmer. Speech at the Second Business Forum on Digital Innovation, IT and Communications Technology. *Newsroom*, 30 September 2016.

Federal Minister of State Niels Annen. Opening Remarks at the SWP Conference on U.S. Foreign Policy under the Trump Administration, 19 February 2019.
Federal Minister of State for Europe Michael Roth. Speech at the Asia Pacific Lunch 'Europe at the Crossroads: The Challenges Europe Is Facing in 2017', 18 May 2017.
Federal Minister of State for Europe Michael Roth. 'The Security of our Citizens Is at Stake'. Published in *Der Spiegel*, 2 August 2020.
Secretary of State at the Federal Foreign Office Antje Leendertse. Inaugural Address to the Cyber Security Summit, Berlin, 26 November 2019.
State Secretary at the Federal Foreign Office Andreas Michaelis. 'Welcome Remarks at the Regional Ambassadors' Conference on ASEAN', 22 May 2019.
State Secretary at the Federal Foreign Office Andreas Michaelis. 'Keynote Speech: EU Retreat on China: A Strategic Approach for Dealing with China'. *Federal Foreign Office News Room*, 2 March 2020.
State Secretary at the Federal Foreign Office Stephan Steinlein. 'Speech at the Asia-Pacific Conference of German Business: "Political Stability and Security in Asia-Pacific"'. Ho Chi Minh City, 22 November 2014.
Vice Admiral Kay-Achim Schönbach. 'The Future of Indo-Pacific Maritime Security'. Speech by the German Chief of Navy, 42nd IISS Fullerton Lecture, 21 December 2021, https://www.iiss.org/events/2021/12/42nd-iiss-fullerton-lecture.

United Kingdom

Chancellor of the Exchequer Philip Hammond. Speech at the Belt and Road Forum, 26 April 2019.
Chief Executive Officer of the National Cyber Security Centre Ciaran Martin, in House of Commons. *Oral Evidence: The Security of 5G*, 30 June 2020.
First Sea Lord Admiral Sir Philip Jones. Speech at the DSEI Maritime Conference, 11 September 2017.
Foreign and Commonwealth Office. 'Chancellor: "Let's Create a Golden Decade for the UK–China Relationship"'. *Speech*, 22 September 2015.
Foreign and Commonwealth Office's Asia-Pacific Director Stephen Lillie. 'The United Kingdom and the Asia-Pacific Region'. Speech at the Carnegie Endowment in Washington, DC, 15 March 2016.
Minister of State at the Foreign and Commonwealth Office Baroness Chalker of Wallasey, in House of Commons, *China: Arms Sales Embargo*. House of Commons Hansard, WA11, 4 April 1995.
Minister of State for Asia and the Pacific Mark Field. 'The UK and All-of-Asia: A Modern Partnership'. Speech at the Center for Strategic and International Studies, Jakarta, 14 August 2018.
Minister of State for Asia and the Pacific Mark Field, in House of Commons, *China and the International Rules-Based System*. Foreign Affairs Committee, HC 612, 15 January 2019a.
Minister of State for Asia and the Pacific Mark Field, in House of Commons Hansard, Westminster Hall, Foreign Affairs Committee, Vol. 657, 4 April 2019b.
Minister of State for Asia at the Foreign and Commonwealth Office Nigel Adams, in House of Lords, *Oral Evidence: The UK's Security and Trade Relationship with China*. International Relations and Defence Committee, 9 June 2021, https://committees.parliament.uk/oralevidence/2329/html/.
Minister of State for the Armed Forces Nick Harvey. Speech at the Shangri-La Dialogue, Singapore, 3 June 2012.

Minister of state for International Defence and Security Baroness Ann Taylor. Speech at the Shangri-La Dialogue, Singapore, 31 May 2009.

Parliamentary Under-Secretary of State for Foreign and Commonwealth Affairs Denis MacShane, in House of Commons. *China*. House of Commons Hansard, Vol. 387, 18 June 2002, https://publications.parliament.uk/pa/cm200102/cmhansrd/vo020618/halltext/20618h01.htm.

Parliamentary Under-Secretary of State for Trade and Industry Melanie Johnson, in House of Commons. *Draft Enterprise Act 2002 (Protection of Legitimate Interests) Order 2003 and Draft Enterprise Act 2002 (Anticipated Mergers) Order 2003*. Third Standing Committee on Delegated Legislation, 21 May 2003.

Parliamentary Under-Secretary of State (Minister for Exports), Department for International Trade Graham Stuart, in House of Lords, *Oral Evidence: The UK's Security and Trade Relationship with China*. International Relations and Defence Committee, 9 June 2021, https://committees.parliament.uk/oralevidence/2329/html/.

Prime Minister Theresa May. Speech to the Lord Mayor's Banquet 2017, 13 November 2017.

Secretary of State for Defence Liam Fox. Speech at the Shangri-La Dialogue, Singapore, 4 June 2011.

Secretary of State for Defence Philip Hammond. Speech at the Shangri-La Dialogue, Singapore, 31 May 2014.

Secretary of State for Defence Michael Fallon. Speech at the Shangri-La Dialogue, Singapore, 30 May 2015.

Secretary of State for Defence Michael Fallon. Speech at the Shangri-La Dialogue, Singapore, 4 June 2016.

Secretary of State for Defence Gavin Williamson, in House of Commons, *Defence*, House of Commons Hansard, Volume 648, 22 October 2018a.

Secretary of State for Defence Gavin Williamson. Speech at the Shangri-La Dialogue, Singapore, 3 June 2018b.

Secretary of State for Defence, the Rt Hon Ben Wallace MP, in House of Commons, *Oral Evidence: The Security of 5G*, 30 June 2020.

Secretary of State for Digital, Culture, Media and Sport Oliver Dowden. Statement on Telecoms to the House of Commons, 14 July 2020, https://www.gov.uk/government/speeches/digital-culture-media-and-sport-secretarys-statement-on-telecoms.

Secretary of State for Digital, Culture, Media and Sport Baroness Nicky Morgan. Oral Statement to Parliament on UK Telecommunications, 28 January 2020, https://www.gov.uk/government/speeches/baroness-morgans-oral-statement-on-uk-telecommunications.

Secretary of State for Foreign and Commonwealth Affairs William Hague. 'Britain in Asia'. Speech, 26 April 2012, https://www.gov.uk/government/speeches/britain-in-asia.

Secretary of State for Foreign and Commonwealth Affairs Philip Hammond. 'China: Diplomatic and Economic Relations', in House of Commons Hansard, *China: Diplomatic and Economic Relations*, Oral Answers to Questions, Vol. 604, 12 January 2016.

Secretary of State for Foreign and Commonwealth Affairs Jeremy Hunt, in House of Lords, *Corrected Oral Evidence—UK Foreign Policy in Changed World Conditions*. Select Committee on International Relations, 15 November 2018a, http://data.parliament.uk/writtenevidence/committeeevidence.svc/evidencedocument/international-relations-committee/foreign-policy-in-changed-world-conditions/oral/92531.html.

Secretary of State for Foreign and Commonwealth Affairs Jeremy Hunt, in House of Commons, 'Oral Evidence from the Foreign Secretary', HC 538, 31 October 2018b.

Secretary of State for International Trade Liam Fox. *Estimating the Economic Impact of FDI to Support the Department for International Trade's Promotion Strategy: Analytical Report*, Foreword, 2018.

United States

Assistant Secretary of Defence for Asian and Pacific Security Randall Schriver. Testimony before the Senate Foreign Relations Committee, 15 May 2018

Department of State. 'Secretary Antony J. Blinken and High Representative for Foreign Affairs Josep Borrell after their Meeting'. Remarks to the Press, 24 March 2021, https://www.state.gov/secretary-antony-j-blinken-and-high-representative-for-foreign-affairs-josep-borrell-after-their-meeting/.

Deputy Secretary of State Robert Zoellick. 'Whither China? From Membership to Responsibility'. Remarks to the National Committee on US–China Relations, New York City, 21 September 2005.

Secretary of State Michael R. Pompeo. 'A New Transatlantic Dialogue'. Speech at the German Marshall Fund's Brussels Forum, Washington, DC, 25 June 2020a.

Secretary of State Michael R. Pompeo. Remarks to the Press. Press Briefing Room, Washington, DC, 29 April 2020b.

Secretary of State Antony Blinken. 'Reaffirming and Reimagining America's Alliances'. Speech at NATO Headquarters Agora, Brussels, 24 March 2021.

Databases

American Enterprise Institute and Heritage Foundation. *China Global Investment Tracker*, https://www.aei.org/china-global-investment-tracker/.

Banque de France. *Foreign Direct Investment: Annual Series*, 17 June 2020, https://www.banque-france.fr/en/statistics/balance-payments/foreign-direct-investment/statistics/foreign-direct-investment-annual-series.

Banque de France. 'Flux d'investissements directs par pays et par secteur, données annuelles (2000-2020)', 2020, https://www.banque-france.fr/statistiques/balance-des-paiements-et-statistiques-bancaires-internationales/les-investissements-directs/investissements-directs-series-annuelles.

Deutsche Bundesbank. Direct Investments and Foreign Affiliates Statistics (FATS), https://www.bundesbank.de/en/statistics/external-sector/direct-investments.

European 5G Observatory. '5G trial', https://5gobservatory.eu/5g-trial/

European Commission. Community Research and Development Information Service (CORDIS), https://cordis.europa.eu.

National Bureau of Statistics of China. *Statistical Yearbooks of China*, http://www.stats.gov.cn/english/Statisticaldata/AnnualData/.

Office for National Statistics. *Foreign Direct Investment Involving UK Companies: 2019*, 21 December 2020, https://www.ons.gov.uk/economy/nationalaccounts/balanceofpayments/bulletins/foreigndirectinvestmentinvolvingukcompanies/2019.

Organisation for Economic Co-operation and Development (OECD). *FDI by Country and Economic Activity_BMD4 and Historical BMD3 Series*, https://stats.oecd.org/Index.aspx?QueryId=82888.

Organisation for Economic Co-operation and Development (OECD). 'FDI Regulatory Restrictiveness Index', https://www.oecd.org/investment/fdiindex.htm.

Stockholm International Peace Research Institute (SIPRI). 'Trade Register', https://www.sipri.org/databases/armstransfers.

Stockholm International Peace Research Institute (SIPRI). *SIPRI Arms Transfers Database.* Available online at https://www.sipri.org/databases/armstransfers.

Stockholm International Peace Research Institute (SIPRI). *Sources and Methods.* Available online at https://www.sipri.org/databases/armstransfers/sources-and-methods#TIV-tables.

United Nations. *UN Comtrade Database.* Available online at: https://comtrade.un.org/data/.

World Bank. 'World Development Indicators', https://databank.worldbank.org/source/world-development-indicators.

World Bank. 'World Integrated Trade Solutions (WITS)', https://wits.worldbank.org.

Secondary Sources

'Chinese Investments in Europe: German EU Commissioner Floats EU Veto Right'. *DW*, 24 March 2019.

'Five Eyes Intelligence Alliance Builds Coalition to Counter China'. *Reuters*, 12 October 2018.

'France Leads Naval Exercise with US, UK and Japan in American Territory of Guam in the Pacific'. *South China Morning Post*, 12 May 2017.

German Chamber of Commerce in China, *German Businesses in China: Business Confidence Survey 2019/2020.*

'German Chancellor Angela Merkel Urges Europe to Stick Together in China Dealings'. *The Straits Times*, 27 November 2019.

'German Ministers Agree Security Law with High Hurdles for Suppliers'. *Reuters*, 16 December 2020.

'Germany Demands More Free Trade Guarantees on China Silk Road Plan: Minister'. *Reuters*, 14 May 2017.

'German Prosecutors Close Case on NSA Spying Scandal'. *DW*, 5 October 2017.

'Huawei Opens Research Center in Paris'. *XinhuaNet*, 10 October 2020.

'Huawei Will Set up its French Factory in Brumath'. *Archyde*, 21 December 2020, https://www.archyde.com/huawei-will-set-up-its-french-factory-in-brumath.

'Japan, France and the United States Conducted a Joint Amphibious Exercise for the 1st Time'. *DefesaNet*, 1 June 2015.

'Japan, US, France Joint Military Drills Set for Kyushu in May'. *Nikkei Asia*, 23 April 2021.

'Jean-Yves Le Drian dénonce "un coup dans le dos" après la rupture du contrat des sous-marins par l'Australie'. France Info, 16 September 2021.

'Limited Number of Weapons in German Military Ready for Action: Report'. *DW News*, 27 February 2018.

'Macron Wants a Balance against China in the Pacific'. Radio New Zealand, 7 May 2018.

'Soupçonnée d'espionnage industriel, une étudiante chinoise est finalement condamnée pour "abus de confiance"'. *Le Monde*, 18 December 2007.

'Vietnam, Germany Expand Defense Cooperation'. *People's Army Newspaper*, 15 June 2019.

'UK Joins the ReCAAP'. ReCAAP, *Press Release*, 2 May 2012.

'UK Will Pay Price If It Carries out Decision to Exclude Huawei: China Daily Editorial'. *China Daily*, 25 May 2020.

'Value Added by the Manufacturing Sector as Percent of GDP in Europe—2019'. *The Global Economy*, https://www.theglobaleconomy.com/rankings/Share_of_manufacturing/Europe/#United-Kingdom (based on World Bank data).

Air & Cosmos International. 'RAF Typhoons Land in Japan for Bilateral Exercise', 24 October 2016, https://www.aircosmosinternational.com/article/raf-typhoons-land-in-japan-for-bilateral-exercise-1998.
'Airbus Celebrates Technology Transfer to China'. China.org, 1 April 2005, www.china.org.cn/english/scitech/124458.htm.
Airbus. 'Malaysia Takes Delivery of its First Airbus A400M'. Media, 10 March 2015.
Akagawa, Shogo. 'Germany to Send Naval Frigate to Japan with Eye on China'. *Nikkei Asia*, 25 January 2021.
Aldrich, Robert. *The French Presence in the South Pacific, 1842–1940* (Basingstoke: Macmillan, 1990).
Allen, Robert Loring and Jan Vansina. *Oral Tradition: A Study in Historical Methodology*, 2nd edition (Abingdon: Routledge, 2017).
Appia, David, President of the French Agency for International Investments (AFII). 'Les investissements chinois en France et en Europe, quel impact sur l'emploi ?', Proceedings of the Conference *Rencontres économiques : Quel impact de l'expansion chinoise sur l'économie mondiale ?*. Institute for Public Management and Economic Development (IGPDE), 18 September 2012.
Artaud, Denise and Laurence Kaplan, eds. *Diên Bien Phu: L'alliance atlantique et la défense du Sud-Est asiatique* (Lyon: La Manufacture, 1989).
Asia-Pacific Defence Reporter. 'Exercise Bersama Lima 2013—Boosting Regional Security', 11 August 2013, https://asiapacificdefencereporter.com/exercise-bersama-lima-2013-boosting-regional-security/.
BAE Systems. 'Hunter Class Frigates', https://www.baesystems.com/en-aus/what-we-do/hunter.
Ballantyne, Iain. *Strike from the Sea: The Royal Navy and US Navy at War in the Middle East* (Barnsley, UK: Pen & Sword Maritime, 2004).
Barber, Lionel. 'MI5 Head Shrugs off Risk to Intelligence Sharing from Huawei Links'. *Financial Times*, 12 January 2020.
Barry, Ben. 'Posturing and Presence: The United Kingdom and France in the Indo-Pacific'. *IISS Military Balance Blog*, 11 June 2021, https://www.iiss.org/blogs/military-balance/2021/06/france-uk-indo-pacific.
Barysch, Katinka, Charles Grant, and Mark Leonard. *Embracing the Dragon: The EU's Partnership with China* (London: Center for European Reform, 2005).
Bazoge, Mickaël. 'Interdiction des équipements Huawei : SFR et Bouygues Telecom réclament 2 milliards d'euros à l'État'. *iGeneration*, 30 November 2020.
Beckley, Michael. 'The Emerging Military Balance in East Asia: How China's Neighbours Can Check Chinese Naval Expansion'. *International Security* 42, no. 2 (2017): pp. 78–119.
Beckley, Michael and Hal Brands. 'Competition with China Could Be Short and Sharp'. *Foreign Affairs*, 17 December 2020.
Benbow, Tim. 'British Uses of Aircraft Carriers and Amphibious Ships: 1945–2010'. *Corbett Paper 9*, no. 1 (2012), https://www.kcl.ac.uk/dsd/assets/corbettpaper9.pdf.
Benhamou, Laurence and Patrick Baert. 'Macron Urges European Unity to Face Rising China'. *Space Daily*, 10 January 2018.
Benner, Thorsten et al. *Authoritarian Advance: Responding to China's Growing Political Influence in Europe* (Berlin: Global Public Policy Institute and Mercator Institute for China Studies, 2018).
Bentley, Zak. 'Chinese Investors End Controversial Toulouse Airport Reign with €500m Departure'. *Infrastructure Investor*, 3 January 2020, https://www.infrastructureinvestor.

com/chinese-investors-end-controversial-toulouse-airport-reign-with-e500m-departure/.

Berger, Axel. 'The China–EU Investment Agreement: Negotiations, Rationale, Motivations, and Contentious Issues', in *China, the EU, and International Investment Law: Reforming Investor-State Dispute Settlement*, edited by Yuwen Li, Tong Qi, and Cheng Bian (New York: Routledge, 2019), pp. 11–25.

Berger, Thomas U. 'The Past in the Present: Historical Memory and German National Security Policy'. *German Politics 6*, no. 1 (1997): pp. 39–59.

Bian, Shuwen and Oliver Emons. 'Chinese Investments in Germany: Increasing in Line with Chinese Industrial Policy', in *Chinese Investments in Europe: Corporate Strategies and Labour Relations*, edited by Jan Drahokoupil (Brussels: Europe Trade Union Institute, 2017), pp. 157–177.

Blainey, Geoffrey. *The Tyranny of Distance: How Distance Shaped Australia's History* (Sydney: Macmillan, 2001).

Blanchard, Jean-Marc F. 'The People's Republic of China Leadership Transition and its External Relations: Still Searching for Definitive Answers'. *Journal of Chinese Political Science 20*, no. 1 (2015): pp. 1–16.

Blanchard, Jean-Marc F. 'Helping Hands for Huawei: Dialing into China's Technology Policy to Understand its Contemporary Support for Huawei', in *Huawei Goes Global, Vol. I: Made in China for the World*, edited by Wenxian Zhang, Ilan Alon, and Christoph Lattemann (Cham, Switzerland: Palgrave Macmillan, 2020), pp. 65–85.

Boateng Agyenim, Wang Qian, and Yang Tianle. 'Cross-Border M&As by Chinese Firms: An Analysis of Strategic Motives and Performance'. *Thunderbird International Business Review 50*, no. 4 (2008): 259–270.

Boland, Bryce. 'The G20 and the New Reality of Cyber Espionage'. *FireEye*, 4 November 2014.

Bongiorno, Frank. 'British Empire: Australasia and Pacific', in *The Encyclopedia of Empire*: Vol. 4, edited by John MacKenzie (Chichester, UK: John Wiley & Sons, 2016), pp. 1–7.

Borger, Julian. 'David Miliband: China Ready to Join US as World Power'. *The Guardian*, 17 May 2009.

Bozo, Frédéric. *La politique étrangère de la France depuis 1945* (Paris: Flammarion, 2012).

Brakalova, Maria. 'Foreign Direct Investments in Germany—Germany Significantly Lowers Threshold to Veto Deals; FDI Screening Mechanism at European Level Is Coming Soon'. *JDSupra*, 20 December 2018.

Brakalova, Maria. 'Update on Foreign Direct Investments in Germany'. *Denton*, 18 February 2020.

Brattberg, Erik and Etienne Soula. 'Is Europe Finally Pushing back on Chinese Investments?'. *Carnegie Endowment for International Peace*, 14 September 2018, https://carnegieendowment.org/2018/09/14/is-europe-finally-pushing-back-on-chinese-investments-pub-77259.

Brattberg, Erik, et al. 'Can France and the UK Pivot to the Pacific?'. *Carnegie Endowment for International Peace*, 5 July 2018, https://carnegieendowment.org/2018/07/05/can-france-and-uk-pivot-to-pacific-pub-76732.

Brattberg, Erik and Philippe Le Corre. *The Case for Transatlantic Cooperation in the Indo-Pacific* (Washington, DC: Carnegie Endowment for International Peace, 2019).

Brattberg, Erik, Philippe Le Corre, Paul Stronski, Thomas de Waal. *China's Influence in Southeastern, Central, and Eastern Europe: Vulnerabilities and Resilience in Four Countries* (Washington, DC: Carnegie Endowment for International Peace, 2021).

Bräuner, Oliver, Mark Bromley, and Mathieu Duchâtel. *Western Arms Exports to China* (Stockholm: SIPRI, 2015).

Breslin, Shaun. 'Beyond Diplomacy? UK Relations with China Since 1997'. *The British Journal of Politics and International Relations* 6, no. 3 (2004): pp. 409–425.

Breslin, Shaun and Pan Zhongqi. 'Introduction: A Xi Change in Policy?. *The British Journal of Politics and International Relations* 23, no. 2 (2021), doi:10.1177/1369148121992499.

Brewster, Thomas. 'Huawei To Invest £1.3bn in UK'. *Silicon.co.uk*, 12 September 2012.

British Chamber of Commerce in China. *British Business in China: Position Paper*, 2020.

Brocheux, Pierre and Daniel Hémery. *Indochina: An Ambiguous Colonization, 1858–1954* (Berkeley, CA: University of California Press, 2009).

Brooke-Holland, Louisa. 'Royal Navy: A Return to the Far East?'. House of Commons Library, 24 May 2018, https://commonslibrary.parliament.uk/royal-navy-a-return-to-the-far-east/

Brooke-Holland, Louisa. 'Integrated Review: The Defence Tilt to the Indo-Pacific'. House of Commons Library, *Briefing Paper* no. 09217, 11 May 2021.

Brown, Kerry. 'Britain's Relations with China under New Labour: Engagement and Repulsion?', in *British Foreign Policy: The New Labour Years*, edited by Olivier Daddow and Jamie Gaskarth (New York: Palgrave Macmillan, 2011), pp. 170–187.

Brown, Kerry. *Erase and Rewind: Britain's Relations with China* (Sydney: The Australia–China Relations Institute, 2015).

Brown, Kerry. *The Future of UK–China Relations: The Search for a New Model* (London: Agenda Publishing, 2019).

Brown, Scott A. W. *Power, Perception and Foreign Policymaking: US and EU Responses to the Rise of China* (New York, NY: Routledge, 2018).

Browning, Steve and Oliver Bennett. 'National Security and Investment Bill 2019–2021'. House of Commons Library, *Briefing Paper*, 16 November 2020.

Bryan, Victoria and Gernot Heller. 'Germany Moves to Protect Key Companies from Chinese Investors'. *Reuters*, 27 July 2018.

Burghart, Nora and Vanessa Rossi. 'China's Overseas Direct Investment in the UK'. Chatham House, Programme Paper IE PP 2009/06, December 2009.

Burton, Joe. 'NATO's "Global Partners" in Asia: Shifting Strategic Narratives'. *Asian Security* 14, no. 1 (2017): pp. 1–16.

Business France. *Annual Report: Foreign Investment in France*, 2019.

Buzan, Barry and Yongjin Zhang. 'Introduction: Interrogating Regional International Society in East Asia', in *Contesting International Society in East Asia*, edited by Barry Buzan and Yongjin Zhang (Cambridge: Cambridge University Press, 2014), pp. 1–28.

Cabestan, Jean-Pierre. 'France's Taiwan Policy: A Case of Shopkeeper Diplomacy'. Paper presented at the conference The Role of France and Germany in Sino-European Relations. Hong Kong Baptist University, 22–23 June 2001.

Campbell, Kurt M. *The Pivot: The Future of American Statecraft in Asia* (New York: Basic Books, 2016).

Caputo, Victor J. 'US, UK, South Korean Air Forces Conduct Strategic Exercise'. US Air Force, 51st Fighter Wing Public Affairs, 8 November 2016, https://www.af.mil/News/Article-Display/Article/999020/us-uk-south-korean-air-forces-conduct-strategic-exercise/

Carbone, Maurizio. *The European Union in Africa: Incoherent Policies, Asymmetrical Partnership, Declining Relevance?* (New York: Palgrave Macmillan, 2013).

Carrai, Maria Adele. 'Chinese Political Nostalgia and Xi Jinping's Dream of Great Rejuvenation'. *International Journal of Asian Studies 18*, no. 1 (2020): pp. 1–19. doi:10.1017/S1479591420000406.
Casarini, Nicola. *Remaking Global Order: The Evolution of Europe–China Relations and its Implications for East Asia and the United States* (Oxford: Oxford University Press, 2009).
Casarini, Nicola, ed. *Brussels–Beijing: Changing the Game* (Paris: EUISS, 2013).
Casarini, Nicola. 'When All Roads Lead to Beijing: Assessing China's New Silk Road and its Implications for Europe', *The International Spectator 51*, no. 4 (2016): pp. 95–108.
Casarini, Nicola. 'Rising to the Challenge: Europe's Security Policy in East Asia amid US–China Rivalry'. *The International Spectator 55*, no. 1 (2020): pp. 78–92.
Cha, Victor D. *Powerplay: The Origins of the American Alliance System in Asia* (Princeton, NJ: Princeton University Press, 2016).
Chang Lao, Nien-chung. 'The Sources of China's Assertiveness: The System, Domestic Politics or Leadership Preferences?'. *International Affairs 92*, no. 4 (2016): pp. 817–833.
Charon, Paul and Jean-Baptiste Jeangène Vilmer. *Les opérations d'influence chinoises* (Paris: Institute for Strategic Research IRSEM, 2021).
Chatzky, Andrew and James McBride. 'China's Massive Belt and Road Initiative'. Council on Foreign Relations. *Backgrounder*, 28 January 2020.
Chazan, Guy. 'Germany Sets High Hurdle for Huawei'. *Financial Times*, 16 December 2020.
Chemillier-Gendreau, Monique. *La souveraineté sur les archipels Paracels et Spratleys* (Paris: L'Harmattan, 1996).
Chen, Dingding, Xiaoyu Pu, and Alastair Iain Johnston. 'Debating China's Assertiveness'. *International Security 38*, no. 3 (2014): pp. 176–183.
Cheung, Tai Ming. *Fortifying China: The Struggle to Build a Modern Defense Economy* (Ithaca, NY: Cornell University Press, 2009).
Cheung, Tai Ming. 'Innovation in China's Defense Technology Base: Foreign Technology and Military Capabilities'. *Journal of Strategic Studies 39*, no. 5–6 (2016): pp. 728–761.
Cheung, Tai Ming et al. *Planning for Innovation: Understanding China's Plans for Technological, Energy, Industrial, and Defense Development*. Report prepared for the US–China Economic and Security Review Commission, 28 July 2016.
Cheung, Tai Ming and Eric Hagt. 'China's Efforts in Civil-Military Integration, its Impact on the Development of China's Acquisition System, and Implications for the United States', in *Proceedings of the 16th Annual Acquisition Research Symposium—Vol. I* (Monterey, CA: Naval Postgraduate School, 2019), pp. 146–171.
China–Britain Business Council. *UK Jobs Dependent on Links to China* (Cambridge, UK: Cambridge Econometrics, 2020).
'China Sector Watch: Automobiles'. *China Briefing*, 29 May 2009, https://www.china-briefing.com/news/china-sector-watch-automobiles/
Christiansen, Thomas, Emil Kirchner, and Philomena B. Murray, eds. *The Palgrave Handbook of EU–Asia Relations* (London: Palgrave Macmillan, 2013).
Christiansen, Thomas, Emil Kirchner, and See Seng Tan. 'EU–Asia Security Relations—Cooperation against the Odds?'. Paper presented at the 16th Biennial Conference of EUSA, Denver, May 2019.
Christiansen, Thomas, Emil Kirchner, and See Seng Tan, eds. *The European Union's Security Relations with Asian Partners* (Cham, Switzerland: Palgrave Macmillan, 2021).
Christiansen, Thomas, Emil Kirchner, and Uwe Wissenbach. *The European Union and China* (London: Red Globe Press, 2019).
Chubb, Andrew. 'PRC Assertiveness in the South China Sea: Measuring Continuity and Change, 1970–2015'. *International Security 45*, no. 3 (2021): pp. 79–121.

Ciorciari, John D. *The Limits of Alignment: Southeast Asia and the Great Powers since 1975* (Washington, DC: Georgetown University Press, 2010).
City of London Corporation and The People's Bank of China. 'London RMB Business Quarterly', Issue 3, April 2019.
Coco, Orazio. 'German Imperialism in China: The Leasehold of Kiaochow Bay (1897–1914)'. *The Chinese Historical Review 26*, no. 2 (2019): pp. 156–174.
Collingridge, John and Jillian Ambrose. 'Ministers Close to Deal That Could End China's Role in UK Nuclear Power Station'. *The Guardian*, 25 September 2021.
Combined Maritime Force (CMF). 'CTF 151 Leads Focused Operation (FO) "DYNAMIC KHARIF" in Further Successful Collaboration with EU NAVFOR', 5 October 2017, at https://combinedmaritimeforces.com/2017/10/05/ctf-151-leads-focused-operation-fo-dynamic-kharif-in-further-successful-collaboration-with-eu-navfor/.
Cornish, Paul, Rex Hughes, and David Livingstone. 'Cyberspace and the National Security of the United Kingdom: Threats and Responses'. Chatham House, March 2009.
Cosnard, Denis. 'Le montage subtil de l'Elysée pour céder le contrôle des chantiers STX à Fincantieri'. *Le Monde*, 27 September 2017.
Cottey, Andrew. 'Europe and China's Sea Disputes: Between Normative Politics, Power Balancing and Acquiescence'. *European Security 28*, no. 4 (2019): pp 473–492.
Crepy, Sébastien and Nicolas Lovas. 'Foreign Investment Control in France: New Derogatory Regime Applicable to Foreign Investment in French Public Companies'. *Paul Hastings—Client Alerts*, 24 July 2020 https://www.paulhastings.com/insights/client-alerts/foreign-investment-control-in-france-new-derogatory-regime-applicable-to-foreign-investment-in-french-public-companies.
Cronin, Patrick M. et al. *Tailored Coercion: Competition and Risk in Maritime Asia* (Washington, DC: Center for New American Security, 2014).
Crookes, Paul Irwin, and John Farnell. 'The UK's Strategic Partnership with China beyond Brexit: Economic Opportunities Facing Political Constraints'. *Journal of Current Chinese Affairs 48*, no. 1 (2019): pp. 1–16.
Danninger, Stephan and Fred Joutz. 'What Explains Germany's Rebounding Export Market Share'. *IMF Working Paper*, WP/07/24, 2007.
Darby, Philip. *British Defence Policy East of Suez, 1947–1960* (New York: Oxford University Press, 1973).
Dassault Aviation. 'Indonesia purchases the Rafale'. Press Kit, 10 February 2022, https://www.dassault-aviation.com/en/group/press/press-kits/indonesia-purchases-the-rafale/
Datenna. 'China-EU FDI Radar', https://www.datenna.com/china-eu-fdi-radar/ (accessed 12 May 2021).
Davies, Rob. 'Government Criticised as Chinese Bid for Northern Aerospace Is Derailed'. *The Guardian*, 9 July 2018.
Débes, Florian and Fabienne Schmitt. '"Il n'y aura pas un bannisement total de Huawei", affirme le patron de l'Anssi'. *Les Echos*, 6 July 2020.
Debevoise & Plimpton. 'UK National Security and Investment Bill'. *Debevoise Update*, 23 November 2020.
De Briganti, Giovanni. 'DCNS Confirms Sale of 10 Gowind Corvettes, Expects More'. *Defense Aerospace*, 31 October 2014.
Defence Industry Daily Staff. 'Malaysia Ordering EC725 SAR Helicopters'. *Defence Industry Daily*, 3 June 2019.
D'Elia, Danilo. 'La guerre économique à l'ère du cyberespace'. *Hérodote 1*, no. 152–153 (2014): pp. 240–250.
Dempsey, Noel. 'UK Defence Industry Exports'. House of Commons Library, 18 May 2018.

De La Bruyère, Emily and Nathan Picarsic. *Made in Germany: Co-opted by China* (Washington, DC: Foundation for Defense of Democracies, 2020).
Denina, Clara and Ron Bousso. 'Neptune Nears Engie E&P Deal after CIC Ups Stake'. *Reuters*, 21 April 2017.
Deutsche Bundesbank. 'Direktinvestitionen und Auslandsunternehmenseinheiten (FATS)' https://www.bundesbank.de/de/statistiken/aussenwirtschaft/direktinvestitionen
Deutsche Bundesbank. 'Germany's External Relations with the People's Republic of China'. *Monthly Report*, July 2005.
Deutsche Bundesbank. 'German Foreign Direct Investment (FDI) Relationships: Recent Trends and Macroeconomic Effects'. *Monthly Report*, September 2006.
Dokrill, Saki. *Britain's Retreat from East of Suez: The Choice between Europe and the World?* (Basingstoke: Palgrave Macmillan, 2002).
Donahue, Patrick. 'German Spy Chief Says Huawei Can't Be "Fully Trusted" in 5G'. *Bloomberg*, 29 October 2019.
Dorient, René. 'Un septennat de politique asiatique : quel bilan pour la France ?'. *Politique étrangère 67*, no. 1 (2002): pp. 173–188.
Duchâtel, Mathieu and Mark Bromley. 'Influence by Default: Europe's Impact on Military Security in East Asia'. *ECFR Policy Brief*, May 2017.
Duchâtel, Mathieu and François Godement. *Europe and 5G: The Huawei Case*. Institut Montaigne, Note, June 2019
Dumortier, Bernard. *Les Atolls de l'atome* (Paris: Marine éditions, 2004).
Dustmann, Christian et al. 'From Sick Man of Europe to Economic Superstar: Germany's Resurgent Economy'. *Journal of Economic Perspectives 28*, no. 1 (2014): pp. 167–188.
Dyan, Brigitte and Hubert Testard. *Quand la Chine investit en France* (Paris: Agence Française pour les Investissements, 2014).
Électricité de France (EDF). 'Agreements in Place for Construction of Hinkley Point C Nuclear Power Station'. *Press Release*, 21 October 2015, https://www.edf.fr/sites/default/files/contrib/en-en/groupe-edf/espaces-dedies/medias-data/pr/cp_20151021_hinkley_va.pdf.
Emmers, Ralf. 'The Five Power Defence Arrangements and Defense Diplomacy in Southeast Asia'. *Asian Security 8*, no. 3 (2012): pp. 271–286.
Emmott, Robin. 'EU Keeps Defence Fund Alive with 8 Billion Euro Proposal'. *Reuters*, 27 May 2020.
Engel, Jeffrey A., ed. *The Fall of the Berlin Wall: The Revolutionary Legacy of 1989* (Oxford: Oxford University Press, 2009).
Erickson, Andrew S. and Conor M. Kennedy. 'China Maritime Report No. 1: China's Third Sea Force, The People's Armed Forces Maritime Militia: Tethered to the PLA'. *CNSI China Maritime Report*, 2017.
Eriksson, Sören. 'China's Aircraft Industry: Collaboration and Technology Transfer—The Case of Airbus'. *International Journal of Technology Transfer and Commercialisation 9*, no. 4 (2010): pp. 306–325.
Esper, Philippe et al. *Défendre la France et l'Europe* (Paris: Perrin, 2007).
Esteban, Mario et al., eds. *Europe in the Face of US–China Rivalry*. European Think-tank Network on China, January 2020.
EY. 'How Will Chinese Enterprises Navigate New Challenges When "Going Abroad" under the New Global Trade Landscape?'. *ChinaGoAbroad*, no. 9, October 2019.
Faizal, Elly Burhaini. 'Lawmakers Ratify Defense Agreements with Germany, China'. *The Jakarta Post*, 21 March 2016.

Fallon, Theresa. 'The EU, the South China Sea and China's Successful Wedge Strategy'. *Asia Maritime Transparency Initiative*, 15 October 2016.
Fallon, Theresa. 'The Strategic Implications of the China–EU Investment Deal'. *The Diplomat*, 4 January 2021.
Federation of German Industries (BDI). 'Systemic Competitor—How Do We Deal with China's State-Controlled Economy?'. *BDI Policy Paper*, January 2019.
Feng, Huiyun and Kai He, eds. *US–China Competition and the South China Sea Disputes* (New York: Routledge, 2018).
Ferdinand, Peter. 'UK Policy towards China', in *Europe, China and the Two SARs: Towards a New Era*, edited by Miguel Santos Neves and Brian Bridges (Basingstoke: Palgrave Macmillan, 2000), pp. 29–62.
Ferdinand, Peter. 'Westward Ho—The China Dream and "One Belt, One Road": Chinese Foreign Policy under Xi Jinping'. *International Affairs* 92, no. 4 (2016): pp. 941–957.
Fisher, Denise. *France in the South Pacific: Power and Politics* (Canberra: ANU Press, 2013).
Fisher, Denise. *One among Many: Changing Geostrategic Interests and Challenges for France in the South Pacific* (Paris: Sciences Po's Center for International Studies, CERI, 2015).
Foley-Friel, Eugene Kevin. 'Commonwealth Defence Cooperation during the Cold War, 1947–1982'. Ph.D. dissertation, University of Bristol, 2019.
Foong Khong, Yuen. 'Primacy or World Order? The United States and China's Rise—A Review Essay'. *International Security* 38, no. 3 (2013/14): pp. 153–175.
Foot, Rosemary. 'China's Rise and US Hegemony: Renegotiating Hegemonic Order in East Asia?'. *International Politics* 57, no. 2 (2020): pp. 151–165.
Ford, Jonathan. 'UK's Reliance on China's Nuclear Tech Poses Test for Policymakers'. *Financial Times*, 14 February 2019.
Forsberg, Tuomas and Hiski Haukkala. *The European Union and Russia* (New York: Palgrave Macmillan, 2016).
Friedberg, Aaron L. *A Contest for Supremacy: China, America, and the Struggle for Mastery in Asia* (New York: W.W. Norton & Company, 2011).
Friedberg, Aaron L. 'Competing with China'. *Survival* 60, no. 3 (2018): pp. 7–64.
Futák-Campbell, Beatrix. *Practising EU Foreign Policy: Russia and the Eastern Neighbours* (Manchester: Manchester University Press, 2017).
Gady, Franz-Stefan. 'Germany to Upgrade Two Indian Attack Submarines'. *The Diplomat*, 14 June 2016.
Gain, Nathan. 'UK-French Combined Staff Assumed Command of Combined Task Force 150'. *NavalNews*, 12 August 2019, https://www.navalnews.com/naval-news/2019/08/uk-french-combined-staff-assumed-command-of-combined-task-force-150/
Gao, Ni and Jan Schaaper. 'Chinese Companies Go Global: The Case of Chinese Investments in France', in *China's Global Political Economy: Managerial Perspectives*, edited by Robert Taylor and Jacques Jaussaud (London: Routledge, 2018), pp. 127–148.
Gee, Austin and Robert G. Patman. 'Small State or Minor Power? New Zealand's Five Eyes Membership, Intelligence Reforms, and Wellington's Response to China's Growing Pacific Role'. *Intelligence and National Security* 36, no. 1(2021): pp. 34–50.
Giegerich, Bastian and Christian Mölling. 'The United Kingdom's Contribution to European Security and Defence'. IISS/DGAP, February 2018.
Gill, Bates and Melissa Murphy. *China–Europe Relations: Implications and Policy Responses for the United States* (Washington, DC: Center for Strategic and International Studies, 2008).

Gilli, Andrea. 'The United Kingdom and the Indo-Pacific: Return of Global Britain?', in *Mind the Gap: Naval Views of the Free and Open Indo-Pacific*, edited by Sharon Stirling (Washington, DC: The German Marshall Fund, 2019), pp. 44–48.

Gilli, Andrea. 'France's New Raison d'Être in the Indo-Pacific', in *Mind the Gap: Naval Views of the Free and Open Indo-Pacific*, edited by Sharon Stirling (Washington, DC: The German Marshall Fund, 2019), pp. 18–21.

Gilli, Andrea. 'NATO and 5G: What Strategic Lessons?'. NATO Defense College, *Policy Brief no. 13*, July 2020.

Glowik, Mario. 'Market Entry Strategies of Huawei in Germany and the Russian Federation from a Network Theory Perspective', in *Huawei Goes Global, Vol. II: Regional, Geopolitical Perspectives and Crisis Management*, edited by Wenxian Zhang, Ilan Alon, and Christoph Lattemann (Cham, Switzerland: Palgrave Macmillan, 2020), pp. 11–36.

Godement, François. 'Une politique française pour l'Asie-Pacifique ?'. *Politique étrangère 60*, no. 4 (1995): pp. 959–970.

Godement, François. 'France's "Pivot" to Asia'. European Council on Foreign Relations (ECFR). *Policy Brief*, May 2014.

Godement, François. *China at the Gates: A New Power Audit of EU–China Relations* (London: European Council on Foreign Relations, 2017).

Godement, François and Abigaël Vasselier. *China at the Gates: A New Power Audit of EU–China Relations* (London: European Council on Foreign Relations, 2017).

Goh, Evelyn. *The Struggle for Order: Hegemony, Hierarchy, and Transition in Post-Cold War East Asia* (Oxford: Oxford University Press, 2013).

Goh, Evelyn. 'Contesting Hegemonic Order: China in East Asia'. *Security Studies 28*, no. 3 (2019): pp. 614–644.

Graré, Bertrand. 'Huawei ouvre un 6ème centre de R&D en France'. *L'informaticien*, 12 October 2020.

Green Michael et al. 'Harassment of the USNS Impeccable'. Center for Strategic and International Studies (CSIS), Asia Maritime Transparency Initiative, 9 May 2017.

Grieger, Gisela. 'Foreign Direct Investment Screening: A Debate in Light of China-EU FDI Flows'. *European Parliamentary Research Service (EPRS) Briefing*, May 2017.

Griffith, James. 'UN Court Ruling Puts Future of Strategic US Military Base Diego Garcia into Question'. *CNN World*, 26 February 2019.

Gueugneau, Romain. 'Huawei mise 1,5 milliard d'euros sur la France'. *Les Echos*, 29 September 2014.

Guo, Sujian. *China's 'Peaceful Rise' in the 21st Century: Domestic and International Conditions* (New York: Routledge, 2006).

Gurkha Brigade Association. 'The Third Battalion The Royal Gurkha Rifles Reformation Parade', 3 February 2020, https://www.gurkhabde.com/the-third-battalion-the-royal-gurkha-rifles-reformation-parade/.

Gutteridge, Nick. '"Ahead of the Curve" British Trade with Global Giant China Booms as Rest of EU Lags behind'. *Express*, 3 November 2017. https://www.express.co.uk/news/politics/875163/Brexit-news-UK-trade-with-global-giant-China-booms-as-rest-of-EU-lags-behind

Haacke, Jürgen and John H. Breen. 'From Benign Neglect to Effective Re-engagement? Assessing British Strategizing and Policies towards Southeast Asia since 2010'. *Contemporary Southeast Asia 41*, no. 3 (2019): pp. 329–363.

Hack, Karl. *Defence and Decolonisation in South-East Asia: Britain, Malaya and Singapore 1941–1968* (Richmond, Surrey: Curzon Press, 2001).

Hall, Peter A. *Governing the Economy: The Politics of State Intervention in Britain and France* (Oxford: Oxford University Press, 1986).
Hammer, Alexander B. and Shahid Yusuf. 'Is China in a High-Tech, Low Productivity Trap?'. US International Trade Commission, *Working Paper 2020-07-B*, July 2020.
Hanemann, Thilo, Cassie Gao, and Agatha Kratz. *Comparing Chinese Investment into North America and Europe*. Rhodium Group and Baker McKenzie, 13 January 2019.
Hanemann, Thilo and Mikko Huotari. 'Preparing for a New Era of Chinese Capital: Chinese FDI in Europe and Germany'. *MERICS Papers on China*, June 2015.
Hanemann, Thilo and Mikko Huotari. 'Record Flows and Growing Imbalances: Chinese Investment in Europe in 2016'. *MERICS Papers on China no. 3*, January 2017.
Hanemann, Thilo, Mikko Huotari, and Agatha Kratz. *Chinese FDI in Europe, 2018 Trends and Impact of New Screening Policies*. Report by Rhodium Group (RHG) and Mercator Institute for China Studies (MERICS), March 2019.
Hanemann, Thilo and Daniel H. Rosen. *China Invests in Europe: Patterns, Impacts and Policy Implications*. Rhodium Group, June 2012.
Hannas, William C., James Mulvenon, and Anna B. Puglisi. *Chinese Industrial Espionage: Technology Acquisition and Military Modernization* (New York: Routledge, 2013).
Harding, Andrew. 'UN Court Rules UK Has No Sovereignty over Chagos Islands'. *BBC News*, 28 January 2021.
Harwit, Eric. 'The Impact of WTO Membership on the Automobile Industry in China'. *The China Quarterly 167* (Sep. 2001): pp. 655–670.
Hawes, Colin. 'Why Is Huawei's Ownership So Strange? A Case Study of the Chinese Corporate and Socio-Political Ecosystem'. *Journal of Corporate Law Studies Studies 21*, no. 1 (2020): pp. 1–38, doi:10.1080/14735970.2020.1809161.
Hawksley, Charles and Rowena Ward. 'Ripples of Decolonisation in the Asia-Pacific'. *Journal of Multidisciplinary International Studies 16*, no. 1/2 (2019): pp. 1–10.
He, Kai and Huiyun Feng. 'Debating China's Assertiveness: Taking China's Power and Interests Seriously'. *International Politics 49*, no. 5 (2012): pp. 633–644.
He, Kai and Huiyun Feng. 'Xi Jinping's Operational Code Beliefs and China's Foreign Policy'. *The Chinese Journal of International Politics 6*, no. 3 (2013): pp. 209–231.
Heisbourg, François. 'NATO 4.0: The Atlantic Alliance and the Rise of China'. *Survival 62*, no. 2 (2020): pp. 83–102.
Hellström, Jerker. *China's Acquisitions in Europe. European Perceptions of Chinese Investments and their Strategic Implications* (Stockholm: Swedish Defence Research Agency (FOI), 2016), Report FOI-R-4384-SE.
Hemmings, John and Milia Hau. 'AUKMIN 2018: The Future of Global Britain?'. *RUSI Commentary*, 14 August 2018.
Hemmings, John and James Rogers. 'Britain and the Quadrilateral'. *Journal of Indo-Pacific Affairs 3*, no. 5 (2020): pp. 118–130.
Hiery, Hermann. *The Neglected War. The German South Pacific and the Influence of World War I* (Honolulu: University of Hawaii Press, 1995).
Higgot, Richard. 'Closing a Branch Office of Empire: Australian Foreign Policy and the UK at Century's End'. *International Affairs 70*, no. 1 (1994): pp. 41–65.
Hill, Christopher, *Foreign Policy in the Twenty-first Century*, 2nd edition (Basingstoke: Palgrave Macmillan, 2015).
Hoehn, John R. and Kelley M. Sayler. 'National Security Implications of Fifth Generation (5G) Mobile Technologies'. *Congressional Research Service In Focus*, 12 June 2019.

Hornung, Jeffrey W. *Allies Growing Closer: Japan–Europe Security Ties in the Age of Strategic Competition* (Santa Monica, CA: RAND Corporation, 2020).

Howorth, Jolyon. 'Implications of the US Rebalance toward Asia: European Security and NATO', in *Origins and Evolution of the US Rebalance toward Asia: Diplomatic, Military, and Economic Dimensions*, edited by Hugo Meijer (New York: Palgrave Macmillan, 2015), pp. 197–222.

Howorth, Jolyon and Anand Menon. 'Still Not Pushing Back: Why the European Union Is Not Balancing the United States'. *Journal of Conflict Resolution 53*, no. 5 (2009): pp. 727–744.

Huang, Betty et al. 'China: Five Facts about Outward Direct Investment and their Implication for Future Trend'. *BBVA Research—China Economic Watch*, March 2019.

Huawei. 'Duisburg Germany and Huawei Sign MoU to Build a Smart City'. *News and Events*, 12 January 2018.

Huawei. 'The Win–Win Relationship between the EU and Huawei'. *Factsheet*, May 2020.

Huawei Investment & Holding Co. *2015 Annual Report: Building a Better Connected World*, 2016.

Huotari, Mikko. 'Germany's China Policy: No Honeymoon Forever', in *Mapping Europe–China Relations: A Bottom-Up Approach*, edited by Mikko Huotari, Miguel Otero-Iglesias, John Seaman, and Alice Ekman (Berlin: Joint Report by MERICS/IFRI/Elcano, 2015), pp. 30–35.

Huotari, Mikko. 'Germany's Changing Take on Chinese Direct Investment: Balancing Openness with Greater Scrutiny', in *Chinese Investment in Europe: A Country-Level Approach*, edited by John Seaman, Mikko Huotari, and Miguel Otero-Iglesias (Paris: French Institute of International Relations, 2017), pp. 61–68.

Huxley, Tim. 'The Future of the FPDA in an Evolving Regional Strategic Environment', in *The Five Power Defence Arrangements at Forty*, edited by Ian Storey, Ralf Emmers, and Daljit Singh (Singapore: Institute of Southeast Asian Studies, 2011), pp. 118–122.

Hyde-Price, Adrian. '"Normative" Power Europe: A Realist Critique'. *Journal of European Public Policy 13*, no. 2 (2006): pp. 217–234.

International Institute for Strategic Studies. *2018 Asia-Pacific Regional Security Assessment* (London: IISS, 2018).

Izambard, Antoine. 'Cyberattaques contre Airbus : pourquoi la Chine est soupçonnée'. *Challenges*, 27 September 2012.

Jaishankar, Dhruva. 'India and Germany: Realising Strategic Convergence'. Brookings Institution, 31 January 2017.

Jianwei, Li and Ramses Amer. 'British Naval Activities in the South China Sea: A Double-Edged Sword?'. Institute for Security and Development Policy, April 2019, https://isdp.eu/publication/british-navy-south-china-sea/

Johnston, Alastair Iain. 'How New and Assertive Is China's New Assertiveness?'. *International Security 34*, no. 4 (2013): pp. 35–45.

Jones, Sam. 'Britain's "Withered" Forces Not Fit to Repel All-out Attack'. *Financial Times*, 16 September 2016.

Jongbluth, Cora. *Is China Systematically Buying Up Key Technologies? Chinese M&A Transactions in Germany in the Context of 'Made in China 2025'* (Gütersloh: Bertelsmann Stiftung, 2018).

Jowitt, Tom. 'German Industrial Giants Attacked by Chinese Hackers—Report'. *Silicon.co.uk*, 24 July 2019.

Keay, John. *Empire's End: A History of the Far East from High Colonialism to Hong Kong* (New York: Scribner, 1997).
Keith, Ronald C. *Deng Xiaoping and China's Foreign Policy* (New York: Routledge, 2017).
Kelly, Tim. 'British Navy Warship Sails near South China Sea Islands, Angering Beijing'. *Reuters*, 6 September 2018.
Kelly, Tim. 'U.S., France, Japan and Australia Hold First Combined Naval Drill in Asia'. *Reuters*, 16 May 2019.
Kendall-Taylor, Andrea. Statement Prepared for the Hearing 'China's Expanding Influence in Europe and Eurasia'. US House Subcommittee on Europe, Eurasia, Energy, and the Environment, 9 May 2019.
Kerr, David and Liu Fei, eds. *The International Politics of EU–China Relations* (Oxford: Oxford University Press, 2007).
Kerr, Julian. 'Attack Class—Plan of Action'. Australian Defence Magazine, 10 October 2019.
King, Julian. 'Europe's 5G Network Will Be Secure—If We Work Together'. *The Guardian*, 28 October 2019.
Kirchner, Emil J., Thomas Christiansen, and Han Dorussen, eds. *Security Relations between China and the European Union: From Convergence to Cooperation?* (Cambridge: Cambridge University Press, 2016).
Kraft, Ina. 'Germany', in *The Handbook of European Defence Policies and Armed Forces*, edited by Hugo Meijer and Marco Wyss (Oxford: Oxford University Press, 2018), pp. 52–70.
Kratz, Agatha, Mikko Huotari, Thilo Hanemann, and Rebecca Arcesati. *Chinese FDI in Europe: 2019 Update—Special Topic: Research Collaborations*. Report by Rhodium Group (RHG) and the Mercator Institute for China Studies (MERICS), April 2020.
Kratz, Agatha, Max J. Zenglein, and Gregor Sebastian. Chinese FDI in Europe—2020 Update. MERICS/Rhodium Group, June 2021.
Krause, Andreas. 'German Navy Chief of Staff: The Naval Force Is Preparing for Challenges Beyond 2020'. *Defense News*, 2 December 2019.
Krotz, Ulrich. *Shaping Europe: France, Germany, and Embedded Bilateralism from the Elysée Treaty to Twenty-First Century Politics* (Oxford: Oxford University Press, 2013).
Krotz, Ulrich. *History and Foreign Policy in France and Germany* (Basingstoke: Palgrave Macmillan, 2015).
Krotz, Ulrich and Richard Maher. 'Europe's Crises and the EU's 'Big Three''. *West European Politics* 39, no. 5 (2016): pp. 1053–1072.
Kuik, Cheng-Chwee. 'Multilateralism in China's ASEAN Policy: Its Evolution, Characteristics, and Aspiration'. *Contemporary Southeast Asia* 27, no. 1 (2005): pp. 102–122.
Kundnani, Hans. 'Germany as a Geo-Economic Power'. *The Washington Quarterly* 34, no. 3 (2011): pp. 31–45.
Kundnani, Hans. *The Paradox of German Power* (Oxford: Oxford University Press, 2015).
Kundnani, Hans and Jonas Parello-Plesner. 'China and Germany: Why the Emerging Special Relationship Matters for Europe'. European Council on Foreign Relations, *Policy Brief*, 2012, pp. 1–16.
Lairson, Thomas D. 'The International Political Economy of Huawei's Global and Domestic Environment', in *Huawei Goes Global, Vol. I: Made in China for the World*, edited by Wenxian Zhang, Ilan Alon, and Christoph Lattemann (Cham, Switzerland: Palgrave Macmillan, 2020), pp. 13–40.
Lanktree, Graham and Anna Isaac. 'Trade Secretary Liz Truss: UK Must Not Become Dependent on China'. *Politico EU*, 26 May 2021.

Lasi, Heiner, Peter Fettke, Hans-Georg Kemper, Thomas Feld, and Michael Hoffmann. 'Industry 4.0'. *Business and Information Systems Engineering 6*, no. 4 (2014): pp. 239–242.

Lau, Stuart. 'Lithuania Pulls out of China's "17+1" Bloc in Eastern Europe'. *Politico EU*, 21 May 2021.

Laurent, Franck and Pascal Nourry. 'Contexte réglementaire pour les opérateurs 5G'. Paper presented at the Computer & Electronics Security Applications Rendez-vous (C&ESAR) on Virtualization and Cybersecurity, Rennes, 19 November 2019.

Lausson, Julien. '5G : la France s'organise pour écarter Huawei des réseaux télécoms'. *Numerama*, 6 July 2020.

Lechervy, Christian. 'La France, l'Europe et l'Asie-Pacifique'. Institute for Strategic Research, *Lettre de l'IRSEM*, no. 2 (2013).

Lechervy, Christian. 'L'ASEM : le début d'un (mini-)pivot européen vers l'Asie-Pacifique ?'. *Relations internationales 4*, no. 168 (2016): pp. 117–130.

Le Corre, Philippe. 'Chinese Investments in European Countries: Experiences and Lessons for the "Belt and Road" Initiative', in *Rethinking the Silk Road: China's Belt and Road Initiative and Emerging Eurasian Relations*, edited by Maximilian Mayer (Singapore: Palgrave Macmillan, 2017), pp. 161–176.

Le Corre, Philippe. 'On China's Expanding Influence in Europe and Eurasia'. Testimony before the House of Representatives, Foreign Affairs Committee, 9 May 2019.

Le Corre, Philippe and Alain Sepulchre. *China's Offensive in Europe* (Washington, DC: Brookings Institution Press, 2016).

Lehne, Stefan. *The Big Three and EU Foreign Policy* (Brussels: Carnegie Europe, 2012).

Lennard, Jeremy. 'UK Boosts Help for Tsunami Victims'. *The Guardian*, 31 December 2004.

Li, Ling. 'China's Manufacturing Locus in 2025: With a Comparison of "Made-in-China 2025" and "Industry 4.0"'. *Technological Forecasting & Social Change 135* (2018): pp. 66–74.

Li, Shenxue, Mark Easterby-Smith, and Marjorie A. Lyles. 'Overcoming Corporate Rigidities in the Dynamic Chinese Market'. *Business Horizons 51* (2008), pp. 501–509.

Li, Yushan. 'China's Go Out Policy: A Review on China's Promotion Policy for Outward Foreign Direct Investment from a Historical Perspective'. Centre for Economic and Regional Studies, HAS Institute of World Economics, *Working Paper no. 244*, September 2018.

Liefnera, Ingo, Yue-fang Sib, and Kerstin Schäfera. 'A Latecomer Firm's R&D Collaboration with Advanced Country Universities and Research Institutes: The Case of Huawei in Germany'. *Technovation 86–87* (2019), pp. 3–14.

Liff, Adam P. 'Whither the Balancers? The Case for a Methodological Reset'. *Security Studies 25*, no. 3 (2016): pp. 420–459.

Lim, Darren J. and Zack Cooper. 'Reassessing Hedging: The Logic of Alignment in East Asia'. *Security Studies 24*, no. 4 (2015): pp. 696–727.

Lippman, Daniel. 'Trump National Security Adviser Heading to Europe for Talks on China'. *Politico EU*, 7 November 2020.

Liu, Wan-Hsin and Xinming Xia. 'China's Investments in Germany and the Impact of the COVID-19 Pandemic'. *Intereconomics 56*, no. 2 (2021): pp. 113–119.

Lunn, Jon and John Curtis. 'The UK–China Relationship'. *Briefing Paper 9004*, House of Commons Library, 14 September 2020.

Maestri, Edmond. *Les îles du Sud-Ouest de l'Océan Indien et la France de 1815 à nos jours* (Paris: L'Harmattan, 1994).

Magee, Tamlin. 'Huawei Controversies Timeline'. *Computerworld*, 24 April 2019.

Mahadzir, Dzirhan. 'PACFLEET Commander: RIMPAC 2020 Will Be More Complex, Feature More Countries'. *USNI News*, 6 March 2020.

Manach, Jean-Marc. 'Comment on peut, en trois clics, découvrir la carte des stations d'écoute des espions de la DGSE'. *Slate*, 7 May 2014.

Marshall, P. J. *Problems of Empire: Britain and India, 1757–1813* (London: George Allen and Unwin Ltd., 1968).

Matlary, Janne Haaland and Magnus Petersson, eds. *NATO's European Allies Military Capability and Political Will* (Basingstoke: Palgrave Macmillan, 2013).

Maull, Hanns W. 'Germany and Japan: The New Civilian Powers'. *Foreign Affairs* 69, no. 5 (1990): pp. 91–106.

Maxwell, Winston. 'France Criticized for New Foreign Investment Rules'. *International Financial Law Review*, 1 March 2006.

McIntyre, David W. *British Colonization, 1946–1997: When, Why, and How Did the British Empire Fall?* (New York: St. Martin's Press, 1998).

Medcalf, Rory. *Contest for the Indo-Pacific: Why China Won't Map the Future* (Melbourne: La Trobe University Press, 2020).

Meijer, Hugo. 'Transatlantic Perspectives on China's Military Modernization: The Case of Europe's Arms Embargo against the People's Republic of China'. Paris Paper no. 12, Strategic Research Institute (IRSEM), 2014.

Meijer, Hugo. *Trading with the Enemy: The Making of US Export Control Policy toward the People's Republic of China* (New York: Oxford University Press, 2016).

Meijer, Hugo. 'Shaping China's Rise: The Reordering of U.S. Alliances and Defense Partnerships in East Asia'. *International Politics* 57, no. 2 (2020): pp. 166–184.

Meijer, Hugo. 'Pulled East: The Rise of China, Europe and French Security Policy in the Asia-Pacific'. *Journal of Strategic Studies* (2021a), doi.org/10.1080/01402390.2021.1935251.

Meijer, Hugo. 'The European Union's China Policy: Convergences or Divergences?'. European University Institute, *Policy Brief*, 2021b, https://cadmus.eui.eu/bitstream/handle/1814/72201/QM-AX-21-032-EN-N.pdf?sequence=1&isAllowed=y.

Meijer, Hugo, Lucie Béraud-Sudreau, Paul Holtom, and Matthew Uttley. 'Arming China: Major Powers' Arms Transfers to the People's Republic of China'. *Journal of Strategic Studies* 41, no. 6 (2018): pp. 850–886.

Meijer, Hugo and Stephen G. Brooks. 'Illusions of Autonomy: Why Europe Cannot Provide for its Security If the United States Pulls Back'. *International Security* 45, no. 4 (Spring 2021): pp. 7–43.

Meijer, Hugo and Luis Simón. 'Covert Balancing: Great Powers, Secondary States and U.S. Balancing Strategies against China'. *International Affairs* 82, no. 2 (2021): pp. 463–481.

Meijer, Hugo and Marco Wyss. 'Beyond CSDP: The Resurgence of National Armed Forces in Europe', in *The Handbook of European Defence Policies and Armed Forces*, edited by Hugo Meijer and Marco Wyss (Oxford: Oxford University Press, 2018), pp. 14–31.

Meijer, Hugo and Marco Wyss. 'Upside Down: Reframing European Defence Studies'. *Cooperation and Conflict* 54, no. 3 (2019): pp. 378–406.

Meunier, Sophie. 'Divide and Conquer? China and the Cacophony of Foreign Investment Rules in the EU'. *Journal of European Public Policy* 21, no. 7 (2014): pp. 996–1016.

Meunier, Sophie. 'Beware of Chinese Bearing Gifts: Why China's Direct Investment Poses Political Challenges in Europe and the United States', in *China's International Investment Strategy: Bilateral, Regional, and Global Law and Policy*, edited by Julien Chaisse (Oxford: Oxford University Press, 2019), pp. 345–359.

Michael, Gabriel. 'Who's Afraid of WikiLeaks? Missed Opportunities in Political Science Research'. *Review of Policy Research 32*, no. 2 (2015): pp. 175–199.

Miko, Francis. 'Germany's "Grand Coalition" Government: Prospects and Implications'. Congressional Research Service. *CRS Report*, 17 January 2006.

Moens, Alexander and Brooke Smith-Windsor, eds. *NATO and Asia-Pacific* (Rome: NATO Defense College, 2016).

Möller, Kay. 'Diplomatic Relations and Mutual Strategic Perceptions: China and the European Union'. *The China Quarterly 169*, no. 169, Special Issue: China and Europe since 1978 (2002): pp. 10–32.

Moore, Charles. *Margaret Thatcher: The Authorized Bibliography, Vol. II* (New York: Penguin Press, 2015).

Morris, Anne. 'France Unlikely to Ban Huawei, But Will Encourage Operators to Steer Clear'. *LightReading*, 7 June 2020.

Mukherjee, Supantha and Helena Soderpalm. 'Sweden Bans Huawei, ZTE from Upcoming 5G Networks'. *Reuters*, 20 October 2020.

Mull, Jörg, Executive Vice President for Finance. Presentation on the Volkswagen Group China, Beijing, 27 November 2012, p. 3, https://www.volkswagenag.com/presence/investorrelation/publications/presentations/2012/03-march/Presentation_Dr_Mull.pdf (accessed 9 June 2021).

Müller, Patrick, ed. *EU Foreign Policymaking and the Middle East Conflict: The Europeanization of National Foreign Policy* (New York: Routledge, 2012).

Nauheim, Markus et al. 'Update on German Foreign Investment Control: New EU Co-operation Mechanism and Overview of Recent Changes'. *Gibson Dunn*, 11 November 2020.

Naval Technology. 'UK Navy Completes Taurus-09 Deployment', 4 August 2009, https://www.naval-technology.com/news/news61264-html/

Naval Today. 'HMS Montrose Heads to Bahrain after Operations in Japan', 20 March 2019, https://www.navaltoday.com/2019/03/20/hms-montrose-heads-to-bahrain-after-operations-in-japan/

Nègre-Eveillard, Nathalie and Orion Berg. 'Foreign Investments in France: New Legislation Expands and Strengthens the National Security Review Mechanism'. *White & Case*—Client Alert, 22 July 2019.

Ng, Teddy. 'British Navy Vessel Passes through Taiwan Strait'. *South China Morning Post*, 7 December 2019.

Nguyen, Thi Lan Anh. 'Origins of the South China Sea Dispute', in *Territorial Disputes in the South China Sea: Navigating Rough Waters*, edited by Jing Huang and Andrew Billo (New York: Palgrave Macmillan, 2014), pp. 15–35.

Nicolas, Françoise. 'Chinese Direct Investments in France: No French Exception, No Chinese Challenge'. Chatham House, *IE Programme Paper IE PP 2010/2*, January 2010.

Nicolas, Françoise. 'France and China's Belt and Road Initiative'. Italian Institute for International Political Studies, *ISPI Commentary*, 8 April 2019, https://www.ispionline.it/en/pubblicazione/france-and-chinas-belt-and-road-initiative-22787.

Nicolas, Françoise and Stephen Thomsen. 'The Rise of Chinese Firms in Europe: Motives, Strategies and Implications'. Draft Paper for presentation at the Asia Pacific Economic Association Conference, Beijing, 13–14 December 2008.

Nienaber, Michael. 'German Minister Ups Rhetoric against Takeovers ahead of China Trip'. *Reuters*, 29 October 2016.

Nienaber, Michael. 'Germany Blocks Chinese Takeover of Satellite Firm on Security Concerns: Document'. *Reuters*, 8 December 2020.

Noboru, Okabe. 'The New Anglo-Japanese Alliance and the "Six Eyes"'. *Nippon.com*, 29 October 2020.
Norton-Taylor, Richard. 'Titan Rain—How Chinese Hackers Targeted Whitehall'. *The Guardian*, 5 September 2007.
Nouwens, Meia and Helena Legarda. 'China's Pursuit of Advanced Dual-Use Technologies'. *IISS Research Papers*, 18 December 2018, https://www.iiss.org/blogs/research-paper/2018/12/emerging-technology-dominance.
Nouwens, Meia and Helena Legarda. 'China's Rise as a Global Security Actor: Implications for NATO'. IISS and MERICS, *Research Paper*, December 2020.
Odgaard, Liselotte. 'European Engagement in the Indo-Pacific: The Interplay between Institutional and State-Level Naval Diplomacy'. *Asia Policy 14*, no. 4 (2019): pp. 129–159.
Oertel, Janka. 'The New China Consensus: How Europe Is Growing Wary of Beijing'. *ECFR Policy Brief*, September 2020.
Osterhammel, Jürgen. 'Semi-Colonialism and Informal Empire in Twentieth-Century China: Towards a Framework of Analysis', in *Imperialism and After: Continuities and Discontinuities*, edited by Wolfgang Mommsen and Jürgen Osterhammel (London: Allen & Unwin for the German Historical Institute, 1986), pp. 291–314.
Oxford Economics. *The Economic Impact of Huawei* (London: Oxford Economics, 2020).
Pajon, Céline. 'France's Indo-Pacific Strategy and the Quad Plus'. *The Journal of Indo-Pacific Affairs 3*, no. 5 (Winter 2020/21): pp. 165–178.
Parameswaran, Prashanth. 'What's in the New Singapore–Germany Cyber Pact?'. *The Diplomat*, 11 July 2017.
Parameswaran, Prashanth. 'Military Exercise Highlights Singapore–Germany Defense Ties'. *The Diplomat*, 24 March 2018.
Parameswaran, Prashanth. 'What's Next for Germany–Vietnam Military Cooperation?'. *The Diplomat*, 18 June 2019.
Pardo, Ramon Pacheco. 'Europe's Financial Security and Chinese Economic Statecraft: The Case of the Belt and Road Initiative'. *Asia-Europe Journal 16*, no. 3 (2018): pp. 237–250.
Park, Sunghoon and Jae-Seung Lee. 'EU's Strategic Partnerships with Asian Countries'. *Asia-Europe Journal 17*, no. 3 (2019), Special Issue.
Parker, George and David Sheppard. 'UK to Shut out China with Revamped Nuclear Funding Model'. *Financial Times*, 26 October 2021.
Patalano, Alessio. 'Days of Future Past? British Strategy and the Shaping of Indo-Pacific Security'. *Policy Exchange*, 1 April 2019.
Patalano, Alessio. UK Defence from the "Far East" to the "Indo-Pacific"'. *Policy Exchange*, 24 July 2019.
Patalano, Alessio. 'The United Kingdom and Indo-Pacific Security'. IISS, *Asia-Pacific Regional Security Assessment 2021* (London: IISS, 2021): pp. 9–26.
Patman, Robert G., Patrick Köllner, and Balazs Kiglics, eds. *From Asia-Pacific to Indo-Pacific: Diplomacy in a Contested Region* (Cham, Switzerland: Palgrave Macmillan, 2022).
Pavlićević, Dragan and Anastas Vangeli. 'New Perspectives on China–Central and Eastern Europe Relations'. *Asia-Europe Journal 17*, no. 4 (2019), Special Issue.
Pedersen, Susan. *The Guardians: The League of Nations and the Crisis of Empire* (Oxford: Oxford University Press, 2015).
Pejsova, Eva, ed. *Guns, Engines and Turbines: The EU's Hard Power in Asia* (Paris: EUISS, 2018).
Pesjova, Eva. 'The EU as a Maritime Security Provider'. *EUISS Brief 13*, December 2019.

Percy, Joseph. 'Chinese FDI in the EU's Top 4 Economies'. *China Briefing*, 8 May 2019.
Philp, Catherine, Lucy Fisher, and Francis Elliott. 'Ditch Huawei and Trade Will Suffer, Warns China'. *The Times*, 7 July 2020.
Poggetti, Lucrezia. 'One China—One Europe? German Foreign Minister's Remarks Irk Beijing'. *The Diplomat*, 9 September 2017.
Poh, Angela and Mingjiang Li. 'A China in Transition: The Rhetoric and Substance of Chinese Foreign Policy under Xi Jinping'. *Asian Security 13*, no. 2 (2017): pp. 84–97.
Public Sénat. 'Huawei, le Sénat pointe des liens avec le pouvoir chinois', 11 October 2020, https://www.publicsenat.fr/article/societe/huawei-le-senat-pointe-des-liens-avec-le-pouvoir-chinois-184978.
Rahn, Wesley. 'South China Sea: France and Britain Join the US to Oppose China'. *Deutsche Welle*, 27 June 2018.
Rascke, Sven. 'Marine-Misere: Deutschlands U-Boote Sind alle Kaputt'. *SHZ.de*, 20 October 2017.
Rath, John. 'Alcatel-Lucent Introduces New Core Routers'. *Data Center Knowledge*, 24 May 2012, https://www.datacenterknowledge.com/archives/2012/05/24/alcatel-lucent-introduces-new-core-routers.
Regaud, Nicolas. 'France and Security in the Asia-Pacific: from the End of the First Indochina Conflict to Today'. Australian Strategic Policy Institute, *Strategic Insights 12* (December 2016).
Regaud, Nicolas. 'France's Indo-Pacific Strategy and its Overseas Territories in the Indian and Pacific Oceans: Characteristics, Capabilities, Constraints and Avenues for Deepening the Franco-Australian Strategic Partnership'. *Australian Strategic Policy Institute*, 25 June 2021, https://www.aspi.org.au/report/frances-indo-pacific-strategy-and-its-overseas-territories-indian-and-pacific-oceans.
Rehman, Iskander. 'The Indian Ocean in France's Global Defence Strategy'. CNA Roundtable Proceedings, 18 January 2018a.
Rehman, Iskander. 'Policy Roundtable: Are the United States and China in a New Cold War?'. *Texas National Security Review*, 15 May 2018b.
Reilly, James. 'China's Economic Statecraft in Europe'. *Asia-Europe Journal 15*, no. 2 (2017): pp. 173–185.
Reilly, James. *Orchestration: China's Economic Statecraft Across Asia and Europe* (New York: Oxford University Press, 2021).
Reiterer, Michael. 'The EU's Comprehensive Approach to Security in Asia'. *European Foreign Affairs Review 19*, no. 1 (2014): pp. 1–22.
Rej, Abhijnan. 'Germany to Deploy a Frigate to Patrol the Indo-Pacific'. *The Diplomat*, 3 November 2020.
Reuters Staff. 'US Intelligence Says Huawei Funded by Chinese State Security: Report'. *Reuters*, 20 April 2019.
Reuters Staff. 'German Security Office Warned German Firms about Chinese Hacking: Report'. *Reuters*, 19 December 2019.
Rhodium Group. 'People's Republic of China/European Union Direct Investment'. *Cross Border Monitor*, 16 January 2019.
Richelson, Jeffrey T. *The Ties That Bind: Intelligence Cooperation between the UKUSA Countries: The United Kingdom, the United States of America, Canada, Australia and New Zealand* (Sydney: Allen and Unwin, 1990).
Riley-Smith, Ben. 'Liz Truss: "Thatcher's Devotion to Democracy Inspires Me to Tackle Today's Global Challenges"'. *The Telegraph*, 22 October 2021.
Rinke, Andreas. 'German Draft IT Security Law Strives for Consensus on Telecoms Vendor Risks'. *Reuters*, 20 November 2020.

Ritchie, Greg. 'Police Shoot Man Dead after London Terrorist Attack'. *Bloomberg*, 29 November 2019.
Roberts, John. *Safeguarding the Nation: The Story of the Modern Royal Navy* (Barnsley, UK: Seaforth Publishing, 2009).
Roblin, Sebastien. 'Germany Does Not Have One Working Submarine'. *The National Interest*, 16 December 2017.
Rogers, James. 'European (British and French) Geostrategy in the Indo-Pacific'. *Journal of the Indian Ocean Region 9*, no. 1 (2013): pp. 69–89.
Rosamond, Ben. 'Brexit and the Problem of European Disintegration'. *Journal of Contemporary European Research 12*, no. 4 (2016): pp. 864–871.
Rosemain, Mathieu and Gwénaëlle Barzic. 'Exclusive: French Limits on Huawei 5G Equipment Amount to De Facto Ban by 2028'. *Reuters*, 22 July 2020.
Rosendahl, Jussi and Leila Abboud. 'Nokia Buys Alcatel to Take on Ericsson in Telecom Equipment'. *Reuters*, 15 April 2015.
Ross, Robert S. 'The 1995–96 Taiwan Strait Confrontation: Coercion, Credibility, and the Use of Force'. *International Security 25*, no. 2 (2000): pp. 87–123.
Ross, Robert S. 'The Domestic Sources of China's "Assertive Diplomacy," 2009–2010: Nationalism and Chinese Foreign Policy', in *China across the Divide: The Domestic and Global in Politics and Society*, edited by Rosemary Foot (Oxford: Oxford University Press, 2013), pp. 72–96.
Ross, Robert S., Øystein Tunsjø, and Tuosheng Zhang, eds. *US–China–EU Relations: Managing the New World Order* (London: Routledge, 2010).
Ruechardt, Felix. *Non-Proliferation and Foreign Direct Investment Reviews: Implications for Reform in the UK*. Report prepared by Project Alpha at the Centre for Science and Security Studies (CSSS), King's College London, 16 April 2018.
Rupprecht, Klaus. 'Germany's Policy towards China and the SARs of Hong Kong and Macau', in *Europe, China and the Two SARs: Towards a New Era*, edited by Miguel Santos Neves and Brian Bridges (Basingstoke: Palgrave Macmillan, 2000), pp. 63–69.
Rynning, Sten. 'Realism and the Common Security and Defense Policy'. *Journal of Common Market Studies 49*, no 1 (2011): pp. 23–42.
Sabbagh, Dan. 'Rebel Tory MPs Put down Amendment to Bar Huawei Technology'. *The Guardian*, 6 March 2020
Sarotte, Mary Elise. *1989: The Struggle to Create Post-Cold War Europe* (Princeton, NJ: Princeton University Press, 2009).
Schmidt, Vivien A. 'Varieties of Capitalism: A Distinct French Model?', in *Oxford Handbook of French Politics*, edited by Robert Elgie, Amy Mazur, Emiliano Grossman, and Andrew Appleton (Oxford: Oxford University Press, 2016), pp. 606–635.
Schnellbach, Christoph and Joyce Man. 'Germany and China: Embracing a Different Kind of Partnership?'. Center for Applied Policy Research, *CAP Working Paper*, September 2015.
Schöning, Falk et al. 'This Time's for Real: German Government Prohibits Acquisition of a Tech Company by a Chinese Acquirer'. *Hogan Lovells*, 4 December 2020.
Schröder, Oliver and Stephanie Birmanns. 'Germany', in *The Foreign Investment Regulation Review*, edited by Calvin S. Goldman and Michael Koch, 8th edition (London: Law Business Research, 2020), pp. 68–83.
Schuetze, Christopher. 'Russia's Invasion Prompts Germany to Beef Up Military Funding'. *The New York Times*, 27 February 2022.
Schwarzenberg, Andres B. 'Tracking China's Global Economic Activities: Data Challenges and Issues for Congress'. *Congressional Research Service, Report R46302*, 14 June 2020.
Scobell, Andrew and Scott W. Harold. 'An "Assertive" China? Insights from Interviews'. *Asian Security 9*, no. 2 (2013): pp. 111–131.

Scott, David. 'France's "Indo-Pacific" Strategy: Regional Power Projection'. *Journal of Military and Strategic Studies 19*, no. 4 (2019): pp. 76–103.

Seaman, John. 'Chinese Investment in France: An Openly Cautious Welcome', in *Chinese Investment in Europe: A Country-Level Approach*, edited by John Seaman, Mikko Huotari, and Miguel Otero-Iglesias (Paris: French Institute of International Relations, 2017), pp. 55–60.

Seibt, Sébastien. 'France Wades into the South China Sea with a Nuclear Attack Submarine'. *France24*, 12 February 2021.

Sendagorta, Fidel. 'The Triangle in the Long Game: Rethinking Relations between China, Europe, and the United States in the New Era of Strategic Competition'. Belfer Center for Science and International Affairs, Harvard Kennedy School, 19 June 2019.

Senkyr, Jan. 'Germany–Indonesia Strategic Dialogue'. Event Reports, Konrad Adenauer Stiftung, 4 December 2018.

Severino, Rodolfo. *The ASEAN Regional Forum* (Singapore: Institute of Southeast Asian Studies, 2009).

Shabalala, Zandi and Tom Daly. 'Germany Blocked Chinese Metals Takeover on Military Concerns—Sources'. *Reuters*, 14 August 2020.

Shambaugh, David. 'China Engages Asia: Reshaping the Regional Order'. *International Security 29*, no. 3 (Winter, 2004/2005): pp. 64–99.

Shambaugh, David. 'U.S.–China Rivalry in Southeast Asia: Power Shift or Competitive Coexistence?'. *International Security 42*, no. 4 (2018): pp. 85–127.

Shambaugh, David. *Where Great Powers Meet: America and China in Southeast Asia* (New York: Oxford University Press, 2021).

Shambaugh, David, Eberhard Sandschneider, and Zhou Hong, eds. *China-Europe Relations: Perceptions, Policies, and Prospects* (New York: Routledge, 2007).

Shen, Qinna. 'Tiananmen Square, Leipzig, and the "Chinese Solution": Revisiting the Wende from an Asian-German Perspective'. *German Studies Review 42*, no. 1 (2019): pp. 37–56.

Shetler-Jones, Philip. 'Britain's Quasi-Alliance with Japan', in *Natural Partners? Europe, Japan and Security in the Indo-Pacific*, edited by Luis Simón and Ulrich Speck (Madrid: Elcano Royal Institute, 2018), pp. 15–19.

Shi-Kupfer, Kristin and Mareike Ohlberg. 'China's Digital Rise: Challenges for Europe'. *MERICS Papers on China no. 7*, April 2019.

Silove, Nina. 'The Pivot before the Pivot: U.S. Strategy to Preserve the Power Balance in Asia'. *International Security 40*, no. 4 (2016): pp. 45–88.

Simón, Luis. *Geopolitical Change, Grand Strategy and European Security: The EU-NATO Conundrum* (New York: Palgrave Macmillan, 2013).

Simón, Luis. 'Europe, the Rise of Asia and the Future of the Transatlantic Relationship'. *International Affairs 91*, no. 5 (2015): pp. 969-989.

Simón, Luis. 'Neorealism, Security Cooperation, and Europe's Relative Gains Dilemma'. *Security Studies 26*, no. 2 (2017): pp. 197–211.

Simón, Luis, and Stephan Klose. 'European Perspectives towards the Rise of Asia: Contextualising the Debate'. *Asia-Europe Journal 14*, no. 3 (2016): pp. 239–260.

Simón, Luis, Alexander Lanoszka, and Hugo Meijer. 'Nodal Defence: The Changing Structure of U.S. Alliance Systems in Europe and East Asia'. *Journal of Strategic Studies 44*, no. 3 (2021): pp. 360–388.

Singh, Daljit and Pushpa Thambipillai. *Southeast Asian Affairs 2012* (Singapore: ISEAS Publishing, 2012).

Sizewell C Supply Chain. 'New Nuclear Update', September 2017, https://www.sizewellcsupplychain.co.uk/wp-content/uploads/2017/09/SZC_New-Nuclear-Update-Sep-17-VL.pdf.
Small, Andrew. 'Transatlantic Cooperation on Asia and the Trump Administration'. *GMF Policy Paper*, 30 October 2019.
Small, Andrew, Bonnie S. Glaser, and Garima Mohan. 'Closing the Gap: US-European Cooperation on China and the Indo-Pacific'. *Policy Paper*, German Marshall Fund, February 2022.
Smith, Julianne and Torrey Taussig. 'The Old World and the Middle Kingdom: Europe Wakes up to China's Rise'. *Foreign Affairs*, September/October 2019.
Sohm, Stefanie, Bernd Michael Linke, and Andreas Klossek. *Chinese Companies in Germany: Chances and Challenges* (Gütersloh: Deloitte/Bertelsmann Stiftung, 2009).
Spiegel, Peter and John Thornhill. 'France Urges End to China Arms Embargo'. *Financial Times*, 15 February 2005.
Spohr, Kristina. *Post Wall, Post Square: Rebuilding the World after 1989* (London: William Collins, 2009).
Stares, Paul and Nicolas Regaud. 'Europe's Role in Asia-Pacific Security'. *Survival* 39, no. 4 (1997): pp. 117–139.
Stashwick, Steven. 'US, UK, and Japan Navies Sign First-Ever Trilateral Cooperation Agreement'. *The Diplomat*, 1 November 2016.
Stec, Grzegorz. 'Central and Eastern Europe and Joint European China Policy: Threat or Opportunity?'. *MERICS Short Analysis*, 1 October 2020.
Stefanini, Sara. 'Theresa May Gives Hinkley the Green Light'. *Politico EU*, 15 September 2016.
Stephenson, Charles. *Germany's Asia-Pacific Empire: Colonialism and Naval Policy, 1885–1914* (Woodbridge: Boydell Press, 2009).
Stern, Philip J. *The Company-State: Corporate Sovereignty and the Early Modern Foundations of the British Empire in India* (Oxford: Oxford University Press, 2011).
Stirling, Sharon, ed. *Mind the Gap: Naval Views of the Free and Open Indo-Pacific* (Washington, DC: The German Marshall Fund of the United States, 2019).
Stockholm International Peace Research Institute (SIPRI). 'Trends in International Arms Transfers 2015'. *SIPRI Fact Sheet*, February 2016.
Stockholm International Peace Research Institute (SIPRI). 'Trends in International Arms Transfers, 2018'. *SIPRI Fact Sheet*, March 2019.
Stockholm International Peace Research Institute (SIPRI). 'Trends in International Arms Transfers 2019'. *SIPRI Fact Sheet*, March 2020.
Stockwell, A. J. 'British Expansion and Rule in South-East Asia', in *The Oxford History of the British Empire, Vol. 3: The Nineteenth Century*, edited by Andrew Porter (Oxford: Oxford University Press, 1998), pp. 371–394.
Stolton, Samuel. 'US Praises German Moves to Sideline Huawei from 5G Networks'. *EurActiv*, 30 September 2020.
Strachan, Hew. *The First World War* (London: Penguin Books, 2004).
Striby, Francis. 'L'Indonésie et la France prêts à signer un accord de coopération en matière de défense'. *Portail de l'intelligence économique*, 23 January 2020.
Stumbaum, May-Britt. *The European Union and China: Decision-Making in EU Foreign and Security Policy towards the People's Republic of China* (Baden-Baden: Nomos 2009).
Stumbaum, May-Britt. 'Impact of the Rebalance on Europe's Interest in East Asia: Consequences for Europe in Economic, Diplomatic, and Military/Security Dimensions', in

Origins and Evolution of the US Rebalance toward Asia: Diplomatic, Military, and Economic Dimensions, edited by Hugo Meijer (New York: Palgrave Macmillan, 2015), pp. 223–251.

Sullivan, Lawrence R. *Historical Dictionary of the People's Republic of China* (Boulder, CO: Rowman and Littlefield, 2016).

Summers, Tim. 'Chinese Investment in the UK: Growing Flows or Growing Controversy?', in *Chinese Investment in Europe: A Country-Level Approach*, edited by John Seaman, Mikko Huotari, and Miguel Otero-Iglesias (Paris: French Institute of International Relations, 2017), pp. 159–166.

Sunesen, Eva Rytter and Morten May Hansen. *Screening of FDI towards the EU*. Report Commissioned by the Danish Business Authority, January 2018.

SWIFT. 'An Inside Look into London's Quest for the Renminbi'. *RMB Tracker*, September 2019.

Swinford, Steven, Lucy Fisher, and Didi Tang. 'China Threatens to Make British Companies Pay for Huawei Ban'. *The Times*, 15 July 2020.

Tang, James T. H. 'From Empire Defence to Imperial Retreat: Britain's Postwar China Policy and the Decolonization of Hong Kong'. *Modern Asian Studies 28*, no. 2 (1994): pp. 317–337.

Taube, Markus. 'Economic Relations between Germany and Mainland China, 1979–2000'. *Duisburg Working Papers on East Asian Economic Studies*, no. 59 (2001): pp. 1–24.

Taussig, Torrey. 'Germany's Incomplete Pivot to the Indo-Pacific', in *Mind the Gap: National Views of the Free and Open Indo-Pacific*, edited by Sharon Sterling (Washington, DC: German Marshall Fund of the United States, 2019), pp. 22–26.

Taylor, Claire. *UK-US Defence Trade Co-operation Treaty*. House of Commons Library, 17 February 2009.

TechUK. 'China's Tech Landscape', 22 January 2021, https://www.techuk.org/resource/china-s-tech-landscape.html.

Terres, Hadrienne. 'La France et l'Asie : l'ébauche d'un "pivot" à la française'. French Institute of International Relations (IFRI), April 2015.

Tertrais, Bruno. 'French Nuclear Deterrence Policy, Forces, and Future: A Handbook'. *FRS Research & Documents 4*, 2020.

Thayer, Carlyle A. 'The Five Power Defence Arrangements: The Quiet Achiever'. *Security Challenges 3*, no. 1 (2007): pp. 79–96.

The National Archives (United Kingdom). 'UK Leads in Asia Rush to Europe', 29 January 1999, https://webarchive.nationalarchives.gov.uk/19990129040048/http://www.dti.gov.uk:80/IBB/GB/1997-02-031.html.

Théophile, Didier, Olivia Chriqui-Guiot, and Guillaume Griffart. 'France', in *Foreign Investment Regulation Review*, edited by Calvin S. Goldman and Michael Koch (London: The Law Reviews, 2017), 8th edition.

Thomas, Leigh. 'France to Nationalize STX Shipyard If Italy Snubs Ownership Deal'. *Reuters*, 26 July 2017.

Thoms, Anahita. 'Germany Widens the Scope of its Foreign Investment Review Regime'. Baker McKenzie, *Insight*, January 2019.

Timothy, Nick. 'The Government Is Selling our National Security to China'. *Conservative Home*, 20 October 2015.

Tōgō, Kazuhiko. *Japan's Foreign Policy, 1945–2009: The Quest for a Proactive Policy* (Leiden: Brill, 2010).

Trachtenberg, Marc. *The Craft of International History: A Guide to Method* (Princeton, NJ: Princeton University Press, 2006).

Ulatowski, Rafał. 'Germany in the Indo-Pacific Region: Strengthening the Liberal Order and Regional Security'. *International Affairs* 98, no. 2 (2022): pp. 383–402.

Uwer, Dirk and Bera Jungkind. 'Reform of Foreign Investment Control in Germany'. *Hengeler Mueller Newsletter*, July 2017.

Van der Putten, Frans-Paul and Chu Shulong, eds. *China, Europe and International Security: Interests, Roles and Prospects* (London: Routledge, 2011).

Vavasseur, Xavier. 'Naval Group Inks Major "Attack-class" Submarine Contract with Australia'. *Naval News*, 1 February 2020a.

Vavasseur, Xavier. 'France and Australia Reaffirm Commitment to the Attack-class Submarine Program'. *Naval News*, 18 February 2020b.

Vavasseur, Xavier. 'Australia, France, India, Japan and the United States Take Part in Exercise La Pérouse', *Naval News*, 6 April 2021a.

Vavasseur, Xavier. 'French SIGINT ship Dupuy de Lôme Makes Rare Taiwan Strait Transit'. *Naval News*, 13 October 2021b, https://www.navalnews.com/naval-news/2021/10/french-sigint-ship-dupuy-de-lome-taiwan/.

Veit-Brause, Irmline. 'Australia and Germany in the Pacific: Aspects of the "New Imperialism"', in *The German Empire and Britain's Pacific Dominions, 1871–1919: Essays on the Role of Australia and New Zealand in World Politics in the Age of Imperialism*, edited by John A. Moses and Christopher Pugsley (Claremont, CA: Regina Books, 2000), pp. 309–336.

Vey, Jean-Baptiste and Michel Rose. 'Macron Wants Strategic Paris–Delhi–Canberra Axis Amid Pacific Tension'. *Reuters*, 2 May 2018.

Viellard, Luc, Mathieu Anquez, and Jean-Pierre Histrimont. *Vulnérabilités de la France face aux flux maritimes*. European Company of Strategic Intelligence, Report Commissioned by the Ministry of Defence, 31 January 2012.

Wacker, Gudrun. 'Changes and Continuities in EU–China Relations: A German Perspective', in *US–China–EU Relations: Managing the New World Order*, edited by Robert S. Ross, Øystein Tunsjø, and Zhang Tuosheng (New York: Routledge, 2010), pp. 77–100.

Wai Ling So, Fion. *Germany's Colony in China: Colonialism, Protection, and Economic Development in Qingdao and Shandong, 1898–1914* (New York: Routledge, 2019).

Wallace, Cynthia Day. *The Multinational Enterprise and Legal Control: Host State Sovereignty in an Era of Economic Globalization* (The Hague: Martinus Nijhoff Publishers, 2002).

Walsh, Kathleen. *Foreign High-Tech R&D in China: Risks, Rewards, and Implications for US–China Relations* (Washington, DC: The Henry L. Stimson Center, 2003).

Ward, Matthew. 'Statistics on UK Trade with China'. *Briefing Paper*, House of Commons Library, 5 November 2019.

Ward, Matthew. 'Geographical Pattern of UK Trade'. *Briefing Paper*, House of Commons Library, 25 November 2020.

Watkins, Peter. 'China and the "Integrated Review"'. *Chatham House*, 23 November 2020, https://americas.chathamhouse.org/article/china-and-the-integrated-review/.

Webber, Mark. 'The Perils of a NATO Rebalance to the Asia-Pacific', in *NATO and Asia-Pacific*, edited by Alexander Moens and Brooke Smith-Windsor (Rome: NATO Defense College, 2016), pp. 83–100.

Wenniges, Tim and Walter Lohman. *Chinese FDI in the EU and the US: Simple Rules for Turbulent Times* (Singapore: Palgrave Macmillan, 2019).

Wikipedia. 'Exercise RIMPAC', 2020 https://en.wikipedia.org/wiki/Exercise_RIMPAC#RIMPAC_2004 (accessed 12 September 2020).

Williams, Glyndwr. 'The Pacific: Exploration and Exploitation, in *The Oxford History of the British Empire, Vol. 2: The Eighteenth Century*, edited by P. J. Marshall and Alaine Low (Oxford: Oxford University Press, 1998), pp. 552–575.

Wolfers, Arnold. *Discord and Collaboration: Essays on International Politics* (Baltimore, MD: Johns Hopkins University Press, 1965).

Wong, Reuben Y. *The Europeanization of French Foreign Policy: France and the EU in East Asia* (New York: Palgrave Macmillan, 2006).

Woodcock, Andrew. 'Senior MP Calls for Safeguards over Proposed Chinese-Built Nuclear Power Station'. *The Independent*, 14 July 2020.

Workman, Daniel. 'United Kingdom's Top Trading Partners'. *World Top Exports*, 19 July 2020.

Wright, Olivier. 'China Blocked from Funding Nuclear Power Stations by Boris Johnson'. *The Times*, 25 November 2021.

Wyelands Bank. *UK Trade Briefing*, 2018, https://www.wyelandsbank.co.uk/media/1089/wyelands_bank_gtr_trade_briefing_2018.pdf.

Xu, William. 'How Huawei Collaborates with Universities'. *Huawei Blog*, 17 December 2019, https://blog.huawei.com/2019/12/17/how-huawei-collaborates-with-universities.

Yahuda, Michael. 'The Sino-European Encounter: Historical Influences on Contemporary Relations', in *China–Europe Relations: Perceptions, Policies, and Prospects* edited by David Shambaugh, Eberhard Sandschneider, and Zhou Hong (New York: Routledge, 2007), pp. 13–32.

Yahuda, Michael. 'China's New Assertiveness in the South China Sea'. *Journal of Contemporary China 22*, no. 81(2013): pp. 446–459.

Zenelli, Valbona. 'Mapping China's Investments in Europe'. *The Diplomat*, 14 March 2019.

Zhang, Raymond. 'Who Owns Huawei? The Company Tried to Explain. It Got Complicated'. *The New York Times*, 25 April 2019.

Zhao, Minghao. 'Is a New Cold War Inevitable? Chinese Perspectives on US–China Strategic Competition'. *The Chinese Journal of International Politics 12*, no. 3 (2019): pp. 371–394.

Zhao, Suisheng. 'East Asian Disorder: China and the South China Sea Disputes'. *Asian Survey 60*, no. 3 (2020): pp. 490–509.

Zysman, John. 'The French State in the International Economy'. *International Organization 31*, no. 4 (Autumn, 1977): pp. 839–877.

Index

Allan, Alex 203
Anti-Secession Law (2005) 40, 75, 228
Armed forces
   end of France's nuclear tests in South Pacific (1995-96) 35
   France's bilateral security partnerships in Asia-Pacific 46–50
   France's multilateral initiatives in Asia-Pacific 51
   Germany's bilateral security partnerships in Asia-Pacific 79–82
   Germany's multilateral initiatives in Asia-Pacific 83
   Germany's regional security regimes in Asia-Pacific 83–84
   United Kingdom presence in Asia-Pacific 90–92, 93
   western security cooperation in Asia-Pacific 51–53
   see also naval deployments in Asia-Pacific
Arms sales
   EU embargo of China (1989) 39–41, 74–75
   France to Asia-Pacific 26, 28
   France to Australia 47–48
   France to India (2005) 42
   France to Malaysia 48–49
   France to Singapore 48
   France to Taiwan 39
   Germany to Asia-Pacific 65
   United Kingdom as global number-two exporter 97
   United Kingdom to Australia 95
   United Kingdom to China 95
   United Kingdom to India 95
   United Kingdom to Japan 95
   United States as global number-one exporter 97
ASEAN Defence Ministers' Meeting Plus (ADMM+) 84
ASEAN Regional Forum 17, 42, 76–77
ASEAN+3 17
Asia-Europe Meeting 42
Asia-Pacific region
   arms sales to 26, 28, 65, 95
   Asia-Europe Meeting 42

'China Factor' in European regional partnerships 49–50, 82–83
China's claims in South China Sea 31
drivers of China's rising assertiveness after 2009 18–19
economic potential 25–26
effects of China's rising assertiveness 4, 5, 127
end of nuclear tests in 35
European awareness of security challenges from China 19
European naval deployments 11–12, 21
European policy goals 21
European powers' policy shifts 127
European threat perceptions of China 20
Europe's responses to challenges from China 19–21
evolution of China's influence and policy in 17
existing literature on 6–7
global economic hub, as 27–28, 95–98
'grey zone' activities by China 33
Indo-Pacific region, and 19
intra-European diplomatic and security cooperation 53–59, 55–56, 122–124
multilateralism 42–43
'nine-dash line' claim by China (2009) 17–18
shift in strategic focus towards 1
see also European Union; France; Germany; United Kingdom
Australia
   arms sales by United Kingdom 117
   France and 47–48, 53
   Germany and 81
   United Kingdom and 90

Bagger, Thomas 69, 182
Beissert, Joern 82
Belt and Road Initiative 130, 149, 180, 199
Bentégeat, General Henri 29, 36, 151
Blair, Tony 104
Blinken, Antony 239
Borrell, Josep 233, 239
Brexit *see* United Kingdom
Brown, Gordon 104
Burn, Richard 201

Cablegate 11
Cablegate leaks *see* Wikileaks/Cablegate leaks
Cables *see* diplomatic cables
Cameron, David 199
Campbell, Kurt 233
Cecilia Malmström 163
China
  2008 financial crisis 18
  Anti-Secession Law (2005) 40, 75
  Asia-Pacific, and *see* Asia-Pacific
  author's approach to analysis of policies 4, 5–6
  author's contribution to literature on 6–12
  Belt and Road Initiative 130, 149, 180, 199
  Belt and Road Initiative (BRI) 130
  challenges to international rules-based order 20, 32–33, 69–70, 99–101
  content and structure of author's analysis 12–14
  core findings of author's analysis 226–230
  economic development 128–129
  Europe's awareness of security challenges from 4
  foreign direct investment *see* foreign direct investment
  foreign policy, rise in assertiveness 2
  future research, areas for 231–241
  global investment 130
  'Go Out' policy 138, 197
  'Great Rejuvenation strategy' 19, 129
  Hong Kong, and *see* Hong Kong
  Japan, and *see* Japan
  lack of literature on European responses to China's security challenges 3
  Made in China 2025 (MiC25) plan 129–130, 149, 157, 176
  military modernization 29–30
  National Intelligence Law (2017) 134
  National Security Law (2020) 18
  'peaceful rise strategy' 17
  Philippines, and *see* Philippines
  rise to great power status 2
  Taiwan, and *see* Taiwan
  technology development 128–129
  Tiananmen Square demonstrations (1989) 74
  'twenty-four-character strategy' 17, 29, 98
  United States, and *see* United States
  US views on transatlantic cooperation on, future research 239–241
  World Trade Organization accession (2001) 94
China National Offshore Oil Corporation 18
Chirac, Jacques 29, 36, 142, 150, 151
Colonialism

France 22–23
Germany 61–62
United Kingdom 88–89
Cowper-Coles, Sir Sherard 200
Cullerre, Admiral Anne 33, 53

Defence policy *see* threat perception
Deng Xiaoping 17, 29, 100
Diaoyu/Senkaku islands dispute (2012) 18
Digital sector, China's investment in European 132–136
Diplomatic cables, Wikileaks/Cablegate leaks 11

Economic interests
  Asia-Pacific as global economic hub 27–28
  China's rise in Europe 4–5
  China-US competition 2–3
  Europe's protectionism from China 3–4, 5
  France in Asia-Pacific 24, 36
  France in China 25–26
  Germany in Asia-Pacific 63–64
  Germany in China 64
  identification of national interests 13
  motive for European engagement with China 1–2
  security challenges 5
  see also foreign direct investment
EU Toolbox for 5G Cybersecurity
  France 138, 166–167
  Germany 191–193
  United Kingdom 223–224
Europe
  author's approach to analysis of policies 4, 5–10
  China's Asia-Pacific policy, and 19–21
  China's economic expansion in 4–5
  content and structure of author's analysis 12–14
  cooperation with US in Asia-Pacific 21
  core findings of author's analysis 226–230
  existing literature on 7–9
  future research, areas for 231–241
  high-threat view of China 2–3
  Huawei and 132–134
  implications of China-US rivalry 2–3
  intra-European diplomatic and security cooperation in Asia-Pacific 53–59, 122–124
  investment by China in 128, 130–132
  investment by China in digital sector 132–136
  lack of literature on responses to China's security challenges 3
  primary sources on 10–12

security challenges from China, awareness
    of 4–5
threat perceptions of China, shift in 3
US retrenchment from 2–3
see also France; Germany
European Union
    arms sales embargo of China (1989) 39–41,
        74–75
    ASEAN Regional Forum, and 76–77
    Asia–Europe Meeting 42
    Asian multilateralism 76–78
    Asia-Pacific policy 24
    China policy 13, 21
    China relations 5, 7
    China strategy cohesion and
        distinctiveness 182–183
    convergence/divergence of China policies,
        future research 231–239
    cooperation in Asia-Pacific 84–86
    digital infrastructure protection 165–167
    'digital sovereignty' 190–193
    EU Toolbox for 5G Cybersecurity 138,
        166–167, 191–193, 223–224
    Indo-Pacific strategy 56
    intra-EU diplomatic and security cooperation
        in Asia-Pacific 53–59, 84–86
    investment screening framework 163–165,
        189–190
    national security competence 6
    post-Brexit cooperation with United
        Kingdom 93
    primary sources on 10–12
    US views on transatlantic cooperation on
        China, future research 239–241

Foreign direct investment
    China in Europe 128, 130–132
    China's global investment 130
    China's 'Go Out' policy 138
    see also European Union; France; Germany;
        United Kingdom
France
    arms sales embargo of China (1989) 39–41
    arms sales to Asia-Pacific 26, 28
    arms sales to Australia 47–48
    arms sales to India (2005) 42
    arms sales to Malaysia 48–49
    arms sales to Taiwan (1991-92) 39
    Asia–Europe Meeting 42
    Asian multilateralism 42–43
    Asia-Pacific action plan (2014) 37
    Asia-Pacific diplomatic and economic ties,
        overhaul of 35–36
    Asia-Pacific policy assessed 59–60

Asia-Pacific policy changes 24, 35
Asia-Pacific policy framework, overhaul of 43
Asia-Pacific policy instruments, overhaul
    of 38–39
Asia-Pacific policy risk assessment of regional
    escalation and crises 33–34
Australia and 47, 53
author's approach to analysis of
    policies 137–138
bilateral cooperation with China 46
bilateral security partnerships in
    Asia-Pacific 46–50
bilateral ties with major Asian powers (China,
    Japan, and India) 39–42
'China Factor' in Asia-Pacific regional
    partnerships 49–50
'China policy' assessed 168, 193–194
'China policy,' changes in 150–154
'China policy' divisions with France and
    United Kingdom 77–78
'China policy' goals 150–154
'China policy,' hardening of 3–4
'China policy' instruments, overhaul
    of 156–163
China's challenges to international rules-based
    order, and 32–33
China's economic interests in 138
China's investment, digital/sensitive
    technologies 144–148, 156–158
China's investment, early growth 138–140
China's investment, economic concerns
    about 148–149
China's investment, new EU policy
    instruments 163–167
China's investment, open investment
    policy 154–156
China's investment, political concerns
    about 149, 179–180
China's investment, restrictions on 156–163
China's investment, restrictions on suppliers
    of concern 158–163
China's investment, subsequent
    expansion 140–142
China's investment, threat
    perceptions 142–149
China-US competition in Asia-Pacific,
    and 37–38
colonial empire in Asia-Pacific 22–23
core findings of author's analysis 226–230
diplomatic engagement with China 150–151
drivers of policy change in Asia-Pacific
    region 24, 49
economic engagement with China 150

France (*Continued*)
  economic interests in Asia-Pacific 24
  economic interests in China 25–26
  economic motive for Asia-Pacific relations 36
  economic motive for China relations 1
  end of nuclear tests in South Pacific (1995-96) 35
  EU digital infrastructure protection 165–167
  EU investment screening framework, promotion of 163–165
  EU Toolbox for 5G Cybersecurity 138, 166–167
  Exclusive Economic Zone 24, 26, 33
  Germany and 55–56, 85–86
  'Go Out' policy 29–30
  'grey zone' activities by China 33
  high-threat view of China, China in Asia Pacific 30–31
  high-threat view of China, China in France 144
  Huawei and 139, 141–142, 145–147, 158–163, 165–168
  India and 41–42, 46–47
  Indonesia and 49
  Indo-Pacific strategy 2, 56–59
  Indo-Pacific strategy development 36–38
  intra-European diplomatic and security cooperation, and 53–59
  investment in Asia-Pacific 27
  investment in China 137
  Japan and 41, 46, 53
  low-threat view of China, China in Asia Pacific 29–30
  low-threat view of China, China in France 142–143
  Malaysia and 48–49
  military presence in Asia-Pacific 43–46
  multilateral initiatives in Asia-Pacific 42–43, 50–51
  naval deployments in Asia-Pacific 11–12, 44–46, 52–53
  presence in Asia-Pacific 22–24
  primary sources on 10–12
  response to China's challenges to Asia-Pacific power balance 31–32
  shift to harder policy on China 1
  sovereignty concerns 33
  strategic partnership with Singapore 48
  threat perceptions, China in Asia-Pacific 24, 28–30, 137, 140–142
  threat perceptions of China, shift in 3
  United Kingdom and 54
  United States and 51–53
  Vietnam and 49
  western security cooperation in Asia-Pacific, and 51–53
  'Westernization of China' as policy goal 151
  see also Europe

Gabriel, Sigmar 179, 182
Gerberich, Thomas 77, 181
Germany
  arms sales embargo of China 74–75
  arms sales to Asia-Pacific 65
  ASEAN Defence Ministers' Meeting Plus (ADMM+), and 84
  Asia-Pacific policy assessed 86–87
  Asia-Pacific policy goals 84–85
  Asia-Pacific policy instruments, overhaul of 70–73
  Asia-Pacific policy, overhaul of 63, 70–73
  Asia-Pacific security regimes 83–84
  Australia and 81
  author's approach to analysis of policies 62–63, 169–170
  bilateral cooperation with China 74–75, 79–80
  bilateral security partnerships in Asia-Pacific 79–82
  bilateral ties with major Asian powers (China, Japan, and India) 74–76
  'China policy' 169–170
  'China policy' assessed 193–194
  'China policy' divisions with France and United Kingdom 77–78
  'China policy,' economic engagement 181–183
  'China policy' goals 180
  'China policy,' hardening of 2, 3–4
  'China policy' instruments, overhaul of 183–184
  'China policy' overhaul 181–183
  China's challenges to international rules-based order, and 69–70
  China's investment, digital/sensitive technologies 175–179
  China's investment, economic concerns about 175–179
  China's investment, growth of 171–174
  China's investment, open investment policy 184
  China's investment, restrictions on 185–189
  China's investment, restrictions on suppliers of concern 187–189
  China's investment, threat perceptions 174–180
  China's key trading partner in Europe 169
  colonial empire in Asia-Pacific 61–62

constraints on foreign and security policy in Asia-Pacific 62
cooperation/competition balance with China 181–182
core findings of author's analysis 226–230
drivers of policy change in Asia-Pacific region 62–63
economic engagement with Asia-Pacific 73–74
economic engagement with China 181–183
economic interests 170
economic interests in Asia-Pacific 63–64
economic interests in China 64
economic motive for China relations 1, 169, 180–181
EU Asian multilateralism, and 76–78
EU China strategy cohesion and distinctiveness, promotion of 182–183
EU cooperation in Asia-Pacific, and 84–86
EU 'digital sovereignty,' promotion of 190–193
EU investment screening framework, promotion of 189–190
EU Toolbox for 5G Cybersecurity 191–193
France and 55–56, 85–86
high-threat view of China, China in Asia Pacific 69–70
high-threat view of China, China in Germany 175–180
Huawei and 171, 173, 177–179, 187–189, 193
India and 76, 80–81
Indonesia and 82
Indo-Pacific strategy 2, 56–59
intra-European diplomatic and security cooperation in Asia-Pacific 55–56
investment in Asia-Pacific 27, 66–67
investment in China 66–67, 170–171
Japan and 75–76, 80
low-threat view of China, China in Asia Pacific 67–69
low-threat view of China, China in Germany 174–175
military capability decline after Cold War 78–79
military presence in Asia-Pacific 78–83
multilateral initiatives in Asia-Pacific 83
naval deployments in Asia-Pacific 11–12, 78–79
Netherlands and 85–86
presence in Asia-Pacific 61
primary sources on 10–12
Singapore and 81–82
threat perceptions, China in Asia-Pacific 67–70
threat perceptions, China in Germany 174–180
threat perceptions of China, shift in 3
Tiananmen Square demonstrations, and 74
trade with Asia-Pacific 65–67
trade with China 66
United Kingdom and 85
United States and 84, 85
Vietnam and 82
Wikileaks/Cablegate leaks (1990–2010) 75
see also Europe
'Go Out' policy 138, 197
'Great Rejuvenation strategy' 19, 129
'Grey zone' activities by China 33

Hagel, Chuck 52
Hong Kong 99
  handover to China (1997) 90, 103–104
  'one country, two systems' 18, 100, 103–104
  United Kingdom and 90, 93, 100, 103–104
Houghton, Lord Nick 203, 211
Hu Jintao 17
Huawei Technologies (Corporation)
  Europe 132–134
  France 139, 141–142, 145–147, 158–163, 165–168
  Germany 171, 173, 177–179, 187–189, 193
  United Kingdom 197–198, 199–200, 202–203, 208–209, 213–214, 217–221
Hum, Christopher 210

India
  arms sales by France (2005) 42
  arms sales by United Kingdom 95
  France and 41–42
  Germany and 76, 80–81
  independence (1947) 89
  United Kingdom and 118
Indonesia
  France and 49
  Germany and 82
Indo-Pacific region
  European Union strategy development 56–59
  France's strategy development 36–38
  reference to 19
  United Kingdom and *see* United Kingdom
International law, China's challenges to rules-based order 20, 32–33, 69–70, 99–101
Investment *see* foreign direct investment

Japan
  acquisition of German colonies in Asia-Pacific 62

Japan (*Continued*)
  arms sales by United Kingdom 95
  China overtakes as world's second-largest economy 18
  Diaoyu/Senkaku islands dispute (2012) 18
  France and 41, 53
  Germany and 75–76, 80
Johnson, Boris 216, 224
Juillet, Alain 142–143, 155
Juncker, Jean-Claude 164

King, Sir Julian 164, 166, 189, 192–193
Kinkel, Klaus 74
Könen, Andreas 178
Kramp-Karrenbauer, Annegret 82–83
Kreft, Heinrich 65, 171

Le Drian, Jean-Yves 53–54
Le Maire, Bruno 158
Lechervy, Christian 42, 50
Liu Xiaoming 220
Locklear, Admiral Samuel 53

Maas, Heiko 182
Macron, Emmanuel 149, 153
Made in China 2025 (MiC25) plan 129–130, 149, 157, 176
Malaysia
  creation 89
  France and 48
  Singapore and 89
  United Kingdom and 89
Martin, Ciaran 209, 219
Martinon, David 145
May, Theresa 100, 204, 206
Merkel, Angela 75
Military forces *see* armed forces
Mitterrand, François 151

National Intelligence Law (2017) 134
National security *see* security challenges
National Security Law (2020) 18
Naval deployments in Asia-Pacific
  China's naval modernization 31
  European increase in 21
  France 44–46, 52–53
  Germany 78–79
  primary sources on 11–12
  United Kingdom 11–12, 54, 113–115
Netherlands, Indo-Pacific strategy 56–59, 85–86
New Zealand: United Kingdom and 90
'Nine-dash line' claim (2009) 17–18

Obama, Barak 239
'Oil rig crisis' (2014) 18

'One country, two systems' *see* Hong Kong
Osborne, George 203

Paracel Islands 18
'Peaceful rise strategy' 17
Permanent Court of Arbitration, ruling on China territorial dispute (2016) 18, 32, 100
Philippines
  PCA ruling on China territorial dispute (2016) 18, 32, 100
  Scarborough Shoal dispute (2012) 18
Policy goals
  analysis of 13
  effects of China's rising assertiveness 3
Policy instruments
  analysis of 13
  effects of China's rising assertiveness 3
Poupard, Guillaume 160

Raffarin, Jean-Pierre 142
Ren Zhengfei 199
Ricketts, Lord Peter 105, 209, 213
Roth, Michael 179
Roule, Jonas 164
Rules-based order *see* international law

Sarkozy, Nicolas 151
Scarborough Shoal dispute (2012) 18
Schröder, Gerhard 75
Sea power *see* naval deployments in Asia-Pacific
Security challenges
  author's contribution to literature on 2, 5, 9–10
  China in Asia-Pacific 20
  Europe's awareness of challenges from China 4, 20
  US retrenchment from Europe 2–3
Singapore
  arms sales by France 48
  arms sales by Germany 82
  Germany and 81–82
  Malaysia and 89
  United Kingdom and 117–118
Smith, Jacqui 203
South China Sea *see* Asia-Pacific region
South Pacific *see* Asia-Pacific region
Stanzel, Volker 174
Steinmeier, Frank-Walter 69, 71, 83, 84, 179, 182

Taiwan
  arms sales by France (1991-92) 39
  Taiwan Strait Crisis (1995–1996) 17
Telecommunications sector *see* Huawei Technologies

China's investment, digital/sensitive technologies *see* France; Germany; United Kingdom
EU Toolbox for 5G Cybersecurity 138, 166–167, 191–193, 223–224
Threat perception
  analysis of European perceptions of China 13
  shift in European perceptions of China 3
  see also European Union; France; Germany; United Kingdom
Tiananmen Square demonstrations (1989) 74
Trump, Donald 239
Truss, Liz 216
'Twenty-four-character strategy' 17, 29
2008 financial crisis 18

United Kingdom
  arms sales to Australia 117
  arms sales to China 95
  Asia-Pacific, intra-European diplomatic and security cooperation 122–124
  Asia-Pacific joint military exercises 119–120
  Asia-Pacific military engagement 112–113
  Asia-Pacific ministerial relations 111–112
  Asia-Pacific multilateral initiatives 119–121
  Asia-Pacific policy assessed 124
  Asia-Pacific policy goals 102–103
  Asia-Pacific policy instruments 107
  Asia-Pacific policy overhaul 105–107
  Asia-Pacific policy post-Brexit 11–12, 55
  Asia-Pacific policy shortcomings 104–105
  Asia-Pacific Western security cooperation 121–122
  Australia and 90, 116–117
  author's approach to analysis of policies 92–93
  'China Factor' in Asia-Pacific regional partnerships 118–119
  'China policy' assessed 224–225
  'China policy,' author's approach to analysis 196
  'China policy' divisions with Germany and France 77–78
  'China policy,' economic engagement 210–211
  'China policy' goals 104, 209–210
  'China policy,' hardening of 2, 3–4
  'China policy' instruments, overhaul of 212–224
  'China policy' overhaul 211–212
  'China policy,' overview of 195–196
  'China policy,' threat perceptions 195, 201–209
  China-Centric policy approach 108
  China's challenges to international rules-based order, and 99–101
  China's cyber-espionage and disruption 207–209
  China's investment, beginning of 196
  China's investment, digital/sensitive technologies 207–209
  China's investment, early growth 196–198
  China's investment, EU FDI screening framework 221–222
  China's investment, Huawei restrictions and ban 217–221
  China's investment, open investment policy 212–214
  China's investment, screening mechanisms 214–217
  China's investment, strategic sectors 205–207
  China's investment, subsequent expansion 198–201
  core findings of author's analysis 226–230
  economic engagement with China 210–211
  economic interests in Asia-Pacific 93–98
  economic motive for Asia-Pacific relations 94
  economic motive for China relations 103, 195
  economic ties with China 108–111
  engagement policy with China 1–2, 103–104
  EU FDI screening framework 221–222
  EU Toolbox for 5G Cybersecurity 223–224
  EU-UK post-Brexit cooperation 93
  France and 54
  Germany and 85
  global number-two arms exporter 97
  high-threat view of China, China in Asia Pacific 93, 99–102
  high-threat view of China, China in UK 203–209
  Hong Kong and 90, 93, 100, 103
  Huawei and 197–198, 199–200, 202–203, 208–209, 213–214
  India and 89, 118
  Indo-Pacific colonial empire 88–89
  Indo-Pacific decolonization 89–90
  Indo-Pacific policy goals 93
  Indo-Pacific policy overhaul 93
  Indo-Pacific presence 88
  Indo-Pacific strategy 105–107
  investment in China 94–95
  Japan and 116
  low-threat view of China, China in Asia Pacific 93, 98–99
  low-threat view of China, China in UK 201–203
  Malaysia and 89
  military presence in Asia-Pacific 90–92, 93
  naval deployments in Asia-Pacific 11–12, 54, 113–115
  New Zealand and 90

United Kingdom (*Continued*)
  post-colonial role in Asia-Pacific 90
  primary sources on 10–12
  Singapore and 117–118
  threat perceptions, China in Asia-Pacific 92–93, 98
  threat perceptions, China in UK 201–209
  threat perceptions of China, shift in 3
  trade with China 94
  United States and 89
  see also Europe
United Nations, 'nine-dash line' claim by China (2009) 17–18
United States
  China's Asia-Pacific policy, and 17–18, 17–19
  cooperation with Europe in Asia-Pacific 21
  Europe and US-China rivalry 226–241
  existing literature on 6
  France and 51–53, 136, 143, 153–154, 162, 163, 166, 167, 168
  Germany and 84, 85, 170, 183, 188–189, 190
  global number-one arms exporter 97
  increased competition with China 2–3
  retrenchment from Europe 2
  United Kingdom and 89, 101, 106, 110, 116–117, 119–124, 195, 212, 219, 220, 221
  USS *Impeccable* 17, 30
  USS *Impeccable* incident (2009) 17, 30
  western security cooperation in Asia-Pacific, and 51–53

Vietnam
  France and 49
  Germany and 82
  'oil rig crisis' (2014) 18
Villepin, Dominique de 142–143
Volkswagen (Corporation) 1

Watkins, Peter 224
Webb, Simon 103, 202
Wiegand, Gunnar 232–233
Wikileaks/Cablegate leaks (1990–2010) 11, 75
World Trade Organization, China's accession (2001) 94

Xi Jinping 19, 99, 129

Zypries, Brigitte 189